BUSINESS
COMMUNICATION

Strategies and Skills

FIFTH EDITION

James M. Lahiff
University of Georgia

John M. Penrose
San Diego State University

Prentice Hall
Upper Saddle River, New Jersey 07458

Library of Congress Cataloging-in-Publication Data

Lahiff, James M.
    Business communications : skills and strategies / James M. Lahiff,
John M. Penrose.
       p. cm.
    Rev. ed.: of Business communication / Richard C. Huseman, James M.
Lahiff, John M. Penrose, Jr.
    Includes bibliographical references and index.
    ISBN 0-13-531112-8
    1. Business communication   I. Penrose, John M.   II. Huseman,
Richard C.   Business communication.   III. Title.
HF5718.H84   1996
658.4'5—dc20   96–16405

Acquisitions Editor: *Elizabeth Sugg*
Editorial Assistant: *Khadijah Bell*
Managing Editor: *Mary Carnis*
Project Management & Composition: *Elm Street Publishing Services, Inc.*
Design Director: *Marianne Frasco*
Interior Design: *Edward Smith Design, Inc.*
Director of Manufacturing & Production: *Bruce Johnson*
Manufacturing Buyer: *Ed O'Dougherty*
Marketing Manager: *Danny Hoyt*
Printer/Binder: *Von Hoffmann Press*
Cover Design: *Edward Smith Design, Inc.*

 ©1997 by Prentice-Hall, Inc.
A Simon & Schuster Company
Upper Saddle River, New Jersey 07458

Earlier editions of this title were published by The Dryden Press,
301 Commerce Street, Fort Worth, Texas 76102, ©1991, 1988, 1985, 1981

Printed in the United States of America

10 9 8 7 6 5 4 3 2 1

ISBN 0-13-531112-8

Prentice-Hall International (UK) Limited, *London*
Prentice-Hall of Australia Pty. Limited, *Sydney*
Prentice-Hall Canada Inc., *Toronto*
Prentice-Hall Hispanoamericana, S.A., *Mexico*
Prentice-Hall of India Private Limited, *New Delhi*
Prentice-Hall of Japan, Inc., *Tokyo*
Simon & Schuster Asia Pte. Ltd., *Singapore*
Editora Prentice-Hall do Brasil, Ltda., *Rio de Janeiro*

CONTENTS

CHAPTER 3   Cultural Diversity   **48**

PART TWO   STRATEGIES FOR WRITTEN COMMUNICATION   **107**

CHAPTER 8   Persuasive Letters   **195**

CHAPTER 9   Memoranda   **234**

CHAPTER 18   **Meetings: Small Group Communication**   **440**

CHAPTER 19   **Communication and Conflict**   **466**

PREFACE

Since the first edition of *Business Communication: Strategies and Skills* was published in 1981, the workforce of the United States has grown from 77 million to 196 million people, and the gross domestic product has increased from $3,030 billion to $7,250 billion. Although those figures suggest a robust economy, that is only a partial picture; during those same years more than 43 million jobs have been eliminated in the United States. Although many more jobs have been created than lost, the competition for well-paying jobs has never been stronger.

Organizations, both business and nonprofit, now exist in an environment in which change has become a permanent characteristic rather than an occasional occurrence. Concepts such as downsizing, decentralization, employee empowerment, and quality management—once considered somewhat exotic—have become mainstream management approaches for improving efficiency and productivity. It is interesting to note that chaos is a central theme of nearly five hundred books that have been published in the United States during the past ten years, and many of these books have dealt specifically with the management of people. The notion of chaos is thought by many to accurately describe the contemporary organization.

As organizations have changed, so also have the expectations of management for its new employees. For example, the opportunity to acquire basic skills on the job has become a luxury no longer made available by most organizations. New employees are now expected to "hit the ground running," by being able to contribute immediately to organizational effectiveness.

This fifth edition has been designed with the new managerial expectations in mind. The focus is on the most consequential aspects of communication, and the intent is to give the reader an edge on the competition by developing those communication skills crucial to success in today's organization.

THE PATH TO A COMPETITIVE EDGE

An underlying premise of this fifth edition is that learning is not a spectator sport, but that it requires commitment and involvement on the part of the reader. The book has undergone an extensive revision, with the intent of increasing its appeal to the student in terms of relevance, ease of understanding, and attractiveness. All of the chapters have been updated and many new examples and assignments added.

The Electronic Office chapter has been completely rewritten and the Cultural Diversity chapter largely so. In recognition of the importance of these topics in establishing a foundation on which to build a repertoire of communication skills, both chapters have been moved to the first section of the book.

Ethical considerations are again integrated throughout the book rather than relegated to a single section. Each chapter includes an "Ethical Dilemma" designed to stimulate class discussion and critical thinking. By the end of their business communication course, students should recognize that ethics and communication are unalterably entwined. While analyzing each Ethical Dilemma, readers should keep these questions in mind:

- Are any laws being broken?
- Is the situation fair to all parties involved?
- Would I feel guilty if my friends and family learned that I was involved in a similar situation?

Knowledge, communication skills, and a willingness to stretch beyond one's former limits characterize those who succeed in today's business environment. The newest edition of *Business Communication: Strategies and Skills* is designed to facilitate development accordingly.

TEXTUAL FEATURES THAT FACILITATE COMPREHENSION

The following features of the fifth edition are intended to promote the development of communication skills of the readers:

- Learning objectives help readers focus on the most important features of each chapter.
- Opening vignettes serve as a bridge between the chapter objectives and content.
- Marginal notes assist in identifying significant ideas.
- Checklists facilitate the review of information.
- Annotated letters illustrate both effective and ineffective writing strategies.
- New cases provide opportunities for discussion and analysis.
- There are many more written assignments. (Eighty percent of them are new.)
- Key terms are highlighted in the text.
- End-of-chapter listing of key terms and concepts provides an opportunity for an immediate measurement of retention of information.
- New Appendix B illustrates and discusses the standard appearance of business messages.

INSTRUCTIONAL SUPPORT PACKAGE

The comprehensive instructional support package is designed to facilitate the educational experience for instructor and student. It is intended to improve teaching by providing resources that will enrich the study of business communication. The instructor may choose among the following supplements.

INSTRUCTOR'S MANUAL   This extensive volume contains the following detailed elements:

- Chapter outlines
- Student learning objectives
- Chapter synopses
- Teaching suggestions for each chapter
- Answers to review questions from the text
- Case notes
- Content-related exercises
- Readings on teaching methods
- Transparency masters emphasizing key points from the text

- PowerPoint disk for computer-driven presentation of transparencies
- Sample mid-term and final exams

TEST BANK   The organization of this collection of approximately 2000 multiple-choice, true/false, and essay questions and answers follows the organization of the book. Test items are divided by chapters and are presented in the same sequence in which the material is covered within each chapter. The level of difficulty of each question is indicated as is the text page on which the answer can be found. One mini-case problem with several related multiple-choice questions is provided for each chapter.

STUDY GUIDE   This supplement was developed to provide additional assistance for students in maximizing their understanding of key principles of business communication and in learning how to apply these principles to real-world problems. This guide provides chapter-by-chapter exercises designed to develop crucial communication competencies.

VIDEOTAPES   A series of JWA videotapes provides instruction in methods for dealing with common problematical communication situations. Included in the series are tapes on telephone communication techniques, making business presentations, conducting meetings, dealing with difficult employees, and methods for improving writing. Each videotape is approximately thirty minutes in length.

POWERPOINT   The files on this disk allow manipulation of transparency content, display, incorporation of graphics and the ability to create an instructor's own transparency program.

ACKNOWLEDGMENTS

Publication of the fifth edition of *Business Communication: Strategies and Skills* is a testimonial to the efforts of many highly skilled individuals. Craig Piercy merits special appreciation for his masterful coverage of management information systems in The Electronic Office (Chapter 4). We would also like to thank the following professional educators who made significant contributions to this edition with their thorough and insightful reviews:

Mary M. Conrad
Iowa Central Community College

Caroll J. Dierks
University of Northern Colorado

James Downs
Metropolitan Community College (CO)

Pamela R. Johnson
California State University, Chico

Jane Knight
East Texas Baptist University

Doris Riley
LeTourneau College

Dona Vasa
University of Nebraska–Lincoln

William B. Woodward, Jr.
University of Alabama–Huntsville

The end-of-chapter cases have proved to be a popular feature of each edition. Thanks to the following individuals, the fifth edition includes additional cases to stimulate thinking and discussion among students:

Donald E. Anderson, Grossmont College

Lynne K. Anderson, Tidewater Community College

Lecia Archer, University of Colorado at Boulder

Richard J. Barnhart, San Francisco State University

Anita Bednar, Central State University

Julie C. Burkhard, Charlottesville, Virginia

Randy E. Cone, University of New Orleans

Amanda Copeland, Southwestern Oklahoma State University

Cara A. Curtis, University of Georgia

Mary Dehner, Clemson University

Carol David, Iowa State University

Glenn B. Dietrich, University of Texas at San Antonio

Judith V.A. Dietrich, Vancouver, British Columbia

Margaret Fitch-Hauser, Auburn University

Marie Flatley, San Diego State University

Mary A. Gowan, University of Texas at El Paso

Beryl D. Hart, West Liberty State College

Heather Honeycutt, Coca Cola Foundation

Susan Tucker Kinney, Wake Forest University

J. Timothy Lake, Equitable Real Estate Investment Management, Inc.

Mildred W. Landrum, Kennesaw College

Anthony S. Lis, University of Oklahoma

Carolena Lyons-Lawrence, San Diego State University

Marsha Mascolini, Western Michigan University

Martha Andrews Nord, Vanderbilt University

Robert J. Olney, Southwest Texas State University

Michael T. O'Neill, Arlington, Texas

David B. Parsons, Lakehead University

Elizabeth Plunkett, West Georgia College

Richard Pompian, Boise State University

Kath Ralston, Chisholm Institute of Technology

Debbie A. Renshaw, Port Townsend, Washington

Anji K. Roy, University of Wisconsin–Oshkosh

William C. Sharbrough III, The Citadel

Chun-Sheng Yu, Hangzbou University

John D. Stegman, The Ohio State University

Jim Stull, San Jose State University

Kathy B. White, University of North Carolina at Greensboro

For their help on previous editions, we thank E. Paul Alworth, Lois Bachman, Martha Bickley, Frankie Clemons, Betty Cochran, Marian C. Crawford, William Damerst, Nancy Darsey, George H. Douglas, Ron Dulek, Nancy Elliott, Lilian Feinberg, Alton V. Finch, Michael Finnigan, Marie E. Flatley, Barbara Miller Gentile, Theresa Gilbert, Lee Goddard, Hal W. Hepler, Herb Hildebrandt, R. Eugene Hughes, Betty Jacquier, Charles Jamison, Betty S. Johnson, Ron Kapper, Paul J. Killorin, Retha Hoover Kilpatrick, Judith Remy Leder, David O. Lewis, Robert Lorenzi, Marcia Mascolini, Iris Mauney, Robert Ochs, Doris Phillips, Virgil R. Pufahl, Mary Ellen Raleigh, Richard David Ramsey, Diana C. Reep, Jeanette Ritzenthaler, Joan C. Roderick, Ron Schlattman, Larry R. Smeltzer, Arthur Smith, Ted Stoddard, Robert Underwood, Dan Viamonte, Ron Weidenfeller, and Charlotte West.

The fifth edition of *Business Communication: Strategies and Skills* would not have been possible without the assistance of Elizabeth Sugg, Mary Carnis, Judy Casillo, and Khadijah Bell of Prentice Hall. We are also grateful to Phyllis Crittenden of Elm Street Publishing Services, who contributed much to the final product.

Suggestions from students have led to many of the changes reflected in previous editions, and the same is true of this one. Students' active participation in the learning process frequently provides them with insights unavailable to anyone else, and we appreciate their suggestions.

This book is intended to prepare students to meet the ever-rising expectations of today's employers. Its value will extend well beyond the completion of any single course and will continue for as long as one pursues personal and professional development.

James M. Lahiff

John M. Penrose, Jr.

ABOUT THE AUTHORS

JAMES M. LAHIFF, PH.D. (Pennsylvania State University), has taught more than five thousand undergraduate and graduate students since coming to the University of Georgia in 1969. During that time he has also conducted training programs involving several thousand supervisors, managers, and executives from many different business and nonprofit organizations, both U.S. and international. As a professor of management, he teaches courses in interpersonal and organizational communication, interviewing, and human resource management. He is the author of many articles and scholarly papers, and he has presented his research findings for various professional associations, foremost of which is the Association for Business Communication (ABC). He has been an active member of ABC for more than twenty years, during which time he has served in a variety of positions, and at present is a member of the board of directors. In addition to this text, he has co-authored books on supervision, management, and communication. The previous editions of this text have also been published in Australian, Canadian, and Japanese editions.

JOHN M. PENROSE, PH.D. (University of Texas at Austin), is Professor in and Chair of Information and Decision Systems Department in the College of Business Administration at San Diego State University. From 1972 to 1988 he was on the faculty of the Graduate School of Business at the University of Texas at Austin, where he served as coordinator of the 11-member business communication faculty. He has also served on the faculties of Southern Illinois University at Edwardsville and of Ohio University. He is the author of many journal articles, book chapters, and six textbooks in business communication. He was president in 1989 of the Association for Business Communication and has served on the editorial boards of three scholarly journals. As a consultant to business, he has worked with numerous business and nonprofit organizations as a trainer and expert on technical writing, written and oral strategies, and organizational communication.

Part 1

INTRODUCTION

1 An Overview of Communication in Business

2 The Nature of Communication

3 Cultural Diversity

4 The Electronic Office

An understanding of the elements of communication is essential prior to seeking to improve one's written or oral skills in business. To accomplish this understanding, we examine communication basics, relate them to business, and review myths about communication. We look at communication in both international and cross-cultural settings, and present electronic communication options available to the modern organization.

Chapter 1

An Overview of Communication in Business

The possibility of a merger between Bell Atlantic Corporation and Tele-Communications Inc. excited many investors. Newspaper, television, and radio accounts of the potential merger resulted in brokers being swamped with "buy" orders for stock in TCI. In minutes, eighty-seven to be exact, the price per share of TCI stock rocketed from $15.50 to $17.75, an increase of almost 18 percent.

After one hour and twenty-seven minutes of chaos, the New York Stock Exchange halted all trading of TCI, which, it turned out, was actually the symbol for Transcontinental Realty Investors. During that brief period of time approximately 55,000 shares of stock in Transcontinental Realty had changed hands. The following day, for purposes of comparison, a grand total of 100 shares of Transcontinental stock were sold.[1]

On Tuesday, June 14, 1994, at 12:51 P.M., the Dow Jones news service mistakenly reported that Bernard Marcus, CEO of Home Depot, had said that second-quarter sales growth was weaker than in the first quarter. At 2:39 P.M. on the same day the same news service sent out a correction. It seems that Marcus had actually expressed concern that other retailers' sales growth was slowing.

Home Depot stock was the ninth most actively traded on the New York Stock Exchange that day. The stock lost 3.6 percent of its value, and closed at $43 per share. By the end of that day, nearly three million shares of Home Depot stock had changed hands. Stock analysts know of nothing other than the incorrect information that could explain the stock's decline.[2]

When she was a junior securities analyst, Carolyn Ziegler was advised by a friend to invest in a particular biotechnology company. She bought a sizable number of shares for herself at $7.00 per share, and she was delighted to see the price quickly shoot up to $15. Shortly thereafter, however, the stock disappeared from the market and could no longer be traded. Then she learned that the future of the entire company in which she had invested had rested on a single cow. Cancer research was being done on the cow. When the cow died, so did the company.[3]

Breakdowns in communication regularly influence the outcome of events, just as happened in the three examples described above. First it was a false assumption regarding the meaning of TCI that led investors astray. Poor listen-

ing resulted in an inaccurate quotation and subsequent financial losses in the second instance. Because an individual failed to probe for relevant information in the third example, an ill-advised investment was made in a one-cow operation. Communication, whether effective or not, strongly influences the lives of individuals and organizations alike. The focus of this book is on developing your communication abilities and thereby equipping you to attain the goals you pursue.

THE PERVASIVE NATURE OF COMMUNICATION

According to T.A. Murphy, former Chairman of General Motors, " . . . the one common denominator in business and in management is people and relationships with people. . . . in the final analysis, communication is all important . . . effective communications can make the difference between success and failure, or at least it can determine the degree of success."[4] Regardless of the type of organization in which you work now or will work in the future, the business of communicating is all important. Communication is significant to organizations and to individuals alike.

Even the monster in the classic *Frankenstein* became aware of the significance of communication. While hiding in the woods, the monster observed the family of a shepherd for several days.

> I found that these people possessed a method of communicating their experiences and feelings to one another by articulate sounds. I perceived that the words they spoke sometimes produced pleasure or pain, smiles or sadness, in the minds and countenances of the hearer. This was indeed a godlike science and I ardently desired to become acquainted with it.[5]

Regardless of where communication occurs or who is involved, the basics of the transaction are identical. To illustrate, Frank Rhodes owned and operated a small wholesale janitorial supplies company. The workforce consisted of five warehouse workers, one secretary, and three outside salespeople. He regularly encountered problems caused by salespeople failing to complete their order forms, warehouse workers losing bills of lading, and the secretary misfiling important papers. Frank found that the more closely he observed his workers and the more he talked with them, the less frequently such problems occurred. No matter how hard he worked at it, however, problems involving information seemed to arise. Sometimes a message did not go where it was supposed to. At other times information was distorted by the time it reached the intended recipient.

Although human communication often appears purposeless, it is not.

Much of the information exchanged on the job has little to do with the job itself but it is vital to the individual. Human beings are sometimes referred to as social animals, for they need to communicate even when there is nothing urgent for them to express. In fact, much conversation may appear purposeless on the surface but actually satisfies the need to interact with others. To recognize the importance of such communication, we need only to consider what is generally regarded as the ultimate punishment for troublesome prison inmates: solitary confinement. The person placed in solitary confinement is absolutely deprived of the opportunity and right to communicate with others.

Organizations devote much effort to improving communication.

Because communication is recognized as crucial, many organizations train employees to become better communicators. Training programs may be structured around many different aspects of communication. For example, an American Management Association catalog of course offerings included the following communication courses or courses that list communication as a key topic:[6]

Strategies for Developing Effective Presentation Skills
Effective Executive Speaking
Advanced Executive Speaking
Effective Presentation Skills for Technical Professionals
Maximizing Presentation Impact
Visual Aids Workshop
Effective Listening/Better Results: Making Communication Work for You
Negotiating to Win
Beyond Negotiating to Win: Practical Applications for Enhanced Effectiveness
Interpersonal Skills
Communication and Interpersonal Skills: A Program for Technical Professionals
Building Interdepartmental Cooperation: Strategies for Workplace Effectiveness
How to Sharpen Your Business Writing Skills
The Grammar Course
Effective Technical Writing
Quick Fix Writing: Think it Write it!
Business Writing: When English Is a Second Language
Writing, Speaking, and Listening for Successful Communication
Communicating for Maximum Results: Building Better Work Relationships
Creativity and Innovation: Getting the Winning Edge
Projecting a Positive Executive Image
Listen Up
Cross-Functional Communication
Listening and Writing
New Techniques for Results-Oriented Communication
Selling Your Great Ideas Inside Your Organization

The list suggests just how varied the nature of communication courses is as well as the many organizational activities in which communication is vital.

THE COST TO ORGANIZATIONS OF COMMUNICATION

Monetary Costs

Business organizations must provide a great deal of information to federal, state, and local governments. This is difficult for the best of communication systems, and the expense involved is high. For example, over 5 million business firms and associations reported detailed information on income and finances to the Internal Revenue Service in 1992. The federal government requires lengthy reports and applications from thousands of businesses, nonprofit organizations, and state and local agencies that must comply with regulatory requirements or that receive federal grants or contracts. In all, American organizations and individuals spent over 6.8 billion hours to meet federal information collection requirements during 1992. This is equivalent to employing 3 million people full time.

Not surprisingly, the single largest paperwork agency in the federal government is the Department of the Treasury, which includes the Internal Revenue Service (IRS). The IRS form 1040 and related schedules impose an annual burden of more than 297 million hours. The Department of Defense required 229 million hours of paperwork in

1992. Demands for information increase each year despite efforts by the government to reduce the amount of paperwork. The total paperwork burden increased 27.7 percent from 1989 to 1992. In an attempt to reduce the incidence of faulty diagnostic tests, the Department of Health and Human Services in 1992 devoted 18 million more worker hours to reporting to the federal government than it had the previous year.[7]

Research has shown that we spend approximately 75 percent of waking time involved in some form of communication. The time spent on one or another phase of communication in a typical manufacturing plant comprises approximately half of an average workday. The cliché "time is money" is true. The tremendous cost of business communication partially accounts for the intense interest in it.

Consider the cost of a single letter to a business organization. The Dartnell Institute began studying such matters in 1930. The total cost of a business letter in 1930, including planning, dictation, writing, materials, and postage, was $0.30. In 1994 the cost of the same business letter ranged from $12.64 to $19.13, depending on the method used to produce it. Research conducted by Dartnell suggests that transcribing from dictation on a personal computer is the fastest and most cost-effective way to generate a business letter.[8]

Effective communication is costly to the business organization, but ineffective communication is even more costly.

Nonmonetary Costs

Monetary costs are important to an organization, but many other less tangible costs of communication are also important. For instance, although it is difficult to compute the cost of communication failures, such failures often cause long-felt repercussions.

To illustrate, when Fred Adkins misunderstood the tolerances required for the pipe fittings he was machining, his mistake was not noticed until he had completed half the order. The completed fittings had to be scrapped. To replace them, other orders were delayed, and the work schedules for some other lathe operators were disrupted. The customer waiting for the fittings was also inconvenienced and may be hesitant to place another order with Fred's employer. Fred believed that his supervisor had given him incorrect instructions, which the supervisor denied. For the next week, Fred was disgusted with his boss and with his job. His friends at work sympathized with him, and shop productivity temporarily dropped. After several weeks, things returned to normal, but Fred continued to talk occasionally about finding another job.

The repercussive nature of communication failures may make it difficult to determine the exact financial costs involved. No doubt exists, however, that ineffective communication results in errors, misunderstanding, poor performance, and negative feelings.

INTERNAL AND EXTERNAL COMMUNICATION

When a major corporation installed an 800 number to provide the news media with a daily recorded update on the status of the company, the majority of the calls came from the company's own managers stationed all over the world. They wanted to know what was going on and what was being said by the home office.[9] This should have caused top management to question how effectively the company was addressing the information needs of its employees.

Internal communication may be either formal or informal.

Messages sent and received within an organization comprise its **internal communication**, which may be formal or informal. **Formal communication** messages are sent through channels developed by management. Much communication in any organization, however, does not go through regular channels. This **informal communication** consists of exchanges between individuals who, although not formally connected, interact by telephone conversation, social or chance meetings, and even on the golf course.

Figure 1.1
Times Square at Night
Advertisers compete for the
attention of the public
through external
communication.
Source: Wayne Eastep,
Tony Stone Images.

Much of the communication conducted by an organization is with individuals or groups outside the organization. **External communication** may involve any of the many different segments of the public with which the organization interacts (see Figure 1.1). Most organizations have their greatest number of public contacts through **advertising**, which is a highly structured form of external communication. Examples include television commercials, printed ads, and brochures sent by the company to persons on a select mailing list. Most external communication is less formal than advertising; for example, management might informally keep the neighboring community aware of how the company contributes to the local economy. Annual reports, news releases, and public speeches by executives are other examples of external communication.

Toll-free 800 numbers may be the fastest growing medium of external communication. Since the introduction of the 800 service in the United States in 1967, the annual volume of calls has increased from seven million to more than ten billion. More than 300,000 businesses now take calls on more than 700,000 toll-free lines.[10]

External communication is not always planned and purposeful. Employees play many different roles in the course of a day, and the roles are sometimes difficult to separate. For that reason all employees are unofficial spokespersons for their employers. Even though you may seldom talk to outsiders about your work or about your employer, you are still representing the organization.

Advertising is the most structured type of external communication.

Not all external communication is planned.

THE CHANGING BUSINESS ORGANIZATION: IMPLICATIONS FOR COMMUNICATION

Organizational growth often leads to communication problems.

For much of the eighties, business organizations experienced significant growth. The end of that decade ushered in a period of organizational restructuring. Layoffs, hiring freezes, and early retirement plans became common tactics of organizations attempting to control the costs of doing business. "**Downsizing**," which originally pertained solely to the size of automobiles, became part of the business lexicon.

Employees typically experience increased workloads following an organizational restructuring, and the importance of communication is especially pronounced at that time. Employees who remain following a downsizing, for example, feel insecure about their jobs and are more likely to trust each other than the organization.[11] As a result, ongoing communication between employers and employees is essential to build trust and to reduce uncertainty. The future success of the organization depends on the remaining employees, and communication is vital to energizing their performance. Restructuring has become so commonplace that, from 1988 to the present, approximately 85 percent of corporate executives reported that some form of restructuring had been implemented in their organizations. These same executives, incidentally, ranked "communicate better" as one of the most important changes, in hindsight, that they would have made.[12]

Despite the fact that many organizations are smaller today than a few years ago, the different levels within the organization and the distribution of responsibilities greatly complicate transmission of information. A comparison of the organizational charts in Figures 1.2 and 1.3 suggests how organizational changes might prevent the organization from performing efficiently.

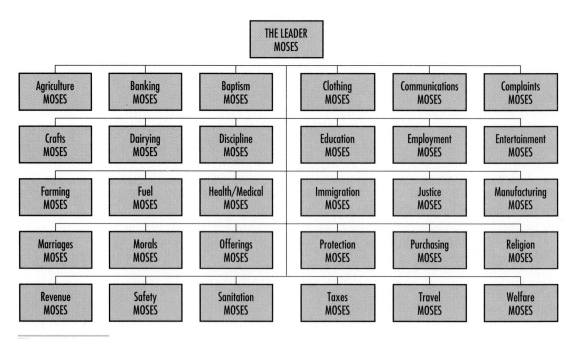

Figure 1.2

Organization in Biblical Times before Expansion
Source: Adapted from *Organization*, by Earnest Dale, pp. 11, 13. ©1967
AMACOM, a division of American Management Association, New York.

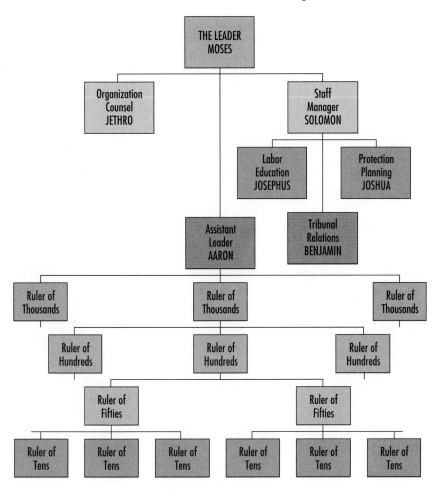

Figure 1.3
Organization in Biblical Times after Expansion
Source: Adapted from *Organization*, by Earnest Dale. ©1967 AMACOM, a division of American Management Association, New York.

International Expansion

Despite the widespread restructuring of organizations, however, many organizations are placing increased emphasis on doing business abroad. International growth makes communication all the more important and at the same time frequently more difficult.

When two people attempt to communicate, each may assume that the other person "shares the code" and that the message sent is very close to the message received. However, individuals from different cultural backgrounds frequently do not share the code and, therefore, must be careful not to miscommunicate. Many language and cultural influences can disturb the process of effectively getting a message across to people from a culture different from the sender's.

Even individuals who share the same language may have difficulty communicating. For example, if British service station attendants wanted to lift your bonnet, they would actually be asking to look under the hood of your car. If you told them that they could look under your hood, they might expect to find a gangster in the car. To most Americans, bonnets are something grandmothers wore at Easter. To buy bonnets, they went to a department store and rode the elevator to the ladies' hat section. In Great Britain grandmothers would have ridden the lift.

Sharing the code involves more than a shared language base; it involves the sharing of a culture. For example, women in the rural United States spoke of their decorative headgear as Easter bonnets, not simply as bonnets. They wore functional bonnets throughout the summer to protect against the sun. Such bonnets were invariably

Sharing the code also means sharing the culture.

homemade rather than purchased at a store with a lift, or elevator. To these women, a lift was a set of metal arms at the rear of tractors used to raise and lower implements. An elevator was a mechanism used to convey grain from a low elevation to a higher one.

Specialization of Tasks

In recent years many companies have become more diversified in the products or services they provide. Such diversification is intended to make a company more profitable by making it less susceptible to the ups and downs of one segment of the economy. As organizations change, whether through diversification or other means, management seeks ways of creating greater and greater efficiency. One way to increase efficiency is to make the individual worker's duties more specific. As duties are narrowed down, the consequences are that (1) the use of sublanguage or jargon increases and (2) individual workers become competent and more productive faster because less training is required for them to master their highly specialized jobs.

> The use of jargon will facilitate communication between specialists.

Business communication is affected significantly by the use of **jargon**, a verbal shortcut that allows specialists to communicate more easily among themselves. An accountant, for example, uses certain terms that are understood by other accountants and, in doing so, is able to be briefer and more specific. Consequently, jargon saves time and achieves understanding readily—as long as both individuals are specialists of the same sort (see Figure 1.4).

> Jargon is functional only when the communicators possess similar occupations and knowledge bases.

Problems occur when a specialist uses jargon to communicate with someone outside the discipline. Economists, for example, sometimes use the term "negative saver" to describe people who spend more than they earn. This term may convey the intended meaning to other economists but not to the general public. As an occupational group, computer specialists are especially criticized, often for good reason, for overusing jargon. Instead of telling the user to "Turn it off and start over," the manual will advise the user, "Deactivate the PC's energy input and then attempt a hard reboot of the system."[13] Instead of calling a computer "a computer," a specialist may refer to one as a "platform" or "server."[14] And the longer specialists work within their chosen fields, the more inclined they become to communicate with everyone else through jargon. When that happens, misunderstandings and frustrations inevitably follow.

At one time management researchers viewed specialization as a solution to many of the problems confronting business organizations. Through specialization many companies become more productive and more efficient.

Years ago, a single carpenter built most of a house alone. This was both time consuming and expensive, however, and work teams were developed. Individual work-

Figure 1.4
Jargon facilitates communication among specialists.
Source: Reginald Wickham.

ers became highly specialized. Rather than work on a single house from start to completion, an individual did one job and moved on to the next building. Through specialization it became possible to construct large housing developments using many workers in the time span formerly associated with building a single house.

Managers now realize that specialization is not the panacea they once thought. When management narrows jobs and turns people into specialists, these people become more dependent upon the efforts of other specialists. For specialization to be effective, whether in construction or in any other endeavor, there must be good communication among the specialists.

Without good communication, specialization will be ineffective.

THE DEVELOPMENT OF COMMUNICATION SKILLS

Many people consider oral communication to be as natural as breathing, eating, and sleeping. They maintain that with maturity humans naturally develop into proficient communicators. Each day we can observe examples of the falsity of that position.

Without training, one cannot reach full potential as a communicator.

Business leaders frequently bemoan the lack of communication skills among many college graduates. Workers often cite the inability to communicate as a prime shortcoming of their superior. The ability to communicate ranks high among attributes that employers seek in all potential employees. In a recent survey, corporate recruiters identified communication skills as the skills they most preferred in job applicants. (Leadership skills came in second.)[15]

Brenda Fernandez, for example, enjoyed working with numbers and was pleased when she was hired as a payroll clerk. She had always thought that a payroll clerk spent most of the day working with numbers. After a few months on the job, she said, "I like my work, but it's different from what I expected. At least half of my time is spent getting and giving information. Mathematical ability is important to this job, but the ability to communicate with others is just as important."

Until recently most people did not realize that effective communication requires that both the speaker and the listener have good communication skills. We spend almost 50 percent of our average workday listening to others. Listening ability can be improved, and several tape-recorded courses are available for this purpose. Listening is also the subject of many training courses conducted in business and governmental organizations.

Many communication problems are the fault of the receiver.

Some companies also provide remedial reading instruction for employees who are unable to read and to comprehend at an acceptable level. Certain employers consider reading to be so important that they provide this instruction completely at company expense. The worker attends these classes at full pay.

Through training, listening ability can be improved.

Companies and individuals daily pay the price for problems caused by a lack of skill in receiving information. For example, the drill press operator who did not listen carefully to the supervisor's explanation of how to work with a new alloy ruined $300 worth of drill bits and wasted $1,000 worth of raw materials. Several weeks after the human resources manager announced in a memo the provisions of a new group health insurance plan, it became apparent that several maintenance workers had misunderstood them.

Improper reception of information can be costly to an organization.

Geoffrey Nightingale, managing director of Burson Marsteller's Syner Genics Division, recommends the following rules for overcoming barriers to effective organizational communications:[16]

1. Always establish the context before trying to communicate anything. If the context is wrong, your communication will not make sense, no matter how bright and attentive you believe your audience to be. If the context is right, if it makes

sense, you will have the audience standing right up there alongside you as you communicate.

2. There can be no communication without both give and take. An internal communications system that allows for one-way communications only cannot possibly be effective. Set up a formal system that encourages two-way communications. Design and install programs and activities that ensure that two-way communications take place. And train your managers to become "active listeners" in their dealings with employees and others.

3. Too much communication is no communication at all. Get rid of the clutter, the "sacred-cow" reports, bulletins, newsletters. Consolidate and streamline. Make sure priority information gets priority treatment.

4. Foster the belief at all levels within your organization that behavior—what a person does, how he or she acts, what the company rewards and what it punishes—is much more important in terms of communicating, than what is formally written or what is said. If you're looking for a crusade, this is it. Make a personal commitment to see to it that the behavior of management matches their words and, then, follow that commitment through.

THE RELATIONSHIP BETWEEN COMMUNICATION AND ORGANIZATIONAL EFFECTIVENESS

The widespread recognition of the importance of communication has spawned much research in business communication. The researchers have discovered that effective communication enhances much of what is considered important in business organizations.

Improved communication usually leads to better morale.

Management considers worker morale to be an important indicator of a healthy organization. Better communication is usually accompanied by better morale. Managers who are concerned about low morale should create additional communication opportunities for workers.

A relationship exists between communication and such factors as job satisfaction and relationships with coworkers.

A close link exists between job satisfaction and morale. Research in business organizations has revealed that interpersonal relationships among workers greatly influence job satisfaction. When workers believe they are actually a part of their work group, they will be more satisfied than if they feel left out. Workers are also more likely to be satisfied with their jobs if they are satisfied with the amount of information that they receive on the job. Communication is therefore a vital part of the manager's job.

Employee Involvement Practices

Communication occurs in a variety of settings and under varying circumstances. The variability in the communication process dictates that a manager must adopt any one of several roles to remain effective. These include **interpersonal roles**, which focus on interpersonal relationships; **informational roles**, which recognize the manager's vital position in the receipt and dissemination of information; and **decisional roles**, which focus on the essential managerial activity of decision making. The one element common to these roles is that effective communication is necessary if the manager is to perform effectively.

The concept of **management by walking around (MBWA)** was intended to enable managers to increase their contact time with subordinates, suppliers, and customers and to improve communication between those parties.[17] MBWA led to informal communication, which became the stimulus for managerial decision making as well as the vehicle for feedback to all of the individuals who contribute to organizational success.

In recent years there has been a move toward increased employee involvement by allowing workers to make decisions rather than merely providing input to managers. Known as employee **empowerment,** it is a practice that is coming to be viewed as crucial if a company is to remain competitive. As of 1993, approximately 89 percent of Fortune 500 companies had established some form of worker involvement program.[18]

This new emphasis on empowerment provides an additional challenge to managers and other employees who seek to communicate effectively. The **self-directed work team (SDWT)**, for example, has become a major component in many empowerment programs. SDWTs are comprised of employees and a team leader who oversees the team activities. Unlike traditional work teams, however, the team leader does not exercise veto power over decisions made by the team. Communication between the team leader and team members ideally is face-to-face and highly interactive in order to optimize the exchange of information. Managing by walking around and employee empowerment programs represent contemporary management thinking, and together they illustrate the direction in which management practices are moving. In 1995 an estimated 3 million Americans were telecommuting to work, and the number is increasing by 20 percent a year.[19]

A Changing Workforce

Some dramatic changes in the workforce have had an impact on communication in organizations. The sheer growth in the size of the workforce has been impressive, as has its growing diversity. In 1970 the civilian labor force in the United States totaled 82.8 million workers; in 1990 it was 125.1 million.

The composition of the labor force has shifted. For example, in 1980, 51.5 percent of all women held a job while 77.4 percent of all men worked. By 1992, the figures were 57.8 percent and 75.6 percent, and they are expected to be 62 percent and 76 percent by 2000.[20] The proportion of African-Americans, Hispanics, and Asians in the workforce will also increase as it increases in the general population (see Figure 1.5).

An increasingly diverse workforce provides new challenges for the communicator.

Such changes plus many others contribute to the dynamism in today's business organizations. Much organizational change, however, can be controlled and managed through effective communication.

> ✔ *CHECKLIST for Employee Involvement Practices*
>
> ____ MBWA is informal.
>
> ____ The focus of MBWA is internal (employees) as well as external (customers, suppliers, and competitors).
>
> ____ MBWA involves actively listening to what others are saying.
>
> ____ It is demanding in terms of time and energy.
>
> ____ It is a mindset that the manager must adopt, not just a "gimmick" to solve particular problems.
>
> ____ Empowerment allows workers to make more decisions.
>
> ____ Self-directed work teams are a component in many employee empowerment programs.
>
> ____ Communication between the team leader and team members is highly interactive.

THE QUALITY MOVEMENT

Since early in the 1980s "quality" has become a watchword in many U.S. business organizations. **Total Quality Management (TQM)** programs have been implemented in thousands of companies of all sizes. Companies such as Motorola, Intel, Hewlett-Packard, and General Electric have sought to make excellence the norm. Approaches to quality improvement vary greatly, but organizations of all types, whether manufacturers or service providers, have raised the banner of quality. Some manufacturers, for example, have initiated "zero-defects" programs. The Hampton Inn organization sought to guarantee quality by offering refunds to customers dissatisfied for any reason with their stay. Surveys of customers showed that they were impressed with the offer. Refunds given in 1993 totaled $1.1 million. It is estimated, however, that the program brought in an additional $11 million. A byproduct of the program was that employee

Figure 1.5

A Changing Population
Source: Reprinted from
*DMA 1994/95 Statistical
Fact Book U.S. Bureau of
the Census*, 221; and from
*DMA 1992/93 Statistical
Fact Book U.S. Bureau of
the Census*, p. 200.

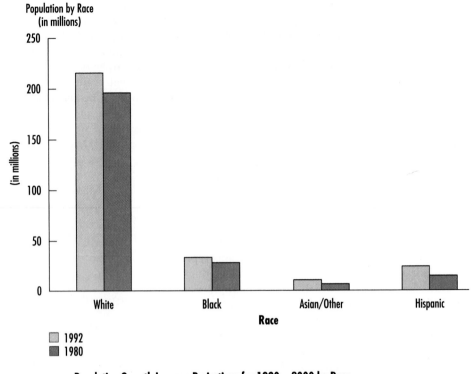

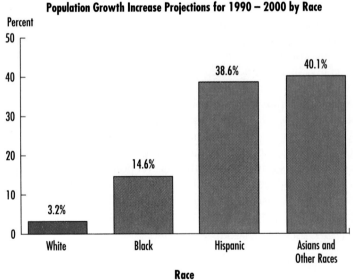

job satisfaction also rose. Employee turnover in 1993 fell to 50 percent, whereas three years prior to that it had been 117 percent.[21]

The success of the U.S. auto industry in recent years is attributed in part to its adherence to the principles of quality management. From its inception in 1981, Saturn empowered its employees and committed the organization to quality.[22] The big three U.S. auto makers are all deeply involved in quality management.

There are several common threads through all quality management programs. Meeting the customer's requirements is of the highest priority, and there must be evidence of continuous improvement. Work teams are heavily used for planning and problem solving. Developing a climate of openness and trust through the organization is a prerequisite for the success of any quality program.[23] It is obvious that all of the common threads involve communication. The success of any quality management program will be commensurate with the quality of the communication practiced within the organization.

In recent years companies have begun to redefine the concept of quality and to focus only on quality changes that their customers actually want. **Return on quality (ROQ)**, which means that any corporate spending on improving quality must contribute to financial performance, is now often being emphasized. For example, AT&T requires that any new quality proposal show that the effort will yield at least a 30 percent drop in defects and a ten percent return on investment.[24]

The Interpersonal Environment

Environmental changes within organizations cause repercussions that extend beyond organizational boundaries. Pressures emanating from the organizational environment affect the interpersonal environment and thereby influence our relationships and interactions with others.

Some of the changes in the workforce have resulted in a greater diversity of workers who possess fewer shared goals and interests. This heterogeneous workforce represents differing frames of reference. With reduced commonalities communication problems are more prevalent.

Changing lifestyles affect us both interpersonally and organizationally. For some workers, a growing interest in leisure-time activities may result in a declining interest in their jobs. On the other hand, the word **workaholic** has become a common part of our language to describe people who become obsessed with their work to the point that other aspects of their lives suffer.

Personal problems, even though removed from the workplace, have an effect on job performance. For example, a person going through a divorce may seek to alleviate pressures through altered on-the-job behaviors. Because family problems in general affect one's work, repercussions from such problems will affect the work environment.

Coping with stress is one of the challenges of modern living. Some sources of stress are occupational; others are not. Regardless of source, however, the effects are far-reaching. The term **burnout** is used to describe exhaustion caused by excessive demands on one's energy or strength.

Social phenomena such as divorce, leisure-time pursuits, or burnout profoundly affect every dimension of life. Such phenomena intensify communication problems of both an interpersonal and an organizational nature.

> Communication problems are intensified in a heterogeneous workforce.

> Personal problems affect job performance.

THE EVOLUTION OF COMMUNICATION TECHNOLOGY

Our society is communication oriented. In the fiscal year 1991, the United States Postal Service (USPS) delivered over 165 billion pieces of mail, an increase of 34 billion pieces in approximately ten years. By the year 2001, the annual volume will have leaped to a staggering 250 billion pieces. The USPS, the nation's largest civilian employer, now has about 750,000 full-time employees.[25] Notwithstanding the present strength of our postal system, competitors such as Federal Express, grossing $7.39 billion in 1993, and United Parcel Service, grossing $17.5 billion in the same year, have grabbed large pieces of the delivery pie.[26, 27] Approximately $11 billion is spent each year on overnight delivery services.[28] And rapidly becoming more popular are electronic messaging services, voice mail, fax, and E-mail. The number of cellular phone subscribers is also growing at ever increasing rates. Between 1991 and 1992 the number of subscribers grew from 7.5 million to more than 11 million.[29]

Evolution versus Revolution

Each technological change that we have witnessed has heralded the coming of a "new age" in communication—the end of communication as we know it, the beginning of an "information revolution." With the advent of radio in 1922 and, again, with television in 1946, oracles predicted the end of the newspaper. More recently, we heard prophecies of the demise of motion picture attendance as home videos made it unnecessary to leave the home for movie viewing. Although we have seen a significant decrease in the

BOXED IN

AN ETHICAL DILEMMA

Terry had been an above-average employee for the three years he had worked at Ellis Laboratories. As an Assistant Technician his job entailed a variety of duties, all of them pertaining to the establishment and maintenance of the laboratory in a manner that met the standards dictated by the nature of the current research project and the wishes of his supervisor, Bill Cowling.

Four months ago two workers had individually complained to Bill that Terry was not doing his fair share of work. When Bill talked to Terry about this he learned that Terry had been diagnosed with a degenerative bone condition that, while not life threatening, would permanently reduce his strength and his ability to do heavy work. Bill then confirmed these details through Terry's doctor. Terry requested that Bill not tell any co-workers of his condition since he didn't want to be viewed as different from the others, and Bill assured Terry that he would tell no one about this.

Since that time Bill has been giving Terry less physically demanding tasks whenever possible. When new supplies were delivered, for example, Terry was given the job of checking the invoice while his co-workers unloaded the delivery truck. In the past the duty of checking the invoice had been rotated among the ten group members, most of whom were by now openly expressing their dissatisfaction with their workloads. Morale of the group has dropped, and the work habits of the other group members have deteriorated.

Questions
1. What do you regard as the main issues in this situation?
2. What options are open to Bill?
3. If you were Terry what would you do? Why?
4. Identify the most likely repercussions of your action. How would you deal with those repercussions?

number of newspaper firms and a stabilization of average weekly movie attendance (1975-1994), during the same time frames we have also witnessed an increase in newspaper circulation.

What we typically see happening is not extinction of media dimensions, but evolution of their forms and how they fit together. This is occurring at faster rates than in the past. The telephone took 70 years and newspapers more than 100 years to reach 50 percent market penetration, but television took just 8 years and VCRs 11 years to do as well. Rather than replacing older forms of technology, new information tools are supplementing and complementing them. Printed media continue to flourish but now we collect, order, edit, print, and sometimes deliver information via computer electronics. The following example illustrates the speed of electronic communication. A question was raised in the *Atlanta Constitution* concerning how an emergency (911) telephone call would be handled if the caller spoke little or no English. The answer:

> When 911 operators determine that the person on the line cannot speak English, they immediately contact the "language line service," and a three-way conversation ensues. This line is subscribed to by the 911 services in most major cities, including Atlanta. The service, based in Monterey, CA, has hundreds of interpreters, speaking more than 140 languages, who are available on a 24-hour basis all over the country. A spokesperson for the service, which is run by AT&T, said a typical call can be handled in less than a minute.[30]

We can anticipate further changes in the use of printed media not only as a result of technological changes, but also in response to growing environmental concerns pertaining to the destruction of trees, energy shortages, and the disposal of wastes.

The Information Superhighway and the Business Organization

Also referred to as "Infobahn" and "I-way," the **Information Superhighway** is a worldwide computer network. It links together the large commercial on-line services (like Prodigy, America Online, and CompuServe) with thousands of smaller networks. The Superhighway, better known as the Internet, is growing at a phenomenal rate. In 1983 there were approximately 33,000 computers in the world that were connected to the Internet. By 1995 the number was 20 million.[31] The growth in the number of networks is equally impressive. In March 1993 there were 10,000 networks on the Internet; by November of that same year the number had grown to 34,000.[32]

In 1969 the U.S. Defense Department developed a computer system to facilitate the exchange of information between the military and university researchers. It eventually provided a worldwide link for universities, government facilities, and corporations. As the relatively small number of users began to use the system for private messages or public announcements, the **Internet** was born.[33]

Computers that process and store tremendous amounts of information have truly detonated an **information explosion**. Equipped with a high-speed printer, a computer can turn out reams of paper daily and, in the process, inundate management with information.

Modern technology has contributed greatly to organizational effectiveness, but problems remain.

As costs of computer hardware and software dropped, as software increased in ease of use, and as people became familiar with its use and capabilities, incorporation of computer technology into the business arena skyrocketed. Estimates for the number of personal computers in U.S. businesses rose from 2.6 million in 1982 to 51 million in 1993.[34]

Modern technology has contributed greatly to management's access to information. It has also enhanced management's ability to transmit information quickly and economically. Modern technology has not, however, replaced the human communicator. If anything, computerization has increased the importance of the human commu-

Because of computerization, a greater need exists for skilled communicators than ever before.

nicator's role, for it is the manager who must ultimately determine the information to be retrieved and those to whom it should be sent.

Growing numbers of organizations now employ a **director of communication**, a job title virtually unheard of until recently. The director of communication is responsible for managing the flow of information within the organization and for solving communication problems. No matter how sophisticated technology becomes, individuals who are skilled in communication and aware of the vital components in the communication process will always be needed.

Telecommunications

Given the importance of time, accuracy, and money in today's business environment, an improved process of mail communication was inevitable. The traditional method of typing a letter and sending it by U.S. mail provides the sender with a confirmed hard copy for transmission but is costly in terms of staff and delivery time. If a document requires input from reviewers in other locations and is sent by Federal Express, transmission and manpower costs will quickly add up in addition to the elapsed time.

In less than 30 minutes a **facsimile (fax) machine** can send a ten-page document to four different locations. With turnaround, all participants can have a copy of the completed document in a reasonable period of time at a reasonable cost. Fax machines use an electronic scanner to transmit graphic images.

The telephone also transmits messages quickly, and it provides a means of immediate feedback to the sender. However, experts estimate that about 50 to 70 percent of all calls are not completed, resulting in games of telephone tag. Telephone discussions are often subject to miscommunication. Additionally, staff must usually prepare follow-up documents.

Computer-based **voice mail** systems process voice messages rather than text messages. The sender records the spoken message into the machine for the receiver to listen to, thereby saving transcribing time. It serves to eliminate telephone tag, to save time by broadcasting messages to a group, and to lower secretarial costs. Disadvantages include high initial costs, the resistance of individuals both to deliver and to listen to recorded messages of substantial length, and the lack of a permanent document.

The generic name for noninteractive communication of text, data, image, or voice messages utilizing telecommunications links is **electronic mail (E-mail)**. Despite its noninteractive nature, E-mail is a means of communication between people and can be responded to immediately upon retrieval of a message. The costs of this technology vary based on time of day and speed of modem.

Both facsimile and voice mail are examples of electronic mail. The benefits of electronic mail include speed (though not as fast as a telephone), low cost, and increased precision and control. When preparing for a meeting, background material (which often constitutes 80 percent of the discussion time) can be distributed ahead of time using E-mail, freeing up the meeting time for more crucial issues.

Videotext is an interactive two-way system for sending and receiving graphic or textual information through a computer interface by electronic means. Examples of videotext include CompuServe, The Source, and Dow Jones News/Retrieval, which offer access to a variety of services for the business user.

The Extended Office

Telecommunications has yielded the means for releasing individuals from the confines of the office while providing them with a way to continue operations from virtually any place and at any time they choose. Sometimes referred to as the **"virtual office,"** it is a business strategy that allows people to work where and when they work best. Gil

Gordon, management consultant and proponent of such flexible work arrangements, believes that " . . . this may be the most radical redefinition of the workplace since the Industrial Revolution. . . ."[35] Freed from the headaches and costs of office dress, commuting, business lunches, and idle chatter, employees can perform more work in less time and feel better about it. Employers save as well in the form of less required office space and more efficient communications with employees. Society in general profits from having fewer people in automobiles on congested highways, using precious fuel and contributing to air pollution.

To illustrate, Jennifer Chiu is a morning person. By 6 A.M., she is in her home office, reviewing her E-mail and either typing in responses or forwarding messages for further action. She works steadily until 10:30, when she breaks to dress for lunch with a client. From her car, she makes calls to her boss and checks on the status of a job she sent to marketing. Having spent so much time alone this week, Jennifer thoroughly enjoys her client's company at lunch and her warmth contributes to making a big sale for her firm. She spends the afternoon completing a major report and faxes it into the office before closing time. Following a two-mile run and a light supper, she takes advantage of lower phone rates and begins downloading needed information from a large commercial information network. She calls it a day at about 9 P.M., having put in nearly 13 hours of steady work. She sleeps well, knowing that one more equally productive day will allow her to enjoy a peaceful four-day weekend in the country.

Initially, telecommuting was an executive-dominated process or a way programmers might choose to do business. Today thousands of employees from such major firms as J.C. Penney, Pacific Bell, and Travelers are participating in company-supported telecommunications. Additionally, self-employed individuals, particularly single parents and handicapped people who would otherwise face daily impediments to employment, are enjoying the flexibility of this alternative work style.

There has been tremendous growth in the number of telecommuters, and that is reflected in the increased use of cellular phones. In 1987 there were 1.2 million cellular phone subscribers. In 1994 there were 24.1 million.[36]

Key Terms

- internal communication
- formal communication
- informal communication
- external communication
- advertising
- downsizing
- jargon
- interpersonal roles
- informational roles
- decisional roles
- management by walking around (MBWA)
- empowerment
- self-directed work teams (SDWT)
- Total Quality Management (TQM)
- return on quality (ROQ)
- workaholic
- burnout
- Information Superhighway
- Internet
- information explosion
- director of communication
- facsimile (fax) machine
- voice mail
- electronic mail (E-mail)
- videotext
- virtual office

Summary

Review Questions

1. What is meant by the pervasive nature of communication?

2. Why are humans sometimes referred to as social animals?

3. Which type of costs, monetary or nonmonetary, can be more accurately computed? Why?

4. Define internal communication.

5. Define external communication.

6. Compare formal channels to informal channels.

7. Explain how task specialization affects communication between individuals within an organization.

8. Explain the relationship between organizational downsizing and empowerment.

CASE

Too Much of a Good Thing

J. Timothy Lake, Equitable Real Estate Investment Management, Inc.

Electronic mail (E-mail) has revolutionized business communication by enabling the sender to transmit information virtually instantaneously and reducing the need for time-consuming paperwork. While E-mail is still in its infancy, it has the potential to be an effective tool for managing communication. Since its founding in 1975, Microsoft Corporation has emerged as a major force in the computer software industry through such popular programs as DOS, Windows, Excel, and Word. It is not surprising, therefore, that such a pacesetter would have successfully integrated E-mail into its communication culture, but the extent of the integration is impressive.

Microsoft encourages its employees to express their views on company matters via E-mail to anyone in the company, including founder and CEO Bill Gates. Upper-level managers and executives have made it a high priority to respond promptly to E-mail messages, and this is intended to give subordinates a stronger sense of connection with senior decision makers. Although this open access sometimes results in long-winded complaints and harsh criticism (known as "flame mail"), the ensuing climate has helped Microsoft deal with many company issues better.

Despite the advantages of E-mail, Microsoft is now faced with a dilemma. Having more than doubled in size in the past four years, the company now (1994) has more than 14,000 employees. Meeting the obligation to respond quickly to E-mail from employees has become increasingly difficult for senior management. Executives can receive as many as 100 messages a day. The situation became particularly cumbersome for Bill Gates in early 1994 after *New Yorker* magazine published his E-mail address. Gates wasthen inundated with more than 5,000 messages from outside the company, in addition to his normal intracompany mail. To deal with the influx, he was forced to develop a "bozo filter" that weeded out or redirected unimportant messages and flame mail.

Case Questions

1. What should Microsoft do? How can it maintain open lines of communication without placing an undue burden on top management?
2. What do you think of using E-mail in the way Microsoft is?
3. What type of companies would benefit most from such openness?
4. Should Microsoft try to curtail "flame mail"? If so, how should it do it?

CASE

What Happened to My Luggage?

David B. Parsons, Lakehead University, Thunder Bay, Ontario, Canada

In June 1990, John and Anne Davis flew from Calgary to Winnipeg, where they were to catch a connecting flight to Thunder Bay. Once they arrived in Thunder Bay, they planned to rent a car and drive 450 kilometers to an isolated northwestern Ontario logging town to attend John's sister's wedding.

In the luggage hold of the aircraft were not only their clothes but also wedding presents and the bridal gown, which John's mother had worn at her own wedding. Approximately ten minutes before the flight was due to land, Jim Richards, a flight steward, noticed wisps of smoke coming through the floor in the rear galley.

Having been notified of the problem, the captain asked all passengers to leave the plane when it landed because a minor technical problem had to be corrected. John and Anne left the plane and waited the scheduled three hours in the terminal for their flight to Thunder Bay. What they didn't know was that all the luggage in the hold was either destroyed or severely damaged by a flash fire that had erupted in the luggage hold during the flight.

When John and Anne landed in Thunder Bay, their luggage and that of 40 other passengers failed to appear on the conveyor belt. When John and Anne explained their dilemma to the airport manager, they were told to report their luggage as lost. The Thunder Bay airport hadn't been informed about the fire in Winnipeg. Consequently, John and Anne had to leave for the wedding without their luggage, the gifts, or the gown. They did not find out about the destruction of their belongings for six days after the incident.

Case Questions

1. Should the passengers have been told about the fire while the plane was in the air? Explain your answer.

2. Should the passengers whose luggage was destroyed in the fire have been told about it while they waited in the airport for their connecting flights?

3. Should the Winnipeg airport have informed the airports of destination about the damaged and destroyed luggage?

4. Assuming the role of John or Anne Davis, write a letter to the airline expressing your concerns about the way the situation was handled.

Notes

1. *The Wall Street Journal*, October 14, 1993, B1.

2. *Atlanta Constitution*, June 15, 1994, F1.

3. *The Milwaukee Journal*, August 14, 1994, D2.

4. Ray Wild, ed., *How to Manage: By More than 100 of the World's Leading Business Experts* (New York: Facts on File Publications), 1985, 89-90.

5. Mary W. Shelley, *Frankenstein* (London: Oxford University Press, 1969), 112.

6. *American Management Association Seminars Catalog*, October 1995–June 1996 (New York: American Management Association, 1994).

7. Office of Management and Budget, U.S. General Services Administration, U.S. Dept. of Commerce, *Information Resources Management Plan of the Federal Government*, December 1993.

8. *Dartnell Institute of Business Research Target Survey* (Chicago: Dartnell Corporation, 1994).

9. William J. Corbett, "Internal Communication: Where It All Starts," *International Public Relations Review* 12 (1988): 15-25.

10. C.L. Martin and Denise T. Smart, "Consumer Experiences Calling Toll-Free Corporate Hotlines," *Journal of Business Communication* 31, no. 3 (April 1994), 195.

11. "HR Paints a Bleak Portrait of Downsizing Survivors," *HR Focus*, May 1993, 24.

12. Diane Filipowski, "Downsizing Isn't Always Rightsizing," *Personnel Journal*, November 1993, 71.

13. L. Paul Quellette, "Why IS Is Not Well Understood," *Datamation* 38, no. 23 (November 15, 1992), 128.

14. John Kavanagh, "Survey of A-Z of Computing," *Financial Times*, April 26, 1994, IX.

15. "Portrait of the Ideal MBA," *The Penn Stater*, September/October 1992, 31.

16. Geoffrey Nightingale, "Communicating from a Standing Position," *International Public Relations Review* 12 (1988).

17. Tom Peters and Robert Waterman, *In Search of Excellence* (New York: Harper & Row, 1982).

18. Editorial, *Journal of Commerce*, March 26, 1993.

19. Scott LaFee, "Computers Keep on Multiplying," *San Diego Union-Tribune*, April 26, 1995, E3.

20. *Statistical Abstract of the United States*, 1993, 393.

21. "Making Quality Pay," *Business Week*, August 8, 1994, 56.

22. David A. Aaker, "Building a Brand: The Saturn Story," *California Management Review*, Winter 1994, 114-133.

23. Watten H. Schmidt and Jerome P. Finnigan, *TQ Manager* (San Francisco: Jossey-Bass, 1993), 5.

24. "Making Quality Pay," 56.

25. *Direct Marketing Association's Statistical Fact Book* (New York: DMA, 1992), 295-310.

26. *Standard & Poor's Stock Reports* (New York: NYSE, August 1993), vol. D-K.

27. *United Parcel Service Annual Report*, December 31, 1994, 25.

28. Jeanette Borzo, "Tools Resurrect Hope for Paperless Office Concept," *Info World* 15, issue 24 (June 24, 1993), 124.

29. U.S. Bureau of the Census, *Statistical Abstract of the United States: 1992* (Washington, DC: 1992).

30. Betty Parham, "Q&A on the News," *Atlanta Constitution*, August 29, 1994, A2.

31. LaFee, E3.

32. Mary Lu Carnvale, "World Wide Web," *The Wall Street Journal*, November 15, 1993.

33. Philip Elmer Dewitt, "Battle for the Soul of the Internet," *Time*, July 25, 1994, 50-56.

34. *Statistical Abstract of the United States: 1995*, 671.

35. Sue Shellenbarger, "Overwork, Low Morale Vex the Mobile Office," *The Wall Street Journal*, August 17, 1994, B1.

36. *Statistical Abstract of the United States: 1995*, 905.

Chapter 2

The Nature of Communication

Item: Commuters in New York City have long complained about how difficult it is to understand announcements made by the driver over the public address system in the subway cars. Riders frequently get off at the wrong stop because they have misunderstood the message. The hum and crackle of the poorly maintained sound systems produce the same clarity experienced at the drive-through window of the average fast-food restaurant. The New York City Transit Authority expressed both an awareness of the problem and hope for the future by placing this message in its subway cars:

"You m ight n t belive this, but we real y are w rking on the public addr ss sy t m.

Item: The owner of a restaurant telephones her supplier and tells him that she wants her order of Thanksgiving turkeys cut in half. When the order arrives, she is shocked to receive the same number of turkeys that she ordered last year—with each bird cut neatly in half.

Item: An employee in an organization is told that his work is outstanding and he is going to receive the highest raise among the five people in the office. Later the employee finds out that his raise was just a few dollars more per month than the others. Even more significant is that the person who got the lowest raise says the supervisor has promised to have a private office built for her. The other four will continue to work in one large open area. What are the rewards for outstanding work?

As these situations show, there are many ways of communicating. Often what we hear is not what the other person said. What we say can frequently be interpreted in an entirely different manner by the listener.

Most of this book will focus on developing effective communication skills. This chapter provides a theoretical framework for the chapters that follow.

THE NATURE AND PURPOSE OF COMMUNICATION

A basic goal of any organization is survival. If campus organizations fail to meet the needs of their members, they cease to exist. Many student government organizations on campuses in the United States have gone out of business because members found that the organization no longer met any particular goals. In private business a major goal is making a profit. When businesses fail to make a profit, they eventually cease to function.

The major factor enabling organizations to meet their goals and continue to exist is the behavior of their people. The judgments, decisions, and efforts put forth by employees determine to a large extent the profitability of a business. Admittedly, some other factors—such as government intervention and regulation, competing businesses, and natural disasters—also affect profits, but the behavior of people in organizations has great influence. The fundamental question is one of motivation. How do we motivate others to behave in the desired manner?

Just as the behavior of others affects us, our behavior affects others. For example, have you ever found an item at a garage sale that really caught your interest? "That's a good deal for the price," you said to yourself, "but it's more than I have to spend." The transaction may have occurred as follows:

"That item over there that you have marked $10—does it work?"

"Sure it works; it's brand new."

"If it works I'd be interested in it for $5, but I don't think it's worth much more than that."

"You kidding? Those sell for $20 new and that's if you can find one. I got a new one for Christmas. That's why I'm selling this one. I'd have to have at least $8 for it."

"Yeah. It's probably worth that, but I only have $7.25 with me. If you'll take that, I'll buy it."

"Okay."

"Wow!" you thought. "I'd have paid the whole $10 if I'd had to. What an opportunity!"

"I'd have let that old thing go for $5. Hope that person comes back," the seller thought.

Just as your behavior influenced the seller, so did the seller's behavior influence you. Interpersonal behavior elicits responses. Communication is not one-way.

The Influencing of Behavior

To understand how we influence the behavior of others we need a brief examination of reinforcing and aversive stimuli.[1] Reinforcing stimuli are pleasant, and in many cases we seek them out. Reinforcing stimuli are experienced through our senses in such forms as the taste of good food or drink, the sight of an attractive man or woman, or the smell of perfume or cologne. This type of stimulus is positive and can have a motivating effect on behavior. It is sometimes called positive reinforcement.

Aversive stimuli have quite the opposite effect on our behavior. Aversive stimuli are also sensory experiences and can include the taste of rotten food, a nasty smell, or the sight of something or someone we find ugly. These stimuli influence our behavior in a negative way in that we seek to avoid aversive stimuli. They are sometimes called negative reinforcement.

Perhaps some of the most forceful stimuli, both reinforcing and aversive, come to us as auditory verbal stimuli, those that arrive through the sense of hearing. For example, the statement "You are doing good work" can be a reinforcing stimulus that will encourage long, hard work. Likewise, "You really muffed that one" can have an aversive effect that will cause the person to reduce effort and perhaps skip a day of work. Frequently, aversive stimuli may cause an employee to explore other employment options.

What is reinforcing to one person may be aversive to another. For example, drinking blood is aversive to most people in this country, but in some parts of the world it is reinforcing. Or perhaps more realistically, some find drinking alcoholic beverages aversive, while others find this activity reinforcing. Any stimulus can be reinforcing or aversive depending on the person and the situation. The basic question is, how does a stimulus become reinforcing or aversive?

Any stimulus paired or linked with a (positive) reinforcer becomes a reinforcing stimulus. Any stimulus paired or linked with an aversive (negative) stimulus becomes an aversive stimulus. An example of a reinforcing stimulus is found in advertisements in statements such as "Eating yogurt leads to a long life." An example of an aversive stimulus pairing is part of the learning process of a young child who puts a finger on the hot stove; the pain in the finger (stimulus) is associated with the stove, which is now avoided (aversion).

Many important pairings take place in conversations. The statement, "Karen thinks you are doing a bad job," will cause you to react less favorably to Karen the next time you see her. Likewise, the statement, "John says you are one of our best sales reps," will be reinforcing to how you behave with John.

There are three important points in this discussion of stimuli. First, it is the behavior of people that enables most organizations to meet their goals.

Communication is the major way we influence the behavior of others.

Second, behavior is greatly influenced by reinforcing and aversive stimuli. Third, some of the most powerful reinforcing and aversive stimuli come to us through the auditory sense, the sense of hearing. Communication is the major way we influence the behavior of our business colleagues. Indeed, the verbal and nonverbal communication of managers influences profits more than any other factor.

✔ CHECKLIST for Influencing Behavior

____ Behavior is influenced by reinforcing and aversive stimuli.

____ Reinforcing stimuli have a positive impact on behavior.

____ Aversive stimuli have a negative impact on behavior.

____ Auditory stimuli are some of the most forceful.

____ A paired stimulus produces either a reinforcing or an aversive reaction.

Superior–Subordinate Communication

Internal communication flows either horizontally or vertically within the organization. **Horizontal communication** is the communication between peers (people on the same level in the organization). **Vertical communication** is between superiors and subordinates. Communication from the superior to the subordinate is called downward communication and that from the subordinate to the superior is called upward communication.

Perhaps the most influential element of the relationship between superiors and subordinates is the communication climate. Several factors affect upward communication. The subordinate's willingness to communicate accurate information to a superior is affected by the subordinate's desire to climb the organizational ladder. Believing that the superior may "kill" the messenger who brings bad news, the subordinate may distort the message to disassociate himself or herself from the bad news. This distortion is a result of the subordinate's upward mobility aspirations. The end product of this behavior is that superiors are often either poorly informed or uninformed about organizational ills.

Subordinates may also distort upward communication if they perceive their superior as having little or no influence with persons higher in the organization, or if they do not trust their superior. If a subordinate thinks the boss cannot influence other superiors, the subordinate is more likely to distort the information passed on to the superior.

Other barriers to upward communication include physical distance between the superior and the subordinate, too many layers of the organization that require the information, and the lack of tradition of upward communication. These barriers give rise to the principle of information inertia: once information has come to rest at a certain level of the organization, it will tend to remain there.

Downward communication is usually job related.

Downward communication is usually job related and not personal. A major shortcoming of downward communication is this depersonalization of the superior-subordinate relationship.

Robert Half International, a large placement firm, polled 150 executives from the nation's largest companies regarding why employees quit their jobs. The executives felt that these were the main reasons:

Reason	Identified By
Lack of recognition and praise	34%
Low compensation	29%
Limited authority	13%
Personality conflicts	8%

According to Half, the firm's founder, "Praising accomplishments provides psychological rewards that are critical to satisfaction in any professional setting."[2] Superiors should sincerely praise, and thereby reinforce, their subordinates in front of other people. This study suggests that it is the absence of such reinforcing behavior that contributes to employee turnover.

SEVEN MYTHS AND REALITIES ABOUT THE NATURE OF COMMUNICATION

To understand the nature of communication, we must confront some of the common misunderstandings, or myths.

1. Myth: We communicate only when we consciously and deliberately choose to communicate.

We may think we control our communication. For example, we decide to send a letter to a prospective employee making a job offer or we decide to call a staff meeting to discuss an important problem. In such instances we consciously and deliberately control the way we communicate. However, we are often surprised when our communication brings a different result than we had anticipated. The prospective employee may reply that he has already accepted a job at a lower salary with a lesser firm. Why? Several days had passed after his employment interview without any word from the company. He assumed he was not going to get an offer or, at least, he was not the company's first choice. He had received a message of disinterest just as if it had been communicated face-to-face.

Reality: We communicate many times when we are not consciously aware that we are communicating.

Continuing the example, the reason that several days passed before the applicant received the job offer was that one secretary was ill and the other was busy preparing a lengthy report. The reality of the situation is that the employer offering the job had communicated a message he was unaware of. Indeed, all of us frequently communicate messages that we do not intend to communicate.

2. Myth: Words mean the same thing to our listener as they do to us.

The basis for this myth is that we assume words have the same meanings for everyone. In a large organization, for example, one of the sales representatives phones in a special order and asks that it be shipped right away. On the following Monday, the customer reports that the order has not been received. The rep learns that it was not shipped until Friday. She complains to the shipping department supervisor, who replies, "We did ship it right away." To the rep, "right away" meant the same day. To the person who receives dozens of calls daily demanding "Ship it now" or "Ship it yesterday," the phrase "right away" meant within the week.

To illustrate further, when the word "apple" is spoken, some will hear or see a red apple, some a yellow apple, still others perhaps will think of an apple pie, and still others will think of a computer. Why does the same word mean different things to different people?

> Reality: Words do not really have meanings; meaning is dependent on our experiences and perceptions.

In the example, "right away" meant different amounts of time to the sales representative and to the shipping supervisor because of their different perceptions. Because of the myth that words have specific meanings, we assume that others will get exactly the same message from words that we do. The reality is that words mean different things to different people.

Words have denotative and connotative aspects. Denotative meanings are those that are commonly agreed upon or standard, such as the definitions in dictionaries. Thus, "chair" yields the denotative meanings of a support one sits on, usually alone, probably having a back and four legs. However, when you internalize—that is, add your own meaning to words—you are introducing the connotative aspect. "Chair," for example, might bring to mind a dentist's chair or a barber chair if your day's activities include them. We seldom share the same connotative meanings.

3. Myth: We communicate primarily with words.

People tend to believe that a communicated message is one that is either spoken or written. For example, assume you go to your professor's office to discuss a topic for your term paper. The professor says, "The outline looks good. Go ahead with the paper." You feel somewhat uneasy, however, because she looked over the outline very quickly and several times glanced at her watch, as if she had something more important on her mind. Nevertheless, you proceed with the paper.

> Reality: The majority of the messages we communicate are based not on words but rather on nonverbal symbols.

The professor in the example communicated nonverbally. In recent years we have become much more aware of nonverbal communication. Books such as *Body Language* and *How to Read a Person Like a Book* show that our tone of voice, eye contact, body movement, or even the clothes we wear communicate much more than the words we use. Albert Mehrabian, an expert on nonverbal communication, has calculated that as much as 93 percent of our attitudes are formed by nonverbal messages, while only 7 percent are the result of verbal stimuli.[3]

Frequently our nonverbal communication undermines our verbal communication. For example, at a lecture the speaker begins by saying, "I am pleased to be here and to talk about my favorite topic—human motivation." However, his nonverbal communication denies it: he wears a wrinkled suit, he looks at his notes instead of the audience, and he speaks in a monotone. The real message that has been communicated is that it is going to be a long and boring afternoon.

When there is a contradiction between what is communicated verbally and what is communicated nonverbally, why do we usually choose to believe the nonverbal message? It is easier for people to manipulate words than to manipulate nonverbal behavior. Most of us believe that nonverbal messages more accurately reflect what a person really is thinking. There is truth in the old adage, "Actions speak louder than words."

4. Myth: Nonverbal communication is the silent language.

The term body language is often misused in place of nonverbal communication. Many think nonverbal communication is never heard—that it is only seen.

Reality: Nonverbal communication is received through all the five senses.

Gestures, body positions, and the way we walk are silent nonverbal messages—and so are tone of voice, the clapping of hands, and the touch of a handshake. Nonverbal messages can be felt, heard, smelled, and tasted, as well as seen.

5. Myth: Communication is a one-way activity.

The basis for this myth is the assumption that our message moves uninterrupted to the receiver and ends there. All of us at one time or another have had people communicate in this fashion, talking at us rather than with us. For example, a supervisor uses a tone of voice that makes you reluctant to ask any questions or to respond other than with a passive, affirmative nod. If you fail to carry out an assignment correctly, the boss may say, "I *told* you exactly how to do it." All of us have been guilty of *telling* people rather than *communicating with* people.

Reality: Communication is a two-way activity.

Most of us have played a parlor game similar to "Pass the Message" in which people sit in a circle and one member of the group whispers a message to the person on the right. The message is passed in turn from one person to the next. Each repeats the message only once, and no one can ask any questions about the message. When the message finally reaches the last person, that person states it aloud. Usually there is little, if any, resemblance to the original message. This game is a classic example of one-way communication. The message is passed quickly but inaccurately.

Using the same group of people, the game can be played so that each member, after hearing the message, is allowed to ask questions about the message. There are two dramatic differences from the first version of the game. First, it takes longer to play the game. Two-way communication always takes longer than one-way communication. The second and more important difference is that the message is passed along much more accurately. The major reason for the increased accuracy is feedback.

Feedback is simply the reaction that the listener has to the sender's verbal and nonverbal message. A major function of feedback is that it allows senders to see how well they are accomplishing the objectives of the original communication. In brief, what distinguishes effective from ineffective communication is the ability to interpret accurately the feedback provided by the other party.

6. Myth: The message we send is identical to the message received by the listener.

We all have a tendency to assume that the message we send is received by our listener exactly as we sent it. For example, suppose you send a letter to a friend in another state inviting that person to be your guest during homecoming next month. When you receive no response to your letter, you become irritated. Why did your friend not respond? Perhaps the problem is not that your friend did not reply, but that the post office lost your letter. Perhaps you inadvertently left out a page of the letter when you sealed the envelope and your friend never received the message.

Reality: The message as it is finally received by the listener is never exactly the same as the message we originally sent.

The message that we send may be perfectly clear to us but not to our listener because of some influence that neither we nor our listener can control, such as a lost letter. Also, as was suggested earlier, no two of us have had exactly the same set of experiences. The message received by one person can therefore never be exactly the same as the message sent by another.

7. Myth: You can never give someone too much information.

People in organizations sometimes say, "Nobody ever tells me; I just work here." Indeed, there are times when people do not receive the information that they need to perform their jobs properly. In an effort to keep employees informed, some organizations have adopted communication policies that send an abundance of information on all types of topics to all employees. We frequently assume that the more information we provide employees, the more productive they will be.

> Reality: There are times when people can be given too much information and thus suffer from an information overload.

A problem more common than most of us realize is **information overload**, that is, having too much information to make intelligent use of it. In the past 50 years the development of copying machines and other types of mechanical reproduction has vastly increased our ability to generate and transmit information. But our capacity as humans to handle and mentally process information has remained virtually unchanged. We speak at about the same rate as we did 50 years ago. We listen and understand at about the same level as we did 50 years ago. It is not surprising, therefore, that information overload is a major problem for people in many organizations. We need to be concerned not so much with the quantity of communication as with the quality of communication.

As these seven myths and realities about the nature of communication indicate, communication can be a confusing activity.

VARIABLES IN THE COMMUNICATION PROCESS

Communication is the transmission of a message between two or more people.

Communication can be defined broadly as the transmission of a message between two or more people. Many writers also discuss intrapersonal communication—occurring within the individual—but our concern here is to examine interpersonal communication.

The communication process includes six variables.

The six major variables in the interpersonal communication process are (1) sender/encoder, (2) message, (3) channel, (4) receiver/decoder, (5) perception, and (6) feedback. The way these six variables interact is illustrated in Figure 2.1, a model of the communication process. Too many of us take the art of communication for granted because we are ignorant of the mechanics involved. This model is intended to increase awareness of the variables responsible for successful communication.

The Sender/Encoder

The sender's basic task is to search for and use communication skills that will bring understanding to the receiver.

The sender has the responsibility for formulating the message in a way that accurately conveys an idea to the receiver. The process of translating an idea into a message is called **encoding**. Because communication is essentially a process of creating understanding, concerted effort on the part of the sender and receiver is needed to arrive at a similar meaning. The sender, however, bears the major burden. The sender must mentally see the communication from the receiver's viewpoint. The sender's task is to search for and use communication symbols and communication skills that will bring about understanding in the mind of the receiver.

Specifically, the sender should use verbal and nonverbal symbols that are on the receiver's level and should secure feedback from the receiver.

The Message

The message consists of the verbal and nonverbal symbols that represent the information we want to transmit. Each message we send is an attempt to convey an idea to the receiver. Some of the messages we attempt to communicate are relatively simple. An

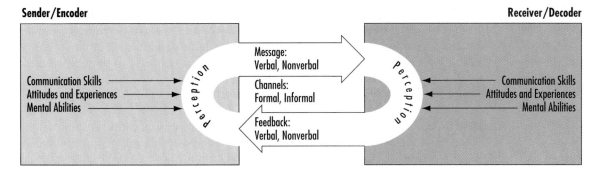

Figure 2.1
A Communication Model

example of a simple message is a stop sign. Although we may not always obey the sign, the message is clear and straightforward. Other messages are more complex and thus are more difficult to impart to the receiver. For example, we may wish to convey to a group of employees that we want simultaneously to increase production and improve quality control. Achieving understanding of that message by the entire group of employees could be difficult because the two components of the message—improve quality control and increase production—seem incompatible on the surface.

The Channel

What is the appropriate channel for any given message? Should it be communicated face to face or on paper? The decision as to whether to use an oral or written channel can be based partially on answers to the following questions:

1. Is immediate feedback needed? Is it important to get the receiver's reaction to your message? Oral communication provides the quickest feedback. Although feedback can be gained from written communication, it generally comes slowly. For many messages there is a need for immediate feedback, and oral communication provides that opportunity.

2. Is there a question of acceptance? Frequently there may be resistance to the message we are attempting to communicate. If acceptance is likely to be a problem, oral communication is better than written communication. When people receive a written communication, they feel they have had no chance for input. In face-to-face communication, the message can be adapted to the receiver to seek feedback.

3. Is there a need for a documented record of the communication? Many times in organizations the messages we send may need to be verified or monitored at a later date. Frequently the receiver of a message is expected to be accountable for information contained in the message. If accountability is important, written communication is superior to oral communication.

4. Is there a need for detailed accuracy? If the message being communicated contains detailed or exacting information, or if it explains a complicated procedure, the written method is a superior means of communication.

No one communication method is universally superior to another method. In many cases the message can best be communicated by a combination of written and oral channels. Frequently individuals will follow a conversation with a written summary. In other cases people will hand carry a written communication so that they can provide a few words of explanation and ensure acceptance of the written statement.

Frequently there is a need for both written and oral communication.

Whatever your choice of communication channel, be sure to weigh both its benefits and its costs. For example, most managers are always short on time, a precious resource. The high cost of time can determine which channel of communication is most appropriate. A company directive announcing an increase in employee health benefits should obviously not be communicated face to face to two thousand employees; it would take too much time. A written memo is the more appropriate channel of communication in light of the number of people and the nature of the message. On the other hand, relaying a new business strategy against competitors to the director of marketing would definitely call for a face-to-face conference to ensure complete understanding of the company's revised approach. Determination of the communication channel depends on its cost (time, people, equipment) and the derived benefits (more effective message and more efficient means of message dissemination).

Formal Channels

Formal channels of communication are those that have been designated by management. The lines linking positions on a company's organization chart will ordinarily represent the formal channels of communication. A policy manual may also specify the formal channels of communication.

In one study employees were asked to identify the "official" communication channel(s) used by their employer. Respondents identified the following formal channels:[4]

Channel	Identified By
Newsletter	71%
Bulletin board	50%
Electronic mail	43%
Regular companywide meetings	36%
Other (memos, other meetings, etc.)	36%
None	14%

While the above channels are all formal, the list is far from exhaustive. In fact, much formal communication is face to face. Formal communication channels are often described in directional terms—downward, upward, and horizontal.

Organizations are structured to facilitate the downward flow of information. Such information usually possesses special credibility since it emanates from the higher levels of the organization. In many organizations today, however, excessive downward communication is contributing to a situation of information overload.[5] The ease with which messages are conveyed results in people being inundated with too much irrelevant and unnecessary information. Victims of information overload are forced to do filtering, which should have been performed by the sender before communicating. If senders would limit their communication to individuals who needed the information, many resources would be conserved.

Downward Channels

Downward channels of communication include several types of information.

There are five major types of downward communication.[6]

- *Job instructions* explain how a task is to be done. The instructions come from written specifications, training manuals, training sessions, or on-the-job training.
- *Job rationale* tells workers how their task relates to other jobs in the organization. Specialization in many organizations has made it difficult for workers to see this.

- *Policy and procedure* communications explain to workers the regulations and personal benefits that are provided by their employer. An example of policy is "Employees receive a three-week paid vacation after three years with the company." Policy and procedure communication may be thought of as "the way we do things around here."

- *Feedback* includes messages that inform employees about whether their work is being performed satisfactorily. Feedback should be provided daily as well as in the form of systematic performance appraisal reviews.

- *Indoctrination* communications seek employee support of a particular organizational objective. For example, "Acme Company would like all employees to participate in the blood drive."

> ✔ *CHECKLIST for Selecting the Appropriate Channel*
>
> _____ Is immediate feedback needed?
> _____ Is there a question of acceptance?
> _____ Is there a need for a documented record of the communication?
> _____ Is there a need for detailed accuracy?

As messages travel downward in organizations, they tend to become distorted. In many cases much of the message never gets through to the intended receiver. One study of downward communications in 100 firms attempted to determine how much of what top management said actually penetrated the organizational structure.[7] The results of that study were:

Much of the message is lost as it is passed down the organizational structure.

Level	Percentage Understood
Vice president	65%
General supervisor	56%
Plant manager	40%
Foreman	30%
Production line	20%

Upward Channels

Upward channels are important because they are the major means of getting information to higher organizational levels where important decisions are made. Essentially, upward communication means following the chain of command. The individual employee communicates a request or a problem to the immediate supervisor; if the immediate supervisor is not able to respond or make the decision, the message is passed to the person at the next higher level.

Communication moving upward in the organization consists of the following types of information: [8]

Upward channels of communication contain several types of information.

- What the employee has done.
- What those under the employee have done.
- What the employee's peers have done.
- What the employee's problems are.
- What the problems of the employee's department are.
- What the employee thinks needs to be done.
- What the employee's perceptions of his or her job performance are.
- What organizational policies and practices need adjusting.

Because upward communication is often viewed as being less important than downward, it is sometimes neglected. For example, an investigation into the disastrous explosion of the space shuttle "Challenger" in 1986, in which the crew of seven perished, revealed that NASA had become an organization unreceptive to upward com-

Figure 2.2
News and rumors spread quickly on the grapevine.
Source: Reginald Wickham.

munication. The immediate cause of the catastrophe had been a flawed engineering design; however, in the words of one investigator, " . . . the real precipitating cause of the accident was a bureaucratic organization that deliberately blocked repeated warning signals."[9] Another writer stated that the "can-do" attitude that had prevailed at NASA had evolved into an arrogant "can't-fail" attitude.[10] Because little attempt was made to solicit or encourage upward communication, a technical problem, which might have been recognized had more minds been actively involved in a launch, went unnoticed and disaster followed.

Horizontal Channels

Horizontal channels of communication have four important uses.

Four major purposes for using horizontal channels have been identified: (1) task coordination, (2) problem solving, (3) sharing information, and (4) conflict resolution.[11] Because horizontal communication occurs among employees of about the same level in the hierarchy, it has a different tone from communication between superiors and subordinates. The tone is likely to be consultative, persuasive, or suggestive rather than directive.

Informal Channels

Informal channels of communication are frequently referred to as the grapevine.

Informal communication in organizations is referred to frequently as the grapevine. While many writers assume that grapevine communication is inaccurate, at least one researcher maintains that between 75 percent and 95 percent of grapevine information is correct.[12] In addition, informal channels usually provide information faster than formal ones and play an important role in coordination of organizational tasks.

In a more recent study of office gossip, only 14 percent of the respondents said that they rarely used the grapevine. All of the other participants claimed to use the grapevine either frequently or sometimes. Most of the topics discussed on the grapevine were work-related, with business changes and office intrigue the most frequently mentioned topics (see Figure 2.2). Fifty-seven percent of the respondents explained their participation in the "rumor mill" by claiming it was the only way to find out "what's really happening."[13]

Informal messages are also called by other names: non-job-oriented, task, social, or maintenance communication. At times communication can follow the chain of command but still be informal; this is especially true when the topic is not related to the organization or the job. An example is when various levels of employees discuss non-task topics on the golf course or at the company picnic.

The Receiver/Decoder

The basic skills employed by the receiver are listening and providing feedback to the sender.

The process of translating a message into an idea is called **decoding**, and this is done by the receiver. The receiver can be viewed in many ways. How much does the receiver know about the topic? Is the receiver likely to be receptive to the message and the

Figure 2.3
Bill Gates, CEO of
Microsoft, recognizes the
importance of
communication to his
organization.
Source: Microsoft
Corporation.

sender? What experience has the receiver had with the sender? These questions and
many others determine the impact of the message upon the receiver.

Specifically, the receiver is primarily concerned with two types of behavior: listening and providing feedback to the sender.

Perception

One of the most important variables in communication is **perception**—our unique
understanding of the way things are. As shown in Figure 2.1, perception is an integral
part of both the sender's and the receiver's involvement in the communication process.
As a perceiver, each of us is a product of all of our experiences. Our attitudes toward the
surrounding environment also modify our perception of what is being communicated.

Of course, our mental abilities, or intelligence, greatly determine our capacity to
discern the communication experience accurately. Finally, communication skills,
whether in the area of speaking or listening, will influence the way we send a message
and the way we receive feedback about that message. In all likelihood each sender and
receiver will bring different attitudes, experiences, mental abilities, and communication
skills to bear on the communication process. This does not mean that an understanding cannot be reached. Rather, an awareness and sensitivity to these differences in perception can facilitate an open and productive communication experience.

The position a person occupies in an organization strongly influences perception.
In one study, 76 percent of the foremen "always or almost always" sought ideas from
subordinates in seeking solutions to job problems. However, only 16 percent of the
workers thought their foremen actually sought their opinions.[14] There can be little
question that perception greatly influences the way we send and receive messages.

*Perception greatly affects
how we send and receive
messages.*

Feedback

As we have said, feedback is the reaction that the receiver has to the message. Feedback
may be verbal or nonverbal; it can be written or oral. Feedback provides guidance for
the next message that we send to the receiver. In brief, we can evaluate the effectiveness of our communication by the feedback we receive. The ability to interpret feedback accurately is an important skill to master.

The significance of feedback is recognized by the many organizations that now
employ the managerial technique of 360-degree feedback. This is an approach that gath-

*Feedback is the reaction the
receiver has to the message.*

ers observations from many layers within the organization, including superiors, subordinates, peers, and self-review, for the purpose of evaluating an individual's performance. If a jobholder is required to interact with external clients, the clients would also be involved in providing feedback. With the growing emphasis on teamwork, the use of multiple evaluators should provide more valid and comprehensive information than a single supervisor could.[15] Many of the leading companies in the United States, such as AT&T, DuPont, Merck, and Northwestern Mutual Life Insurance, are using the technique.[16]

COMMUNICATION BARRIERS

Several barriers to communication affect the six major variables in the communication process. One of the earliest and most complete lists of these barriers includes seven major categories.[17]

* *Meaning barriers:* problems with meaning, significance, and the sending and reception of the meaning of the message.
* *Organizational barriers:* problems with physical distance between members; specialization of task functions; power, authority, and status relationships; and information ownership.
* *Interpersonal barriers:* problems with the climate of the relationship, values held, and negative attitudes held by the participants.
* *Individual barriers:* problems with individual competencies to think and act, which would include physical ailments or handicaps, and problems with individual skills in receiving and transmitting information, which would include poor listening and reading skills and psychological considerations.
* *Economic, geographic, and temporal barriers:* problems with time and dollar costs, different locations, and the effects of time upon reception of the message.
* *Channel and media barriers:* problems that confront the issue of how to best communicate a message. (For example, is it best to transmit a message face to face rather than in writing?)
* *Technological barriers:* problems with too much information for the capacity of the recipient.

ENCODING-DECODING SKILLS

Imagine that you want to write a letter to a company about possible summer job openings. You have certain ideas you want to communicate in the letter. For example, you should offer reasons why you chose that particular company. Also, you should provide some general information about your qualifications in the letter accompanying your resume. As these ideas form in your mind and you put them on paper, the encoding process is occurring. Encoding includes your decisions whether to use verbal or nonverbal channels; which communications channels, such as writing or speaking, are within your selection; which words to use and with how much emphasis; and when and how to deliver the message.

Imagine the personnel manager of the company you have written as she opens your letter of inquiry. She notes that you are asking about a summer job. At the same time she makes decisions about you and your qualifications. She decodes information about your work by how neat and attractive your letter and resume are. She decodes information about your work experience, courses you are taking, and interests you seem to have. All the decisions the personnel manager makes about your messages are the end result of the decoding process.

Perhaps the descriptions of encoding and decoding make them appear to be simple processes. They are not. Anywhere in the encoding-decoding processes, breakdowns in communication can occur. Three main encoding-decoding skills can help overcome common breakdowns: (1) analyzing the other person, (2) getting and giving feedback, and (3) understanding perception.

Encoding-decoding skills help avoid communication breakdowns.

Analyzing the Other Person

As a sender, we should know that different receivers react to the same message in different ways. Imagine a basketball coach criticizing a player's performance: "Wilson, you couldn't catch that ball with a bushel basket!" How will Wilson react? Some people will try harder because their pride is hurt, or they want to avoid future criticism. Other people might stop trying altogether and quit the team. Many of us at one time or another have "quit the team," whether quitting involved basketball, playing the piano, attending a class, or any other activity where someone important criticized our work. Still others have succeeded in an activity in part because someone prodded them to improve. We react differently to the same message.

Receivers of our messages are unique. They are of different races and sexes. They have different family backgrounds and come from different parts of the country or the world. Their personalities are different. Therefore, they will react in individualized ways to what we encode.

As a receiver we should analyze the sender's frame of reference, too. Consider this telephone exchange:

Martha: Jim, I've got to have that report on my desk by 9 A.M. tomorrow.
Jim: Impossible. I'll be up all night working on it.
Martha: I'm sorry, but I've got to have it by nine.

As Jim puts his phone back on the receiver, he thinks, "This is terrible. . . . I can't believe how unfair she is. . . . She'll get her report all right . . . but it's the last time." At the same time Martha is thinking, "If he doesn't get that report to me by nine, I'll never be ready for the board meeting. . . . It's unfair. . . . Why can't they give us more time?"

It's easy for Jim to be angry. Martha hasn't told him why the 9 A.M. deadline is so important. Would he feel different if Martha had justified the deadline? Perhaps not. He would need to work all night anyway. However, Jim needs to understand why Martha acts in such an adverse manner. She is pressuring him, but she also has pressures on her.

The receiver analyzes the sender's frame of reference—and responds accordingly.

When receiving messages, we must analyze our senders. They are just as individual as we are and, consequently, they encode messages in different ways.

Getting and Giving Feedback

Feedback is important because it is the only way we can know how we are performing. Think a minute about the varied ways Boris Becker gets feedback during a match on center court at Wimbledon. First, he gets immediate visual feedback about his shot: he sees the ball land either in or out on the opponent's court. Even if something blocks his vision, Becker can also hear the call of the line judge if the ball lands out or wide. If he makes a particularly spectacular shot, he hears the roar of the crowd and perhaps even the groan of his opponent.

Feedback lets the sender know how he or she is performing.

If Boris Becker were alone on center court at night with portable lights for only his side of the court, his serve would vanish across the net. No visual contact, no line judge, no opponent, no crowd: in essence, no feedback. Although Becker may be confident enough in the accuracy of his serves to continue serving into a darkened court, most of us would quit immediately. Feedback is a critical element that motivates people

Feedback is crucial to organizational success.

to continue. As a member of the organization, you need to ensure that you, your peers, your boss, and your subordinates receive adequate feedback.

As a sender, we need to create a climate in which the receiver will feel comfortable and be willing to provide feedback. Immediate feedback seldom occurs when we use written communication. That is one of the disadvantages of writing letters or memos instead of speaking face to face with our receiver. In verbal situations we must try to get as much immediate feedback as possible to determine whether we have created the understanding we want.

The recipient of a message has certain obligations, too. As receivers, we should try to apply the guidelines to better listening that are presented in Chapter 14. We should avoid giving false feedback and should seek agreement on message meaning.

Many managers ask questions such as these to get feedback about instructions or directions: Do you understand? Repeat that to me, will you? Got any questions? What'd I forget to tell you?

For each of these questions, think about three things. Will the question get useful feedback? How will the receiver react to each question? Is the receiver likely to return false or expected feedback?

For example, "Do you understand?" is a very common question that might follow this set of instructions: "Here, type this double-spaced except for tables. I need one-inch margins all around, two inches at the bottom. Don't forget the enclosures. Do you understand?" We say it almost unconsciously. At the same level of consciousness our secretary responds, "Yes."

In some organizations, "Repeat that" is used as a matter of policy, especially in areas where misunderstood instructions might endanger the safety of employees. Yet what would you think if your own supervisors asked you to repeat them every time they gave you instructions?

Getting useful feedback involves more than phrasing questions. Feedback is a receiver's responsibility.

There is no one sure way of getting accurate and willing feedback. In many situations, though, if we ask questions or perhaps pause momentarily, our receiver will give us the feedback we need.

Feedback is the way we tell senders about the understanding or misunderstanding they have created. There are several characteristics of effective feedback:

- *It is specific rather than general.* To be told, "You are dominating," is not as constructive as to be told, "You did not listen to what others said and thereby curtailed their suggestions."
- *It is descriptive rather than evaluative.* By avoiding evaluative language, such as, "You handled that badly," you reduce the need for the individual to react defensively.
- *It takes into account the needs of both the receiver and the giver of feedback.* Feedback can be destructive when it serves only your needs and fails to meet the receiver's needs.
- *It is directed toward behavior the receiver can do something about.* Frustration is increased when people are reminded of some shortcoming over which they have no control.
- *It is well-timed.* In general, feedback is most useful at the earliest opportunity after a given behavior—depending on the other person's readiness to hear it. There are occasions when a cooling-off period should occur.
- *It is two-way.* You get feedback about the feedback.
- *It is tailored to the individual.* A successful communicator recognizes the different needs and abilities of each person and interacts with each accordingly. You must guard against the desire to remake others in

your own image. Changes in behavior must be within the framework of each individual's personality and skills.

Understanding Perception

Perception occupies a central role in the communication process. Perception is the process of assigning meaning to a message and illustrates the reality that meanings are in people. Consider the following statement: "Ned is a middle-aged, moderate drinker." Now estimate how many drinks he has on an average day (1? 2? 4?). Estimate his age (30? 40? 50? 60?). If the statement had been "Carol is a middle-aged, moderate drinker," would you estimate that Carol drinks as much as you estimated for Ned? Is Carol as old as you estimated Ned to be? In your estimates, you were perceiving the words moderate and middle aged. You assigned meaning to the message.

Misperception is the major cause of communication breakdowns. We are simply not careful when we perceive other people and their messages. For instance, Chevrolet was a victim of misperception when it attempted to market its Nova line in Latin American countries. Sales were dismal, and company officials were baffled. The cause of the low sales came to light when Chevrolet officials realized that, in Spanish, "no va" means "does not go."[18] Chevrolet's lack of analyzing the cultural dimension of its marketplace plus the misperception of the Latin American consumers cost Chevrolet many sales.

Perception is the filter through which all communication passes, as Figure 2.1 showed. The element that separates communication from miscommunication is perception. Accurate perception results in communication; misperception results in miscommunication. Unfortunately, we misuse our perceptual skills in several ways.

First, our experiences influence our perceptions of messages. Consider this old riddle: A father and his son are driving to work one morning. A terrible accident occurs. The father is killed instantly, and the son is badly injured. An ambulance arrives at the accident scene. The attendants place the son in an ambulance and rush him to the hospital. When they carry him into the emergency room, the nurse says, "He's in terrible shape. We've got to get him to surgery." They rush him down the hall to surgery. The surgeon walks in, takes one look at him, and says, "I'm sorry. I can't operate on him. He's my son." How can this be?

Perhaps he is the father's stepson. Perhaps the "father" is a Catholic priest. Perhaps the boy was adopted. Other explanations abound. Yet actually the surgeon was the boy's mother. At one time, we couldn't think of the correct answer simply because our experiences and stereotypes had convinced us that surgeons are male.

Receivers interpret messages according to their past experiences.

In another case of perception, read aloud the sentences in the two triangles pictured in Figure 2.4. Did you notice that "the" was repeated by mistake in the first triangle and "a" was repeated in the second? If not, then your experiences ("I've read this before") are controlling your ability to perceive and, in this case, to read.

Second, we often fill in missing information about messages we receive. Consequently, we sometimes perceive them wrongly. For example, what appears in Figure 2.5 is the Roman numeral nine. Your instructions are to add one line to this Roman numeral and make six out of it. Possibly, you placed an *S* in front of the *IX* and created *SIX*. If you tried to create a Roman numeral six, then you filled in missing information. Reread the instructions. They do not specify that you must use Roman numerals.

Receivers fill in missing information.

Many times when we are faced with an unclear message, we fill in information and hope for the best. In our earlier example of the sales representative who asks for an order to be shipped right away, the shipper assumed the rep meant by the end of the week. Without feedback and further information, the shipper simply assigned his own meaning to the sales rep's message.

Figure 2.4
A Test of Visual
Perception

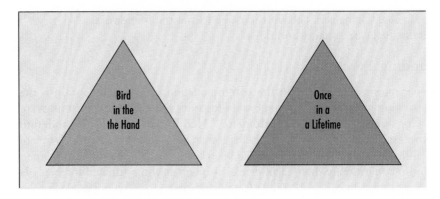

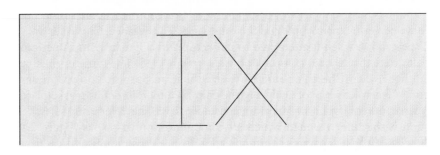

Figure 2.5
A Test of Mental
Perception

Receivers interpret messages
according to their own attitudes and beliefs.

Third, we often perceive messages so that they are consistent with our own attitudes and beliefs. Tom and Bill are playing tennis:

Tom: You play much tennis?
Bill: Every day.
Tom: Wow. Don't you miss a lot of class?
Bill: Yeah, I only went to Math 104 twice last quarter.
Tom: How'd you do?
Bill: Flunked.
Tom: You failed?
Bill: Yeah. Prof gave really tricky tests. Besides that, I don't think she liked me.

We are often inclined to interpret messages so that they satisfy our impression of
the world and see the world through rose-colored glasses, shaded the hue of personal
attitudes about ourselves, others, and life in general.

COMMUNICATION STYLES

Effective communication often depends on assuming the appropriate communication
style for the occasion. The trick is to correctly analyze the occasion and to have the ability to modify your communication to meet that situation.

There is no agreed-upon number of categories of communication styles. Some
authorities find as few as one, while others list as many as eight. Most of the styles cluster around four dimensions: blaming, directing, persua-
sive, and problem solving.[19]

A person who uses the **blaming style** is trying to find
fault or discover who is to blame for a problem. At the
extreme, the tone is accusatory and negative. "This is
what you did wrong" is a typical blaming expression. This
tone evokes a negative feeling in the receiver, and the
results are not likely to be positive. Usually this style is to

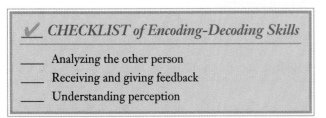

✓ *CHECKLIST of Encoding-Decoding Skills*

____ Analyzing the other person
____ Receiving and giving feedback
____ Understanding perception

BOXED IN

AN ETHICAL DILEMMA

Marcia Hartwell is a junior account executive in the commercial accounts division of a telephone company. It is a competitive and lucrative division in which there is constant pressure to exceed the previous month's billing. The only way to increase billing enough is to win new customers. Merely maintaining existing clients and selling them new services was not enough.

Jill Weinstein was the star account executive in Marcia's division. Jill's sales record was the benchmark for the division. She consistently had the highest sales. The only month in the last six that she did not have the highest sales figure was when she took a two-week vacation. Even then she was second highest. Her record was no small accomplishment in a division comprised of intelligent and motivated employees. Jill arrived at the office early and left late. She was pleasant to all, but did not spend much time socializing. Jill stopped working only at lunch, and she made a point of leaving the office for her lunch hour. She considered skipping lunch or eating at the desk to be unhealthy.

In an effort to pattern herself after Jill, Marcia began arriving when Jill did and not leaving until after Jill left. She also invited Jill to lunch a few times in order to learn the key to her success. Jill told her it was hard work and experience, but Marcia felt Jill was holding back on her. Marcia suspected that Jill had access to private, inside information on prospective clients.

One day when Jill was at lunch Marcia saw a folder labeled "Prospects" on her desk. Marcia paused. "That file may contain the secret to Jill's success," she thought, "and there it is on top of her desk." Marcia told herself that if Jill really wanted to keep the information private she would have put the folder away, but on the other hand it was *Jill's* desk. Marcia feels boxed in.
What would you do?

be avoided; it might be selected when all other styles have failed or when the facts of the situation are absolutely clear.

The second style is the **directing style**. A directing person tells others, particularly subordinates, how to do their jobs or how to solve problems. Discussion is minimized; communication is predominantly one-way. "This is the way you'll do it" exemplifies a directing tone. Don't confuse the directing style with the more positive instructional tone that involves more feedback. Keep in mind the unidirectional aspect of the directing style.

The directing style can be effective in certain situations. The school teacher who finally becomes exasperated with whispering in the fourth-grade class orders "Be quiet!" and reestablishes authority. The acceptance of the command may not be heartfelt, but the command is followed.

The **persuasive style** employs information sharing and acceptance techniques. Instead of directing the audience to do something, the sender presents the message for their evaluation and active acceptance. The goal of the message may be to have the receivers want to do what you present because they *choose* to. Because the recipient makes the decision, much greater acceptance of the action is likely than with the blaming or directing approaches. Frequently the truly persuasive person is able to establish a need in the receiver and present a plan of action that meets that need. The action is the original goal.

The **problem-solving style** seeks mutual acceptance from both sender and receiver of the final action; compromise is frequent. Two-way communication is

Figure 2.6
Degree of Interaction
in Four Communication
Styles

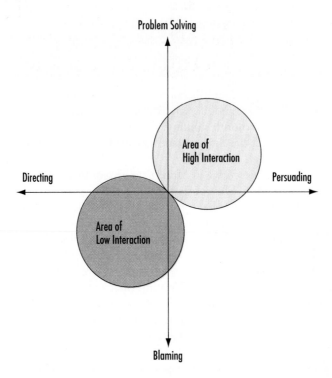

required. Ideas are jointly explored and evaluated. Personalities may emerge but are not used in deciding the final action, as they are in the other three styles. Discussions between the parties may lead to fruitful plans of action and mutual respect. On the other hand, they may also lead to disagreements, confusion, and frustration when consensus is evasive. This style is especially valuable when group behavior change is sought.

The blaming and problem-solving approaches, from the sender's viewpoint, are almost opposites; and the directing and persuasive approaches are bipolar. Further, the blaming and directing techniques have little feedback whereas the persuasive and problem-solving methods build on this interaction, as Figure 2.6 illustrates.

SELF-ASSESSMENT

If you know which style is your dominant style, you can better prepare for the occasion with the correct style—whether it is your first choice or another one. The self-assessment instrument in Figures 2.7 and 2.8 measures the tendency to use blaming and problem-solving styles. Having evaluated these, you should be able to determine your abilities on the styles between these extremes.

If your score for the left column in Figure 2.8 is between 21 and 28, you are probably a moderate blamer; a score of 29 or higher suggests you rely somewhat heavily on the blaming style.

If your score for the right column is from 21 to 28, you fall in the moderate problem-solving style category. A score of 29 or higher indicates a strong leaning toward problem solving as your dominant technique.

Blaming is not always bad and problem solving is not always good. There are occasions when you need to be directive and perhaps even blame. Problem solving can be both tedious and time consuming; it is not a panacea for all ills. Become familiar with the four styles and with your own strengths and weaknesses, then try to select the appropriate style for the occasion.

Figure 2.7
Self-Assessment of
Communication Style

Indicate the degree to which you do the following:

		Very Little	Little	Some	Great	Very Great
1.	Make judgments early in the conversation.	—	—	—	—	—
2.	Share my feelings with others.	—	—	—	—	—
3.	Talk about the issues.	—	—	—	—	—
4.	Have analyzed others' motives.	—	—	—	—	—
5.	Talk about the person.	—	—	—	—	—
6.	Use clear and precise language.	—	—	—	—	—
7.	Decide on the action before the conversation.	—	—	—	—	—
8.	Encourage the other person to discuss feelings.	—	—	—	—	—
9.	Am open for new information.	—	—	—	—	—
10.	Ask questions which seek agreement with me.	—	—	—	—	—
11.	Talk the majority of the time.	—	—	—	—	—
12.	Ask questions which get others to describe events.	—	—	—	—	—
13.	Talk half the time or less.	—	—	—	—	—
14.	Allow others to defend their position to me.	—	—	—	—	—

Source: The Manager as Communicator by Sandra E. O'Connell, p. 25. Copyright 1979 by Sandra E. O'Connell. Reprinted by permission of Harper & Row, Publishers, Inc.

Key Terms

- **horizontal communication**
- **vertical communication**
- **feedback**
- **information overload**
- **encoding**
- **decoding**
- **perception**
- **blaming style**
- **directing style**
- **persuasive style**
- **problem-solving style**

Figure 2.8
Score Sheet for
Self-Assessment

Item No.	Score	
1	_____	
2		_____
3		_____
4	_____	
5	_____	
6		_____
7	_____	
8		_____
9		_____
10	_____	
11	_____	
12		_____
13		_____
14	_____	
Totals	_____	_____

Total column 1 _____
Total column 2 _____
Interpretation of scores: very little = 1 point, little = 2 points, some = 3 points, great = 4 points, and very great = 5 points

Source: The Manager as Communicator by Sandra E. O'Connell, pp. 25–26. Copyright 1979 by Sandra E. O'Connell. Reprinted by permission of Harper & Row, Publishers, Inc.

Summary

Reinforcing and aversive stimuli   p. 25

Horizontal and vertical communication   p. 26

Communication process   p. 30

Determinants of an appropriate channel   p. 31

Formal channels   p. 32

Grapevine   p. 34

Perception   p. 35

360-degree feedback   p. 35

Barriers to communication   p. 36

Encoding and decoding   p. 36

Characteristics of effective feedback   p. 37

Styles of communication   p. 40

Review Questions

1. How can reinforcing or aversive stimuli have an impact on behavior?

2. In the superior-subordinate communication relationship, what do subordinates want from their superiors? Discuss why most downward communication is job related.

3. Discuss the seven myths and realities about the nature of communication.

4. What is the sender's major responsibility in the communication process?

5. Comment on the statement, "The more information we provide employees, the more productive they will be."

6. What important criteria determine whether an oral or written channel of communication is the most appropriate form of a message?

7. What are downward, upward, and horizontal channels of communication? Suggest several situations in which these channels should be used.

8. Name the encoding and decoding skills that both sender and receiver should master to prevent communication breakdowns. Within the context of a business setting, give an example of each.

9. What are the characteristics of good feedback? Who bears the primary responsibility for good feedback? How can good feedback facilitate an accurate and willing information exchange?

10. How do your experiences with the grapevine compare with the way it is described in this chapter?

11. What do you consider to be the advantages of using 360-degree feedback to evaluate employees rather than the traditional evaluation by one's immediate superior? Any disadvantages?

CASE

Real Estate and Real Time

Anji K. Roy, University of Wisconsin–Oshkosh

Jeffrey King, a real estate developer, had acquired some land in Oshkosh, Wisconsin. He wanted to build condominiums, but needed partners.

He called his brother, John, an orthopedic surgeon in Chicago, who was looking for some investment opportunities. John expressed interest. He also talked about it with his friend from Baltimore, Richard Morrison, who was visiting him at the time. They decided to drive together to Oshkosh during the weekend.

Jeffrey, however, had one problem. He had planned to attend a conference on Saturday in Madison, 80 miles from Oshkosh. Jeffrey indicated that he would return late Saturday night if they decided to come on Saturday. John told Jeffrey that instead, they would come early in the morning on Sunday since Oshkosh is only 160 miles from Chicago.

After the conference, Jeffrey stayed in Madison Saturday night. He remembered his brother had said they would be coming early Sunday morning. He thought he could reach Oshkosh before his brother and his friend arrived from Chicago.

John and Richard started from Chicago at 10:00 P.M. on Saturday. Richard wanted to have time to visit his grandmother in Ripon, 20 miles away from Oshkosh, before catching his plane from O'Hare Sunday evening. John recalled Jeffrey mentioning that he might be coming back Saturday night from Madison.

They arrived at Oshkosh at 2:00 A.M. on Sunday. Because of the annual EAA (Experimental Aircraft Association) convention then in progress, they could not find any accommodations within a sixty-mile radius of Oshkosh. They pulled the seats back and slept in the car. Jeffrey reached home at 7:30 A.M. on Sunday.

Case Questions

1. Who is at fault in the breakdown of the communication?

2. What could have prevented the misunderstanding?

3. What were the assumptions on which the actions of John and Jeffrey were based?

4. How responsible is Richard in the communication gap created between John and Jeffrey?

CASE

Whom Can You Trust?

David B. Parsons, Lakehead University, Thunder Bay, Ontario, Canada

Joan Duncan is a registered nurse. One day she took her son to the family physician because he was experiencing difficulty in breathing. After diagnosing a bronchial infection, Dr. Smithers prescribed an antibiotic. Duncan decided to have the prescription filled at the pharmacy in the neighborhood mall.

Being a registered nurse, Duncan read the prescription before she took it to the pharmacy. She told the pharmacist that her husband would pick up the prescription later in the day.

When Mr. Duncan brought the prescription home, Mrs. Duncan read the instructions on the label. Immediately, she realized that the pharmacist had indicated the wrong dosage and frequency of administration on the label.

Therefore, she phoned the pharmacy to question the apparent discrepancy between the doctor's orders and the instructions on the bottle. Making certain that she was speaking to the pharmacist, she asked him to check the prescription order. The pharmacist's first response was the Connors Drug Mart does not make mistakes and that the instructions on the label were correct.

However, Mrs. Duncan insisted that the pharmacist check the original order. Reluctantly, and somewhat indignantly, he agreed to do so. When he returned to the phone, he admitted that, in fact, the instructions were wrong. However, he passed off the error as a typographical mistake, refusing to admit that someone on his staff had made a medication error.

After discussing the situation with several friends who deal with this pharmacy, Mrs. Duncan discovered that they had also experienced similar problems. For example, just the week before, Mrs. French had been dispensed and had used the wrong eye drops. Fortunately, no serious complications had arisen.

Case Questions

1. How would you describe the communication problem involved in this situation?

2. Assuming the role of Mrs. Duncan, write a letter of concern to the physician, to the pharmacy, or the Society of Professional Pharmacists.

3. What would be the appropriate steps to take to correct this problem?

Notes

1. For a more detailed discussion of reinforcing and aversive stimuli, see David Thompson, *Managing People—Influencing Behavior* (St. Louis: Mosby, 1978).

2. Jay Mathews, "It's Praise, Not a Raise, That's the Big Motivator," *Washington Post,* September 8, 1994, B10.

3. Albert Mehrabian, *Silent Messages* (Belmont, CA: Wadsworth, 1981), 77.

4. "FAX Forum Results," *Training and Development*, October 1994, 20.

5. Robert C. Greco, "Information Overload," *Office Systems*, February 1994, 28.

6. Daniel Katz and Robert Kahn, *The Social Psychology of Organizations* (New York: Wiley, 1978), 440.

7. Ray Killian, *Managing by Design...for Executive Effectiveness* (New York: American Management Association, 1968), 254.

8. Katz and Kahn, *The Social Psychology of Organizations*, 446-448.

9. Laurence Barton, *Crisis in Organizations* (Cincinnati: South-Western, 1993), 4.

10. Henry Migliore, "The O-Ring Syndrome and Other Painful Lessons About Listening," *Management World*, November/December 1987, 4.

11. Gerald M. Goldhaber, *Organizational Communication*, 5th ed. (Dubuque, IA: William C. Brown, 1990), 160.

12. Keith Davis, "Care and Cultivation of the Corporation Grapevine," *Dun's Review* (July 1973): 46.

13. "FAX Forum Results."

14. E. Jacobson, "Foremen-Steward Participation Practices and Work Attitudes in a Unionized Factory," unpublished doctoral thesis (Ann Arbor: University of Michigan, 1951).

15. Robert Hoffman, "Ten Reasons You Should Be Using 360-Degree Feedback," *HRMagazine*, April 1995, 82-85.

16. "Companies Where Employees Rate Executives," *Fortune*, December 27, 1993, 128.

17. Lee Thayer, *Communication and Communication Systems* (Homewood, IL: Irwin, 1968), 195-203.

18. David A. Ricks, *Big Business Blunders* (Homewood, IL: Dow Jones-Irwin, 1983), 38.

19. Much of this discussion is taken from Sandra O'Connell, *The Manager as Communicator* (San Francisco: Harper & Row, 1979).

Chapter 3

Cultural Diversity

When United Machine Parts, Inc., built a plant in Genoa, Italy, John Fanning was selected to manage the operation. He seemed a logical choice because of his proven record of success during the past fourteen years with the company. For six of those years he had been a plant manager, first in central Pennsylvania and then in Liverpool, England. It was the latter experience that was thought to have especially prepared him for the job in Italy.

Upon arriving in Genoa, John soon recognized that many of those abilities that had ensured his past success as a plant manager did not transfer easily to the new environment. His minimal grasp of the language presented problems, as expected, but language differences were not the main source of his problems. He found the people to be different from any he had ever worked with before. His efforts to motivate workers fell flat, as did the emphasis he attempted to place on self-directed work teams.

After nine months on the job, during which the Genoa plant did not meet a single quota, John began to recognize that it would take more than his superior technical skills to create a successful operation. It was at this point that he started listening and observing more, and talking less. As he became a student of the local culture, he stopped considering his way of doing things as the only way. Ultimately becoming effective as manager of the operation, he was transferred back to the United States three years later. He attributes much of his success to his "teacher," a twenty-five-year-old high school graduate who was his secretary.

In 1909 Israel Zangwill contributed a phrase to the American lexicon that continues to be widely used. The phrase is "The Melting Pot," and it was the title of a play he wrote.[1] In the play, which became a Broadway hit, he compared the United States to a melting pot because of the transformation that occurred to the streams of immigrants attracted to U.S. shores. As Zangwill described it, the immigrants, predominately European, would lose much of their ethnic identity as they were transformed into Americans. While many people feel that the melting pot analogy continues to describe the immigrant experience, others maintain that it is Balkanizing, not melting, that now occurs. Rather than striving to become a part of one homogenous mass, immigrants today are more likely to seek to retain their ethnic identity, and U.S. society, therefore, is becoming a collection of distinct groups. Whether you accept the melting pot or Balkanization as being most accu-

rate, the end result is that cultural diversity is growing, and with it the importance of under-standing intercultural communication.

As cultural diversity grows, so does the importance of understanding intercultural communication.

THE GLOBAL MARKETPLACE

International business was once considered the province of a small number of multina-tional organizations. That is no longer true, as companies of all sizes are now engaged in international trade. The percentage of sales that come from the international sector indicates the significance of international trade to some companies. International sales account for 77 percent and 67 percent of total sales of Exxon and Coca-Cola, respec-tively. In 1994 American Family Life Assurance Company (AFLAC), with its home office in Columbus, Georgia, had total sales greater than $6 billion, of which 82.5 per-cent came from foreign sales.[2] The growth of exports and imports in the United States also illustrates the significance of international business. In 1980 exports by U.S. com-panies totaled $344 billion; in 1992 exports were worth $726 billion. The value of imports rose from $334 billion in 1980 to $758 billion in 1992.[3]

Despite the dramatic growth in international business, the untapped potential remains staggering. According to Edward D. Jones & Company, a Wall Street investment firm, half of the world's population has never made a telephone call. At present two out of three people in the world would have to walk more than a day to reach a telephone.[4]

At one time only large orga-nizations engaged in interna-tional trade, but companies of all sizes do so now.

The rate at which employees are transferred abroad is another indicator of how significant international business has become. In 1993, for example, there were 82,781 citizens of foreign nations transferred by their employers to the United States, with the greatest number, approximately 16,000, coming from Japan.[5] Total foreign invest-ment in the United States for 1980 was $83 million; for 1991 it was $407 million.[6] The large number of familiar companies that are owned by foreign interests provides addi-tional evidence of the international nature of business. What could be more American than Vaseline™, Alpo™, and Ball Park Franks™? All are owned by foreign companies.[7]

Foreign investment in the United States continues to grow.

The immigration that Zangwill dramatized in 1909 continues today, however, the patterns of immigration continue to change. Table 3.1 describes a major source of the growing cultural diversity in the United States.

According to the U.S. Census Bureau foreign-born people now make up 8.7 per-cent of the population, the highest proportion since World War II. Nearly one third of the nation's foreign-born reside in California.[8]

TABLE 3.1 IMMIGRANTS BY PLACE OF BIRTH			
	1961–1970	**1971–1980**	**1981–1990**
Europe	1,200,000	801,000	705,000
Asia	445,000	1,600,000	2,800,000
Canada	286,000	114,800	119,200
Mexico	443,000	637,000	1,600,000
Carribean	519,000	759,000	892,000
Central America	97,000	132,000	458,000
South America	228,000	264,000	455,000

Source: Statistical Abstract of the United States (Washington, DC: Department of Commerce, Bureau of the Census), p. 11, table 8.

Governmental actions here
and abroad have facilitated
international trade.

Governmental actions in recent years have done much to facilitate international business. The **North American Free Trade Agreement (NAFTA)** was significant because it eliminated trade barriers between the United States and its major trading partners: Canada and Mexico. The **General Agreement on Tariffs and Trade (GATT)** is another multinational trade agreement. The formation of the **European Economic Community (EEC)** in 1993 eliminated long-standing trade barriers by creating a free-trade zone comprised of twelve European countries.

Learning about other
cultures leads to better
understanding of people.

Widespread involvement in international business by U.S. companies, foreign ownership of American companies, changing immigration patterns, and far-reaching trade agreements have all contributed to a more culturally diverse society. Learning about other cultures is essential if one is to become more proficient in intercultural communication.

CULTURAL DIVERSITY

Many people consider cultural diversity to be synonymous with and limited to racial differences; some would also include gender differences. Others maintain that it is geographic boundaries that determine cultural boundaries. The fact is, however, that the concept of cultural diversity is not restricted to race, sex, and geographic boundaries.

Webster's Third New International Dictionary defines **culture** as:

> the total pattern of human behavior and its products embodied in thought, speech, action and artifacts and dependent upon man's capacity for learning and transmitting knowledge to succeeding generations through the use of tools, language, and systems of abstract thought.[9]

Culture deals with the way people live by providing a framework for living. Some cultures are broad in scope and include large numbers of people. Other cultures are comprised of smaller groups of people who are set apart by some shared characteristic or interest. The thousands of special-interest groups represented on the World Wide Web suggest just how many micro-cultures, often called subcultures, exist.

Culture provides a frame-
work for living.

Contrary to popular belief, one need not even travel abroad to encounter different cultures. In fact, U.S. society is comprised of many cultures, and most people are members of more than one. Whether your interest is line dancing or paleontology, all who share that interest comprise a culture. Cultures may be categorized in many different ways. In the movie, *What about Bob?*, Bill Murray's character has a simplistic view of the cultures in U.S. society; he feels that there are two types of people: "Those who like Neil Diamond and those who don't." Regardless of how narrowly or broadly culture is perceived, culture embodies thoughts and actions that are learned, shared with others, and conveyed to future generations.

COMPONENTS OF CULTURE

A culture is made up of many different components, including everything that a society thinks, says, does, and makes. The value system, roles, religious traditions, decision-making patterns, language, and time orientation are especially strong determinants of a culture.

Value System

The value system constitutes the foundation of a culture, and it provides guidelines for behavior. That which is proper, acceptable, and significant in any culture is identified by its value system.[10] In the United States, managers are expected to calculate what must be done in order to accomplish their job-related goals and then to act on the calculations. They are trained to remain conscious of the goals at all times. Goal orientation is not such a significant part of many foreign cultures, however; individuals in other cultures commonly allow nonurgent family matters to take precedence over business. Efficiency and productivity, which are common goals of American managers, are alien notions in many foreign cultures.

Not all cultures produce managers who are as goal-oriented as Americans.

American values are not readily transferable to other cultures. For instance, Jane Scarborough accepted an assignment as compensation consultant to a mid-sized textile producer in South America. She convinced management that more generous pay would increase employee loyalty and reduce absenteeism. Pay was increased by 25 percent. Jane returned to the United States. Absenteeism worsened as many workers discovered that the increased pay enabled them to subsist on an even shorter workweek. Some workers began to take every Wednesday off and others left at noon on Wednesday.

Many American managers define themselves by their jobs, but this is seldom true in foreign cultures. Foreign managers frequently place a high priority on getting to know individuals before doing business with them. Small talk and socializing routinely precede getting down to business. This dismays American representatives, who regard such use of time to be wasteful, if not pointless.

Roles

The role a person plays and the status accorded to that role is indicative of the culture in which that person functions. As the volume of international business travel continues to increase, more people will have to modify their role-playing on the basis of the culture in which they are doing business. Since the role of women varies so dramatically around the world, businesswomen are especially challenged to be aware of the cultural expectations of their clients. In some countries female business executives have traditionally been taken less seriously than are males. There is, however, a growing acceptance of women in the international business arena, and international business executives seem to accept things from their clients that they might not tolerate within their own culture.[11]

The status of a role in a culture indicates much about that culture.

Women make up slightly more than 10 percent of international business travelers based in the United States and approximately 40 percent of business travelers within the United States.[12] Following the lead of U.S. business in the promotion of women to executive positions, a similar upgrading of the role of women is slowly occurring in much of the world. According to the Human Development Report of the United Nations, however, in many less developed nations women still trail far behind men in literacy and employment.[13]

Compensation is another indicator of the status of a person's role, especially in the United States, where the average starting salary of a public school teacher in 1993 was $22,505, the lowest salary for any of the eleven categories of college graduates reported.[14] When the Dallas Cowboys agreed to pay Deon Sanders $35 million for a seven-year contract to play football, that also revealed much about the U.S. culture.[15]

The manner in which a person is referred to is another measure of respect for that person's role. In many international cultures respect is demonstrated by addressing people by their job title, such as "Editor," or "Manager." Since age is equated with wisdom in many cultures, older people are often shown special respect. Thus sex, occupation, financial status, and age are among the factors that pertain to role.

Religious Traditions

Many early colonists came to America in search of a sanctuary in which religion would be a matter of personal choice. Regular or semi-regular attendance at weekly religious services is the most obvious evidence of membership in an organized religion. Americans assume that religious beliefs influence their morals and ethics in everyday matters. Little additional tangible evidence exists of the practical impact of religion.

Religion exerts a strong influence on business in some cultures.

In many foreign countries, however, religion directly influences the manner in which business is conducted, including business communication. In Muslim countries, for example, everything stops five times a day for prayers. Non-Muslims, though not expected to pray, are expected to honor the practice, despite delays in business matters.

Every culture has its own holy days. Business travelers need to refer to a calendar that includes, for example, Ramadan (in Islamic cultures), Lady of Guadalupe Day in Mexico, and Chinese New Year.

In many countries businesses follow religious dicta.

Decision-Making Patterns

In the goal-oriented, time-is-money culture of the United States, decisions are usually made and implemented as quickly and efficiently as possible. Often this efficiency depends on the accepted strategy of delegation of authority. In other countries, approaches vary; some are more participative than the United States and others are less so.

In many countries, companies are run from above, with all decisions, even on routine matters, made at or near the top of the organization. French, German, and Italian executives tend to make most decisions themselves rather than to delegate, and they direct rather than persuade.

Arab executives rely on one-to-one consultation rather than on committees or on simple delegation of decision-making responsibility. Decision-making patterns in Arab culture are unstructured and informal.

Japanese managerial principles emphasize the role of the group in decision making. In this **bottom-up style**, subordinates are actively involved in all phases of arriving at decisions. There is much give and take between top management and subordinates. This approach is time consuming but, once made, decisions are implemented quickly because all of the details have already been considered.

The most successful managers assume the decision-making patterns of the host culture.

Patterns of decision making vary throughout the world. A manager who considers his or her own approach to be superior and attempts to mandate its use in another culture is unlikely to succeed. American managers can work toward maximizing their effectiveness by accepting and employing the decision-making patterns of the **host culture**—that is, the culture of the country in which they seek to do business.

To illustrate, Jeff Turner strongly believed in letting workers make as many decisions as possible. When transferred to Germany, he continued to ask workers to make group decisions. He soon learned, however, that they simply polled the group and reported the findings. The German workers expected Jeff, as manager, to make the decision.

Language

Many Americans justify their lack of a second language by pointing out that English is rapidly becoming the language of international business. This attitude can lead to problems, as Holly Norton learned during a 30-day assignment abroad. She had been unconcerned about going to Germany, because everyone there must study English in school. She soon discovered that the English language requirement did not necessarily mean overall fluency or that American English was being taught. The night she drove 60 miles in the wrong direction in a heavy rain before realizing that she had misunderstood directions, Holly vowed to acquire a second language.

Foreign nationals are likely to nod in agreement over this old joke:

Q: What do you call a person who can speak two languages?
A: Bilingual.
Q: How about three?
A: Trilingual.
Q: Good, how about one?
A: Hmmmm . . . American![16]

Even while depending on English-speaking foreigners to transact business in English, Americans tend to use jargon in their speaking and writing that is intelligible only to other Americans. Those who assume that their English will always be understood as intended are in for a shock.

Language and intercultural issues impact not only those who travel abroad. Linguistic and cultural problems abound within the United States where, according to the Census Bureau, more than 300 different languages and dialects are spoken. Of a total student population of 42 million, 5.5 percent of them have a limited proficiency in English. Spanish is the native language of three-quarters of the limited-English-proficiency students in the United States.[17]

Concerns that immigrants would maintain their own language rather than learn English has led to a movement to make English the nation's official language. If such a movement were to succeed, the government would ban bilingual education and require that most government documents be printed in English only. This movement, although largely symbolic, illustrates a long-standing national concern about immigrants. Prior to the American Revolution Ben Franklin warned that immigrants would never learn English. During the time of World War I attempts were made to ban the teaching of German in the United States.[18]

One should not make many assumptions, even when communicating with a person for whom English is the native language. A business traveler in Australia during the World Soccer Cup finals tried to fit in with her clients by discussing soccer with them. Each time she would ask a client, "Which team are you rooting for?" she would receive a quizzical look and little in the way of conversation. Finally an older businessman sternly informed her that in Australia "root" was a term for a sexual act.[19]

A common language does not ensure understanding.

A shared language ties people together, but it does not ensure complete understanding. Language is a vital component in the concept of culture because it is difficult to understand a particular culture without understanding the language.

Time Orientation

Many businesspeople in the United States consider time to be the scarcest natural resource, and they treat it accordingly. "Time is money," is a statement that has been repeated in U.S. business circles for generations. It stands to reason that in any society in which books with titles like *How to Control Your Life and Your Time*,[20] *Overcoming Procrastination*,[21] and *The One Minute Manager*[22] become best-sellers, there must be strong feelings on the subject of time. In both North America and northern Europe punctuality is considered to be essential; it is equated with efficiency and courtesy. To be late for a meeting or appointment is thought to be disrespectful of the party who is kept waiting, and such behavior also suggests disorganization.

Time is more important in the United States than in many other places.

On the other hand, some cultures are characterized by a different attitude toward time. When doing business in Latin America, southern Europe, or parts of Asia, U.S. executives discover that they are not able to fit as many appointments into the day as they do in the United States because there is a more casual attitude toward time. While we are taught to set a schedule and stick to it, schedules are more likely to be viewed as a loose guide in many cultures. In Africa or the Middle East it is not uncommon to keep people waiting for an hour or more.[23] Differing perceptions of time have been the cause of many misunderstandings in international business.

CHARACTERISTICS ATTRIBUTED TO AMERICANS

The United States is an insulated country, sharing borders with only Canada and Mexico. Because of the country's huge size, many of its citizens, especially those in the heartland, are unaware of the significant differences that exist among cultures. However, this lack of cultural awareness will gradually subside as dealings with other countries become more routine.

The United States exports its popular culture all around the world through movies such as *Jurassic Park* and entertainers like Whitney Houston. Many of the television shows that are popular in the United States have a viewing audience that spans the globe, sometimes to the chagrin of much of the local adult population. *The Suddeutsche Zeitung* bemoaned the popularity of *Beavis and Butt-head* in Germany among "adolescent loudmouths with a developed feeling for guitars and a still undeveloped feeling for taste."[24] Whether or not the culture conveyed by the United States bears any resemblance to reality, non-Americans tend to attribute certain characteristics to Americans, and some behaviors of Americans tend to validate these perceptions.

When shown abroad, U.S. movies and television shows teach many about the U.S. culture, for better or for worse.

Individualistic

Diverse people have immigrated to America for religious, economic, and political freedom throughout the country's history. U.S. citizens have always valued their independence. Strength is often measured by the ability to stand alone; for many years actor John Wayne was viewed as the epitome of rugged individualism. Today Ted Turner is widely admired for his individualism and for his drive for self-realization through the American business process.

In keeping with this heritage, the United States sets global standards for human rights, particularly as related to employment. Foreign companies operating within U.S. borders are likely to encounter difficulties in following American laws written to protect women, minorities, older citizens, and the handicapped. They often perceive these laws as unreasonable, counterproductive, and contrary to their own views of social order.

Arrogant

Many American businesspeople tend to act as if they believe everyone wishes he or she were American. As a result they deal with foreign nationals in a manner perceived as offensive. By conveying an attitude of superiority and displaying an unwillingness to accept the worth of others, Americans construct obstacles that hamper their intercultural effectiveness.

The enthusiastic patriotism of Americans stems from certain basic beliefs. For example, Americans assume that all people—male or female, rich or poor, regardless of race or creed—can become successful if they work hard enough. Americans also view with pride the system of advancement based on merit. Their confidence in the free enterprise system is a topic that Americans expound on to an extent that may alienate others.

Aggressive

Americans respect the ability to confront problems head on. They are taught to answer challenges directly through clever and quick verbal exchanges. Consider that there are 15 times more lawyers per capita in America than in Japan. Given the Japanese mistrust of the legal system, particularly the U.S. legal system, the presence of lawyers can severely disrupt negotiations between Japanese and American business people.

American business operates in an environment of high pressure. Successful business people in the United States are able not only to cope with the pressure but to flourish under stress. When they are assigned to a foreign country, however, these same abilities often become dysfunctional. The aggressiveness that leads to accomplishment in the United States may contribute to failure abroad. An aggressive and direct communication style will be viewed as unmannerly and inappropriate in many foreign countries.

Intolerant of Silence

As children, Americans are frequently put on display and are taught by their parents to entertain and to show other adults what they have learned. They are instructed to focus on external communications and how these communications move them toward predominately materialistic goals. Contrast this with Eastern cultures that hold spiritual growth in higher regard and stress the mastery of inner communication. Rather than view periods of silence as an opportunity to reflect on the situation at hand, Americans feel uncomfortable with silence and feel pressured to fill the void with conversation. This puts them at a significant disadvantage when negotiating with many foreign executives, especially Asians, who are comfortable with silence.

Americans tend to be overly talkative in the eyes of many foreigners.

Money Oriented

American businesspeople are commonly viewed as having a bottom-line mentality, that is, they base their actions primarily on the effect the actions will have on the finances of the operation. When a choice must be made between people and profits, Americans are expected to opt for profits. Indeed, U.S. companies often view their people and social institutions as resources to be cultivated. An American manager based in an undeveloped country may strive to mechanize as a means of reducing labor costs; foreign managers may view such an action as contrary to good business practice because it will take away jobs. Any business communicator whose messages focus solely on money will enjoy little credibility in many foreign countries.

Preoccupied with Time

American businesspeople tend to view time as a scarce natural resource, as something not to be wasted. For that reason they set deadlines for themselves and operate to meet them. In many other parts of the world, however, time is viewed as the servant rather than the master. The expression "laid back" describes many cultures' attitudes toward time. Signs of impatience by a U.S. sales representative kept waiting for a scheduled appointment reduce the probability of success.

A race with the clock is how many Americans spend every business day.

    The focus of Americans is often criticized, too, as being too narrow and present oriented. Rather than develop broad strategies, which requires recognition that organized change takes time, Americans act to bring about rapid change. The long-term results of this approach are being questioned by Americans themselves.

Obsessed with Talking Shop

Americans, it is alleged, do not discriminate between appropriate and inappropriate settings in which to transact business. Instead, they are likely to violate the norms of a host country by talking about business matters in settings in which social conversation is expected. Good business communication practices dictate that message content be appropriate for the situation.

Informal

Although highly structured with their time and goal-oriented behaviors, Americans tend to be relaxed in dress and in their relationships with others. Picture the stereotypical California talent agent as characterizing this position at an extreme. His clothing is casual, faddish, and gaudy. He delights in calling people by their first names and

☑ *CHECKLIST for Changing the Way Americans Are Perceived Abroad*

_____ Tone down the image of rugged individualist.

_____ Resist the temptation to feel that American ways are superior.

_____ Learn the art of patient compromise.

_____ Be aware that silence can be a strategy.

_____ Understand the impact on other cultures of putting money before people.

_____ Do not press for immediate action or decisions.

_____ Restrict shop talk to appropriate settings.

_____ Avoid excessive informality.

_____ Learn to speak the language of the country in which you are doing business.

In today's business environment Americans need to speak the language of countries in which they do business.

may tack on a "sweetheart" or "my man." He leans back in his chair with his feet on the table in front of him. When meeting people for the first time, he is likely to vigorously clasp their hand and shoulder as though being reunited with a long-lost buddy.

Few American businesspeople carry informality to this length, but in the eyes of foreigners they are still too unceremonious. No other country tolerates such relaxed exchanges between superiors and subordinates, nor do many of them accept the use of first names in business. In Japan, for example, first names are used only among family members and close friends. Even long-time business associates and coworkers are hesitant to use first names.

Unwilling to Learn Host Language

Many foreign nationals are fluent in several languages. In contrast, as indicated in the section on cultural diversity, American managers historically have expected business communication to be conducted in English. Unwillingness to take the time to learn a host language reinforces the negative impression Americans make.

As early as 1958 a book called *The Ugly American* indicted representatives of the United States, both official and unofficial, for their behavior abroad.[25] The negative impressions created by their behavior, according to the authors, would ultimately damage the image of the United States. Many of the allegations made in that book are still relevant. With inappropriate behavior and questionable communication practices, American business representatives abroad damage themselves, their employers, and their country.

CULTURAL PROFILES OF LEADING TRADE PARTNERS

English is spoken by only about 10 percent of the world's population. Even if a global language were to exist, cultural differences would preclude complete understanding among people. The more businesspeople can learn about a foreign culture, however, the more effectively they will operate within it. This section focuses on the cultures in which readers are most likely to find themselves doing business.

Canada

Canada and the United States are the world's largest trading partners. When measuring cultural diversity, the differences between Canada and the United States seem slight, but they are noteworthy. The similarities between the two countries lead many U.S. businesspeople to view Canada as identical to the United States. Although most Canadians live close to the U.S. border and are familiar with American ways, they do not necessarily like the American way of doing things.

The close proximity of the United States to Canada is both an asset and a liability. We tend to take Canada for granted, and this often weakens relations between the two countries at all levels—government, business, and interpersonal. Businesspeople who display an awareness of Canada's uniqueness are better able to communicate with Canadians.

Two primary cultures dominate Canada: English and French. Canada is officially designated as a bilingual nation and many of its citizens are truly bilingual. This bilingualism contributes to the cosmopolitan atmosphere of the Canadian business community. French is recognized as the official language in the province of Quebec. Anyone who is able to conduct business in French when in Quebec holds a definite advantage over a competitor who lacks that ability.

The Canadian business culture is more formal than that of the United States. European styles and manners prevail and people are more aware of etiquette than in the United States.

Canadians appreciate business communication that is direct and to the point. Presentations that are both clear and thorough are likely to be well received. In the traditional business culture, a conservative approach to communication is appropriate. Gimmickry and showmanship will go unrewarded; decorum is expected.

In Canada the system for dating correspondence is like that in Europe. May 1, 1997, is written 5/1/97 in the United States; it is 1/5/97 in Canada and Europe. Business relationships have soured as a result of this difference. Imagine discovering that the order expected to arrive on January 5 would not arrive until May 1!

Canadians have long felt that most people from the United States are both ignorant of and indifferent toward Canada. They will be more receptive to the U.S. manager who communicates a knowledge of Canadian current events, political units, and geography.

> The ability to speak French is an aid to doing business in Quebec.

Mexico

Like Canada, Mexico sometimes seems to exist in the shadow of the United States. This proximity sometimes causes identity problems for Mexicans, who do not like for their country to be compared to the United States. Even implied comparisons should be avoided in business communication.

Neither Canadians nor Mexicans like to hear U.S. citizens referred to as "Americans." They share this sentiment with the citizens of most of the other nations in Central and South America, all of whom rightfully consider themselves to be Americans as well.

The warmth and personalism of the Mexican people pervade all areas of that culture, including the business community. Anyone who fails to devote attention and time to personal relationships will not do well in this culture. U.S. businesspeople should get to know the people with whom they are dealing and establish a rapport with them.

Until trust is developed, little business will be transacted in the Latin culture. Developing trust is a gradual process, and Mexicans do not like being rushed. Hard-sell approaches are not effective.

> The first step in doing business with Mexicans is to develop sincere interpersonal relationships and trust.

> Doing business in Latin America is like getting married in a formal, old-fashioned way. First there's a period of courtship. It's a time of testing, a proving ground. If the two of you can manage to fall in love with each other, the rest becomes easier and things take on a logic and momentum of their own. If you don't take the time for a romance, the wedding will probably be called off. The business will go to a competitor who has the patience to cultivate a relationship first.[26]

Friendships are important in this culture, although they may take considerable time to cultivate. Casual conversation and sociability, likely to be perceived as unprofessional and inefficient in some cultures, is an important dimension of any business relationship in Mexico.

Mexicans like to make people happy and they show deference to those of higher status. This tendency results at times in their saying what they think the other person wants to hear. This same tendency also sometimes results in oral agreements that are subsequently broken in writing. Written agreements are necessary in business dealings in this type of culture.

Mexicans, and Latinos in general, disclose much about themselves in their dealings with others, and they expect others to reciprocate. Hard-driving U.S. executives who attempt to avoid such rituals are rarely effective in this culture. The best strategy is to reveal your personal side. Latin businessmen strive to develop a *simpatico* relationship—characterized by a sincere empathy such as old friends might share—before doing business together. The most effective U.S. business communicators recognize the value of empathy and work to develop it.

For individuals who manage foreign nationals in this culture, the style that seems most effective is one that demonstrates **machismo**—a strong sense of power and pride. Machismo is conveyed through forceful and self-confident dealings with others.

Germany

In Germany, as in most of Europe, people are introduced by their last names and titles. Referring to a person by first name is considered impolite unless you have been invited to do so. Individuals who have known each other—perhaps worked side by side—for many years, still often address one another by title.

Unlike Latin Americans, Germans devote little time to developing relationships with business associates. A social conversation may precede business dealings, but it will be kept brief. German business executives tend to get down to business quickly.

Germans prefer logical rather than emotional arguments.

To be well received, a business presentation should be factual, explicit, and thorough, yet concise. A business presentation that is perceived as informative will be viewed more positively than one seen as being mainly persuasive. Logical appeals are more effective in this culture than emotional appeals. Jokes, a part of many presentations in the United States, should be excluded for two reasons: (1) cultural differences make it unlikely that jokes told by a U.S. representative will be understood and (2) business communication, including whatever small talk accompanies it, is regarded as serious.

One German proverb defines America as "a place where an hour is 40 minutes." This may suggest that the pace in the United States is much faster than in Germany, but there is not much difference between the two, especially in urban areas. Punctuality is as important to German executives as to their U.S. counterparts. Appointments should be made well in advance, and business calls should not be made without appointments.

Northern European nations in general take pride in their longevity and admire it in other institutions. The date of the founding of any older firm should be included on the business cards of the representatives of the firm. Holders of advanced educational degrees also receive high esteem. Business representatives' advanced degrees should be indicated on their business cards.

Currently, pride in native languages is growing in many countries. This pride is sometimes reflected in an insistence that the local language be used. In Germany, for example, government contracts must be written in German; this policy has significant implications for any organization seeking to do business with any unit of the German government.

Although few U.S. executives may become fluent enough to write contracts in a second language, a basic knowledge of the language of the host nation is invaluable. Most European languages distinguish between a familiar and a polite form of "you." Learning to distinguish between the two forms and mastering the use of the polite form, which would ordinarily be used in business communication, are important so as to avoid embarrassment.

The German workforce is comfortable with an authoritarian management style. Communication is direct and managers who are most effective in this culture direct rather than persuade. In Germany, policy, decisiveness, and breadth of knowledge give a manager stature.

Business communication should be direct and task-oriented, but hard-sell approaches are rarely effective. Logical, rather than emotional, messages are more likely to be successful.

China

China covers a land area the same size as the United States, but its population of one billion is approximately four times that of the United States. From 1949 until the mid-1970s the Chinese government kept the nation isolated from the rest of the world. Since then the doors have been open to foreign trade, and organizations in the United States, as well as in other nations, have been transacting business with the Chinese. In 1993 China exported approximately $31.5 billion worth of goods to the United States while importing $8.7 billion.[27]

In the Chinese business community, organization and punctuality are important. Directness, however, is one characteristic on which the Chinese culture differs from those of the United States and northern Europe. In fact, the prevailing communication style is indirect, extremely polite, and bordering on the evasive. This evasiveness can be both frustrating and charming. In their book *Going International,* Copeland and Griggs tell of a rejection slip that a Beijing publication sent to a British journalist:

> We have read your manuscript with boundless delight. If we were to publish your paper, it would be impossible to publish any work of a lower standard. And as it is unthinkable that, in the next thousand years, we shall see its equal; we are, to our regret, compelled to return your divine composition, and beg you a thousand times to overlook our short sight and timidity.[28]

Obviously, the Chinese tend to use hyperbole in their communication.

Formality is another significant characteristic of the Chinese culture. Etiquette is more important than in most cultures in which U.S. business operates. A very reserved people, the Chinese do not like to be touched. A brief handshake and bow is the usual greeting or farewell. The stereotypical backslapping U.S. salesperson would be met with quiet disdain.

The Chinese are very slow in establishing business relationships with outsiders. They are willing to devote inordinate amounts of time to social relations before getting down to business, much to the dismay of U.S. executives. Salespeople from the United States who have done business with the Chinese will attest that it seems to take forever to reach a decision. Once the decision is made, however, the Chinese may become as impatient to implement it as a North American.

A group orientation pervades every aspect of the Chinese culture. A Chinese businessperson uses "we," even when talking about himself or herself. U.S. business executives should do likewise and avoid the use of "I," which is viewed as evidence of self-centeredness, a characteristic the Chinese view with contempt.

Involving the worker is a key to effective management. Senior and middle-level employees are encouraged to make suggestions, and in the process management seeks to develop some common goals. Because an authoritarian style of management is likely to succeed, managers should seek to establish a cooperative work environment.

The Chinese are very formal, reserved, and slow in developing business relationships.

Japan

Japan is a small country, destitute of natural resources, a part of Asia but not like Asia. In Japan contrasts abound, both visually and idealistically—for example, the modern Seto Ohashi bridge stands in sharp contrast to ancient Shinto shrines. The furious pace of technological development seems to contradict the fervent attempts to preserve centuries-old customs, rituals, and social structure. The conflicting desires of the Japanese people are causing their culture to change haltingly. Foreign visitors still find Japan to be one of the least accommodating of all the industrialized nations.

The Japanese value conformity—in dress, education, roles, language, and values. Japan's education system is considered to be one of the best in the world, with well-qual-

The Japanese, like the Chinese, focus on conformity, group values, and harmony.

ified teachers commanding high respect and significant salaries. Students in Japan attend school 240 days a year compared with approximately 180 days in the United States.

Japanese children are taught that they must develop inner strength and peace in order to be able to use these values to benefit society. Meditation is encouraged. The Japanese people believe that communication can occur through sensory channels other than hearing, seeing, and physically touching. Silence can therefore be used as a means of communication. Japanese parents value this "silent rapport" with their children. Adults in group situations feel no need to self-disclose or use space-filling conversation in order to be at ease.

The primary unit of value in Japan is the group. Attention to the individual is required only for its value to the group. Identity is found, not through individual virtue, but through collective excellence and strength. The Japanese support consensus decision making and group responsibilities and rewards. Managers do not single out individuals for recognition because outstanding individual effort is considered to be a necessary part of group participation.

Communication patterns are very different from those seen in most other cultures. In a conflict situation, Japanese will typically choose silence as their response. As conflict increases, their withdrawal becomes even more pronounced. Their primary goal is harmony and they will allow as long as necessary for the relationship to develop in order to support this goal.

BOXED IN

AN ETHICAL DILEMMA

A cardboard box on the corner of the desk holds photographs and other personal possessions John will take with him after 16 years with the company. The memories are rich and bring a smile to his face. But, like many companies today, Lovecraft Importers is having to downsize, and many long-term employees are being let go. After two years of wondering when his number would come up, John is glad the waiting is over. He is ready to start a new career that will renew his passion for work.

He picks up a document from Jiang Silk Inc., a Chinese exporting firm, and quickly scans its familiar contents. This document represents over six months of negotiations on a project that John has personally supervised and that has resulted in a substantial contract for Lovecraft. He takes pride in a job well done and also recalls with pleasure the foreign friends he has made in the process.

He discovers that this final contract, complete except for his signature and that of his superior, contains a major error. Despite care to ensure that the communications between the two companies were clear and exact, the agreement drawn up by Jiang Silk reflects a translation error that would cost the Chinese company thousands of dollars in fees. John knows that if he points the misunderstanding out to his superior, he will be told to sign the contract anyway—his company cannot afford another delay. John is weary of the rat race. He knows that all he has to do is sign his name, pick up his box, and walk out the door, and these hassles will be behind him.

John feels boxed in. What would you do?

European Union

The Common Market—a coalition of France, West Germany, Italy, Belgium, The Netherlands, Luxembourg, and later Denmark, Great Britain, Ireland, Greece, Portugal, and Spain—was founded in 1958. It was formed to improve economic activities and political relationships between the member countries. Now known as the **European Union**, or **EU**, it also includes Austria, Sweden, and Finland, and its goals have broadened to include improved cooperation in science, education, and cultural matters (see Figure 3.1). The EU is now the second largest trading partner of the United States. In 1993 U.S.-EU trade totaled $195 billion. Twenty-one percent of total U.S. exports went to the EU, and the EU provided 17 percent of U.S. imports.[29] The EU hope is to enhance Europe's global competitiveness and improve the citizens' standard of living.

International business will change dramatically as a result of Europe's combined economic power.

Specific communication obstacles that interfere with smooth operations between EU countries include ten different languages and hundreds of different cultures and subcultures. Additionally, telecommunications in the EU is archaic, inefficient, and expensive.

Although the diversity in people and customs will not be immediately affected by the EU, business strategies certainly will. The increased business activity will require other nationals to have greater international communication skills.

INTERCULTURAL DIFFERENCES IN BODY LANGUAGE

Only 7 percent of what is communicated between people is transmitted through words. As will be discussed in Chapter 15, the bulk of what is communicated is a function of interpreted physiology, both body language and tone of voice. Individuals who are skilled at observing and interpreting the physiology of others, and who can adjust their viewpoints of the world in such a way as to accommodate the perspectives of others, will find that they are able to communicate rather effectively with people with whom they have no common language. However, this task is complicated not just by the absence of a shared vocabulary, but also by the radically different meanings that common body movements can have. Drawing primarily on the work of Peter Marsh, this section will explore some of these differences in terms of distance, eye contact, facial expression, and time.

Distance

Each individual varies in the size of the bubble of personal body space that surrounds him or her, but cultural patterns can be seen. The people of the **contact cultures** of Latin America, Southern Europe, and the Arab states touch more often and stand much closer than do Northern Europeans. North Americans fall somewhere between these two extremes. Marsh reported a study done on the differences:

> One researcher observed 180 touches on average between pairs of acquaintances spending an hour together in San Juan, Puerto Rico, and 110 in Paris, France. In Gainesville, Florida, the average was less than twice. In London, England, it was 0. When people touch each other during conversation, their contact commonly includes control touches such as tapping your listener on the arm to emphasize a point, as well as touching on the arm or shoulder to amplify expression of support and appreciation.[30]

Visitors to foreign cultures can also be startled by the different types of touches. In the Middle East or Southern Europe, two men might walk with their hands clasped or with their arms around each other's shoulders. Westerners would regard this behavior as acceptable for women but effeminate in men, preferring to greet each other with a handshake. Mexicans embrace companions upon meeting them, Japanese bow, and

Map Inset shows the continent of Europe in relation to the rest of the world. Europe's area is about one-third larger than that of the United States (excluding Alaska and Hawaii) and its population is more than double that of the United States.

Figure 3.1
The European Community

Malaysians press their noses against each other's cheeks. Without knowing what is acceptable distance in a culture, businesspeople can easily violate a social norm or misinterpret the behavior of others as being either distant and cold or as being overly aggressive, depending on their point of view.

The most common form of greeting among Westerners is the handshake, and how one shakes hands will influence an initial impression. By U.S. standards, the ideal handshake is firm, just as is true in Germany and Korea. There is considerable variety, however, in what constitutes an appropriate handshake in other cultures. In England and France the handshake should be softer, and even more so in much of Asia.

Eye Contact

Culture influences what is considered acceptable or expected eye contact. People in the contact cultures not only stand physically closer; they also tend to exchange more eye contact. Although Americans view direct eye contact as a sign of power and honesty, they feel that unbroken eye contact is too aggressive to be used in normal business dealings and personal interactions. They may interpret the directed gaze of Latin Americans as being threatening or insulting. At the same time, a Southern European may view a North American's broken eye contact as insincere or impolite.

The gazes of the French and Middle Easterners are direct and prolonged, while Asians, who consider prolonged eye contact to be impolite, engage in minimal eye contact. Lowered eyes are thought to convey respect.[31] In some cultures people listen while completely avoiding eye contact.

> People of the contact cultures touch more often, stand closer, and have more eye contact.

Facial Expressions

Cultural differences in smiling are found even within the United States. The highest incidence of smiling is in the Southeast, specifically in Atlanta, Louisville, Memphis, and Nashville. A Southerner smiling and walking down a New England street may be seen as crazy or scorning. On the other hand, a New Englander, who typically smiles the least, might be seen as annoyed or dejected in the South.[32]

Even something as subtle as raising eyebrows can have different connotations in different cultures. According to Marsh:

> Darwin reported that if (eyebrow raising) accompanied a head-toss it meant "yes" in Ethiopia and Borneo. In Greece and Turkey, however, a similar gesture means "no." The difference between the two expressions may lie in the eye opening wide for "yes," resembling the pleasure of a surprise; narrow, resembling a supercilious expression, for "no." In Japan the eyebrow flash has sexual connotations and decency requires its avoidance in Japanese meetings.[33]

PRINCIPLES FOR EFFECTIVE INTERCULTURAL COMMUNICATION

Communicating effectively in English with people who do not share your culture or for whom American English is a second language requires careful use of the language. By adhering to certain principles you will enhance your intercultural communication skills, both as a writer and as a speaker.

Written Communication

1. Avoid idioms, abbreviations, acronyms, and jargon. When you tell a friend from Dubuque that it is "raining cats and dogs," the news is likely to be greeted with a yawn. When you make the same statement to an associate from Caracas you may see a look of astonishment, and perhaps, a dash to the window. Such an expression is an **idiom**. Although each word may be understood by an English-speaking foreigner, the intended meaning may not be. Idioms complicate international communication.

   Technical writing often relies heavily on jargon. Consider this printed information that accompanied a hair dryer manufactured in China:

   > Choosing subferalle high temperature and hard plows materials, it cannot be easily broken more thom its inner part has heatproof equipment and not change the sapl of outride for a long time ure[sic].

The message, which was meant to attest to the durability of the hair dryer, was lost in the translation into English.

An **acronym** is a word comprised of the first letters from each of a series of words in a phrase. Using acronyms allows people to save time in their writing or speaking, provided everyone is familiar with the acronyms. Anyone employed in a U.S. business organization knows what a CEO is, for example, but foreign nationals would not. Acronyms should be avoided in international communication.

2. Learn the appropriate format for letters in the culture in which you are attempting to transact business. A letter that does not meet the expectations of the receiver is unlikely to be effective.

3. Be brief in words, sentences, and paragraphs. Make the first sentence of each paragraph the topic sentence, and use the rest of the paragraph to provide clarification and elaboration.

4. Use concrete words whenever possible. A word with a specific meaning is much more likely to be understood than is an abstract term.

5. Use visual aids whenever possible to reinforce your written message. Frequently a graphic will clarify a point that was not clear.

6. Have a knowledgeable second party read and evaluate the document.

Recent marketing history is rich with examples of advertising campaigns that backfired because of problems with semantics. "Come alive with Pepsi," went over well in the United States. The German version, "Come out of the grave with Pepsi," and the Asian interpretation, "Pepsi brings your ancestors back from the grave," understandably failed to increase sales in those countries. Incidentally, the phrase "The spirit is willing but the flesh is weak" becomes "The ghost is ready but the meat is rotten" in Russian. All ads, speeches, slogans, and important letters should be checked with a local translator.

Oral Communication

1. Speak slowly. Anyone listening to a conversation in a foreign language marvels at the participants' ability to understand such rapid speech. You may recall hearing an unfamiliar language and thinking it sounded like gibberish. Rapid English sounds the same way to those for whom it is not a primary language. For that reason, speak slowly. When the other person is speaking in English, never interrupt. He or she may need time to think about how best to express a thought.

2. Avoid the use of slang or profanity. Slang is likely to be misunderstood, and profanity may be thought to be offensive.

3. Encourage feedback from the other party. Make it easy for that person to ask questions or make observations.

4. Don't interrupt when the other person is speaking. Not only are interruptions discourteous, they are likely to inhibit that individual from further participation.

5. Watch the other person for nonverbal cues. If confusion or misunderstanding appear to be occurring, modify your approach and continue to monitor nonverbal messages.

Extra Efforts That Pay Dividends

1. Learn as much as possible about the other person's culture. The more you know about the background of a person the easier it will be for that person to identify with you.

2. Learn appropriate greetings and other practical phrases in the other person's language. Such actions will be greatly appreciated, and mispronunciations will not matter.

3. Be willing to admit it when you do not understand something. Ask for clarification, and ask again if necessary.

4. Be patient. Don't be in a hurry, and avoid the temptation to talk louder. The problem is rarely one of not enough volume. It takes time to achieve mutual understanding, even under the best of circumstances. When significant cultural differences are present, it may take somewhat longer.

AMERICAN MANAGERS ABROAD

In the past several decades, the volume of international business has increased greatly. In 1991 there were 12,741 foreign-owned companies operating in the United States, and together they employed more than 2 million U.S. citizens. International travel continues to increase. The Travel Data Center projects that during 1997 more than 46 million internationals will visit the United States, and more than 50 million U.S. citizens will travel abroad.[34]

Employees of multinational organizations are routinely transferred to foreign countries. Each successive year's college graduates are increasingly likely to spend time living and working in foreign cultures.

Researchers have identified two skills they think contribute most to intercultural effectiveness. They are (1) the ability to establish interpersonal relationships and (2) the ability to communicate effectively. Individuals who possess these skills cope better in foreign environments than do those who lack them. Unfortunately, U.S. companies may send these employees abroad with no intercultural or language training and with no consideration for how the individual employee will fit in with the cultural expectations of the new setting.

> Growing numbers of graduates are likely to spend time living and working in foreign cultures.

Preparing for Travel Abroad

Prior to departing for a foreign assignment, managers should learn as much about the culture as possible. No matter how rigorously they have prepared for the foreign assignment, however, they will experience some culture shock. This shock will be cushioned in proportion to the extent of their preparation.

Some business organizations provide intercultural training for employees anticipating overseas transfers. Such programs are intended to reduce the uncertainty the employee experiences on being thrust into a different environment. Whether or not you have access to such formal training, you can do much to reduce your degree of culture shock. In learning about a country's culture, you will gain the ability to anticipate patterns of behavior to which you will be exposed abroad as well as the reasons for the behavior. Equally important, you will learn the sort of behavior that will be expected of you in unfamiliar surroundings.

> Some U.S. businesses provide employees with intercultural training before sending them abroad.

Using Foresight in Planning Negotiations

Businesspeople who negotiate international business in their own country have the home-court advantage. When planning critical meetings on foreign ground, they should visit the country and their business counterparts ahead of time. This visit can facilitate their understanding of the people and reduce uncertainty surrounding the issues.

Indeed, the term "issues" points up a crucial cultural difference in negotiations. Westerners negotiate issues. From their perspective, each issue is to be discussed and agreed upon individually before moving on to the next issue. In the Soviet Union and Japan, however, agreement comes only after all issues have been discussed. No issue is settled in and of itself. This presents a problem to the Western negotiator.

American negotiators, for example, may become frustrated by what they perceive as a lack of progress when meeting with the Japanese and may be tempted to make concessions. The Japanese perspective, however, may be that negotiations are moving appropriately and the stage for making demands or concessions has not been reached. The Americans can easily lose power and respect by not recognizing the Japanese viewpoint.

Presenting to Groups

By following the following steps, a speaker can make it easier for listeners not highly proficient in English to follow and understand a business presentation:

1. Arrange to have two overhead projectors.
2. With one projector you will show a general outline of the major details of the presentation. Use the general outline to preview the main details to be covered in the presentation and continue to display it throughout the presentation.
3. With the other projector you will display suboutlines. These will be changed as the presentation progresses.
4. When moving from one main topic to the next, refer to the general outline to keep listeners aware of the structure of the presentation.
5. Remove the suboutline temporarily if you must present charts or other visuals.[35]

Attending to Details

Meetings and telephone contact among businesspeople from diverse cultures are more likely to be successful if these suggestions for planning and follow-up are observed:[36]

1. *Use of interpreters.* Be sure that all interpreters are familiar with both languages and both cultures so that they will be able to offer an interpretation that conveys the meaning of what you are saying and not just a translation of the words. These interpreters should also be familiar with the business to be discussed and should know the terminology or language of the business.
2. *Written summary.* Follow up every meeting with a written summary. Include in this summary what was discussed and what was agreed to.
3. *Use of confirmation.* To be sure that meanings and not just words have been communicated, use the telex to confirm the content of telephone conversations and to have a backup written statement of the communication.

MAINTAINING PERSPECTIVE

The competitive spirit between countries and cultures can be assumed to be an inherent part of the human drive. This does not mean, however, that all or even many business negotiations are win-lose situations. The emphasis should be on understanding and communicating for the purpose of satisfying mutual goals. Both parties in international business transactions should strive for win-win outcomes.

The U.S. population is heterogeneous and is, itself, comprised of multiple cultures. Businesspeople, therefore, need not go abroad to interact with foreign cultures. Some 600,000 legal immigrants arrive in the United States yearly, many more than go anywhere else in the world. These people restore national energy and enthusiasm and bring new talents. The flexibility and perspectives gained by growing up with and interacting with diverse cultures on a daily basis become the foundation for developing the needed skills for international business.

Key Terms

- **North American Free Trade Agreement (NAFTA)**
- **General Agreement on Tariffs and Trade (GATT)**
- **European Economic Community (EEC)**
- **culture**
- **bottom-up style**

- **host culture**
- **machismo**
- **European Union (EU)**
- **contact culture**
- **idiom**
- **acronym**

Summary

Global marketplace   p. 49
Governmental actions to facilitate international business   p. 50
Components of a culture   pp. 50–53
Influence of value systems on culture   p. 50
Significance of roles   p. 51
Characteristics attributed to citizens of the United States   pp. 53–56
Major trade partners of the United States   pp. 56–61
Role of the European Union in international business   p. 61
Intercultural differences in body language   pp. 61–63
Writing effectively for intercultural communication   pp. 63–64
Speaking effectively for intercultural communication   p. 64
Planning for doing business abroad   p. 65
Presenting to international groups   p. 66

Review Questions

1. What are six significant components of culture?

2. In what ways are foreign nationals' perceptions of Americans inaccurate?

3. Discuss the difficulties English-speaking natives of other countries would have working in the United States.

4. Choose a country discussed in this chapter and describe how you would prepare for a year-long assignment to that country.

5. Are there industries within the United States in which strict adherence to timetables is not as important? When foreign businesspeople set up business in the United States, do they necessarily have to adapt to American time standards?

6. What two skills contribute most to intercultural effectiveness?

Exercises

1. Your company is sending you to Japan to negotiate a contract for importing art objects to the United States. Although you speak no Japanese, the representatives from the other firm speak limited English. What steps should you take in preparing for this meeting?

2. Ask an international student what kinds of things Americans do that make it harder for him or her to understand and fit into the American culture. What kinds of things are helpful?

3. Form groups of two to four people and experiment with different distances and eye contact. At what distance do you feel as if someone is too close to talk to? Too far away? Vary the topic of conversation from something impersonal (such as the weather) to something personal (for example, what you find embarrassing) and note whether eye contact changes.

4. Briefly describe the most recent U.S. movie you have seen. When that movie is shown abroad, what image of the U.S. culture do you think it will convey?

CASE

Lou's New World

Chun-Sheng Yu, Hangzhou University, Hangzhou, Zhejiang, P.R. China

Lou got off the airplane and stood near the exit of the International Airport in Atlanta. It was 8:55 P.M., the arrival time Lou told his uncle in his letter. This was Lou's first visit to the United States. He continued to wait for his uncle to come and pick him up.

Lou had graduated from Beijing University in China and received his master's degree in management. Having been a university instructor for two years, he recognized that it would help in his professional development to do additional study abroad. Fortunately, Lou had an uncle who had been living in the United States almost 40 years. Because of his uncle's support, Lou was accepted by a university located in the city where his uncle lived.

Nearly an hour passed and Lou's uncle still had not appeared. Lou was wondering whether his letter had reached his uncle. Finally, he decided to telephone. To his surprise, his uncle told him over the phone that he had arranged with a Chinese restaurant to hire Lou and also provide Lou a place to live. Lou's uncle told Lou to go directly to the restaurant.

Lou was puzzled. He was the only nephew of his uncle. According to Chinese tradition, he would be warmly welcomed into his uncle's home and attend a big banquet in his honor his first night in the new country. Looking at the two big pieces of baggage, he felt lonely and helpless. He could not imagine carrying them with him and searching for the location of the restaurant in a large city that was totally new and strange to him.

Three weeks after his arrival, Lou was busy working as a waiter in the restaurant. He had made some friends in the city. One of them was Tom, a graduate student in the same business school where Lou was soon to begin his studies. Tom also worked in the restaurant. That day Lou saw several professors come into the restaurant. As he quickly approached them, one of them leaned toward him and said politely: "If you don't mind, I would like my son, Tom, to come and serve us." Tom came up, smiling. Lou heard the professor introduce Tom to his friends proudly and later saw that they put a tip on the table when they left. Lou spoke to Tom about it. "It's unimaginable in China, a father should bring his friends to the restaurant where his son was a waiter and pay a tip to his son!" Tom took Lou's comment quite casually and said it was common in the United States. Lou told him people in China would look down on a waiter. Certainly nobody would let his or her friends know that his son was a waiter. Tom responded, "Maybe you would be even more surprised if you know who my father is. He is president of your university!" Lou was utterly at a loss for words.

Lou's first quarter began. Within a few days, he noticed several things he could not understand. Students in the United States were very active in class. They seemed to have an endless number of questions every day. Some of the questions sounded facetious or silly. Lou thought, "Why are they not afraid of losing face before others?" Even more puzzling, a student raised a question and the professor simply said, "You've got me there. I cannot answer it right now. That's a really insightful question." In China it was unacceptable for a professor to admit his or her ignorance so openly, and students would despise such a professor. A professor should know everything.

What Lou found even stranger was that another professor took his dog into the classroom and introduced himself as a single man. Many students were enjoying soft drinks and snacks during the class. Soon Lou's advisor called him into his office and asked why he was so silent in class. He told Lou his lack of participation in class activities might affect his grade.

Lou was frustrated. He had been in the United States only a month and many strange things had happened in that short period of time. Lou wondered what else he would encounter.

Case Questions

1. What do you think of Lou's uncle? Why do you think the uncle introduced Lou to the restaurant owner instead of having Lou stay with him?

2. What is the hidden reason for Tom's work in the restaurant?

3. Why was Tom's father proud of his son?

4. Is there any relationship between the class behavior and culture? Please explain.

5. What suggestion could you make to Lou to help him adjust to his new world?

CASE

Business Is Business Wherever You Are

Susan Tucker Kinney, Wake Forest University

The weather in Minneapolis was a frigid -3 degrees as Jennifer opened the massive doors at Old World Spice. She was insensitive to the cold, however, as she thought about her new appointment. Imagine! She was soon to be Jennifer Sanders, regional manager, for the district office in Kerala, India.

She had worked hard for this level of responsibility and this assignment. In the seven years she had been with the organization, she had accepted all assignments without complaint. Admittedly she was tired from working 60-hour weeks and taking work home on weekends and on vacation. She could not say that she had made many friends in the company, but that was not important to her. She had proven to management that she was a "company player" and willing to sacrifice her personal life for the good of the company.

For a while Jennifer had been worried that she would not get the Kerala post. She was in competition with a relatively new member of the firm. John Krishna, a 1994 graduate of the University of Minnesota, had majored in international business and spoke four languages fluently. Although he did not have much of a track record with the company, he was well liked and was quickly gaining respect for his ability to communicate with the increasing number of foreign suppliers the company worked with. Apparently management had decided to reward Jennifer for her dedication to the company.

The day after the appointment was announced, she found on her desk a folder labeled *India: A Study of the Culture and the People*. The author was John Kirshna. The index listed such topics as traditions, religion, languages, dress, climate, and industry. "What nerve," she thought. "Does he believe I need to read one of his old essays?" She threw the report into the trash together with a packet of information on company training programs. Her time before leaving for India would be taken up with paperwork and reports. Besides, she had got by quite well so far on her own resources. "Business is business no matter where you are and I am a proven winner," she thought. She began to set an agenda for making the move.

Case Questions

1. Compile a list of criteria Old World Spice might use in selecting employees for overseas assignments.

2. Given the selection instrument you designed in response to Question 1, how might John and Jennifer compare?

3. You are Jennifer's immediate supervisor. What action will you take at this time to ensure that she is prepared for the move?

4. Assuming that Jennifer goes to India with no real understanding of the society, what kind of problems is she likely to encounter?

5. Find a recent article on India and note the ways the culture is different from your own.

CASE

A Rough Start
Margaret Fitch-Hauser, Auburn University

Sandra Lewis had been with Takabishi USA for a week when it was announced that the chairman of Takabishi Inc. would be coming from Japan to visit the U.S. locations. Sandra's boss, Jackie, needed every available minute to do the paperwork involved and asked Sandra to coordinate and schedule the events for the visit. She told Sandra to check the company's library for information on Mr. Takabishi, on the parent company, and on Japanese social and business customs. This trip would be Mr. Takabishi's first visit to the new plant and it was crucial that everything go smoothly.

Sandra found the material in the company library that Jackie had recommended. After carrying it to her office, she decided to begin by making a list of the tasks that she needed to complete in order to be ready for Mr. Takabishi's visit. This done, she picked up a book on Japanese customs and glanced at the table of contents. She noticed a section on gift giving. Oh yes, she thought, I remember that the Japanese like to exchange gifts. Immediately, Sandra put the book down and added gifts to her list.

Once Sandra had made all of the arrangements for Mr. Takabishi's visit, she wrote him a letter and enclosed the itinerary. She signed her letter "Sandra."

On the big day Sandra was undecided about what to wear. Finally satisfied with her appearance, she hurried to her car. If she caught all of the lights just right, she would be only a fashionable five minutes late.

Unfortunately, finding a parking place took longer than she had expected and she was 20 minutes late. Near the arrival gate she saw a group of Japanese men talking with some American officers of the company. They were all waiting for her, because she had scheduled herself to escort the party to the first stop on the itinerary.

Sandra wished she had taken more time to look at the company reports so that she would know which man was Mr. Takabishi. Unfortunately, she had not, and so she approached the nearest of the blue-suited men and shook hands and introduced herself. She failed to notice that the young man seemed embarrassed as he bowed to her. Sandra, not accustomed to bowing, decided not to return the bow. She did notice that a distinguished-looking man at the end of the line appeared to be shocked at her behavior.

After introductions, she opened her briefcase and gave each member of the party one of the gifts that she had selected for the occasion. As she handed each unwrapped box to a recipient, beginning with the guest standing nearest to her, she noticed they all looked uncomfortable. In an attempt to put everyone at ease, she urged that they open the boxes. Inside each box was a shiny pen with a digital clock near the clip. On a band around the pen were the words "made in Japan."

Sandra then gave them all a copy of the day's schedule of events and led them to cars waiting to take them to the hotel. As soon as they were settled, Sandra returned to her office. There Jackie was waiting for her, clearly unhappy.

Case Questions

1. Why did Jackie suggest that Sandra read about Mr. Takabishi, the company, and Japanese customs?

2. What mistakes might Sandra have avoided if she had taken the time to read the material Jackie suggested?

3. Why do you think the young man that she first shook hands with was uncomfortable?

4. Of what significance are the words "made in Japan" on the gift pens?

5. Of what significance is Sandra's late arrival at the airport?

Notes

1. Israel Zangwill, *The Melting Pot* (New York: AMS Press, 1969).

2. *Hoover's Handbook of World Business 1995-1996*, eds. Patrick J. Spain and James R. Talbot (Austin, TX: Reference Press, 1995), 90.

3. *Statistical Abstract of the United States* (Washington, DC: Department of Commerce, Bureau of the Census), p. 794, table 1328.

4. "American Utilities See Big Markets in Other Nations," *Atlanta Constitution*, September 18, 1995, D2.

5. *1993 Statistical Yearbook of the Immigration and Naturalization Service*, p. 123, table 144.

6. *Statistical Abstract of the United States*, p. 798, table 1323.

7. Milton Moskowitz, *The Global Marketplace* (New York: Macmillan, 1987), 8.

8. "Immigrant Population Rising Across Country," *Atlanta Constitution*, September 14, 1995, D3.

9. *Webster's Third New International Dictionary* (Springfield, MA: Merriam-Webster, 1993), 552.

10. Lillian H. Chaney and Jeanette S. Martin, *Intercultural Business Communication* (Englewood Cliffs, NJ: Prentice Hall, 1995), 10.

11. Judith Schroer, "Fewer Barriers Overseas," *USA Today*, September 4, 1993, 13E.

12. Schroer, "Fewer Barriers Overseas."

13. Carrie Teegardin, "Equality Still Elusive in Most Poor Countries," *Atlanta Constitution*, September 14, 1995, D3.

14. *Statistical Abstract of the United States*, 1995, p. 165, table 246.

15. "Money Talks: Sanders Signs with Cowboys," *Atlanta Constitution*, September 10, 1995, E1.

16. Roger E. Axtell, *The Do's and Taboos of International Trade* (New York: John Wiley, 1994), 215.

17. "Linked by Language," *Atlanta Constitution*, September 15, 1995, A14.

18. Steven Thomma and Angie Cannon, "English-Only Campaigns Seen as Wasteful, Weak," *Atlanta Constitution*, September 15, 1995, A14.

19. "Travelers' Bouts of Foot-in-Mouth Disease," *USA Today*, September 14, 1993, 5E.

20. Alan Lakein, *How to Control Your Life and Your Time* (New York: Wyden, 1974).

21. Albert Ellis and William J. Knaus, *Overcoming Procrastination* (New York: Signet, 1977).

22. Kenneth Blanchard and Spencer Johnson, *The One Minute Manager* (New York: William Morrow, 1982).

23. Colin Coulson-Thomas, *Creating the Global Company* (London: McGraw-Hill, 1992), 199.

24. "Channel Surfing Through U.S. Culture in 20 Lands," *New York Times*, January 30, 1994, H-30.

25. William J. Lederer and Eugene Burdick, *The Ugly American* (New York: Norton, 1958).

26. Neil Chesanow, *The World-Class Executive* (New York: Rawson, 1985), 268.

27. *U.S. Foreign Trade Highlights 1993* (Washington, DC: Department of Commerce, 1994).

28. Lennie Copeland and Lewis Griggs, *Going International* (New York: Random House, 1985), 109.

29. U.S. Department of State Dispatch, *Fact Sheet: European Union* 6, No. 6, January 26, 1995, 524.

30. Peter Marsh, *Eye to Eye* (Oxford: Andromeda Oxford Ltd., 1988), 90.

31. Sondra B. Thiederman, *Bridging Cultural Barriers for Corporate Success* (Lexington, MA: Lexington Books, 1991), 137.

32. Marsh, *Eye to Eye*, 87.

33. Marsh, *Eye to Eye*, 86.

34. *Foreign Direct Investment in the U.S.* (Washington, DC: Department of Commerce, 1992).

35. The 3-M Meeting Management Team, *How To Run Better Business Meetings* (New York: McGraw-Hill, 1987), 198.

36. Nina Strietfeld, "How To Communicate in Other Cultures," *Public Relations Journal* 42 (February 1986), 34–35.

Chapter 4

The Electronic Office*

Imagine being able to do housework during your coffee break or replacing the rush-hour commute with a leisurely stroll down the hall from the breakfast table. For many workers, including a medical transcriptionist from Marietta, Georgia, this is becoming reality. The transcriptionist is one of more than 9 million Americans called **telecommuters**. *By using a personal computer and advanced telecommunication technology, telecommuters can perform part or all of their work at home.*

Our transcriptionist cites several advantages derived from telecommuting. Besides allowing her more time for relaxation and household chores, she claims that, without the distractions of the office, her productivity has increased by 25 percent. "Some people just pound the keyboard like you wouldn't believe," she says. Her employers have seen similar increases with their other telecommuters. In addition, many urban areas are encouraging telecommuting as a possible means of reducing rush-hour traffic and thus improving air quality.[1]

Telecommuting would not be possible if it were not for advances in office technology. These advances allow the work to be performed where the people are located instead of bringing the people to work. All it takes is a computer, a phone line, and a connection to a computer network. But what seems simple today would have been just a dream ten years ago.

INTRODUCTION

The modern office, regardless of the size of the organization, is being equipped with complex electronic machinery at a faster and faster rate. The luxuries of the past decade—word processors, personal computers, facsimile machines, multipurpose phone systems, and color copiers—are relatively commonplace now. New advances in office equipment improve productivity and reliability while requiring increased technical competence from those who use the equipment. Office professionals are required to become more "computer literate" in order to weather the fantastic rate of change. Managers are increasingly able to perform their own office tasks. As roles and job descriptions are modified, the traditional secretary who types, files, and takes dictation is hard to find.

*This chapter was written by Craig A. Piercy, Terry College of Business, University of Georgia, Athens, GA 30602.

As the opening story illustrates, technology is not only changing the look and efficiency of the corporate office. New opportunities arise as a result of continuing trends in information technology, the decreasing price of technology and telecommunications equipment, and the enhanced performance and ease of use of office products and services. These advances have also made possible the growth of a new trend: a workforce that no longer requires a traditional corporate environment in order to be effective. This workforce includes: mobile professionals who spend a large amount of time away from the office; telecommuters who work at home at least three days a month; and small office/home office workers who now have access to the same advanced office technology that was once reserved for large corporations.

Everywhere you look, new technologies have changed the way people work. These new technologies have changed the basic flow of information and in turn have changed the ways that companies are organized. With new technologies, one can communicate with remote offices in other time zones or even other countries. Communication with customers is easier. One can easily communicate with the office while traveling. Primarily the new communication technologies allow more people to share information with greater ease. In many organizations, these facts have led them to believe that the time has come to use these technologies to change the basic way that work is done. Companies are beginning to reengineer their processes. **Reengineering** is a term for a process of changing basic business procedures in order to make more efficient use of people, technology, and information resources. With the constant development of new technologies and the accelerating pace of change, companies will develop a reengineering cycle to meet these changes.[2]

Technology increases the efficiency of communication. The ultimate effectiveness of communication remains a human responsibility, however, and the challenge is one of integrating human skills and electronic technology. This chapter will provide you with a description of some of the advances in office technology and how they affect communication.

THE EVOLUTION FROM TRADITION TO TECHNOLOGY

The paperwork explosion, ever-increasing costs, and the declining availability of skilled employees have combined to exert heavy pressure for higher productivity rates in the office. The office has been called the most labor-intensive and least cost-effective domain.[3] The percentage of information workers versus the combined total in agriculture, services, and industrial classifications in the United States has grown steadily since the turn of the century. Information workers have been the largest group since 1955, and their numbers are still rising. Business must maximize electronic technology to remain competitive. Fortunately, this technology is becoming easier to use and less expensive to purchase.

The Traditional Office

In the traditional office, one manager employed one secretary who performed a variety of duties. They included answering the phone, greeting visitors, taking dictation, typing, running errands, filing, arranging meetings, and keeping records. Desktops were covered with file folders, loose papers, calendars, and telephone message reminders. The office supply cabinet held a large quantity of typewriter erasers, correction strips, white correction fluid, carbon paper, file folders, and labels, along with several different types of office paper.

At times, work piled up. As the secretary typed a report, the manager often found information to add or change. The revise-and-retype exercise might go through many

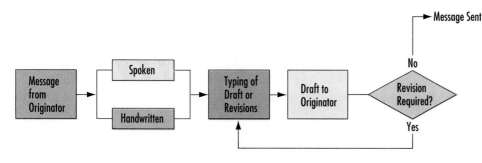

Figure 4.1
Traditional Method of
Originating and Sending a
Written Message

cycles. In any case, the secretary had to totally retype the text, use correction fluid on the typed copy, or cut-and-paste the text of each revision. In most cases, at least the final copy was retyped for quality (see Figure 4.1).

In the mid-1960s storage was added to office typing systems. IBM developed the MT/ST (Magnetic Tape Selectric Typewriter), a very specialized, and expensive, type-writer-based system. The characters keyed in were stored on a cassette tape and later on a magnetic card. Meanwhile companies such as Lanier and Smith-Corona were developing stand-alone **word processing systems** designed especially to capture and store words, revise them, and print them. These systems were specialized computers that could do only one task, word processing.

The evolution of word processing has had interesting effects on the nature of office duties—for example, the development of typing pools, in which people with excellent typing skills utilized those skills eight hours a day. This was primarily an efficiency move, as experts believed that the office, like the factory, could benefit from separations of duties based on skills. Before long the emotional effect of such separation became apparent. Changing a secretary's job to two jobs—office assistant and clerical typist—was received enthusiastically by some people and less enthusiastically by others. With time, and with the decline in equipment price, it became obvious that the word processor could support both tasks, making each more interesting.

These duties have continued to change as word processing has moved from type-writers and word processors to personal computers. Each day the capabilities of computers are increasing. For example, the movement away from special computer languages means that the new electronic tools are more accessible. Many managers now operate their systems directly rather than use support staff. In the electronic office, all employees are responsible for, and take part in, improving office productivity.

Word processing and other office duties will continue to be handled via computer. On July 5, 1995, Smith-Corona, one of the largest manufacturers of typewriters and word processors, filed for bankruptcy. They had been struggling to sell their products in the booming personal computer market.[4] This marks a turning point in the evolution of the electronic office, as one of the most basic elements in office technology approaches extinction. It also demonstrates how the future evolution of the office will be driven by computer technology.

THE MODERN OFFICE

The major tasks of any office are centered around the processing of information. These tasks include, but are not limited to: generating business documents; processing and filing documents; and communicating with clients and colleagues. The information technology of today has been designed to make the performance of these tasks more efficient. In some cases, traditional tasks have been completely automated. In almost all cases, computer technology of one form or another is used.

OFFICE HARDWARE AND SOFTWARE

In technological parlance, **hardware** refers to the physical, electronic machinery, while **software** refers to the programs and routines that provide the instructions for the machinery. Office hardware includes personal computers, copiers, fax machines, telephones, and other devices. Many of these can be classified as smart machines. A **smart machine** is one that contains a small computer enabling it to make simple decisions and provide information to the user. This increased machine intelligence makes the machinery easier to use and increases its capabilities. Here we will describe the various capabilities of some of these devices.

THE PERSONAL COMPUTER

The personal computer has become the backbone of the modern electronic office. The pervasive nature of the computer in business is related to several trends. First, the power and speed of personal computers continue to increase, and this increase in processing power has led to an expanding number of tasks that the personal computer is capable of performing. In addition, the cost and the size of computer equipment continue to decrease. These trends have led to computers on individuals' desks that have as much or more power as the much larger, mainframe computers in use only a few years earlier.

The hardware and software of a personal computer system work together to perform many office tasks, including: word processing, desktop publishing, document generation and storage, database processing, graphics presentation and generation, business calculation and budgeting, scheduling, and communications. In addition, more capabilities are being introduced every day through the availability of new hardware and software. Because of the computer's ability to process information in numerous ways it has been called an **information tool.**[5]

Personal Computer Hardware

Computer hardware performs five functions: input, output, processing, storage, and communications. These functions are directed by software that enables them to work together to process data into information. Most basic systems today contain all five functions, but communications is a relative newcomer. It allows the computer to communicate with other computers via network connections or modem.

The Central Processing Unit

The "brain" of the computer is the **central processing unit (CPU),** which is where the processing of information occurs. The CPU is made up of two parts: the **arithmetic-logic unit (ALU)** and the **control unit.** The **arithmetic-logic unit** carries out the actual processing of information. The **control unit** guides these operations by supplying the data and instructions to the ALU. The CPU is located on a computer chip called a **microprocessor,** which is located along with other chips on the main circuit board in the computer.

The power of the microprocessor is the main determinant of the power and speed that the computer system will posses. Two types of microprocessors are in common use today: those made by the Intel Corporation and those manufactured by Motorola. The microprocessors developed by Intel are primarily used in **compatible computers.** These are computers that are based on a computer architecture developed by IBM. The most common Intel microprocessors in use are the 80386, the i486, and the Pentium—the newest and most powerful microprocessor in the Intel line. Motorola microprocessors are used in computers based on a computer architecture developed by Apple and are used primarily in Apple Macintosh equipment. Motorola chips in common usage include the 68020, 68030, 68040, and the PowerPC—the latest microprocessor from Motorola. The PowerPC uses a new microprocessor technology to increase the power and speed of the processor. It also provides the capability of running software designed for either the Apple Macintosh or the IBM-compatible computers. In 1995, Intel accounted for about 91 percent of the microprocessor market while Motorola accounted for only 9 percent.[6]

Computer Input

For a computer to process information there must be some method for providing it with the data it needs. Input devices are used to enter the necessary data and instructions into the computer for processing. The most common methods of computer input are the keyboard and the mouse. A computer keyboard is used for typing the data and instructions into the computer. It looks very similar to a typewriter keyboard, but it usually contains additional keys such as special function keys, cursor control keys, and/or a numeric keypad. While it is the most common form of input, the keyboard is also one of the most complicated to use. A **mouse** is a small device that is connected to the computer by a long cord (see Figures 4.2a and 4.2b). The small size and the cord give it the appearance of a rodent, hence its name. By moving the mouse over a flat surface, usually a mouse pad, the user can manipulate a pointer on the screen. The user communicates instructions to the computer by moving the pointer to various locations on the screen and then pressing a button (called *clicking*) on the mouse. The computer will then determine what to do based on the location of the pointer at the time the button was pressed. Other types of computer input include trackballs, joysticks, touch screens, pens, and bar-code readers. Voice and handwriting recognition are also in use but their full potential has not as yet been realized.

Computer Output

Output devices provide a means for the information processed by the computer to be presented to the user. The two most popular output devices are the computer monitor and the printer. A **monitor** is the medium by which the instructions and data that are inputted using a keyboard or a mouse are displayed. The monitor also provides an immediate outlet for the results of computer processing. Monitors can come in various sizes and with various features. A monochrome monitor presents output in only one color while a color monitor can present information in many colors. Another important characteristic of a computer monitor screen is its resolution. **Screen resolution** is a measure of the quality of the picture and it is calculated by the number of picture elements, or pixels, that the screen contains. A **printer** is used when a permanent printed copy of computer output is desired. Printers also come in various sizes and produce a varying quality of output. Probably the most popular printer for the office is a **laser printer,** which uses a laser beam to write dots on a drum that is coated with light-sensitive material. These dots are then transferred to paper using ink. A laser printer provides printed output of near professional quality at a relatively low cost. Other types of printers in use include dot-matrix printers and ink-jet printers. Other types of output devices include: pen plotters, speakers for audio output, magnetic tape or disk storage, and signals to smart machines. The price of output devices varies directly with the speed and the quality of output.

Figure 4.2a

A New Kind of Mouse
When its famous mouse
broke the million-unit sales
barrier in 1988, Microsoft
used presentation graphics
to publicize the event.
This graphic uses seductive
trivia to create a memorable
impression.
Source: Reproduced with
permission from Microsoft
Corporation.

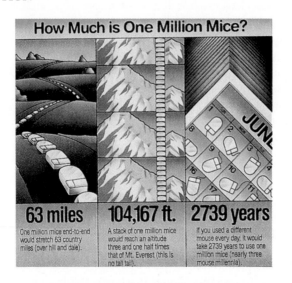

Figure 4.2a

A New Kind of Mouse
When its famous mouse
broke the million-unit sales
barrier in 1988, Microsoft
used presentation graphics
to publicize the event.
This graphic uses seductive
trivia to create a memorable
impression.
Source: Reproduced with
permission from Microsoft
Corporation.

Figure 4.2b

This graphic uses a
photograph with a
combination bar-chart
and pictograph format.
Source: Reproduced with
permission from Microsoft
Corporation.

Computer Storage

If the CPU is the "brain" of the computer, then storage is the computer's "memory."
There are two types of storage for a personal computer system: primary storage and
secondary storage.

Primary storage is the working memory for the computer and consists of ROM
and RAM. **ROM**, or **read-only memory,** is a set of chips that stores the instructions
needed for the computer to start when the power is turned on. The instructions that
are stored in ROM are permanent and cannot be changed or lost, even when the
power is turned off. **RAM, random access memory**, is used to store the data and
instructions required for immediate tasks when the computer is working. RAM is temporary memory, and the data and instructions in RAM are lost when the power is
turned off or when they are replaced by new data and instructions. Since the
computer uses RAM to store the items it is currently working with, the amount of
RAM in a computer is very important. The more RAM available, the more data that is
immediately available for processing and the better the processing speed of the computer. Software available for IBM-compatible computers in late 1995 required at least
8 megabytes of RAM to perform well.

When we wish to save our work for the future, we then use secondary storage. **Secondary storage** media include floppy disks, hard disks, magnetic tape, and CD-ROM. The capacity of external media can vary from 720 kilobytes on a standard 3½" floppy disk to about 1 gigabyte on the newest hard drives. A **floppy disk** is the most widely used method of external storage. With a floppy disk information is saved on a small, plastic magnetic disk using a device called a **floppy disk drive**. Most personal computer systems produced today include at least one floppy disk drive. The primary advantages of a floppy disk are that information can be saved indefinitely and that a disk can be carried from one computer to another. A disadvantage is that the amount of storage available on a single floppy disk may not be adequate for a large program or a large number of files.

Information from a computer can also be stored on **magnetic tape,** much like audiotape. A disadvantage of tape storage is that access is sequential, meaning that each item on the tape can only be read by the computer when the tape is unwound to the point at which the information is stored. This is not the case with disk storage, which allows for access to any point on the disk at any time. For personal computer systems, magnetic tape is typically used to back up the hard disk.

A **hard disk** is a secondary storage device—a metal disk—that is usually housed in a system unit and utilizes the hard drive. Advantages of hard disks include the high capacities and speeds at which data can be stored and accessed. One disadvantage is that it is difficult to move a hard drive from one computer to another. Many computer users store their information and programs on the hard disk and use floppy disks or magnetic tape to back up the information.

The newest type of secondary storage for the personal computer is **CD-ROM (Compact Disk–Read Only Memory)**. CD-ROM is a form of optical storage in which a laser is used to "read" information from a disk very similar to an audio CD. Because the CD-ROM is a read-only medium, information cannot be written on it from the personal computer. With very large storage capacities, a single CD-ROM can hold up to 650 megabytes of information, enough for an entire encyclopedia. Organizations are finding many uses for CD-ROM technology. Their high speed and storage capacities make them well suited for such applications as storing large amounts of archival information, video and images, large databases, and large software programs (see Figure 4.3).

Computer Communications

The fifth element of computer hardware, communications devices, has rapidly become a necessity for office personal computer systems. Communications devices allow the user to connect to other computers, communicate with other users via E-

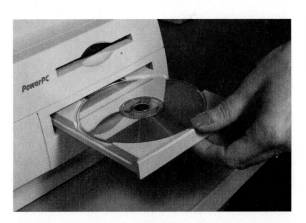

Figure 4.3
CD-ROM and Drive
Source: Photo by Reginald Wickham.

mail, share work with colleagues, share peripheral devices with other users, and connect to global information networks. The two most common types of communication devices for PCs are the modem and the network card. A **modem** is used by a computer to communicate information over a phone line. A computer uses information in a digital format: that is, every piece of stored information is coded as a set of ones and zeros. With a modem and the appropriate software, digital information from the computer is converted to analog information that can be sent over the phone line. A modem can also convert the analog information that is received from a phone line into a digital form that the computer can understand. Modem speeds are measured as the number of bits per second (bps) that can be transmitted. Common modems for PCs can send and receive information at rates of 2,400, 9,600 and 14,400 bps. Newer models allow for even higher transmission rates. The cost of a modem varies directly with the transmission rates. **Fax-modems** can also be combined with circuitry that enables the computer to send and receive documents from facsimile machines.

A **network card** allows a computer to connect to a computer network. A **computer network** is a combination of two or more computers and other devices that allows information to be exchanged between the devices. The network card and the appropriate software convert the information into the required form for network transmission and handle the communication between the networked devices. A more detailed discussion of computer networks appears later in this chapter.

The hardware devices that have been discussed so far make up the bare minimum required for an office personal computer system. Much other equipment can be included in a computer system for handling special needs. This might include other types of input devices, such as a voice recognition system or a video camera, and output devices, such as audio speakers, robotics, and monitors of all shapes and sizes. Also many specialized circuit boards, called *cards*, are available for computers. These include cards for handling additional memory, video and audio, and advanced communications. Every day new hardware devices are invented to increase the capabilities of personal computer systems.

Personal Computer Software

Computer hardware cannot function without computer software to provide it with instructions. *Software* is a generic term for the programs and instructions provided to the computer by the user. While prices for hardware devices have dropped dramatically, the prices of many common software tools have remained virtually constant. Software can be found for almost any application imaginable—from designing a wooden deck for a house to manipulating complex mathematical functions to playing video games. Not surprisingly, the software products with the highest sales figures are for office applications.

Operating System
One type of software that is necessary for any computer to function is called the operating system. The **operating system** provides the basic instructions to the computer for controlling the hardware, providing an interface between the user and the computer, handling files and storage, and running other software. The most common operating system for IBM-compatible machines has been **MS-DOS**. DOS stands for disk operating system and was so named because of the PC's use of secondary storage devices. Other operating systems for IBM compatibles include **UNIX** from various developers, **OS/2** from IBM, and various versions of **Windows** from Microsoft. A recent version of Windows, Windows 95, provided a more "intuitive" user interface, the ability to run several programs at one time, automatic setup for hardware devices,

and support for more complicated programs and multimedia. The standard operating system for Macintosh computers is **System 7** from Apple. Many of the features available in Windows 95 have long been standard features of System 7.

Word Processing

As we have seen, word processing has evolved from a stand-alone system to a software package on a personal computer. *Word processing software* is generally used for the generation and editing of business documents, letters, and memos. It allows the user to input and edit text using the keyboard and a mouse, define the format of the document, save the document to secondary storage, and print the document. Advanced features include the ability to add graphics such as tables and graphs to a document, the ability to search the document for a specific word and replace it with something else, the ability to check the document for spelling or grammatical errors, and the ability to share data with other users and applications. Common word processing packages in use include WordPerfect, Microsoft Word, and Wordpro. Some features of word processing systems software follow:

- Delete/insert: allows text to be deleted or inserted anywhere in the document.
- Copy/move: allows any part of the information to be copied or moved to another location in the document.
- Page formatting: allows the user to specify the overall format of the document such as number of lines per page, spacing, margins, justification, etc. These settings can usually be varied throughout the document.
- Merge: allows the user to combine previously keyed text and data.
- Search and replace: allows the user to search the document for specific words and replace them with different spellings or specified text if necessary.
- Headers and footers: allows, for instance, section titles to be placed at the top of each page and consecutive page numbers to be placed at the bottom of each page.
- Fonts: allows the characters to be printed in different styles and allows for such special fonts as subscripts, superscripts, boldface, or italics.
- Graphics: allows graphics from other sources to be inserted into a document.
- Footnote tie-in: automatically allows footnotes to be inserted into a document.
- Document output: allows documents to be saved to a secondary storage device or sent to a printer.
- Special utilities: includes special tools such as a spelling checker, grammar checker, and thesaurus that aid the user in creating and editing the document.

Efficiencies through Innovation

Not all of the advances in office efficiency occur with the purchase of expensive equipment or software. Often, we can dramatically affect productivity simply by changing the way we do our jobs.

A former president of Bell & Howell related an incident that demonstrates this point. When he first went to work as an entry-level office employee, his job was to dictate letters to customers who had complained about products. At the end of the first day, he had dictated a large number of individual letters. As he was carrying the glass dictation records to the typing pool, he tripped and broke the entire day's efforts. As he had been dictating the letters, he recognized strong similarities among the complaint situations. The accident caused him to find a better, and safer, way to fulfill his duties. He cataloged the 137 letters and gave each a number. Then, when he had to respond to a complaint, he simply wrote the number of the response on the bottom of the letter and

Figure 4.4
Example of a Boilerplate Letter

A B C COMPANY
Main Street Office
Anywhere, State

Date: _____

Dear Valued Customer:

    This office recently received correspondence from you concerning your difficulty with our product:

_____.

    We strive to sell products that work and are easy to use. I have sent your letter to our office at _____ for action. You should be hearing from the manager there within ____ days.

    Please excuse this form of communication; we have found it to be the fastest way to support our valued customers and hold costs to a minimum, allowing us to keep our prices the lowest in the industry.

    Please don't hesitate to write again if our solution is not adequate and timely.

Sincerely,

Manager, Customer Relations

gave it to the clerk to type a response. He had created a supply of letters, each of which was well worded and could be reused, saving time and mental energy. His colleagues quickly determined that he had thought his way out of employment, which of course he had, on the way to the top of the corporation.

    The Bell & Howell story illustrates that reusable communications are a way to improve content and save time. With word processing software, you can create individual paragraphs, possibly with missing key words, and then use the paragraphs in the necessary order and insert the proper special words. Standard paragraphs of text that are reusable are called **boilerplate** (see sample boilerplate letter in Figure 4.4). The editing and storage capabilities of PC word processing software lend themselves ideally for the use of boilerplate material. With such a system a letter that appears to be unique can be created in a short time. Many of today's word processing packages come with sample letters of various types. In addition, specialized software is available with boilerplate material for common letters and forms.

Database Software

Many times businesses require the access to and manipulation of large amounts of data. When this is the case, database software is required. A **database** is information that is stored in a way that makes it easily manipulated and retrieved by a user. Customer mailing lists, product inventories, library book catalogs, and point-of-sale data are just a few examples of the types of information commonly stored as a database. Information is stored in a database in an organized manner called a data hierarchy. The typical data hierarchy consists of three elements—fields, records, and files. A field is a single item or piece of data under consideration. A particular customer's telephone number or the price of a specific product in inventory are examples of a field. A record is a collection of fields that pertain to a particular person or object. A record for a particular customer might include the fields for name, street address, city, telephone number, and so on. A file is a collection of records that have some relationship or special use. For instance, a customer mailing list database might have a file that contains records of the customers from the southeast region and another containing records for customers from the western region.

Database software for personal computers allows users to design, create, and work with a database. In working with a database, the software permits the user to enter information, edit information, and extract information from the database. To extract information from a database the user typically frames his or her information needs in the form of a query. A **query** is a question about the database that is presented to the database software in a format that it can understand. An example of a query for a customer mailing list might be to ask the computer to list all customers who reside in a particular state. The database software could then find the data of interest in the database and present it to the user in the form of a report. Popular database software packages include: FoxPro and Access by Microsoft, Borland's Dbase, and Novell's Paradox.

Spreadsheet Software

The most popular form of software for business calculations and financial management is called **spreadsheet software**. Common uses of spreadsheet software are financial analysis, budgeting, and forecasting but it has many other applications as well.

A spreadsheet is basically a table on the screen that consists of numbered columns and rows. The intersection of a row and a column is a cell, which can be identified by its column and row number, called a **cell address.** The user constructs the spreadsheet by placing labels, values, or formulas into the cells. A label is a word that is usually written in a cell to describe or label various parts of the spreadsheet. A value is a number that is placed in a cell to represent some quantity of interest. The real power of a spreadsheet comes from the use of formulas, which can be constructed using values, cell addresses, and mathematical operators. If a cell address is used in a formula, whenever the value of the referenced cell is changed the result of the formula will be updated automatically. With this capability it is easy to set up a spreadsheet that can be utilized over and over by changing only a few values each time.

It is very easy to make changes to spreadsheets. Whole ranges of cells can be moved or copied at once. Numerical values can be displayed in many desired formats such as currency or as percentage values. Specific ranges or an entire spreadsheet can be printed or saved to a file. Advanced features of spreadsheets include the ability to generate charts based on data in the spreadsheet, the ability to automate often-used commands with programs called **macros**, the capability to perform database functions with the data, and the ability to share information with other applications such as word processing or database software. One popular spreadsheet package, Lotus 1-2-3, is the all-time sales leader for application software. Other popular spreadsheet software includes Microsoft Excel and Quattro Pro.

Presentation Software

Presentation graphics software aids the user in preparing professional-quality slides and graphics for business presentations. Lotus Freelance, Harvard Graphics, Microsoft PowerPoint, and Novell Presentations are some of the more popular packages for PCs. With this software, the user can easily design slides for overhead projectors complete with color charts and graphics.

The more advanced software packages also allow the user to create *screen presentations*. These are presentations that the computer displays on a terminal or projects onto a movie screen. In this format the presentation can be more creative and include elements such as animation, sound, and video. A presentation that includes these elements is called **multimedia.**

In addition to the software packages listed above there are several packages that are specifically designed for multimedia.

Scheduling Software

Another office need that is prominent in the attention of software developers is the scheduling of appointments and projects. The developers of software have tried to fill this need with software called **personal information managers (PIMs)**. Typical capabilities of PIMs include scheduling of appointments, tracking to-dos, managing calendars, and an electronic Rolodex feature. Day-Timer Technologies has compiled figures showing that 85 percent of those who use PIMs daily also carry paper-based planners. Realizing this, the developers of PIMs have programmed a feature whereby output can be formatted and printed in sizes that fit the standard paper-based planners. Some popular PIM software includes Lotus Organizer, Day-Timer Organizer and Microsoft Schedule+.

Integrated Packages

Since several types of software packages are commonly used as a group in many offices, some companies have combined selected projects into integrated packages called **software suites**. A software suite typically includes word processing, spreadsheet, database, presentation, and scheduling software. There are several advantages to using a software suite over individual software packages from various vendors. First, a software suite is generally cheaper as a bundle than the components would be if bought separately. Second, the entire package can be covered by the same customer support services. Finally, the major advantage is that information can be easily shared between the various applications of the suite. For example, the spreadsheet can use information from a database to calculate values for a table. The table can then be used in a word processing document or incorporated into a presentation. Lotus Smartsuite, Microsoft Office, Microsoft Works, ClarisWorks and Novell Perfect Office are popular integrated software packages.

Desktop Publishing

The user of desktop publishing can be highly creative and obtain typeset quality at a lower cost and in less time. **Desktop publishing** is extremely high-quality word processing, made possible by faster personal computers and lower cost, high-quality laser printers.

If your only communication is letters and memos, word processing is adequate. If, however, you create brochures, newsletters, advertisements, programs, and the like, and you work within tight budgets and time constraints, desktop publishing is a possibility. This technology allows you to use the power of words, graphics, pictures, and style to create high communication impact. As noted in Aldus Corporation's manual, Pagemaker, a popular desktop publishing package, does in minutes what it formerly took hours to do with traditional typesetting, layout and paste-up methods.[7]

Typically, a desktop publishing document is created in several steps. First, the text for the document is created using a word processor. Next, the desktop publishing package is used to develop the format for the document called a *stylesheet*. The stylesheet is used to define the margins and the spacing of the text, the size and shape of the print, and the general look of the document. During this step, frames or spaces are left in which graphics are to be placed. Next the graphic elements—clip art, drawings, charts, or photographs—are inserted. Finally, the document is printed on a high-quality laser printer.[8]

The ease of use and the low cost combine to make high-quality publishing a possibility for almost anyone with a computer and a laser printer. The lower cost has also been attractive to professional publishers. *Folio* reported in 1993 that 58.6 percent of magazine companies had set up desktop and electronic publishing systems and that 7 percent more planned to make the conversion to desktop publishing. According to the survey desktop publishing software packages are QuarkXPress, Aldus PageMaker, and Ventura Publisher.[9]

CD-ROM and computer network technologies have made possible electronic publishing, by which multiple forms of media such as video, animation, and audio can be incorporated into the published document. As mentioned previously, because many forms of media are used, the term for this type of document is *multimedia*.

BOXED IN
AN ETHICAL DILEMMA

Susan has worked in the corporate office for seven months and is comfortable with the equipment and systems. She has her own microcomputer that is everything she could hope for. The computer contains enough storage to hold all of her work, a color monitor, and a variety of software packages. She has WordStar word processing, Lotus 1-2-3 spreadsheet, the latest version of MS-DOS, and a fancy printer. Susan has become so knowledgeable about the software that she is asked questions by coworkers almost every day.

Jim and Susan are at lunch discussing the computer Jim is thinking about ordering. He has a catalog of computer equipment and software and is trying to put together a system with software and stay within his budget of $2,500. "It's amazing what they offer," Jim tells Susan, pointing to a system like hers for $2,500. "I wish I could afford that, but there would be no money left over for software. If I get the software, I will have to drop the color monitor and either the hard disk or printer."

All of a sudden Jim's face lights up. "Susan, if I get the $2,500 system, is it all right for me to copy your software? That would save me a lot of money and you would still have the original software. In fact, no one is hurt."

Susan thinks about Jim's question. If she says yes, she will be agreeing to let Jim violate the software copyright and place both their jobs in jeopardy. She has seen other people copy software from their machines for their computers at home and has not really thought about it much. But this is her software on her machine. What if she is caught? In any case, is it right to let Jim make a copy of software that cost several hundreds of dollars, even if no one knows?

Susan feels boxed in. What would you do?

Multimedia products are widely available on CD-ROM, covering applications from encyclopedic information to video games to fancy product catalogs. Multimedia documents are also used on the global computer network, the Internet, which will be discussed later in this chapter.

Telecommunications Software

Telecommunications allows large organizations to share resources and communicate as if they had a single location. Telecommunications software allows a user of a personal computer to communicate with another computer system or device. This communication takes place by way of a modem and phone line or a network connection. Using this software a user can send **electronic mail (E-mail),** access remote databases, and download software from remote computers. The telecommunications software handles the tasks of establishing communications with the remote device and translating signals between the computer and the device. Communication between very different machines is possible through the use of a set of standard signals called **protocols.**

Suppose you could take stored text from the word processor and send it electronically, without ever printing it on paper. This procedure would eliminate the cost of the paper and envelope as well as the postage, and, most important, would reduce the delay in delivering the message. This is the objective of E-mail, the process of capturing text on an electronic device and transmitting it to another electronic device. With E-mail a person can send mail at any time. The message will be stored in the electronic "in-box" of the addressee. When it is convenient, the addressee will check the "in-box" and find the message. Typical E-mail systems allow users to send mail to lists of users, forward or reply to a message with just a click of the mouse button, and automatically include electronic signatures on all correspondence. The newest office applications software, such as word processors and spreadsheets, has built-in commands for sending documents in conjunction with the E-mail system (see Figure 4.5 for a sample E-mail message).

Figure 4.5

An E-Mail Message
Source: Figure 16-8 from *Understanding Computers and Information Processing: Today and Tomorrow,* Third Edition, by Charles S. Parker, p. 514, copyright 1990 by the Dryden Press, a division of Holt, Rinehart and Winston, Inc., reprinted by permission of the publisher.

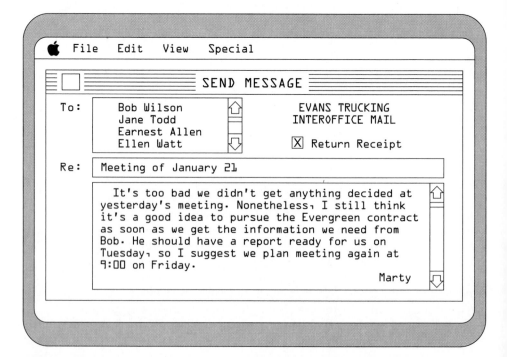

The first corporate electronic mail systems were installed in the 1970s. Users soon began to notice a downside: unwanted mail. Walter Ulrich, a partner at Coopers & Lybrand, monitored ways to cope with the problem of overuse while serving as chairman of the privacy and security subcommittee of the Electronic Mail Association. He described a typical case of information overload in a private corporate electronic mail system:

> Someone in a branch office hires a new salesman and sends a message to everyone in the company, including the chairman. That clutters everyone's mailbox. It is so simple to address the message to "everyone" that there is abuse. Without electronic mail that branch manager would never think of making the same announcement, running off 10,000 Xerox copies and mailing it out.[10]

Since the 1970s, E-mail has become extremely popular. Over the Internet (to be discussed later in this chapter), it is possible to send E-mail all over the world. It is not uncommon these days to find a person's E-mail address printed on a business card or as part of a published mailing address.

IMAGING TECHNOLOGY

Imaging technology is concerned with the making of document reproductions. These reproductions can be in the form of printed copies from a copy machine or a facsimile machine, or images on micro-media storage, or they can be stored as an electronic image on a computer disk.

Copy Machines

Found in traditional offices for several decades, the **copy machine** makes duplicate copies of a page of text, drawings, or pictures. Its purpose is to make copies of paper documents for storage, use, or transmittal to other people for storage, use, or transmittal to still other people. Secretaries of the 1950s remember less than fondly going home with black and blue arms and stained clothing after having used spirit duplicating machines and carbon paper—the only ways to make copies at that time, other than retyping the document. Although Xerography was invented and patented in the late 1930s, it was not until the late 1950s and early 1960s that use of Xerox machines became routine. This was the plain-paper copier, still in use today. With the expiration of the Xerox company's patent, the plain-paper copier is now available from dozens of companies and is even used in many homes.

Today's machines produce copies of far greater quality and at higher rates of speed than did the early equipment. Many models have advanced capabilities such as two-sided copies, collation of documents, and automatic stapling. Other features are listed in Figure 4.6. In addition, high-quality, multicolor copiers are available, albeit for a high price.

Facsimile Machines

A technology that is commonplace in offices and in many homes is the **facsimile machine** (or **fax**), which is used to send copies of a document from one place to another electronically. The fax can transmit anything that is printed. You can send copies of pictures, graphics, handwritten notes, or a signed contract. While E-mail can be treated as a document for further processing (that is you can edit a received E-mail message

Figure 4.6
A Few Features to
Think About
Source: From "Choosing the
Right Copier for Your
Situation," *Managing Office
Technology*, March 1995, 56.

A Few Features to Think About

The list of copier features can go on and on. How do you know what you need, and what do these features do? Here is a list of some of the most useful, productivity-enhancing features that should be considered when making a copier purchase.

- Auto job start: Allows users to program settings while the machine is warming up so that when the copier is ready, the preset job will begin automatically.
- Automatic document feeder (reversing and semi-automatic): Feeds a stack of up to 50 one-sided or two-sided originals.
- Automatic magnification selection: Detects different size originals and adjusts to copy them all onto a single paper size.
- Automatic paper selection: Automatically selects a copy that is the same size as the original.
- Computer forms feeder: Feeds unseparated computer paper continuously.
- Copy access codes: Codes for billing copies to designated departments or clients.
- Dual page copying: Copies facing pages of a book or report onto a single sheet.
- Duplexer: Makes two-sided copies from one-sided or two-sided originals.
- Edge eraser: Erases black borders that sometimes appear when copying facing pages of books.
- Image editing: Eliminates cutting and pasting by deleting sections of an original.
- Interrupt memory: Allows a user to interrupt a long copy run for a quick copy without disrupting the original copier setting.
- Job memory: Maintains in memory frequently copied jobs and recalls the settings instantly.
- Long run paper selection: Senses the size of the paper in each drawer and automatically switches to that drawer to continue the job when the original paper source becomes empty.
- Multiple paper drawers: For increasing a machine's paper supply.
- Quick copy: To make a few copies quickly by repeatedly pressing the "Print" key for the desired amount of copies instead of searching for the appropriate quantity selection key.
- Reduction/enlargement (zoom 50%–200%): To reduce or enlarge originals from 50 to 200 percent.
- Remaining paper volume indicator: Indicates remaining paper volume in the copier.
- Sorter/stapler sorter: For sorting and/or stapling documents for organized high-volume copying projects.
- Stack sheet bypass: For bypass copying onto varying size sheets of paper.
- Weekly timer: Turns the copier on and off each day.
- Zoom indicators: Show the copying area for a job to enable a user to determine whether the original needs to be repositioned in order to capture the entire area to be copied.

and send it to someone else) this is not as easy with a regular fax. What you receive with a fax is a picture. Until recently, the fax has been quite useful for sending nontextual information quickly over a distance, but the received document has been difficult to reprocess. With the introduction of the plain-paper fax machine, which prints the reproduction on ordinary paper, the quality of the fax has improved. Also, with the use of a fax-modem and the appropriate software, faxes can be sent or received directly via a computer.

Scanners

A **scanner** is a computer peripheral that is used for making an image of a hard, paper copy and storing it in the computer as an electronic image (see Figure 4.7). All scanners convert areas of light and dark into digital data for the computer. Two widely used types of scanners are flatbed and handheld. Scanning an image on a flatbed scanner is similar to using the ordinary office copier.

To use a flatbed scanner you place a document facedown on the glass of the scanner and close the cover. The scan head moves underneath the document along the bed of the scanner. A light bar moves over the image, and the reflected light falls on a bed of photosensitive cells. The cells read the image, interpreting it as a series of dots, called pixels. When the document has been scanned, its image appears on the monitor. It can then be printed as it appears on the screen, filed on disk for storage, or manipulated with graphics software. For a document that consists of text, special software for **optical character recognition** can be used to convert the image into standard text for use with a word processor. Because of the high quality of the image and the low storage requirements, scanning and storing images on disk is quickly replacing other methods of document storage, such as file cabinets full of paper or drawers of micro-media.

Handheld scanners are moved manually over the page image. The scan head is limited in size, usually to about four inches. Also, it is difficult to piece an image together and to avoid distortions when using the handheld variety.

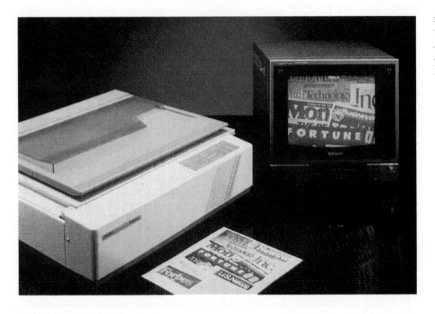

Figure 4.7
An Image Scanner
Source: Courtesy of
Howtek, Inc.

Figure 4.8

The Canon Multipass 1000
Multifunction Unit
Source: Courtesy of Canon
U.S.A., Inc.

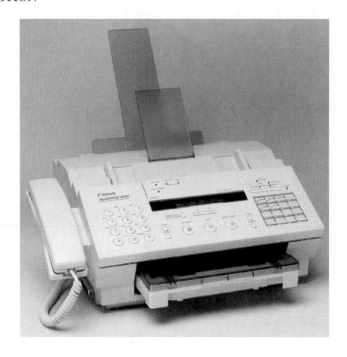

Multifunction Units

Since the copy machine, fax, and scanner all use the same technology for imaging a document, it is not surprising that devices are now on the market that perform the functions of all three of the machines in one unit. Mary Peller, an executive office administrator at Varian Associates, says that she enjoys the benefits of having one machine perform a variety of office functions. According to Peller, the unit has improved office productivity by replacing a laser fax and a dot-matrix printer and adding a copier to her workgroup. This increases the offices' document-processing capabilities. Besides improving her productivity other benefits include the need to stock only one kind of toner cartridge, an energy savings from one machine versus three stand-alone machines, and the need to purchase only one service contract.[11] Popular models of multifunction units include the Ricoh MV715 fax/copier/printer multifunction unit, the Hewlett-Packard OfficeJet, and the Canon Multipass 1000 (see Figure 4.8).

OFFICE COMMUNICATION TECHNOLOGY

Voice Processing Technology

If you have recently called a large corporate office, an airline reservation office, the IRS during the first two weeks in April, or a company that takes orders on the phone, you most likely encountered a machine before a human. The phone system that answered either held the call or directed it to the person who would talk with you. In some cases, no person was available and you were directed to leave a voice message. In this situation the phone system had a dictation capability available. With this experience you encountered a technology known as voice processing.

Voice processing is a collective term that encompasses voice messaging, speech recognition, speech synthesis, and interactive voice response services. In American businesses voice processing has become indispensable to the efficient office. Cost restrictions on travel and reductions in the number of employees limit the opportunities for customer contact, and voice processing offers an alternative method to keep customer service levels high. The most common application found in the office is voice messaging which can be divided into telephone answering, voice mail and automated attendant. Each application is different and addresses different needs and audiences.

A **telephone answering system** is simply an answering device that allows callers to leave messages in individual voice mailboxes. It is the simplest and oldest form of voice processing—reminiscent of the days when the systems could only answer the telephone and record messages. Telephone answering systems are limited in growth potential and they have few bells and whistles. However, for a small office with modest needs, telephone answering may be all that is needed.

With **voice mail,** users are assigned a personal mailbox from which they can access information at any time, and they can place detailed messages in the mailboxes of other subscribers without having to telephone them directly. Messages can be coded as "private" or "urgent," giving the recipient an idea of how to prioritize their retrieval. Voice mail allows users to telephone at their own convenience regardless of work hours or time zones. In addition voice mail provides the ability to record a message and send it to a distribution list as well as the convenience of forwarding of messages to other users.

Voice mail systems can be very reliable. In August of 1995, parts of the main building for the Terry College of Business at the University of Georgia were destroyed by fire. Besides losing much of their work and personal belongings, for several weeks many of the faculty lost their ability to contact colleagues and associates outside of the university. Some of the professors had been using answering machines on their desks, while others used a voice mail system to receive incoming messages. Since the electricity (and access) to the building had been cut off, users of answering machines were out of luck. However, those professors who used voice mail could still access their voice mailboxes from other phones on campus.

The third type of voice messaging system is automatic attendant, a type of specialized system that routes a call to a specific department or individual depending on the caller's response to a series of questions. Questions from an automatic attendant are usually in the form of a verbal "menu." For example, when calling an airline recently, a caller heard the choices: "For automated flight departure and arrival schedules, press 1 or say one. For reservations within the U.S., press 2 or say two. For international reservations. . . ." You can also use advanced systems to access individuals if you know their extension. The earliest automatic attendant systems worked only when called from a Touch Tone telephone, but with the addition of speech recognition any phone can be used.[12]

Voice messages contain more information than written mail—loudness, inflection, tone and so on—have the least time delay, are the easiest to create, and require no intermediary person or paper. Voice processing has undoubtedly increased the speed and reduced the cost of communication.

Integrated Services Digital Network

Science fiction stories have long described gadgets like video telephones, remote control of house appliances or climate control, and access to film libraries on the computer. With **integrated services digital network (ISDN)** all of this is now possible. ISDN is a high-speed telephone connection that operates over existing phone lines and can change the way that phones are used. ISDN is the first major change in phone line technology in many years. Customers can now get ISDN through existing phone lines in virtually every business and household.

A basic ISDN line connected to a single phone can have as many as 64 telephone numbers and can use features such as multiple holds and conference calls. A major change is that a single line can handle a voice call and send computer information simultaneously. This lets the user carry on a conversation while logging on to an on-line service or sending a fax. Using the newest modems, computers can send information at unprecedented speeds. The feature that might prove most popular from ISDN is video. The large amount of information in a video transmission requires a very high speed to display in real time. ISDN should make it possible to receive a video call from a colleague or download an entire movie from an on-line service (see Figure 4.9).[13]

Cellular Communications

In the story that opens the chapter we saw how technology is making it possible to move the office out of the headquarters and into the home. Technology is also making the office portable. With devices based on cellular technology, workers can perform office tasks on the run. Cellular technology allows signals and messages to be sent through the air without the constraints of wire connections. With this technology, people can work in airplanes, on customer visits, and even in their cars—talking to colleagues, sending faxes, or preparing computerized documents. These devices are allowing for the evolution of a new workplace called a **mobile office**.

A mobile office provides several advantages over a traditional office for certain employees—while introducing new concerns for their managers. Salespersons and customer representatives are the primary users of mobile office equipment because of the necessity of providing fast, efficient customer service to clients. With this technology, they can make visits with clients while remaining in almost constant contact with the home office. They can send and receive messages while at the customer's site or while en route. This in turn makes them more responsive to the customer's needs and provides a quicker turnaround time of sales information. In addition, the mobile office

---

The Speed of ISDN

ISDN offers incredible leaps in computer speed for on-line users. The time it takes to transfer files using different modems and phone lines:

Plain old telephone line			
Modem speed	25-PAGE MICROSOFT WORD FILE	1 MB GIF picture	X-ray image
9,600 bps	42 seconds	14 minutes	11 hours, 48 minutes
14,400 bps	28 seconds	9 minutes	7 hours, 47 minutes

ISDN			
Modem speed	25-PAGE MICROSOFT WORD FILE	1 MB GIF picture	X-ray image
64,000 bps	6 seconds	2 minutes, 4 seconds	1 hour, 44 minutes
128,000 bps	3 seconds	1 minute, 2 seconds	52 minutes

Figure 4.9
The Speed of ISDN
Source: From "Revolution on the Phone Line," by Todd Copilevitz of *The Dallas Morning News;* article reprinted in *The Atlanta Journal-Constitution,* August 6, 1995, H1.

worker can transport more material and cut down on the time required for shipping material from the office to the client.

The increased use of mobile office technology has several ramifications for managers. The local office may become radically downsized as the traditional infrastructure for supporting "at-office" workers becomes unnecessary. Managers will have to learn how to motivate and coach workers whom they rarely see face to face. Moreover, more efficient communication technologies may allow for fewer layers of management, and those layers will have increased responsibilities. Many companies, however, are finding ways to cope with these changes and are beginning to take full advantage of cellular technology.

The most basic and affordable device in a mobile office worker's arsenal is the **pager**, a small device that is worn on the belt or carried in a pocket (see Figure 4.10). Its main function is to notify the user that he or she has received a message. The earliest pagers utilized a beep, signaling the user to call the paging service to receive the message. Pagers have since undergone a few changes. One modification affects the pager's means of notifying the user of a message. Many pagers now use a vibration in place of a beep. In this way, the user can receive a message while in a meeting or presentation without disturbing other participants. Many newer pagers are equipped with a small screen. The phone number of whoever is calling and even short messages can be displayed on the screen. One pager can store up to 20 messages totaling close to 1000 characters.

The devices now causing most of the excitement surrounding cellular technology are cellular telephones. The **cellular telephone** is a wireless telephone that can be carried in the automobile, briefcase, or even a jacket pocket (see Figure 4.11). It is a major step up from pagers because it allows full voice communication. It has become common to see people carrying on conversations on commuter trains, as they head down the highway, or as they walk through an airport. One almost expects someone to be "beamed" to the nearest starship at any moment. Because of the massive popularity of cellular telephones, metropolitan areas have required new area codes in order to handle the large demand for telephone numbers.

Cellular telephones and cellular technology in general are made possible by large antennas and satellites that can receive and pass along cellular transmissions. These are

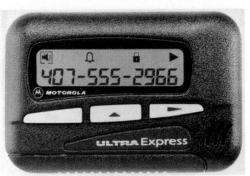

Figure 4.10
A Personal Pager
Source: Courtesy of Motorola, Inc.

Figure 4.11
The Cellular Phone
Source: Photo by Reginald Wickham.

placed in strategic locations in such a way as to provide service to a specific area. Usual coverage has been in major metropolitan areas, but the technology has improved to allow cellular service to rural areas as well. In some places service is not limited to above ground. For example, in Hong Kong it is possible to make cellular telephone calls while traveling 60 kilometers per hour on the subway.

Cellular telephones are shrinking in size and growing in ability. Besides the basic function of outgoing and incoming calls, cellular phones can be equipped with a variety of features. These features can include answering machine capabilities, storage and automatic dialing of frequently used numbers, call screening, and call waiting. Speaker phones are available for cars, along with a "horn alert" function that will honk the horn if you receive a message while out of the car. A newer trend is data traffic, or the transmission of data by radio waves, which permits one to send and receive E-mail and faxes via cellular phone.

Cellular phones can also be useful at the company headquarters. Many corporations, like United Services Automobile Association (USAA), have headquarters in large, sprawling campus complexes. Often workers are required to leave their desks to visit other parts of the complex that could be many minutes away by walking. USAA has issued cellular phones to 350 of the 10,000 employees located at their home office in San Antonio. This allows these employees to be reachable at all times. Also, a person receiving a message does not have to leave a work project to place a call, which is an advantage over a pager. With this system, USAA has implemented what is known as an in-building cellular phone system. With the success of the initial group of 350, USAA plans to expand the system in the near future.[14]

Portable Computers

Small, portable computers have been around for several years, but thanks to cellular technology they can now be used to send electronic documents over the airwaves. The differences between these smaller computers and the personal computers that are on the desktop are primarily just differences in size and portability. Portable computers work in the same manner, have the ability to use the same types of peripheral devices, and in many cases have the same power, speed, and storage capabilities as the larger desktop units. With the addition of a cellular-based modem they can connect to many of the same information resources from almost anywhere. These smaller computers can be divided into two sizes: laptop (or notebook) computers and palmtop computers, which are sometimes called personal digital assistants (PDAs).

Laptop computers are small versions of personal computers that are about the size of a phone book and weigh from 5 to 9 pounds (see Figure 4.12). The name "laptop" is derived from the fact that the computer can be operated while sitting on

Figure 4.12
Laptop Computer
Source: Photo by Reginald Wickham.

one's lap in an airplane or meeting. As mentioned above, these systems typically have the same capabilities as desktop models, with the additional feature of portability.

Most of these systems use a 486 processor, and many are beginning to incorporate the Pentium processor. This keeps the processing power on a par with the desktop machines and allows the portable computer to run the same software. Apple corporation has a line of portable computers based on the PowerPC chip. For input, laptop computers include a keyboard and one of several possible pointing tools—a mouse, a trackball (which is like an upside-down mouse), a light-pen, or other device. The portable computer also includes either a monochrome or color screen for output. Small portable printers can also be used. For storage, laptops typically include a 3½" drive and a hard drive. Newer models can be found with CD-ROM drives. Another device that is unique to laptop computers is a docking station. One can place a laptop in a docking station, which can connect it to normal-size monitors, a keyboard, and printers. This in effect turns the laptop into a desktop computer.

With all of the advantages of laptops it might seem that desktop computers would be obsolete. While the small size and weight of portables make them easy to transport, they also make them more difficult to use. A small keyboard can be difficult for large fingers and the smaller screens can strain the eyes. Since they run on a battery, the actual time available for use may be less than is needed while away from a power source. Also, the average lifetime of a laptop computer is less than that of a desktop because they are more easily dropped, lost, or stolen.

Palmtop computers are hand-held computers that weigh a pound or less and fit into a jacket pocket (see Figure 4.13). Their smaller size allows for greater portability, but at a sacrifice of computing power and storage. Also the smaller keyboards and screens can be more difficult to work with. Some makers have tried to get around the small keyboard's limitations by incorporating a light-pen and handwriting recognition capabilities, but this has not been altogether successful. Because of their limitations palmtop computers have primarily been used to store such information as contacts' telephone numbers and addresses; personal schedules, memos and reminders; and small documents for E-mail and fax. The personal nature of this information has prompted some to call these computers **personal digital assistants (PDAs)**. Probably the most powerful features of PDAs are a result of the inclusion of cellular technology. With this technology, PDAs can be used as pagers or to send and receive faxes and E-mail.

Figure 4.13
Palmtop Computer
Source: Photo by Reginald Wickham.

Computer Networks

Throughout this chapter we have discussed various gadgets for communicating with remote locations. Technology such as phone systems, facsimile machines, modems, and cellular communications all falls under the general heading of telecommunications.

The telephone is considered vital and central to organizational functioning. Audio, however, is but one form of telecommunications. We also want to communicate graphics, text, data, and video. We have fax networks for graphics; direct data communications networks for text and data; cable TV, satellite radio, and microwave radio for video; and ISDN lines with the capability of transmitting all data types.

With the emphasis on digital devices, it is routine to convert all of the communication forms mentioned into a digital format as discussed in the section on computer modems. AT&T, MCI, and Sprint convert all telephone calls that they carry over distances to digital forms. Computer-stored text and data are already in digital form, and graphics and video can be converted much like audio telephone calls. When we place all of these forms in a digital mode, not only can we carry them on any digital network, but also we can intersperse them, and the network cannot tell the difference.

In addition to the telephone system, a form of telecommunication used most directly in the electronic office is a **local area network (LAN).** This is a small telecommunications network for connecting computers that are located close together. A LAN uses telephone-like wires, coaxial cables, or optical fiber to connect computers or workstations in a work group, department, area, building, or campus. The people so connected work together and share common business interests (see Figure 4.14).

The LAN network has three basic configurations. In the star configuration, individual computers or workstations are all connected to a central switching station or

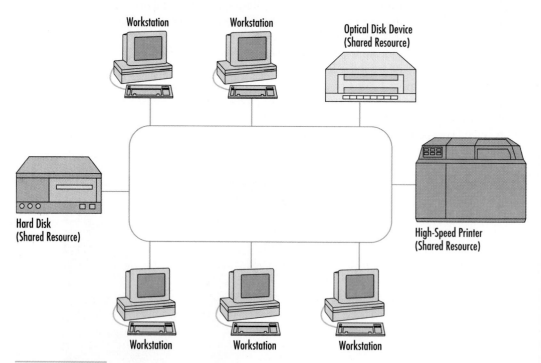

Figure 4.14

Local Area Network (LAN)

Source: Figure 7-13 from *Understanding Computers and Information Processing: Today ad Tomorrow,* Third Edition, by Charles S. Parker, p. 236, copyright 1990 by the Dryden Press, a division of Holt, Rinehart and Winston, Inc., reprinted by permission of the publisher.

computer. In the ring configuration, they are all connected in a closed loop or circle, and information is passed along the loop until it reaches the receiver. In a bus configuration, they are all connected to the main line so that additions can be made at the end of the network without interruption.

Traditional LANs use a powerful computer such as a mainframe as the main file server. The mainframe would handle all of the work, including both the storage and processing of information. The computers at each desk serve only for input (from the keyboard) and output (to the screen). A computer that is used for only input and output when connected to the network is referred to as a dumb terminal. However, the latest LANs use what is known as a client/server architecture. With client/server both the main file server and the desktop computer are capable of processing information. The desktop computer—the client—presents and processes the information. The server handles the tasks of storing, retrieving, and protecting the data. In this manner the tasks are shared between the client and the server. The main difference is that the client terminal now has "intelligence."

The LAN may be further connected to other LANs and WANs (wide area networks), allowing resource sharing and communications. For example, all members of a LAN can use the applications stored on a single disk (file server) instead of having individual copies, use data from a single up-to-date source, and share a single high-quality laser printer.

Wide area networks (WANs) are similar to LANs but they connect computers that are much farther apart. While a LAN connects computers that are located in the same building or in nearby buildings, WANs can connect computers that are located all across the world. This enables organizations with offices located in different states or countries to provide a network for sharing computing resources and information. WANs are usually a collection of local area networks that are connected using leased phone lines and a special connecting device called a **gateway.** With a wide area network the employees of large organizations are brought closer together.

The greatest advantage of a computer network is the ability to share information. While the primary method for sharing information over a network is via electronic mail, other methods are also available. For example, files that are stored on a central server can be accessed by anyone with the proper password. Information can also be shared with customers or suppliers.

Electronic Data Interchange (EDI), a method for exchanging data with customers and suppliers, has been in use for several years. A case in point is the du Pont corporation's use of EDI with customers of their fibers division, which has been successful in reducing paperwork and making deliveries more efficient. When a load of material is shipped to a customer, du Pont can send information about the contents of the truck, the quality of the materials, and the expected delivery time electronically. Armed with this information the customers can be ready to receive the shipment and easily update their inventory. EDI eliminates the need for paper invoices and bills of lading. It also improves delivery times, making possible such programs as JIT (just in time) inventory.

With the emphasis on organizational work groups, new software and hardware have been developed for computer networks that help people work together. The general term for this technology is collaborative computing and the software is called **groupware.** A collaborative system furnishes an environment where people can share information without being constrained by time or location. With groupware, people can be linked to the same applications in the same building or around the world. The software provides a group with a common, on-line venue for meetings, and it allows all members to work on the same data simultaneously. Groupware applications include schedule and project management, teleconferencing, integrated team support, and support for meetings. Electronic mail and messaging systems are the most basic type of

Figure 4.15
Videoconferencing
Source: Courtesy of IBM.

group software.[15] Other types of groupware include: group decision support systems, which are designed to facilitate face-to-face meetings; operating systems such as Windows for Workgroups; and communications environments like Lotus Notes.

Lotus Notes by Lotus Development Corporation has been the preeminent, defining force in the category of groupware software. In fact, it has become so much of a groupware standard that IBM bought Lotus Development Corporation in the summer of 1995, primarily for the Notes software. Notes can be described as a group communications environment that lets you access and create shared information. Its tools give a group E-mail, distributed databases, bulletin boards, text editing and document management, and other applications development tools. It also provides a means of creating group conferences. Many other developers are presently trying to create group software that will challenge Lotus Notes in the enormous groupware market.

Electronic mail and telephone conferencing have been a great aid in allowing people to communicate over distances. But some information, such as visual cues and body language, just cannot be conveyed in an E-mail message or by voice alone. When these types of information are important, **videoconferencing** can help (see Figure 4.15). Videoconferencing has been around for almost as long as television, but despite its advantages it has seen limited use. In the past the high prices of specialized equipment and special phone lines have confined the use of videoconferencing to big companies and special occasions.[16] More recently, the lower price of equipment and the increasing use of computer networks are making videoconferencing more affordable and available on the desktop.

Videoconferencing is especially useful for sharing visual and time-sensitive information. By videoconferencing from desktop-to-desktop, participants can interact by sharing words, video pictures, and computer data. It reduces the time and travel costs of face-to-face meetings and can help minimize the language barriers that are often encountered in a telephone call. A conference begins when a caller brings up the conferencing application on the desktop or portable computer. The application usually consists of a user interface and functions for supporting the videoconference. Several products have been developed that work over normal phone lines and network connections. In addition, newer software has been designed to take advantage of the high-speed ISDN lines. One limitation is that most of the current software is designed to connect from one desktop to another. This limits the number of participants in the conference. As the software improves, this limitation should be taken care of.

The Global Information Network

Due to society's insatiable need for information, a global information network is emerging. One overused term for this global network is the information superhighway. With this network, a person using a computer at home or at work can access information from a seemingly infinite variety of resources. For example, stock quotes and financial reports may be downloaded in real time; late-breaking news reports can be accessed from news and sports services complete with sound and video; and computer programs such as games or utility software can be obtained and used. This information resource is a two-way street. A business can also use this network to broadcast information about its services and products.

The backbone of this global information network is the **Internet**. In the simplest terms, the Internet is a collection of interconnected mainframe computers, personal computers, LANs, and WANs. In the United States these are connected by high-speed, long-distance data lines that were built by the National Science Foundation. The Internet began as a research network, but it has recently expanded to become a consumer and business network. Restrictions on commercial use of the Internet were removed by Congress in 1991. Since then many companies and individuals have clamored to gain access. As mentioned earlier, it has become fashionable to include a user's Internet E-mail address on business cards and in mailing lists. The rate of growth since 1991 has been phenomenal. The Internet Index, an on-line report that keeps statistics on the Internet, reported in September of 1995 that, at the then-current growth rates, everyone on earth would be connected to the Internet by the year 2004.[17]

Businesses usually connect to the Internet through their own gateway or from one owned by a service provider. Each user is provided with a unique address, which is based on the user's computer ID, the computer used to access the network, and the organization that owns the computer. For example, Jane Doe who works for the XYZ Corporation who uses the corporate computer HAL might have an address JDOE@HAL.XYZ.COM. Here JDOE stands for Jane's computer ID and COM is the Internet code for a commercial organization. All Internet addresses are written in a similar format. Other organization codes include GOV for government, EDU for educational institutions, and MIL for military installations; and there are codes for countries, such as FR for France.

Once one is connected, there are many different types of resources available. Besides the capability to transmit E-mail all across the world, commonly used features include listservs, Usenet news groups, file transfer protocols, gopher systems, and the World Wide Web. In addition, special programs exist for searching the Internet. These programs can be used to find documents that relate to just about any topic requested.

A **listserv** is a group electronic mail program. It allows users to subscribe to special-interest electronic mailing lists. Messages about a particular subject are posted to the listserv and sent out to all subscribers as E-mail. This allows for many interesting discussions about a variety of topics. Listservs exist for almost any topic. **Usenet News Groups**, like listserv, also allow for on-line discussions about particular topics. The main difference between the two is how they are managed. News Groups are accessed using special programs that can be used to maintain, monitor, access, and post to the discussion. Listservs, however, can be implemented using just about any electronic mail system but they are more limited in their functionality.

File transfer protocols (FTPs) allow users to download documents and programs using a standard set of methods. These files can be found using a search pro-

Figure 4.16
A Web Home Page

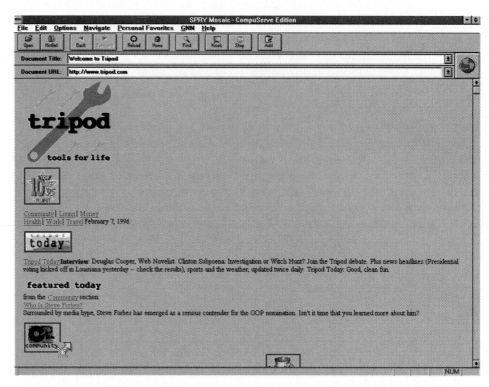

gram and then obtained using FTP. Another method for accessing information on the Internet is called **Gopher.** The primary goal of Gopher is to provide an organized method for navigating the Internet. Gopher uses a method based on menus to move from site to site. It is especially useful for finding information from public databases and libraries or obtaining files from remote computers.

One of the fastest growing areas of the Internet is the **World Wide Web.** The Web provides a rich multimedia environment that includes text, images, sound, and video information. Information on the Web is provided by web "publishers" in the form of "pages." The initial page of a site is called the **home page** (see Figure 4.16 for a sample web page). These pages are accessed using a special program called a browser. The popularity of the Web was dramatically demonstrated when the company that makes Netscape, a popular web browser, announced the initial public offering (IPO) of its stock. Its stock price shot up so fast that it set a Wall Street record for an IPO.

The popularity of the Web is due to two main factors—the multimedia capabilities available and the ease with which a user can navigate from site to site. A feature known as a **"hot link"** can be incorporated into web pages. A user simply points to a hot link with a mouse and clicks. The user can then be connected to another page from the same site or a site located on a computer anywhere in the world.

Businesses are using the Web in many interesting ways. Using its multimedia capabilities, companies are finding new and exciting ways to advertise. Most are creating pages that promote their products and services. Many even allow users to place orders on-line. The Web provides a relatively inexpensive and easy-to-use forum for promotion. For this reason, smaller corporations can use the Web to better compete with the bigger organizations.

The global information network is providing many opportunities for business. New companies have been set up specifically to provide information on the network. Many other companies have been created just to provide access to the network or to provide software for navigating it. Whether or not a company takes advantage of the global network's new business opportunities, it still provides a valuable service with the almost instantaneous access to information and its communications capabilities. The ability to use the network will be an increasingly valuable tool for the electronic office.

THE OFFICE OF THE FUTURE

With the pace of technological developments ever faster, one thing is certain: Office technology will continue to change. In fact, change seems to be the only thing that today's office worker can count on. To be prepared for change, it is important to have some idea about what developments are possible. Following is a list of a few trends that may affect the electronic office of tomorrow:

- The capabilities of computer systems will continue to increase. This will come about as software and peripherals become "smarter" and network capabilities are expanded. Because of this computers will take over more of the functions of office equipment such as messaging, faxing, and document storage. New computer technology could include: storage devices based on optics that will increase storage capacity, reduce disk failures, and improve portability; improvements in computer input such as voice and handwriting recognition; and improvements in video and sound.
- Improved communication technology like cellular communication, computer networks, and ISDN will continue the trend of office relocation. More employees will work at home, in remote locations, and on the run.
- Ergonomics will improve the ease and the comfort of using office technology. **Ergonomics** is the science that studies the relationship between efficiency and comfort in a worker's use of machines. Newer machines will be designed with the user's comfort in mind, which will in turn improve productivity. This may extend to all aspects of the office environment.
- The global information network will continue to become an everyday tool in the office. It can be used for applications ranging from improved remote communications to multimedia advertising.
- New technologies, such as virtual reality, will continue to find applications. **Virtual reality** is the use of computer technology to create a simulated environment. Possible applications include: workers using the technology to visit a "virtual office" from home; "virtual tours" and demonstrations to customers; training simulations; and "virtual conferencing."

Key Terms

- **telecommuter**
- **reengineering**
- **word processing systems**
- **hardware**
- **software**
- **smart machine**
- **information tools**
- **central processing unit**
- **arithmetic-logic unit (ALU)**
- **control unit**
- **microprocessor**
- **compatible computers**
- **mouse**
- **computer monitor**
- **screen resolution**
- **printer**
- **laser printer**
- **primary storage**
- **ROM**
- **RAM**
- **secondary storage**
- **floppy disk**

- floppy disk drive
- magnetic tape
- hard disk
- **CD-ROM**
- modem
- fax-modem
- network card
- computer network
- operating system
- **DOS**
- **UNIX**
- **OS/2**
- **Windows**
- **System 7**
- boilerplate
- database
- query
- spreadsheet software
- cell address
- macros
- presentation graphics software
- multimedia
- personal information managers (PIMs)
- software suites
- desktop publishing
- telecommunications
- electronic mail (E-mail)
- protocols
- copy machine

- facsimile (fax) machine
- scanner
- optical character recognition
- voice processing
- telephone answering system
- voice mail
- integrated services digital network (ISDN)
- mobile office
- pager
- cellular telephone
- laptop computers
- palmtop computers
- personal digital assistants
- local area networks (LANs)
- wide area networks (WANs)
- gateway
- **Electronic Data Interchange (EDI)**
- groupware
- videoconferencing
- **Internet**
- listserv
- **Usenet News Groups**
- **file transfer protocols (FTPs)**
- **Gopher**
- **World Wide Web**
- home page
- hot link
- ergonomics
- virtual reality

Summary

CASE

Miscommunication in an Electronic Office

Carolena Lyons-Lawrence, San Diego State University

AMS College is a nationwide, home-study computer literacy school headquartered in California. AMS has sales representatives in 50 states. The home-study course enables students to work at home with textbooks, study guides, computers, and software and then mail completed lessons to the college. Students can receive assistance over the telephone by calling a toll-free 800 number.

The AMS school, when it opened, had neither computers nor personnel with experience in using computers. A student from a nearby university was hired to direct the company's efforts to computerize. Initially, computerization included only the creation of a student record database on a microcomputer. The person who was hired did not stay with AMS long enough to write documentation for the operation of the database system he created.

The owner of AMS decided on an even more ambitious plan for using computers in the business office. He hired another university student with experience in computer networking. Given the title of technical service support director, this student was instructed to "computerize AMS." Unfortunately, he went about this task without analyzing the environment or consulting with any of the staff. Instead, he relied solely on his previous experience installing a local area network (LAN). The LAN he installed at AMS College consisted of a 386-network file server with workstations attached in a star topography using coaxial cable.

Two programmers were also hired to assist in the creation of application software. Under the supervision of the technical service support director, the programmers wrote programs that allowed the workstations to access the students' record database stored on the network file server. Once this task was completed the director resigned from AMS to take a job with another company. He departed without leaving documentation or anyone knowledgeable enough to supervise and to maintain the LAN.

Case Questions

1. Discuss the computerization pitfalls at AMS.

2. Are the problems at AMS technical problems or communication problems?

3. What written communication should have taken place at AMS with the implementation of the new system?

4. As the newly hired technical service support director, what would you do to get AMS on track?

5. What are some questions the owner should have asked before hiring the other director?

CASE

Internal Communication at a Large Insurance Company

Glenn B. Dietrich, University of Texas at San Antonio

Midwest Insurance Company has experienced rapid and steady growth for the past 10 years. The company began business as a casualty insurance company that restricted its customers to one segment of the population that the founders considered to be a low-risk group. Until 10 years ago, the organization had one office, and its customers were required to communicate with this office for all business activities, including claims adjustments. Business transactions were conducted through the mail or by telephone.

Changes in the policies of the company resulted in the expansion of the population segment that Midwest considers to be its primary market segment. Additionally, the number of insurance products was increased to include life and health insurance. As a result of these changes, along with an aggressive marketing campaign, Midwest has become one of the 20 largest insurance companies in the country. Midwest has 476 offices throughout the United States, Europe, and the Far East. Customers now conduct most of their business with a Midwest employee at a local office.

The impact on internal communication has been significant. No longer can a document be delivered to another employee in a matter of minutes; in fact, overseas memos frequently require a week or more for delivery. Fred Marshall, the manager of information systems, estimates that internal communication has increased twentyfold in the past 10 years and sees this as the most important problem facing the company in the immediate future.

Fred formed a task force to study the internal communication requirements of Midwest. This group concluded that many of the intraoffice and interoffice communication requirements could be satisfied if an electronic mail system was installed, with all of the offices included in the system. Essentially, anyone with access to a computer terminal would be on the electronic mail circuit.

Fred thought that the electronic mail system could be used to satisfy the internal communication requirements of Midwest. However, before committing the organization to the investment required to implement this recommendation, he requested that the task force determine answers to the following questions.

Case Questions

1. How would the ability to send memos electronically affect communication traffic?
2. Would the ease of sending memos result in information overload to key managers?
3. Would there be a shift in the work associated with answering a memo? For example, would the person viewing the memo type a reply while sitting at the keyboard rather than compose the reply and have a secretary type it?
4. Would there be a saving of clerical personnel?
5. Is there any way in which the recipient of the electronic mail could be affected negatively?
6. Would the proposed system be enhanced if other technologies such as voice recognition were included?

Notes

1. Patti Bond, "The Growth of Telecommuting," *Atlanta Journal-Constitution*, July 17, 1995, E1.

2. Michael J. Miller, "The Changing Office," *PC Magazine*, June 14, 1994, 112–122.

3. "Stepping into Tomorrow's Office," *The Office*, November 1981, 119.

4. Jonathan Auerbach, "Smith-Corona Files Under Chapter 11;Typewriter Maker Loses Ground to PCs," *Wall Street Journal*, July 6, 1995, A4.

5. Patrick G. Mckeown, *Living With Computers: Version 5.0* (Fort Worth, TX: The Dryden Press, 1995), 6-11.

6. Louise Kehoe, "Apple Prepares to Do Battle with the Macintosh Killers: The PC Pioneer Is Facing Up to the Threat of Windows 95," *Financial Times*, August 10, 1995, 15.

7. Rick Wallace, *Using Pagemaker 5 for the Mac* (QUE Corporation, 1988).

8. Patrick G. Mckeown, *Living With Computers: Version 5.0*, (Fort Worth, TX: The Dryden Press, 1995), 136–139.

9. Jean Marie Angelo, "Desktop Changes Reshape Publishing Environment," *Folio*, September 1, 1993, 55-62.

10. David Churbuck, "Prepare for the E-mail Attack" *Forbes*, January 23, 1989, 82–87.

11. "Multifunction Unit Simplifies Office Life," *Managing Office Technology*, May 1995, 68.

12. Lura K. Romei, "Voice Processing—Improving Your Productivity," *Managing Office Technology*, January 1995, 15.

13. Todd Copilevitz, "Revolution on the Phone Line," *Atlanta Journal-Constitution*, August 6, 1995, H1.

14. David C. Jones, "Cellular Phones Helping USAA Boost Productivity," *National Underwriter–Life & Healthy/Financial Services*, April 4, 1994, 44.

15. Jeffrey Hsu and Tony Lockwood, "Collaborative Computing," *Byte*, March 1993, 113–120.

16. Bill Husted, "Teleconferencing: Get the Picture," *Atlanta Constitution*, July 19, 1995, E2.

17. Win Treese, *The Internet Index* 9 (September 2, 1995).

Part 2

STRATEGIES FOR WRITTEN COMMUNICATION

In Part 2 we examine the characteristics of all effective business communication, and then break forms of written communication in business into categories, such as length, objective, and formality. We look at strategies for writing effective memos, letters, short and long reports, instructions, and procedures. Some of these messages have a persuasive intent, others instruct or deliver good or bad news. Knowing the appropriate strategy for each type of message enhances your chances of achieving your goals.

Chapter 5

A Systematic Approach to Effective Written Communication

Learning Objectives

1
TO KNOW **10** CHARACTERISTICS OF EFFECTIVE WRITING.

2
TO RECOGNIZE WRITING THAT DOES NOT HAVE THE **10** CHARACTERISTICS.

3
TO UNDERSTAND HOW THE **10** CHARACTERISTICS WORK IN COMBINATION TO MAKE WRITING EFFECTIVE.

4
TO LEARN TECHNIQUES TO BUILD THE **10** CHARACTERISTICS INTO YOUR OWN WRITING.

One of the first things Brad Whitlow did after he was elected president of the Student Government Association was to appoint a committee to investigate student grievance procedures on the campus. During his three earlier years on campus Brad had observed an absence of uniformity concerning how grievances were resolved. The handling of grievances seemed to depend as much on who the aggrieved knew as on the relevant facts of the situation. Eventually a student-faculty committee developed a grievance procedure for all undergraduate students. It was published in the student handbook:

> *In order to provide a mechanism by which students may air their problems concerning academic courses, the university has established the following grievance procedure for all undergraduate students. First, the student should attempt to resolve his grievance with the course instructor. If not satisfied, then he may petition the head of the department in question, who will respond to the grievance in writing. If the student is not entirely satisfied, then his grievance may be submitted to the Undergraduate Petitions Committee, a three-man panel composed of two faculty members and one student who will render a final decision concerning the grievance.*

Jim Malone received his final term grades, and one of them was an unpleasant surprise—a grade two letters lower than he had expected. He called the course instructor, who declined to see him. Angered by this response, Jim called the dean of student affairs and was told to consult the student handbook.

Reread the grievance procedure. As you do, make a mental list of the things you find wrong with it. Remember that whatever you think is wrong probably is. After all, it was written for students: you're the audience.

This chapter introduces 10 characteristics that make written communication effective. Each one will be discussed and the grievance procedure will be rewritten to incorporate it. The goal is to help you see how written communication, if approached systematically, can be improved.

CHARACTERISTIC 1: TACTFUL

People who possess tact know the right thing to do or to say in a given situation. This is especially important in business communication. Unfortunately, too many of us assume that what is inoffensive to us is inoffensive to everyone else. Not every person enjoys off-color jokes, nor does everyone appreciate ethnic jokes or religious anecdotes. As Chapter 2 pointed out, one skill the effective encoder of messages has is the ability to analyze the receiver. Such audience analysis, which may include visualizing your reader or anticipating the reader's level of education or expertise, can be crucial for successful communication. Audience analysis is covered more thoroughly in Chapters 6 and 15. One outcome of such an analysis should be more tactful writing.

Appeal to the Reader's Intelligence

Writing at too high or too low a level may insult the reader.

Write *to* your reader, neither above nor below. Tactlessness occurs when writers seek to impress rather than express. The reader becomes baffled and loses interest or, even worse, misinterprets the information and responds inappropriately.

After several years of successful teaching at the undergraduate level for a college of business, a young instructor felt she had effectively phrased her expectations regarding plagiarism. She had wanted to be clear and firm and she knew that some students had been educated in a system that was tolerant of cheating. The following appeared in her syllabus for her sophomore course:

> Cheating in any form will not be tolerated. While group work in other courses (and in business) may be required and rewarded, efforts for this course must be your own. This policy includes the sharing of computer databases and computer diskette files. If you have any questions about plagiarism at this university, review pages 18 and 19 of the University Code of Conduct, which includes punishments for infractions.

For the most part, the instructor's students seemed to understand the policy and adhered to it. Major problems did not occur, at least not until the instructor was asked to teach her specialty to the prestigious Executive MBA group at her university. This group was made of 40 highly motivated, fast-track, exceptionally bright mid- and upper-level executives, mostly in their late thirties and forties. The average student in this group supervised a dozen direct reports, and paid about $15,000 a year in tuition. Classes met all day, every Saturday, for two years.

Because she was teaching similar subject matter as for her undergraduate class and had a history of success doing so, the instructor used the same phrasing regarding cheating.

The first class meeting opened with a nasty confrontation between the students and the instructor. The students made clear to the instructor that they were above reproach, were interested in learning to better themselves and their organizations, were "paying" to learn not only in dollars but in substantial personal costs, and had never been accused of cheating by any other instructors, most of whom they considered friends and who were referred to by first names.

By insulting the students' intelligence, as well as their integrity, the instructor was never able to gain a comfortable rapport with the students, and removed herself from the program when her course was finished.

Appeal to the Individual

Tactful writing appeals to the individual rather than to categories. Consider the following:

> People such as you like a good bargain. That is why we're offering you these fantastic discounts on . . .

As the sender of this message, you might be assuming that all customers like good bargains. However, many of our customers will think of themselves as being different from other customers. "People such as you" puts the customer in the same category with everyone else. The extent to which you offend one, two, or several customers with your categorization is the extent to which your potential sales could decline. In a different type of categorization, imagine being a personnel manager who receives several hundred resumes from potential employees each year. Many of these resumes are accompanied by a cover letter with the salutation "Dear Personnel Manager." Some managers react quite differently to this salutation than to one containing the manager's name.

The reader may consider it insulting to be categorized.

Avoid Sexism

We can insult at least half our readers by using sexist language. The student grievance procedure at the beginning of this chapter, taken literally, was written only for males: the student should attempt to resolve *his* grievance; the petitions committee is "three-man." Whether you as the sender are offended by sexist language is irrelevant. Someone in your audience could be.

Sexist language may insult the reader.

One problem in removing sexist language is that changes from gender-specific words, such as *he*, to nonsexist language, such as *he or she*, can become cumbersome unless done sparingly. With this problem in mind, here are some ways of removing sexist language from your writing:

1. Use the word *person*. For example:

   Sexist: When you schedule a meeting with a businessman, be aware of the importance of time.

   Nonsexist: When you schedule a meeting with a business person, be aware of the importance of time.

2. Use plurals. For example:

   Sexist: An employee will be promoted based upon his ability and seniority.

   Nonsexist: Employees will be promoted based upon their ability and seniority.

   Sexist: A good manager develops his subordinates.

   Nonsexist: Good managers develop their subordinates.

3. Use the words *you* and *your*. For example:

   Sexist: An employee should punch his time card promptly each morning.

   Nonsexist: Punch your time card promptly each morning.

Some other ways of removing sexist language that you may wish to consider are to alternate feminine and masculine pronouns, to use "one" instead of "person" for the offensive pronoun, or to edit out the personal pronoun.

Many commonly used words in business communication are potentially sexist. Here are some examples of those words and their more contemporary replacements.

Don't Say	Say
Businessman	Business person, business executive, manager
Chairman	Chairperson, moderator, chair
Waitress	Server
Salesman	Salesperson, sales agent, sales representative
Spokesman	Spokesperson, representative
Workmen	Workers
Foreman	Supervisor
Manhole cover	Maintenance cover, utility cover

Finally, avoid falling victim to sexual stereotypes when writing about people who have assumed roles once reserved for a single sex. Such terms as *male nurse*, *female attorney*, and *woman manager* merely call attention to the sex of the role occupant rather than the role itself.

Avoid Offensive Language in General

Sexist writing is not the only offensive use of language.

Other uses of language are just as offensive to some readers as sexist terms.

Stereotypical Language

Included in this category are words that stereotype or create negative perceptions of those being mentioned. If your message is to be accepted, it cannot be offensive to the reader; therefore, be especially careful with topics that relate to ethnicity, religion, or handicap. Recent laws such as those relating to hate crimes and the Americans with Disabilities Act stress treating others equitably in language and action. Changes in our language reflect changes in our society; for those with a disability, for example, we now avoid such terms as afflicted, crippled, deformed, deaf, or invalid, and use such terms as disabled, wheelchair-user, physically impaired, hearing impaired, or multi-handicapped.

Notice how the following sentence is demeaning to Mr. Lee and to others, and how it demonstrates the author's perceptions of those who are disabled:

Mr. Lee is a *crippled teacher* and *confined to a wheelchair*. All of his students are *normal*.

This sentence could be rewritten as follows:

Mr. Lee is a *teacher with a disability*. He is a *wheelchair-user*. None of his students is *disabled*.

Humor in Bad Taste

Even a weak joke is not a good opening for a collection letter; for example:

Maybe you've heard this one: Why are little birds so sad in the morning? Answer: Because their little bills are all "overdew." It may remind you that we have a little bill that is overdue. If you feed it a check . . .[1]

An Accusatory Tone

When your writing contains an accusation, whether implied or expressed, you risk offending your reader. Compare these two sentences:

Perhaps you did not follow the instruction manual that accompanied your Expresso Coffeemaker. (accusatory)

Please recheck the instruction manual that accompanied our Expresso Coffeemaker. (nonaccusatory)

Focus on the Receiver's Perception

As you work toward increasing tact in your writing, remember that your own perception of tact is not what counts. All that really counts is the meaning your receiver assigns to the message.

To make the grievance procedure paragraph at the beginning of this chapter more tactful, we need to remove the sexist language (*his* and *man*):

In order to provide a mechanism by which students may air their problems concerning academic courses, the university has established the following grievance procedure for all undergraduate students. First, the student should attempt to resolve the grievance with the course instructor. If the student is not satisfied, the grievance may be filed with the head of the department in question, who will respond to the grievance in writing. If the student is not then entirely satisfied, the grievance may be submitted to the Undergraduate Petitions Committee, a panel composed of two faculty members and one student who will render a final decision concerning the grievance.

> **✔ CHECKLIST for Tactful Writing**
>
> ____ Appeals to the reader's intelligence.
> ____ Appeals to the individual rather than to categories of readers.
> ____ Avoids sexism.
> ____ Is not offensive.

CHARACTERISTIC 2: PERSONAL

What you write should convey a "you" attitude, which means focusing on the receiver's needs and interests—not on yourself. In terms of writing technique, this means de-emphasizing the use of *we* and *I* and emphasizing *you* and *your*. Here are some examples:

The "you" attitude puts the reader first.

We and I	You
We've mailed a check.	You'll receive your check in the mail.
Our savings accounts pay 6 percent interest.	You'll earn 6 percent interest from your savings account.
I want to express my appreciation for . . .	Thank you for your help with . . .

Using *you* and *your* makes the reader the center of attention in the message. Writing with the "you" attitude can be done on two levels. The first is fairly mechanical and easy. Go through your draft and spot each *I*-type reference. Then work on the elimination of these words. You won't be able to remove all references, but the tone improves with each removal. Now go through that same draft and insert some *you*-type references. Up to the point when the use of *you* becomes bothersome and noticeable, it is a valuable interest developer. Once or twice in a letter the person's name can be spliced into the message for special emphasis. Since interest is more likely to wane in the middle or end of a letter, these may be good locations for the individual's name.

The second level of applying the "you" attitude is more elusive and difficult. This level goes beyond the mere substitution of pronouns and seeks a between-the-lines tone that the message is to the reader rather than from the author. This is the level and tone you should strive toward. Compare these two short messages:

> The company wishes to encourage employees to take part in the suggestion system that it has provided; the system has produced many money-saving ideas in the past.

> Employees are the heart of XYZ Company, and each employee's ideas are enthusiastically sought and carefully evaluated. Many employee-volunteered ideas have produced time- and effort-saving changes.

Neither passage has an *I* or a *you*, but the second one has a tone that is directed to the employee rather than from the company.

Tactful and personal writing are related. As you have probably already discovered, using the "you" attitude is also a convenient way to avoid sexist language. However, tactful writing sometimes requires that you avoid the "you" attitude in order not to offend the reader. Consider the following:

We and I	You
We did not receive a check.	You did not send your check.
Employees who are late three days with no excused reason will be dismissed.	If you are late three days with no excused reason, then you will be dismissed.

Figure 5.1
Signs in Two Auto
Service Areas

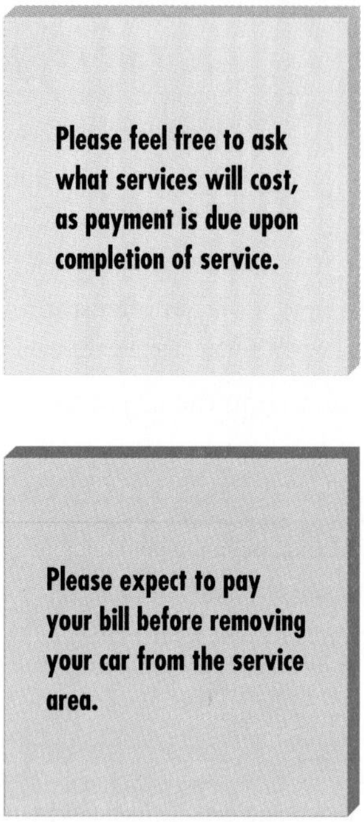

> **Please feel free to ask what services will cost, as payment is due upon completion of service.**

> **Please expect to pay your bill before removing your car from the service area.**

In the first example, "You did not send your check" contains an accusatory tone. The *we* and *I* approach implies that the check did not arrive for reasons other than the reader's not having sent it. The second example is less tactful. The "you" version communicates an expectation that every reader is considering taking three free holidays. The more appropriate *we* and *I* version successfully communicates the company's policy but avoids the implication that all employees are irresponsible.

If the "you" attitude might offend the reader, *we* and *I* should be used instead.

Generally, you'll want to put the reader first. Write from his or her point of view. However, if making the reader the center of attention might bring offense, then shift to the *we* and *I* approach. An alternative to *we* or *I* is to blend in the use of the company's name or reference to the department, as in "XYZ Company values your contributions," or "The department knows you are a skilled worker."

Here, then, is a further revised (but not perfect) version of the grievance procedure paragraph at the beginning of the chapter.

> In order to provide a mechanism by which you can air your problems concerning academic courses, the university has established for you the following grievance procedure. First, you should attempt to resolve your grievance with your course instructor. If you are not satisfied, your grievance may be filed with the head of the department in question, who will respond to your grievance in writing. If you are not then entirely satisfied, request that your grievance be submitted to the Undergraduate Petitions Committee, a panel composed of two faculty members and one student who will render a final decision concerning your grievance.

CHARACTERISTIC 3: POSITIVE

A positive tone develops a positive relationship.

Effective written communication has a positive tone. How people react to your writing depends in part on the climate of communication you establish with them. Such a climate can be positive or negative. Compare the two messages in Figure 5.1. Both messages have the same meaning, yet they convey different ideas about the relationship the auto service firm wants to establish with customers.

When writing for business, we want to create as positive a climate and as much good will as possible. We need to avoid using negative words such as *delay, can't, impossible, inconvenience, trouble, disagreement,* and *misunderstanding.* Here are some examples:

Negative: You *failed* to enclose a check with your order; therefore, it is *impossible* to send you the merchandise.

Positive: As soon as your check arrives, we'll send your order via parcel post.

Negative: There can be *no* exceptions to this policy.

Positive: This policy must apply equally and fairly to everyone.

Negative: This oven *doesn't* come with a 40-inch cooktop.

Positive: The oven is available with either a 30-inch or a 36-inch cooktop.

Negative: The paint is guaranteed not to *dull, chip,* or *scratch* for two years.

Positive: The paint is guaranteed to stay bright and smooth for two years.

Negative: We *regret* having *forgotten* to include your refund check.

Positive: You will receive your refund check by the end of the week.

Negative: We *cannot* meet until Monday morning.

Positive: We can meet on Monday morning.

The tone we employ sets the climate for our communication. A positive climate means we use a positive tone.

Other than careful word selection, there are two other ways to enhance a positive message; both relate to emphasis. The first approach employs the concept of **reversal words.** These words change the direction or tone of a message from positive to negative or from negative to positive. When they occur at a transition point they identify the upcoming change. This identification can be valuable when you are moving from bad news to good news, for the reader knows that the negative is finished.

> Reversal words change the direction or tone of a message.

The change from a positive message to a negative message is unpleasant. For this reason, try not to add extra emphasis to the negative information by saying, in effect, "Brace yourself, here it comes."

In summary, we might wish to use reversal words between negative and positive thoughts, but we should always avoid reversal words prior to negative thoughts. Examples of reversal words and phrases are *however, on the other hand, but,* and *unfortunately.* Of these, *unfortunately* should especially be avoided because it is a negative word that is used only before a negative thought.

The second approach to gain maximum benefit from your message is emphasis through location. In **place emphasis** we place our information at either the beginning or the end of the message because those are the locations of maximum emphasis. The opposite of this works, too; putting negative information in the middle of a message—away from the beginning or ending emphasis locations—draws as little attention to it as possible.

The technique of using repetition for emphasis is called **mass emphasis**. A positive message might be repeated in both similar and different ways throughout the piece of writing.

CHARACTERISTIC 4: ACTIVE

Of the two sentences that follow, which seems more emphatic to you?

> Effective business writers use the active voice.
> The active voice is used by effective business writers.

The first sentence is written in the active voice, meaning that the subject performs the action expressed by the verb. The second sentence is in the passive voice; the subject receives the action expressed by the verb. The active voice helps make sentences come alive. Because people usually talk in the active voice, they are more accustomed to deal-

> The active voice emphasizes ideas.

ing with it. Active is strong because the subject is acting. Passive is weak because the subject is being acted upon. Consider the following:

Passive:	A refund will be sent to you.
Active:	You will receive a refund.
Passive:	The report was written by Jim.
Active:	Jim wrote the report.
Passive:	The product's safety has been shown by laboratory tests.
Active:	Laboratory tests show the product's safety.

The passive voice de-emphasizes ideas.

Sometimes you'll want to use the passive voice, especially if you want to de-emphasize a point. Again, we are concerned about tact in writing:

Passive:	Your payment has not been received.
Active:	You didn't send in your payment.
Passive:	Your credit was checked.
Active:	We checked your credit.

The passive voice need not always be used to de-emphasize an idea. We can rewrite "Your credit was checked" in the active voice and still be tactful: "To assure that the use of credit is in the best interest of the applicant, we do check all credit references."

Using the active voice guideline, we should make two changes in the grievance procedure paragraph at the beginning of the chapter. "Your grievance may be filed" should be changed to "You may file your grievance." And "Your grievance may be submitted" should read "You may submit your grievance."

CHARACTERISTIC 5: UNIFIED

Sentence unity requires limiting each sentence to one idea.

Each sentence in business communication should contain only one idea. When writing a sentence, the goal is to make sure that two unrelated ideas do not appear. Meeting this goal is easy if you write nothing but simple sentences. Limiting yourself to simple sentences, however, will result in a choppy writing style characteristic of a first-grade reader: "See Dick. See Jane. See Spot run."

Experienced writers combine simple, compound, and complex sentences to vary the rhythm. Yet using compound and complex sentences brings the danger of lack of unity:

Poor:	Thank you for placing your order, and your new Beachcraft Towels should reach you by July 15. (compound sentence)
Better:	Thank you for placing your order. Your new Beachcraft Towels should reach you by July 15. (two simple sentences)
Poor:	When you start the engine, adjust the motor speed immediately, and check your owner's manual if you have any further problems. (compound-complex sentences)
Better:	When you start your engine, adjust the motor speed immediately. If you have any further problems, please check your owner's manual. (two complex sentences)

Paragraph unity requires limiting each paragraph to one central idea.

Unity applies in much the same way to writing paragraphs. In this case our goal is to be sure that no paragraph contains more than one central idea. However, many times our thoughts get mixed together:

> We need to talk about expansion plans tomorrow. The report is due next month, and I'm afraid we're running short on time. I can't figure out last month's profit statement. Need to go over it with you. We're over budget. Enclosed is a bill from the printer. Impossible! Did you authorize this?

You can see that this writer is dealing with three separate ideas—expansion plans, the profit statement, and the printer's bill. The paragraph can be improved by making three paragraphs out of it:

We need to talk about expansion plans tomorrow. The report is due next month, and I'm afraid we're running short on time.

I can't figure out last month's profit statement. Need to go over it with you. We're over budget.

Enclosed is a bill from the printer. Impossible! Did you authorize this?

Besides reading more smoothly, the material is presented so as to tell the reader that these are three important ideas, as opposed to only one.

Perhaps the best way to make sure that your paragraphs are unified is to begin each of them with a topic sentence (see Characteristic 7). Then do not write any other sentence not related to the topic sentence. Save unrelated ideas for future paragraphs.

The grievance procedure material at the beginning of the chapter is so brief that paragraph unity is not a problem. In practice, however, you will find that many paragraphs are quite lengthy and require careful attention to unity.

CHARACTERISTIC 6: COHERENT

Writers should achieve a logical connection between ideas as well as a smooth flow of ideas within a document. Referred to as **coherence,** this is important to both sentences and paragraphs. If sentences or paragraphs are coherent, the ideas in them are clearly tied together and easy to understand.

Sentence Coherence

Sentences often lack coherence because we use pronouns such as *this, that,* and *it* ambiguously.

> Coherent sentences and paragraphs are understandable because they stick together.

Unclear:	Your Grasscutter electric mower will operate quietly and quickly; this will save you money.
Clear:	Your Grasscutter electric mower will operate quietly and quickly. Its speed will save you money.
Unclear:	They rented furniture for their apartment that cost $100 per month.
Clear:	For their apartment, they rented furniture that cost $100 per month.

Dangling constructions also make sentences incoherent. Dangling constructions occur when verbal phrases (such as "While doing the laundry," "Sitting at my desk," or "Using a computer") at the beginning or end of a sentence do not clearly and logically refer to the proper noun or pronoun. Here are some examples:

Unclear:	The miscalculation was found using a computer spreadsheet program.
Clear:	We found the miscalculation by using a computer spreadsheet program.
Unclear:	Being a preferred customer, I am sure you'll be interested in this.
Clear:	Because you are a preferred customer, I'm sure you'll be interested in this.
Unclear:	Having been run through the adding machine, the clerk rechecked his figures.
Clear:	After running figures through the adding machine, the clerk rechecked them.

Problems with parallel sentence structure are yet another way sentences become incoherent. Items in a series must be presented in parallel fashion, such as each starting with a verb or with an infinitive. Thoughts compared or contrasted should be in parallel grammatical form as well. Here are examples:

Not parallel:	Our Continuous Improvement Program will fail unless we empower employees, identify problems, and we must have management's blessing.
Parallel:	Our Continuous Improvement Program will fail unless we *empower* employees, *identify* problems, and *obtain* management's blessing.

> Not parallel: Employees wanting to take vacation time this summer must begin now to verify possible dates, to receive their supervisor's approval, and they must make sure no major jobs are logged at the desired vacation time.
>
> Parallel: Employees wanting to take vacation time this summer must begin now *to verify* possible dates, *to receive* their supervisor's approval, and *to make* sure no major jobs are logged at the desired vacation time.
>
> Not parallel: The CEO's message will not only rally the employees behind her, but it will also influence stockholders.
>
> Parallel: Not only will the CEO's message rally the employees behind her, but it also will influence stockholders.

Paragraph Coherence

Four devices for improving paragraph coherence are parallel structure, linking words, enumerating, and signposting.

Paragraphs can be coherent if we make a conscious attempt to use certain devices to help the reader along. Unfortunately, we too often assume the reader can read our mind along with our writing, and we produce paragraphs like this:

> You'll want to own a Washamatic clothes dryer for several reasons. It costs only 9 cents for the average load and has a one-year guarantee on all parts. It comes in three brilliant colors—harvest gold, fresh green, and sunflower yellow.

One device for improving the coherence of this paragraph is the use of parallel structure. **Parallel structure** consists of the repetition of sentence patterns. It adds clarity and readability to ideas.

> You'll want to own a Washamatic clothes dryer for several reasons. It costs only 9 cents for the average load. It comes with a one-year guarantee on all parts. And it comes in three brilliant colors—harvest gold, fresh green, and sunflower yellow.

Parallel structure emphasizes all three of the reasons equally.

Another way to improve coherence is to use **linking words**, which serve as transitions or bridges between ideas. In the following paragraph, "also" and "in addition" are linking words.

> You'll want to own a Washamatic clothes dryer for several reasons. It costs only 9 cents for the average load. Also, it has a one-year guarantee on all parts. In addition, the Washamatic comes in three brilliant colors—harvest gold, fresh green, and sunflower yellow.

Other examples of linking words are *however*, *and*, *consequently*, and *therefore*.

A third device for enhancing paragraph coherence is called **enumerating**. Here we give a specific numeric or chronological label to each of our ideas:

> You'll want to own a Washamatic clothes dryer for several reasons. First, it costs only 9 cents for the average load. Second, it has a one-year guarantee on all parts. And, third, the Washamatic comes in three brilliant colors —harvest gold, fresh green, and sunflower yellow.

Finally, we can incorporate **signposting**; that is, assigning brief headings to our major ideas:

> You'll want to own a Washamatic clothes dryer for several reasons:
> Cost—only 9 cents for the average load.
> Guarantee—one year on all parts.
> Colors—three brilliant colors: harvest gold, fresh green, and sunflower yellow.

If you examine the grievance procedure paragraph at the beginning of the chapter, you will find that coherence was achieved when we made other wording changes. Coherence can also be brought about through careful outlining, which will contribute to improved clarity as well. Coherence and clarity tend to go hand in hand.

Coherence through Careful Outlining

The better you organize your written material, the easier it will be to understand. And the better you outline your ideas, the more organized they will become as you put them on paper. Outlining is one key to reader understanding.

Outlining will be discussed in detail in Chapter 10 in relation to report writing. However, you can use an outline for any written communication—memos, letters, policies, and procedures. The more complex the information, the more it benefits from outlining.

An outline is a convenient way to organize paragraphs and groups of paragraphs into a logical arrangement. Imagine that you need to write a memo to employees about timeliness. They are late reporting to work in the morning, they take extended breaks, and their 30-minute lunch breaks often last from 45 minutes to one hour. Somehow, you need to communicate to them and influence them to abide by company policies. The first step in writing this memo is to outline your ideas on paper. You might, for example, follow the AIDA (Attention, Interest, Desire, Action) sequence, a formula for persuasive writing discussed in more detail in Chapter 8 on persuasive letters, and construct an outline similar to this:

   I. Attention
      A. Some statistics about output per hour
      B. Some statistics about lost output because of lost time
  II. Interest
      A. Employees' role in company success
      B. Reference to time policies
         1. Tardiness
         2. Break time
         3. Lunchtime
 III. Desire
      A. Consequences of conforming to time policies
      B. Consequences of not conforming to time policies
 IV. Action
      A. Simple call for conformity
      B. Expression of appreciation for conformity

Because we have outlined four basic ideas (Attention, Interest, Desire, and Action), at least four paragraphs are needed in our memorandum. Also, we might easily have two paragraphs under Interest and perhaps two under Desire. In any case, we are planning our memo logically. If the material is well organized, our chances of having it understood are increased.

CHARACTERISTIC 7: CLEAR

Clarity in writing applies to word choice, to sentence and paragraph structure, and to the overall organization of whatever you write, be it a letter, a memo, or a report. Clarity is a general concept meaning that what we write is understandable to the reader. Readability, the ninth characteristic, is important to clarity. Unity and coherence are also important. Moreover, clarity involves several additional techniques we have discussed: choosing your words carefully, using topic sentences in your paragraphs, and outlining your ideas before you begin writing.

> ✔ *CHECKLIST for Coherent Writing*
>
> ____ Carefully outline your ideas before putting them in writing.
>
> ____ Use parallel structure to emphasize all points equally.
>
> ____ Use linking words to provide transitions between points.
>
> ____ Enumerate—that is, give a specific numeric or chronological label to the points being made.
>
> ____ Signpost—that is, assign brief headings to major points.

Clear writing exhibits readability, unity, and coherence.

Avoiding Technical Jargon

Technical jargon may be impressive but meaningless.

Every field has its own special language. A blow to the head is a subdural hematoma to a doctor. What the military calls a protective reaction strike is nevertheless the dropping of bombs. And if you do poorly in school, you will probably be called an underachiever. Figure 5.2 humorously illustrates the principle of avoiding jargon except with fellow specialists.

Read the material in Figure 5.3 and notice how the jargon that is probably familiar to those in retailing or marketing can be difficult for others to understand.

Avoiding Unfamiliar Words

Using familiar words can improve reader understanding.

Jargon basically consists of words that are unfamiliar to all but specialists. Other unfamiliar words, although not jargon, create just as much misunderstanding. Try this paragraph:

> Fully cognizant of the inoperative nature of his vehicle, George's initial response was to institute repairs. Prior to modifying the timing, he found a defective wire in the anterior portion of the engine.

See whether these changes make the paragraph more understandable:

Figure 5.2
Technical Jargon as a Barrier to Communication
Source: Copyright International Paper Company.

Figure 5.3
The Problem with Jargon (from a J.C. Penney flyer)
Source: Consumer Reports, January 1993, p. 59.

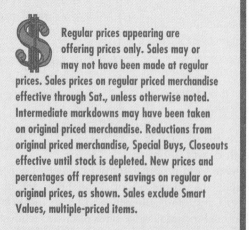

Regular prices appearing are offering prices only. Sales may or may not have been made at regular prices. Sales prices on regular priced merchandise effective through Sat., unless otherwise noted. Intermediate markdowns may have been taken on original priced merchandise. Reductions from original priced merchandise, Special Buys, Closeouts effective until stock is depleted. New prices and percentages off represent savings on regular or original prices, as shown. Sales exclude Smart Values, multiple-priced items.

Knowing well that his car was not working, George's first response was to begin repairs. Before changing the timing, he found a faulty wire in the front part of the engine.

Even the simplest ideas can be made almost unintelligible with unfamiliar words. See if you can translate these old sayings into their familiar form:

- He who expresses merriment subsequent to everyone else expresses merriment of most superior quality.
- Precipitation entails negation of economy.
- Pulchritude is not evinced below the dermal surface.*

To help make your writing clear, use words that will be familiar to your reader. Here are some examples:

Don't Say	Say
Prior to	Before
Subsequent to	After
Accomplish	Do
Reimburse	Pay
Determine	Find out
Transmit	Send
Advantageous	Helpful
Locality	Place
Facilitate	Help
Encounter difficulty in	Find it hard to
Pursuant to your request	As you asked

Using Topic Sentences

A unified paragraph has only one central idea, which is usually expressed in the topic sentence of the paragraph. The topic sentence should be placed at either the beginning or the end of the paragraph. In business communication it usually appears at the beginning. However, you might place your topic sentence at the end of the paragraph if (1) the main topic of your paragraph will be unclear unless the reader is first exposed to some details or (2) you are attempting to persuade the reader, and his or her reaction might be unfavorable. In the second case, presenting details first will help you support the position you take in the topic sentence.

> The topic sentence presents the main idea of the paragraph.

These two examples should help you understand how the topic sentence (in italics) can make writing clearer:

Burns Brick Company has several employee relations problems. The turnover rate is 39 percent, up 10 percent from last year. Absenteeism has increased almost 25 percent this year. And the number of grievances has more than doubled during the past 6 months.

The turnover rate at Burns Brick Company is 39 percent, up 10 percent from last year. Absenteeism has increased almost 25 percent this year. And the number of grievances has more than doubled during the past 6 months. *Obviously, the company is faced with several important employee relations problems.*

By our using topic sentences and ensuring that every sentence in the paragraph is related to the topic sentence (unity), the reader better understands our written message.

*Hints: "He who laughs last . . .," "Haste makes . . .," and "Beauty is only. . ."

CHARACTERISTIC 8: CONCISE

You can become a concise writer if you will avoid wordy expressions, trite phrases, useless repetition, and abstract words. **Conciseness** is saying what you want to say in the fewest possible words. The opposite of conciseness is wordiness.

Avoiding Wordy Expressions

Wordy expressions are deadweight in a sentence. Many sentences beginning with *there are*, *it is*, or *there is* are wordy. You can say the same thing without phrases that make your sentences begin slowly:

Don't Say	Say
There are three fine restaurants on Broad Street.	Broad Street has three fine restaurants.
It is important that all employees read the company handbook.	All employees should read the company handbook.
There is little time left us to make a decision.	We have little time left to make the decision.

In just these three examples we have saved seven words at no expense to understanding.

"More matter, with less art" were Queen Gertrude's words to the rambling, wordy Polonius in Shakespeare's *Hamlet*. As she encouraged him to speak more concisely, we encourage you to write more concisely with the following changes:

Wordy	Concise
A long period of time	A long time (or two weeks)
At the present time	Now (or today's date)
Consensus of opinion	Consensus
Due to the fact that	Because
During the month of November	During November
For the purpose of	For
For the reason that	Because
In many cases	Often
In some cases	Sometimes
In the near future	Soon
In the event that	If
In the state of Illinois	In Illinois
In view of the fact that	Because
With regard to	About
With reference to	About
The jar which is blue	The blue jar

Avoiding Trite Phrases

Trite phrases are worn-out, commonplace expressions. Because they are overused, trite phrases have lost their meaning and can reduce your credibility as a writer.

Some trite phrases can simply be deleted from a sentence; others have fresher replacements. Here are some examples:

Don't Say	Say
Advise	Tell
Enclosed please find	Enclosed is
Numerous and sundry	Many
Permit me to say	(nothing)
It has come to my attention	I have learned
Under separate cover	Separately
Please be advised	(nothing)
Up to this writing	Until now
In accordance with your request	As you requested
Kindly	Please

Avoiding Useless Repetition

Sometimes we repeat ideas for effect—to impress them in the reader's mind. Television advertisements repeat the product's name many times so that we will not forget it. When you write, you might also repeat ideas. Yet one careless mistake we sometimes make is useless repetition of the same idea, as the following examples show:

- The two cars were *exactly* identical.
- His pay raise was small *in size*.
- We join *together* in wishing you well in your new job.
- If you can't use the new typewriter, return it *back* to me.
- What we need are some *new* changes.
- Please see me at 3:30 P.M. *in the afternoon*.

The words in italics can be omitted from each sentence with no loss of understanding.

Avoiding Abstract Words

Abstract words contribute to unclear writing because they are so vague that the reader is not sure what we are trying to say. Concrete words, the opposite of abstract words, have clear, specific meanings. They help readers create the image that we want created in their minds.

"Vehicle" is an abstract word. When we say, "A vehicle was parked at the curb," the reader is not sure just what kind of vehicle we mean—truck, bus, car, or other vehicle. To create a more vivid image for the reader, we should move from the abstract to the concrete:

Vehicle→Car→Pontiac→1997 Pontiac→1997 Pontiac Grand Prix→Brown and gold 1997 Pontiac Grand Prix

Saying "A brown and gold 1997 Pontiac Grand Prix was parked at the curb" creates a much clearer image.

Here are some examples of the use of abstract versus concrete language:

Abstract	Concrete
Your savings account will earn the *highest possible interest*.	Your savings account will earn the *maximum 6.5 percent interest each year*.
The *majority* of our stockholders voted for the new plan.	*Sixty-four percent* of our stockholders voted for the new plan.
Your new, *lightweight* Electro Typewriter can be carried easily from *room to room*.	Your new Electro Typewriter is *feather light*. *Weighing only 12 pounds*, it can easily be carried from *office to office*.
You will receive your refund check *soon*.	You will receive your *full $132.19* by July 15.

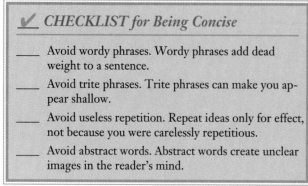

✔ *CHECKLIST for Being Concise*

_____ Avoid wordy phrases. Wordy phrases add dead weight to a sentence.

_____ Avoid trite phrases. Trite phrases can make you appear shallow.

_____ Avoid useless repetition. Repeat ideas only for effect, not because you were carelessly repetitious.

_____ Avoid abstract words. Abstract words create unclear images in the reader's mind.

In summary, you can write concisely if you avoid using wordy expressions, trite phrases, useless repetitions, and abstract words. Writing more concisely usually means using fewer words, thus saving the reader time and energy. When abstract words are replaced, however, conciseness may require increasing the number of words to create a more vivid image.

CHARACTERISTIC 9: READABLE

Saying that something is readable means that it is understandable because of its clear style of writing. Many of us purposefully choose long words and write lengthy, complicated sentences in order to show off our command of the language. Any idea, no matter how simple, can be written in such a way as to make it difficult or even impossible for our readers to understand. The writer of the following paragraph could not have been interested in achieving understanding.

> This chapter's primary purpose is to facilitate and otherwise enhance an individual's proficiency in translating cognitions into appropriately presented written material which effectively satisfies a minimum of 10 salient criteria.

When readers become aware of our writing style, they no longer concentrate on the meaning of our message. The best writing style is one that does not draw attention to itself.

What is your impression of the original form of the grievance procedure paragraph? It is more complicated than it needs to be, yet the style of writing is fairly typical of much communication in business, including handbooks for students.

Readability has been a popular topic since the late 1940s, when mathematical formulas were developed to judge the degree of complexity of written material. One of these formulas is Robert Gunning's Fog Index.[2]

Applying the Fog Index

Gunning's Fog Index is intended to gauge the grade level of written material: What level of education will the audience need to have in order to understand something that is written? It works best with text of at least 200 words. Only prose can be evaluated. The Fog Index does not work on nonsentence material, such as letterheads, inside addresses, or balance sheet information.

The once-tedious process of calculating the readability of a piece of writing has been dramatically reduced by computer software designed for that purpose. Such software falls into two major categories: stand alone and integrated with a word processor. Although the most widely used readability formulas are similar in approach, they do not always give the same results, even on the same sample prose. Further, many of the software packages that calculate readability—and the software that often accompanies the readability software that critiques grammar and punctuation—are much less than 100 percent accurate in their analyses. An understanding of the internal workings of a readability formula, such as the Fog Index, allows a much richer understanding of what the readability numbers mean. Therefore, we examine here one of the more easily applied formulas—the Gunning Fog Index.

Try your hand at using the Fog Index by applying it to the grievance procedure paragraph at the beginning of the chapter, even though that passage is rather brief. The steps to take are as follows:

1. *Count the number of words in the passage.* There are 100 words in the grievance procedure material.

2. *Count the number of complete thoughts in the passage.* A simple or complex sentence has one complete thought; a compound sentence has two thoughts. We counted four complete thoughts.

3. *Compute the average sentence length.* To do this, divide the number of words in the passage (100) by the number of complete thoughts (4); the answer is 25.

4. *Compute the percentage of "hard words."* These words have three or more syllables. Some types of longer words should not be computed:

   a. Proper names (Kennedy, Carolina)

   b. Combinations of short, easy words (bookkeeper, homemaker, however)

   c. Verb forms made three syllables by adding *ed* or *es* (created, trespasses).

   To compute the percentage, divide the number of hard words (we counted 15) by the total number of words in the passage (100). The answer is 15 percent.

5. *Add the average sentence length and the percentage of hard words.* The average sentence length (25) plus the percentage of hard words (15—with no decimal point) equals 40.

6. *Multiply the answer in Step 5 by 0.4.* The answer, 16, is the Fog Index.

Interpreting the Fog Index

We can interpret the Fog Index by comparing it to a grade level. For example, if the index is 6, then the material is written at the sixth-grade level. Our index of 16 for the material from the grievance procedure means that it is written at the level of a senior in college.

The readability index corresponds to a grade level.

Is this level appropriate? Hardly. Gunning states that anyone who writes at a level greater than 12 is inviting misunderstanding.[3]

Using Readability Formulas

In determining the readability of the material from the grievance procedure, you might have realized two things that raise a readability index—long sentences and long words. Use the Fog Index or other readability formula output, be it calculated by hand or computer generated—with care. Applying the formula too strictly in your own writing might result in short, choppy sentences that could become monotonous and perhaps offensive to your readers. Also, longer words often add precision to what we are saying. Yet the readability formula can serve as a guide in your writing—a warning that you may be trying to impress rather than communicate for understanding.

Readability formulas are only guides to better writing.

Try to write at a level at or below your audience's educational level. Always avoid writing above their level. When writing below their educational level, never allow your message to sound as if you are writing down to your audience. Your goal is quick understanding and easy comprehension. Insulting members of your audience by writing too far below them, however, is quite detrimental.

If the Fog Index is low, that does not necessarily mean the material sounds childish or immature. One mark of an effective writer is the ability to write clearly at a low index while maintaining an intelligent tone. Journalists, for example, sharpen these skills. *Time* and *Newsweek* do not sound immature to most of us, yet they regularly average a level of advanced high school (grades 10 to 12).

Using the Fog Index goes beyond applying the formula. There are three steps: (1) quantitative evaluation through the Fog Index formula; (2) interpretation and analysis of the index score; and (3) revision as necessary. Once you have determined your typical index level or the level for a specific piece of writing, compare it to the educational level of your intended audience. If your level is higher than their educational level, make adjustments in your writing.

Gunning shares 10 suggestions for clearer writing, many directly influence the Fog Index:

- Keep sentences short. Aim for an average of 20 words or fewer.
- Use the simple over the complex; this suggestion applies to sentences as well as words and thoughts.
- The familiar word is best.
- Avoid unnecessary words.
- Use action verbs; avoid the passive voice.
- Write the way you talk. Your writing should have a conversational tone rather than a stilted or affected tone.
- Use terms your reader can picture. Avoid abstract words.
- Try to relate to your reader's experience.
- Vary your words, sentence length, and sentence construction to sustain interest.
- Write to express ideas, not to impress the reader.

For its many values, the Fog Index has several shortcomings. First, it is oblivious to the connotations of words; only the number of words and the number of difficult words are noted. Second, the index works only with text. Third, the index is English-language oriented. Finally, reader interest in the material is not determined. An interested reader will put up with difficult writing more than will a disinterested reader.

Readability tests, such as the Fog Index, are widely used both in business and in government. The federal government, for example, sometimes requires organizations producing equipment for the government to apply readability tests to the users' manuals that accompany the equipment.

Measuring readability must be kept in perspective. A readability test is simply a tool intended to give feedback to writers. When you write, you should not limit your attention to achieving a low readability score. You should still focus your primary attention on meeting the needs of your readers.

The grievance procedure paragraph has been revised once again, this time to improve readability:

> So that you can air your problems about your courses, the university has adopted the grievance procedure below for you. Please help us by following each step. Try to resolve your grievance with your instructor. After talking with your instructor, if still unsatisfied, you may file your grievance with the head of the department in question. The department head will respond to you in writing. If you want further consideration, you may submit your grievance to the Undergraduate Petitions Committee. This committee is made up of two faculty members and one student. Its decision will be final.

The Fog Index of the revised material is as follows:

1. 97 words
2. Seven complete thoughts
3. Average sentence length = 13.9
4. Percentage of hard words = 8
5. $13.9 + 8 = 21.9$
6. $21.9 \times .4 = 8.8$

CHARACTERISTIC 10: MECHANICALLY SOUND

Mechanically sound writing is free of two kinds of defects—errors in grammar and format problems. You may have wondered how an English teacher you once had could have been so cruel as to reduce your grade on a theme by three points for every comma splice. Phrases such as dangling construction, faulty reference, and subject-verb agreement may annoy you. Yet one reason standard grammar is so important is that, at the very least, it helps ensure reader understanding. Consider these examples:

Standard grammar enhances understanding.

AN ETHICAL DILEMMA

Shortly after Paula Winston was hired as the copywriter at Champion Appliance, she began to think about someday becoming advertising manager. Owner Warren English promoted her to the position two years later, when his cousin retired.

Warren founded Champion in 1978 by opening one appliance store. It prospered in a highly competitive field, and eventually he owned six stores in a single urban area. Warren attributes the company's success to aggressive advertising. Champion has also benefited from rapid population growth in the area where the stores are located.

As advertising manager, Paula meets regularly with Warren to discuss ads for the following week. Warren usually decides the products to feature and the prices. Paula and her one subordinate, a copywriter, then prepare the ads, subject to Warren's approval. Paula is also responsible for local radio and television advertising.

Paula has questioned some of the claims that Champion regularly makes in its advertisements. Champion had always billed itself as "The House of Lowest Prices and Highest Quality." When Paula suggested this was not entirely true, Warren became upset. Paula maintained, "Our prices are the lowest and our quality is the highest, but only in some cases." She feels that the ads should specify which products are truly the lowest priced and which are truly of the highest quality. She also feels that advertising "Same Day Delivery" is misleading because purchases have to be made before noon to ensure delivery that day.

Warren and Paula no longer discuss ad content during their meetings. Instead, they argue about ethics, and Warren always wins. Paula maintains that some of the advertising is deceptive. Warren's position is that Champion's ads are "no worse than anyone else's." Today Paula described the phrase "Guaranteed Quality" as meaningless and deceitful. Warren threatened to fire her unless she does what she is told.

Paula feels boxed in. What would you do?

Questions
1. What does it take for a message to be deceptive?
2. Is advertising a line of business where ethics can be bent a bit since people don't really believe what they see and hear?
3. How could Paula keep her job and still prepare the ads the way Warren wants them prepared?
4. What could Paula do to change Warren's attitude regarding the wording of the ads?

- City Council Bans Gambling behind Closed Doors (a newspaper headline)
- Your speech will be followed by dinner, to begin promptly at 7:30 P.M. (from a letter to an invited speaker)
- Never withhold herpes from a loved one (newspaper headline)

Standard grammar enhances credibility.

Written communication can often be understood in spite of grammatical errors. However, a second reason for standard grammar is it improves your credibility as a writer. No matter how good your ideas are, if they are presented on paper with poor grammar, many readers will discount the ideas because the grammar detracts from them. Advertisers know that the package sells the product. Many business people are just as concerned about standard grammar as your English teacher was. Grammar is the package that helps sell your ideas. (Appendix A contains material to help you refresh your grammar skills.)

As you read the following chapters about letters, memos, policies and procedures, and reports, you will find that there are certain formats for each. Business letters, for example, typically have a heading, inside address, salutation, body, and complimentary closing. As a writer of business letters, you are expected to adhere to this format. (Appendix B shows formats for business correspondence.)

Format is the physical arrangement of written material.

One format requirement for procedures is that they be written in step-by-step fashion. We should alter the format of the grievance procedure so that it has an orderly appearance. Our new product is this:

So that you can air your problems about your courses, the university has adopted the grievance procedure below for you. Please help us by following each step:

1. Try to resolve your grievance with your instructor.

2. After talking to your instructor, you may, if still unsatisfied, file your grievance with the head of the department in question. The department head will respond to you in writing.

3. If you want further consideration, you may submit your grievance to the Undergraduate Petitions Committee. This committee is made up of two faculty members and one student. Its decision will be final.

Figure 5.4

Evaluation of Grievance Procedure Final Draft

_____ Tactful	We've removed the sexist language. The material does not insult the reader's intelligence.
_____ Personal	Very "You" oriented.
_____ Positive	As positive as possible for a grievance procedure, in which we must use some negative words.
_____ Active	Only one sentence in passive voice.
_____ Unified	Sentences appear to have only one major idea.
_____ Coherent	All sentences and paragraphs are clearly tied together. Enumerating is used to enhance coherence.
_____ Clear	Much more understandable than the material at the beginning of the chapter.
_____ Concise	Deadweight has been removed.
_____ Readable	The material now has an index of 9.1.
_____ Mechanically Sound	Meets all the format specifications for a procedure. Grammar correct.

In Figure 5.4 we evaluate this final draft of the grievance procedure against the 10 characteristics of effective written communication.

Key Terms

- **reversal words**
- **place emphasis**
- **mass emphasis**
- **coherence**
- **parallel structure**

- **linking words**
- **enumerating**
- **signposting**
- **conciseness**

Summary

In this chapter you learned about 10 characteristics of effective writing:

tactful p. 110	coherent p. 117
personal p. 113	clear p. 119
positive p. 114	concise p. 122
active p. 115	readable p. 124
unified p. 116	mechanically sound p. 127

As each characteristic was discussed, you learned to recognize writing outside the characteristics, to understand how the characteristics work together to make writing effective, and to work the characteristics into your own writing.

Review Questions

1. How do we interpret Gunning's Fog Index?
2. What do we mean by tactful written communication?
3. What are some ways of avoiding sexist language when we write?
4. Why should we adopt the "you" attitude when we write?
5. Why is standard grammar important to mechanically sound written communication?
6. When should we use the passive voice? Active voice?
7. How can we ensure paragraph unity?
8. What are some ways of improving paragraph coherence?
9. How can we enhance the clarity of our writing?
10. Suggest some ways of writing concisely.
11. What is meant by positive tone?

Exercises

1. Evaluate part of the student handbook for your college or university against the 10 characteristics of effective written communication, as we have done in this chapter. Then rewrite the part you have evaluated and try to improve it.
2. Compute the Fog Index of three randomly selected paragraphs from *Time* and *Reader's Digest.* Compare the average index for the two magazines. Are there readability differences? If so, why?
3. Select an essay or column from your school paper or other school publication. Rewrite the material using each of the four devices for improving paragraph coherence.
4. Write a 300-word essay on something you consider to be a major problem of the day.

Describe the problem as you see it and suggest solutions. Exchange papers among students, each of whom will then identify mistakes and rewrite another student's article.

5. Imagine that you end a particularly bad day by getting a parking ticket. When you parked the car, you had tried to insert a coin, but the meter would not accept it. You were aware of the city's policy of ticketing cars at expired meters even though the meter is broken. However, parking spaces are not plentiful and parking meters have been poorly maintained. Moreover, you had been parked only long enough to buy some stamps at the nearby post office. You are upset. Write a completely tactless letter to the Chief of Police. (Letters will be read aloud in class and desirable changes suggested. An award may be given for the most tactless letter.)

6. Examine the following memorandum about customer refunds. It was circulated among employees only. Customers did not see it.

   a. Compute and interpret readability.

   b. Find at least five other writing problems in the memo.

   c. Rewrite it so that all writing problems are removed.

   Customer Refunds

   Teaneck Department Store will refund a customer's money in the event that the customer is dissatisfied with his merchandise. If the merchandise is being returned by the customer, it should be accompanied by a sales slip. The merchandise should be examined by the salesman for potential abuse. Subsequent to merchandise inspection, the salesman should fill out a retail credit check form and acquire the appropriate approval (in the form of a signature) from his supervisor. The customer should be asked to sign the credit check and then refund the money. The credit check should be placed beneath the cash drawer.

7. Rewrite the following sentences so that they conform to the 10 characteristics of effective written communication. Each sentence contains at least one error.

   a. Our regional director, a girl with substantial years of experience, will audit your accounts.

   b. If you don't pay promptly, a substantial discount won't be received by you.

   c. In view of the fact that you've had the merchandise for only 6 months, it goes without saying that your warranty covers the repair.

   d. If the employee has a grievance, the employee should take his grievance to the grievance committee.

   e. Smelling of liquor, the policeman arrested the driver.

   f. It is believed by the Board of Trustees that the new plan will work.

   g. Despite your delay in paying the bill, we will not cancel the account.

   h. I can say at this time that a lawyer could provide a solution to this problem, but that he would necessarily need to be a tax specialist.

   i. There can be no exceptions to this policy.

   j. A full report will be sent to you by the department chairman.

   k. Decentralization of the word processing center was suggested by the report to improve work flow and reduce noise.

   l. You are not allowed to miss work if you don't have a good reason.

   m. At the present time the consensus of opinion is that employee turnover will increase during the month of May.

n. Your performance was totally unsatisfactory.

o. The purposes of the meeting was: (1) to communicate personnel policies; (2) encouragement of participation in inservice training programs; and (3) introducing several new employees.

p. The report was intended for Fred and I, not for John and Susan.

q. Each of the following pages have been proofread by the editorial staff.

r. In accordance with your request, attached herewith is the surplus inventory report.

s. Smoking is not permitted anywhere except in the lobby.

t. We beg to inform you that unless you act soon, the contract will expire.

CASE

Schmitz Clothing Company

Dr. Beryl D. Hart, West Liberty State College

Schmitz Clothing Company, your employer, is a West Virginia clothing manufacturer that specializes in tailor-made dress shirts for both men and women. The firm has been in business for 15 years. Some of the company's shirts are sold through specialty men's stores across the United States. However, most are made to order and sold directly to customers who appreciate high-quality tailoring.

This morning you received a letter from an influential customer, Yvonne Cocoa of Huntington, West Virginia. Her November 1 order for 10 tailor-made dress shirts, which she wants to give to her husband for Christmas, totaled $550. Her letter reported that when the shirts were delivered by carrier, the box was damaged and all of the shirts were stained with blue. Naturally she is furious. She has requested immediate replacements so she will have them in time for Christmas. You have been with the company for all of its 15 years, and this is the first time the carrier has lost or damaged an order. After inspecting the shipping cartons, the carrier reported they were in bad condition and agreed to pay the company $250.

Your dilemma is that you cannot duplicate the entire shipment in the 5 weeks until Christmas. You will try to complete half of the order.

Case Questions

1. Considering the above information and the feelings of the customer, determine how you will write the letter. Use the effective letter-writing principles that you have learned.

2. What is the purpose of the letter? What will be your opening paragraph? What will be your explanation? What will be your closing paragraph?

Notes

1. Herta A. Murphy and Charles E. Peck, *Effective Business Communication* (New York: McGraw-Hill, 1976), 457.

2. Robert Gunning, *The Technique of Clear Writing* (New York: McGraw-Hill, 1952). Gunning's Fog Index is only one of many formulas for measuring readability. You might be interested in another classic source: Rudolph Flesch, *The Art of Readable Writing* (New York: Harper & Row, 1949).

3. Gunning, *The Technique of Clear Writing*, 38.

Chapter 6

Good-News and Neutral Letters

Suzie Sanchez wanted to tell her large, extended family the news about her great new job. It was tempting to create a form letter to send to the multitude of aunts, uncles and cousins. However, Suzie knew her relatives would be offended by such impersonal correspondence. Although she had basically the same thing to say to all of them, she decided to write individual letters.

Suzie owned a personal computer and had made good use of it. She realized she could write a form letter and then, using the computer, make variations of it to suit each of her family members. Suzie was surprised she had not thought of this before. She had used the same principle when she was applying for jobs. She would keep certain paragraphs and sentences constant in the cover letters while changing sentences that were specific to the company or job. This use of the computer had saved her a lot of time. She also did not have to worry about the format or the date and other aspects of the letter that she did not need to change.

This method would not always be appropriate, but in this instance it was. She had momentous news she wanted to share with many people. Suzie had found a personalized, yet efficient solution. No wonder she had been offered such a terrific job!

THE IMPORTANCE OF APPROPRIATE LETTERS

The most frequent contact many people have with certain business organizations is through the written word. Printed advertisements and, perhaps, correspondence constitute whatever link is formed between the public and the organization. Letters that are readable and thorough contribute to building and maintaining good will. Letters that are vague and poorly organized have the opposite effect. Letter by letter, a company's written communication influences public perception of the company.

To illustrate, when Robert Hill was no longer able to find air filters for his 20-year-old mower, he wrote to the manufacturer, who replied with the letter in Figure 6.1. Robert did not like the letter for several reasons. The suggestion for finding some air filters was pretty well buried. Besides, having owned a Kleenkutter for 20 years, he hardly had to be sold on the product. Robert said to his wife, "They must think I'm an idiot, telling me

Figure 6.1
An Inappropriate Letter

STELLAR LAWN PRODUCTS, INC.
645 High Street
Troy, MI 48007

March 3, 1997

Mr. Robert Hill
1215 Oakdale Drive
Trenton, NJ 08600

Dear Mr. Hill:

We are pleased to learn of your satisfaction with the Q-11 Kleenkutter. Although our products may cost a little more than the products of some of our competitors, they are designed to last longer and perform better.

Opening ignores the customer's complaint.

Since the Q-11 was finely tuned at the factory, it should require very little in the way of maintenance. When servicing is required, however, one must be sure to follow all of the instructions provided on pages 12–19 of the owner's manual. For the best in servicing and repair, it is advisable that you deal with a registered company technician.

The company's self-interest is emphasized in trying to convince the customer to use registered technicians.

Since the Q-11 went out of production 15 years ago, it has become difficult to find some of the parts for it, but air filters designed for the Q-13 or Q-14 are readily available and may be adapted to the Q-11. Any one of our registered technicians is able to do this, and the cost would be moderate.

The main message is finally stated.

The next time you visit a Kleenkutter dealer, why not inspect the Q-14, our newest and most efficient mower? You'll find that it has the same basic design as the Q-11 with some advanced features intended to simplify its operation.

Sales promotion is unlikely to influence an already frustrated customer.

Yours truly,

William W. Dunbar
William W. Dunbar
Customer Service

to read the owner's manual. In 20 years of operating this mower I've practically memorized it." Robert did not like the tone of the letter and resented that the writer ignored his status as a long-time satisfied user.

We seldom receive a personalized letter that has no effect on us: Some letters are pleasing; others are displeasing. Robert was definitely displeased. Sometimes we are impressed with the cleverness of a letter we receive; we marvel at the writer's ability to select just the right word. Sometimes we are so aware of the writer's flair that we may remember a certain phrase but forget the purpose of the letter. At other times a letter may be so dull that we remember nothing about it at all. We may even throw it away after reading the first line.

A company's written communication influences public perception of the company.

While the advent of electronic communication has caused a decline in the writing of letters for business purposes, letters remain an important vehicle of communication. In a survey on the forms of communication most likely to get their attention, 80 percent of the congressional staff members who were polled identified letters as being most important.[1] According to the staff members, **transitory communication**, such as phone calls, postcards, and form letters, is simply tallied and forgotten, but personalized letters and personalized telegrams represent greater concern and, consequently, receive more consideration. The electronic revolution does provide instant access, but it is apparently viewed by some as "too easy, too transitory, too open to manipulation."[2]

In a national survey, 500 executive secretaries were asked about the best way to get their bosses' attention. According to the survey, sponsored by Parker Pen, 33 percent of the executive secretaries said that letters, memos, and notes written by hand got the most immediate attention from top executives. Computer-printed messages came in second (29 percent), followed by voice mail (24 percent), and E-mail (14 percent).[3] Both the congressional staff and secretarial studies suggest that a recipient does give a letter special attention.

Writing letters that work is not easy, but the process can be made easier through a systematic approach. This chapter, building on the basic techniques presented in Chapter 5, provides a systematic approach to writing good-news and neutral letters of various kinds.

THE PLANNING PROCESS

Planning provides focus to a message.

Sometimes referred to as prewriting, planning contributes significantly to a message that is clearly written and easily understood. Written messages that were not planned are identifiable by their lack of clear focus.

Managers sometimes claim not to have enough time to plan their written messages. Careful planning will actually result in a savings of time, however, both for the sender and for the receiver. To illustrate, Brenda Robb, as a part of her internship with a large midwestern bank, was assigned to a project measuring the volume of bank correspondence that required additional follow-up messages. She learned that written follow-up was necessary for nearly 10 percent of the letters sent by the bank. She also discovered that writers who wrote without planning were much more likely to have to send follow-up letters. They were needed either to explain the initial message or to provide information that should have been included originally.

The **planning process** involves these four steps: (1) Determine the objectives. (2) Consider the audience. (3) Choose the ideas to include. (4) Select the appropriate medium.

Determining the Objectives

Unless a message has an obvious purpose, it is unlikely to elicit the response sought by the writer. Some messages, such as sales letters, seek overt responses. Most sales letters seek to get the reader to purchase the good or service, or at least to request a brochure on the item that is being offered. Other messages seek covert responses, such as a changed attitude toward the notion of leasing rather than purchasing an automobile. Whether the desired response is covert or overt, however, the objective must be clear in the writer's mind if it is to be transferred to the mind of the reader.

Considering the Audience

The more that you, the writer, know about your readers, the more able you will be to frame your message to elicit the desired response. Audience characteristics that require careful analysis include expertise, hierarchical position, age, educational level, occupation, and attitudes.

Audience Expertise

How much do the various receivers know about the topic? When writer and reader(s) possess the same degree of expertise, problems in achieving understanding should be minimal. When the audience is large and the range of expertise is broad, multiple messages may be the most appropriate approach, because a single message is unlikely to appeal to a widely diverse group of readers.

Hierarchical Position

Is your written message being directed at a subordinate or a superior? If a subordinate, will that individual have any choice about accepting the message? If a superior, how familiar is the superior with you and your work? If you do not already have credibility in the eyes of the superior, you must devote some effort to creating it.

Audience Age

Writers frequently reveal their age by the examples and illustrations they use in their communication. Effective business communicators are careful to select examples and illustrations on the basis of the age of the intended receivers. Professors who fail to update their notes ignore the need to appeal to the interests of their receivers and persist in using examples that hold little meaning for students. For example, what does the Bay of Pigs mean to you? How about the War on Poverty? Such topics, meaningful and interesting to the middle-aged professor, are ancient history to the average college student.

Educational Level

Effective communicators may acknowledge the educational level of their audience, but they need not communicate on that same level. The writer or speaker who is easily understood is most likely to get a quick and favorable response. As discussed in Chapter 5, mathematical formulas are available for determining the readability level of written material.

Occupation

Language and occupation influence each other. For that reason a knowledge of the occupation(s) represented in any group of listeners or readers will help you tailor your message to them. As long as you limit the use of jargon to audiences that share the same occupation, the practice is beneficial to all concerned.

Attitudes

The five audience characteristics just discussed will influence the attitudes that the audience will hold toward you and your message. Is the overall attitude positive, negative, or neutral? If your message is to be appropriate, you must consider the attitudes of the receiver when drafting your message. The frustration experienced by employees who claim that nobody ever listens to them results to some extent from unawareness of audience attitudes on the part of management.

Choosing the Ideas to Include

Novice writers sometimes try to create a polished and finished message at the start. Resist this urge and concentrate on generating as many ideas as possible on the subject. Only then should you edit the list to include the most important ideas based on objectives and audience.

For example, the director of human resources asked Pam MacDonald to report on whether their bank should become involved in providing day care for the children of employees. Having already received a cost study, he wanted Pam to research the non monetary aspects. She generated the following ideas:

* Effect on maternity leaves
* Recruitment
* Turnover
* Development of children
* Morale
* Image of the bank
* Productivity

The report she eventually wrote centered on these ideas.

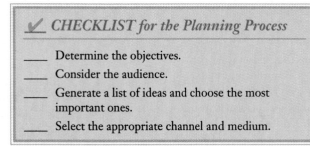

Selecting the Appropriate Channel and Medium

Business communicators have two basic channels and a wide variety of media from which to choose when determining how to convey a message. Messages may be either written or oral. Communication should be in writing when any of the following circumstances are important:

* Information is detailed and complex.
* The audience is geographically dispersed.
* A permanent record is important.
* Immediate feedback is not necessary.

Memos, letters, reports, and proposals are some of the commonly used media of business communication.

THE WRITING AND REVISION PROCESS

The moment of truth arrives as you complete the final step of the planning process. You have selected the appropriate medium, in this case the letter, and it is now time to create a first **draft**—that is, to write a preliminary version of your message.

Stories abound about writers who are whirlwinds at planning but who freeze up when it is time to begin the draft. This is sometimes attributed to **writer's block**, a widely researched condition that prevents a communicator from writing. No one seems to be completely immune. You may have already found yourself frozen in front of a word processor (see Figure 6.2) or vacantly staring at a writing pad. Some writers seek inspiration by sharpening pencils, rearranging their desks, or taking a break, all to no avail. If you carefully plan your message, however, writer's block should not be a problem.

If the initial draft satisfies you, your standards are probably too low. Should you be tempted to skip the revision stage, remember that careless writing is costly to the business organization. It can also be costly to employees in terms of jobs lost and promotions denied.

A **revision** is simply an altered version of the draft. The changes made may be additions, deletions, or substitutions. Some revisions entail significant changes or major rewrites in the pursuit of accuracy and clarity. In an analysis of letters written by the Internal Revenue Service in December 1992, the General Accounting Office found 15 percent to be incorrect, unclear, or incomplete. Flaws had been found in 48 percent of the correspondence in 1987.[4] While most business letters do not possess the impact

Figure 6.2
Frustrated Computer User
Problems in getting started
on a writing project are
sometimes blamed on
"writer's block."
Source: Photo by Reginald
Wickham.

> ✔ *CHECKLIST for Revising Content*
>
> _____ Include all necessary information.
> _____ Make sure the information is accurate.
> _____ Be sure it is clear and well-supported.
> _____ Include answers to likely questions of readers.

of a letter from the IRS, accuracy and clarity are just as important. Other revisions consist of little more than correcting a few errors in grammar or word usage.

All written messages do not deserve the same amount of attention. Some messages are less important than others and can be written, by the experienced writer, with little or no modification. As a novice business communicator, however, you should plan to revise everything you write. For that reason, when you begin to write you should do it rapidly, realizing that this is not the final version. Make sure that you allow yourself enough time to both write and revise. Keep in mind, as you write, the objectives and intended audience that you previously identified.

> ✔ *CHECKLIST for Revising Language*
>
> _____ Adhere to rules of grammar and punctuation.
> _____ Be sure the language is tactful and clear.
> _____ Use the active voice where appropriate.
> _____ Use a professional tone.
> _____ Use concise and readable language.

Approaches to revision vary with the writer and the situation. Some prominent authors anticipate eight to ten major revisions before satisfying both themselves and their publishers. Mark Twain reportedly advised deleting every third word, on principle, to achieve more vigorous writing. [5]

Business writing is unquestionably improved through careful revision. Important reports and ultra-sensitive letters routinely go through multiple revisions. Word processors have simplified the task of revising immeasurably, but the process remains mentally taxing.

Revising is an especially demanding task because it requires objectivity. Students have been known to ask, "How do you improve on perfection?" Try to place yourself in the role of the intended receiver and read the message from that person's viewpoint. If possible, have a colleague read your initial draft and make suggestions.

Some writers equate revising with proofreading. From the standpoint of the business communicator, however, the revision process extends beyond proofreading. It requires focusing on content, language, and organization.

In today's business organization messages are often the product of a team effort. Sometimes a superior and a subordinate work together to produce a document. At other times it may be a team comprised of representatives of several different depart-

Figure 6.3
A Study of Concentration
Whether playing sports or
preparing a message, one
must keep his eyes on the
ball and focus on the goal.
Source: David Madison,
Tony Stone Images.

✔ *CHECKLIST for Revising Organization*

____ Introduce ideas in logical sequence.

____ Include a topic sentence in each paragraph

____ Be sure that purpose and structure are clear.

____ Smooth out transitions to make reading easier.

ments who have been assigned to a special project. Unlike a message prepared by an individual, **collaborative writing** ordinarily reflects the view of all who together created the message. It is not unusual for important documents to go through multiple revisions, and in many instances these revisions continue right up until the deadline. Time management is an important consideration in every aspect of business communication, but it is especially significant in the planning, writing, and revising processes as they pertain to collaborative writing.

Revising is a skill that is developed through practice (see Figure 6.3). The accompanying checklists are intended to help you, but they are not exhaustive. The more familiar you are with the characteristics of effective writing, as presented in Chapter 5, the better able you will be to perform a revision likely to strengthen the original draft.

WRITING GOOD-NEWS AND NEUTRAL LETTERS

Neutral and good-news letters should be arranged deductively: the main idea should precede the secondary details.

In many letters you will transmit either good news or routine, neutral information. These letters are relatively easy to write because of the nature of the message. Some typical situations in which such a letter is written are: placing an order, receiving an order to be filled promptly, making an adjustment requested by a customer, granting an application for credit, and supplying information. When writing a good-news or neutral letter, present your ideas in a direct or **deductive arrangement**:

1. *Start with the main idea.* Because you are conveying positive or neutral information, resistance or disagreement is unlikely. Get right to the point. Such an approach elicits the goodwill of the reader while saving time—both yours and the readers.

2. *Present the secondary details.* In a good-news or neutral letter, secondary details are usually explanatory. If you are acknowledging an order, the secondary details may pertain to method and time of shipment. In a letter of adjustment, the secondary details may explain why the problem occurred in the first place. Respond to whatever questions the reader may have asked. At the same time anticipate and respond to other likely questions.

3. *Close on a positive note.* The letter should end in as straightforward a fashion as it began. If you are acknowledging an order, a reference to future business would be appropriate. Be brief and direct. Avoid clichés such as "Do not hesitate to contact me if I can be of further help." Either omit the close, or, better, end with a brief and direct statement such as "Write me again when I can help."

The main difference between a good-news letter and a neutral letter is found in the first paragraph. A **good-news letter** begins with the good news, the main point of the letter. For example, to respond to a customer's request for a full refund on the purchase price of a five-pound package of grass seed, Rhonda Davis arranged her ideas in this sequence:

A good-news letter differs from a neutral letter primarily in the first paragraph.

Main idea:	Here is a check for the refund you requested.
Secondary details:	Slight soil irregularities occasionally minimize the effectiveness of any grass seed.
Close:	Your satisfaction is important to us.

The **neutral letter**, as the name suggests, presents a message that is neither good nor bad. It begins with the main idea, which is neutral rather than good news. Frank Loftor, to request information for a term paper, arranged his ideas in this sequence:

Neutral letters transmit a nonthreatening and often pleasant message.

Main idea:	Please send information on the products manufactured by Amco, Inc.
Secondary details:	(1) I want the material for a term paper. (2) I am especially interested in products developed in the last 10 years.
Close:	Thanks for your help.

In responding for Amco, Beth Johnson also used a direct approach. She presented this sequence of ideas in her letter:

Main idea:	I am enclosing a brochure describing each of our products.
Secondary details:	(1) The products described on pages 3–8 and 11 were developed during the past 10 years. (2) We are pleased that you selected Amco as a subject for your paper.
Close:	Good luck with your project.

CHARACTERISTICS OF GOOD-NEWS LETTERS

In a good-news letter, you are complying with the wishes of the other party. The reader will be pleased with the message, so get right to the main point. Among the more common types of good-news letters in business are those in which the writer approves an adjustment, grants a routine request, extends credit, or acknowledges the receipt of an order. Responses to such letters are usually positive.

Directness is appropriate when relaying good news.

Approving Adjustments on Claims

When merchants are able to approve an adjustment sought by a customer, they should respond promptly and directly. This approval is positive, and the letter should also include an attempt at another sale. Figure 6.4 is an example of such a letter.

Letters granting an adjustment should be prompt and direct.

When a customer seeks an adjustment on the basis of an error made by a business, most firms grant the adjustment immediately. Many cases are not that clear-cut, however. Sometimes neither party appears to be at fault. A third party may be responsible, or responsibility may be impossible to determine.

Many firms, not wanting to lose a customer, will assume responsibility even though responsibility may be unclear. For example, a woman who ordered a dozen plants through the mail received only two that appeared healthy; the others had died.

Many firms will assume responsibility for an error even when responsibility is unclear.

Figure 6.4
Adjustment Approval Letter

November 20, 1997

Mrs. Lois Hammond
2314 N. 21st Street
Metairie, LA 70006

Dear Mrs. Hammond:

You will receive a brand-new Deluxe Glide steam iron later this week. We are happy to be of service to you.

Thank you for returning the other iron to us. Our technicians are analyzing its performance in order to learn how to improve our inspection procedures. By calling the problem to our attention, you are helping us to serve you better.

You should receive our summer sale catalog next week. It is full of high-quality products that we are pleased to stand behind.

Sincerely,

R. A. Sumner
R. A. Sumner
Customer Service

The good news is stated immediately without fanfare.

The writer expresses appreciation and a desire to improve customer service.

The excellent service makes the reader receptive to this sales promotion.

She had not done business with the company before. She requested replacements for the plants. Figure 6.5 shows the company's response.

Granting Routine Requests

Directness is a desirable characteristic in any good-news letter. When you can answer yes to a request, you should do so enthusiastically. Because yes is the answer that the reader is hoping for, say it immediately, as in Figures 6.6 and 6.7. The plant manager in Figure 6.7 is obviously enthusiastic and sincere about donating scrap materials to a charity drive.

Figure 6.5
Claim Approval Despite Unclear Responsibility

Worldwide Flowers P.O. Box 40080 Lafayette, LA 70504 (318) 504-3750

February 12, 1997

Ms. Margo Boggs
1987 Maple Avenue
Iowa City, IA 52240

Dear Ms. Boggs:

A dozen healthy plants are being mailed to you today at no expense to you. — *Honors the customer's request immediately.*

Under normal circumstances, plants from Worldwide Flowers are extremely resistant to those conditions likely to harm lower-quality plants. In the five years we have been shipping plants in our patented stay-moist containers, more than 99 percent of the plants shipped have arrived in greenhouse condition. — *Assures this new customer that such problems rarely occur.*

To ensure that plants will arrive in good condition, it is important to remove them from the carton and transplant them within 24 hours of receiving them. Doing this will result in healthy plants that will add much to your gardening pleasure. — *Reminds reader how to handle newly arrived plants.*

From now on you will receive our "Green Thumb" newsletter each month. It features unadvertised specials that are likely to enhance your garden at a fraction of the usual price. — *Points to the future positively.*

Yours truly,

Winnie P. Ivy
Winnie P. Ivy
Sales Correspondent

When granting routine requests, you should always view the reader as a potential customer. This does not mean your good-news letter must always be sales-oriented; it does mean your letters should display characteristics that are likely to instill a positive image of your firm.

There are certain pitfalls to avoid if you are to convey a positive image. The writer of the letter in Figure 6.8 on page 144, unfortunately, did not avoid them in responding to an inquiry about when a specific course would next be offered. The writer could have made a better impression and conveyed the information more efficiently by using a direct arrangement. Following is a better version of the letter:

Writers granting routine requests should give an immediate, enthusiastic yes answer.

The direct arrangement is appropriate for granting a routine request.

Our course, Auto Repairs for the Layperson, will begin on September 8. The class will meet on Monday and Wednesday evenings from 7:00 to 10:00 during the fall quarter.

You may register by completing the attached form and returning it to me by September 5. By enclosing tuition payment of $75.00, you will avoid delays often encountered when paying tuition on the first night of the quarter. Many have already expressed interest in Auto Repairs for the Layperson.

Congratulations on taking a significant step in your personal development. Please call me if I can be of assistance.

Extending Credit

Few business organizations insist on cash payment from customers. The extension of credit has become the rule rather than the exception. Consumers are applying for credit in increasing numbers, and the degree to which it is extended grows proportionately.

Figure 6.6
Routine Request Grant

Electro Flex, **INC.** 2162 Industrial Blvd.   Ypsilanti, MI 48197

March 19, 1997

Mrs. Rachel Levine
Barrow Elementary School
Ypsilanti, MI 48197

Dear Mrs. Levine:

Yes, I will be happy to give your sixth-grade class a tour of our plant on the afternoon of March 27.   *Agrees to reader's request.*

Your students will especially be interested in the assembly line, but I will also show them one of our research labs, if they care to see one.   *Extends an additional offer.*

The enclosed brochures will acquaint your students with our full line of products. If you will have them read and discuss the brochures before your visit, it may make the tour more interesting.   *Provides helpful secondary details.*

I look forward to meeting you and your class in the lobby of Building B at one o'clock next Wednesday afternoon.   *Uses positive ending.*

Sincerely,

Lance Elrod
Lance Elrod
Industrial Relations Manager

Encls.

Figure 6.7
Request Acceptance

FOREMOST MANUFACTURING INC.
Midville, OH 43601
(614) 549-0102

November 3, 1997

Ms. Estelle Rawls
Tri-County Connection
P.O. Box 245
Midville, OH 43601

Dear Ms. Rawls:

    Yes, we will gladly contribute the scrap materials from our mill for the next four weeks to the Tri-County Charity Drive. — *Presents good news with enthusiasm.*

    Many of the poor and elderly of the community will benefit from the Tri-County blanket-making project. It is certainly worthwhile, and we are pleased to be a part of it. — *Recognizes the worth of the project.*

    We will deliver the remnants to your temporary warehouse on each of the next four Fridays at 2:00 in the afternoon. — *Describes future action.*

        Yours truly,

        Frank Zeeman
        Frank Zeeman
        Plant Manager

    When a person seeks credit and a business organization sees fit to extend it, the situation calls for a good-news letter. As with all such letters, directness is appropriate. What applicants want to know is whether or not they are going to be given credit. The main purpose of such a letter is to extend credit to the reader; however, this is not the sole purpose. In writing such a letter the writer should try to do the following:

1. Tell the person seeking credit that it will be granted.
2. Compliment the person for meriting the faith implicit in any credit approval.
3. Explain the terms of the credit plan.
4. Point toward future business with the customer and express appreciation for the credit request.

Figure 6.8
Ineffective Routine Response

MID-COUNTY TECHNICAL COLLEGE
P.O. Box 4104
Madison, NJ 07940

March 5, 1997

Mr. Fred Bradwell
1240 Elm Street
Madison, NJ 07940

Dear Mr. Bradwell:

Thank you for your letter of February 28, in which you requested information concerning Auto Repairs for the Layperson.

Unnecessary—letter is a response to a request.

This is one of our most popular courses, and you are one of many who have expressed an interest in it. The practical nature of the course and the present shortage of auto mechanics seem to explain the popularity of this course.

Irrelevant information, not oriented to the reader.

You will be happy to learn that we will offer Auto Repairs for the Layperson in the fall quarter. Classes begin on September 8 and will meet Monday and Wednesday evenings from 7:00 to 10:00.

Should be in the first paragraph—it is what the reader wants to know.

I have enclosed the necessary registration form. Please complete the form and return it to me as soon as possible, along with the tuition payment indicated on the registration form.

Necessary but vague—give specific date.

Sincerely,

Debra J. Bennett

Debra J. Bennett
Associate Director

Encl.

A letter offering to extend credit to an applicant should contain positive phrasing. It should welcome the applicant to a preferred group of customers, and it should express acceptance and trust of the new charge customer. This is an example:

In extending credit the writer should express acceptance and trust.

We are pleased to send you a Rusk Brothers credit card. Thank you for thinking of us when you decided to open a charge account. It is through your intelligent use of credit in the past that you have earned this account.

Bills are mailed on the 20th of each month and are payable by the 15th of the next month. There is a finance charge of $1\frac{1}{2}$ percent on the unpaid balance each month.

The enclosed brochure describes many of the special services we offer our charge customers. As a charge customer you may easily shop by telephone, and you will receive advance notification of sales.

We appreciate the opportunity to serve you, and we hope to merit your patronage for a long time.

AN ETHICAL DILEMMA

Jim Schwartz was a department head for a closely held, large national corporation. The major stockholders were the founder and his son and daughter. The son had recently gained control of the company by forcing his father off the board. Jim felt the founder had been a fine leader for the company. He had built it from nothing and had proven to be a superb businessman.

Jim didn't know the son very well, but he knew he was young and inexperienced. Jim also believed the son must be a nasty person to force his own father out of the company he created. As Chairman of the Board, the son called a meeting of all the department heads. He wanted each to write a letter to his or her staff informing them of the change of management.

Specifically, the son wanted them to assure their respective staff that his father had gone into a long awaited retirement and had chosen his son to succeed him as chairman. He also wanted the department heads to express support for the new chairman and optimism for the future of the company under his leadership. The managers were to write these things in their own words.

Jim spoke with some of his colleagues after the meeting. In general, they were still loyal to the father and didn't trust the son. Jim knew he could be fired for refusing to write the letter and it was unlikely he would find a position as interesting and well-paid elsewhere. On the other hand, if he wrote the letter he would be lying to his staff.

Jim feels boxed in. What would you do?

A company that extends credit takes a risk. Through a careful selection of applicants the risk is reduced but still present. However, once the decision to extend credit is made, the company has determined that the customer has the capacity to use credit wisely. At this point the letter writer should not mar a pleasant occasion with overtones of distrust and apprehension. Contrast the positive tone of the previous example with the negative tone of this one:

> We are pleased to grant you credit as you requested January 3. Bills are sent monthly on the 20th and must be paid by the 15th. It is our policy to charge 1½ percent interest on the unpaid balance on the 15th. Therefore, if you are wise and wish to protect your credit rating, you will be sure to pay your bill by the 15th. We appreciate the opportunity to serve you.

The first letter was optimistic and hopeful; the second was neither. In each case the applicant's request was honored, but the impression created was quite different. In extending credit a company has an opportunity to develop a positive relationship with a customer. An effective letter will capitalize on this opportunity.

This is how a furniture factory informed a retailer that credit was being granted and the goods were being shipped:

> ### ✔ CHECKLIST for Adjustment Approval
>
> ___ Indicate immediately that the adjustment is being granted.
>
> ___ Grant the adjustment wholeheartedly.
>
> ___ Play down the negative aspects by avoiding negative words.
>
> ___ Briefly explain the reason for the problem or imply it when describing the measures.
>
> ___ Specify any action the reader must take.
>
> ___ Look forward to future business in the close.

The Deltina cane-back chairs you ordered on May 1 are being shipped to your store via Statewide Motor Company. They should arrive in Augusta by May 5. The amount of this merchandise has been debited to your new account.

Your excellent record with other creditors allows us to extend to you our regular terms of 2/10, n/30. As a new customer you may carry as much as $3,500 worth of our products on account.

Included with your order are some suggested window and floor displays that other dealers have found helpful in attracting customers. Once customers pause to look at the chairs, they recognize their stylishness and proven durability.

Use the enclosed order forms for placing your next orders. You can always count on prompt deliveries and our full cooperation.

Unlike the earlier credit-extending letter, this one was written to a dealer. A dealer is generally interested in the sales potential of a product and ways to display a product; a consumer will be more interested in price and durability.

A credit extension message should be adapted to the interests of the reader, whether dealer or consumer.

In writing to extend credit you should certainly adapt your message to the interests of the customer. Whether writing to a dealer or to a consumer, however, the same principles apply. In either case the structure of the message is the same.

Acknowledging Orders

Many business organizations live or die according to the volume of orders received. The link between orders received and business success is a clear one; the link between acknowledgments and success is less clear. For that reason, business people have a tendency to play down the importance of letters of acknowledgment.

Some acknowledgment of an order is desirable: a letter is preferable.

Many people look upon acknowledging orders as nothing but a time-consuming chore. Some organizations send only preprinted postcards in acknowledgment. Other sellers, reasoning that the promptly shipped order will soon be delivered to the buyer, send no acknowledgment. Although the postcard is preferable to no acknowledgment at all, a letter is desirable and personal.

Letter writers should recognize that orders are routine for the seller, but may not be routine for the buyer. Future business with the buyer often depends on the way the seller handles the present order.

At regular intervals a company should change the order-acknowledgment letters it uses.

One practice that suggests the seller is uninterested in the customer is the tendency to overuse an order-acknowledgment message. Whether the message is in the form of a letter or postcard, it should be changed at regular intervals. When a seller persists in sending the same message for a long time, customers may begin to feel they are being taken for granted. Customers most likely to feel this way are those who are most important—your best customers.

To illustrate, Francis Genet has worked as a purchasing agent for three companies for a total of 18 years. During that time he has observed a wide variety of business practices on the part of suppliers. One of the most irritating practices, he believes, is the repeated use of the same acknowledgment letter. "In some cases," Francis says, "a company will send out the same letter for years. After a while you start thinking that your business means nothing to the supplier."

No matter how small the order being acknowledged, its potential may be considerable. If handled properly, today's new customer may be tomorrow's major purchaser. Customers—whether old and valued or brand new—are receptive to a statement of appreciation and an assurance that the order will be sent promptly. Consider

---

✔ CHECKLIST for Credit Extension

____ Indicate at the start that credit is being extended.

____ If goods are being shipped, give the details immediately.

____ Specify the goods and the method of shipment.

____ Mention how the reader earned the credit.

____ Resell the reader on the wise choice.

____ Point to future orders in the close.

____ Avoid sarcasm, name-calling, and threats.

the impression likely to be made by each of these kinds of acknowledgments: letter, preprinted fill-in postcard, and completely preprinted postcard.

Letter of Acknowledgment

A good letter of acknowledgment gets down to business immediately:

> Your order for one X-365 workbench is being processed and will be shipped within 48 hours.
>
> Since you included a check for the full purchase price, we are pleased to pay all of the shipping expenses. We know you will be pleased with the workbench, just as thousands of other customers have been. We believe, Mr. Morris, that you will find the table surface truly resists all types of scratches, dents, and burns. This feature, plus the stability ensured by the four sturdy legs, means you will enjoy it for many years to come.
>
> When you decide to order tools, remember that Harris, Inc., carries a full line of manual and power tools. These tools, like the workbench, are designed to provide good service and take hard use. The drawers and shelves of the workbench were designed especially for Harris tools.
>
> Use the enclosed order blank and postage-paid envelope for placing your next order. We look forward to serving you again.

This letter immediately identifies the item ordered and commits the company to a shipping date. It seeks future orders and remains personal throughout.

Preprinted Acknowledgments

A preprinted fill-in postcard, such as the one in Figure 6.9, informs the buyer that the order has been received and action is being taken. If the buyer happens to have placed several orders with Harris recently, however, this postcard does not show which order

---

> ✔ *CHECKLIST for Order Acknowledgment*
>
> ____ Tell the buyer that the order was received and is being filled according to directions.
>
> ____ Identify the order clearly enough to prevent the reader from confusing it with another order.
>
> ____ Give the buyer the details of shipment - how it is being shipped and when the buyer should receive it.
>
> ____ State the financial arrangement if it was not made clear prior to shipment.
>
> ____ Express appreciation for the order.
>
> ____ Encourage more orders in the future.

Individualized letters of acknowledgment provide a personal touch and are appreciated.

Figure 6.9
A Preprinted Postcard

Dear _____ :

    Your order for _____ has been received and will be shipped within 48 hours by United Parcel Service. You should receive it no later than _____.

    Thank you for your business.

                Robert Bates
                Harris, Inc.

is being filled. Although such a postcard is impersonal, it does answer the buyer's most likely question about whether the order is in process.

Certain merchandise occasionally may be out of stock, especially when the seller does a sizable volume of business. In acknowledging the out-of-stock status of an order the seller must inform the buyer that the merchandise will be available soon.

Many organizations that receive a tremendous volume of orders do not acknowledge orders unless shipment will be delayed. Many major retailers such as Sears fill most orders almost immediately: The goods arrive as quickly as any acknowledgment would.

When a delay does occur, some companies acknowledge it with the form in Figure 6.10. The customer's address, along with the information identifying the order, is written on the front of the postcard. Without this information customers who have placed several orders do not know which order was delayed. On the other side of the card is a sales message.

Even the most impersonal order acknowledgment is preferable to none, because it tells the buyer that the order is being filled.

Figure 6.10
Postcard Informing the Consumer of a Delay in Shipment
Source: Lee's, Inc.

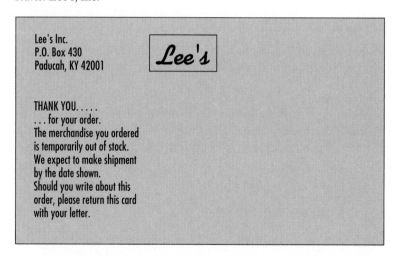

Any of the three kinds of acknowledgments is better than no acknowledgment. Even when an order is filled promptly, unless an acknowledgment is made, the customer is left wondering until the shipment actually arrives.

The benefits of a personal letter of acknowledgment must be weighed against its cost. Such letters are expensive, but they can be justified if an opportunity for significant further business exists.

In many cases a form letter will suffice, but it is unwise to rely solely on forms to acknowledge orders. An organization will be most effective in acknowledging orders if it uses a combination of completely preprinted forms, fill-in forms, and personal letters.

CHARACTERISTICS OF NEUTRAL LETTERS

A neutral letter conveys neither good news nor bad news. Such letters are usually met with cautious interest on the part of the receiver. As with the good-news letter, a neutral letter should be direct. Some of the more common types of neutral letters make routine claims, request routine information, request credit, or place orders.

Making Routine Claims

Consumers evaluate stores partly according to how the stores treat them. The way a store responds to a request for an adjustment is greatly influenced by the manner in which the customer seeks the adjustment. Although the letter in Figure 6.11 on the preceding page does make a claim, it does not do so effectively. This letter is wordy and rambling. It is arranged in an **indirect sequence**, from general (seen on television) to the specific (a full refund).

When writing to make a routine claim, you should use the **direct sequence**, from specific points to general ones. As you expect the claim to be readily satisfied, tell the reader the action you seek and the reasons for the request. If persuasion seems necessary to get a claim satisfied, the persuasive sequence presented in Chapter 8 is appropriate. The approach in making a routine claim is straightforward, as in this letter:

> Will you please send another *Flora and Fauna Dictionary* to replace the one I am returning in the attached package?
>   This book arrived with many of the illustrations blurred, especially those between pages 200 and 300. I have enclosed the invoice that accompanied the book.
>   If an unsoiled copy is unavailable, I shall appreciate a full refund.

The indirect sequence is not appropriate for good-news and neutral letters.

Requesting Routine Information

When you read an advertisement in a magazine about a product in which you are interested, you may have some unanswered questions. Like many other consumers, you may write directly to the company for answers. Business organizations receive and send numerous requests for routine information. The more specific a request is, the more likely it is to elicit the desired response.

In requesting routine information, state the request in the first sentence. In that way you will leave no doubt about what information is desired. Next, provide whatever other details might be necessary. Last, point to the future by stating what you want the reader to do. Note the differences between the letter in Figure 6.12 and the following one:

> Can the gas water heater (model HN422) be installed in a horizontal rather than vertical position? I would like to install it in the space under my workbench. It would be in a clean environment, and there would be no tools or equipment in direct contact with it. The room in which I hope to install it is heated. Since I am in the midst of remodeling my house, I would appreciate a prompt reply.

Requests should be specific.

Requests for credit should get to the point immediately.

Figure 6.11
Ineffective Routine Claim

286 Greencrest Drive
Athens, OH 45701
September 4, 1997

Appliance City
1012 Main Street
Athens, OH 45700

Dear Sales Manager:

When I saw your humidifier advertised on television, I thought it was just what I needed. You said that it would solve the problems of dry air and static electricity, and both of these are real problems in my house.   *— Unnecessary information that does not clarify the problem.*

One thing I didn't anticipate was the way its color would clash with most of the furnishings in my house. I thought that gray would blend in with the surroundings, but it doesn't.   *— Wordy and beside the point.*

After using it for one week, I've decided that I can't get used to it. None of the colors in which it comes would be any better for my house.   *— States the problem, but gives no relevant specifics such as model or size.*

I would like to return my humidifier to you. If I do so, would you please send me a full refund? I would certainly appreciate it.   *— Finally requests a specific action.*

Sincerely,

Kenneth Adams
Kenneth Adams

✔ CHECKLIST *for a Routine Claim*

____ When making a claim, write promptly.

____ Request a specific action in the first sentence.

____ Explain why such action would be desirable.

____ Express confidence in the reader's judgment and appreciation for the action you are seeking.

____ Avoid sarcasm, name-calling, and threats.

Requesting Credit

When you request credit by letter, the sequence of ideas is identical to those in the standard order letter. As with an order letter, you should get to the point immediately and then provide the necessary details.

Please open a charge account for me. My name and address follow:

Marcia O. Bonner
1400 Tiffany Avenue, Apt. 980
Orlando, FL 32802

Figure 6.12
Request for Routine Information

1813 Violet Avenue
Midview, TN 38238
June 12, 1997

Mayor Heather Lange
City Hall
Midview, TN 38238

Dear Mayor Lange:

On the six o'clock news last night, they showed a brief portion of the speech you gave yesterday.

Unclear purpose—most politicians give more than one speech each day.

It sounded interesting, and I would like to learn what else you said in your speech.

Presents no new information.

Please send me a copy of the speech you gave.

The request doesn't indicate whether note cards or a handout would suffice if no copy of the speech is available.

Yours truly,

Robert J. Rasmussen
Robert J. Rasmussen

Prior to moving to Orlando I lived for three years at:
1011 Live Oak Lane
Building C
New Orleans, LA 70113
While living in New Orleans I had charge accounts with Axel's Emporium, Carson's Department Store, and Michelle's Boutique.

I have worked for B&J Electronics for the past five years as a sales representative. I earn more than $25,000 per year.

My Orlando bank is Sun City Bank & Trust, where I have a checking and savings account. In New Orleans I banked at Tri-State Bank.

✔ **CHECKLIST** *for an Information Request*

___ Make a specific request immediately.

___ Ask whatever specific questions are necessary to get the desired information.

___ Avoid wordiness by asking direct questions. "Will the machine..." is preferable to "I am interested in..."

___ Make a positive and an appreciative reference to the action desired of the reader.

Most requests for credit are made on application forms.

Most requests for consumer credit are made by completing an application form furnished by the organization from which credit is sought. Even the person who writes a letter requesting credit will probably be asked to complete such a form . The information requested, however, will be very similar to that provided in the letter.

A person opening a new business will most likely request credit by letter. The sequence of ideas is identical to those presented by an individual consumer.

> Please open a credit line of $1,500 for my company, Schief Clothiers, Inc., formerly known as Threads Unlimited.
>
> On July 1, 1996, I purchased Threads Unlimited from the estate of Waldo Gillis. I plan to feature your Falcon line of sportswear as our highest quality offering.
>
> I have 12 years of experience in men's clothing, the last four of which were spent owning and operating Suit City in Boise, Idaho. The Greater Boise Credit Bureau has my complete credit history on file.
>
> The grand opening of Schief Clothiers will be held September 1-3, Labor Day weekend. By that time, I hope to have a complete inventory of Falcon sportswear.
>
> Please send me a confirmation of a $1,500 line of credit and the payment plan you offer. Also indicate the date by which I must place an order so that I will receive it by late August.

✔ *CHECKLIST for a Credit Request*

_____ Make request immediately.

_____ Provide necessary details regarding type of account and line of credit desired.

_____ Describe your recent credit history.

_____ Provide current banking and credit references.

Placing Orders

In the absence of an order blank, the good-news and neutral letter plan should be followed in placing orders.

When you order something from a supplier of any sort, the process is simplified if you have an order blank from the company. When you do not, you should follow the good-news and neutral letter format.

In your letter, indicate exactly what you are ordering, the instructions for shipping, and the manner in which you intend to pay.

> Please send me one X-365 workbench. I have enclosed a check for the total amount, $249.95.
>
> Since I intend to give the workbench as a birthday gift, it is important that it arrive before May 30. If, for any reason, the workbench is unavailable, please notify me immediately.

Robert Palmer works as an assistant purchasing manager for a large company. For many of the purchases he makes, he simply completes an order blank. Frequently, however, he must write letters of order. When Robert writes a letter of order, he provides enough information so that the seller does not have to request additional details. The following excerpt from one of his letters shows his approach.

> Please ship the following goods to reach our Silvertown plant by December 2, 1996.

Quantity	Catalog Code	Unit Price	Total Price
12	A-812-0610	$167.99	$2015.88
12	A-842-1914	79.99	959.88

Total $2975.76

Charge these goods to our account on the regular 1/10, net 30 terms.

It is important that the goods arrive by December 2. We appreciate the promptness with which you always fill our orders.

Whether using an order form or writing an order letter, you must include all of the necessary details. Delays often occur because information in the order letter is incomplete.

Using Prewritten Messages

In many situations a reply tailored to a specific individual is not needed. The expense of an individualized letter simply cannot be justified in other instances. Still other situations are so routine that it is impractical to compose individual letters. A suitable alternative is often a **form letter**—a very general letter that may be sent to many people without change.

Two approaches may be used with form letters. One is to prepare individual paragraphs in advance for use in situations that frequently occur. The other approach uses complete letters prepared in advance for use in certain routine situations. These prewritten messages allow an organization to respond more quickly to much of the correspondence it receives.

Form messages allow for immediate responses to predictable requests.

Form Paragraphs

After determining the kinds of information usually sought in incoming routine correspondence, writers can save time by preparing appropriate paragraphs in advance. Often organizations have computerized form paragraphs, each with a reference number. The correspondent need only key in the numbers of the paragraphs to be used and the sequence in which they are to appear.

To illustrate, Coach Hank Sloane found that interest was growing in his summer basketball camps as he became better known through his successful basketball teams. The great number of inquiries about the camps made it difficult for him and his secretary to keep up with their work. On the basis of a careful record of the kinds of inquiries he received, Hank prepared a series of paragraphs that answered the most commonly asked questions. He numbered the paragraphs and, after reading a letter, he would tell the secretary which paragraphs to send in response.

✔ *CHECKLIST for an Order Letter*
____ Start with your main point. "Please send" or "Please ship" are appropriate openings and are likely to result in a fast response.
____ Provide all the details necessary for the seller to fill the order now. If details such as catalog number, size, color, and price are omitted, further correspondence will be necessary and a delay will result.
____ Indicate the payment plan you will follow.
____ Include shipping instructions if you have a preference.
____ Close with your expectations of an appropriate delivery date.

When asked by a potential participant about the size of the camp and the possibility of tuition grants, for example, he told his secretary to send paragraphs 2 and 5. This is the letter that resulted.

Yes, there are openings available in the July basketball camp. Enrollment is limited to 25 participants per session. As a participant, you will receive intensive coaching that will help you sharpen your skills.

Yes, partial grants are available for a limited number of participants. Please complete the enclosed application and return it to me in order to be considered for a grant. The enclosed brochure describes our camp in greater detail.

Form Letters

Inquiries are sometimes so predictable that it is more efficient to go beyond form paragraphs and prepare complete form letters. The only types of information that need be added to a form letter are name, address, and date.

Figure 6.13

Form Letter
Source: Jeff Denberg, "Three's a Crowd," *Atlanta Journal*, December 17, 1979, 13-B.

XYZ SPORTS, INC.
P.O. Box 4440 • Grand Central Station • New York, NY 10017

November 6, 1979

Mr. T. V. Viewer
1422 Any Street
Any City, NY 10001

Dear Mr. Viewer:

I appreciate your taking the time to write to express your feelings about _____. While your comments and pointed criticisms do not pass by unnoticed, I would like to state the feelings of XYZ Sports regarding this matter.

Main idea—appreciation to a viewer for having written.

Mr. _____ is an expert commentator with a vast knowledge and total recall of many sports and sports personalities. We feel his intelligence and keen mind far outweigh his sometimes controversial statements. The precision and articulation of Mr. _____'s sports presentations rank him among the best of all sports broadcasters.

Secondary details that support employing the subject of the complaint while acknowledging its validity.

Nevertheless, we do not like to alienate our viewers. In the interest of improving all our telecasts to the greatest possible extent, we take into consideration your comments and the comments of all viewers in connection with future programming. We look forward to winning your full support.

Closes on a positive note and looks to the future.

Yours truly,

I. M. Worthy
I. M. Worthy
Public Relations

Most form letters in business cover routine matters, but there are some exceptions to this rule. According to one newspaper columnist, for example, a television network responded to viewers' complaints about a sports commentator with the form letter in Figure 6.13.

Another unusual instance in which a form letter was used occurred during a recent football season. Many fans of the Atlanta Falcons were irate when National Football League officials penalized their team when Billy "White Shoes" Johnson danced in the end zone after he scored touchdowns. So many fans wrote to the National Football League office that the NFL supervisor of officials responded with this form letter:[6]

We have received a number of postal cards from your area asking that Billy "White Shoes" Johnson be permitted to "do his dance."

Please be advised that we will forward your suggestion to the Rules Committee for its review prior to the start of the 1986 season. This is a routine procedure we follow whenever we receive suggestions from clubs, fans, and members of the media.

However, for the remainder of the 1985 season, the officials will continue to enforce the rules prohibiting such actions. We will have to see what develops in 1986.

Form letters are even more efficient than form paragraphs because they are completely prepared in advance. They are more economical than form paragraphs, and they can be dispatched more quickly. An organization's best writers should be assigned to develop the necessary form letters, for these letters are circulated widely.

This prepackaged approach to written communication has some disadvantages. Form paragraphs and form letters are intended for use in highly specific situations, but they are sometimes used in situations for which they were not designed. Care must be exercised to prevent this tendency, because an inappropriate form letter may be more irritating to the receiver than no response at all. Another disadvantage of the prepackaged approach is that form paragraphs and form letters tend to become outdated quickly. Organizational policies and practices are constantly changing, and management should ensure that its prepackaged messages reflect the changes.

Form messages tend to become outdated quickly.

Appropriateness of Prewritten Messages

Careful thought should be given as to when form letters are appropriate. Most form letters are used in situations that occur so frequently that the cost of individual letters would be prohibitive.

Form letters should be used with discretion.

Department stores, for example, often use form letters to extend credit privileges to those who have sought them. Colleges may use form letters to acknowledge applications for admission. These are among the many situations in which form letters may be used effectively. However, an organization should be careful in sending out form letters, because there are always possible exceptions to their use. For example, a company may routinely use form letters to acknowledge orders. This is good procedure, but a form letter certainly would be inappropriate to acknowledge the initial order from a new customer whose business has been long sought.

Consider two college students who received identical form letters denying them permission to substitute one course for another.

> Bill Thompson, an excellent student, asked permission to take another accounting course in place of a required cost accounting course. He had two years of cost accounting experience. Also, the required course was scheduled for a time when Bill had to be at work. He was the sole support of his wife and two small children.
>
> Jill Hennessey, an average student, requested permission to make a similar substitution. The required course was offered at a time that would conflict with her duties as a volunteer photographer for the school yearbook. Although photography was only a hobby, she hoped to make it her profession eventually.

When Bill received a form letter, he felt that he had been treated with cold indifference. His excellent grades and individual circumstances certainly deserved more personal treatment and consideration. Jill, on the other hand, did not find the form letter offensive. Form letters constitute an aid to communication as long as they are used with discretion.

A major criticism of form letters is that they are too impersonal. Through the use of word-processing software, it is now possible to individualize form letters and to insert special wording for a personal touch. Although the best form letters are not as effective as individual letters, they are expedient. Most readers prefer a prompt and clear reply and thus will overlook any impersonality.

Personal matters deserve personal, rather than form, letters.

As the volume of business communication increases, there will be still greater reliance on form messages. As long as management exercises good judgment, form letters are an effective communication tool.

Key Terms

- transitory communication
- planning process
- draft
- writer's block
- revision
- collaborative writing

- deductive arrangement
- good-news letter
- neutral letter
- indirect sequence
- direct sequence
- form letter

Summary

The impact of letters   p. 134

Determining the objective of a message   p. 134

Identifying important characteristics of the recipient(s)   pp. 134–136

Recognizing the most important ideas   p. 135

Selecting an appropriate channel and medium   p. 136

Revising content, language, and organization   pp. 136–137

Steps for conveying positive or neutral information in writing   pp. 138–139

Uses for preprinted messages   p. 153

Review Questions

1. Why does the transitory nature of electronic communication make it less acceptable to congressional staff members?

2. What are the advantages and disadvantages of collaborative writing?

3. Describe the four steps of the planning process.

4. What types of letters do you think merit the most careful planning?

5. What are the main differences between writing a draft and revising?

6. What are the main areas on which the writer should focus when revising?

7. What is meant by the term bad-news letter?

8. State the arguments for and against an organization's acknowledging every single order received.

9. In what ways is a completely preprinted postcard as effective as an individual letter for acknowledging orders?

10. Describe the outline for a letter in which credit is extended to a new customer.

11. In extending credit to a new customer, should the writer state the penalties for late payment? Why?

12. If the seller is clearly at fault and is giving the adjustment sought by the buyer, why is it desirable to explain the problem that necessitated the adjustment?

13. Why is the direct or deductive arrangement most appropriate for good-news and neutral letters?

14. What criteria determine the appropriateness of a form letter for a particular situation?

15. Why has the wider use of the telephone not made letters less important?

Exercises

1. **Singing for Your Supper.** Last year, you opened a moderately priced restaurant featuring continental cuisine in the pedestrian mall of downtown Charlottesville. The restaurant has become popular for business lunches and other mid-day meals, but you now want to attract more dinner customers.

   You have been considering adding karaoke entertainment to liven up the evenings. After visiting the other karaoke restaurant in town, you recognize that this form of entertainment is growing in popularity and you want to find out more about it.

   Your mission is to write a letter to the American Karaoke Association. Ask specifically about what karaoke equipment you will need and any other recommended renovations you should make to your facility. The Association is located at 100 Martin Circle, Cleveland, OH 30528.

2. **The Customer Is Always Right.** You have been helping your Uncle Bob at his car dealership this summer and handling some administrative tasks involving business communication. Currently, Bob Billet sells more used cars than new cars, and he wants to know if he should continue to do so. He is interested in how the used car customers feel about their purchases, and he asked you to develop a survey that he could distribute to customers.

   After researching effective survey formats and techniques, you developed a fifteen question survey that focuses on the customers' overall satisfaction with their used car purchases and the helpfulness of the Bob Billet staff.

   Your mission is to compose a standardized letter to accompany each survey. In this letter, stress the importance of feedback from the customers and urge them to return the survey in the stamped envelope provided.

3. **Dancing in the Streets.** You are producing a music video for a new band. This production will be the debut video for the group formerly known as Princess, and you want to have a very trendy approach to the piece. Since the song has a thumping bass line and a hard-driving rhythm, you have decided that the video should be set in the harsh environment of the meat-packing district in New York City. You have obtained permission to film the video at Turner Meat and Fish Company on West 7th Street, and you want to find 40 or 50 extras to wander around on the sidewalks while the band is playing.

   In order to find the extra actors to appear in the video, you have contacted a Manhattan casting agency. You are looking for men and women, ages 16 to 25, with an "urban look."

   Your mission is to write the form letter that you would like the casting agency to distribute. In this letter, use your imagination to describe the video's storyline and what the extras' roles will be in the video. Ask the actors to send their resumés and photographs to Evan Erikson, P.O. Box 9235, New York, NY 10023-9235.

4. **Fly the Friendly Skies.** Throughout your life, you have been a risk taker, and recently you have become interested in taking up skydiving as a hobby. You have already tried bungee jumping and cliff diving, and you are looking for a greater thrill.

   Your mission is to request information from Sky San Diego, P.O. Box 5353, San Diego, CA 93125. In your letter mention you have specific concerns about the expense of the sessions, the safety precautions taken, and the requirements for certification.

5. **Debit or Credit.** You are interested in learning more about business, and you feel the best way to begin your pursuit is to learn the language of accounting. Therefore, you are looking into taking an introductory accounting course by correspondence from Janesville City College.

   When contacting the school, you have several questions. You are particularly interested in how much the course will cost, how many credits you will receive for it, and if there are prerequisites. You also want to complete the work during your summer break, so be sure to ask what the typical time frame is for completing an accounting correspondence course.

   Your mission is to write for an application and information about the course. Your request will be sent to: Janesville City College, Admissions Office, 1005 Campus Drive, Janesville, WI 40705.

6. **Here's to Your Health!** Two months ago, you ordered vitamin supplements from Vita-Health, and you were informed that the vitamins were on back order. You have been awaiting their arrival because you feel that they will be an added benefit to your exercise and diet regime. Yesterday you received the vitamins in the mail, along with a notice mentioning that their product lines will expand to include the latest in health and fitness aids.

   Your mission is to write a letter acknowledging receipt of the vitamins and request additional information about availability of new products. Send this letter to the Mail Order Department, VitaHealth Inc., 20 Dunberry Rd., London, England, RM11 1EX.

7. **The Lure of Politics.** You have spent the last few summers working in the pizza parlor on Main Street, and you have decided that you want to find something more stimulating to do this year. You have been following the news and anticipating the upcoming presidential and senatorial elections, and you are very excited about the possibility of working on one of your senator's summer intern staff on Capitol Hill.

   Your mission is to request information from one of your senator's office concerning summer internship opportunities in Washington, DC. Include the time period during which you will be able to work and mention that you will be sending a resumé at a later date. You should obtain your senator's address from the library.

8. **The Deluge of Mail.** As Robert Villa, the legislative correspondent for your state senator, you have the responsibility of personally answering the mail from the constituency. You are sometimes overwhelmed with the daily volume of letters that pass through the senator's office, but you are diligent in answering every one. Among other letters, you have received the internship information request from question 7.

   Your mission is to answer this letter by stating that the senator hires interns for two standard six-week sessions each summer. Provide the dates of these sessions. Since you are working for the senator, sign the letter with his/her name, and be sure to mention the internship application.

9. **Nobody Brews It Better.** For a few years, you have been experimenting with brewing your own beer at home. You've discovered some delicious recipes and your friends can never get enough of your creations. Because beer-making is your favorite hobby, you are thinking about expanding your operations and opening a micro-brewery. You are not sure how to proceed, and you would like some advice—both general information about starting your own business and specific information about the beer industry.

Your mission is to write to the Small Business Administration, Food and Beverages Division, 2000 Independence Avenue, Washington, DC 20585. Ask for basic information about how to set up shop and include any other questions you may have about micro-breweries.

10. **Let It Snow, Let It Snow.** As the director of the billing department of Northwest Heating Oil Company, you have authorized a rate reduction for the upcoming winter season. You have noted that the cost of providing power to your customers has dropped incrementally and you want to pass this savings on to the public.

    Your mission is to compose a form letter that will be sent to all customers, announcing the reduction in rates for the upcoming winter. Be sure to thank them for their continued patronage.

11. **Hitting the Slopes.** For your annual vacation, you would like to go skiing in Argentina during the South American winter. This summer all of your friends will be traveling to the beaches to bask in the sun, and you think it will be exciting to do something different. Since you have never been to the southern hemisphere, you are not sure which month would provide the best skiing and which ski resorts cater to foreign tourists.

    Your mission is to request information from the Argentinean Tourist Bureau, 500 Esperanza, Buenavista, Argentina A5-E223. Mention that you would like to stay in accommodations where English is spoken but you would like to sample the native cuisine and gain some familiarity with local customs.

12. **In the Big Apple.** You have successfully completed an arduous job search and you have accepted a position at an investment firm in New York City. You are thinking about living in Brooklyn Heights and commuting to Manhattan and you will have to rely on the subway system and/or the bus system to get to work. You specifically need to know the cheapest and quickest ways to commute to Manhattan from Brooklyn.

    Your mission is to write the New York City Board of Public Transportation to obtain subway and bus schedules. You will address your letter to New York City Board of Public Transpiration, Customer Information Services, P.O. Box 1155, New York, NY 10036-1155.

13. **Stay under Cover.** After locating an apartment in Brooklyn Heights, you need to inform your insurance company that you would like to transfer your renter's insurance policy to your new address. (You will be moving to a two-bedroom, fourth floor apartment at 3456 Columbia Ave., Apt. 4A, Brooklyn Heights, NY 11022.) You think that your insurance rates may increase, so inquire about the change in fees and ask if you should increase your coverage since you are relocating to an area with a higher crime rate.

    Your mission is to request the above information from your insurance company: Northeast Insurance, 701 Pine Road, Hartford, CT 07654.

14. **Quick Response.** As a customer service representative at Northeast Insurance, you must respond to the letter written for question 13. Your company has been writing personal responses to customer requests as a part of its new Total Quality Management program. In your response, you will inform the customer that annual insurance rates for renting a two-bedroom apartment in Brooklyn range from $300-$500.

    Your mission is to respond quickly to the customer's letter and suggest contacting the New York City Northeast Insurance office in New York City to transfer the policy and get specific local rates and further information.

15. **An Earthy Education.** You are a fourth-grade elementary school teacher in Cartersville, GA, and you would like to take your students on a field trip to the Natural History Museum in Atlanta.

    In science class, the children have been studying geological history and plate tectonics, and you have heard that the museum provides an excellent overview of the concepts you have been teaching. You want to be sure to relate the museum experience to your class.

    Your mission is to find out what the museum has to offer and if there are relevant current exhibitions at the museum. Direct your request to Ann Moyer, Director of Museum Education, Natural History Museum, Atlanta, GA 31232.

16. **Discovering a Taste Sensation.** When you went to the supermarket yesterday, you purchased a new MegaSweet candy bar and you believe it is the best candy bar you have ever eaten. You've decided to write to the Henley Chocolate Corporation and let them know how much you enjoy their new product.

    Your mission is to inform Henley Chocolate Corporation that you think the MegaSweet bar is a real "winner." You are writing them an enthusiastic letter of appreciation. You saved the candy bar label and you write to the address listed there: 60 Chocolate Avenue, Henley, PA 17606.

17. **Calls for All.** As the Vice-President of Human Resources, you have become aware of low morale among employees in your organization. You have checked with the company president and he has agreed to let you offer a new perk to employees—free long distance telephone calls from the office. The employees can now call their friends and family on the WATTS line—but only after 5 P.M.

    Your mission is to write a brief letter to all employees informing them of this new benefit and asking them to enjoy the privilege but not abuse it.

18. **Fun in the Sun.** You are the Director for Recreational Projects at the Public Works Department of the Springdale City Government. Recently the department finished building an interactive playground in a suburban neighborhood, and you want to let nearby schools and clubs know that the park has been completed and the public will have access from sunrise until sundown. You also want to mention the free recreational activities for children that will be offered at the park during summer vacation.

    Your mission is to draft a standardized letter that will be sent to local schools and clubs providing them with relevant information about the park. Be sure to describe the park and encourage them to visit.

19. **Sink or Swim.** As the president of the American Innertube Water Hockey Association, you are trying to promote the popularity of the sport among intramural college programs. You have become aware of the hazards of flying pucks in the heat of competition, and you want to advise all players to wear their goggles during games and practices. In addition, you want the current members of your organization to help educate people about the sport.

    Your mission is to write a form letter that you will distribute to all members of your organization, as well as other universities you have identified as having active intramural sports programs. The purpose of this letter is simply to inform people about the sport and the necessary safety precautions.

20. **The Aggrieved Viewers.** You are employed at a television station in a large urban area. The programming at the station, which is not affiliated with any network, consists mainly of popular reruns. The station has been inundated with

phone calls and letters following an announcement that *The Beverly Hillbillies* will be moved from its 6:30 P.M. daily time slot to 11:30 P.M. The reason is that advertisers are reluctant to pay high, early-evening rates for that program. Advertising rates for the 11:30 slot are much lower.

Your mission is to prepare a form letter to send to viewers who complain that the new time will be too late for children to watch. Many of these viewers also complain about the shortage of programs on your station that are "fit for a family to watch."

21. **The Computer Did It.** As circulation manager of *Contemporary Living* you have received several complaints in the past month about improper billing. The cause of the problem is a new computer system; it had been malfunctioning, but the situation has now been corrected.

    Your mission is to write a response to a subscriber who has complained about incorrect billing. The letter should be sent to Robert Strong, 1210 4th Avenue, Villas, CO 81087.

22. **If It Works in the Alps.** As the owner of a chain of three sporting goods stores, you are always looking for new products to give your business an edge on the competition. While vacationing in the French Alps you learn of a new type of ski, aerodynamically designed and constructed of a newly developed alloy that is lighter and stronger than anything now on the U.S. market. Upon returning from vacation you write to the company in order to get all of the particulars on the skis. You would like to become the U.S. distributor. If your request for a U.S. dealership is denied, you want to at least establish a relationship with the company and sell its skis at your store.

    Your mission is to write to Francois Levant, President, Levant Aero Products, 184 Rue du F.g. Saint Antoines, 75012 Paris, France.

23. **Something to Crow About.** Inspired by the success of the San Diego Chicken, you purchased an appropriate costume and have become the Rochester Rooster. For $25 you will make an appearance at any sort of gathering. For $50 you will present a 20-minute act including singing and dancing. You are not especially talented, but people don't seem to expect much talent from a rooster. Recently you were hired by Big Bill Bluss, President of Bluss Imports (4848 Lake Freeway, Rochester, MN 55901) to appear at the store and present a birthday gift to one of his long-time employees. When you arrived, a birthday party was in progress and the partygoers insisted that you entertain. Because you could not exit gracefully, you presented your complete show.

    Your mission is to write a letter to Big Bill requesting $50 rather than the agreed upon $25.

24. **Power to the People.** As credit manager for Walsh Specialties (P.O. Box 143, Conyers, GA 30207), you approve Harold Smith's request for credit. He has just opened a lamp store called Let There Be Light (P.O. Box 840, Atlanta, GA 30304) in an Atlanta shopping center. You are sending him the following items on terms of 3/10, n/30:

3 solid brass shell floor lamps @ $65	$195.00
6 solid brass 6-way lamps @ $75	450.00
1 Cathay table lamp @ $40	40.00
1 clear glass hexagon table lamp @ $35	35.00
	$720.00

These lamps are fashionable as well as functional and have been popular in all parts of the country. Harold recently came to Georgia from Durham, North Carolina, where he had operated and sold a similar business. A credit report described Harold as "generally prompt in meeting financial obligations." As with all new accounts, you limit his credit to $1000 until he proves himself to be a responsible individual.

Your mission is to write Smith confirming the order and extending credit up to $1000. Point out the 3 percent discount available for payment within 10 days. Mention the desirability of maintaining a good credit record. Also tell him to watch for the new Walsh catalog, which he will be receiving in approximately 30 days.

25. **In the Interest of Time.** You are planning a week's vacation two months from now, and you are considering taking a Windjammer Cruise. You have learned the schedule and rate information from advertisements, but you have several questions: How many tourists will there be on the ship? How many of them are likely to be single like yourself? You are aware that each tourist must perform some work on the ship each day, and you do not object to that. You wonder, however, how many hours per day and what kinds of duties you would have to perform.

Your mission is to write a letter seeking the above information to Windjammer Cruises, P.O. Box 1111, Miami, FL 33101.

CASE

Not So Picture Perfect

Randy E. Cone, University of New Orleans

You are Assistant Customer Service Manager for a nationally known film-processing company, and you have worked in that capacity for about two years. Your duties are many and varied but involve primarily helping the Customer Service Manager (your supervisor) resolve conflicts and disagreements between retailers and customers (photographers). You enjoy your work and hope to ultimately be promoted to Customer Service Manager when your supervisor—an older person of great influence in the company—retires in one year.

In the last three months you have been confronted with a situation that you feel really tests your mettle. A number of letters and telephone calls have reached you, complaining about the contents of a form letter that your supervisor routinely sends to customers on the relatively rare occasions when their film has been lost. Irate and often profane as the photographers have been when writing or calling your office, you have to agree with them. In your opinion, the letter *is* awful and is doing a lot to create ill-will toward your company. You have shielded your supervisor from those complaints partly because you know your supervisor took pride in that letter.

In short, the letter is replete with negative words and poor excuses. It begins immediately by saying that the writer is "sorry not to have good news but we regret to advise you that as of the above date, we have not been able to find your lost film. Even though we take great pains to care for each and every roll of film entrusted to us, yours has apparently gone astray somewhere. We will continue looking for it, but we must admit that we sincerely doubt if we will ever find your missing film. Here is another roll; and though it will probably never be possible to take the same pictures again, we hope you will use the film to take pictures of a like interest. Once again, we are very sorry for the loss of your treasured film." The letter is reproduced on sophisticated equipment and doesn't appear to be a form letter. Your supervisor, in fact, personally signs each one before mailing.

Case Questions

1. Rewrite the letter so that the customer-photographer whose film has been lost will regain confidence in your company.

2. How will you convince your supervisor that yours is the letter that should be sent to these often angry customers?

CASE

Easy to Judge, Hard to Correct

Lynne K. Anderson, Tidewater Community College, Chesapeake, VA

Professor Karen Cook teaches a course in business letter writing at Coastal Community College. Instead of giving a final exam, she asks students to collect letters from businesses and organizations throughout the area served by the college. They organize the letters into a report consisting of a title page, letter of transmittal, table of contents, the letters themselves, and critiques of each of the letters based on the criteria developed throughout the course. Finally, each letter is assigned a grade by the student.

Every quarter many of the students' reports include letters that were written by employees of the college. Invariably these letters receive grades of C, D, or even lower.

Karen concurs with these grades. The letters very often are typed with many unnecessary indentations, thereby adding to the cost of producing them. They are full of *I* and *We* with little emphasis on the reader. Some of the letters are so disorganized that they leave the reader wondering why they were written. Tired phrases abound; and an insincere "thank you" is tacked onto the end of many letters even when there really is nothing for which to thank the reader. Fill-ins on form letters are not aligned and often are done in a different size type from the form itself.

It would be a simple matter to recommend an in-house seminar for the staff on improving letter-writing skills. However, the college already employs an administrative assistant to the president who screens and approves all of the form letters that go out from the college. This assistant does not screen communications that are not mass produced. This assistant's background and experience are unrelated to business communication.

Case Questions

1. Would you recommend that Professor Cook change the content of her course to be more in line with the letters sent out by various staff people in the college?

2. Should she request that students not include college letters in their term projects?

3. Should she agree with the students' critiques of college letters and still do nothing to suggest improvements?

4. What other alternatives does she have?

Notes

1. Greg Miller, "Best Way To Get Ear of Congress? Send a Letter," *Athens Banner-Herald*, September 8, 1993, A-9.

2. Ibid., A-9.

3. "Write On," *USA Today*, January 26, 1994, D-1.

4. "That Dreaded Letter," *Atlanta Constitution*, June 22, 1994, A-6.

5. Kenneth Roman and Joel Raphaelson, *Writing That Works* (New York: Harper & Row, 1981), 97.

6. Chris Mortensen, "NFL Can't Calm White Shoes' Dance Fever," *Atlanta Journal Constitution*, November 2, 1985, 3-D.

Chapter 7

Bad-News Letters

Learning Objectives

1
TO RECOGNIZE THE STRATEGIC DECISIONS THAT MUST BE MADE IN PLANNING MESSAGES OF REFUSAL.

2
TO LEARN THE SEQUENCE OF THOUGHTS TO BE CONVEYED IN A LETTER OF REFUSAL.

3
TO LEARN THE REASONS FOR THE THOUGHT SEQUENCE PRESENTED IN A LETTER OF REFUSAL.

4
TO IDENTIFY THE CHARACTERISTICS OF EFFECTIVE LETTERS OF REFUSAL.

5
TO LEARN TO WRITE REFUSALS THAT READERS WILL UNDERSTAND, AS WELL AS LETTERS THAT WILL ACCOMPLISH THE INTENDED PURPOSE.

Rick Campbell opened his mailbox with a mixture of hope and dread. He was in the last month of his senior year in college and his job search was becoming intense. He had sent out at least 50 resumés with cover letters to companies he wanted to work for. Rick had already received a few brief, impersonal rejection letters. They thanked him for his interest, informed him there were no suitable positions available, and wished him luck in his job search. That was the pattern. He wondered if anyone even read his letters. However, Rick would learn as the waiting and searching continued that sometimes bad news is better than no news. Also, some bad news is better than other bad news.

The companies that made the worst impression on him were the ones that did not even deign to respond to his inquiries. It left him feeling that these organizations, which he had previously respected, were unprofessional and discourteous. Although he was merely a college student he felt he should be treated better. Even the postcards with an address label attached were an improvement.

Rick knew the importance of written communication. He knew that it gives the receiver a lasting and tangible impression of the sender. This is especially important in business matters, when the parties involved likely do not know each other personally. Correspondence should create goodwill, not diminish it. It should also be intelligently and competently written. Unfortunately, some of the companies Rick wrote to fell in his esteem. He wondered why some successful firms with millions of dollars in profits could not communicate effectively or, in some cases, at all.

The letter of refusal is difficult to write because it denies the reader's request. The reader is unlikely to respond favorably to such a message, and so the directness of the good-news letter is inappropriate. Most authorities suggest that **bad-news letters** be written in an indirect or inductive manner.

The indirect sequence of ideas makes the message more palatable to the reader because it allows writers to convey their thought processes on the subject prior to presenting their decision. The reader can look into the mind of the writer and, ideally, is convinced of the reasonableness of the decision.

The indirect sequence will be either strengthened or weakened by the wording used in the letter. In many bad-news letters the wording throughout is negative, and the overall impression on the reader is negative. Even

Bad-news letters are made more palatable by the indirect sequence and positive words.

though the purpose of such a letter is to convey something other than what the reader wishes to receive, it can be done in a positive manner.

PLANNING THE BAD-NEWS LETTER

In recent years the expression "winging it" has become a part of the vocabulary of most of us. Students wing it when they come to class not having prepared the day's assignment. Business people wing it when they make presentations or perform any of their other duties without benefit of customary preparation. People who wing it are gambling that their performance will be acceptable; many times the gamble pays off and their performance does meet minimum standards.

A lack of planning dooms many bad-news letters.

For anyone who is not content with merely meeting minimum standards, however, planning must become routine. This is especially true for challenging tasks—such as conveying bad news. Unless this is done properly, it threatens the relationship that exists between the writer and the reader. In the absence of careful planning it is unlikely to be done properly.

Careful attention to planning differentiates effective business communication from ineffective communication. The following paragraphs describe two different reactions to bad-news letters. Which letter do you suspect was the better planned?

> When Arlene MacEnzie's application for a charge account was turned down by a local clothing store, she was irate. She ripped up the letter of rejection, vowing never again to set foot in that store.
>
> When Evan Slade received word that he had been denied a charge account with a local building supply company, he was displeased but philosophical. Because he recognized that the goods sold by that company were of high quality and priced fairly, he intended to continue doing business there.

Chapter 6 described the four steps in the planning process. Now we will tailor those steps to situations in which the writer must convey bad news, using the following example:

> Bob Costner, fraternity president, recently had to face the task of writing a bad-news letter when the fraternity was sponsoring a sale of 5-pound cans of pecans. Bob had placed an advertisement in the local newspaper that resulted in more than 4,000 orders for the pecans. Unfortunately the fraternity had greatly underestimated the demand and had purchased only 1,000 cans of pecans. Because no more would be available this year, the situation called for a bad-news letter. Bob planned the letter according to the four steps of planning described more thoroughly in Chapter 6.

Determining Objective(s)

Writers must decide what it is they intend to accomplish with their message. Some bad-news letters have more than one objective. If so, decide which is the most important. Although it is not necessary to belabor the bad news, you must ensure that the reader will receive the intended message. Bob felt that the main objective of his letter would be to inform the readers that their orders could not be filled. Another objective would be to retain the goodwill of those whose orders could not be filled.

Considering the Audience

Unless the writer looks at the issue from the standpoint of the readers it is unlikely that the letter will have the desired effect. The audience for Bob's letter consists of local townspeople who were anticipating a genuine bargain. The price of the pecans was approximately half of the usual retail price. Not only was the audience pleased with the notion of a bargain, it was also pleased with the fact that the pecans were guaranteed to be fresh. Virtually all who had placed orders were permanent residents of the community and, therefore, potential customers for future fraternity projects.

Choosing the Ideas to Include

After identifying the objective and the audience to be reached, the writer is ready to determine the ideas that should be included in the message. Sometimes writers list ideas before specifying the objective; this practice usually results in a message with an unclear purpose. Writers who do not identify the audience prior to choosing ideas produce messages that do not appeal to the needs or interests of the readers. Bob felt that these ideas should be included in his letter:

* Thanks for your order.
* Unfortunately we won't be able to fill it.
* We would like to consider you as a possible customer for future fraternity projects.

Selecting the Appropriate Channel and Medium

In selecting the appropriate channel and medium the writer must consider the best way to reach the intended audience. Seeking to maintain a positive relationship with the disappointed individuals, Bob decided to send out letters. He felt that mail would be the most effective medium because his audience was geographically dispersed.

The letter that resulted from this planning is presented later in the chapter.

STRATEGY FOR THE BAD-NEWS LETTER

The general strategy for a letter of refusal is to induce the reader to read the entire letter so as to understand the reasons for the refusal. In this way the writer may be able to retain the reader's approval and business. A continuing relationship might be possible if the reader suspends judgment until the entire message is understood.

The writer should prepare the letter so that it has as little negative effect as possible. Before beginning to write, writers must place themselves in the reader's position. They must decide how to lead the reader to accept their decision.

Imagine that you are the plant manager of an electrical parts manufacturing company. You receive a letter from a sixth-grade class requesting a plant tour for a 40-member group. According to company policy, tours are available only to persons 16 years of age and older and group size is limited to 10. The company benefits from this policy because it greatly restricts the number of individuals likely to take a plant tour. There is, therefore, less disruption of plant operations. Those excluded from such tours may benefit by not being exposed to the potential dangers of the plant's machines, noise, and fumes.

An effective letter writer will strive to point out how the reader will benefit even though the request is denied. In some cases the writer may be able to make a helpful suggestion or offer an alternate plan. The plant manager, for example, might recommend a film that would introduce the students to manufacturing processes and could substitute for a tour.

Occasionally it may be impossible to point out any benefit. However, a writer who looks at the situation from the reader's point of view will generally find a way either to show a benefit or suggest some alternative.

If possible, the letter writer should point out how the reader may benefit from a refusal.

The key to writing letters of refusal that accomplish the intended purpose is to know the facts of the situation. Situations that require such letters are sometimes similar, but they are rarely identical. By knowing the relevant facts, a writer can develop a line of reasoning that the reader is likely to understand and accept.

STEPS IN TRANSMITTING BAD NEWS

Situations requiring letters of refusal vary greatly. However, following certain steps will produce letters that are appropriate and effective.

Neutral Opening

A neutral opening should indicate an area of agreement between writer and reader.

Start with a neutral comment that includes some form of agreement. Your opening comment should let the reader know the subject of the letter, but it should not imply either a yes or a no. After reading the first paragraph, the reader should be aware that the letter is a response to a request. Ideally the writer will indicate some form of agreement with the reader. For example, when a customer wrote to complain about auto repair service, the dealer began his response by stating, "You are certainly right to expect service work that is done properly the first time." This opening accomplishes two things. It indicates the subject of the letter and it points out an area of agreement.

The opening should be consistent with the message that is to follow. Readers who are led to expect acceptance and are then denied it tend to be unhappy and unlikely to continue any relationship with the writer. "We at Baily Motors take pride in the service we provide our customers" would be inappropriate if the writer did not intend to comply with the reader's wishes.

The opening should be objective. Express neither pleasure nor displeasure in responding to the request. "We at Baily Motors are always pleased to hear from our customers" suggests that the writer is enjoying the difficulties the customer is experiencing.

The subject of the letter should be indicated in the opening. "For the past 50 years Baily Motors has been a leader in sales and in service" will leave the reader uncertain as to the subject of the letter. That opening would probably lead the reader to expect a sales letter.

The opening should be written in a positive manner. Don't signal that a rejection is coming. Words such as "however," "although," or "but" signal rejection, as do negative words such as "won't," "can't," and "unable."

Positive Explanation

Present an explanation in a positive manner. The reader will be interested enough to continue reading your letter if you have succeeded in your neutral statement. Next you should give the reasons for your decision. The reasons precede the actual denial of the request. By getting the recipients to read the reasons, you increase the likelihood that they will understand those reasons. It may be true that understanding does not guarantee acceptance, but acceptance seldom occurs without understanding.

Explain rather than apologize. When a writer apologizes, the reader begins to suspect that the decision was not well thought-out. Another shortcoming of writing in an apologetic fashion is that it emphasizes the negative rather than the positive. "We at Baily Motors regret to tell you" reeks of insincerity and negativism.

Whenever possible, cite reasons other than company policy. When the writer must fall back on policy as a reason for not complying with the reader's wishes, it appears that the writer made no attempt to recognize the reader's uniqueness. "For 50 successful years Baily Motors has had a policy that prohibits" is not an adequate explanation.

Communicate on the reader's level. Few things irritate people more than being talked down to. When a writer says, "Our experience in 50 years of serving the public has taught us," it sounds like a parent addressing a child. Readers will not respond favorably.

Provide enough information so that the reader will understand, but not so much that it numbs the reader's mind. An overly brief explanation suggests a lack of concern. When a writer says "Our present exchange policy, which has been in effect for 58 years, originated when a man tried to exchange a saddle," it is overexplanation.

Whenever possible, emphasize reasons that might possibly benefit the reader. To inform a customer that a service contract would not pay for certain auto repairs, one correspondent wrote:

> Your service contract pays for all necessary engine repairs as long as the car is brought in for inspection every 6 months. In the absence of a 6-month inspection, the contract ceases to provide coverage. Regular inspections are intended to identify minor automotive problems before they become major and costly ones. Regular inspections help us to balance our workload so that each workday is quite predictable.

The writer explained not only how customers benefited from service contracts but also how the auto dealer benefited. By describing how the dealer will benefit, the writer comes across as candid and honest, and it makes the whole message more believable. Although the explanation is based on organizational policy, the writer never refers to policy. Policies are cold and impersonal, and it is difficult for people to relate to them. On the other hand, when the writer presents reasons that are clearly stated and plausible, the reasons are better received.

In some instances, the only reasons for refusing a request are, plainly and simply, company reasons. In these instances the writer should not go to great lengths to dream up imaginary benefits for the reader. Instead, just state the company's reason or reasons and let it go at that.

The Refusal

In the third part of the bad-news letter the writer gets to the heart of the matter, the actual refusal. If the reasons were explained clearly, the reader can probably infer a refusal even before actually reading it. Ideally the refusal flows logically from the reasons.

Sometimes it is not necessary to state the refusal directly if it can be implied. When a personnel director writes to tell job applicants that they are unsuitable for the position, a statement such as "We need a person who has had actual supervisory experience" will transmit the bad news. It is unnecessary to say "You do not meet our requirements" or any highly directed equivalent.

De-emphasize the refusal. Convey it without belaboring it. In most well-written bad-news letters, the refusal is embedded in a paragraph—the refusal is neither at the beginning nor the end of a paragraph.

Phrase the refusal in a positive manner. Telling the reader, "Since you forgot to oil the motor, we are unable to give you a refund," conveys the message; however, its accusatory tone may alienate the reader. "We would refund the purchase price if the maintenance instructions had been followed" is preferable.

Use the passive voice when stating the rejection. The active voice is overly blunt and calls undue attention to the refusal. For example, instead of "The admissions committee voted against your application for membership," "Your application for membership was denied by the admissions committee" is more muted but still conveys the refusal.

If there is any chance that the message may be misunderstood, the refusal should be stated directly. The clearer the relationship between the reasons and a refusal, the less necessary it is to state the refusal explicitly.

Positive Note

A letter of refusal should end on an upbeat and should leave the reader favorably disposed toward the writer (and the business). After conveying the refusal, the writer should try to regain some of the goodwill that may have been lost. This can be done in a number of ways. A department store, for example, may suggest its layaway service when it rejects a person's credit application.

Write about something of interest to the reader other than the refusal. Rather than remind the reader of the refusal, offer a counterproposal or some other helpful suggestion.

End in an unapologetic manner. The tendency to apologize suggests that you may have some doubts about the decision, which may encourage the reader to persist in seeking some adjustment or action.

Write positively without relying on clichés. Clichés are tired, overused expressions that may suggest an absence of thought on the part of the writer. Clichés often also suggest insincerity.

The purpose of the ending is to show the reader that you remain interested.

ADJUSTMENT REFUSALS

Adjustment refusals are difficult to write because the writer is denying a request that the customer considers reasonable.

Customers who request adjustments generally consider themselves and their requests reasonable. Most companies take pride in their equitable adjustment policies. No matter how liberal a company's attitude toward claims is, however, certain requests are bound to be refused. Writing an adjustment refusal letter is a delicate process; the writer implies that the request, viewed by the customer as reasonable, actually is not.

In writing an adjustment refusal you should follow the four steps just described for refusals. As with all letters of refusal the two main purposes are (1) to state the refusal and (2) to maintain a positive relationship with the reader. The second purpose is especially important when customers seek adjustments, because they are more likely to remain customers if they are treated well. The writer must strive to maintain a positive relationship.

Imagine that you are the sales manager of a company that manufactures sporting goods. A retailer writes to ask if she might return a sizable number of skateboards that she purchased from your company. Although interest in skateboarding had been high across the nation, the sport never grew very popular in Green Bay, where the retailer's store is located. Because interest in skateboarding is declining nationally, the skateboards would take up valuable warehouse space for some time. You decide that it is

---

✔ CHECKLIST for Transmitting Bad News

_____ Start with a neutral comment that includes some form of agreement. The opening should be consistent with the main message, objective, relevant to the interests of the reader, and written in a positive manner.

_____ Present an explanation in a positive manner. The explanation should explain rather than apologize, cite reasons other than company policy, communicate on the reader's level, and provide enough information so that the reader will understand.

_____ Convey the refusal. When stating the refusal, the writer should embed the refusal in the paragraph, phrase the refusal in a positive manner, and state the refusal in the passive voice.

_____ End on a positive note. The writer should write about something of interest to the reader, end in an unapologetic manner, write positively without relying on clichés, and make the reader aware of the writer's concern rather than of the refusal.

unwise to grant her request, and you write her accordingly. Figure 7.1 shows how one correspondent did it.

As mentioned earlier, the indirect approach is appropriate for most bad-news letters. The manager of a convention hotel used the following approach in responding to a request for an adjustment. The president of a national student government association had written to complain about the quantity of food the hotel provided for its Keynote Night banquet.

In refusing adjustment requests the writer should take the indirect approach.

Pleasing our customers is the foremost goal of the Elliot Plaza. Our success depends upon your satisfaction, and we appreciate your comments regarding the banquet services provided for your group.

Having catered banquets for more than 200 groups during the past year, we have established a reputation for offering quality meals at reasonable prices. Our standards

---

Figure 7.1
Adjustment Refusal

***OMNI SPORTS*, INC.**
P.O. Box 3546
Athens, OH 45701

March 12, 1997

Ms. Grace Trent
Games Aplenty, Inc.
3612 Main Street
Green Bay, WI 54301

Dear Ms. Trent:

You were right to expect our Rollfree skateboards to be a popular item among your customers. After all, they have been shown to be superior both in durability and in safety. Sales figures have shown the Rollfree to be one of the most popular skateboards in the country. — *Neutral comment that confirms the store's good judgment.*

One of the many challenges in the leisure goods field is the speed with which consumers' interests change. The public's changing tastes frequently leave us with excess inventory. We're always willing to make adjustments if there are quality problems in our merchandise. In the absence of such problems, all sales are final. — *Reasons for the decision with an implied refusal.*

Some analysts already predict a resurging interest in skateboarding. This resurgence and Rollfree's upcoming national advertising campaign should help boost your sales. Also, I am sending you separately some new mats for newspaper advertisements that have stimulated sales in cities like Green Bay. — *Ends on hopeful note with focus on the future.*

Sincerely,

Ramon Evans

Ramon Evans
Sales Correspondent

mb

ensure that food will be served in generous portions. Our records show that the dinner prepared for your group was identical to portions served similar-sized groups, most of which have praised our food service. We would certainly make an adjustment if our standard servings had not been available for your group.

Many organizations are already reserving rooms for holiday banquets, and most of them are repeat customers. We would appreciate the opportunity to count you and your group among them.

When a rock concert promoter was forced to make a substitution for a warm-up group she had advertised, she received a complaint following the concert. She sought to reject the request for a refund without sacrificing future business by writing the letter reproduced in Figure 7.2.

Figure 7.2
Request Denial

Star Productions Inc.
2006 Mainline Avenue, Suite 2000
Newark, NJ 07102

October 15, 1997

Randolph Scott
1646 12th Street
Perth Amboy, NJ 08861

Dear Mr. Scott:

We can certainly understand why you had expected Abject Failure to be the warm-up act at the concert last Friday. We begin to advertise a concert only when all of the acts on the program have agreed to perform.
Neutral statement that confirms the original expectation.

Occasionally something happens that we cannot control. Two members of Abject Failure were hospitalized the night before the concert, and there was little time to advertise the change. Most of the spectators seemed to think that the Scavengers did an excellent job as the replacement warm-up group. Our surveys show that most spectators attend concerts to see the headliners. Since the headline acts appeared as advertised, everyone seemed pleased with the concert.
Explains the cause of the unusual occurrence and subtly justifies the decision.

We take our responsibilities to the public very seriously. If ever an advertised headliner is unable to appear, you can be sure that you will receive a full refund.
Describes the organization's policy and conditions that would warrant a refund.

Loyal fans like you may soon be able to see Abject Failure headlining a concert here. Our schedule for the next three months is enclosed. You're sure to find some of these concerts to your liking.
Compliments the complainant's good judgment and looks ahead to doing business again.

Yours truly,

Whitney Dallas
Whitney Dallas
Promotion Specialist

nf

Enc.

Although a small number of requests for adjustments may border on the fraudulent, most do not. Sometimes correspondents who regularly handle adjustments grow cynical, and cynicism is reflected in their letters. Such letters often may read like this:

> You claim that the hair dryer did not work as advertised. We cannot understand how this quality-checked appliance could possibly malfunction. According to you the dryer never worked as it was supposed to.

The writer should avoid cynicism in letters of refusal.

Letters written by cynical correspondents are tinged with distrust and suspicion. They may convey the message but lose a customer. An effective bad-news letter clearly conveys the message yet retains the trust and business of the customer.

Occasionally a writer faces a situation in which the indirect approach is either inappropriate or unworkable. If a customer has already received a written refusal and explanation yet persists in requesting an adjustment, the direct approach may be suitable for a second letter. If the reader ignores the first letter refusing adjustment and simply repeats the request, the writer is justified in becoming more blunt.

A direct approach is sometimes taken in bad-news letters, but only after careful consideration.

To ensure that the message is unmistakably clear the writer might present the denial in the first sentence. (For example, "Until you complete the travel expense form properly, you will not be reimbursed for your business trip.") This approach may make

BOXED IN

AN ETHICAL DILEMMA

Carl Hammerstrom was in a dead-end job. He had been in the same position for over two years and his firm routinely hired from outside rather than promoting from within. Carl was ambitious and wanted a more challenging and interesting job, so he decided he needed to begin a job search.

The first thing he needed to do was update his résumé, which he hadn't even looked at in over two years .He needed to add his current position, continuing education courses, and volunteer work. He also thought the format and wording of the older information could be improved. He went for help to a friend of his named Lisa who was a human resource specialist. As a human resource specialist she saw hundreds of résumés every year and was regarded by her friends as a résumé expert. She had advised many of their friends.

After reviewing Carl's résumé, Lisa conceded it was adequate, but it needed work. First, she told him to modernize the layout, to make it more dynamic. She also advised him to use active rather than passive verbs. After these routine changes Lisa and Carl discussed how he would describe his current position.

He described his responsibilities to Lisa and she wrote them down in language appropriate for a résumé. She handed the page to Carl. As he read it he barely recognized his own job. Although he assisted the department manager with almost everything, he felt uncomfortable being described as "assistant department manager." No such job title existed in his company and he didn't feel it was proper to create it. He was also uncertain about some of the wording in the description.

He voiced his concerns to Lisa and she said, "Don't worry about it. No one expects you to be completely honest on your résumé. You're trying to impress people. I always assume half of what I read is pure exaggeration. Modesty will get you nowhere, Carl." Carl considered this and he thought about his future. He really wanted a better job. Maybe Lisa was right. After all, she was the expert.

Carl feels boxed in. What would you do?

the reader realize that the problem is serious. It is a risky approach, however, and may alienate the reader. For this reason the direct approach should be used only after careful consideration of how the reader is likely to respond.

After buying a lightweight suit on sale, Bob Norris had second thoughts and wrote to the store:

> Two weeks ago I purchased a lightweight suit at your half-price sale. Now I realize that the color isn't right for me and I'd like to return it. I wore the suit only once.
>
> As you can see from your records, I am a longtime customer of Grenier's. In fact, almost once a month I make the 60-mile drive to shop at your store. Since I plan to go shopping within the next two weeks, please inform me promptly of your decision.

The store conveyed the bad news of an adjustment refusal in this way:

> As a smart shopper you know that taking advantage of sales makes sense. You saved 50 percent by buying your suit at our recent end-of-the-season sale. Your willingness to drive 60 miles to shop at Grenier's shows that you appreciate quality, too.
>
> Customers like you benefit from our end-of-the-season sales in several ways: not only do you enjoy tremendous savings, you also have the opportunity to select from the newest styles. Our end-of-the-season sales allow us to change our stock often and to be up-to-date.
>
> You can be sure that any clothing you buy at Grenier's will be brand new and that you are the original purchaser. We feel that we owe that to our customers. Although sales items are nonreturnable, the purchase price would, of course, be refunded on any defective merchandise.
>
> We appreciate your loyalty and we hope to continue to earn it.

After reading the letter, Bob:

- Knew that he couldn't return the suit.
- Understood why the store was unable to take it back.
- Believed that the store was aware of the facts.
- Believed that he had been treated fairly.
- Intended to continue shopping at Grenier's.

These are the kinds of responses sought by the writer of a letter refusing a requested adjustment.

✔ *CHECKLIST for an Adjustment Refusal*

____ Make your opening comment neutral and relate it to the subject of the letter.

____ Imply neither yes nor no in the opening.

____ Keep the opening brief.

____ Convey a positive tone rather than an apologetic one in presenting the reasons for your decision.

____ If possible, show how the reader may actually benefit from the decision because of the reasons.

____ Present the reasons so that the reader anticipates a refusal.

____ Make your refusal clear, but don't overemphasize it.

____ Avoid mentioning the refusal in the ending. End the letter on a positive note.

CREDIT REFUSALS

Some authorities maintain that every single business letter is a sales letter. No matter what the stated proposal of a letter, the writer must also try to sell the reader on the organization.

Denying a person credit while keeping that person's business is a challenge to the writer of credit refusals.

When you write a refusal of credit, you face a real challenge. Although you are denying a request, you should take a positive approach and try to retain the goodwill of the reader. Many people today regard credit as a right that cannot be denied them. This attitude complicates the task facing the writer.

Many writers seem to ignore the challenge of a letter of refusal. Writers who believe that you cannot deny credit and at the same time keep a friend write uninspired letters, such as this:

> Thank you for applying for a charge account at Wilson's Department Store. We regret to state that we are unable to extend credit to you at this time.
>
> We appreciate your patronage.

A credit refusal like this suggests that the company has little hope of retaining the applicant's business. The letter is cold and impersonal. The writer presents the obvious message but pays no heed to the applicant's feelings or continued patronage. The person who receives such a letter is likely to become frustrated and angry.

By changing the thrust of the letter, the writer may be able to turn a negative situation into a more positive one. The applicant might be persuaded to become a cash customer. Another department store stressed in its refusal letter the advantages of shopping there:

When denying credit, the writer might strive to sell the reader on becoming a cash customer.

> Thank you for your recent application for a charge account at Astor Brothers.
>
> Much information is considered before opening a new charge account, and your application was carefully evaluated. Once you are employed on a full-time basis, it may be possible for you to receive an Astor Brothers credit card.
>
> Until that time please allow us to serve you on a cash basis. As our fall fashions are about to arrive, you may also enjoy our convenient layaway plan.

Of the many possible reasons for refusing a request for credit, a poor credit record is number one. Other common reasons may be that the applicant has too small or unsteady an income or, perhaps, no credit experience upon which to base a decision.

Whether the credit applicant is an individual consumer or a business organization, the letter of refusal is organized in the same way. In either case the writer will probably refer to the advantages of paying cash or making cash-on-delivery purchases. The writer should follow the four steps for transmitting unpleasant news. The letter to the organizational applicant may be somewhat more forthright. A letter that refuses credit to a business follows the usual pattern of neutral comment, explanation, refusal, and positive ending. In Figure 7.3 the writer incorporates a bid for cash business in the ending.

The writer follows the same steps whether rejecting credit to an organization or an individual.

Those who seek credit cannot be expected to be pleased when their applications are rejected. Many people think a rejection of credit is a rejection of personal worth. Refusing credit is a delicate matter meriting thoughtful consideration. Writers often err by emphasizing the refusal rather than developing a cash customer. By de-emphasizing the refusal and stressing the advantages of cash payment, a writer can often retain customers who might otherwise be lost.

The refusal should be de-emphasized.

Beyond this, a person who is refused credit has a legal right to know the reason for the refusal. If it is based on information provided by a credit-reporting agency, the writer should say so. Although the writer is not required to give the specific reasons in the refusal letter, according to the Fair Credit Reporting Act, customers are entitled to an explanation if they request one within 60 days of receiving the credit refusal. In order to avoid having to write an additional letter of explanation to rejected credit applicants, many organizations include the reasons in the initial credit refusal letter. Some organizations use forms such as the one in Figure 7.4 for refusing credit applications.

Sometimes the volume of credit applications is so great that they cannot be handled individually. Using a refusal form serves a useful purpose in that the reader receives the necessary information more promptly than might otherwise be the case.

Figure 7.3
Credit Refusal to a Business

NATIONAL HARDWARE SUPPLY 4000 Industrial Parkway Tell City, IN 47586

February 28, 1997

Mr. Paul Friendly
Friendly Hardware
1002 S. Adams Street
Letts, IA 52754

Dear Mr. Friendly:

Thank you for your order for four dozen Evenflow seed and fertilizer spreaders. Your large order suggests that you are expecting a profitable spring.
We are glad to hear that.

Your credit references unanimously agree that you are a person of integrity
and sound business principles. At this time the information about your hardware operation, however, is somewhat less positive. It is obvious that the
competition for hardware customers is indeed intense, and this always has an
adverse impact on one's financial position. Current economic conditions
lend additional uncertainty to the general business environment.

The upturn in the economy that is expected this spring will most likely
improve your position considerably. For the present, however, we'll be
pleased to continue serving you on a cash basis. You, in turn, will continue to
receive a 2 percent discount for cash purchases. Another advantage of cash
payment is that orders may be of any size; no minimum order is required.

By reducing your present order by as much as one-half, you will still have
adequate stock to meet the early spring demand.

Please send us your instructions on the enclosed order form. Your shipment
will be sent as soon as we hear from you.

Sincerely,

Rankin Jones
Rankin Jones
Credit Analyst

na

Enc.

*Introduces the subject
objectively.*

*Simultaneously presents a
positive personal profile of the
customer and a rationale for
the decision.*

*Points out positive aspects of
the refusal.*

*Ends on a positive note and
requests specific action.*

Figure 7.4

Example of Credit Refusal Form

Date _____ 19 _____
☐ Statement handed to Applicant
☐ Mailed
by: _____
Authorized Signature
Telephone: 546-1866

We would like to thank you for your recent loan application. We have given it careful consideration. However, we regret to inform you that your application has been denied.

We have provided the reason(s) for our decision in the section below. This notice is given in accordance with the various consumer credit laws and regulations applicable to our bank.

Description of account, transaction, or requested credit: _____
_____

Description of adverse action taken: _____
_____

Reason(s)
☐ Credit application incomplete
☐ Insufficient credit references
☐ Unable to verify credit references

☐ Insufficient income
☐ Excessive obligations
☐ Unable to verify income

☐ No credit file
☐ Insufficient credit file
☐ Delinquent credit obligations

☐ Length of employment
☐ Temporary or irregular employment
☐ Unable to verify employment

☐ Too short a period of residence
☐ Temporary residence
☐ Unable to verify residence

☐ Garnishment, attachment, foreclosure, repossession, or suit
☐ Bankruptcy
☐ Inadequate collateral

☐ We do not grant credit to anyone on the terms and conditions you request

☐ Other-(specify) _____

DISCLOSURE OF USE OF INFORMATION OBTAINED FROM AN OUTSIDE SOURCE
☐ Disclosure Inapplicable   ☐ Information obtained in a consumer report from: Credit Bureau of Athens, 400 College Avenue, Athens, Georgia 30601.
☐ Information obtained from an outside source other than a consumer reporting agency. Under the Fair Credit Reporting Act, you have the right to make a written request within 60 days of receipt of this notice, for a disclosure of the nature of the adverse information.

The Federal Equal Credit Opportunity Act prohibits creditors from discrimination against credit applicants on the basis of race, color, religion, national origin, sex, marital status, age (provided the applicant has the capacity to enter into a binding contract), because all or part of the applicant's income derives from any public assistance program or because the applicant has in good faith exercised any right under the Consumer Credit Protection Act. The Federal Agency that administers compliance with this law concerning this creditor is

COMPTROLLER OF THE CURRENCY   CONSUMER AFFAIRS DIVISION   WASHINGTON, D.C. 20219

PROBLEM ORDERS

The success of any business organization depends to a considerable extent on the speed with which the organization can satisfy its customers. The term **turnaround time** is often used to describe how long it takes for business firms to provide customers with their goods and services.

Even the most efficient organization sometimes experiences delays in handling orders. Regardless of who is responsible for the delay, it often calls for a letter in which the writer must convey information likely to displease a customer.

Items Not in Stock

When an item is temporarily out of stock but will be available soon you should so inform the customer. Because the customer will experience a delay, you will be transmitting bad news. At the same time you want to retain the customer's business. Here is an example of a letter of refusal that suffers from misplaced focus:

> Thank you for your order of April 7. Unfortunately, we are presently unable to fill your order for one Classic circulating fan.
>
> We pride ourselves on our speed in filling orders, and we usually order in ample quantities. Skyrocketing energy costs combined with customer recognition of a genuine bargain may help explain why customer demand has outdistanced our supply.
>
> We're working hard to remedy the situation, however, and by May 15 you should be enjoying the economy and comfort that accompany a Classic circulating fan. If, due to the delay, you wish to cancel this order, please notify us promptly. We hope you won't do that, however, since we know you'll agree that a Classic circulating fan is worth waiting for.

This letter is ineffective for several reasons. The first paragraph shows no attempt to indicate an area of agreement between writer and reader. The writer presented the bad news immediately, so it is unlikely that the disappointed reader will finish the letter. When notifying a customer of a delay in an order, you should focus on the order rather than on the delay. The example focuses on the delay in the first paragraph.

Knowing that the company takes pride in filling orders quickly provides little consolation for the customer who is not benefiting from this speed. If anything, the customer will be skeptical of an organization that boasts at such an inopportune time. The second paragraph, therefore, serves no useful purpose.

The third paragraph states that the situation will be remedied soon and reminds the reader of the product's superiority. This statement is completely appropriate. Suggesting that the order could be canceled, on the other hand, is not in the company's best interests. The customer may choose to cancel the order, but the writer need not suggest it. The request that the customer not cancel is weak and unnecessary. By ending the letter with a reminder of the delay, the writer incorrectly makes it the parting thought.

A letter that informs a reader that an order will be delayed has two main purposes: (1) to convince the reader to wait for the order and (2) to retain the reader's business in the future. These purposes are accomplished better in this way:

> Your order for a Classic circulating fan identifies you as a person who recognizes both quality and value.
>
> A growing volume of orders for the Classic indicates that the public has also become aware of the superiority of the Classic. Production is increasing, but the quality you associate with the Classic is being maintained.
>
> You will be enjoying the comfort and economy of a Classic circulating fan by May 15, well before the onset of hot weather. The Classic will make the heat and humidity of summer disappear in a breeze.

When Bob Costner learned that his fraternity would be unable to fill many of the orders for pecans, as described earlier in this chapter, he wrote this letter:

> Dear Patron:
> Do you realize how many friends you have? It was only after the TZ fraternity house was swamped with orders for pecans that we realized the number of our friends.
>
> In each of the past five years our pecan sales have increased by approximately 10 percent. For that reason we felt comfortable in increasing our total order by 10 percent this year. We intended to keep our order realistic so that we would not have to pay for shipping any unsold pecans back to the wholesaler. Such shipping expenses would eat into the amount earned for the Family Shelter, this year's project. We are still wondering if

A letter of refusal should not end with a reminder of the bad news.

it was the quality of the pecans, the fair price, or the importance of the Family Shelter that caused the avalanche of orders. Whatever the reason, we received orders for 300 percent more pecans than last year.

As we have always done with this project, the orders were filled in the sequence in which they were received. Each of the other patrons is receiving this letter.

This has been a learning experience for us. When you place your order with us next year, we plan to have enough fresh pecans on hand to fill it.

Sincerely,

Discontinued Items

In the best of all possible business worlds, as soon as a company stopped handling a certain item, all orders for that item would cease immediately. What actually happens is that orders continue to trickle in for the item long after its discontinuation.

In response to an order for a discontinued item, you must inform the customer of the discontinuation while offering an appropriate substitute. Do not, however, offer a substitute that is not clearly appropriate. It is better to lose one sale and to retain the goodwill of a customer than to provide a substitute with which the customer will be displeased.

The writer should offer an appropriate substitute, if possible, for a discontinued item.

When a retailer ordered some T-450 tapes from a wholesaler who had stopped carrying the T-450, the wholesaler offered an appropriate substitute.

Thank you for your order of March 17. Your customers apparently associate high quality with the Superchron name as do most people who take pride in their video investment.

As a result of its ongoing research program, Superchron has now developed a videotape that is significantly superior to anything formerly available. This new product offers 30 percent higher picture quality and 50 percent longer life than does the T-450. By refining high-energy tape particles, Superchron has created the T-900, a tape that is mirror smooth and which provides perfect pictures for replay after replay. Although you may be able to order some T-450 tapes directly from the Superchron Company, your customers will prefer the T-900 once they learn of it.

Your customers will agree that the T-900 is worth an additional $1.50 for a 60-minute cassette. Call me at (601) 592-1313 any weekday between 9 and 5. I'll fill your order that same day at a price of $15.25 per tape on orders of one dozen or more.

The savings your customers will enjoy through the longer life of the T-900 will make them glad you acquainted them with the T-900.

Too Small an Order

Many different types of misunderstandings may occur in the process of placing and filling orders. One instance happens when a customer places an order for a quantity too small to merit the discount expected by the customer.

In order to stimulate sales, the Green-Gro Company offered a 5 percent discount on purchases of 100 or more 50-pound bags of lawn fertilizer. When a retailer requested the 5 percent discount on an order of only 50 bags, the wholesaler responded this way:

This year marks the 12th year you have purchased your supply of Green-Gro products from us. The growth of your orders over these years suggests that your customers enjoy dealing with you as much as we do. Your adherence to sound business practices in placing orders, making prompt payment, and customer follow-up have been appreciated.

For the first time ever, the Green-Gro Company has offered a special 5 percent discount on its lawn fertilizer, and we are passing this discount on to our customers. The one stipulation made by the Green-Gro Company is that orders must be for at least 100 50-pound bags in order to get the special discount.

> ### ✔ *CHECKLIST for a Problem Order*
>
> ____ Begin with a noncommittal statement to which the reader is likely to respond positively.
>
> ____ Present the reasons for the decision.
>
> ____ If possible, show how the reader would benefit from the decision.
>
> ____ Present the refusal without belaboring it.
>
> ____ Avoid additional references to the refusal and point to future business in the closing.

By increasing your order to 100 bags, you will be ready for the upcoming seasonal rush and you will qualify for the special discount. Regardless of the size of your order, you will still receive our regular terms of 2/10, n/30.

You will be receiving our new catalog within three weeks. It features several new garden products that your customers will soon be seeking.

Many problems in ordering can be resolved face to face or over the telephone. When a letter is necessary, however, remember to use the indirect arrangement.

FAVOR REFUSALS

When refusing or modifying problem orders, the writer should use the indirect arrangement.

Business organizations routinely receive requests for favors of various types. Some of the favors may be business-related, such as a special discount or preferential treatment for a particular order. Other favors may be sought by complete strangers. Charities may seek contributions. Students may write for information for research papers. A list of the types of favors sought from business organizations would be endless.

It is easy to write a letter granting a favor—that's good news! Denying a favor is somewhat more difficult, but it is best accomplished through a carefully considered letter of refusal. If it is possible to offer a counterproposal, the writer will soften the refusal.

A counterproposal will soften the impact when a request for a favor is refused.

One of the authors of this book asked several business organizations to provide some actual letters to serve as examples in this book. Although Delta Air Lines would not grant the request, it made a generous and attractive counterproposal. The letter in Figure 7.5 follows the four steps: neutral comment, explanation, refusal (with a counterproposal), and a positive ending.

Sometimes you receive a request that you are unable, or do not choose, to honor, and no counterproposal is possible. Nevertheless, you should follow the four steps. Try to convey the refusal clearly while retaining the reader's goodwill. This is how one corporation responded when solicited for a financial contribution:

> You and the other members of the Committee to Preserve the Strand should be commended for your efforts to have the theater designated as a historic site. The lives of future generations will be enriched through the success of such projects.
>
> We at the regional headquarters of Turflo are impressed with the large number of worthwhile projects such as yours. Several times each week we receive requests for financial support, and invariably the causes are worthy ones. Determining the worthiest recipients is a task precluded by our own time constraints.
>
> One way in which we try to meet our social responsibility is through our financial support of three major health-oriented organizations and the United Way. By targeting our contributions in this way we balance our support between social action goals and quality of life improvement.
>
> Your efforts to preserve a genuine landmark deserve widespread support. Best wishes on this project.

WRITING THE LETTER OF COMPLAINT

While the primary focus of this chapter is on how to turn down the requests or applications of others, the role of the complainant should not be ignored. Everyone, at some time, will feel that he or she has a legitimate complaint, and knowing the special impact of a personal letter, should write one.

Figure 7.5
Letter Offering a Counterproposal to a Request
Source: Courtesy Delta Air Lines

 DELTA AIR LINES, INC.
GENERAL OFFICES/HARTSFIELD ATLANTA INTERNATIONAL AIRPORT/ATLANTA, GEORGIA 30320 U.S.A.

September 5, 1987

Mr. James M. Lahiff
Associate Professor
Department of Management
College of Business Administration
University of Georgia
Athens, Georgia 30602

Dear Mr. Lahiff:

This is just the helpful sort of reply to your good letter (of August 30th)
that you imagined you'd receive. College students are likely correct in
their complaints that classrooms are "far-removed" from the real world. And
too many of us "out here" in the private sector must share the blame.

Unfortunately, Delta's correspondence must be considered as confidential
between the company and those to whom we address letters. So, we can't
"lift" from our files, forwarding copies of actual letters. However, we
might be able to draft several "sample-type" examples, if you'd give us some
subject ideas, and if you agree that such samples would suffice.

I have a special place in my heart for the University and its excellent
College of Business Administration. My late son, Lane, graduated from your
college, magna cum laude, in 1975. He thought very highly of Georgia and
its faculty.

You see, Professor, because of your nice comments about Delta and my special
affiliation with you all, I can't let you down! Let's hear from you soon
and we'll supply your sample business letters.

Thank you so much for your interest in Delta, and with best wishes, I am

                    Sincerely,

                    James L. Ewing, III
                    Staff Director-National Media Relations

JLE/dw

A major reason that consumer activism has become such a potent force in society is
that consumers have more options than ever before. Recognizing the many choices that
are now available to their customers, and knowing that it is at least as important to keep
the present customers as it is to attract new ones, business organizations are growing ever
more receptive to the wishes of the customers. Not only do businesses proclaim that the
customer is always right, they demonstrate their acceptance of the idea by paying close
attention to customer complaints. In short, well-written letters of complaint get results.

A well-written letter of complaint gets to the point quickly. Since people whose job involves handling complaints are usually overworked, they do not appreciate rambling letters. State the most relevant details and indicate what you expect to be done to correct the situation. Include such information as the date and place of purchase, serial number of the product, and what went wrong. Avoid making threatening or belittling remarks. Such conduct will not motivate the reader to be helpful. A well-organized letter of complaint that is presented in a reasonable manner is likely to elicit the desired action.

The U.S. Office of Consumer Affairs included the sample letter of complaint, shown in Figure 7.6, for guidance in its most recent *Consumer's Resource Handbook*.[1]

Figure 7.6
Sample Complaint Letter

(Your Address)
(Your City, State, ZIP Code)
(Date)

(Name of Contact Person, if available)
(Title, if available)
(Company Name)
(Consumer Complaint Division, if you have no contact person)
(Street Address)
(City, State, ZIP Code)

Dear (Contact Person):

Re: (account number, if applicable)

On (date), I (bought, leased, rented, or had repaired) a (name of the product with serial or model number or service performed) at (location, date and other important details of the transaction). — *Describe purchase / Name of product, serial numbers / Include date and place of purchase*

Unfortunately, your product (or service) has not performed well (or the service was inadequate) because (state the problem). I am disappointed because (explain the problem: for example, the product does not work properly, the service was not performed correctly, I was billed the wrong amount, something was not disclosed clearly or was misrepresented, etc.). — *State problem / Give history*

To resolve the problem, I would appreciate your (state the specific action you want—money back, charge card credit, repair, exchange, etc.). Enclosed are copies (do not send originals) of my records (include receipts, guarantees, warranties, canceled checks, contracts, model and serial numbers, and any other documents). — *Ask for specific action / Enclose copies of documents*

I look forward to your reply and a resolution to my problem, and will wait until (set a time limit) before seeking help from a consumer protection agency or the Better Business Bureau. Please contact me at the above address or by phone at (home and/or office numbers with area codes). — *Allow time for action / State how you can be reached*

Sincerely,

(your name)

Enclosure(s)
cc: (reference to whom you are sending a copy of this letter, if anyone) — *Keep copies of your letter and all related documents*

✔ *CHECKLIST for a Letter of Complaint*

_____ Keep the letter short.

_____ Clearly state what you want done.

_____ Control anger and belligerence.

_____ Write in short paragraphs.

_____ Include all relevant details.

_____ Save a copy of the letter you send.

_____ Include copies, not originals, of all relevant documents.

_____ Include details on how you can be reached
(e.g., telephone numbers for work and home).

RETRACTING AGREEMENTS

Situations sometimes arise that require a writer to cancel or retract a decision already accepted by both parties. The retraction may be necessitated by the unexpected action of a third party, and an apology to the injured party is often appropriate. A well-written letter of apology, however, does not belabor the apology, but seeks to maintain a relationship by ending on a positive note.

Consider the problem confronted by Jack Smith, General Manager of the Metropolitan Congress Center (MCC), when the state legislature decided not to fund the expansion of the huge convention center. In anticipation of doubling the size of the MCC, Jack had begun approaching various large associations before all of the details for the planned expansion had been finalized, and he successfully persuaded eight large groups to schedule national meetings at the expanded MCC four years from now. (It is customary for large bodies to schedule gatherings years ahead of time.)

How would you break this unpleasant news to the Executive Directors of the eight associations, each of which had approximately 10,000 members? It wasn't until Jack had written the fourth version of the letter that he was satisfied. Here are all four versions, with marginal notes identifying problems with the first three. Each of the four versions was addressed to the Executive Director by name and signed by Jack Smith, MCC General Manager.

The first three letters include a variety of mistakes. The fourth version is informative, persuasive, and apologetic. Of the four versions, it alone is likely to leave the reader with a favorable impression of Jack and of the MCC.

Version 1

The Metropolitan Congress Center planned to begin an expansion of 320,000 square feet this year, but recently the state did not approve funds for this expansion. In order to provide the finest convention space possible, we felt that this expansion was necessary and imminent, and we booked your conference under the assumption that the expansion would be completed.

Blaming the state for MCC's current dilemma.

We requested $69.4 million from the state's supplemental budget, but this budget was allocated to other projects such as highway development, children's aid programs, teacher benefits, and prison improvements. The state should maintain a high quality of life for its citizens, and these programs will meet some previously unaddressed needs in local communities. We certainly do have children to protect and potholes to fill! While all of these projects may be worthy recipients of state funds, we wish that some of the discretionary funds could have been reserved for the MCC.

Unnecessary editorializing.

Due to the denial of additional state monies, we will be unable to expand the Metropolitan Congress Center at this time. We will reapply for funding next year and, if other state projects are not so pressing, we will hopefully be able to serve your conference needs.

Does not directly address the booking error. Provides no solution to the problem.

Version 2

We are pleased that you chose to book your convention at the Metropolitan Congress Center. MCC was scheduled to begin a sizable expansion later this year, but recently we were denied state funding, so we regret to inform you that this expanded space will not be available for your scheduled event. However, we firmly believe that Atlanta is a tremendous city for conventions, with a growing number of intellectual and recreational opportunities.

De-emphasizing the "real" message of the letter by hiding it in middle of paragraph.

Atlanta is a wonderful place to visit or to live. It has a thriving business district, bountiful shopping opportunities, engaging museums, and beautiful parks. Atlanta's growing urban center provides the southeast with a cosmopolitan area rivaling northeastern cities, but with a much more pleasant climate. The weather is particularly beautiful in spring and autumn, with average temperatures ranging between 50 and 80 degrees Fahrenheit. It rarely snows in winter, and this appealing climate attracts visitors from around the United States and beyond.

Irrelevant information.

Although we will not be able to accommodate your needs for the previously scheduled convention, we hope that you will consider Atlanta as a site for future events. The Peachtree City has so much to offer!

Inappropriate conclusion.

Version 3

We regret to inform you that the Metropolitan Congress Center will not be able to complete its scheduled expansion due to a denial of state funding. We had intended to utilize the 320,000-square-foot expansion well before your scheduled meeting. A monumental mistake was made when we booked your convention under the assumption that the space would be complete. We fully expected to receive the necessary $69.4 million from the state's supplemental budget. We are extremely sorry to let you know that we will be unable to host a convention of your organization's size, given our current space limitations.

Belabored explanation of the "mistake."

Unfortunately, when we attempted to gain additional funding from other sources, we were unsuccessful. Again we apologize for our inadequate convention center accommodations, and we regret any rescheduling inconvenience we may have caused your organization.

Overly apologetic tone.

Version 4

In January, the Metropolitan Congress Center applied for $69.4 million of state funding to complete a 320,000-square-foot expansion project, and recently this request was denied. Due to the long-term planning perspective of convention centers, we have been scheduling conventions for four years from now under the assumption that the MCC expansion would be completed by that time. Unfortunately, without the necessary state funding, we will be unable to meet this goal.

Factual and informative.

We regret to inform you that we will be unable to accommodate the convention which you previously booked at the MCC, and we apologize for any inconvenience this may cause you.

Apologetic.

By whatever means, we feel confident that the expansion will be funded soon. After the planned expansion, the Metropolitan Congress Center will be the second largest convention space in North America, and the thriving Atlanta business community welcomes visiting organizations with real Southern hospitality! Therefore, we would like to suggest that you keep the MCC in mind when planning future conferences.

Persuasive.

Key Terms
- **bad-news letter**
- **turnaround time**

Exercises

1. **A Hair-brained Idea.** You are the programming director for York Cable Access Television, the local network and cable provider. On Channel 4, you schedule half-hour slots with area talent, and you have been extremely successful finding quality programming for afternoons and evenings.

   One of your original programs was a hair-styling segment produced by Craig's Hair Designs. In this show, Craig's stylists would demonstrate the latest looks, as well as provide enlightening information about manicures, tanning, and electrolysis. The show no longer has a large audience. You would like to fill this slot with a more popular topic and your supervisor has suggested doing a show about car maintenance.

   Your mission is to write to Craig Devins, 7865 Mount Rose Blvd., York, PA 17659, and inform him that "Craig's Hair Design Showcase" will be discontinued as of next month. Explain to him that the viewers are not responding to this show, and perhaps he should look into a different advertising venue.

2. **Par for the Course.** As the Assistant Manager of Fair Oaks Golf Club, one of your responsibilities is to review new applications for membership, determine if the applicants are eligible, and assign them to a position on the waiting list. Fair Oaks' waiting list has been growing at a phenomenal rate, and your boss has just informed you that you should not add any prospective applicants to the list for at least the next six months. You feel that it is unfortunate to turn away interested parties, but you recognize that the golf course is packed virtually every day, and perhaps people should feel free to join another competing country club.

   Your mission is is to write a form letter that you will send as a reply to prospective applicants. Let them know that you are not accepting applications at this time and the waiting list is also filled to capacity. Encourage them to check back with you next year if they are still interested in applying for membership.

3. **Two Artists, One Job.** You are Director of Human Resources for a small ad agency specializing in hospital and health care advertising campaigns. You have been seeking a new graphic artist, and you narrowed the search to two highly qualified candidates. Both individuals participated in extensive interviews and submitted excellent portfolios, and you wish that your agency had the funds to hire both candidates. At this time, however, you need only one new designer, and you must inform Sarah Cooke that you are unable to offer her a position.

Your mission is to write a tactful rejection letter to Ms. Cooke. You could have sent her the standard rejection letter you developed for other, less-qualified job applicants, but since Ms. Cooke impressed you highly, you decide to write a personalized response to her. Explain your agency's budget constraints and try to avoid the clichés that often appear in rejection letters. Address this letter to: Sarah Cooke, 91 Sea View Lane, Portland, OR 87650.

4. **Convenient Recycling.** As the Coordinator of Sanitation Engineering for Clarkville City Government, you organize trash pick-up for all city residents. You have received numerous letters from people who would like to implement a curbside pick-up recycling program for plastics and glass. Currently, the city provides curbside pick-up for only newspapers and aluminum, and Clarkville residents must take their glass and plastics to a recycling center located ten miles west of the city. You understand that few people are willing to drive so far in order to recycle these items.

You have conducted a budgetary analysis study and determined that it is not feasible for the city to take on additional recycling responsibilities this year. You anticipate an expanded curbside service within the next three years, but it will be contingent on the funds being available. The city needs to make recycling a higher priority before the expanded service will become a reality.

Your mission is to respond to the stack of letters you have accumulated from people who are asking for curbside glass and/or plastic recycling. You feel that the most efficient way to respond to these citizens is by writing a detailed, concise form letter in which you explain the need for expanded curbside services, but you are currently unable to provide these services. Include enough relevant data to make a convincing argument, and be sure to thank these people for their suggestions.

5. **Running on Empty.** Four months ago, you purchased a pair of Evion running shoes from Flying Feet in the Carolina Square Mall. This brand of shoes is new on the market, but they seem remarkably similar to the Nike shoes that you typically use, and since the Evions were on a special promotional sale, you thought you would try them out.

You run five miles every other day and normally your running shoes last almost a year. This pair, however, has worn out very quickly; the shoes have lost most of their traction and the soles are becoming unglued. You feel that, in the course of daily wear, these shoes should last at least six to eight months, and you want to inform the company that you do not think their product is comparable with other shoes on the market.

Your mission is to compose a letter to the Customer Service Department, Evion Inc., 2941 Airport Parkway, Seattle, WA 86755. Explain your situation and let the company know that perhaps they should implement a more rigorous program of quality testing, in order to produce a more durable shoe. Suggest some ways in which they could improve their product.

6. **Soup Is Good Food.** As a marketing executive for Healthy Alternative Foods Inc., you are excited about introducing a new line of soups for your label. The soups are being manufactured by Hanover Foods and then sold to you for distribution. All of the Healthy Alternative products guarantee low sodium, low cholesterol, and low fat content, and you want to maintain your current reputation as an innovative provider of good-for-you foods. This week you received initial samples of vegetable soup and black bean soup from the Hanover Foods factory. You were informed by your in-house research and development lab that due to

high fat and cholesterol content, these two soups did not meet Healthy Alternative's healthy standards. You thought that your Hanover contact had understood that the soups must meet certain requirements, and you want to inform him as soon as possible that some recipe revisions will have to be made.

Your mission is to write a letter to Bill Haversham, Soup Production Manager, Hanover Foods, 78 James Road, Hanover, ME 01348. Remind Mr. Haversham that Healthy Alternative Foods has standards to maintain, and suggest that he respond quickly to your concerns that Hanover is not producing a product that Healthy Alternative Foods can market. Stress that you want to work together to create the tastiest, most healthful soup for the public.

7. **Rising Parking Rates.** As the Vice President of Finance of AmeriPark, a chain of parking garages in northwest Washington DC, you are responsible for forecasting corporate revenues for the upcoming fiscal year. You realize that your firm is not operating at a profitable level, due to increased utilities and taxes in the District. In response to higher costs, you would like to raise parking rates, particularly the monthly parking rates, which are primarily used by people who work in nearby office buildings. Six months ago, you raised the monthly rate to $100, and now you are upping the rate to $120.

Your mission is to write a standardized letter to your many monthly customers informing them of the rate increase. State that rising costs necessitate this increase, but you will attempt to keep rates at the new level for at least one calendar year.

8. **Bug Off!** Recently you moved into an apartment complex in the suburbs of Richmond, VA, and you are experiencing a horrible problem with cockroaches in your kitchen and bathroom. Although you are an extremely clean person, you feel that your neighbors must be attracting the roaches, or perhaps the roaches have completely infested the building and are living in every wall. You have asked the maintenance crew to fumigate your apartment twice, but you have not noticed any improvement. You really like the location and layout of the apartment and you don't want to terminate your lease, but you feel that something must be done to eliminate these pests.

Your mission is to draft a letter that you will send to the management company representing your apartment complex. Let them know that you attempted to deal with this cockroach problem through your on-site maintenance crew, and you have not achieved adequate results. You feel that the pesticide they were using was simply not strong enough or extensive enough to reach all of the roaches living in your building. In your letter, insist that something more drastic be done to alleviate the problem, or else you will take legal action. Address this letter to: Ms. Jane Brodinger, Grady Management Corporation, 5400 Paul Blvd., Richmond, VA 23530.

9. **Made to Order.** You are chair and sofa salesperson for "Your Way," a special-order furniture company that prides itself on the variety of styles and patterns available. Last week a customer named Bob Greenwood requested a sofa-bed to be covered with an off-beat iridescent material. Today the manufacturer has informed you that this fabric was discontinued because virtually no one had ordered it.

Your mission is to write a letter to Mr. Greenwood (87 James Avenue, Hightown, ND 67950) to let him know that the sofa he ordered is not available in the material he preferred. Suggest a few alternatives that might please him, and ask him to contact you as soon as possible to revise his order.

10. **Clearing the Air.** As a part of your duties as an inspector for the state Department of Environmental Safety, you visit industrial sites to determine if

the levels of smokestack pollution are within the state's minimum requirements. Earlier this morning, you analyzed samples from the Oslo, Oklahoma, plant of Intercontinental Paper Inc., and you have found their air pollution to exceed allowable levels. Historically this plant has met all of its safety requirements and you believe that a malfunctioning filter may be causing the excess pollution.

Your mission is to draft a letter to Tim Simonson, Plant Manager of Intercontinental Paper Inc., to inform him of your findings and give him the opportunity to correct the problem by next week. Let him know that you will be testing again on the following Friday and suggest that he examine the plant's filter system because you suspect it is the source of the problem.

11. **Fowl Play.** While taking a walk through your neighborhood yesterday afternoon, you noticed that one of your neighbors has built a chicken coop in his front yard and has four chickens in it. You serve on the Residents' Committee for your subdevelopment and you know that keeping livestock is a violation of your neighborhood's Standards Code. You contacted the Committee president, Martha Grimes, and she suggested that you inform this neighbor that he is not permitted to keep the chicken coop according to the rules of the subdevelopment.

Your mission is to write a letter to Russell Anderson at 501 Briarcliff Road, West Coconut Beach, FL 39055. Be as diplomatic and cordial as possible, so that Mr. Anderson does not feel defensive, since he may not have been aware of the Standards Code rule prohibiting chickens and other livestock in your neighborhood.

12. **Quality Clothes.** You are the Marketing Director for Boston Cotton Company, a manufacturer of fine cotton casual clothes. Your company has experienced healthy sales in its 35 retail stores, but you have observed a steady decline in catalog sales. At a meeting of top executives, a decision was reached to discontinue mail-order operations and focus entirely on generating profits through the retail outlets.

Your mission is to compose a form letter that you will send to every customer on your catalog mailing list. In this letter, explain that the mail-order division has been phased out and you regret any inconvenience that this may cause your loyal customers. Mention that you are including a complete list of all retail locations and you hope that these stores can now provide your customers with Boston Cotton's quality clothing.

13. **Breaking the News.** As the Director of Admissions for San Diego School of Art, you also have the responsibility of choosing the recipients of full scholarships to be provided by the school's endowment. This year you considered the top 20 applicants for the five endowment scholarships, and you have already informed the five scholarship winners by telephone.

Your mission is to write a letter to send to the fifteen people who did not receive the scholarship this year. Inform them that they were among the best applicants of this school year, and encourage them to apply for other scholarships and grant monies.

14. **Take Care of Your Health.** You are a Statewide Insurance agent, and your national headquarters has recently instituted a policy of routine blood testing for new applicants for health insurance. The corporation would also like all currently insured parties to undergo these tests to update and standardize their records. You have approximately 250 people to whom you have provided health insurance since you began working for the company, and you would like to urge them to make an appointment with your office to have this brief but necessary testing done.

Your mission is to write a standardized letter to be mailed to all insured parties informing them of the new statewide health care policy. Suggest that the clients contact your assistant, Jan Brody, to set up an appointment for the testing some time in the next two months.

15. **Bad Credit.** As a Customer Service Representative for National Trust Bank, you review people's requests for credit cards and credit line increases. You evaluate their past credit histories to determine what credit level they are eligible for and you make recommendations to your supervisor. You already have standardized letters that you send to approve or deny credit cards, as well as to approve credit line increases, but you must write a personalized letter to each customer when you do not approve a credit extension. Management feels that this personal touch will maintain good customer relations, even though you are delivering "bad news."

    Your mission is to write a letter to Maria Jones, 6478 Twin Oaks Blvd., St. Louis, MO 45677. Inform her that she will maintain her current credit limit of $2500 and let her know that her credit history did not allow you to extend her line of credit at this time. Encourage her to make her minimum payments and explain that she may reapply for the extension in eighteen to twenty-four months.

16. **No Gain, Too Much Pain.** One month ago, you purchased a High Climber exercise machine, which is modeled after the best-selling Stairmaster. You began working out for twenty minutes a day on the new machine and, within three days, you started to experience excruciating pains in your lower back and on the backs of your thighs. For a few years, you have been using the Stairmasters at your local fitness center, and you have never felt such pains as a result of this kind of exercise. You have determined that the High Climber is not properly designed for your use because the pedals are tilted backward and you cannot balance your weight correctly on the machine.

    Your mission is to write to the Consumer Services Division of High Climber Inc. to complain about your physical discomfort. Explain that you have been using stair-climbing machines for years and you believe their product to be very inferior. You recognize that the product was not guaranteed, but you are going to attempt to return it and you want to let the company know that you are an extremely dissatisfied customer.

17. **Hitting the Books.** For extra money, you have been working as an instructor of an SAT study course that meets on Saturday mornings. The course is sponsored by Scholastic Partners Inc., and they employ college students like yourself to prepare high school students living in the area for the upcoming SAT exams. You have been teaching the course for over a year, but due to your increased course load and extracurricular activities, you will be unable to continue working for Scholastic Partners.

    Your mission is to write a letter to James Antony, President of Human Resources, Scholastic Partners Inc., 6590 North Lakeshore Drive, Chicago, IL 45093. Explain your situation and tell him that you will finish teaching the current five-week course, but that after this session, you will no longer be able to teach the course.

18. **. . . Keeps on Ticking.** As the Customer Relations Director for Timella, a small, high-quality wristwatch manufacturer, you respond to customers' complaints and suggestions, as well as handle any watches returned for repairs or replacement. For the past three decades, your company has advertised that all of its products have a lifetime warranty, and since you took this position six years ago, your company has replaced or fixed every watch that has been sent to your department. You recently received a watch that was made when the company was first established in the late 1940s, and you know that you will not be able to fix this watch because the parts are no longer available.

Your mission is to write a letter to the woman who sent back this watch for repairs. Explain to her that Timella has been able to fix or replace every watch manufactured in the past thirty years, but since this watch was made before 1960, the company cannot repair it. Offer to send a brand new watch to replace this one if she wants to accept it in return for her "antique" watch.

19. **Ode to Billy Joe.** You are reservations manager for the Extravagancia, a 900-room oceanfront hotel in Florida. The Extravagancia has an annual occupancy rate of 88 percent, and it is strongly oriented toward families. In fact, 90 percent of its guests bring at least one child with them. In recent years there has been a growing influx of college students who spend their spring break at the Extravagancia. In several instances boisterous college students have upset some of the more sedate guests.

    Your mission is to discourage the college trade, but you realize that today's undesirable college students will be tomorrow's desirable customers. For that reason you do not want to alienate the students when you decline to allow them to stay at the Extravagancia. Today you received the season's first request for a reservation from a college student. Send your response to Billy Joe Harrison, 120 Finnegan Hall, Central State University, Eclipse, VA 23349.

20. **The Impossible Dream.** You have just received a request from the seniors at Martin High School to allow them to conduct a sales campaign among the employees and on the premises of Rampart Insurance Company. The proceeds will be donated to a nearby children's hospital. Company policy prohibits such soliciting, and the firm's liability insurance policy would not cover solicitors.

    Your mission is to write a letter of refusal to Robert Hocking, president of the senior class, Martin High School, Beaufort, SC 29902. This is the tenth consecutive year you have had to reject their request.

21. **Cutting It Close.** When you received a check from Gilson Hardware Company on November 10, you discovered that Gilson deducted the 2 percent discount that is available only for payment within 10 days of delivery. Gilson received an order of 12 lawn mowers from your company on October 12 and was billed $1,788.00. The check dated November 8 is for $1,752.24. Gilson Hardware has been a good customer for 10 years.

    Your mission is to write a letter to Gilson Hardware Company (1400 Clayton Street, Farley, MO 64028) requesting a check for $35.76, the amount incorrectly deducted from the recent payment.

22. **Preventing a Breakout.** Imagine that you are the manager of Vittles Super Store, a huge ultramodern supermarket that includes a pharmacy, bank, beauty salon, florist, and bakery. The store is located in a college town and you employ 120 part-time employees, almost all of them college students. Last year, the first year of operation, you encountered many personnel problems during the week of spring break. A number of employees who were given the week off did not return when they were scheduled to. Several phoned from out of town to tell you that they were quitting. Some simply did not show up again. About 60 percent fulfilled their obligations completely. You have decided to avoid problems this year by allowing no one to take time off during spring break. It is only 6 weeks from now, and some employees are already asking to be away.

    Your mission is to write a letter to all employees in which you convey your decision.

23. **Trash Talk.** You are the owner of Trash Master Inc., a refuse collection firm that picks up trash from both residential and commercial customers. Trash Master is 15 years old, the oldest such firm in town. Until 3 years ago you had no competitors.

Since then Trash Wiz, a national firm, arrived in the community and has taken 15 percent of your customers. You have resisted raising your rates for the past 3 years but you must now do so. Your own rapidly increasing expenses dictate that rates must be raised by 15 percent. For residential customers the new monthly rate will be $9 for the usual twice-a-week pickups. The rates for commercial customers vary according to the number and size of the pickups. For example, fast-food restaurants will pay $50 per month for daily pickups. There are several differences between Trash Master and Trash Wiz: (1) Trash Master is locally owned and operated. (2) Trash Master offers residential customers two pickups per week while Trash Wiz—which uses containers one-and-one-half times larger than those used by Trash Master—offers a single weekly pickup. (3) Trash Wiz has curbside pickup only, while Trash Master customers need not carry their trash containers down to the street. (4) As a result of the rate increase, Trash Master residential rates will be 20 percent higher than those of Trash Wiz, while the commercial rates of the two will be the same.

Your mission is to (a) write a letter to all of your residential customers, announcing the rate increase while trying to retain their business, and (b) write a letter to your fast-food clients.

24. **What Price Liberty?** Eighteen members of a German tour group of 40 complained individually to Liberty International Inns Inc., about the poor service, dirty rooms, and discourteous treatment they received at a Liberty Inn while visiting the United States. Each one of the 18 writers is requesting a 50 percent refund as a result of the unpleasant experience. The president of Liberty International sent this form letter to each complainant:

Thank you for your letter regarding your recent stay at the Liberty Inn in the Big Apple. We are always happy to hear from our customers and we thank you for letting us serve you.

We think that your complaints might have some merit; however, we can't truly imagine how any of our well-trained employees could make such mistakes. We at Liberty International take pride in the courteous and efficient manner in which we treat our guests. The fact that we do a good job is evident from the 86 percent annual occupancy rate we have enjoyed for the past three years. Incidentally, according to the research of the H.A.A., that is the highest occupancy rate in the entire lodging industry.

When you look at the wide variety of organizations that stay with us on a regular basis, everything from NFL teams to MADD conventions, it's obvious that we must be doing something right. Just last week, for example, our site in the Windy City hosted the national convention of Trekkies.

We hope that you will give us another try because we expect that you will become as satisfied as our regular customers.

Even though we have been unable to verify your complaints, we have decided to give you the benefit of the doubt. It is contrary to our policy to provide refunds for such complaints; however, on your next visit to the United States, please be our guest at any Liberty Inn, absolutely free for two nights.

Thanks again for your letter.

Your mission is to evaluate the form letter and to rewrite it.

25. **A Credit Crunch.** You are a building supply wholesaler. You receive an order from King Hardware for one dozen Vent Lights, a plastic-domed ventilating skylight that wholesales for $185 each. The balance due on the King account is already $1,400, and $2,200 for the Vent Lights will raise the balance over the $3,000 credit limit allowed Ken King, owner of the store.

Your mission is to write to him (225 Main Street, Joplin, MO 64810) and refuse the order because his account must stay below the credit limit, or you might ask that part of the bill be paid in cash. Whatever you do, remember that you want to retain his business.

C A S E

Children Are Customers, Too

David B. Parsons, Lakehead University, Thunder Bay, Ontario, Canada

Jane and Billy Harris, 11-year-old twins, saved up $130 from their paper route to buy their mother a cordless telephone for her birthday. Filled with excitement, they walked down to their local department store to look at its selection of cordless telephones. They decided to buy a white Sanyo model that cost $129.84, including sales tax.

The salesclerk, however, not only refused to wait on them until all of the adults had been served, but he also questioned the ownership of the $130. Blinking back tears, the children told him they had earned the money delivering papers. The clerk then sold them a floor model in an unsealed box.

One week after their mother had opened her present, the telephone's antenna would not extend properly, a problem created by the abuse the telephone had taken while on display. The children decided to return the telephone and ask for a replacement or a refund. The clerk refused to replace the damaged telephone or to refund their money, accusing the children of breaking the antenna through carelessness.

The children returned home, hurt and bewildered, after being thoroughly intimidated by the rude and abusive clerk. After hearing the details of the entire incident, Mrs. Harris decided to write two letters, one to the salesclerk (whose name was on the receipt) and one to the store manager.

Case Questions

1. Identify and discuss the communication barriers involved in this situation.

2. Write the letter to the salesclerk.

3. Write the letter to the store manager.

C A S E

A Matter of Grave Concern

Randy E. Cone, Department of Management, University of New Orleans

It has been a tough week for Edna Crawford, co-owner of Eternal Monuments, which manufactures and sells cemetery monuments.

First, there was the visit of Ruby Jane Sweetack, wife of the late Peter Sweetack. Ruby Jane had been married to Peter for 11 years after his first wife of 47 years (Frances) went to her Greater Reward. Although Peter had purchased a double monument for Frances and himself after her death 12 years ago, three years into his marriage to Ruby Jane he bought a second double monument with his and Ruby's names engraved thereon. It was at the second monument that he was laid to rest.

Ruby Jane, though, was aggravated that Peter's name and birth date appeared on the first monument, next to Frances's name and birth and death dates. She ordered Edna to have Peter's name removed from that monument and paid for the service. Since Peter had no children by either of his two wives, Edna agreed to have the name removed.

In the meantime, Peter's blood nephew, Bruce Allen, telephoned from another city to arrange for the purchase of a monument for himself. Single, with no living relatives, he wanted to take care of that part of his last arrangements. In the discussion of where Bruce's monument would be (in the Sweetack family plot), Edna mentioned that she had "another order for work in that plot." Bruce was surprised and assured Edna that she was mistaken—"My uncle was buried in another section of the cemetery, not with his first wife." Edna then explained Ruby Jane's wish to have Uncle Peter's name and birth date removed from the Sweetack marker.

Bruce was livid! His grandmother had purchased *all* the lots for the family years ago and had erected a large monument with "SWEETACK" emblazoned thereon. Although Bruce had never liked his uncle or either aunt, he felt that Frances deserved some recognition for 47 years with Peter; and he forbade Edna from having Peter's name removed.

Edna immediately called her craftsman and, to her chagrin, learned that the name had been removed yesterday. The man did a wonderful job. All that appeared in the square, alongside Frances's name, was a blank spot. It would appear that Frances had been a maiden lady who died at 78, still hopeful of acquiring a husband.

Edna must now write to Bruce giving him the news that his uncle's name appears nowhere in the Sweetack family plot. She dreads this as Bruce threatened legal action "if any work whatsoever is done on that stone or if it's touched by anyone." His last words, before slamming down the telephone, were "You have no business being in business. And Ruby Jane had no right to touch a marker that was bought by *my* grandmother, before Ruby Jane was ever in the family."

Case Questions

1. Write a letter to Bruce Allen explaining that the worst-case scenario had occurred. Edna had agreed to Ruby Jane's request only because she knew no other blood relatives who may be concerned about the marker. Try to regain his confidence in you and your firm (after all, he has ordered a monument of his own).

2. Is there anything else that Edna can do, aside from apologizing, for this incident? Is she, her firm, or Ruby Jane legally liable for defacing a cemetery monument in a public cemetery? How can Edna prevent such happenings in the future?

3. Does Mr. Allen have any recourse against Edna or Ruby Jane, or should he just let it rest, as his uncle is doing?

Note

1. United States Office of Consumer Affairs, *1994 Consumer's Resource Handbook*, (Washington, D.C.: 1994).

Chapter 8

Persuasive Letters

Sophia Perniski was a volunteer at the children's hospital. Her job was to convince people to donate money to the hospital, and she had initially made telephone calls. Now she had been given the task of writing the season's fundraising letter. Sophia was a good writer, which was why she had been given this job, but she had never written anything quite like this. She was not sure what sort of approach would be most effective. Over the telephone, Sophia could alter the tone of the pitch to match the reaction of the person on the other end. One could tell a lot about someone even during a brief telephone conversation. In a letter one did not have the same option.

Sophia decided to write several prototype letters and test them on her friends. One letter was a logical request for assistance, and it cited several figures attesting to the success of the hospital and gave some idea of the financial requirements. Another was a compassionate plea and related the stories of several children whose lives had literally been saved by the hospital. These children could not have been treated without donations from private individuals. Sophia wrote another sample letter, although she did not feel the hospital administrators would approve of it. This letter had a more strident tone and attempted to raise funds by making the reader feel guilty for his or her good fortune. Sophia prepared this letter because she was curious what the reaction would be among her friends.

Sophia's friends disliked the last letter intensely, and said that it made them feel hostile toward the hospital because they felt they were being coerced. Subsequently, Sophia found that the most effective method was a combination of elements of the first two letters. That way she would appeal to those who are more emotional and those who are more logical. The letter was balanced, as well. Monday morning, when she presented the letter to her supervisor, it was approved.

Throughout our waking hours we are inundated with messages attempting to persuade us. In fact, the average American is subjected to 1600 commercial messages a day, but only 12 of these are effective enough to get some kind of a reaction.[1] Television, radio, magazines, and newspapers bombard our senses with a multitude of appeals. We are urged to buy products and services, prevent forest fires and tooth decay, and, whatever we do, vote on election day.

Some of the more blatant attempts to persuade are found in advertising, but we receive many other persuasive messages as well. Ministers,

Figure 8.1
According to a survey by American Sports Data, Michael Jordan is the most influential athlete with consumers.
Source: Ralf-Finn Hestoft, SABA Press Photos, Inc.

priests, and rabbis urge us to live a better life and suggest ways we might do so. Police officers remind us to watch our speed. Our friends seek favors from us.

Our responses to persuasive messages vary. We barely pay attention to some, and so advertisers continue their search for better ways to get and hold our attention—bright colors, attractive people, catchy music, pleasing situations (see Figure 8.1). Other messages attract our attention but have very little effect. Some products we simply do not want or cannot afford to buy, but the commercials for them are nevertheless entertaining.

Other messages change our behavior. We purchase the product or service. We slow down as we drive, especially when we near the place where we earned our last speeding ticket. We do help our friends in need, perhaps at great inconvenience to ourselves.

GOALS OF PERSUASION

Although for some of us the process of persuasion is so mysterious that it is threatening, persuasion is nothing new. Aristotle, Plato, and Cicero wrote about persuasion almost two thousand years ago. Popular treatments of persuasion abound today in such books as Vance Packard's classic *The Hidden Persuaders,*[2] and Fisher, Kopelman, and Schneider's *Beyond Machiavelli.*[3] David Ogilvy's *Confessions of an Advertising Man*[4] and *Ogilvy on Advertising*[5] look at the commercial aspects of persuasion. Each of these writers takes a different approach to persuasion, but they are all concerned with one central idea—shaping the behavior of others.

How the behavior of people enables an organization to meet its goals was discussed in Chapter 2. The essence of persuasion is to shape the behavior of others so that goals can be reached more easily. Simply defined, **persuasion** is the art of getting people to do something that they would not ordinarily do if you did not ask. By asking in a persuasive manner, we shape behavior.

Persuading and threatening are two distinct approaches to shaping behavior. Effective persuasion results in willing compliance. Threats may elicit grudging compliance. People usually become defensive when threatened, and whatever the outcome, their relationship with the threatening party is adversely affected.

The primary goal of persuasion is to shape behavior.

When shaping others' behavior, you will often want to influence not only what they do, but also when they do it. The next time you receive an invitation to enter a sweepstakes from a mail-order advertiser, see if there are extra rewards for winners who enter the contest by an early deadline. Television commercials offering such consumer goods as tapes, records, books, and kitchen gadgets almost always provide a toll-free number for you to call in your order. They may also remind you to call immediately: "The supply is limited, so act now!" Many salespeople in department stores are instructed never to let a customer leave without having signed on the dotted line. In each case the persuader is aware that delay in shaping behavior could mean no shaping at all.

Some persuaders also want to influence how (or where) you perform the behavior. Although the League of Women Voters simply encourages you to vote, politicians are obviously interested in controlling the way you cast your ballot: "Don't forget to vote in the October 3 primary. And when you do, vote for George Jenkins." Some owners of fast-food restaurants would prefer that you never prepare meals in your kitchen and now offer every meal of the day. When they tell you, "You deserve a break today," they clearly want to influence where it is you take that break.

Goal clarification is a vital prerequisite to persuasion. Many persuasive efforts fail because their goals have never been clarified. Shaping the behavior of others should be based on the more specific goal of influencing at least one of the following:

- What the behavior should be
- When the behavior should occur
- How (or where) the behavior should be performed

THE PERSUASION PROCESS

After selecting your specific goals, you are prepared to develop your persuasive message. As in any form of communication, certain factors will influence the success of your persuasive attempt. The four important factors are (1) the sender of the persuasive message, (2) the receiver of the persuasive message, (3) the persuasive message itself, and (4) the channel through which the persuasive message is sent.

Sender

"Consider the source," we often say if we doubt the truthfulness of a message. The source of a persuasive message has an enormous impact on how well the message shapes behavior. This impact is one reason why baseball players sell aftershave lotion on television and why the picture of an Olympic champion is on the front of thousands of breakfast cereal boxes. You are more apt to respond favorably to persuasive messages when the sender is someone you respect or admire. Your response is based on the key sender concept of source credibility.

The more credible the source, the more persuasive the message will be.

To understand how credibility works, try this exercise: Think of the best supervisor you have ever worked for (if you have never had a job, then think about the best teacher you have had). Respond to the following statements about that person by answering *yes* or *no:*

1. This person really knew the work. (expertise)

2. This person always told the truth and kept his or her word. (trustworthiness)

3. This person was active and energetic. (dynamism)

4. This person would always level with me. (objectivity)

5. This person was always interested in my personal welfare. (goodwill)

How many *yes* responses did you give? The more you gave, the more credible the person is. **Credibility**—the quality of inspiring belief—is based on the overall image of the message sender.

The exercise you just completed points out five important components of credibility. A receiver's image of you involves how competent, trustworthy, dynamic, objective, and well intentioned the receiver perceives you to be. The more favorable this perception is, the more likely you are to shape the receiver's behavior.

The relative importance of these components varies from one situation to another. Here are some persuasive situations that might apply to you now. Which components of credibility do you think are most important in each situation?

- You're turning in a term paper to your instructor one day late. The lateness is not your fault, and you want to avoid losing points because of tardiness.
- You're trying to convince a friend not to drop out of school.
- You're asking someone for a date.
- You're running for office in school government.

As a sender of persuasive messages you should evaluate your own credibility. What is the receiver's perception of you? The word "source" may refer to more than you as an individual. When you communicate in business, the credibility of your organization may be just as important as your own personal credibility. The first step in shaping the behavior of others is to consider your credibility as a sender of persuasive messages. Both within and outside of business your receivers will usually consider the source before they act. Self-image also appears to be related to persuasiveness. One researcher found that salespeople who perceive themselves as being effective communicators are more successful than those who do not perceive themselves in that way.[6] In another study it was shown that precision and friendliness on the part of a salesperson will result in greater persuasiveness and a higher level of sales.[7]

Receiver

An important encoding skill is the ability to analyze your receiver, as was pointed out in Chapter 2. In persuasive situations this ability is critical. Two sets of factors to consider in analyzing the receiver of your persuasive message are attention and motivation. Before motivating the receiver you must first gain the receiver's attention.

Attention Factors

In any persuasive situation—a letter, speech, or advertisement—your first function is to get and hold your receiver's attention. Knowing several things about receivers will help you to do this.

The unexpected will get attention.

First, people pay attention to the unexpected. Several years ago a man toured the country giving speeches on driving safety to high school assemblies. He began every speech this way:

> Look around you. Look at the person on each side of you. Ten years from now one of the three of you will be dead.

The original, startling, and personal way he used those statistics caught the receivers' attention.

There are many examples of using the unexpected. The New York Racing Association, seeking buyers for its horse manure, advertised:

> Our horses leave a lot to be desired.

The owner of a service station and restaurant along a busy highway posted a sign outside his establishment reading:

Eat Here and Get Gas

An orphanage for boys began its solicitation letter with:

How much is a homeless boy worth?

People heed the unexpected, and once they do, they're easier to persuade.

Second, people pay attention to what is pleasing. Many persuaders use reinforcing stimuli to get the receiver's attention. Look at the advertisements in one of your favorite magazines. You will immediately notice that many products are shown in elegant surroundings—physically attractive men and women, cheerful settings, pleasing colors. Such attention-getters are used in television commercials as well. Besides the surroundings, reinforcing words and phrases are often used to get attention:

Reinforcing stimuli will get attention.

Make Anyone Do Anything You Mentally Command—With Your Mind Alone
One Pill Blocks 600 Calories
How to Find Someone to Love
Factory-Direct Savings to You

Once attention is gained, the real persuasive message begins.

Third, people pay attention to messages related to their own goals and objectives. Receivers will heed your persuasive message if it concerns something important to them. People who have dentures are more likely to watch denture-cleaner commercials on television than are people who have their natural teeth. The latter pay more attention to toothpaste commercials. Pet owners pay more attention to pet food commercials than do viewers who have no pets.

Emphasizing the relevant will get attention.

The three attention factors are thus the unexpected, the reinforcing, and the relevant. Which factors you use in developing a persuasive message depends on your analysis of the receiver. Will he or she respond more favorably to an attention getter that is not expected, one that is reinforcing, or one that emphasizes his or her important goals?

You should also consider your own credibility when choosing an attention factor. Low credibility can weaken any attempts at getting attention to persuade.

Motivation Factors

Once you have gained the receiver's attention, you need to know what will make that person respond favorably to your persuasive attempt. Many theories have been developed to explain what motivates people both at work and in their personal lives. One of these theories, developed by Abraham Maslow almost 50 years ago, states that people do things to satisfy certain needs.[8]

- Physiological needs: lower order survival needs, such as food, sleep, and air.
- Safety and security needs: lower order needs for personal security (for example, a safe home) and financial security (for example, a steady income or a savings account).
- Belonging needs: higher order needs to be included in other people's activities and affection.
- Esteem and status needs: higher order needs to feel self-respect and respect from others.
- Self-actualization needs: higher order needs for self-realization or fulfillment in a vocation or avocation.

The first two needs are lower order and the last three needs are higher order. Maslow maintained that you progress from the first need to the fifth; that is, you first satisfy your physiological needs. You then satisfy the safety and security needs, and so on, until you reach the self-actualization needs. This progression from lower to higher order needs is the reason why Maslow's theory is sometimes called Maslow's **hierarchy of needs**. It is illustrated in Figure 8.2.

To incorporate Maslow's theory into your attempt to persuade, you must (1) estimate the receiver's level of needs at the time of your attempt; (2) create a message relevant to those needs; and (3) tell the receiver that the behavior you desire will satisfy the needs. The following three persuasive messages involve the same product, yet are adapted to different needs.

> Your new Phantom will be the safest car on the highway. Heavy-duty bumpers, specially molded fenders, and our exclusive invisible roll-bar frame will protect you better than any other car on the market. (safety and security needs)
>
> The Number 1 car in America—that's the Phantom. More than 30 million people drive Phantoms. Maybe you should think about owning one, too. (belonging needs)
>
> For the discriminating driver, Phantom's Marquis de Luxe is a step above luxury. It's a sign you've arrived. (esteem and status needs)

Direct and Indirect Rewards

Maslow's hierarchy is only one way to analyze what motivates your receiver. Another way is based on the assumption that people do things for reasons. In your persuasive message you show how these reasons can be rewarded in two ways—direct and indirect.

Direct rewards come from the actual, shaped behavior.

Direct rewards come from actually buying the product or using the service; that is, these rewards come directly from the consumer's involvement with the behavior the persuasive message prompts. Think for a few moments about the rewards a consumer gets from purchasing a washing machine. There's the convenience of not having to visit a Laundromat once or twice a week. It's more economical because it costs less to use a home washer than a coin-operated machine. Perhaps the clothes are washed better because the consumer can control the cycle, temperature, and water level of each wash. Clothes might even wear longer, because the home washer treats them more delicately than the commercial Laundromat washer. These rewards all come directly from the consumer's having bought a washer. In that sense they are direct.

Figure 8.2

Maslow's Hierarchy of Needs

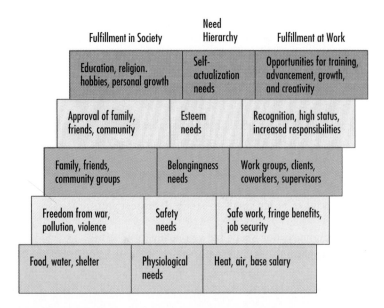

Our consumer might also receive some indirect rewards from having purchased the washer. Indirect rewards come from other people as a function of the consumer having performed the behavior. Assume that the clothes washer is the top of the line of a name brand and that our consumer is the first person in the neighborhood to own this superior machine. Among the indirect rewards our consumer might receive are status, prestige, respect, and approval from others in the neighborhood. You don't give these rewards to yourself. Doctors and lawyers have status only because others in the community assign that status to them. You may have heard conspicuous consumption used as an explanation for why many people purchase expensive consumer goods—large automobiles, color television and stereo combinations, elaborate computers and electronic equipment, and so on. These people buy expensive items so that others will notice their accomplishments and assign them various kinds of indirect rewards.

> Indirect rewards come from other people as a result of shaped behavior.

You can choose from a multitude of both direct and indirect rewards when analyzing your receiver. Here are some examples:

Direct Rewards	Indirect Rewards
Comfort	Affection
Convenience	Appreciation
Enjoyment	Approval
Entertainment	Belonging
Health	Friendship
Less work	Pay increase
Money saved	Popularity
Personal improvement	Prestige
Problem solved	Promotion
Safety	Recognition
Satisfaction	Reputation
Sense of achievement	Respect
Variety	Status

Which of these rewards can you find in the persuasive message that follows? (You should find at least eight.)

Lonely? Never again!

Are you a wallflower at parties? Are you afraid to approach strangers? Do you have trouble with conversation openers? Starting today, you can meet and date dozens of interesting, attractive people.

WINNING PEOPLE will show you more than 50 proven techniques for being successful with the opposite sex. For example, you will find out: How to tell immediately if someone is attracted to you. . . .How to be the life of the party without making a fool out of yourself. . . .How to say you find someone attractive without appearing weak or foolish . . . and much more. WINNING PEOPLE will teach you how to win others and, in doing so, become a winner yourself.

For persuasive messages like this one, the writer carefully analyzes the characteristics of the intended receivers. These messages are put together to bring certain rewards to the receiver's mind as the message is read. The words are not selected haphazardly. Rather, they are carefully chosen to meet the needs of the receiver.

The more you learn about the needs and interests of your receivers, the more likely you are to persuade them. One authority on advertising described the effects of different approaches to persuasion in this way:

I have seen one advertisement actually sell not twice as much, not three times as much, but 19½ times as much as another. Both advertisements occupied the same space. Both were run in the same publication. Both had photographic illustrations. Both had carefully written copy. The difference was that one used the right appeal and the other used the wrong appeal.[9]

Message

A third variable in the persuasion process is the message. The type of persuasive message you create depends, in part, on the channel (for example, sales letter, speech, advertisement) you intend to use. In constructing a persuasive message you should pay careful attention to both the organization of that message and the kinds of persuasive appeals you use within it.

No matter what channel you use, your message should contain at least three essential ingredients: (1) an attention step; (2) a need step (in which you emphasize needs or direct and indirect rewards); and (3) an action step (in which you specify the behavior the receiver should perform).

The organizational pattern provides the skeleton for your persuasive message, but the persuasive appeals you use flesh out the skeleton and give the message substance. These appeals are like tools in a toolbox. You pick the ones most appropriate for your specific persuasive task. The two kinds of appeals used in persuasive messages are emotional and logical.

Emotional Appeal

> Emotional appeals are directed to the receiver's emotions or feelings.

Most widely used in shaping consumer behavior, **emotional appeals** are directed to the feelings (rather than the intellect) of the receiver. Such appeals promise the direct and indirect rewards described earlier. Some examples of how emotional appeals work are given in Table 8.1.

Some emotional appeals are technique oriented. For example, the bandwagon technique appeals to a need to belong. This emotional appeal says, in essence, "Everybody is doing it." For years a certain automobile was advertised as the number-one car in America (meaning, of course, that everyone was buying this car). A well-known car rental agency advertises: "We're number one."

Logical Appeals

> Logical appeals, directed to the receiver's rational thinking, are used most often in persuading other business people.

Appeals may be directed toward the receiver's rational thinking. These **logical appeals** are used most often when persuading other business people. One reason is that people in business (for example, purchasing agents) must be able to clearly justify the behavior that the persuasive message suggests. This need to justify behavior calls for appeals such as the examples in Table 8.2.

Most persuasive messages are positive—that is, the message describes a reward to be attained through some positive action. Occasionally, however, a persuader will use a negative appeal to arouse emotions of fear or of self-interest. Avoiding social disapproval is sometimes the reward when a negative appeal is used.

> Negative appeals may suggest an unfortunate occurrence unless some action is taken.

Insurance companies try to sell policies by pointing out that, in the event of your death, your family will be left destitute unless you have insurance. This is a negative appeal. The persuader is predicting an unfortunate occurrence unless some action is taken. A company advertising a mouthwash may play on your fear of rejection. Health care organizations publicize the fact that smokers do not live as long as nonsmokers. In other words, unless you quit smoking you will die at an earlier age. Collection letters, described later in this chapter, may sometimes include negative appeals.

The appeals used in persuasion can be either positive or negative. Positive appeals are used more frequently, but in some situations negative appeals are appropriate. If

TABLE 8.1 EXAMPLES OF HOW EMOTIONAL APPEALS WORK

Shaped Behavior	Rewards	Message
Purchase of a pair of sunglasses	Personal improvement, prestige	How good-looking can you get? Watch for those second looks as you stroll the beach in your new Sundowners. They're a sure sign you live the good life.
Joining a computer dating service	Belonging, friendships, problem solving	Why spend time waiting when you'll find that perfect someone at Date-A-Match? Love is just around the corner at 100 Houston Drive.
Signing up for a cruise	Entertainment, friendships, enjoyment	There's dining, dancing, swimming . . . or, if you'd like, lounging on our spacious sundeck with the most interesting people you'll ever meet.

TABLE 8.2 EXAMPLES OF HOW LOGICAL APPEALS WORK

Shaped Behavior	Rewards	Message
Using a collection agency for overdue accounts	Convenience, saving money	Let us show you how we can help you reduce your uncollectible bills by 25 percent. Our service also means you won't have to spend your own time dealing with delinquent accounts.
Purchasing a new computer	Convenience, efficiency	The AEI laptop computer is so light (only 5 pounds) that you can easily move it from office to office. Its memory system allows you to always be close to the office.
Purchasing a prefabricated building	Money saved, durability	The aluminum siding on Brock buildings means you'll get years of economical and long-lasting service.

you have any misgivings about the appropriateness of an appeal, it's best to heed that warning bell. When the sender questions the ethical value of a message, the recipients will usually find fault as well. Imagine, for example, that you received a letter that began:

I am sorry to have to tell you this, but your tests have come back. You have AIDS.

It was not until you unfolded the letter that you saw a second paragraph, which asked readers to "try to imagine what impact these words would have on you if they were true." Such an appeal is both fraudulent and unethical, and readers will feel as though they have been manipulated. The responsible organization publicly apologized after having mailed nearly 5,000 of the letters.[10] Had the writer exercised better judgment, the problem would have been avoided.

> **Emotional appeals are used more often than logical appeals in consumer advertising.**

Many persuasive messages contain a mixture of emotional and logical appeals. If you carefully analyze television commercials and magazine advertisements, you will notice that emotional appeals are made more frequently, especially to consumers. You will also begin to recognize the various organizational formats used in constructing persuasive messages.

Channel

As a business communicator you will probably use the persuasion process in many different situations. Some typical uses are these:

Written	Face to Face	Orally
In a collection message	In a public speech	On the telephone
In a job application	In an interview	
In a sales letter	In a small group conference	Audiotaped presentation
In a magazine or newspaper advertisement	In everyday conversation	With dictation equipment
In a claim letter		
In a request for a favor		

Sometimes you have a choice between oral or written channels. For example, if you want to persuade a credit customer to mail an overdue payment, should you telephone or write a brief collection message? If you want immediate feedback and better acceptance, perhaps the oral channel is preferable. But if you need documentation, or if your message is fairly detailed, a written message might be better. Chapter 2 discussed when to use each type of communication.

Several factors discussed in this chapter should also enter into your decision. First, you might show more goodwill through an informal telephone conversation. Or perhaps you would be more objective in a letter. Also, your decision should be based partly on your analysis of the customer. An unexpected telephone call might get attention, but it might be better to communicate in a letter so that you can more easily control both the organization and the types of appeals you use in your message. In the matter of **channel selection**, you should weigh benefits carefully when beginning your effort to shape behavior.

PLANNING TO PERSUADE

The four steps in the planning process introduced in Chapter 6 can be tailored to the planning of persuasive messages. Ray Williams' experience will be used to demonstrate.

Ray Williams took an expensive leather jacket to Peerless Cleaning, a company that specialized in leather goods. He was upset when it was returned with a large spot on the back. He made repeated visits to the cleaner, who was unable to remove the spot. In fact, the local manager denied any responsibility for it. Ray knew that the spot was not on the jacket when he initially took it to Peerless. He decided that he must write a letter to persuade someone in upper management that Peerless, not he, caused the spot and was therefore responsible for it.

Determining Objectives

The first step in planning is to recognize the reason for writing. Decide whether you are seeking a covert or an overt response. Are you trying to change the way the reader feels about a problem or issue, or are you asking the reader actually to do something about it? Ray decided to seek $295, the full purchase price of his leather jacket, from the cleaning company. The jacket was only 6 months old, and this had been its first cleaning.

Considering the Audience

When trying to persuade, think of the audience as being actively involved in the communication process. Even when using a written message to persuade, imagine the reader responding either positively or negatively to each of your statements. Knowing the needs and interests of the audience, whatever its size, makes it more likely that the audience will respond as desired (see Figure 8.3). Ray decided to send his letter to the vice president of customer relations at Peerless Cleaning. He believes that this person, although far removed from day-to-day cleaning operations, will be vitally interested in keeping customers satisfied.

Choosing the Ideas to Include

At this stage, based on your impression of the intended reader or readers, decide which ideas have the most reader appeal. Ray felt that the following ideas might be included in his letter:

He is a long-time customer of Peerless. The spot had to have been caused by the cleaner. The jacket was practically new. This is his first problem with Peerless, and he is

Figure 8.3
Lands' End, Inc.
The company conveys a rural American emphasis on values and quality through its sponsorship of "The Prairie Home Companion" on NPR.
Source: Photo by Teri Stratford.

AN ETHICAL DILEMMA

During the past 10 years the fortunes of Imperial Caterers have soared. The business that Ray Hilton started as a sideline consumes all of his time. In fact, most of his efforts are now devoted to administrative detail. The assistant managers he hired several years ago, Bruce Thornton and Ernest Nettles, are responsible for managing the catered events.

Bruce and Ernest are both competent but have very different personalities. Bruce is outgoing and gregarious; Ernest is quieter and serious. Customers are equally pleased with the services provided by the two; however, they are initially more impressed with Bruce. For that reason customers who know Bruce request him for their catered affairs. Several have expressed disappointment when Ernest has been sent when Bruce was expected. These customers have agreed that Ernest handled his duties well. No business has been lost.

Ray was pleased when Northern Industries, a major local employer, approached him about catering a company event. Ray had been calling on the company, seeking its catering business, for a long time. Ray and the Northern representative sat down together and worked out the arrangements for the event. The representative then asked if Bruce could be scheduled to manage it. Not wanting to jeopardize a new account, Ray said, "I don't see why not," although he knew that Bruce was already committed elsewhere on that day.

Ray's contracts for catered meals cover many details, but not the name of the on-site manager. He words his contracts to allow himself flexibility on that point. He reasons that his two assistants are equally competent and it should not make any difference which one is assigned to a job.

The Northern Industries event is only days away. Ray is beginning to have second thoughts about misleading the Northern representative. He can't decide whether it really matters. Ray feels boxed in. What would you do?

familiar with the company's reputation for customer satisfaction. He hopes to be able to continue to do business with Peerless; however, this depends on how the problem of his jacket is resolved.

Selecting the Channel and Medium

Communicators have many different channels and media available. They must decide which is most likely to help accomplish the predetermined objective. Ray decided to write a letter.

Selecting an appropriate channel and medium is crucial, and for that reason researchers have investigated the topic in a variety of settings. Among the findings are these:

- Face-to-face communication with one's supervisor leads to the acceptance of change.[11]
- Team briefings are effective for getting all levels of the company to communicate with each other.[12]
- Informal channels of communication are generally evaluated more highly than formal channels.[13]

WRITING PERSUASIVE LETTERS

The **persuasive letter** is one in which you seek to modify the thought and action of others in a certain direction. The types of persuasive letters most frequently encountered in the business setting are sales letters, collection letters, and letters of special requests. Whether you are writing an individualized persuasive letter or a letter that will be widely distributed, the same basic principles apply. Whenever you seek to persuade someone, you should follow four steps:

1. Get the reader's *attention*. (A)
2. Stimulate the reader's *interest*. (I)
3. Awaken a *desire* in the reader. (D)
4. Encourage the reader to take a specific *action*. (A)

These steps are known as the **AIDA sequence**. They are discussed and developed in the section on sales letters under "Writing."

Persuasive writing is not limited to letters, of course. Persuasion is frequently employed in memos and reports. Many reports, for example, include recommendations that are presented persuasively.

The persuasive letter seeks to modify others' actions and thoughts.

SALES LETTERS

Millions of unsolicited sales letters are mailed each year to consumers. Many of these letters are routinely discarded and disparagingly referred to as junk mail. What may be junk mail to many consumers is called direct mail advertising by advertisers, and it is big business. Almost as much is spent annually on direct mail advertising as is spent on television advertising.

Direct mail advertising is considered to be more precise than either television or newspapers, which are ordinarily directed at the general population. Direct mail advertising can be tailored and sent to a narrow segment of the population. Another attractive feature of direct mail advertising is it can be scientifically tested. Sales results can be easily related to a specific letter, and various versions of a letter can be compared for effectiveness.

Large organizations often send sales letters by the thousands. Composing an individual letter for each reader is impractical, and so a form letter may be developed. A credit account application typically accompanies such a letter.

Writing good sales letters is an art. For some people it is a full-time occupation—and a well-paying one at that. Some of the best-known practitioners of direct mail advertising are paid extravagantly to develop a single packaged sales letter that will produce the desired results. Because such letters are mailed in tremendous quantities, a response rate of 1 to 2 percent is considered good.[14]

You may never become a part of the direct mail advertising business, but much of your writing will be aimed at persuading your reader. The obstacles you face will be similar to those encountered by the direct mail writer. In the split second that a reader may actually look at your sales letter before discarding it, you must grab the reader's attention.

When you try to persuade someone, you are trying to sell that person on an idea or a course of action. By becoming familiar with the strategy of the sales letter you can become a more effective persuader.

The principles governing sales letters pertain to all persuasive writing.

The reception a sales letter gets is considerably different from the reception for other types of letters. The good-news and neutral letter is easy to write because it tells readers what they want to hear. The letter of refusal, on the other hand, delivers an unfavorable response. No one wants that type of news, but a well-written letter of refusal will be read because it contains information that interests the reader.

Sales letters generally fall into two categories, unsolicited and solicited. The unsolicited sales letter does not have the advantages of other types of letters. It does not present information that the reader is likely to consider good news. In fact, the reader may not even be interested at first. To succeed, the writer must create a message that, although unsolicited, will stimulate a relatively uninterested reader.

The solicited letter is easier to write because the reader has expressed interest, sought information, or made specific inquiry. The writer is responding to some needs of which the reader is already aware.

Preparation

Before beginning to write persuasively you should learn as much as possible about the idea, service, or product to be offered. You should thoroughly understand all aspects of a product before trying to sell it. You should certainly have the following information about the product:

- Exactly what it can do
- Materials from which it is made
- The expertise that developed it
- Outstanding features of the product
- Ways it differs from its competitors
- Price of the product
- Extent of the maintenance required and the expertise required to perform it
- Warranty, if any, that accompanies the product

Without this basic information you are unlikely to sell the product successfully. This information by itself, however, is not usually enough because physical characteristics are only one dimension of a product.

Buyers will be as interested in the benefits they will derive from a product as in its physical characteristics. For that reason you should learn as much as you can about those to whom the letter will be sent. The more you know about the readers, the more likely you are to appeal to their interests and the more successful the resulting letter will be. You will understand the readers better if you have this type of information about them:

The writer of a sales letter should become familiar with the product and the intended customers.

- Income level
- Whether homes are owned or rented
- Urban or rural location
- Occupations represented
- Educational level attained
- Marital status
- Family size
- Age of family members

At times you may have to write a sales letter with little specific advance knowledge about the readers. In those instances, the product or service itself may indicate the kind of person who will read the letter. For example, if you are trying to attract customers for a lawn-care service, the letter will be geared to homeowners who live in the suburbs.

After you are fully aware of the product or idea and the potential customers, you can plan the sales message. You must determine how best to link the intended customer with what is being offered. In other words, exactly how will the reader benefit from the physical characteristics and capabilities of the product? For example, the physical characteristics of a certain brand of running shoes are lightweight rubber, canvas, and color. The benefits to the purchaser of such shoes, however, would be factors such as these:

- The purchaser saves money because the shoes last longer than other running shoes.
- The shoes make the runner faster because they are very lightweight.
- The shoes improve the runner's appearance because they are stylish and available in many different colors.
- The shoes provide more comfort because of the specially designed arch.
- The shoes provide more safety through the unique double-deep tread.

Potential buyers are interested in the physical features of a product, but they are more interested in how they would benefit from them. David Ogilvy recognized this fact when he said, "Advertising which promises no benefit to the customer does not sell." He also referred to a study that showed "advertisements with headlines that promise a benefit are read by an average of four times more people than advertisements that don't."[15] The likely benefits, or psychological features, convince the reader to buy.

Writing

Whether you are trying to sell something or tying to convince the reader to pursue a certain course of action, the four steps in the AIDA sequence discussed earlier have proven to be effective. Although the terminology has varied somewhat, persuasive writers have used these same steps for years. Here they are applied to sales letters.

Attracting the Reader's Attention

The first sentence of an unsolicited sales letter must grab readers while leading them on to the remainder of the letter. In order to accomplish this, the letter should identify one of the most significant features of the product it is trying to sell. If possible, it should suggest how the reader stands to benefit from using the product.

> The first sentence of a sales letter must attract the reader's attention.

Many writers attempt to include in the first sentence the aspect of the product that will interest most readers. The manufacturer of an energy-efficient water heater, for example, considered economy to be the most important characteristic of the product. For that reason economy was emphasized in this opening:

Want to cut your water heating expense by 30 percent?

An auto dealer who believed that the product's new styling was its most interesting aspect stressed this newness:

Test drive the all-new C-7 now. Be the first in the neighborhood to own one.

There is no one right method of getting the reader's attention. Only after becoming familiar with both the product and the intended reader will you be ready to select an appropriate method. Some of the more common methods used are these:

- Make a thought-provoking statement: "The best thing about our new line of purses is something you can't see."
- Present a startling fact: "Ninety-five out of 100 families would be bankrupt if they missed just three paychecks."
- Offer a bargain: "Imagine, two pairs of shoes for the price of one!"
- Describe something that currently is happening: "Today more than 500 families enjoyed the *Press Journal* with breakfast."
- Present a direct challenge: "Try to tear the enclosed piece of rubberized plastic and you'll understand why our seat covers won't wear out."

- Tell an interesting anecdote: "Until I was 25 years old I thought you had to be rich to afford a new car. The day I visited Bill Smith's Auto Market was the day I learned otherwise. That was also the day I bought my first new car."

Originality is an important characteristic of a sales letter.

An opening is more likely to attract attention if it is written in an original manner. When the writer uses clichés and timeworn phrases, the reader is likely to discard the letter. The reader is more likely to continue reading if the opening paragraph is short. Brevity and conciseness are vital to an effective opening in an unsolicited letter.

While striving to make your approach unique, you risk making an error that may cause the reader to lose interest. These are some of the most common errors to avoid:

- Avoid asking a foolish question. The writer will lose the reader's attention with a question that has an obvious answer, such as "How would you like to double your income and shorten your work week?"
- Avoid emphasizing the writer instead of the reader. Readers want to know how they will benefit. "It looks like WKUR will be number one in the ratings soon" virtually ignores the reader.
- Avoid presenting an irrelevant statement. A sales letter that begins, "There's at least one thing in life that you needn't be a millionaire to enjoy," sounds intriguing until the reader discovers that the product is a new deodorant soap. A direct link between the opening statement and the product being sold should always be made.
- Avoid phrasing an idea in an unoriginal way. Do not use clichés such as "a stitch in time saves nine" or anecdotes that are already widely known.

Stimulating the Reader's Interest

The interest section of the sales letter should make the reader want the product.

Having attracted the reader's attention, you must now strive for a receptive reaction. In this section of your letter you usually introduce the product and provide the reader with good reasons for buying it. Some authorities recommend that at this point the reward that will be derived from the product should be emphasized rather than the actual product. For example, instead of selling the reader on a lawn mower, stress the pride associated with having an attractive lawn. In this way the reader goes beyond the product to the pleasure that results from its use. In the interest step, therefore, you are both describing the product and suggesting its value to the reader.

Once you have the reader's attention, you must link the attention-getting step to the interest step. Unless the interest step flows naturally from the attention step, the reader will probably stop reading the letter. In this letter the writer failed to link the steps:

Why carry paperwork when you can pocket the office? The new Omni palmtop computer frees you from some of the burdens of business travel. You can download data from your PC and work at your convenience, using its built-in software. Easy to use and powerful, it has four slots for extra memory and software. Try it and you'll agree that it is truly on the cutting edge.

The key idea of the attention-getting step is that this palmtop is small and manageable. The writer makes the point but never returns to it. There is no continuity between the attention and the interest steps.

To stimulate the reader's interest, the writer should emphasize a **central selling point** of the product. A central selling point is the prime reason why a person would

---

✔ *CHECKLIST for Attention Getting*
____ Present what the reader will view as the major benefit of the product that you seek to sell.
____ Relate the product to the reader rather than to the writer (the "you" attitude).
____ Write an original opening statement.
____ Make the first paragraph interesting enough to appeal to the reader and so short that the reader will have to read subsequent paragraphs to get the important details.

want what a seller is offering. Any product or service has many possible central selling points. What kind of person is the customer? What are the customer's needs and interests? Answering these questions will help you identify a likely central selling point.

Developing Desire within the Reader

In the desire section the writer moves the reader from the "like to have" category to the "really need" position. By relying on an appropriate emotional or logical appeal, the writer helps readers justify the desire for the product. The product being sold will usually suggest whether to use logical or emotional appeals. Sometimes a combination of the two is preferable.

The desire section of the sales letter should make the reader feel a need for the product.

One automobile dealer may try to sell a car on the basis of its complete warranty. This appeal is logical. Another dealer may try to sell the product through an emotional appeal: The reader will be the first one on the block to own this distinctive new model.

If price is mentioned, it will appear in the desire section. Rather than emphasize it, however, the writer should bury it within a paragraph.

Sales letters must usually be longer than other types of business letters. The greater length is required to develop a successful persuasive appeal. However, sales letters sent to dealers are usually shorter than those sent to consumers because appeals to dealers are more direct, generally emphasizing the profit to be made.

Encouraging the Reader to Take a Specific Action

The writer has pointed out the most significant features of the product as well as how the reader will benefit from its use. All that remains is for the reader to take the desired action. The writer must now tell the reader what action to take. If you want the reader to complete an enclosed form and mail it, say so as specifically as possible. Some otherwise good sales letters are rendered ineffective by the lack of a clear action closing.

The action close should indicate the specific action the reader should take.

It is not enough to have a clear action close, however. Before suggesting a specific action, give it a trial run and make sure it works as intended. Imagine that you had received a letter that said, "We invite you to be our guest for an exciting test drive of the magnificent new BMW 7401." The letter also gave an 800 number and the name of the person who would arrange a test drive. Imagine that you decided to accept the offer, called the 800 number, and had the following experiences:

Call #1: Phone rang 31 times and was never answered.
Call #2: Busy signal.
Call #3: Busy signal.
Call #4: Answered and put on permanent hold.
Call #5: Answered and put on permanent hold.
Call #6: Call was answered, put on hold for 50 seconds, then the caller spoke to the person named in letter, who treated the caller as if he "were a new killer virus."[16]

An example of a sales letter in which the four steps are used is presented in Figure 8.4. The steps are not always as separate and distinct as this. In some sales letters the interest and desire steps may be indistinguishable. You may not recognize the point at which one step ceases and another begins, but the sequence of ideas is obvious. Following this idea sequence is more important than keeping the steps separate.

A letter sent to office managers by a large office equipment supply company is shown in Figure 8.5.

> ✔ *CHECKLIST for a Sales Letter*
>
> _____ Begin with a brief statement or question that is likely to attract attention.
>
> _____ Be sure the opening statement clearly relates to the product offered.
>
> _____ Gain the reader's interest by emphasizing a central selling point that appeals to him or her.
>
> _____ In the desire section try to develop a need within the reader by providing additional evidence of the product's value. Also remind the reader of the central selling point.
>
> _____ Minimize price resistance by de-emphasizing it. Mention some of the strong points of the product while referring to price.
>
> _____ Indicate briefly and specifically what the reader should do, and restate the reasons the reader should take the desired action.

Figure 8.4
Sales Letter for a Trade School

TROTTER INSTITUTE   *P.O. Box 1981   Baltimore, MD 21233*

July 30, 1997

Mr. Charles Dunbar
286 Greencrest Street
Anita, PA 15711

Dear Mr. Dunbar:

Did you know that you don't need a college degree to get a good job? ——————— *Gets attention by suggesting a benefit for the reader.*

You've probably read newspaper articles about how job opportunities are declining today. At the same time, however, there are occupations in which opportunities are expanding. The U.S. Bureau of Labor Statistics reports that in the next 10 years the demand for electronics technicians will increase by 21 percent. That means that for every 10 electronics technicians now working, two more will be needed. As an electronics technician, you can expect to have your choice of many high-paying jobs with excellent working conditions. ——————— *Stimulates interest by emphasizing the reward to be derived from the product.*

One of the best aspects of an electronics education is that you don't have to leave home to get one. The Trotter Institute of Electronics offers a one-year correspondence course that leads to a Certificate of Electronics. You could soon be on your way to a career in electronics. ——————— *Points out desirable features: introduces but de-emphasizes price by linking it with another product strength.*

You probably think that any course offered by the Trotter Institute would have to be expensive. You're in for a surprise! You get textbooks, assignments, and consultation with our excellent instructors for only $450.00, and this includes employment counseling after you graduate. You can see now that getting a better job is easier than you thought. ——————— *Encourages specific actions and reminds the reader about benefits.*

To prepare for a better job with a great future, complete the enclosed registration form. Within 10 days you'll be progressing toward an interesting and rewarding new career.

Yours truly,

Michael T. Langford
Michael T. Langford
Admissions Counselor

Enc.

COLLECTION LETTERS

An effective collection letter will collect the money due and also maintain the customer's goodwill.

In most organizations relationships between salespeople and customers are carefully cultivated. These same relationships are often threatened by the company's efforts to collect unpaid bills. Collecting the unpaid balance should not be the only goal of the collection process. Another important goal is to retain the goodwill and the business of the delinquent customer. Many collection letter writers alienate the same customers in whose loyalty the company has heavily invested. Much of what has been accomplished through advertising, public relations, and skilled sales personnel can be undone through inept collection procedures.

Collection letters become more direct in tone as the account becomes further past due.

Virtually every type of business relies at least occasionally on collection letters to prod past-due accounts. These letters comprise the collection campaign, and they are written

Figure 8.5
Sales Letter for Office Equipment

ACE OFFICE EQUIPMENT, INC. • 2814 17th Avenue Gary, IN 44407 • (800) 555-2101

May 29, 1997

William C. Sams
Office Manager
Calumet Insurance Agency
5146 N. 56th Street
Calumet Park, IL 60643

Dear Mr. Sams:

Blurred vision and headaches are considered to be normal occupational hazards for video display terminal (VDT) operators. In fact, research by the National Institute for Occupational Safety and Health shows that up to 90 percent of VDT operators complain of such problems.

Identifies the problem and documents how widespread it is.

Other studies have shown that such complaints lead to a variety of adverse effects. Sore, burning eyes will make it difficult for your VDT operators to concentrate; consequently, productivity is diminished. Absenteeism and insurance claims often increase. The lowered job satisfaction that accompanies such conditions leads to higher rates of turnover.

Explains how the problem makes the office manager's job more difficult.

Some specialists suggest that rearranging the office layout to avoid glare from windows and installing customized lighting systems is the only way to prevent these problems. However, there is another less disruptive and less expensive solution. The Contrast Control® antiglare filter can be mounted on any VDT screen in seconds. Its thin-film optical coating will eliminate over 90 percent of the glare that results in eye fatigue and irritability.

Describes an expensive solution.

Presents a simple and inexpensive solution and documents its effectiveness.

You'll be amazed at the way your VDT operators will respond to this tangible evidence of your concern. You'll be even more amazed at its low price.

Describes an additional important benefit.

Call us today on our toll-free line for additional details and a price list. Act now to protect the health and productivity of your valued employees.

Suggests a specific action.

Sincerely,

Diane C. Fast

Diane C. Fast
Sales Associate

and mailed in a predetermined sequence. The early letters, sent when an account is slightly late, are mild in tone. As the account becomes more delinquent, the letters become more direct. Collection letters should never, however, become as direct as this one:

Your bill is overdue. Pay us immediately or I'll see that you never get credit in this town again.

Reasons for Collection Problems

A blacksmith shop in a one-story building in northern Wisconsin displayed this sign prominently: "Interested in credit? See our credit manager. Please take elevator." With a credit policy like this a company would have no collection problems.

The underlying reason for collection problems is that we extend credit. If a business were to revoke the credit privileges of all its customers, collection problems would disappear, but this almost surely would be accompanied by a decline in sales and profits. People expect credit. It has become a part of life both for the creditor—the organization extending credit—and for the debtor—the customer purchasing on credit.

In the quest for greater profits business organizations often extend credit to customers who, in an earlier time, would probably have been refused credit. As the number of these questionable accounts increases, so do collection problems increase.

Debtors become delinquent in paying their bills for many reasons, and many of these reasons are completely valid. Some credit managers refer to nonpayers as deadbeats, and they impute the motives and character of these debtors. Although some customers may use credit in bad faith, their number is small.

Many collection problems may be explained by such factors as illness, loss of job, or some other unexpected occurrence. In some cases collection difficulties can be traced to a debtor's misunderstanding the terms of the credit agreement. By taking greater care in explaining the operation of a charge account, companies can prevent some future collection problems. No matter how much care is taken in extending credit, however, there will be some problems.

The Collection Campaign

Company efforts to collect past-due accounts can best be described as campaigns. As in any campaign there is a series of stages. The stages in the collection process are (1) reminder, (2) strong reminder, (3) inquiry, (4) urgency, and (5) ultimatum. You must approach each stage somewhat differently. The assumptions you make about a debtor change as the account becomes more overdue, and you write differently on the basis of the new assumptions.

Although we divide the campaign into five stages, this division does not mean that only five letters will be sent to a delinquent debtor. For any single stage, more than a single letter is usually sent.

Reminder

The first collection letter is a reminder.

When a customer is first recognized as delinquent, collection efforts are restrained and mild. The assumption guiding the collection correspondent at this point is that the customer has merely overlooked the bill and needs only a reminder. When the account is about two weeks late, many companies merely send a duplicate of the original bill with some reminder that it is overdue.

The approach in the early stages of collection is low key. This approach continues into the first actual collection letter. Many people require only slight prodding, and the initial letter should only prod:

> Have you overlooked your unpaid balance with us? Please accept this friendly reminder and send us your check for $97.50.

The number of reminders that are sent to a delinquent customer varies from one company to another. A creditor will likely send several reminders to a customer who has a good credit history. To a customer who is viewed as a poor risk, the creditor might send only one reminder and then move to the strong-reminder stage. The process moves to the next stage quickly when it appears that the customer is not likely to respond.

Strong Reminder

In a strong reminder the writer may call the customer's attention to the value of the company's services.

The second stage consists of a strong reminder, yet the assumption remains that the customer has simply forgotten to pay the bill. Some companies use this occasion to remind the customer of the value of the company's services and to point out that the customer is held in high regard despite the oversight. This letter from a department store exemplifies such an approach:

> You will like the wide array of merchandise we now have in stock. You are sure to find something that suits your taste and your needs throughout each department.
>
> At the time you come in, you may pay your bill of $180, which is 45 days past due. Then, let us help you look and feel great this summer.

Besides reminding the customer of the past-due account, the writer has reassured the customer that credit will not be a problem. The customer is reminded that this store is a reasonable place to do business.

Inquiry

If the reminders do not have the desired effect, you as the writer must take a stronger position. Rather than continue to attribute the past-due status of the account to oversight, you now assume that some other reason has kept the customer from paying. This stage is called inquiry because you ask why the past-due account is not being paid. If it is not possible to elicit payment through this letter, you seek at least an explanation. If the customer responds with an explanation, there is a good chance that a payment plan will eventually result. In short, you seek customer action, preferably to pay the bill, but at least to give an explanation.

In the inquiry stage the writer asks the customer why the bill is past due.

When you write a letter in the inquiry stage, you should also appeal to the reader's pride, sense of equity, or self-interest.

By appealing to the reader's pride, you encourage self-esteem. You may point out the pride of satisfying financial obligations. Some writers emphasize pride in terms of avoiding the embarrassment of a bad credit record.

An alternative is an appeal to the reader's sense of equity. The thrust of an equity appeal is that the creditor provided what the customer had requested. In all fairness, the customer should acknowledge the creditor's trust by paying the bill.

Some readers may not be swayed by appeals to their pride or to their sense of equity. They may, however, respond to an appeal to their self-interest. Many people take credit for granted. If you can remind the reader of how valuable credit is, you may get a positive response. When readers realize how credit contributes to their self-interest, they may be more inclined to pay their bills and protect their credit rating.

This is how one writer approached the inquiry stage:

> Because payments have not been received on your clothing account for either July or August, the account is delinquent.
>
> In the past you have met your obligations promptly. We believe that something unusual has temporarily disrupted your payments. May we assist you in solving the problem?
>
> Please send the balance due of $180 or let us know of your plan for satisfying the account.

Usually only one letter is sent in the inquiry stage. By this time the account will be approximately 60 days late. As in the example, the writer seeks to reestablish contact with the customer by making a reply easy. By suggesting that an unusual situation has caused the delinquency, the writer makes it easy for the customer to save face. At no point, however, should the writer suggest the possibility that there was any problem with the merchandise.

Urgency

If the inquiry did not result in positive action by the customer, the collection process moves into the urgency stage. At this point the account has been delinquent for at least 90 days. A very small percentage of accounts remain delinquent for this long; however, the collection writer must be prepared to deal with the problem.

In the urgency stage the writer indicates that payments must be made at once.

At this stage you must impress upon the customer the seriousness of the situation. To signify the gravity of the situation a higher level executive will often sign the letter instead of a collection correspondent. You should convey the idea that this is the end of the line, although hope for a reasonable solution still exists. Avoid threats, however, for they may have an adverse effect on goodwill and usually elicit defensiveness rather than compliance.

At this point you might refer to the possibility of legal action, although not in specific terms. If several letters comprise the urgency stage, you should not mention a specific date for action until the final letter. One writer wrote the final letter in the urgency stage in this way:

> Based on your credit record we were sure that you would have contacted us regarding your delinquent account. The time has come for us to take stronger action in order to collect the $180 balance of your account.
>
> We will expect full payment of your account within the next ten days. We hope to avoid having to present your account to the Interstate Collection Association. Neither of us wishes to get involved in court actions, but it is a definite possibility.
>
> Please send your check for $180 by October 31. By doing so you will avoid legal entanglements that will be expensive and damaging to your credit record.

In the urgency stage the tone of the letter is more demanding than persuasive. You should emphasize the need to pay rather than the reasons the customer has not paid. In that way you avoid the stridency that destroys goodwill, but leave no question in the reader's mind about the need for immediate action.

Ultimatum

This is it—the last chance the customer will have to avoid the embarrassment and expense of legal problems. Convey the seriousness of the predicament explicitly and describe in detail what will be the consequences for nonpayment. This is the least subtle of the letters in the collection sequence. State the amount owed and the date by which it must be paid. As was true of the urgency stage, the situation is too serious for the letter to be signed by anyone other than a high-level executive. Resist the urge to name-call or to question the motives of the customer. Whether the financial problems of the customer are temporary or chronic, retaining that person's goodwill is desirable. By now the bill has been owed for 100 days or more. Writers will often use the deductive arrangement to communicate the seriousness of the situation. One writer presented the ultimatum in this way:

> Unless you pay your balance of $245 within the next five days we will turn your credit record over to Tri-State Collections. The lowered rating that will result from this adverse information will severely limit your ability to receive credit in the foreseeable future. Since it is the policy of Tri-State Collections to enforce collection in a court of law, you will also be obligated to pay all court costs.
>
> Your bill is now more than 100 days past due, and your credit record will soon be transferred from this office. Paying your balance of $245 within the next five days, however, will allow you to retain your good record and avoid the expense and frustration of legal proceedings.

The letter of ultimatum is direct and unequivocal. It is subject to only one interpretation, and that is "Pay now to avoid severe consequences." The impact of such a letter is heightened by its brevity.

A series of collection letters used by a department store follows. Each letter represents one of the five stages of a collection campaign.

Reminder—A Gentle Prod

This is a gentle reminder that a portion of the unpaid balance on your account is overdue. This is more than likely an oversight that you will correct by making a payment within the next few days. Perhaps you have mailed your remittance already. If so, we would like to thank you for your patronage.

Strong Reminder—A Direct Prod
Most of our customers appreciate a reminder when their account is overdue.

Therefore, we would like to remind you of your overdue account. Listed below is your present balance as well as the minimum amount due if you prefer monthly payments.

You may have already mailed a payment within the past few days. If not, won't you please do so?

Inquiry—To Reestablish Communication
We recently wrote to you regarding the past-due balance on your charge account. With your revolving charge account you have the option of a 30-day account or monthly payments of as little as 5 percent of the balance. At any time, of course, you may pay more or all of your balance.

Please contact us immediately if you are unable to pay the $225 now due. Together we will be able to resolve your problem.

Use the enclosed envelope for your prompt reply.

Urgency—A Genuine Crisis
Twelve years ago this October you opened a charge account with us. Since that time we have worked hard to meet your needs. Apparently we have succeeded because you have been a regular customer.

Because you have been such a loyal customer, it's all the more surprising that we have not heard a word from you. It's a mystery to us why you have allowed your account to become overdue after such a good credit history.

We are waiting for your check for $260 and we must have it. If your credit record is to be protected, you must act now.

Please send us a check today, or at least contact us so that a payment plan can be arranged. By acting immediately you may save your valuable credit record.

Ultimatum—Severe Problems Await
Your account is now more than 120 days overdue. Because you have not responded to any of our letters, we are unaware of the reasons why you have so seriously jeopardized your credit record. It is essential that you send us your account balance of $260 within the next five days. Unless payment is made within five days your account will be turned over to our attorney, and legal proceedings will begin immediately.

Time is truly running out. By making payment of $260, however, you will be able to retain the excellent credit record you have developed over the past twelve years.

> ✔ *CHECKLIST for a Collection Letter*
>
> _____ Be aware of the assumption under which each letter should be written.
>
> _____ Get what is owed without sacrificing the goodwill of the customer.
>
> _____ As a collection campaign progresses, letters should become more demanding and stress collection rather than any additional sales.
>
> _____ Keep the reminder letter low-key and matter-of-fact.
>
> _____ In the strong reminder letter you may make the customer aware of the benefits of having credit.
>
> _____ Appeal to some interest of the reader in the inquiry stage when seeking a payment or an explanation.
>
> _____ In the urgency stage you should convey the seriousness of the situation and the fact that time is running out.
>
> _____ The ultimatum is that, unless payment is made immediately, the customer's credit record will be damaged and legal proceedings may commence.

Collection strategies differ somewhat from one organization to another. In general, however, the collection correspondent's approach follows the progression from reminder to stronger reminder to inquiry to urgent appeal to ultimatum. Collection campaigns require thorough planning so that past-due bills are collected without sacrificing the goodwill of the customer.

SPECIAL REQUESTS

Large organizations may send sales letters by the hundreds of thousands. If research shows that a particular sales letter is effective, it may be used for a long time. The same is true of collection letters. Another kind of persuasive letter, however, is not normally used in mass mailings; this is a letter in which you ask a favor of someone. You will write many such letters during your career.

Because the reward for complying with such a request is small or nonexistent, writers tend to dispense with the proven sales approach. In this example the writer seems to think that the reader is either going to comply or not and that persuasion will have no effect:

> The Public Library Guild is in the midst of its annual drive for volunteers.
>
> Your name has been submitted as a possible volunteer. Please join us for an orientation session at the Woodword Library on Wednesday, September 8 at 7 P.M.
>
> Through the involvement of volunteers professional librarians are freed from clerical duties and can concentrate on performing the duties for which they were actually hired. Volunteers help make the Woodword Library run more efficiently.
>
> Please let us know that you are interested in enhancing the quality of the services provided by the Woodword Library. Your help will make a difference.

The first paragraph is more likely to elicit a response of "who cares?" than the reader's attention. In the second paragraph an invitation is extended; however, the writer made no attempt to motivate the reader to accept it. The writer points out in the next paragraph that volunteers make it possible for professional librarians to perform their intended duties but does not explain why this is important. The closing paragraph implies that the reader's unwillingness to volunteer would be evidence of disinterest in the library's services. Such a close is unlikely to make the reader receptive to future contact with the writer.

When a writer takes a fatalistic approach and assumes persuasion will have no effect, the resulting letter will be bland, and a positive response is unlikely. By adhering to the persuasive sequence, this writer was much more effective:

> You have demonstrated, through your civic mindedness in the past, the effect one dedicated person can have on a project. Now you have the opportunity again to significantly improve the services provided by one of our most important institutions.
>
> Thomas Carlyle described the founding of a library as "one of the greater things we can do." Our entire community has enjoyed the benefits of the Woodword Library, yet one obstacle prevents its continued development. A reduced budget has resulted in staff reductions, and our professional librarians must now spend most of their time on clerical tasks.
>
> Misusing professional librarians is a waste of tax money. Equally important, librarians are less accessible to those who come to learn and grow. You can help the library serve the public by performing some of the clerical duties necessary for efficient operation. There will be an orientation for new volunteers on Wednesday, September 8 at 7 P.M. in the conference room at the Woodword Library. As a Woodword volunteer you will enjoy being part of a team so clearly devoted to the public good.

The writer recognized past contributions of the reader and then described a problem that the reader could do something about. By following the AIDA steps, the writer presented the reader with good reasons for helping prior to actually requesting assistance.

Too many writers try to avoid wasting the reader's time by leading off with the request. When a letter begins, "Please send me a packet of the materials that you used to try to enlist public support for the recent bond referendum," the reader may immediately begin to think of reasons for not complying and may never read the rest of the letter. In contrast, this is the opening of a letter in which the recipient is asked to give a public speech:

> Effective public relations practitioners are able to influence the attitudes of the public on virtually any issue. You demonstrated this ability by persuading more than 40 percent of the voters to support the recent bond referendum.

The writer presented a statement with which most public relations practitioners would agree and followed that with an acknowledgment of the reader's abilities. Because no request has yet been made, there is nothing for the reader to refuse. The writer has established a common ground with the reader; the reader will continue reading:

> Most students preparing for a career in public relations are unaware of all that such a career entails. Their knowledge of the field is limited to the advice of professors, many of whom are long removed from the public arena. It is only through greater contact with successful practitioners that students will become more attuned to the realities of public relations.

The writer has laid out the problem, which is of concern to practitioners such as the reader. As a practitioner the reader is uniquely qualified to alleviate the problem:

> By speaking to the Mid-City Public Relations Society on Wednesday, March 15, you will contribute greatly to the development of public relations students. The meeting will begin at 7:00 P.M. and will be held at the Downtowner. All of our 75 members hope you will share your expertise with us.

In this paragraph the writer provided the reader with an opportunity to make a valuable contribution. This is a request that the reader will find hard to refuse.

Note the subtlety of the letter in Figure 8.6. At no point is an actual request made, yet it is certainly a request for support. It was sent on the letterhead stationery of a prestigious law firm and signed by the chairman of the board of trustees of St. Jude's House. The writer emphasized the attention and interest steps with some specific examples. The examples will stimulate the desire of the reader to provide continued support. The same organization took a different approach in another letter, shown in Figure 8.7 on page 222. It follows the AIDA sequence and is more explicit.

Many of the requests you write will be briefer and more explicit than either of these examples. However, the sequence of ideas will be the same. Note that Ray Williams followed the AIDA sequence in his letter about a jacket damaged by the dry cleaners:

> Imagine that one of your most prized possessions was ruined through no fault of your own.
>
> When you are putting yourself through college you think twice before parting with your hard-earned money, especially for luxuries, such as the leather jacket I purchased six months ago for $295. This jacket is the most expensive piece of clothing in my wardrobe. Because I was so proud of it, I gave it the best of care.
>
> Last month when the weather became too warm for leather, I took my jacket to the Peerless location in Abeline. Because I was aware of Peerless's excellent reputation in cleaning leather, I did not object to the premium price.
>
> When I picked up my jacket and discovered a large spot on the back, I was upset. I was even more upset when the Peerless manager was unable to remove the spot and then denied any responsibility for it.
>
> Please recognize that I have been too careful with my jacket to allow it to get soiled. If such had occurred I would certainly have recognized it. Since my jacket, which had been in perfect condition, is now unwearable, I believe that I am entitled to $295, the price I paid for it.
>
> For three years I have been a satisfied customer of Peerless. For even longer than that I have been aware of the excellent record of Peerless for customer satisfaction. I look forward to hearing from you.

Among the countless purposes for writing letters of special request, some of the more common ones are recruiting a guest speaker, seeking financial contributions, recruiting a chairperson or a member for a committee, requesting a letter of recommendation, and seeking cooperation for a survey. Competition is keen for the attention and cooperation of the reader. Letters that follow the persuasive strategy are more likely to elicit the desired response.

Figure 8.6
Letter Making a Special
Request: Subtle Appeal
Source: Reprinted with
permission of St. Jude's
House, Inc.

October 9, 1997

Dear St. Jude's Benefactor:

In an effort to give you a report in the most human terms of
the return on your monetary investment in St. Jude's House, it
seemed appropriate to share the following vignettes with you.

Mr. D., a long-time resident of St. Jude's House, simply could not
function outside a structured environment. He is now employed
by a hospital, pays his own way, and was recently able to spend
his vacation in his hometown—sober!

St. Jude's director has supper once a month with a former resident
with eight years' sobriety, and he is a working, taxpaying citizen
now. College educated, he came to us at St. Jude's after living in
cardboard cartons under a bridge and delivering handbills to
finance the next drink.

Mr. C., a former resident of St. Jude's House, has remained sober
for over four years. He now is an active member of Alcoholics
Anonymous. He has secured a high-paying job as a computer
programmer. His last four Christmases were sober ones, the first
in over twenty years!

Ms. B. has a long history of nonalcoholic drug abuse. She was
admitted to St. Jude's House because we needed bed occupancy.
Although she is on legal probation, last month she obtained a job
as a clerk typist, the first job she has had in a very long time.

Mr. A., a person we have worked with over the last five years,
had a kidney transplant. He was the donor—he saved his brother's life! He now has something to be proud of, and he is sober
for the first time in twenty years! Both are recovering well.

Figure 8.6
Continued

St. Jude's Benefactor
October 9, 1997
Page 2

Mr. E. is in his late twenties and has been an alcoholic since he
was fourteen. After two aborted residences, he is now settling in
and making use of the community that St. Jude's makes available
to him. His progress is good and his outlook positive for the first
time since he was fourteen.

Mr. F. was once a prominent Atlantan. He now suffers brain
damage from his alcoholism, but he has been able to "hang in" at
St. Jude's House. He now works as a parking lot attendant.
Although his family feels this job is beneath him, he is beginning
to come to grips with the fact that he will never be able to return
to his earlier profession. But he can pay his own way and become
a valued member of his community. He now has self-respect.

Although I have only scratched the surface of the human
drama that unfolds day in and day out at St. Jude's House, I hope
this insight will indicate the tremendous return on your financial
help at St. Jude's House. Your money is wisely garnered and
spent. Human suffering is alleviated, and the hope you provide is
the most touching thing in the world!

Sincerely,

E. Reginald Hancock
E. Reginald Hancock
Chairman of the Board of Trustees
St. Jude's House

ERH/sts

cc: Reverend Canon Herbert J. Beadle
       St. Jude's House Board Members

Figure 8.7
Letter Making a Special Request: Explicit Appeal
Source: Reprinted with permission of St. Jude's House, Inc.

October 16, 1997

Dear St. Jude's Benefactor:

In past years, you have generously supported St. Jude's House, and I hope you will do so again this year.

As responsible, affluent citizens we are all asked to respond to many good causes. These range from our church, handicapped children, the elderly, finding a cure for cancer and MS, Jerry Lewis Telethons, the Atlanta Symphony, the High Museum, and more. Depending on our loyalties and dispositions, we make our charitable gifts. Whose heartstrings have not been touched by a little blonde, blue-eyed girl about 5 years old with her legs in braces? It's easy to give to her.

Now, contrast that with a sloppy, falling down, filthy, bug-ridden, sour-smelling drunk who has not shaved in weeks. Some think that if he were not so damned sorry, he could stay off booze and earn a good living. Of course, this overlooks the fact that he or she is a victim of a disease, too, called alcoholism.

All those other diseased folks are going to get their share of the funds. But who is going to help that dirty drunk, who will cheat, lie, and steal for another shot of red-eye? St. Jude's does by providing a home, hope, and health for the alcoholic whose family and friends have given up. The result in many cases is little short of miraculous.

It doesn't take much to give to those other needful people. I think it takes real guts, real character, to work for and give to St. Jude's House.

St. Jude's is not perfect. Anyone who knows the frustration of fighting alcoholism will appreciate that, but we do save lives

St. Jude's Benefactor
October 16, 1997
Page 2

and we do give men and women an opportunity to regain their respect and return to our community. Moreover, while at St. Jude's, these men and women pay for a substantial portion of the cost of the house and, with the help of job location assistance, find jobs where they become taxpayers, no longer a drain on the taxpaying citizens of the city and country.

St. Jude's makes no pretense to being a large institution. It is modest in its size and scope, but it is the best thing that ever happened to many people who have been victimized by alcoholism. We receive no government aid and are not a United Way agency. Rather, we have served for 18 years because of the faithful support that you and our other friends have given us. In this fall of 1997, we ask again for your support and pledge our continued work to the alcoholics who turn to us for help.

Please help in whatever way you can and know that we are grateful.

Sincerely yours,

E. Reginald Hancock
E. Reginald Hancock
Chairman of the Board of
Trustees

St. Jude's House

ERH/sts

Key Terms

- persuasion
- credibility
- hierarchy of needs
- emotional appeal
- logical appeal
- channel selection
- persuasive letter
- AIDA sequence
- central selling point

Summary

Shaping behavior through persuasion   pp. 196–197

Four key factors in the persuasion process   p. 197

Factors of attention   pp. 198–199

Maslow's theory of motivation   p. 199

Indirect and direct rewards   pp. 200–201

Choosing the most appropriate channel   p. 204

Planning a persuasive message   pp. 204–205

AIDA sequence of ideas   p. 207

Sales letters   pp. 207–211

Writing letters to collect past due bills   pp. 212–213

Five stages of the collection process   pp. 214–217

Review Questions

1. What is the primary goal of persuasion? What more specific goals does this goal encompass?

2. What is meant by source credibility? How can we use it in constructing persuasive messages?

3. What factors can you use to gain and hold the attention of a receiver?

4. Compare and contrast Maslow's theory of motivation with the direct and indirect reward approach to motivating receivers.

5. How do the four steps in the planning process relate to the four steps in writing a sales letter?

6. Explain the difference between the interest step and the desire step.

7. Four common errors in seeking attention are presented in this chapter. Describe another error and provide an example of it.

8. Describe the five stages of a collection campaign.

9. In which ways is the reminder stage in the collection campaign similar to the strong-reminder stage? How are they different?

10. What is meant by central selling point?

Exercises

1. **Give Peas a Chance.** Del Monte Foods, a major manufacturer of canned goods, is worried about its aging customer base. People who enjoy canned foods are getting older, and younger consumers tend to pass over canned products and choose fresh or frozen fruits and vegetables. Like all brands of canned foods, Del Monte products have decreased in popularity, but you feel the company is now ready to make a comeback.

   As a Del Monte marketing executive, you have been developing catchy advertising strategies to make canned foods seem more appealing. Your boss has told you, "We're not old-fashioned. We don't use additives and preservatives in the canning process." This is a very important ad campaign, because sales of canned fruit and vegetables peaked in 1969 and have experienced a steady slow drop in supermarket sales. In order to combat this negative trend, you have decided to run commercials on MTV and E!, The Entertainment Network, to attract younger customers. You are also buying air time on the major networks with the exception of CBS, the one network with a statistically older viewing audience.

   To complement the television advertising blitz, you have developed a snazzy promotional display that will be installed in supermarkets in California, your initial test market area. The canned food display will echo the themes of your commercial spots.

   Your mission is to write a form letter addressed to the managers of supermarkets in California. This letter will accompany the display, highlighting the advantages of canned foods, including the quick preparation time and the flexibility of these products. You should emphasize how you want to promote canned foods to a more contemporary customer base.

2. **Give a Hoot, Don't Pollute.** As you rush across campus each morning on your way to class, you have noticed dozens of promotional flyers scattered along the walkways. You pick one up and see that it is an insert that appears in your college's free student newspaper, and it is an advertisement for General Motors. The car manufacturer boasts a subscription audience of one and a half million nationwide for its flyers, but you realize that most of these "subscriptions" are never read.

   You recognize that General Motors could advertise in a much more effective way. You feel that they should know that their inserts are not really reaching the intended audience and that they create a noticeable litter problem at your school, as well as an unnecessary waste of paper.

   Your mission is to persuade General Motors to stop using the newspaper inserts as their primary way of advertising to college students. You could suggest that they develop radio spots for popular college stations, or at least print ads inside the newspaper pages, rather than use the insert format. Address your letter to: Marta Simmons, Vice President of Public Relations, General Motors Corporation, P.O. Box 1000, Detroit, MI 47076.

3. **Rock On.** Your roommate and four other friends have formed an alternative rock band called The Suicide Clowns. Because of your shrewd business sense, they have asked you to help them promote their music and find places to play, and as the band's new manager, you have been thinking of ways to get greater exposure for the band. You think that The Suicide Clowns should offer to play

at local establishments on Wednesday and Thursday nights, for considerably less than you would charge for a weekend performance.

The band members have been playing together for a few months and they have recorded a promotional tape that you will use to drum up business. Featuring a unique combination of Latin rhythms and hard-edge guitar sound, you feel that The Suicide Clowns could gain widespread popularity—with the proper marketing strategies.

Your mission is to write a letter to attach to the demo tape, which you will send to various bars and restaurants. In this letter, give a brief description of the band members and their music, and be sure to include a fee schedule, with a reduced rate for weeknights. Emphasize that The Suicide Clowns have a growing listening audience, and since the band will attract more customers to a particular night spot, the situation could be mutually beneficial for the band and the business owners.

4. **The Gift of Life.** You are the American Red Cross representative at your university, and you are organizing a series of blood drives throughout the school year at different locations on campus. You want to set up the blood donation facilities at the Law School and the Business School, as well as the larger department buildings in the university. The first blood drive this year is scheduled in the Business School, and in past years, the business students have not participated at the same level of the other students. You feel that this year you should distribute a brief letter to this group of students in order to show them the merits of giving blood.

Your mission is to develop a catchy letter so that the business students will be motivated to give blood to the American Red Cross. You should appeal to the often competitive nature of the business world by suggesting the idea of competing with other schools within the university to have the highest participation rate. Inform the students how necessary and valuable their blood donation will be, and encourage them to give the gift of life.

5. **Tennis Anyone?** Avery Dimming, a New York inventor, has recently developed the Avery Swinger, a large curved device that can be attached to your tennis racket to create wind resistance. Tennis players can modify the level of drag by adjusting the Avery Swinger on the racket. This invention can help tennis players warm up, work out, or practice more powerful strokes, and its curved surface provides ten times more wind resistance than a standard racket cover.

As the store manager of the Sports Authority in Rockville, Maryland, you stock a variety of sporting goods equipment. You read about the Avery Swinger in the newspaper, and because tennis is the most popular sport in your area, you would like to order this product for your store. You read that the product is difficult to sell in mail-order catalogs since shipping costs are high due to its large size, but you feel that the Avery Swinger would sell much better in stores and you should seize the opportunity to be among the first to sell it.

Your mission is to write to Don Mendelssohn, Director of Purchasing, Sports Authority, Inc., 750 Remington Road, Columbus, OH 34800. You want to inform him about this invention and suggest that the Avery Swinger be sold in all Sports Authority stores. Describe the advantages of the product and attempt to convince Mr. Mendelssohn to stock this product.

6. **Keeping the Streets Safe.** You have become very worried about safety issues on your campus since there has been an increase in violent attacks. You are especially concerned because women area often studying very late and leave the library alone. The area surrounding the library is not very well lit and you feel that the University should provide street lamps in this are, as well as in other poorly lit areas near the student dorms.

Your mission is to formulate a letter to University Utility Improvements division. You want to persuade them to install good-quality lights along the paths near the library because at night these paths are the most commonly used walkways in the entire university. Be sure to cite the recent incidents of attacks in the area to emphasize your points. Address the letter to: Ms. Ann Marie Benton, Utility Improvements Coordinator, Central University, Fenwick Hall, Valley, IA 54928.

7. **Better Safe than Sorry.** After you drafted your letter to improve campus lighting (question 6), you recognized that, even with better lighted pathways, students must be increasingly careful and help each other. There is safety in numbers, and you want students to be aware that they never need to walk any distance at night alone. The Student Union recently started a Student Escort Service, and you have offered to help promote this service. The Escort Service will provide an escort for a walk from the library to any of the nearby parking lots, in addition to providing an Escort Service van that will take students home, within a three-mile radius. You feel that this service is much-needed and you are thinking up ways to let others know about it.

Your mission is to write a letter to Mabel Smith, Director of the Rape Crisis Center and Women's Clinic, 3 University Way, Valley, IA 54928. You want the Center to know about the Student Escort Service and encourage people to use it. Explain how it works and that anyone can call 4ES-CORT to get in touch with the service operators.

8. **Running Is Good for the Heart.** A few years ago, you began running to get into shape and now you have become an avid runner. You always look forward to the various road races held in nearby communities because these races are an opportunity to set goals and have a little friendly competition. You believe that the races inspire more people to exercise, especially if the race entry fees help provide funds for a charitable organization. When your sister, a volunteer for the American Heart Association, asked for your advice in planning a 10-kilometer race to support the local AHA branch, you agreed to chair the race planning committee.

Through radio and newspaper advertisements, you have generated considerable interest in the event. Prominent area businesses, like Pete's Pet Palace and Office Works, are already sponsoring the race, and you anticipate that hundreds of people will participate. You would like some more sponsors, and you have decided to contact local sporting goods stores to see if they would like to donate some small item that race participants would receive after they cross the finish line. You feel that this would be a great way for these stores to promote themselves to people who could really use their products.

Your mission is to write a form letter to the owners of sporting goods stores in your area, asking them to support this event. First describe the race and how it will benefit the American Heart Association. Then suggest that the business owners can promote their stores within the runners' community by donating their products to the cause. Be sure to tell them that you will include their company logo on the race T-shirts and other promotional items. Also mention your general goal—to get more people involved in running and exercising—and mention your own personal experience.

9. **Refreshments on the Run.** In response to your letter in question 8, you have obtained two sporting goods stores who are providing towels and key chains to race participants. Now you are working on the final details of the race day, and you would like to provide free refreshments to all race participants and have concession stands where onlookers could purchase food and drinks.

Your mission is to draft a form letter that will be distributed to approximately twenty local restaurants, asking them to set up concession stands during race day festivities. Mention that the restaurants could have the chance to sell their products at concession stands, making this event a good business opportunity. Since it is a charitable event, however, you would appreciate it if the restaurants would consider donating refreshments to the race participants. Make an appeal similar to the one you made to the owners of the sporting goods stores in the previous question.

10. **PCs—For Play or Profit.** As the parent of two children, you decided to purchase a home computer to supplement their education. When you bought the computer, you also believed it would help you manage your finances and organize your household. Now that your family has been using the computer for a few months, you realize that the kids mainly use it to avoid their schoolwork by playing endless hours of video games.

    You made a trip to the downtown software store, and you were surprised to find out how many computer games were available. Exciting adventure games are displayed prominently in the store, and you had difficulty finding the software that would be useful in aiding your children's education. The educational software you found looked rather drab and unappealing, compared to the impressive graphics on the games software.

    Your mission is to write a letter to Digital Pictures Inc., a major manufacturer of video games located at 400 Seaward Drive, San Mateo, CA 98760. You decided to write to this particular company because your children really like Digital Pictures games, but you would like the company to consider using its graphic capabilities to enliven mathematics or grammar lessons. Explain that you think that a gamelike format could be used to educate children and that you would like to see children learning more at home with the computer.

11. **Hike or Bike?** You live in northern Virginia and, to escape from the frantic pace of the Washington, DC, metropolitan area, you like to go hiking on the trails in the Shenandoah Valley. Recently you and your friends were hiking peacefully at White Oak Canyon Park, when you were overrun by speedy mountain-bike riders going along the narrow trail. You actually like to ride your own bike, so you are not opposed to biking in general, but like many hikers you feel that the bikers are making the trails unsafe. The bikers can be inconsiderate to the hikers as well as to the environment. You have noticed that the bike tracks create ruts that accelerate erosion on many trails.

    Your mission is to inform White Oak park rangers about this problem. You want to persuade them to consider opening some trails only to hikers, and perhaps other trails to bikers. Describe your experiences in this park and suggest real solutions to the hiker/biker conflict. Address your letter to Barbara Johnstone, Director of Park Services, White Oak Canyon Park, P.O. Box 345, Madison, VA 24293.

12. **A Different World.** Last semester you agreed to be a companion for a foreign exchange student from Madrid, Spain. Originally you thought that the opportunity would help you improve your Spanish and you wanted to become more fluent. You decided to meet with Juan Hernandez every Monday and Friday for lunch, but after a few weeks of getting to know each other, you became good friends and started going out together on weekends and studying together. Juan went back home over winter break, and because of your positive experience you have volunteered to sponsor another student this spring.

Since you are an international relations major, you enjoy teaching others about cultures and you feel that other students in your department would benefit from the chance to spend time with foreign students.

Your mission is to write a letter to distribute to 75 international relations majors at your college. Tell them about the great experience you had when you met Juan last semester and urge them to befriend an international student. Interested people should contact the Society at Student Union, P.O. Box 34.

13. **Get a Job!** In your job as the assistant to the Career Development Counselor at your university, you persuade the students you meet to start thinking about planning their courses and preparing for their future careers. You want to help others with their job searches and, from your previous experiences, you have determined that liberal arts majors, especially, sometimes lack direction.

Your supervisor has instructed you to write a form letter to all juniors asking them to start thinking about their job options before their final year of college. You should inform them of all of the resources available in the Career Center library, including the University's Alumni Databases as well as Industry and City Directories.

Your mission is to write a special letter containing the above information directed only toward liberal arts majors. Be sure to emphasize the benefits of a broad-based liberal arts education and how students can apply their analytical and writing skills to a variety of careers. Suggest that the students become involved with the Career Center and, if they need further guidance in determining a suitable career path, inform them of the aptitude tests and other resources available in your office.

14. **Satisfy Your Sweet Tooth.** You own a candy company that makes and distributes chocolate bars and gourmet jelly beans. The candies come in festive holiday packaging for the December gift-giving season, and you have compiled a catalog of your products which you want to make available to local schools. The schools can sell your candies for a fund-raising project, and each school will receive 20 cents' profit on every dollar of candy sold by the students.

Your mission is to write a letter to the principal of your neighborhood's school, Ms. Elizabeth Higgins, Clark Hill Elementary School, 500 N. Main St., Youngsville, PA 15467. You will first write to Ms. Higgins to see how receptive she is to the fund-raising idea before distributing your catalogs to other nearby schools. Be sure to emphasize the guaranteed profits the school will make from selling your products, and suggest that the school consider undertaking the fund-raiser in time for the upcoming holiday season.

15. **A Little Goes a Long Way.** As a well-known student athlete at your university, you want to maintain a high standard for academic and athletic excellence. Two years ago, the university began construction of a modern new sports fitness facility, but the project has encountered many difficulties and the costs have skyrocketed. You recognize that the new facility, with its indoor swimming pool, track, racquetball courts, and aerobic and weight-lifting rooms, could really benefit the entire population of 40,000 students. But the funds to complete the facility are dwindling and the state government cannot allocate any more money to this project.

Your mission is to write a letter to the general student body, which you will submit for publication in the university's daily newspaper. In this letter, suggest that every student contribute at least one dollar to a capital project fund to complete the sports facility. Even if each individual contributes only one dollar, you could raise $40,000. Suggest that it would be worth even five or ten dollars to students who would no longer have to pay over $100 to join a local gym. Offer to administer collection of the money and suggest that students drop off their dollars in the centrally located Coliseum box office.

16. **Expanding Cultural Horizons.** You are serving on a special committee to promote awareness of cultural diversity at your school. The committee meets twice monthly and plans cultural events that focus on different ethnic groups within the university community.

    Until this point, the Cultural Diversity Committee has had only student members, but due to recent concern about cultural sensitivity, you have suggested that the committee ask some faculty members to get involved. You have determined that Dr. Louis Hammond, a professor of Asian studies, would be a very valuable faculty advisor for the committee, and you would like to approach him about serving on the committee.

    Your mission is to compose a letter to Dr. Louis Hammond, Department of Asian Studies, Willow Hall, Oliver State University, Yardley, PA 17303. You will describe the activities of the committee and tell Dr. Hammond that the group would be honored to have his guidance. Let him know that you will set up an appointment with him next week, but you wanted to give him time to consider the position before talking to him in person.

17. **California Dreamin'.** As an employee of the California Tourist Bureau, you read all of the trade publications, and in the latest issue of *U.S. Travel*, you found a survey showing that your state has fallen dramatically in popularity polls. California is no longer the most popular tourist spot in America, due to the frequent natural disasters and negative publicity related to urban problems.

    In this survey, Americans named Florida as the most desirable vacation destination. Since you recognize that California, like Florida, has sun, surf, and amusement parks, you have decided to emphasize these aspects of the state when you promote California as a tourist haven.

    You feel that the survey results accurately reflect people's desires to vacation elsewhere, since your statistical resources also note a drop in tourism during the past two years. You have decided to take action by writing an informative letter to prominent travel agencies in states west of the Mississippi River.

    Your mission is to draft a form letter to send to travel agents urging them to encourage their clients to visit California. Be very positive and emphasize all of the exciting attractions that the state offers. Be sure to discuss the possibilities of visiting northern and/or southern California and what tourists can do in these different areas.

18. **Seeing Double.** You are working for a chef in an unusual Manhattan restaurant to help pay for your college education. The restaurant is called Twins, and it is owned by Lisa and Debbie Ganz, 27-year-old identical twins. The sisters employ only identical twins on the restaurant's wait staff and the restaurant is becoming increasingly popular because many people are intrigued by the novel idea.

    When Lisa and Debbie hire twin waiters or waitresses, the twins must agree to work all of the same shifts, and if one twin is sick or otherwise unavailable, both twins must find a substitute pair to work for them. Lisa and Debbie have been having some logistical problems staffing the restaurant, and you found out that there is a National Twins Association, which distributes a quarterly newsletter. The twin owners have asked you to help contact the NTA for help.

    Your mission is to write a letter to Dan Brownwell, Editor of the National Twin News, P.O. Box 7564, Memphis, TN 49786. Suggest that the newsletter run a story about the restaurant in order to gain publicity, but, more importantly, to ask any twins (or triplets!) in the greater New York City area to think about working at the restaurant.

19. **Juicy Information.** Last month, you opened a vegetarian restaurant and juice bar in the downtown shopping district in Athens, Georgia. You believe in the therapeutic powers of healthy eating and you are aware that many college students have poor diets and drink excessive amounts of caffeine. You would like to inform the students that they can improve their health by eating and drinking better, and you would also like to encourage them to try your restaurant.

    Your mission is to write a letter to Jeanie Davis, Chief Nutritionist of the Gilbert Health Center, University of Georgia, Athens, GA 30601. Let her know that your restaurant is now open and tell her some of the items on your menu. Explain that you would like to promote healthy eating in the university community and you would appreciate it if she would try your restaurant in the hope that she will recommend it to others.

20. **Let the Flicks Begin.** You are sales manager of Columbia Cable Television Corporation. You must persuade the public to subscribe to Living Room Theatre, a channel featuring movies 24 hours a day. Many of the movies are recent films; none is more than one year old. The cost of Living Room Theatre is $5.50 per month or $55 per year if paid in a single payment at the time of subscribing. There are no commercials on this channel, and free maintenance is provided to any subscriber. Living Room Theatre has just become available in Huntington, West Virginia.

    Your mission is to write a sales letter in a form that could be sent to all the residents of that area. (If you wish to name some of the movies scheduled to be shown in the near future, use your imagination.)

21. **Walk Don't Run.** As owner-publisher of *Global Running* magazine you have observed a significant decline in running as a pastime during the past two years. During the same time period the number of subscribers has declined 45 percent. Walking appears to be the sport of choice for an ever-increasing segment of the population. For that reason, you have started *Healthful Walking* magazine and are planning to discontinue *Global Running* in February.

    In recent years favorable publicity for walking has emphasized that, unlike running, it is not harmful to ankles, knees, or the skeletal system. It has been shown to strengthen the cardiovascular system, and people of any age can do it. Different age groups have different interests, and when you write to present subscribers about discontinuing publication of *Global Running*, you plan to tailor your message to three age groups: 16–30, 31–50, and over 50.

    Your mission is to prepare a letter for one of the age groups. Offer either to send a refund for the unfulfilled portion of their *Global Running*, subscriptions or to substitute issues of *Healthful Walking*. Those who elect to receive *Walking* will receive double the number of issues remaining on their *Running* subscriptions.

22. **Local Color.** Your favorite course work, with the exception of business communication, is international business. You have become aware of the importance of understanding people from other cultures, and, with that in mind, you have decided to embark on a project. Every other week during the summer your community is visited by a group of 30 to 40 German tourists. These tours are sponsored by the German–American Friendship Association and are conducted by a major U.S. bus company. Although each group spends 2½ days in your community, the members rarely meet any of the residents, nor, to your way of thinking,

do they get much of a feel for the area. The individual tour guides, who are invariably from northeastern cities, know only what is in the tour guide manual.

Your mission is to write a letter to the German–American Friendship Association and offer your services as a guide for the 2½ days each group spends in your community. Suggest also that the association seek out knowledgeable individuals in each community to serve as guides. You feel that better understanding between people would result and that the tours would be more enjoyable for the tourists. Your fee for serving as a local guide would be $100 per day. The address of the German–American Friendship Association is 2 Hamburg 13, Hafenstrasse 28, Germany.

23. **Don't Hibernate.** You own a sporting goods store and have completed a mailing list of the members of the various bicycle clubs in your area.

    Your mission is to prepare a sales letter to be sent to the club members in late October, when a typical Minnesota winter is about to begin. Try to sell the readers on continuing to enjoy the benefits of cycling exercise by purchasing a new Exer-Bike. The Exer-Bike is manufactured in the United States, weighs only 22 pounds, and sells for $210. It is a stationary bike, 40 inches long and 30 inches high, and the handlebar is 22 inches long. The handlebar is easily adjusted, without tools, for persons of any height.

24. **Get the Picture.** You volunteered to take pictures at your cousin's wedding to save the newlyweds the expense of hiring a photographer. You took approximately 150 pictures and gave them to a local camera store for processing. More than half of the photographs were badly blurred. Because you are an accomplished photographer, you know that you are not at fault. The owner of the camera store disclaims responsibility, because he merely sent the films to another for processing. The store owner has offered to give you free film equivalent to the amount of film that was blurred.

    Your mission is to write a letter to the photo laboratory that processed the film. You have suffered considerable embarrassment, and you believe that the photo laboratory should pay you at least $100 in damages. You intend to give whatever payment you get to your cousin. Write your letter to Slic Pics Inc., P.O. Box 1212, Hilda, MO 65670.

25. **Correcting an Injustice.** While you await your flight home after a two-week tour of Europe, an announcement is made that the flight is overbooked. You volunteer to take a later flight in exchange for the airline's offer of a free six-course dinner at an elegant French restaurant. The airline guarantees that you will have a seat on the next flight, which is scheduled to depart 10 hours later. When you arrive for the later flight, having enjoyed a sumptuous meal, you learn that, in order to get enough volunteers for a later flight, the airline paid some passengers as much as $400 in exchange for their seats. You are upset with what you regard as unequal treatment, and you feel that you should get additional payment.

    Your mission is to write a letter to Jean-Paul Langlois, Vice President of Customer Service, Air Marseilles Inc., Marseilles, France.

CASE

Fishing for a Break

David B. Parsons, Lakehead University, Thunder Bay, Ontario

Mr. Parker McCart is a fisherman who sails out of Channel-Port aux Basques, Newfoundland. Parker just spent $10,000 refitting his trawler, which had been severely damaged during a brutal storm that battered the southwestern coast of Newfoundland. Parker spent $5,000 of his own money and $5,000 borrowed from his brother Ian, a lobster fisherman in Pictou, Nova Scotia.

Parker also owes $800 to McDonald's Department Store for two cribs, two carriages, two playpens, baby clothes, and other assorted items purchased soon after his wife, Annie, presented him with twin girls three months ago. Because of the damage to his trawler, Parker is unable to pay the account, in spite of McDonald's demands for payment.

Assuming the role of Parker McCart, write a letter to McDonald's requesting some consideration regarding the account. Create whatever conditions you perceive to be fair.

Case Questions

1. Do you think McDonald's should consider Parker's request?

2. How would McDonald's benefit?

3. Should Parker use an emotional appeal?

4. What strategy should Parker adopt?

CASE

The Broken Heel

Anita S. Bednar, The University of Central Oklahoma

You recently represented your company at a conference in Ft. Worth, Texas. The conference was held in the Imperial Hotel, a three-star hotel that you had stayed in before. The service had always been excellent—good food, friendly professional atmosphere, and fast check-in and checkout. You were pleased when the business meeting was scheduled for the Imperial again this year.

Unfortunately, some construction was underway at the hotel; in fact, a contractor was refurbishing most of the meeting rooms. Plastic sheeting was being used as dividers, and this made hearing the speakers nearly impossible. Going from one meeting room to the next, you stepped in a space that was normally covered by carpet and broke the heel of your shoe. You had to hobble around for a couple of hours before buying new shoes to wear during the remainder of the three-day conference. The shoes cost $65.

When you arrived home from the meeting, you attempted to have your shoe with the broken heel repaired. The Tyler Shoe Shop did repair the heel for $10.50, but did not match the heel on the other shoe. One of your colleagues suggested that you write the Imperial Hotel for some kind of reimbursement. You decide that you will.

Case Questions
1. Should this be considered a persuasive letter or a routine claim letter?
2. Should you ask the Imperial Hotel to reimburse you for your new shoes, the repair of the broken heel, or both?
3. To which of the following should you send the letter?

    The general manager of the hotel

    The convention director

    The reservation clerk
4. How much detail should you give about the circumstances?
5. Should you use your personal stationery or your company letterhead?
6. Should you also complain about the disruption of the meetings because of the construction going on?
7. What kind of goodwill statement can you include?

Notes
1. Ferd Nauheim, "Society's Changes Require New Approaches to Persuasion," *Direct Marketing*, November 1978, 40.
2. Vance Packard, *The Hidden Persuaders* (New York: D. McKay, 1957).
3. Roger Fisher, Elizabeth Kopelman, and Andrea Kupfer Schneider, *Beyond Machiavelli* (Cambridge: Harvard Press, 1994).
4. David Ogilvy, *Confessions of an Advertising Man* (New York: Atheneum, 1963).
5. David Ogilvy, *Ogilvy on Advertising* (New York: Crown, 1983).
6. John Parrish-Sprowl, Rod Carveth, and Marshall Senk, "The Effect of Compliance-Gaining Strategy Choice and Communicator Style on Sales Success," *The Journal of Business Communication*, October 1994, 305.
7. Paul A. Dion and Elaine M. Notarantonio, "Salesperson Communication Style: The Neglected Dimension in Sales Performance," *The Journal of Business Communication*, Winter 1992, 74.
8. Abraham Maslow, *Motivation and Personality* (New York: Harper & Row, 1954).
9. John Caples, *Tested Advertising Methods* (Englewood Cliffs, NJ: Prentice-Hall, 1975), as quoted in David Ogilvy, *Ogilvy on Advertising* (New York: Crown, 1983).
10. "Nation in Brief," *Atlanta Constitution*, April 3, 1992, A4.
11. Stuart M. Klein, "Communication Strategies for Successful Organizational Change," *Industrial Management*, January/February 1994, 28.
12. Eric Sandelands, "Channels of Communication," *Work Study*, September/October 1994, 3.
13. J. David Johnson, William A. Donohue, Charles K. Atkin, and Sally Johnson, "Differences between Formal and Informal Communication Channels," *The Journal of Business Communication*, April 1994, 120.
14. Jim Powell, "The Lucrative Trade of Crafting Junk Mail," *The New York Times*, June 20, 1982, F-7.
15. Ogilvy, *Ogilvy on Advertising*, 60.
16. James R. Rosenfield, "In the Mail," *Direct Marketing*, April 1995, 39.

Chapter 9

Memoranda

Gary Ferguson had been in his current position for about three months and he was extremely eager to make a favorable impression on upper management. In order to get noticed, he began writing memoranda on the subject of efficiency in the company. He knew this was a particular concern of the CEO, and he sent copies to all the managers through interoffice mail. He had learned in school that writing makes a lasting impression on people, that it is much more permanent than oral communication. Gary took the opportunity to capture the attention of upper management as often as possible. His memos were very detailed because he knew how the company valued thoroughness.

One day Gary accidentally overheard two middle managers talking by the water cooler. One said how ironic it was that Ferguson wasted so much company time with lengthy and boring memos about efficiency of all things. The other laughed and said maybe Ferguson was trying to teach by negative example. Gary was stunned. The criticism really hurt because he realized these managers were right. He had made an impression all right, a bad one.

Gary went to the library that night after work and looked at a book about effective writing. He found that memos should generally be one page or less. Otherwise, few people are likely to read them. Also memos should be used sparingly. The more memos a person sends, the less of an impact each one has. Gary thought back to his first months on the job, and wondered how long it would take for his co-workers to forget his earlier bombardment-by-memo campaign.

Some people call it "memoitis," and others talk about "memomania." Many refer to it in terms that would never appear in textbooks. Managers who overuse memos are called "memomaniacs." What they are all talking about is the excessive use of memoranda. In many organizations employees complain that they are swamped with memos. "If I read every memorandum that I received, I wouldn't have time for anything else," is a frequent complaint.

Complaints about the excessive use of memoranda are not new. Over 40 years ago Robert Benchley described the problems in this way:

> When the mail is disposed of we have what is known as Memorandum Hour. During this period everyone sends memoranda to everyone else. If you happen to have nothing in particular about which to dictate a memorandum, you dictate a memorandum to someone, saying that you have nothing to suggest or report. This gives a stimulating exchange of ideas,

and also helps to use up the blue memorandum blanks which have been printed at some expense for just that purpose.[1]

Such statements are exaggerations. It is true that memoranda are widely used, but mostly for good reason.

CHARACTERISTICS AND USES OF MEMORANDA

A **memorandum** is a message written for use within the organization. Traditionally letters are used for external communication; ordinarily the memorandum is intended solely for internal communication. Researchers have found that approximately 90 percent of the writing done by business people is in the form of letters or memos. The same researchers also found that business people write more memos than letters.[2]

The main explanation for the popularity of memoranda is that within large organizations there is a great need for communication. As organizations grow, problems of coordination become more severe. Memoranda can help to keep the various parts of the organization in touch with one another. They have many different uses: to convey information from one department to another, to communicate between branches, or to file as records and reference. In fact, the memorandum is the most widely used form of written communication within the organization.

Memoranda influence the personal and professional lives of most business people simply because they are the primary means of updating employees on what is going on in the organization. Policy and procedural changes as well as details of internal operations in general are usually conveyed via memoranda.

Because memos are highly visible in most organizations, employees have definite opinions about them. In a poll of 1,000 executives conducted by Robert Half International, the following major complaints were registered:[3] 76 percent felt that most memos are too long; 58 percent believed that copies are distributed too broadly; 55 percent believed that most memos are too self-serving; and 20 percent think that memos are too often written in haste or anger. Not too surprisingly, four out of ten executives said that memos were a waste of time. The management of United Technologies Corporation felt strongly enough to purchase the full-page ad in the *Wall Street Journal* shown in Figure 9.1.

The memorandum is used primarily for internal communication.

Memo To Those Who Write Memos:	Art Buchwald tells of the kid who visited his father's office. When asked what his father did, the kid said, "He sends pieces of paper to other people and other people send papers to him." When you draft a memo, remember other people love to "correct" drafts. The more textually taut you keep it, the less chance for others to pounce on it. The Lord's Prayer has 71 words. The Ten Commandments has 297. The Gettysburg Address has 271. The legal marriage vow has two. General McAuliffe at the Bulge made his point in one: "Nuts!" For practice, send your memo to yourself as a straight telegram at your own expense. Chances are, the less your telegram costs, the more effective your memo is.

Figure 9.1
A Public Statement on Memorandum Writing
Source: United Technologies Corporation, 1986.

THE ADVANTAGES OF MEMORANDA

Memoranda have several advantages over oral communication.

Because memoranda are intended for internal communication, it might appear easier to talk to the other person than to write a memorandum. This is sometimes true, but using a memorandum has distinct advantages:

1. A memorandum provides a written record. Unlike a conversation, a memorandum can be filed for future reference. It serves as a written record for the writer or for the reader or for both. The more important the subject of the memorandum, the more likely that copies will be filed. By referring to the memorandum at a later date, both receiver and sender are reminded of specifics, such as date, individual responsibilities, and deadlines.

2. A memorandum is suitable for transmitting complex information. When a spoken message contains a lot of very specific detail or is in some other way complex, the listener has difficulty remembering it. Complicated instructions are easily misunderstood under the best of circumstances, but when they are spoken, the chances for error are manifold. Consequently, a memorandum becomes an accurate memory jogger.

3. A memorandum can reach many persons simultaneously. If you must transmit some information to a number of coworkers, contacting each one individually is time consuming. Schedule conflicts may make it difficult to assemble the group for a meeting. A memorandum, however, can reach a large number of individuals easily.

Memoranda were once economical but now may cost almost as much as a letter.

At one time memoranda were considered to be economical. They were routinely handwritten and usually designated for individuals who were difficult to contact by telephone or face to face. Many memoranda are now prepared on a word processor, however, and the expense is almost as great as for actual letters. There is a savings in postage and envelopes, perhaps, but little more than that.

Since the electronic revolution, described in Chapter 4, first began to impact business communication practices, the prospect of a paperless office has been debated. The idea of no longer having to face a desk piled high with paperwork, much of it memoranda, has a certain allure to it; such a transformation is occurring, however, it is very gradual. In many organizations messages that formerly were conveyed as traditional memos are now routinely sent via E-mail, especially if the message is a brief one. Longer memoranda continue to be sent on paper and, of course, there are many organizations not yet using E-mail.

THE SIGNIFICANCE OF MEMORANDA TO THE WRITER

People are judged in part by the memoranda they write.

In larger organizations the impression you make on your coworkers is determined partially by the memoranda you write. Your manner of communicating influences what others think of you. The further removed the other person is from you, the stronger the effect of your memoranda. For example, when Brenda Thornton sent a memorandum suggesting a change in pricing procedures, her superior, Bill Hawley, did not have the authority to act on it. For that reason she provided more detailed information than Bill, who was familiar with the topic, would have required. Bill forwarded the memorandum to his superior, Max Whitcomb, who had never met Brenda and knew little about her. His perception of her was created largely by her thorough memorandum.

When you are working in a large organization, the impression you make upon others goes beyond those with whom you personally interact. It extends to all who read your memoranda. For some, their sole link with you may be through your memoranda. In the example, Brenda's managerial potential was recognized in part through her efficient use of the medium.

THE SIGNIFICANCE OF MEMORANDA TO THE ORGANIZATION

Occasionally a memo intended for a small number of receivers within the organization is released to the public, either inadvertently or intentionally. Such occurrences, while rare, have sometimes been covered by the mass media. For example, in September 1989, when Bryant Gumbel, "Today Show" host, wrote a memo to his boss in which he evaluated other people on the show, its release triggered a public outpouring of feelings, many negative toward Gumbel.[4] The incident led to a live on-the-air public apology by him.

In another instance, Georgia Pacific Corporation's bitter takeover battle with Great Northern Nekoosa Corporation was further inflamed by Great Northern's contention that it had "uncovered" one of Georgia Pacific's internal memos. In it Georgia Pacific is alleged to have been planning an action contrary to what it had been publicly proclaiming.[5]

Fortunately most of the memos you will write during your career will be unlikely to result in such major repercussions. Nevertheless, you should write them with care.

PREPARATION OF MEMORANDA

The memorandum has evolved to simplify communication within the organization. Some of the niceties of letter writing are sacrificed for the sake of conciseness.

BOXED IN

AN ETHICAL DILEMMA

The Cumberland Corporation has experienced problems in retaining good employees since Uniframe Inc. opened a plant in the same town two years ago. Uniframe recently announced the addition of a third shift. This meant to Ben Thomas, plant manager at Cumberland, that he could expect even greater problems in retaining his best workers.

Today Ben received in his company mail packet a memo from division headquarters that was actually intended only for the vice presidents. It details a sizable layoff scheduled in two months to last for an indefinite period. Readers are cautioned to honor the secrecy of the memo because Cumberland must complete several major orders before the layoff.

Ben knows that he should not have received the memo in the first place. He also knows that, unless he alerts good, loyal workers to the coming layoff, they will miss the chance to be hired by Uniframe. To whom does he owe the greatest allegiance: his loyal employees or the company?

Ben feels boxed in. What would you do?

Figure 9.2
Example of a One-Page
Memorandum

MEMO

TO: All Department Heads

FROM: Wayne Kasten,
           Compensation Manager

DATE: December 2, 1996

SUBJECT: Holiday Schedule for Salary Submission

Because of the abbreviated work schedule for December 23 through December 27, all salary request forms must be received at this office no later than December 16. Any adjustments in pay that are requested between December 16 and December 23 will be represented in the January payroll.

Format

The format of the memorandum ensures consistency in internal communication.

The format of the memorandum is intended to simplify and speed up internal communication by ensuring consistency. A typical form for memoranda appears in Figure 9.2.

Some organizations provide employees with preprinted forms that have the basic elements of any memorandum printed at the top of the page:

To:
From:
Date:
Subject:

By providing this format, a company can ensure that certain types of information always appear in the same place in memoranda. Finding a particular memorandum in a file is easier if all the memoranda are uniform in the placement of this information. You will know precisely where to look to find the subject of each memorandum.

Some organizations provide more structured forms to further simplify the process of memorandum preparation. Some structured forms consist of an original and two color-coded carbon copies and include space for the recipient to reply. This is the usual sequence of steps in using such a form:

1. The initiator writes the message, addresses the form, and removes one of the copies to keep as a reminder.

2. The recipient replies in the space provided, removes the second copy, and returns the original to the initiator.

3. The initiator now has the message and its reply on one form and can take whatever action is necessary.

Although such forms are intended primarily for internal communication, in exceptional instances they are sometimes used more broadly. Some organizations use such forms for routine correspondence with people outside the organization. For example, suppose that you order a lightweight tent from a sporting goods company. Although the company does not have the model you ordered in stock, a comparable model is available. The company might use such a form to notify you and await your response.

Memoranda vary considerably in length. Some, such as Figure 9.2, are brief, perhaps no more than a few sentences, while others may be three or four pages long. Some companies provide half-sheet memorandum forms for short messages, thus reducing the expense of paper. (Others feel that the savings from smaller forms are offset by the problems in filing and finding these smaller forms.) When a memorandum is more than one page long, each subsequent page should have a heading showing the addressee's name, the page number, and the date, similar to the continuing page of a letter. In some organizations the subject of the memorandum is also included, as shown in Figure 9.3.

Planning and Writing

Generally, business writers agonize less over wording and other stylistic matters when they write memoranda than when they write letters. Intended for internal communication, memoranda are usually less formal and more direct. Exceptions occur, however. For example, after Becke Longman's research convinced her that a training

Figure 9.3
Example of a Two-Page
Memorandum

MEMO

TO: All Exempt Employees

FROM: Bill Wendall, Chairperson, Evaluation Committee

DATE: September 30, 1997

SUBJECT: Explanation of Delphi Technique to Measure Clarity and
          Equity of Personnel Procedures

On October 1, 1997, 20 percent of the exempt employees will be invited to participate in an evaluation of personnel procedures within the company. This memo is an explanation of the Delphi technique, which will be used in investigating the subject.

Purpose of the Delphi Technique

The Delphi technique is a method of combining the knowledge and abilities of a diverse group to reach conclusions when true values are not known. Exempt personnel from all departments will be involved in presenting their thoughts on all aspects of personnel procedures. It is expected that such company practices as recruitment, selection, performance evaluation, and promotion will be among the topics considered.

This study is intended to result in some modifications in current personnel practices within the company. It is expected that subsequent personnel operations will better meet the needs of exempt employees once the personnel practices needing improvement are identified.

Advantages of Delphi Technique

The Delphi technique is an upward communication format that has several advantages over the questionnaires used in previous surveys. The Delphi technique is less structured than the questionnaire and thus allows for greater input from employees. Feedback is more immediate than it is from questionnaires, and unlike questionnaires the Delphi technique allows respondents to refine their thinking.

In earlier studies within the company, interviews and group meetings have been used to elicit employee attitudes and opinions. The Delphi technique is not only less expensive, but it also provides the anonymity that is lacking in interviews and group meetings.

program was the most likely solution to the materials waste problem, she devoted three days to preparing the report for her boss. She knew that he would not be willing to spend the sizable amount of money necessary for the program unless she could show that the training program would be likely to solve the problem. In short, she had to persuade him.

Figure 9.3
Continued

Memo to All Exempt Employees
(Explanation of Delphi Technique)
September 30, 1997
Page 2

The feedback present in the Delphi technique exposes all of the members to other points of view and stimulates everyone's thinking. The participants' anonymity means that the respondents need not take conventional viewpoints nor follow a policy dictated by their superiors. The Delphi technique allows a participant to safely abandon long-defended stands, and the participants cannot be pressured into following the opinions of a well-known expert in the field.

Procedures

1. On October 1, 1997, 20 percent of the exempt employees will receive several open-ended questions concerning personnel practices. Participants will be asked to comment on those practices and to list the strengths and weaknesses of the practices. Participants may also suggest possible changes. Responses to these questions should be sent to me no later than October 8.

2. On about October 22, the participants will receive returns from the first round of questions. Responses will be arranged according to the frequency in which they were given. Participants are urged to reconsider and possibly modify their previous statements. Suggestions previously given will be voted on according to desirability and feasibility. Participants should return their responses to me no later than November 3.

3. On about November 17, the participants will receive returns from the second round of questions. Responses will again be arranged in order of frequency. Participants may modify their previous responses if they wish and return their responses to me by November 25.

4. On about December 2, participants will receive results of the third round in summary form. Appropriate action will be taken shortly thereafter.

If you are selected to participate, you will be able to do so at your convenience. Each round will require only 30 to 90 minutes of your time. Through the cooperation of those selected to participate, company personnel practices will become more attuned to the needs of the employees.

Regardless of the situation in which the memo is written, planning is essential. A knowledge of the planning process, described in Chapter 6, is crucial to the success of any kind of business communication. The characteristics of effective business writing presented in Chapter 5 also pertain to memos.

Figure 9.4
Memo Conveying
Good News

MEMO

TO: All Employees

FROM: Gabe Harrison, President

DATE: November 14, 1997

SUBJECT: Successful Halloween Fund-Raiser

For the third consecutive year, the proceeds from our haunted house project have exceeded our goal. This year's goal of $6,000 had seemed unrealistically high; however, the project's final accounting shows receipts of $6,875.

Thanks to the involvement of every Harrison International employee, the project was a complete success. We should all be pleased with the knowledge that our efforts have provided this year's beneficiary, the Mid-Town Shelter, with the resources necessary to complete its renovation.

As in letters, ideas in a memo conveying good or neutral news should be arranged in the direct or deductive manner described in Chapter 6. Figure 9.4 is an example of such a memo.

Bad-news memos, like bad-news letters, are made more acceptable by using the indirect sequence.

Memos must sometimes provide negative information. Ideas in bad-news memos should be arranged in the indirect sequence described in Chapter 7. Ed Percival used this sequence when he notified the members of the maintenance crew, all of whom were avid hunters, that they would have to work on the first day of hunting season. His memo is presented in Figure 9.5. Ed followed the bad-news sequence. What do you think of his approach? Should he have mentioned that he realized that it was the first day of hunting season?

Figure 9.5
Memo Conveying
Bad News

MEMO

TO: All Members of Maintenance Crew

FROM: Ed Percival, Personnel Director

DATE: October 30, 1997

SUBJECT: Weekend Maintenance Schedule
               Change for November 8–9

You have been involved for the past two years in providing your expertise to Engineering regarding the long-awaited new generator. After more than a year of planning and construction, we are almost ready to put the new generator on line. The installation will be completed over the weekend of November 8–9.

All production will cease at 6:00 a.m. on November 8, and all maintenance personnel will be expected to work on the 8th and 10th. Because it so rarely happens that all production equipment is down at the same time, it is important that we take advantage of the opportunity to perform as much routine and nonroutine maintenance as possible.

The work we will be able to accomplish over that weekend should ensure that the maintenance schedule for the rest of the year, including the holiday season, will not necessitate any unexpected weekend work.

Bob Alexander, on the other hand, did not believe in the bad-news sequence. "Gilding the lily" was what he called it; he always preferred the direct approach. He prided himself in "telling it like it is." When he became upset with employees listening to Walkmans while on the job, he hurriedly wrote the memo in Figure 9.6. Some criticisms of the memo are included in the figure. What are some other possible criticisms?

✔ *CHECKLIST for Planning a Memo*

_____ Determine your objective(s). Why are you writing?

_____ Consider your audience. To whom are you writing?

_____ Select your main ideas. What do you especially want the reader to remember?

Figure 9.6
An Inappropriate Memo

TO: Check-Processing Clerks

FROM: Bob Alexander, Human Resources Director

DATE: June 27, 1997

RE: Use of Walkmans While Working

It has come to my attention that a majority of clerks in the check-processing department now listen to music on Walkmans while processing documents. In my opinion, it appears that productivity has decreased as a result of this distraction. When using Walkmans, employees are tapping their feet, snapping their fingers and even humming or singing. Listening to music isolates individuals, making it impossible for them to communicate with their managers or each other about relevant work-related issues. In addition, it provides the appearance of leisure in our offices, and we want to project a "strictly business" image. Nobody seems to care about the job anymore, and this "don't care" attitude is extremely unprofessional.

From now on, any employee wearing a Walkman during normal business hours will be reprimanded by his/her supervisor. Walkmans should be used ONLY during the designated break times. If the employee does not refrain from using the Walkman, more serious actions will be taken. I will not tolerate an unproductive workforce.

Personal opinion. No attempt to give verifiable information. Wordy—unnecessary information.

Overly strident tone.

Finally gives consequences.

Purposes

Memorandum are prepared for many different purposes. Among their routine purposes are: (1) requesting information, (2) giving instructions, (3) serving as covers (transmittals) for other messages, and (4) making announcements.

Requests for Information

Memoranda requesting information are a part of organization life. Sometimes the requests will require hours of research by the reader. At other times the reader may

Figure 9.7
A Memorandum
Requesting Information

```
                          MEMO


      TO:          Faculty, Business Education Department

      FROM:        Y. A. Young, Chairman, Business Education Department

      DATE:        January 8, 1997

      SUBJECT:     Film Catalog for Faculty Use

            In order to reduce the time it takes to screen and select
      appropriate films, we are putting together a catalog of films that have
      been used effectively in business education classes.

            Please submit to this office the following information, using a
      separate sheet of paper for each film:

      1.  Film title and approximate length.
      2.  One-paragraph description of the main points made in the film.
      3.  One-paragraph description of how the film relates to the course in
          which it was used.

            Please provide this information by January 31.  Shortly thereafter
      you will receive your copy of the completed catalog.  Through the
      cooperation of all faculty members in this project, all of us will benefit.
```

be able to write a paragraph in reply on the original memorandum and return it to the sender. An example of a memorandum requesting information is presented in Figure 9.7.

The three steps in preparing memoranda requesting information are:

1. State the key idea, the request.

2. Present the details.

3. Remind the reader of the request and provide additional specific information.

The effectiveness of a memorandum requesting information is determined largely by the clarity and reasonableness of its message as well as by the writer's explanation of

Figure 9.8
A Memorandum Giving
Instructions

MEMO

TO: Faculty, Sinclair College

FROM: J. R. Easton, Assistant Circulation Manager, College
           Library

DATE: March 14, 1997

SUBJECT: New Procedure for Reserving Books for Class Use

A new procedure for putting books on reserve will begin at the start of the summer quarter. Follow these guidelines:

1. Submit a list of books on the attached form to the Reserve Department at least four weeks before the start of the quarter in which the books will be assigned.
2. Do not include more than ten books on a form.
3. Include the following for each entry:
   a. Call number
   b. Book title
   c. Author's name
   d. Course number and name
   e. Type of reserve desired—two-hour or overnight
   f. Anticipated class size
   g. Instructor's name, campus address, and office telephone number

By following these procedures, you will be contributing to library efficiency.

---

purpose. The readers of the message in Figure 9.7 knew what they were to do and why they were to do it. They also recognized that their task would be accomplished easily and would result in benefits for them.

Giving Instructions

In giving instructions through a memorandum you must try to cover the subject so that the reader will not have any unanswered questions. At the same time you should avoid overwriting or belaboring the obvious. Figure 9.8 shows a sample memo of this type.

Transmittals

A memorandum of transmittal covers another message.

A **transmittal memorandum** introduces the reader to a longer, accompanying message. At times you may go beyond a mere introduction and interpret the message for

Figure 9.9

A Transmittal Memorandum

MEMO

TO: James Bellamy,
          Human Resource Manager

FROM: Sharon Wilcox,
          Logistical Support Coordinator

DATE: August 1, 1997

SUBJECT: Research Report on Turnover among Custodial Workers

Here are the results of the research I conducted pertaining to turnover among custodial workers.

My report is divided into four parts, and each part is preceded by a brief abstract of its contents.

Part I clarifies the problem and its effects on operations; Part II presents a compilation of the custodial supervisors' perceptions of the problem; Part III presents a compilation of the custodial workers' perceptions of the problem; Part IV presents conclusions based on the findings of the survey.

If Wilcox thought Bellamy might not remember the problem (much less her assignment to do the research), she might have begun the memo as follows: "I have done some research on the high rate of turnover among custodial workers."

the reader or at least describe the main points of the message. Regardless of its length or brevity, however, the transmittal memorandum introduces something.

When her boss asked her to learn the reasons for the high turnover among custodial workers, Sharon Wilcox did extensive research and prepared a memorandum on the subject. The transmittal memorandum she wrote to accompany the report appears in Figure 9.9.

Announcements

Memoranda may be used to announce such matters as personnel transfers, meetings, or policy changes. **Announcement memoranda** are sometimes disseminated widely within the organization; in other instances they are sent only to a select few. They are often posted prominently on company bulletin boards.

Memoranda are used to announce a great variety of matters of interest to one or to many.

Key Terms

- **memorandum**
- **transmittal memorandum**
- **announcement memorandum**
- **paperless office**

Summary

Advantages of memoranda   p. 236
The extended audience   p. 236
Format of the memorandum   pp. 238–239
Planning to write a memorandum   pp. 239–243
Purposes of memoranda   pp. 244–245
Sequence of ideas in an effective memorandum   p. 242

Review Questions

1. What is a memorandum?

2. What are the advantages of the memorandum?

3. For what reasons do business people express strong feelings on the subject of memoranda?

4. What might a writer do to overcome the complaints most frequently made about memoranda?

5. What might an organization do to overcome the complaints most frequently made about memoranda?

6. In what ways does a memorandum differ from other business communication formats? In what ways are they similar?

7. How do the steps to the planning process apply to the memorandum?

8. Describe a situation in which a memo might be used for external communication.

9. When preparing a memo for internal communication, what assumptions can the writer ordinarily make about the reader(s)?

Exercises

1. **Productivity Problems.** As the Vice President of Human Resources at NetWorks Software Inc., you have been concerned that the company's 65 employees recently have been less productive than they were in past years. NetWorks prides itself on an informal office environment and flexible work schedules, but many members of the senior staff feel like the employees are taking advantage of the company's laid-back management approach.

   Specifically, you have noticed that employees are consistently working less than eight hours per day so that they are not averaging the required forty hours per week. Each employee is asked to work forty hours, based on the honor system, but all of the managers say it is impossible to determine if their employees work at times other than the standard eight-to-five schedule. Socializing at work is encouraged, to foster teamwork and compatibility, but this also seems to be detracting from productivity. In addition to these problems, NetWorks office is located in a vibrant downtown district with cafes and boutiques where employees often spend long lunches, eating and shopping. You feel that there are too many distractions in and around the office, and that employees are not able to focus properly on their work.

Your mission is to write a memo to all NetWorks Software employees reminding them that they should be responsible and work diligently for forty hours a week. State that you have been concerned due to recent declines in productivity, and as of next Monday, you would like the employees to sign in and sign out. Time logbooks will be located in every department for this purpose. Mention that this procedure may only be temporary, but you would like employees to be thinking about their time commitment to the company. Feel free to make other brief suggestions that could encourage employees to be more productive.

2. **In Search of Big Bucks.** You are the fund-raising coordinator for The Urban Partnership, a nonprofit organization that works to combat problems of inner city crime and substance abuse. Your organization is based in Newark, New Jersey, and it has been successful in focusing its attention on the metropolitan area south of New York City. The director of the organization, Mary Beth Whiteberg, has asked you to try to increase corporate donations by soliciting more new businesses in New York and New Jersey. She asked you to research some possible contacts and let her know the results of your research.

Your mission is to compose a memo describing two or three local corporations you would like to approach for contributions. You can either invent likely companies for this exercise, or look in *The Wall Street Journal* or other publications for possibilities. Provide Ms. Whiteberg with a brief description of each corporation, an address, and a contact name at the company.

3. **Too Hot, Too Cold, or Just Right?** Most of your college courses meet in one particular lecture room, Room 302 in Bryant Hall. You and the other students have noticed that this room is extremely cold in the summer months and unbearably warm in the winter months. Not only does this temperature control problem make it difficult to dress for indoor/outdoor discrepancies, but also it wastes resources by using excessive amounts of air conditioning or heat. It is very distracting, since the students constantly complain about the temperature, and there is no way to control it within the room.

Your mission is to write a memo to William Wright, the Director of University Utility Services, to inform him of the temperature control problem in Bryant 302. Suggest that someone from his staff install a control unit in this room, or suggest that something else be done to regulate the unpleasant conditions in the room and prevent the wasteful use of energy.

4. **Never Stop Learning.** You are the human resources director of Pacific Scientific, a high-tech engineering firm, and you want to recommend that employees keep current with their knowledge of chemistry and physics. You also want to encourage people to pursue advanced degrees in the fields of science, engineering, or business. To meet these goals, your company has established a tuition reimbursement program, which will provide employees with 80 percent of their tuition upon completion of a course, if they receive a grade of C or higher.

Your mission is to write a memo to Pacific Scientific employees, at all seven plant sites, informing them about the tuition reimbursement program. Provide them with all of the relevant details. Before enrolling in a class, the employees should get approval from personnel, but you want to mention that the program is very flexible, and course work from any university or college could be eligible.

5. **Type-Casting.** As the Office Manager at a busy real estate firm in Los Angeles, you have noticed some personality conflicts between various members of your staff and you would like to improve the working environment in your office. To reduce the tension, you feel you would like to encourage all members of the staff to get to know each other better. You feel that the employees would better understand each other's personality traits if everyone would take the Myers-Briggs Type Indicator, a test that categorizes people as one of 16 personality types.

   Your mission is to inform the employees that you will administer the Myers-Briggs Type Indicator on Monday, February 10th, at 10:00 A.M. Draft a memo explaining that the Myers-Briggs test identifies whether people are introverted or extroverted, sensing or intuitive, thinking or feeling, and perceiving or judging. Stress that the MBTI has proven itself to be very effective in helping employees improve their internal communication skills, as well as improving customer relations. Also mention that there will be a follow-up session on Monday, February 17th, when a management consultant will go over the MBTI results with the staff.

6. **Give Yourself a Pat on the Back.** You are the Executive Assistant to Ben Cohen, CEO of Ben and Jerry's, a successful ice-cream manufacturer based in Vermont. One reason that you wanted to work for this company is the fact that Ben and Jerry's is committed to the environment and recycling efforts. You also appreciate the company's humanitarian efforts; Ben and Jerry's gives an average of 7.5 percent of its pretax earnings to nonprofit organizations every year, in addition to donating "One Percent for Peace" from every carton of ice cream to help feed and house the homeless.

   Ben Cohen has just informed you that the corporation has received a prestigious Business Enterprise Trust Award, recognizing Ben and Jerry's efforts to encourage social responsibility and conduct a for-profit enterprise in ways that benefit the community. The award was presented in light of all of the company's efforts to help the environment and the underprivileged.

   Your mission is to write a memo (from Ben Cohen) announcing that the Business Enterprise Trust Award was recently given to Ben and Jerry's. Acknowledge that this honor could not have been achieved without the support and commitment of every employee, and encourage them to keep volunteering their personal time and assisting the corporate efforts to help others.

7. **Ideas Welcome!** As the Director of Product Development at 3M Corporation, you want to ensure that the company continues to produce new and necessary office and household supplies. In the past, 3M has developed many simple ideas that have revolutionized office environments—most notably, the development of the special adhesive on Post-it brand notes.

   3M corporate policy allows that employees can spend up to 15 percent of their time working on new product ideas. The corporation is divided into small divisions that function as tightly knit teams working together brainstorming and sharing resources and information. You want to provide an additional incentive to employees to come up with brilliant new ideas, so you have decided to hold a "contest" that will award a year-end bonus to the division coming up with the best new product idea.

Your mission is to write a memo for distribution to all employees in the product divisions to explain the contest idea. Mention that the entries will be judged by a panel of five members of the 3M Board of Directors, and each division should submit its entry by the end of the third quarter.

8. **In Need of a New Look.** You have been promoted to Office Manager of Little & Dunn, a progressive advertising agency located in the old Sears Building in downtown Richmond, VA. In addition to your administrative tasks overseeing the daily operations of the agency, you have been assigned the task of updating the office interior—without spending too much money. You have decided that the best "face-lift" for the office would be to paint the dingy walls. You want to coat the office with a bright white paint, and then invest in a few good pieces of local artwork to enhance the reception area.

Your mission is to draft a memo to prepare the employees for the minor renovations. You need to let the employees know that the painting will occur on the evening of Wednesday, June 25. On Wednesday afternoon, everyone should take all items off the walls in the areas in and around their offices, and they should move all furniture away from the walls. Dropcloths will be provided to protect the items left in the offices. Also mention that you will be purchasing some paintings or prints for the reception area and, if the employees have suggestions, you would like to hear them.

9. **A Panel of Judges.** As the Director of the MBA program, you are responsible for conducting a case competition in which teams of second-year students present detailed business policy strategies. You have decided to hold this event on the weekend before Thanksgiving, and you want to invite all of the faculty members who teach MBA students to serve as judges for the competition.

Your mission is to compose a memo that will be distributed to the MBA faculty. In this memo, briefly describe the competition and give the date and time specifics. Since you want to determine whether the professor can or cannot serve as a judge, you will end your memo with a detachable portion on which professors can check one of two options: (1) Yes, I can serve as a case competition judge; or (2) No, I will be unable to serve as a judge. Be sure to make the memo as "user-friendly" as possible in order to obtain the best response.

10. **Abusing a Privilege.** It has always been your company's policy to allow employees to "borrow" from the petty cash fund if they need a few extra dollars for some reason. You ask those who borrow money to place an IOU in the petty cash box and to replace the money within a week. As the comptroller, you are frustrated with the increased frequency with which the employees are borrowing petty cash. A few times when you have needed the fund's resources, the money remaining has been inadequate to cover your expenses, and you have had to replenish the fund immediately.

Your mission is to direct a memo to all employees, reminding them that the reason that the petty cash fund exists is to cover *business*-related expenses, although you have previously allowed employees to "borrow" from the fund. State that many people have been abusing the privilege, either by not leaving IOU notes in the box, or by never paying back the borrowed funds. These practices have disrupted your accounting policies, and you want the employees to know that you have been authorized to discontinue this privilege. Employees should now borrow money from each other if they need some extra pocket cash.

11. **A Request for Funds.** You are the marketing director of L.L. Bean, of Freeport, ME. You have been given $100,000 for direct marketing in Japan to tap the huge demand for high-quality outdoor wear, especially clothing that bears the sought-after American label. Your research shows that annual direct-marketing sales, such as catalogue sales, in Japan reached only $18 billion compared to $300 billion in the United States. Ten percent of these sales were from American companies. A U.S. trade association in one Japanese city offered 125 different U.S. catalogues, and thousands were purchased each week at $2 and $3 each. Direct-marketing experts believe that Japan is in a position similar to that of the United States 15 years ago and that direct-marketing sales will skyrocket over the next decade.

    Your mission is to write a memo to convince your company that the opportunity is enormous in Japan. You need an increased budget to reach more potential customers at this stage so you can foster brand loyalty before the market becomes saturated.

12. **Bargaining for a Brewery.** You are Hans H. Meerloo, the chief executive officer of Interbrew, a Belgium brewery that has roots dating back to 1366 and is now one of the world's larger producers of beer. You are looking to expand your market share of your most popular lager, Stella Artois, by entering the North American continent. Marketing a new product in North America would take years and cost millions of dollars. The opportunity that presents itself is purchase of Labatt, a well-established Canadian brewery that has a 45 percent market share in Canada and a rapidly expanding market in the United States and Mexico. In fact, last year Labatt showed an operating profit of 22.8 percent, one of the highest in the industry. Experts agree that the best way to enter the beer market in the United States is through a well-known name. With the Labatt purchase, your company would become the fourth-largest producer of beer in the world, producing 31 million barrels per year, behind Anheuser-Busch at 88 million, Heineken at 51 million, and Miller at 45 million.

    Your mission is to write a memo to your board of directors to encourage them to pay the $2 billion price tag for Labatt.

13. **The Scent of Success.** You are a U.S. Customs Service agent in charge of monitoring contraband coming into Key West, FL. You are in charge of 50 agents and several drug- and bomb-sniffing dogs. Your operation has been running well over the past few years, due largely to the abilities of your men and women and their use of your highly skilled dogs to quickly investigate thousands of suspicious situations each day. However, a new contraband has increasingly been infiltrating your territory over the last few years and there is nothing your dogs can do about it because the substance is perfectly legal—tobacco. The problem is that this tobacco is banned in the United States because it is from Cuba—in the form of high-quality, hand-rolled Cuban cigars. The rebirth of America's love of the cigar in recent years has put a higher demand on the illegal "Cubans" and smuggling is on the rise. *Cigar Aficionado* magazine estimates that up to 10 million Cuban cigars per year enter the United States in defiance of the ban on Cuban products.

Your mission is to write a memo to your staff describing the increased incidence of smuggling of cigars and to make some suggestions for how to catch smugglers in the act in airports and in dock areas.

14. **Storm Warning.** You are the head lifeguard of an exclusive beach club in Waimea Bay, Hawaii. A tropical storm is expected to pass within 500 miles of the Hawaiian Islands within two days. Although, due to the ocean's current, the probability of a direct hit from the storm is minimal, forty-foot ocean swells have been observed near the storm and the Coast Guard predicts "extreme wave activity" for Hawaii over the next several days. This typically means 20- to 30-foot waves and potentially deadly situations for anyone attempting to go into the water, due to rip tides, tumbling waves, and coral reefs. Normally your beach is designated "members only," but during "extreme wave activity," local custom allows anyone interested, be it tourists, photographers, or surfers, to have free access to the beach and waters.

    Your mission is to write a memo to your ten lifeguards informing them of the situation. Include all relevant information. Also write a similar memo to the club members.

15. **Getting a Jump.** You are an Olympic official in charge of steroid testing of athletes in the next Olympic games. Although the women's swim team from one country had won no gold medals in the eighties, in 1992 they won 16 of 21 gold medals at the world championships in Rome. Recently, at the Asian Games, seven swimmers, two canoeists, a hurdler, and a cyclist were tested positive for steroids. Making matters worse, there is a state-of-the-art drug, dehydrotestosterone (DHT), that is very difficult to detect, and it becomes more difficult to detect each hour after it has been last administered. Your governing board has directed you to change the testing procedure from pre-event to pre-Olympics as a result of the DHT that some swimmers are suspected of using.

    Your mission is to write a memo to your staff of volunteer doctors to inform them of a scheduling change in the drug testing. They will still get free tickets to events they have requested, but only if they can give eight hours of their time in early July to test all Olympic athletes as they get off their planes. Explain the reasons for the change but do not name specific teams suspected of drug abuse.

16. **Undesirable Behavior.** When the Marton Corporation was founded in 1929 it was based on the philosophy of its founder J.W. Marton, "Happy employees make happy customers." This philosophy has been maintained within the company even after his death. You are the restaurant manager of J.W.'s Grille, in the Newport Marton in Rhode Island. You observe a situation one lunchtime of two servers arguing over the ownership of a table. Although the table was in another section, one of the servers was convinced that it should have been in his section. This argument took place in the dining room, and the guests at the table were uncomfortable because they could hear the conversation, and the servers could be overheard by other guests as well. This is obviously not desirable because unhappy employees probably result in unhappy guests. You talked to the serving staff then and there but you think that you must do more.

    Your mission is to write a memo to the staff outlining dining room etiquette and Marton's philosophy on customer satisfaction, and giving the consequence of any such behavior in the future.

17. **A Crying Need.** You work in a large office as a supervisor, and one of your employees has recently been taking a lot of time off work due to child-care problems. She is a single parent and has been leaving early to pick up her child at her day-care center; her ex-husband has recently been banned from doing so because of his disruptive behavior. The problems she is having have started to affect her work. You are sympathetic to her troubles, but are aware that other employees are wondering why she is receiving preferential treatment. Supervisors in other departments have mentioned to you they are also having problems with employees who are having day-care problems. Your research shows there are nearly 100 employees in your firm with children who need day care.

    Your mission is to write a memo to the office manager explaining the need to have a corporate-sponsored day-care program. Mention that employees are paying for it elsewhere and may be willing to have money deducted from their pay to offset the company expense.

18. **Starting a Turnaround.** Pamerelli's Restaurant, in the downtown of a large city, has been suffering from a slump in business over the past few months. Because tourism is continuing to grow, it is apparent that the problem is not due to the lack of potential customers. Pamerelli's has a wonderful reputation as a fine dining restaurant, and in July of this year it received a glowing review in *Where* magazine. It is apparent that the quality of food is not the problem, so it must therefore be a lack of successful marketing. Staff morale is low due to the lack of business, and you as the manager must, therefore, find a way to improve this as well as increase the flow of customers into your restaurant.

    Your mission is to write a memo to your employees explaining the problem and asking for their help and contributions to a marketing scheme. Ask them to outline solutions and inform them how their efforts will benefit them.

19. **The Auto Show.** As manager of Tri-State Merchants Mall, which consists of 150 retail establishments, you are responsible for identifying and soliciting promotions that are likely to attract more shoppers to the mall. You have been approached by Statewide Auto Association about holding an auto show at the mall. The show would feature most of the latest model automobiles and could be held in the enclosed pedestrian area of the mall. Salespeople from the local dealers would be available to assist interested shoppers. Mall policy is that decisions on large promotions must be made by the members of the Promotions Committee, 10 merchants who represent all of those at the mall. In order to make the best decision about the proposed auto show, the committee will need more information.

    Your mission is to write a memo to Brian Benson, head of the Promotions Committee, in which you ask him to do some research on the effects of auto shows on shopping centers: Do auto shows attract customers who would not otherwise come to a shopping center? What possible disadvantages accompany having an auto show in an enclosed shopping center? Would additional liability insurance be desirable for such an event? Include several other questions that you think would be appropriate for such a situation.

20. **National Holidays.** You are employed by HH Manufacturing as a plant manager in a foreign country (you select the country). You receive a request from your boss, Morris Corrales, for a list of the national holidays celebrated in that country. (These are days on which most business organizations in that country

would ordinarily be closed.) Corrales wants this information in order to facilitate the scheduling of visits and meetings during the upcoming year.

Your mission is to get the necessary information from a library and prepare an appropriate memo. Morris Corrales is based at the home office in Marinette, WI 54143.

C A S E

Analysis of the Membership of a City Chamber of Commerce

Anthony S. Lis, University of Oklahoma

You are vice president for membership of the Chamber of Commerce in a city with a population of over 85,000. Chamber members total 153.

Within the city limits are located a state comprehensive university with an enrollment of over 16,000, a state mental health hospital with over 1,000 patients, a 230-bed municipal hospital, and two manufacturing plants employing over 900 workers combined.

The Chamber of Commerce secretary has given you the following data about the composition of the membership of your organization:

		Sex		**Employment**								
				Govt./Ed.		*Retail*		*Mfg.*		*Service*		*Other*
Age Group	*Total*	*Male*	*Female*	M	F	M	F	M	F	M	F	M	F
35 and under	3	3	0	1	0	2	0	0	0	0	0	0	0
36–44	37	22	15	4	1	11	9	3	1	4	4	0	0
45–54	68	41	27	4	2	26	13	8	1	3	11	0	0
55–64	36	21	15	4	0	9	10	7	2	1	3	0	0
65 and over	9	9	0	0	0	4	0	1	0	1	0	3	0

Case Questions

1. Prepare an appropriate table giving the percentages for the various characteristics according to the sex and the employment categories.

2. What conclusions can be drawn on the basis of the data about the nature of the current membership?

3. What recommendations could you as the vice president for membership offer to the board of directors concerning any appropriate and desirable changes in the membership?

4. In your opinion, how should any changes be implemented?

5. Should the members of the Chamber of Commerce be told about this study and any changes that you will be proposing? Why?

6. Prepare a two-page memorandum to the board of directors with an appropriate table and your recommendations for changing the composition of the membership.

C A S E

Management Memo

Carol David, Iowa State University

You are the plant manager of a food-processing company with about 1000 employees. Your plant is located in Pleasantville, Iowa, and the corporate headquarters in St. Louis, Missouri. You have a good relationship with your employees and often spend time on the floor talking to workers. They call you by your first name. Your plant is in continual competition with sister plants located throughout the Midwest, and ordinarily you excel in volume of production. This year, however, your safety record is not good, and safety is a value strongly supported by corporate. Unless some definite improvements are made in the next quarter, you expect that you will hear from corporate when the reports are made at the end of the fiscal year.

First of all, you know that employees in all departments have been lax in following the safety regulations. For instance, office employees walking through the plant do not observe the rules for staying between yellow lines. In addition, the production workers do not follow all of the procedures for machine maintenance. These daily procedures take time, and the workers know them so well that they assume that they can catch any problems when they arise. They look upon the daily procedures as unnecessary busywork. Many other procedures are also not rigorously followed. You feel that you want to contact all employees to let them know about the poor current record and to set goals for the upcoming period.

Write a memo to all employees that informs them that safety standards have slipped. You have already recorded 12 accidents and 33 reportables (minor accidents) for this six-month period. In the following period the plant must experience no more than 6 accidents and 12 reportables if Pleasantville is not to gain negative attention from corporate. The memo will tell employees that safety will become a part of their individual evaluation criteria. Regulations will be more strictly enforced and an all-out follow-up campaign will take place.

Case Questions

1. What is the main purpose of the memo?
2. What are the secondary purposes?
3. How will the public posting of the memo influence its content?

CASE

A Disturbing Trend

David B. Parsons, Lakehead University, Thunder Bay, Ontario, Canada

Three days ago, Polly Darton received a letter of complaint from a senior citizen who was extremely upset about the quality of service she had received in Kitchen Appliances. As the Supervisor of the Customer Service Department at Hoover's Home Furnishings and Appliances, Polly has to ensure that her employees are always courteous and tactful.

In this instance, she was more than concerned because this complaint was the third complaint about poor service lodged by a senior citizen in the past two weeks. Polly decided to phone each of the three complainants to apologize directly (she had already sent a standard form letter of apology) and to find out exactly what had happened.

All three seniors reported the same things: sales clerks being impatient, badgering customers to buy something, ignoring them if they didn't seem interested in the merchandise, and talking to one another rather than tending to the needs of the customer. So Polly spent three days walking throughout the store, observing the behavior of the sales staff. She soon discovered that the seniors' complaints were justified.

Polly decided to write a memo to all department heads outlining the problem and suggesting ways to improve the situation.

Assuming the role of Polly Darton, write the memo.

Case Questions

1. Has Polly handled this communication situation effectively?

2. What constraints is she under in this situation?

3. What should her rhetorical strategies be?

4. How would you describe Polly's audience?

Notes

1. Robert Benchley, *The Benchley Roundup* (New York: Harper & Row, 1954), 28.

2. William H. Baker and Larry D. Hartman, "A Follow-Up Study of Business Students with Good and Poor Writing Abilities," paper presented at a meeting of the Association for Business Communication (Las Vegas, 1989).

3. Marcy Eckroth Mullins, "USA Snapshots," *USA Today*, March 25, 1987, 1-A.

4. Barrett J. Mandel and Judith Yellen, "Gumbel's Bumble Redux," *Working Woman*, September 1989, 136-138.

5. Bill Hendrick, "Memo Heats Up the Battle between Great Northern, Georgia-Pacific," *Atlanta Journal and Constitution*, December 15, 1989.

Chapter 10

Short Reports and Proposals

Learning Objectives

1
TO RECOGNIZE THE UNDERLYING PURPOSE OF INFORMATIONAL MEMORANDUM REPORTS.

2
TO DEVELOP EFFECTIVE PROGRESS REPORTS AND PERIODIC REPORTS.

3
TO DEVELOP EFFECTIVE JUSTIFICATION REPORTS AND ROUTINE MEMORANDUM REPORTS.

4
TO IDENTIFY SITUATIONS FOR WHICH A LETTER REPORT WOULD BE APPROPRIATE.

5
TO IDENTIFY SITUATIONS FOR WHICH A FORM MESSAGE WOULD BE APPROPRIATE.

6
TO LEARN THE PURPOSE AND STRATEGIES UNDERLYING SOLICITED AND UNSOLICITED PROPOSALS.

The same format should be used for all progress reports in a series.

In his business communication classes, Enrique Fernandez heard horror stories about costly mistakes resulting from poor communication. Through the courses he became familiar with the different types of reports and the functions of each. He spent countless hours on the exercises assigned. All the while he suspected that professors sometimes exaggerate the importance of topics that interest them. Enrique earned a degree and took his first full-time job. There he soon learned for himself the importance of being able to write a good report. What he knew about planning and writing reports helped him to get the job and then to do it well.

As assistant purchasing director, Enrique reviewed many proposals submitted by organizations seeking to provide goods and services to his employer. He was astonished by the wide variation in the quality of the proposals he received. Some were well-planned and carefully written. Others showed a complete lack of understanding of what a proposal should be. Few of the latter were ever accepted. Enrique wondered why people would give so little thought to documents that were so important to the success of their business.

REPORTS WITH A MEMORANDUM FORMAT

Many short reports are intended for internal use, and their writers often use the memo format. Writers must be aware, however, of the differences between a memorandum and a memorandum report. A **memorandum report** is usually more structured; it will have a recognizable introduction, body, and conclusion, which a memorandum does not necessarily have. The memorandum report has the same advantages as the memorandum. Progress reports, periodic reports, and justification reports are among those that are often presented in the memorandum format. The broad purpose of all types of memorandum reports is to supply the information needed to keep the organization operating smoothly.

Progress Reports

Progress reports are informational and are widely used throughout business, industry, and government. Depending upon the nature of the organization and the project being reported, a progress report may be made only one time or as one of a series. If there is to be a series of progress reports, the same format should be followed throughout the series for the reader's convenience.

Ordinarily sent upward in the organization, **progress reports** inform management of: (1) rate of progress as compared to the schedule and (2) goals for subsequent time periods and a forecast for completion of the project. The more specifically this information is presented, the more helpful a progress report will be. In Figure 10.1, a banker describes the progress being made in a campaign through a memorandum report to upper management.

Progress reports compare progress on a project to the schedule and also forecast future progress.

Periodic Reports

In any organization some reports must be prepared on a regular basis. Whether daily, weekly, or monthly, the purpose of these **periodic reports** is to keep others informed of some aspect of operations. Because they are ordinarily directed regularly to the same reader, the writer may assume the reader is generally knowledgeable about the

Periodic informational reports are prepared on a regular basis.

Figure 10.1
Progress Report

MEMO

TO: Roger Davis, Director of Marketing

FROM: John Dartley

DATE: November 19, 1997

SUBJECT: Monthly Progress Report on Card-Bank Usage –
              Oakdale Branch

<u>Summary</u>

    In this reporting period, the percentage of customers using Card-Bank has risen from 7.1 percent to 7.9 percent. Of customers with accounts for less than six months, 70 percent have used Card-Bank at least once.

<u>Present Usage</u>

    There has been a 6.8 percent increase in the number of customers using Card-Bank. Our goal for this date had been set at 8.0 percent. Among new customers with accounts for less than six months, 70 percent have used Card-Bank at least once. The goal for new customer usage for this date is 50 percent. The increased usage might be a result of our policy of personal instruction of new customers.

<u>Usage Forecast</u>

    Our customer usage goal for the next period is 10 percent. A local media blitz is scheduled for early December. Advertisements will emphasize that card holders can access their accounts from their computers and conduct a wide variety of banking activities. Our surveys have shown that computer interconnectivity is the least-known feature of Card-Bank.

subject. For that reason the writer need not provide much introductory information.

An example of a periodic report on absenteeism in a manufacturing plant is presented in Figure 10.2.

Justification Reports

You may at some time have to write a memorandum report in order to justify something—a change in procedure, an increase in budget, or perhaps reasons for resisting any new policy. For whatever reason it may be written, and there are many, the **justification report** is a common type of memorandum report.

When Nancy Lew sought to justify a change in operating procedures, she took the direct approach. She organized her memorandum report in this way:

1. Proposal

2. Description of present system

Figure 10.2
Periodic Report

MEMO

TO: R. T. Bowen, Plant Manager

FROM: Bill Hughes, Assistant Personnel Director

DATE: February 4, 1997

SUBJECT: Monthly Plant Absenteeism Record

During January the average rate of absenteeism was 6 percent. The average rate of absenteeism last January was 7.5 percent. The average rate of absenteeism during the past twelve months was 6.8 percent.

Here is a breakdown of absences according to shift and department. An asterisk indicates those absences for which the absentee submitted a written excuse from a doctor.

Shift	Production	Shipping	Yard Crew
1st	8 of 202	1 of 28	1 of 20
2nd	10 of 202	2 of 28	2 of 80
3rd	19 of 200	N/A	1 of 10
	*8	*3	*1

Supervisors are being urged to persuade workers to call in when they are unable to come to work and to persuade workers to bring an excuse from a doctor. Here is a breakdown of the absentees who did phone in advance.

Shift	Production	Shipping	Yard Crew
1st	6 of 8	0 of 1	0 of 1
2nd	10 of 10	0 of 2	2 of 2
3rd	12 of 19	N/A	1 of 1

If you have any questions about the records, please give me a call.

Figure 10.3
Justification Report

MEMO

TO: John T. Bowers, Director of Personnel Research

FROM: Nancy Lew, Manager of Production

DATE: June 18, 1997

SUBJECT: Communication Problems at Shift Changes

Proposal

My proposal for improving the transmittal of instructions during shift changes is for the company to require a five-minute overlap of all production employees at shift changes.

Present System

At present the supervisors are responsible for communicating job-related information. Much of it is done through work logs that each supervisor maintains. They make entries each day regarding orders and equipment functioning. At the time of the shift change, the incoming supervisor first reads the log and seeks any necessary clarification before the outgoing supervisor leaves.

There are several problems with this system. A supervisor will often forget to record vital information, and the incoming supervisor will not be aware of it. Workers do not always tell their supervisors about equipment problems, so such problems cannot be recorded. Some supervisors are in such a rush to leave work that they are of little assistance to the incoming supervisor.

Advantages of the Change

A five-minute overlap would make the exchange of information at shift changes easier and more thorough. Not only would the supervisors exchange work-related information, but individual production workers also would. Supervisors would no longer have to depend on the work log for information from those on the previous shift.

Each production employee would be paid for eight hours and ten minutes per day rather than for eight hours. The benefits to the company would be worth it. Unclear instructions in the work log plus order changes that were not conveyed to the succeeding shift have cost the company much in terms of both dollars and frustrated workers.

3. Advantages of the change versus its costs to the organization.

Because her report is directed upward in the organization, Nancy begins by reminding the reader of the problem, as shown in Figure 10.3. The remainder of the report is devoted to suggesting a change and to indicating the advantages to be derived from it.

If Nancy had anticipated strong opposition to her plan, she might have taken an indirect approach. If the receiver, John Bowers, had a reputation for resisting change, Nancy might have been less direct. No rigid formula exists. The writer must look closely at the situation and adapt the approach to fit it.

REPORTS WITH A LETTER FORMAT

Many short reports intended for external communication are presented in the format of a **letter report**. As is generally true of short reports, the letter report is usually less formal than longer reports.

Just as in any letter, the nature of the message and the response expected from the reader will determine the plan to be followed. If the reader is likely to approve of the

Figure 10.4
Letter Report

NATIONAL INSURANCE ANALYSTS   P.O. Box 940   Red Bank, NJ 07701

May 1, 1997

Mr. Elbert Cunningham
Director of Employee Benefits
Falwick Industries
Camden, NJ 08101

Dear Mr. Cunningham:

Having analyzed the health-insurance plan provided by Falwick Industries as you requested, I'm now reporting my findings, which you may find helpful.

Forecast of the Cost of Employee Benefits

Your concern over the spiraling cost of employee benefits is justified. During the last decade the cost of providing employee benefits has increased at an average rate of 14 percent each year. Your employee benefit plan is intended to cover growing medical costs and to replace lost job income. As long as inflation continues to reduce the real income of employees, benefit payments will rise proportionately. In other words, this rate of increase is expected to continue for the foreseeable future.

One Option: Pay-as-Go Insurance

In this direct self-funding approach, the company pays claims directly from the company's cash flow. The firm actually becomes its own insurer and does not set aside any reserves for future claims. Most companies using this plan purchase stop-loss insurance to protect against unexpectedly severe claims. Since your company does not require employee contributions to its plan, Falwick Industries is eligible, under ERISA restrictions, to initiate such a plan.

---

message, take the direct approach described in Chapter 6. Begin the letter with the main point, because the reader agrees with it, then construct the message as a good-news or neutral letter.

If the reader is likely to disapprove of the message, you should follow the letter of refusal sequence described in Chapter 7. Rather than state your main point at the start of the letter, you should build up to it. In this type of letter a buffer and one or more reasons usually precede the main point.

A letter report is similar to a letter in appearance and includes many of the same features.

A letter report is similar to a letter in appearance. Because letter reports usually are sent outside the organization, they are prepared on stationery with the company letterhead. Letter reports usually include many of the features of a letter: date, inside address, salutation, body, and signature. Some writers insert a subject line between the greeting and the body of the letter report.

Most letter reports are comprised of introduction, body, and close.

The body of a letter report, like the body of the business letter, has three basic parts:

1. *Introduction.* In this part the purpose of the report is described. If the report concerns a problem, the problem might be presented at this point. For longer reports

Figure 10.4
Continued

Falwick Industries
May 1, 1997
Page 2

Another Option: Tax-Exempt Trust

In this self-funding approach, a plan must be drawn to meet the unique needs of the individual company. A tax-exempt trust is then set up, and employer and employee contributions are deposited into it. Claims and expenses are paid from the trust, and excess funds are invested to build up reserves. There are several tax advantages of this trust. It may be administered so as to qualify for exemption from federal income tax. The contributions of the employer may be deductible as a business expense. Usually the benefit payments are not taxable to the employees who receive them.

Administration of Self-Funding Benefit Plan

Either of these self-funded plans can be administered within the organization. Some companies prefer to have a professional outside the company handle the administration. Companies that hire outside administrators often find that employees more readily accept the claims decisions. Whether the benefit plan is administered by an employee or by an outsider, a company such as Falwick Industries will enjoy considerable savings.

I hope that this report gives you a satisfactory picture of two options open to your company. I shall be pleased to answer any questions that you may have.

Sincerely,

Roberta Simmons

Roberta Simmons
Employee Benefit Analyst

---

a description of the way the report is organized is included in the introduction; however, a description is not necessary for most letter reports.

2. *Body.* This is the meat of any report. Here the reader's attention is directed at the findings or conclusions. If the report is somewhat involved, it may be divided into sections with headings to aid the reader in following the flow of information.

3. *Close.* In most reports this is simply an offer of additional assistance if the reader desires it. The closing paragraph may deal with the relationship between the writer and the reader rather than with the contents of the report. If the letter report is for internal use, closing comments are not necessary.

Elbert Cunningham hired National Insurance Analysts to appraise the health insurance plan provided by Falwick Industries for its employees. After investigating the plan, National responded with the letter report in Figure 10.4.

REPORTS USING PREPRINTED FORMS

Short reports perform many functions in the business organization. Listing all of the different types of short reports would be a monumental task.

The most common type of short report in most organizations is the informational report that is required on a regular basis. At the end of each week, for example, each sales representative for Falcon Products must send a customer contact report to the sales manager. The number of customers visited, sales made, and service problems are included in the report. Because this **form report** is submitted so frequently and by such a large number of representatives, Falcon Products provides a preprinted form for the purpose, shown in Figure 10.5. The form specifies the information needed and clearly indicates where the completed form should be sent.

From the company's perspective, the form ensures that the information provided will be uniform and hence easy to compile. From the individual respondent's perspective, it simplifies the process by indicating clearly what is to be provided. Although the number of forms that must be completed is a source of complaint for many workers, preprinted forms can save a great deal of time. If the workers had to develop and prepare individual reports instead of using preprinted forms, there would be much more complaining.

Preprinted forms constitute the greatest volume of short reports, and they play an important role in the smooth operation of any business. Without them the routine transmitting of information would be greatly complicated. Because this kind of report requires no particular expertise to complete, it has not been emphasized in this chapter.

> The most common type of short report uses preprinted forms to transmit routine information on a regular basis.

MISCELLANEOUS SHORT REPORTS

Most organizations have no shortage of short reports. These reports are very functional, and are therefore heavily used. Examples include credit reports, reports of meetings, end-of-month production reports, and some reports to stockholders. Many companies put forms on a network server; the user accesses the form, fills it in, and sends the response electronically. As is generally true of short reports, each one has a distinct purpose and contributes significantly to organizational operations.

PROPOSALS

A **proposal** is an attempt to persuade someone that you are especially qualified to fill one of his or her needs in exchange for compensation. Proposals are usually written documents and come in a variety of sizes and formats. A contractor may be called in to examine a house in need of remodeling. He may then submit a statement in which he identifies what will be done, the cost of labor and materials, and the date of completion. That is one example of a proposal.

Proposals vary in the degree of formality as well as in the planning that goes into them. Imagine that a man comes to your house and asks if you want any of your trees removed. When you inquire about the cost he does some quick calculations on the back of an envelope that he then gives to you.

At the other extreme are proposals that require extraordinary amounts of preparation. The attempt by the City of Atlanta to host the 1996 Summer Olympics is one such example. The Atlanta Organizing Committee was formed early in 1987 and drafted a proposal for the U.S. Selection Committee. After many months of preparation, their proposal, approximately 100 pages long, secured for Atlanta the right to rep-

> Proposals are usually submitted in writing.

> Proposals are not uniform and vary in formality.

Figure 10.5
Form Report

Customer Contact Report

Enter all visits with customers and potential customers each week. Indicate your time of arrival and departure as well as product(s) discussed. Describe any sale you made or service problem of which you learned. Describe any follow-up which you intend to perform.

Date	Time	Name of contact and company	Product discussed	Sales made	Service problems	Follow-up
Mon.	Arr. Dpt.					
	Arr. Dpt.					
	Arr. Dpt.					
Tues.	Arr. Dpt.					
	Arr. Dpt.					
	Arr. Dpt.					
Wed.	Arr. Dpt.					
	Arr. Dpt.					
	Arr. Dpt.					
Thurs.	Arr. Dpt.					
	Arr. Dpt.					
	Arr. Dpt.					
Fri.	Arr. Dpt.					
	Arr. Dpt.					
	Arr. Dpt.					

_____
Signature of Sales Representative

NOTE: Complete this form at the end of each work week and mail it immediately to the Sales Manager.

resent the United States in the competition to host the Olympics. Following their initial success they then set about preparing a proposal for the International Olympic Committee. This 600-page proposal was divided into five separate volumes. Approximately seven months after the deadline for submission, the members of the International Olympic Committee selected the winning proposal.[1] In terms of formality and complexity, most proposals fall somewhere between the one submitted to the Olympic Committee and the one prepared on the back of the envelope.

The two basic types of proposals are the solicited and the unsolicited. A **solicited proposal** is written in answer to a request. An **unsolicited proposal** is initiated by the proposer; no motivation is provided by the intended recipient. The contractor and the tree-removal specialist both provided solicited proposals. The first proposal of the Olympic Committee would be considered an unsolicited one. Its subsequent proposals were solicited.

Solicited Proposals

Changes frequently occur as a result of solicited proposals. Contracts may be awarded, funds may be dispensed, or any of a multitude of other actions may be taken. Proposals play a major role in the operation of many business organizations of all sizes.

Requests for solicited proposals may come from many different sources. Sometimes the solicitation is nothing more than a casual comment or an encouraging word. Bob Reynolds, for example, had never even considered seeking a refrigeration maintenance contract with any hotel until a neighbor in the hotel business encouraged him to do so. Had his neighbor not made him aware of such possibilities, he would have continued to limit himself to the residential refrigeration market. Now Bob has contracts with almost half of the local hotels and motels.

An RFP is a request for a proposal.

A formal solicitation for a proposal is often called a **request for proposal (RFP)**. Many requests for proposals from various units of the federal government appear in the *Commerce Business Daily (CBD)*, a publication of the U.S. Department of Commerce. The *CBD* has been published for many years and is widely read in organizations that wish to provide goods or services to the government. An electronic edition of the *CBD* is now available for computer on-line acquisition. Here is a typical RFP as it appeared in the *CBD*:

> CONFERENCE FACILITIES SOL 52SBNB0C6122 DUE 030190 POC Joan Smith (301)/C.O. Pauline Mallgrave. Contractor shall supply facilities, labor, material, equipment and food to provide formal and informal meeting services for National Institute of Standards and Technology (NIST) conferences—Contractor shall be able to provide informal outdoor banquet services and facilities—Facility shall be less than 5 miles of NIST, Gaithersburg, MD—The proposed contract will be an Indefinite Delivery Indefinite Quantity type contract—The Base period will be approximately 7 months with four one-year options for renewal—Significant Evaluation Factors are: 1) experience in providing similar types of supplies/services 2) understanding the requirements in the statement of work and 3) ability to respond to last-minute changes regarding equipment and space—Please request solicitation in writing—All responsible sources may submit a proposal which shall be considered by the agency.

Most requests for proposals specifically state the goods or services that are wanted. You should therefore read the request carefully before beginning to write a proposal. Also note whether a certain kind of organizational scheme is suggested for the proposal. Solicitors often give guidelines in the RFP in order to make it easier to compare the proposals that are received. Many proposals are rejected because the writer did not specifically address all of the factors included in the RFP or did not organize the proposal as instructed, or because of errors. In one case, a company lost a $64,000 contract because there were two misspelled words in the proposal.[2]

Proposals are expected to provide a rational analysis of how the writer's organization can satisfy the needs described in the RFP. Even though the writer may consider a proposal to be primarily a sales document, the persuasion should not be blatant. Solicited proposals should let the facts speak for themselves.

Figure 10.6
Short Proposal

Kiddie Corral, Inc.
1812 Shady Lane Abilene, KS 67410

July 14, 1997

Mr. Warren Downs, President
Plastic Castings, Inc.
2818 Industrial Parkway
Abilene, KS 67410

Dear Mr. Downs:

There have been several articles in <u>The Gazette</u> in recent months about the high rate of employee turnover and absenteeism in the local work force. According to authorities on the subject, turnover and absenteeism are invariably accompanied by increased training costs and lower employee morale. With those thoughts in mind, I am pleased to present you with this proposal.

The writer provides a context for this unsolicited proposal and points out a problem in the local business community to awaken the reader's interest.

<u>Problem Statement</u>

During the past decade there have been dramatic changes in the U.S. work force. The two-job family has become the norm, and finding satisfactory child care is an ongoing concern. Fifty-one percent of all mothers of infants are now in the work force. It is expected that throughout the late 1990s, fully two-thirds of all new job recruits will be women.

The writer documents the problem, confirms that the problem is likely to grow, and shows that a growing number of employers are addressing it.

Approximately 4 1/2 billion hours are lost each year due to tardiness, sickness, and absenteeism, much of it attributable to problems employees experience in trying to balance their jobs

Unsolicited Proposals

Unsolicited proposals resemble solicited ones in most ways. The most significant difference is that, with the solicited proposal, the solicitor has already recognized a need to be filled. In contrast, the writer of the unsolicited proposal must persuade the recipient that a need exists. For that reason the sequence of ideas will be less direct, more closely resembling the sequence presented in Chapter 8. An example of an unsolicited proposal is presented in Figure 10.6.

Persuasion is usually more obvious in an unsolicited proposal than in a solicited one.

Writing the Proposal

Whether the proposal is solicited or unsolicited, the information presented will be very similar. What will differ will be the emphasis placed on the various factors. After analyzing the needs of the solicitor or intended recipient, the writer should focus especially on the needs that appear to be most crucial.

Figure 10.6
Continued

Plastic Castings, Inc.
July 14, 1997
Page 2

with the demands of being a parent. During the last decade, there
was a **3,000 percent** increase in the number of companies that
provide some form of help for employees' offspring as a means of
stemming absenteeism and turnover with its attendant skyrocket-
ing cost of training new employees.

Objectives

One objective of this proposal is to alert you to the wisdom
of assisting your employees in solving their child-care problems.
A second objective is to introduce you to Kiddie Corral as a possible solution. A third objective is to help you reduce the expenses incurred by such problems as absenteeism, turnover, and
dissatisfied employees, as well as the expense of recruiting and
training new employees.

*The objectives are written
from the reader's standpoint
without predicting possible
survey results, and focus on
how both the employer and
employees might benefit.*

Method

1. We will survey your full-time employees, both hourly and
   salaried, who have children younger than age 16, concerning
   their current child-care arrangements and how they think these
   arrangements could be improved.
2. Results of the survey will be compiled and presented to you
   within ten days of the completion of the survey.
3. You and any associates you select will be given a tour of
   Kiddie Corral to see what it has to offer to your employees.

*The writer tells the reader
specifically what kind of information will be sought and how
it will be used, including a
time frame.*

**Internal proposals are often
in the form of memos.**

The destination for a proposal determines the appropriate format. The proposal that is intended for in-house use is written as a memorandum. Writers usually use the letter format when preparing short proposals for external use. The long report format is used for longer proposals, whether directed internally or externally. Most proposals are relatively short.

Proposals vary greatly in such characteristics as formality, length, and format. Good proposal writers attempt to respond to the needs of the solicitor or intended recipient by tailoring the proposal to that person or organization. The characteristics of effective writing presented in Chapter 5 are all relevant for writing proposals. The use of frequent headings is especially helpful in guiding the reader through such documents, no matter how complicated. The following sections usually are included in a proposal:

Figure 10.6
Continued

Plastic Castings, Inc.
July 14, 1997
Page 3

<u>Facilities and Personnel</u>

    The newly enlarged and remodeled Kiddie Corral has the equipment and personnel necessary to provide for the comfort, security, enjoyment, and intellectual stimulation for your employees' children. We have been in business for 12 years and have earned a reputation for the highest quality in child care. We always maintain a ratio of at least 1 adult for every 8 children, and there is a registered nurse on site at all times.

This section justifies selecting the writer to satisfy the need described and details the resources that are most relevant for the task.

<u>Cost</u>

    The administration of the survey, the compilation of its results, and an extensive tour of the facility will be provided at no cost to you. Should you choose to offer our services as a fringe benefit to your employees, many options are available. Enrollment costs are $125.00 per child for five 8-hour days. Some employers offer the service to employees for free, believing that it is a fair price to pay for reduced turnover and training costs, not to mention the heightened employee satisfaction that accompanies such a benefit. Other employers share the cost of the program with their employees.

The writer emphasizes the value of the service more than its cost. A detailed budget is not necessary in an unsolicited proposal.

<u>Summary</u>

    By providing company-sponsored child care, an employer reaps the rewards of increased employee loyalty, productivity,

The writer reminds the reader that accepting the proposal is the first step to solving the problem.

- Introduction
- Statement of the Problem
- Objectives
- Method or Plan
- Materials/Equipment/Personnel Available for Use
- Cost or Budget
- Summary

    An unsolicited proposal that was written in response to a problem about which the recipient had displayed no awareness or concern is shown in Figure 10.6. Two of the main challenges for such a proposal involve convincing the other party (1) that there is a problem and (2) that you are uniquely qualified to solve the problem.

Figure 10.6
Continued

Plastic Castings, Inc.
July 14, 1997
Page 4

and satisfaction. Because Kiddie Corral is located less than one mile from your plant, its convenience will also be appreciated.

I am available to answer any questions you may have about this proposal.

Sincerely yours,

Regina Grantham
Regina Grantham
President

✔ CHECKLIST for Writing a Solicited Proposal
____ Clearly define the problem.
____ Propose a reasonable approach.
____ Describe your company's expertise for solving the problem.
____ Provide a time frame.

✔ CHECKLIST for Writing an Unsolicited Proposal
____ Persuade the reader that a problem exists.
____ Clearly define the problem.
____ Propose a reasonable approach.
____ Convey expertise persuasively.
____ Provide a time frame.

BOXED IN

AN ETHICAL DILEMMA

George Stuart has read the Request for Proposal (RFP) from Candler County and has decided to submit a proposal. The project involves the building of an addition to the county courthouse. In general, the specifications in the RFP are ones that George feels Coastal Contractors Inc. could meet. In fact, the only specification about which he is uncertain is the completion date for the project. The building has to be turned over to Candler County in 18 months.

A possible obstacle to finishing the courthouse addition in 18 months is Coastal's current major project, Mid-Iowa Mall. As George tries to calculate the likely number of days necessary to complete the mall, he recognizes that the winter weather is an unknown factor. Even if no days are lost to inclement weather, he would be cutting the time close on the courthouse project.

January and February are traditionally the worst months of the winter for lost workdays. Looking over his calendar for the past five years, George sees that in four of the years days were lost in both January and February. The average number of days lost in January was three. In February the average was two days. George has read, however, that this winter is supposed to be unusually mild with little snowfall.

From past experience with the county, George knows that Coastal will not be considered for the courthouse job if his proposal suggests any uncertainty about meeting the deadline. Always optimistic, George is inclined to accept the long-range weather forecast and assume that everything will go without a hitch. On the other hand he knows that if he gets the job and fails to meet the deadline, Coastal's reputation will be tarnished.

George feels boxed in. What would you do?

Questions

1. Is there any way to better predict the weather?

2. What could George do to meet the deadline even with some bad weather?

3. In addition to the damage to reputation, what else might happen to Coastal if it does not meet the deadline?

Key Terms

- **memorandum report**
- **progress report**
- **periodic report**
- **justification report**
- **letter report**
- **form report**

- **proposal**
- **solicited proposal**
- **unsolicited proposal**
- **request for proposal (RFP)**
- *Commerce Business Daily (CBD)*

Summary

Progress reports   p. 258

Periodic reports   p. 259

Justification reports   p. 260

Letter format reports   pp. 261–263

Preprinted form reports   p. 264

Solicited proposals   p. 266

Unsolicited proposals   p. 267

Review Questions

1. In what ways does a memorandum differ from a memorandum report? How are they alike?

2. How do memorandum reports differ from letter reports?

3. What kinds of information might be included in a progress report?

4. What is a periodic report?

5. What are some possible purposes of justification reports?

6. Give two examples of routine memorandum reports.

7. What are the purposes of letter reports?

8. What are the advantages to an organization of providing preprinted forms for short reports? What are the disadvantages?

9. In what ways do solicited proposals differ from unsolicited proposals?

10. What is the main purpose of any proposal?

Exercises

1. You are branch manager employed by a multinational organization. Your boss requests a short report in which you detail the involvement in the foreign culture of those of your employees who are U.S. citizens. You are manager of German Operations and you have four subordinates who are U.S. citizens. You conduct an informal survey and learn the following: (a) Bill Henry and Thornton Aldrich and their families have joined local churches; (b) Suzanne Langer belongs to a community chorus; (c) Bill and Thornton are members of a local golf club; (d) Thorton and his family and Suzanne belong to a local swimming club; (e) Suzanne and Bill and his family belong to a social club in their respective neighborhoods; (f) although Tom Nettles has not joined any formal organizations, he has volunteered his expert advice to the town council regarding two engineering problems that arose in recent months. Bill and Thornton have lived in Germany for ten months, Tom for six months, and Suzanne for four months. Prepare your report for William

Fitzsimmons, manager of international production, 3T, Inc., Bangor, ME 04401.

2. As Director of Student Life you have been swamped with complaints about the lack of convenient parking for students on campus. You are seeking someone with the competence to help you solve such problems. Prepare an RFP for a consultant who is qualified to advise you on what must be done.

3. Imagine that you are a consultant with the necessary expertise and are responding to the RFP developed in Exercise 2. Prepare a proposal for the Director of Student Life.

4. As personnel research director of Metro Bank, a large urban bank with many branches, you were assigned six months ago to investigate why there is such high turnover among the tellers and the clerks. You implemented an exit interview program and learned that of the 60 tellers and clerks who quit during that period, 32 gave the heavy rush hour traffic as the main reason; 20 said they wanted to work part time instead; 8 others gave personal reasons.

   It seems to you that a good solution would be to introduce a more flexible schedule. By altering work schedules you believe that some workers could avoid rush-hour driving. Another possibility might be to hire more part-time employees and to allow full-time employees to work part time if they wish.

   The cost of training new employees is very high. Anything that can be done to reduce turnover and training costs would be worthwhile, you believe. Prepare for Willard Petrol, vice-president of personnel, a report in which you present your findings and make recommendations. Willard has a reputation for being against change. He believes that most modern personnel practices are actually harmful to the organization.

5. As head of the student activities committee you are in the process of developing a booklet for new students. You hope to include a section on free things students can do. To compile this information you plan to contact the presidents of the social, civic, and all other clubs on the campus. You hope to come up with a long list of free things to do on campus and in town. Prepare a memorandum report to be sent to the club presidents. In it you will seek as much information about free activities as possible.

6. Students and faculty alike usually believe that registration procedures could be improved at their schools. List whatever changes you consider to be desirable; then prepare a memorandum report in which you detail the steps a student must follow in registering for classes under your improved system. This memorandum report will be sent to all students who are accepted by your school. If you are pleased with present registration procedures, your memorandum report should describe them.

7. You are a management trainee in a large (4,000 employees) manufacturing plant. The plant manager, Tom Collins, has asked you to write a report on the use of quality circles in business and industry. He wants to learn what quality circles are, their uses, how widespread their use is, and their benefits. Use the *Business Periodical Index* to locate several articles on quality circles in order to gain the knowledge necessary to write the report. Tom has little patience with long reports and will not read a report longer than three pages.

8. Prepare an informational report on the "Man of the Year" selected by *Time* magazine for the past 20 years. In this report indicate the recipients, the year each was selected, the main reason each person won the award, and any trend that appears to be developing in bestowing the award. Finally, predict the next recipient of the award and briefly defend your prediction.

9. Prepare a progress report describing the progress you are making in your education. Describe your goals, and detail your plan for accomplishing these goals. Also,

describe the major obstacles to accomplishing your goals and what you are doing to overcome the obstacles. Address this report to your advisor.

10. You are a member of a professional association in your area of interest. You have been asked to suggest an appropriate topic for a 90-minute session at the national convention. You will not be responsible for giving a presentation but merely for suggesting an appropriate topic. Prepare a justification report in which you suggest a topic, and present a rationale for its being a part of the convention. Indicate clearly why you believe this topic would appeal to the members of the professional association.

11. In order to actively include as many association members in the convention in Exercise 10 as possible, it is decided that each 90-minute session will feature four presentations. Prepare a justification report in which you suggest a topic for a session. Also, explain how the topic could be divided into four parts and what each speaker would cover. Explain in what ways the topic would interest the membership and defend your suggested division of the topic.

12. Keep a time log for one week. At 30-minute intervals throughout each day stop and write down what you did during the prior 30-minute period. At the end of the week prepare a letter report in which you describe your time use. Divide your report into sections on the basis of your major uses of time. Conclude with a list of recommendations of how you could improve your use of time. Address the report to yourself.

13. Prepare a preprinted form that could be used for keeping a time log as described in Exercise 12. Prepare this form for college students to use.

14. Locate an RFP in a copy of the *Commerce Business Daily* or in the classified section of another newspaper. (Sometimes they are listed under "Requests for Bids.") Prepare a proposal in response to it.

15. Write an RFP for some need that you consider to be currently unfilled. (Don't make it too personal.) Bring your RFP to class. Your instructor will collect all of them and redistribute them within the class. Write a proposal in response to the RFP you are given.

CASE

Selecting the Winning Proposal

Martha Andrews Nord, Owen Graduate School of Management, Vanderbilt University

Towsen Corporate Services works as an independent contractor to develop software documentation, procedures manuals, and business proposals. Starting as a one-person shop with three clients five years ago, TCS now has 25 clients, 10 contract writers, and a new full-time marketing director. Elizabeth Towsen, president, is wrestling with the rapid growth. Her original five-year plan did not anticipate the current need for office space and equipment. To keep up the high-quality service to her clients, within the next quarter she must purchase additional computer equipment, office furniture, and a copy machine.

Her immediate goal is to identify a few vendors and then choose from that list. Among the steady stream of vendors with whom she has met, three sell copy machines. This past week she received proposals from all three. She knows that each offers comparable equipment and some level of support service, but she is not sure which equipment and service will best meet her needs. Feeling some pressure to make a decision, she skims the beginning of the three proposals:

Vendor One: Our Model DB4825 Copier has simple, easy-to-read digital controls that put all the copier functions at your fingertips. It makes 14 copies per minute on a variety of stock including address labels and most letterheads. For special applications, you can reduce or enlarge the copy size in one percent increments from 65% to 122%. . . .

Vendor Two: *Micshoba DB4825 System Cost*
24 Month Lease/Purchase: $189.00 plus tax per month
Micshoba DB4825 System Includes
Micshoba DB4825 Copier
Matching Console Cabinet
Paper Cassette
Reduction and Enlargement
50 Sheet Stack Sheet Bypass

Vendor Three: Although sporadic, your copying needs are complex. The nature of your business requires that copies have a consistently high quality and that the machine be able to
  –collate
  –duplex
  –copy in 2 colors

After her hurried review of the three documents, she quickly narrowed her choice to one and picked up the phone to call.

Case Questions

1. Specifically, what was Elizabeth Towsen looking for in the proposals?

2. Which vendor came out on top? Why?

3. What focus did the other two proposals use that caused them to miss the needs of their reader, Elizabeth Towsen?

CASE

American Forged Hand Tools

John D. Stegman, College of Business, The Ohio State University

You are pleased! Only a month out of the state university with a degree in business administration you have landed a super job. You are a new salesperson for the Authentic Automotive Parts Company. This warehouse distributor of automotive parts for the automotive aftermarket serves the state of Indiana. Warehouse distributors (WDs) keep large inventories of parts and accessories and serve automotive jobbers. Jobbers sell to mechanics, garages, and do-it-yourselfers. The automotive aftermarket is quite profitable because there are always cars that need repairs, and in most cases mechanics as well as car owners are willing to pay top dollar for a part that is always available from the jobber. Jobbers get overnight delivery from their WD. In addition to parts and accessories, WDs and jobbers also carry automotive, or mechanic's, hand tools.

   Your boss, Pat Sekoll, the sales manager at Authentic, wants you to go after additional—or what she calls "PLUS"—sales in your well-established territory. One way is to sell the jobber on stocking and displaying a line of mechanic's hand tools. Authentic is the WD in the state for American Forged Hand Tools. Tools are a profitable item and mechanics especially want a tool *on the spot*. They may have a car engine torn down and discover they do not have the right tool(s) to put it back together. Time is money for mechanics and garages.

Snappy Car Parts is a medium-sized jobber with several locations. Upon investigation, you discover that Snappy does not carry a line of tools. When they get calls for tools they promise them for the next day and get them overnight from Authentic. They probably lose many tool sales because customers need them today, not tomorrow. The investment in inventory of tools is substantial, but it has always paid off for jobbers as well as WDs. You make a breakfast appointment for next week with Frank Kopas, the president, and Randy Jacobs, the sales manager, at Snappy. Now you begin to worry about your proposal. Perhaps you should have taken better notes in your business communication class at the university. You do not remember how to structure business proposals; should this one be an oral presentation, in writing, or both?

Case Questions

1. What are the elements in a business proposal?
2. Which would you use in this proposal to Snappy?
3. How would you structure the oral pitch to Frank and Randy?
4. How much detail would you include in the written proposal?
5. What would you emphasize, and how?

C A S E

He Did It His Way

Don Anderson, Professor Emeritus, Grossmont College, San Diego, CA

Pat Brandon landed an excellent job with Made-Well Corporation after fewer than a dozen interviews. Considering the tight economy and job market, he felt particularly fortunate. Although his grade point average from Podunk University was certainly commendable, he was fairly convinced his communication skills played a large part in securing a good position.

In the first six months with Made-Well, Pat had only occasional opportunities to demonstrate these skills to John Gilbert, his branch manager. Pat's writing consisted of one or two memos per week and an occasional letter. He had yet to make a significant presentation, either in writing or in person.

Now, at last, he was called to Mr. Gilbert's office and given his first significant writing assignment: Reorganize and rewrite portions of the corporation's style manual where necessary and update the information to reflect current technology being used at Made-Well. Since he was convinced he wouldn't have been given the responsibility without the manager's complete confidence, he was happy to accept the assignment. After a 15-minute meeting with Mr. Gilbert, he proceeded with the task. Although Pat's other duties were reduced only slightly while he undertook the revision, he felt comfortable with a 6-week due date.

Pat's recent writing successes in college papers provided the impetus to make substantial changes. He totally rewrote the section on internal communications so that it barely resembled the original. He added a new chapter on "Communicating in the 1990s." He discarded the transmittal letter and wrote his own version, in which he explained that this manual was now very readable, concise, jargon-free, and devoid of gobbledygook. The revised version was on Mr. Gilbert's desk three days in advance of the due date.

The praise Pat anticipated was not forthcoming. Apparently the original author, Jan Wiley, was still with the company but working in a different division. Mr. Gilbert showed her the camera-ready copy to solicit her thoughts. She felt somewhat offended by the implication that her writing style had been considered verbose, stilted, and with antiquated phrasing to boot. Mr."G" called Pat to his office and thanked (not praised) Pat for his efforts but said little else. As much as anything, Pat felt slighted as well as confused. He was proud of his revision.

Case Questions

1. Do you feel Pat received acceptable recognition for his efforts?

2. How might he have proceeded to ensure a favorable reaction from both Mr. Gilbert and Ms. Wiley?

3. What points needed to be covered in the initial meeting of Pat and Mr. Gilbert?

4. As Pat's revision progressed, how might a further meeting or two with Mr. Gilbert have been useful?

CASE

The Team That Writes Together

Deb Renshaw, M.A., Ed.D., Psychotherapist and Trainer, Port Townsend, WA

As a result of your having demonstrated well-developed abilities in coordinating collaborative projects, you have recently been hired by an Atlanta-based consulting firm to head up a major project involving seven people. Five live in the greater Atlanta area close to you, while two live out of state. You've made contact with all of them by phone and have learned that none of them has experience in collaborative work on a project of this size. However, they all are up-to-speed on the latest technology including fax, E-mail, and computer systems (several using Macintosh systems and several using DOS systems).

The end product of this project is an in-depth proposal discussing the feasibility of developing a Mediation Training Program for the firm and securing grant moneys for the development and implementation for the program. You and your project team have nine months to complete the research and go to print on this project.

As project coordinator and editor, you have decided that two meetings taking place in your Atlanta office are necessary. You've had one, and everyone involved with the project has had an opportunity to meet. You're now having your second meeting, and the purpose of this meeting is to determine who is responsible for what part(s) of the project, to develop a time line for the project, and to work out any currently present and/or anticipated glitches.

(Note that all correspondence among the project team members from now until the review of the final draft of the proposal will be handled long distance. The next meeting of the full project team will be one month prior to submission of the final document.)

One and a half months following your last project team meeting in Atlanta, you've received some E-mail from several team members concerning J. Harrison, another team member. The thrust of the E-mail is about Harrison's inability to meet deadlines and complete small research tasks, and his seeming overall lack of desire to work as a "team member." In the meantime, other project team members' ability to proceed with their tasks is being held up because of the situation with Harrison—and the deadline for project completion is rapidly approaching.

Case Questions

1. Write a memo to your project team explaining the collaborative process. You'll send the memo to each of them prior to your second project team meeting, so they can be prepared to contribute and ask questions coming into the meeting.

2. Since Harrison is not working out well, how do you handle this situation? In writing? In person? Do you communicate with Harrison individually, or do you communicate with the entire project team simultaneously or individually? Explain how and why you chose your particular course of action.

3. Describe your thinking about how you and your project team will construct a time frame for the life of the project. Begin by describing how decisions are made about how the work is shared by the project team members through the remainder of the life of the project.

4. In your opinion, what do you consider difficult when working with multiple authors? How do you think through and work out difficulties?

Notes

1. From an interview with Ginger Watkins of the Atlanta Olympic Committee, January 16, 1990.

2. Wicke Chambers and Spring Asher, "Make Sure Your Proposal Stands Out," *Atlanta Journal and Constitution*, January 10, 1994, p. E7.

Chapter 11

The Long Report: Planning

Stephanie McQuiston is anxiously waiting to see her boss at Atlantic Electronics, Scott Millan.

Several weeks ago she turned in a report on employee relations problems and is confident that she researched the topic well. Her solutions to the problems were, she believes, logical and desirable; she said as much in her report. But now Scott is meeting with Louise Alexander, who is his superior, and the vice president to conduct Stephanie's first semiannual review. She had known the meeting was to take place today, and she had known who would be participating. What caught her off guard was that she saw the vice president carrying her report to the meeting. It was going to be used in the evaluation.

Stephanie is worried that some parts of the report—other than her research and recommendation sections—might not be correct. Although she believes she had the right information, perhaps it could have been better organized.

In the six months she has been with Atlantic, she has written a dozen or so reports of various lengths, and Scott has been gracious in guiding her in preparing the type of reports he wants. Although her business-degree background included some report-writing instruction, she quickly found that she had a lot to learn. Now she is wondering about the organization of her report, the clarity of her conclusions, and whether she should have included more visual support, such as charts, to illustrate her findings.

Well, she thinks, I'll know soon. Here comes Scott.

You may have had the same uneasy feeling about a term paper that Stephanie has about her business report. Of course, term papers differ from business reports, but both are used in performance evaluation; therefore, afterthoughts are likely. Chapters 11 and 12 will describe what Stephanie might have done to be more self-assured in her report preparation. An effective and appropriate report on her topic appears in Chapter 12 (Figure 12.1).

Much of the material in Chapter 11 and 12 can be applied to term paper assignments. However, several major differences between reports and term papers exist. (1) Many term paper assignments identify the specific purpose, such as an assignment to describe the influence of technology on office workers. The business report writer will often need to identify the purpose of the report. In other words, many business reports are self-initiated. (2) Most term papers are written for a single audience, usually the instructor, whereas business reports typically are written for many readers. Some reports that are written for a single reader are viewed by many more than the one intended reader. (3) Business reports typically have standard parts that are seldom used when writing term papers.

CHARACTERISTICS AND CATEGORIES OF BUSINESS REPORTS

Decisions about report characteristics are made during planning.

The characteristics of the finished report result from decisions made during the planning stage. They include:

1. *Level of formality.* Some reports, such as for government or high-level management, have an extremely formal tone and appearance.

2. *Length.* Reports may be as long as several hundred pages, depending on the topic and the purpose of the report.

3. *The time interval.* Reports may be periodic, such as annual financial reports, or they may be prepared only once.

4. *Destination.* Does the report go downward to subordinates or upward to superiors? Is the report directed internally—that is, will it be used within the organization? Is the report directed externally to an audience removed from the organization, such as a local government?

5. *Research category employed.* The presentation of information differs depending on whether primary or secondary research is used.

6. *Intent.* Is the goal of the report to justify some action, to establish progress toward an objective, or to recommend a change?

7. *Number of authors.* Team-written reports frequently have a different tone than individually prepared reports. Further, team reports may incorporate individually written sections into one package, or the team may work together, in both writing and editing, on each sentence in the document.

8. *Contribution to decision making.* Reports range from straightforward statements of fact to highly structured analyses that include recommendations and discussion of implications.

The three types of business reports differ in their contribution to the decision-making process.

All business reports, whether short or long, can be categorized by the extent of the contribution they make to the decision-making process. The **informational report**, which presents data without interpretation, is valuable and ever present. However, it has little application in decision making. An example is a weekly absenteeism report that indicates only who was absent, when, the employee's department, and number of absences to date.

A step above the informational report, the **interpretive report** adds meaning to the data. The facts presented in the informational report are examined and implications are drawn. To the absenteeism report already described, the writer would add an explanation: which employees are absentee problems, whether some departments experience higher rates than others, and what cost in time, dollars, or materials is attributable to absenteeism.

The third level of decision-making reports—and the one that makes the most contribution to the decision-making process—is the **problem-solving report**. Because the problem-solving report not only informs with data and interprets the data, but also analyzes the problem situation, reviews alternatives, examines implications, draws conclusions, and makes recommendations, it is frequently referred to as an **analytical report**. The absenteeism report already described might, for example, include a recommendation that two employees be interviewed by their supervisors to determine the cause of their extreme absenteeism.

The problem-solving report is obviously the most involved and difficult of the three types; it encompasses the other two. Thus, generally speaking, anyone who can write an effective problem-solving report can probably write the others as well. Chapters 11 and 12 therefore focus on the problem-solving report.

THE PLANNING PROCESS AND THE LONG REPORT

The first step in the planning process, as presented in Chapter 6, is to determine the objective of the message. A clear understanding of the objective, or purpose, is especially important in planning a report, which typically takes much more effort and time than a letter or a memorandum. Further, the purpose of a long report is often stated in an early section so that the reader can anticipate the direction of the report.

A clear understanding of purpose is important in planning.

Suppose that three members of the marketing department are asked to write problem-solving reports. They might define the problems in problem statements such as these:

- Sales of Product X have fallen 37 percent in 14 months.
- Competitors are taking approximately 1.7 percent of our market share each quarter.
- Sales of our best-selling products are falling because the quality of our competitors' products is better.

The purpose statements that members of the marketing department develop to describe a desired outcome might be similar to these:

- This is a plan for stopping the sales decline for Product X.
- I propose this design for an aggressive advertising campaign that will recapture our market share.
- The purpose of this report is to propose improvements in our quality control program.

Other steps in the planning process presented in Chapter 6 are to consider the audience—expertise, interests, opinions, and hierarchical position—and to generate a list of ideas and choose the important ones. For the long report, this involves conducting research, evaluating results, and outlining the report.

CONDUCTING THE RESEARCH

Doing the research for a report means answering two questions: (1) what do I need? and (2) where can I get it? In planning her problem-solving report, Stephanie used a procedure most good report writers employ in answering the first question. She broke down her problem into three areas of need and created a checklist for herself, as shown in Table 11.1. A similar chart can help you clearly define your information needs and also serves as a feedback device—you can check items as you acquire the information.

You are now ready to answer the second question, Where do I get the information? This involves choosing between two kinds of information sources—primary and

Information may come from primary or secondary sources.

TABLE 11.1 A SAMPLE NEEDS CHART		
Need 1: What Is the Problem?	**Need 2: What's Causing the Problem?**	**Need 3: What Are Some Solutions?**
Turnover information	Why high turnover?	More money
Absenteeism information	Why high absenteeism?	More fringe benefits
Grievance information	Why so many grievances?	Better working conditions
Morale information	Why such low morale?	What else?
Unionization information	Why talk of unionization?	

secondary. **Primary sources** are generally unpublished; you get them firsthand. **Secondary sources** are publications. Following are some examples:

Primary Sources	**Secondary Sources**
Questionnaires	Newspapers
Experiments	Government documents
Interviews	Books
Personal observations	Magazines
Organization files (in some cases)	Pamphlets

Your choice of sources depends on how much time you have to complete the report, the budget, and your ability to use the sources. You should try first to use secondary research. If the information is incomplete, inaccurate, or outdated, primary research may be required. In some cases, a combination of secondary and primary research builds a stronger report.

Sometimes writers assume that secondary research is easier and quicker than primary research. Although this may often be the case, it is not always true. You should not select a secondary research technique just because it appears to be the quickest method. A better rule of thumb—one that comes from scientific inquiry—is to do secondary research first. If others have already researched your topic, rely on their findings. However, you must be careful not to assume that because something is in print, it is correct, complete, or current.

In examining secondary research, it is wise to ask: (1) Is the information complete? (2) Does it appear reasonable and logical? (3) Is it biased? (4) Is it recent? A weakness in any one of these areas may suggest the need to conduct your own (primary) research. Raise these same four questions before secondary research is included in the report.

Secondary Research

Secondary research is sometimes called library research, but this does not mean that all secondary research is done in a library. Some items, such as newspapers, magazines, or pamphlets, you may have at home or at your office. However, a thorough secondary research project will likely mean a trip to the library. Although you probably know how to use the library effectively, here are a few hints and reminders:

- Do not focus your search exclusively on books and neglect periodicals, or vice versa.

- Use the *Guide to Periodic Literature*, which may be in magazine, hardbound, or microfilm form, to find <u>citations</u> by title, author, or subject. The *Business Periodical Index* serves the same function but lists only articles related to business. Also consider using *The Wall Street Journal Index* and *The New York Times Index*.

- Remember to use computerized databases such as *InfoTrac*® or *Lexis/Nexis*, which can quickly and thoroughly search hundreds of periodicals for key words.

- When you find a book on your topic, use both the table of contents and the index to locate information. Skim both completely because you may not know the exact term the author uses to refer to your topic.

- Pay special attention to the footnotes in the books and articles you find to guide you to other related sources.

- Look for sources that survey your topic. Books of this type are sometimes entitled, *The Handbook of . . . , The . . . Manual*, or *An Analysis of. . . .* These sources often break the topic into outline form, may give its history, and frequently have many valuable footnotes.

- Watch for sources with bibliographies. Sometimes entire books are bibliographies, and these can be most helpful.

- If you become frustrated or confused, seek help from a librarian, who is an expert in locating information.

- As you locate information that you think may be of some value to you, put the information on notecards.

> Notecards are better than paper for recording information obtained during secondary research.

(Of course, instead of using notecards, entering the information in a computer database on your computer is even more efficient.) You can save time later by taking several steps as you make notecards. At the top of the card write the complete citation of the source in bibliographic form. (The differences between footnotes and bibliographic citations, with examples of each, are found in Chapter 12.) By using separate cards instead of notebook paper, the cards can be sorted by topic, which can be helpful in developing a working outline. Further, an additional sourcecard can easily be placed between two existing cards.

An alternative to the physical trip to the library is to make an electronic trip. With a computer and a modem at home or from a university computer laboratory connected to the library, students today regularly and efficiently search the electronic card catalog, which probably tells whether the book is currently in the stacks, or reviews electronic databases. Some databases hold business periodicals, legal sources, medical information, or financial data. See Table 11.2 for a list of major databases that support business students' research.

Databases typically can be searched by author, subject, title, or key words. Once found, the citation may include full text or an abstract. They usually are updated monthly.

There are several alternatives to connecting to a library's databases; one is to use national on-line services, such as CompuServe, America On-Line, or Prodigy. For those without access to a university database, these services are powerful and convenient. A disadvantage is that they charge monthly fees, plus each database accessed may add a fee as well—sometimes a very large fee.

A second alternative is to use the Internet to find your information. With relatively little instruction or computer expertise, you can research your topics in a variety of ways.

- Join an E-mail discussion group. You can browse the discussion occurring in a specific group or become an active member by posing a question, such as, "I read a statistic that 47 percent of Toyota's cars are

TABLE 11.2 REPRESENTATIVE ELECTRONIC DATABASES
ABI/Inform is the most complete index to articles in business research journals and important trade publications. It includes lengthy abstracts.
Applied Science and Technology Index is an index, with abstracts, to articles in major technology and applied science periodicals.
ERIC contains references and summaries of journal articles and other materials related to all aspects of education and training.
Expanded Academic Index is an index to articles in scholarly and general-interest periodicals focusing on topics in the social sciences, humanities, and nontechnical general science areas.
Lexis/Nexis is an index to, and collection of, mostly full-text documents such as law reports, company filings, newspaper articles, and trade magazine articles. The focus is on current events, business, and law.
National Newspaper Index is an index to articles, reviews, speeches, editorials, and interviews in *The New York Times*, *The Washington Post*, *The Christian Science Monitor*, *The Los Angeles Times*, and *The Wall Street Journal*.
PsycLIT is the most comprehensive index to the world's journal and book literature in psychology and related disciplines.
UnCover provides table of contents information for over 16,000 journals in all subject areas. Coverage for most journals begins with 1989.
Wilson Business Abstracts is an index, with abstracts, to articles in basic business journals and magazines and in recent issues of *The Wall Street Journal* and *The New York Times*.

Source: Courtesy Malcolm A. Love Library, San Diego State University.

built in the United States, but now I can't find the source. Can anyone help me find the source?" Such a question would have to be posted to a group (also "news network" or "bulletin board") that is relevant, such as cars/Japanese or business/manufacturing/automobiles/Japanese.

- A spin-off of the news group is to search information from commercial services, such as wire services or syndicated columns. On the Internet, within USENET, Clarinet is one such source.
- Use Archie. Archie is a system that allows you to search indexes to locate files on public servers; in 1994, there were about 1,200 servers and 2.5 million files.[1]
- Use USENET's User List to see if a specific individual, such as an author of an important article or someone whose quote is relevant, is an Internet user. If so, use the Internet much like a phone call, to contact him or her.
- Select Gopher to find Internet resources. This interface uses hierarchical menus linked to files. Use Gopher to view computer resource manuals, libraries throughout the world, or connect to the National Weather Service. Within Gopher, use Veronica to search for files.
- Search indexed databases with Wide Area Information Server (WAIS). WAIS scans the full text of indexed articles in specified databases.
- Pick the World Wide Web (also "WWW" or the "Web"), which creates a hyperlink interface for Internet information. Use the popular Mosaic browser to view graphical Web documents. With Mosaic, for example, a user could move to San Diego State University's home page, click on the highlighted word colleges, departments, or programs, and then select College of Business Administration,

Information and Decision Systems Department, or Information Systems program, respectively. From any of these choices access the Information and Decision Systems Department's home page. Clicking on highlighted students would take the user to organizations, job seekers, and other choices. Picking job seekers would give the viewer choices of home pages for individual students by type of job they are seeking.

The power of the Web is that the user could have ended with an individual's home page having followed any of a variety of paths from SDSU's home page—through Student Services or Career Services, for example. A national organization with a home page to which the student belongs might provide yet another way of "pointing" to the job-seeking student's home page.

In addition to its hypertext feature for text, Mosaic can handle audio, static pictures, and moving pictures.

If you are dealing with notecards, with the bibliographic citations at the top, the bibliography at the end of your report will be easy to prepare. Alphabetize your cards by authors' last names. Put only one piece of information on a card, even if this means using several cards to represent one source, because it allows for easy sorting and cross-referencing. Make sure your handwriting is legible. If someone else types your report, that person can type the bibliography directly from your cards.

The information you write on the card may be a direct quote, your own summary, or how the information relates to other sources. You may wish to put the card catalog listing on the other side of the card so you can quickly locate the source again. A sample card may look like the one in Figure 11.1.

Be sure to relate your secondary research activity to the objective of your report. If you seek a specific person's opinion on a topic, finding a single source that gives that opinion may conclude your research. If you bring together a variety of opinions about a topic, a number of sources will need to be examined. You should continue to review sources until one of the following occurs: (1) You exhaust your search (and perhaps yourself); to be thorough is to locate everything you can find on the subject. (2) You work until what you find starts to cluster; once you reach the point where you find nothing new, you may be at the end of your search. (3) You have thoroughly answered the specific question you set out to answer; this assumes you have a specific question, such as, "How many cars for four or more passengers were imported from Japan in 1996?"

Figure 11.1
Sample Notecard

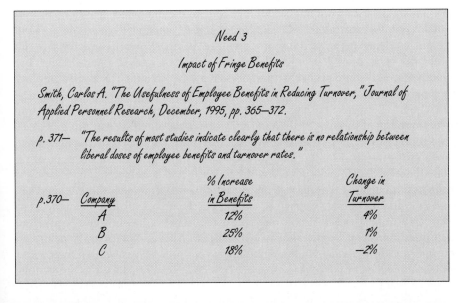

Primary Research

The primary research sources listed earlier are the most frequently used; questionnaires, experiments, interviews, personal observation, and organization files. Familiarity with primary research sources can be useful not only in writing reports but also in other activities, such as consumer behavior, research, feasibility studies, and employee attitude measurements.

Questionnaires

Properly developed questionnaires can provide an enormous amount of useful data. Improperly developed questionnaires can give misleading and often uninterpretable information. Proper use of questionnaires includes selecting an appropriate sample of respondents, carefully writing the questionnaire, administering the questionnaire in such a way as to encourage response, and accurately tabulating the results.

Sample Selection. When you hear the results of political opinion polls, you might wonder how information obtained from as few as one thousand people can accurately reflect the opinions of sometimes millions of individuals. Because many opinion pollsters carefully select their samples, their predictions of election results are frequently accurate within several percentage points. Such accuracy occurs because these pollsters have clearly defined their population and, using scientific sampling guidelines, have chosen their sample from that population.

A **population** (also called a **universe**) is some definable group—every item, person, or thing is either in or out of the population. For national opinion pollsters in the United States, the population consists of more than 250 million citizens. On your college campus, it might be all the students or perhaps just the female undergraduate students. In an organization such as Stephanie's, the population might be all full-time employees or perhaps all hourly employees. Your first step, then, is to define your population. What group of people should the data you gather represent?

Selecting a sample involves choosing a group to represent the whole population. Ideally questionnaires would be administered to the entire population. This, however, might be time consuming and expensive. A well-conducted sample should give us similar results by contacting only a subgroup. The important assumption is that the sample represents the population.

A convenience sample is not statistically defensible.

Several types of sampling techniques exist. First, in Stephanie's report-writing problem, she might use a convenience sample. She might administer questionnaires to any available employees from the 500 employees in the company. Because she works in the operations department, she might distribute 50 questionnaires to the first 50 employees she encounters during the lunch hour. Such a sample is convenient, but Stephanie's findings would probably not represent all the Atlantic Electronics employees. She might miss employees who go out for lunch or executives who do not keep regular lunch hours. Convenience sampling generally is not an appropriate way of selecting a sample. Sampling of this type is also referred to as **nonprobability sampling** because there is a good chance the sample selected does not represent the larger population.

Probability sampling, on the other hand, assumes the elements in the population have some known chance or probability of being selected as subjects. Three types of probability sampling are random, systematic random, and stratified random sampling.

A random sample requires careful control.

Using random sampling, Stephanie would place the names of all 500 employees in a box and draw out 50 names. Employees whose names were drawn would be asked to complete questionnaires. Despite the inconvenience of having to prepare 500 names on slips of paper for the drawing, random sampling is appropriate because each member of the population (each employee) has an equal chance of being included in the sample.

This chance of being part of the sample is what makes random sampling scientifically useful and defensible. With a convenience sampling, Stephanie cannot say for sure that her findings represent the opinions of all Atlantic Electronics employees. Using a random sample, Stephanie can make that important assertion.

Systematic random sampling draws from a list and takes every nth name. Assume that Stephanie has a list of all 500 Atlantic employees. If she randomly picks a number between 1 and 10, such as 4, and picks every fourth person from the list, she would be conducting a systematic random sample. As with random sampling, each population member has an equal chance of being part of the sample.

Stratified random sampling is the most sophisticated of the techniques. Again, random sampling is used, but sample members are also selected based on some important demographic characteristics (e.g., sex, race, or age). The sample is stratified according to some important characteristics and usually reflects the same proportions found in the population. For example, if 47 percent of the population is female, then 47 percent of the sample should be female also. Of course, not all characteristics are important. For example, in a campus political election, sample members' hometowns may not be important. Stephanie might decide to use the following stratifications: hourly or salary, management or nonmanagement, male or female, and more than five years with Atlantic or less than five years.

Stratified random sampling is a powerful sampling technique because it ensures that sample members are selected according to one or more characteristics that might influence the findings of the questionnaire. In fact, most opinion pollsters use this technique to stratify their samples by age, income, socioeconomic status, political party affiliation, and a host of other important characteristics. Such stratification adds precision to their polls and explains why their predictions are often so accurate. Generally speaking, a stratified sample uses fewer people in its sample but requires much more sophisticated development.

Writing the Questionnaire. The terms questionnaire and, later, interview are used in this book instead of survey because of the need for clarity. A questionnaire is always a paper-and-pencil activity completed by the respondent. An interview is always oral.

A well-developed questionnaire has three basic parts: introduction, instructions, and questions. The objective of the introduction is to motivate the respondent to complete the questionnaire. If you have but a few comments to share in your introduction, you may wish to include them immediately before—or as part of—your instructions. On the other hand, as the introduction becomes lengthy or the situation more formal, you may present your introduction as a cover letter or memorandum.

> A questionnaire has an introduction, instructions, and questions.

The Introduction. The introduction identifies the purpose of the questionnaire. Unless you are concerned that stating the actual purpose for the questionnaire will bias the respondents' answers, state specifically why you are administering the questionnaire.

> The questionnaire introduction covers six points.

Second, the introduction discusses anonymity. Because you will rarely be interested in identifying individual respondents, a statement guaranteeing their anonymity will help prevent biased responses. If their names are needed, explain why. If you need to be able to identify them, but identification will not be used in the report or shared with others, emphasize this; the emphasis may be almost as beneficial as complete anonymity in gaining their response.

Third, the introduction tells respondents what to do with the questionnaire once they have completed it. In the case of mailed questionnaires, for example, this section might contain instructions for returning the questionnaire through the mail.

Fourth, the introduction may explain why a response is important. If you are using a sample of 100 from a population of 1,000, you may explain that each respondent's opinions reflect the feelings of 10 people.

Fifth, particularly when questionnaires appear time consuming but actually are not, the introduction should indicate the amount of time required. "Only about two and one-half minutes of your time are required" is the type of statement that may be helpful in gaining cooperation.

Finally, the introduction should identify the sender by name and title. This humanizes the message and enhances the response rate. An example introduction, as well as the balance of a questionnaire, is found in an appendix to Stephanie's report, which is reproduced in Chapter 12.

The Instructions. If instructions are not thorough and clear, respondents may misunderstand what they are to do. The need for clear instructions cannot be overemphasized. Assume that your reader is going to misinterpret your questionnaire—where will the error occur? Help yourself and the quality of your responses by giving clear instructions.

You may find that one set of instructions, at the beginning of the questionnaire, will guide the reader through the entire questionnaire; this is particularly true when you ask only one major category of questions, such as several rank order questions. In more complex situations, however, you may need a set of instructions at the beginning and additional instructions before each new category of questions. For example, you may need new instructions as you move from a series of rank order questions to multiple choice questions.

The Questions. Some novices present the questions without introductory comments or instructions. Such an approach is doomed to failure. Six major categories of questions exist. Deciding when, where, and how to use these categories is both an art and a science.

Demographic questions seek information on respondents.

Each category of questions has its own purpose, strengths, and weaknesses. **Demographic questions,** which frequently appear first, seek information on characteristics of the respondent. Age, sex, income, race, department, college major, and hometown are examples of demographic questions. Demographic questions have two major values: first, they can be used to break down answers to other questions. For example, you may seek a difference by sex (demographics) in the way respondents feel toward the president's foreign policy. A second value is to test the appropriateness of a random sample. If you know that your population is 35 percent college-educated but your sample includes only 10 percent college-educated respondents, your demographic question of education indicates that your sample appears not to be random.

Dichotomous questions have two possible answers.

A second category of question is the **dichotomous question**—a question that elicits one of only two possible answers. Yes/no, male/female, and true/false are examples of responses to dichotomous questions. You may have noticed that dichotomous questions may also be demographic questions: "What is your sex?" fits both categories. Other categories of questions may overlap somewhat, too. Dichotomous questions allow respondents to branch or skip irrelevant questions. An example of a branching question and instructions is, "Have you earned a bachelor's degree as of today? _____ Yes _____ No (if yes, answer Questions 2 through 9; if no, skip directly to Question 10).

List and rank order questions are common.

A **list question** presents a list of items and asks the respondent to select one. The selection may be the greatest or the least, the largest or the smallest, the most or least important, or the best or worst. Here is an example of a list question:

Which of the following do you feel is most important in determining your job satisfaction?

_____ Money

_____ Praise from superiors

_____ Doing job well

_____ Respect from peers

_____ Fringe benefits

Similar to the list question is the **rank order question**. It, too, presents a list; however, it differs because a response is given for each item in the list instead of just one item. Furthermore, the items are ranked according to some request, such as best to worst or largest to smallest. Here is an example of a rank order question:

Rank the following five items, from 1 for most important to 5 for least important, in terms of their importance to your job satisfaction:

_____ Money

_____ Praise from superiors

_____ Doing job well

_____ Respect from peers

_____ Fringe benefits

Although rank order questions can gather substantial information, be careful in analyzing the rankings. Remember that the rankings determine a hierarchy among the items, but that the distances between the items are not known. That is, Selections 1 and 2 may be close to each other, but there might be a large gap between 2 and 3. The rankings are ordinal numbers rather than interval numbers.

A major category of questions used in questionnaires is the **attitude question**. These questions may be direct or indirect. The direct attitude question seeks a clear or obvious attitude. Because attitudes usually are not dichotomous (yes or no) but are found on a scale, a five- or seven-position type of direct attitude question is often prepared. This type of question is called a Likert question. The respondent gives a single reaction to each stimulus on a scale that most likely has five positions. Here is an example of a Likert question:

Attitude questions may be direct or indirect.

I enjoy my marketing classes.

Strongly agree	Agree	Neutral	Disagree	Strongly disagree
_____	_____	_____	_____	_____

The semantic differential question, as opposed to the direct attitude question, seeks a deeper or more indirect attitude. Figure 11.2 shows a sample question. For each stimulus there will be a number of responses, usually about 10. A scale of five or seven positions is used between bipolar adjectives or scales.

This category of question elicits responses that respondents might not have considered on their own. Semantic differential responses can be compared group against group by which side of the neutral center they fall on or by time period, such as current responses versus answers from a year ago.

The sixth and final question category is the **open-ended question**. When you are unsure about how your respondents might answer a question, when you do not want to limit them to your wording, or when you seek answers with richness and depth, consider an open-ended question. One open-ended question is, "How do you feel about your company?" The strength of such a question lies in the richness of the answers; the weakness is that it is difficult to analyze the answers statistically. You will have unique

Figure 11.2

Semantic Differential
Question

(Stimulus:)		My Marketing Classes	
(Scale and Responses:)	rewarding	___:___:___:___:___:___:___	unrewarding
	difficult	___:___:___:___:___:___:___	easy
	relevant	___:___:___:___:___:___:___	irrelevant
	messy	___:___:___:___:___:___:___	tidy
	active	___:___:___:___:___:___:___	passive
	weak	___:___:___:___:___:___:___	strong
	good	___:___:___:___:___:___:___	bad
	unnecessary	___:___:___:___:___:___:___	necessary
	required	___:___:___:___:___:___:___	elective
	illogical	___:___:___:___:___:___:___	logical
	fun	___:___:___:___:___:___:___	work

responses and therefore cannot tabulate percentages because responses may defy definite categorization.

In contrast, a closed question is one that limits the respondents' depth of answer. Thus, rank order, dichotomous, and other categories of questions can be considered closed questions.

Lack of clarity in the wording or goal of a question can lead to problems of interpretation. Here are examples of several common problems in phrasing and design:

Overlapping Answer	Age: _____	Younger than 20
	_____	20-30
	_____	30-40
Leading Question	You do like your boss, don't you?	
Multiple Questions in One Question	Do you like ham and eggs?	
Confusing-Categories Question	Marital status: _____	Widowed
	_____	Divorced
	_____	Single
	_____	Married
Multiple-Interpretations Question	Are you an honest person?	

Chapter 20 presents a thorough analysis of questions used in interviews.

Experiments

A second major primary research technique is experimentation. When you use an experiment to gather primary data, there are some implicit assumptions. First, you manipulate something and pay attention to the result. Second, you start with a specific research question or hypothesis that you test. Third, you are objective and unbiased in your technique. Finally, most likely you will test your findings with well-defined statistical procedures. These major assumptions, plus many other guidelines and conditions, mean that experiments can be rigorous. However, if the experiment is to have meaning, the assumptions and guidelines must be met.

Describing important methodology in any depth is beyond the scope of this text. A few guidelines follow, and you are encouraged to seek additional direction elsewhere if you need it.

- Often you will need to sample some population for your experiment. Follow the rules for sampling.

- Always try to be unobtrusive; your presence alone can affect the data you are collecting.
- Be careful not to overgeneralize your findings—the results you observe for a sample of 50 reflect only those 50 and not necessarily the balance of the population. Conditions may have changed, for example, in the time between the start of your experiment and when you draw conclusions.
- Examine the secondary literature first to see if similar research has been conducted already. The mistakes of others may help you.
- Keep your experiment simple. Try to control as many variables as possible. For example, if you wish to know the effect of raising the price of hamburgers by 10 cents in the company cafeteria, do not raise the price of other items at the same time.

Interviews

When using interviews to gather data for a business report, you are likely to use one of the following interview types: persuasive, information giving, or information gathering. Persuasive interviewing might be conducted to encourage students to take part in an experiment. Information-giving interviewing might be used to instruct

> ✔ **CHECKLIST** *for Planning a Questionnaire*
>
> ____ Be sure to thoroughly define the universe and correctly select the sample.
>
> ____ Include all necessary information in the introduction.
>
> ____ Provide instructions that are thorough and clear.
>
> ____ Select the correct type of question to generate the desired data.

BOXED IN

AN ETHICAL DILEMMA

Joachim Hoang wants to measure employees' indirect attitudes toward the company's new benefits package. He is reasonably sure that the type of question he needs to ask in his questionnaire is a semantic differential question. However, he is not comfortable with the process of selecting the bipolar adjectives for his questions. His initial research has led him into an overwhelming array of complex issues. He does not understand the statistical process by which the adjectives usually fall into three main factors of evaluation, activity, and potency, nor does he know why it is important to have adjectives from each of these factors in his pilot test.

What's more, he is running out of time to complete the project.

Most discussions of semantic differential questions show adjectives such as hot/cold, friendly/unfriendly, and so on. Joachim is beginning to think he could pick up some of these common adjectives and avoid doing any more time-consuming research on how to select them. No one else in the company seems to know much about the correct use of the semantic differential. Chances are good that he would not get caught.

Joachim feels boxed in. What would you do?

Questions

1. What is the value to an organization of shoddy research?

2. Where could Joachim turn to learn more about the correct development of semantic differential questions?

3. How much research exists in business today that bends the rules of scientific inquiry, randomness, statistical interpretation, or accuracy? Where is the best research being done? The worst?

selected subjects in how to function during an experiment. However, in terms of data gathering, you are most likely to use the information-gathering type of interview.

Two chapters in this book examine the interviewing process. Chapter 20 looks at interviewing as a management tool. Chapter 22 examines the applicant's role in the job interview. These chapters discuss types of questions, the interview structure, and styles of interviewing. The following is a summary of major concerns:

- Sometimes only one or a few individuals need to be interviewed. This is particularly true when the individuals are experts. The opinion of one dietitian may be far more valuable than the opinion of many employees about the nutrition of cafeteria food.
- If many people need to be interviewed, do you need a random sample? Must you meet the criteria of random sampling?
- If you are sampling and interviewing many people, are you conducting a scientific experiment, and are you therefore required to meet all the relevant scientific criteria? Not all studies need to be scientific.
- Because interviews are such obtrusive data-gathering techniques, should you consider an alternative collection method?
- Is interviewing, which is individualized and flexible, able to justify the sometimes extensive personnel time and effort it requires?
- Would telephone interviewing, which has its own strengths and weaknesses, serve better than face-to-face interviewing? Telephone interviewing can gather more honest answers than face-to-face interviews because the interviewee does not have to look you in the eye. But be careful—for the same reasons telephone interviewing yields honesty, it can result in dishonesty. Telephone interviewing usually takes longer to conduct than you plan. Wrong numbers, busy signals, no answers, and number changes are part of the time to account for in telephone interviewing.

The development of interviewing skills requires training and practice.

Data-gathering interviewing has these strengths: flexibility, potential for uniformity, individualization, and ability to be enacted quickly. However, interviewing is expensive when many respondents are used, it is obtrusive, and it requires skill and training to execute properly.

Personal Observations

A data-gathering source that is frequently overlooked is personal observation. You may be observing as you conduct an interview or run an experiment, but observation can be a formal approach to answering your research question.

Along with meeting the same rigorous guidelines as sampling and experimentation, observation must also be unobtrusive. Is your presence modifying what you are observing? Can you overcome this problem by becoming a participant within the group? Can you objectively observe the effect of raising hamburger prices in the company by joining the regular group of employees who use the cafeteria? This might have a different effect than a stranger walking about the cafeteria during lunch with a clipboard and pencil.

The benefits of observation are that it is inexpensive, quick, adjustable, and capable of individualization. On the other hand, observation is often biased, nonscientific, or incomplete.

Organization Files

Organization files can be either primary or secondary forms of research. The form of research is not so important as how to use organization files.

Sometimes you can find the answer to your research question in readily available organization files. Because you are not affecting the existing data, this technique is the least obtrusive of the primary source techniques. If you raise the price of hamburgers in the cafeteria on a certain date, are you selling more or fewer hamburgers? Records may indicate the pounds of hamburger purchased before and after the change. Did the 10 percent salary increase affect output? Look to the production reports, absentee reports, tardiness reports, or number of grievances filed for possible changes.

Frequently some ingenuity is necessary in locating the record that meets your needs. Because the information is gathered and your presence does not affect it, using organization records can provide better quality data and take less time and effort than other research methods.

EVALUATING THE RESULTS

After having determined your purpose, considered your audience, and conducted your research, the next step is to evaluate your results. To help in this evaluation—whether primary or secondary sources were used—test your data against these questions. You should be able to respond *yes* to each.

- Are my findings reasonable and logical? If not, why?
- Was my sample size adequate?
- Did I apply appropriate statistical tests to my data to make it more meaningful?
- Did I achieve appropriate depth in my research?
- Did I answer the initial research question?

OUTLINING THE REPORT

A discussion of outlining is really about the organization of the report. Organization is important and will affect how the report is received. For purposes of outlining, you need be concerned about only three of the parts of the report: introduction, body, and conclusion. Together, they make up the bulk of the report.

Arrangement of the Parts

You have three choices for presenting the introduction, body, and conclusion:

Choice 1	Choice 2	Choice 3
Introduction	Introduction	Conclusion
Body	Conclusion	Introduction
Conclusion	Body	Body

In Choice 1, the indirect order arrangement, you save the conclusion (which might contain a summary and recommendations) until last. This is appropriate when the receiver might tend to resist your conclusions or will not understand them until the rest of the report is read. However, many executives will find the conclusion, no matter where it is in the report, and read it first.

Choices 2 or 3 are direct order arrangements. Using this type of arrangement, you present conclusions either second (Choice 2) or first (Choice 3). Whether conclusions are first or second is not important. Either is appropriate when (1) the report contains good news, (2) the receiver has enough background to understand the conclusions without reading the rest of the report first, (3) the conclusions provide a framework around which to interpret the detailed information in the body, or (4) the reader needs the conclusion first.

The introduction, body, and conclusion may be arranged in direct or indirect order.

Presentation of the Body

The body of the report is almost always the longest section. You should make sure that it flows smoothly and has the kind of impact you want.

Writing the Headings

A good outline will help you write more clearly, check that all important concepts are included, and that they are logically placed, thereby enhancing reader understanding. When you write your outline, you must use a common set of numerals and letters that many other writers use:

    I. Major concept
       A. Main point
          1. Supporting point
          2. Another supporting point
             a. Additional support
             b. Additional support
       B. Another main point
    II. Another major concept
       A. Main point
       B. Another main point

At each level in the outline, a minimum of two headings must occur.

A major rule of outlining is that at least two headings must occur within the same level. Thus, I requires II, and A under I must be matched with B under I.

Two types of headings are appropriate for your outline: topic and sentence. Topic headings contain single words or short phrases; sentence headings are complete sentences. Here are some examples:

Topic Headings	*Sentence Headings*
I. Employee problems	I. Atlantic Electronics has several employee problems.
A. Turnover	A. Turnover is high.
1. Electronics industry rates	1. Turnover rates in the electronics industry are decreasing.
2. Atlantic's rates	2. Atlantic's turnover rate is increasing.
a. 1992-1996	a. From 1992 to 1996 Atlantic controlled turnover.
b. 1996-present	b. Since 1996 turnover has increased dramatically.
B. Absenteeism	B. Absenteeism is at a new high.
1. Etc.	1. Etc.

The topic outline can be prepared more quickly than the sentence outline. However, the sentence outline will make the actual writing go faster. In fact, some of the sentences in the outline example might be good paragraph topic sentences.

Notice the importance of parallelism: equivalent parts are the same part of speech, have the same suffix, and the same structure. For example, in the sentence heading outline above, parts I-A-1 (Turnover rates in the electronics industry are decreasing) and I-A-2 (Atlantic's turnover rate is increasing) are similar in structure.

Organizing the Headings

Chronological order is often used for an informational report.

One approach to organizing the outline headings for the report body is chronological—that is, according to time. This chapter uses chronological order to describe the step-by-step procedure for planning a long report. The chronological order is especially useful for writing an informational report with a topic that can be time sequenced. Be cautious, however. The chronological approach often is not justified. So much of our lives is time sequenced that we may be tempted to force our reports into this outline as well.

A second way to organize the report body is by topic order. Using this outlining method, you organize the body around important topics. For example, if you were writing a report to help your employer choose a location for a new plant, you could organize the report around the potential sites. Some first-degree headings for such an outline are:

    I. Columbus, Ohio
    II. Dover, Delaware
    III. Montgomery, Alabama

Or you might organize your report using the criteria your employer uses in selecting a new plant:

    I. Labor market
       A. Columbus, Ohio
       B. Dover, Delaware
       C. Montgomery, Alabama
    II. Community support
       A. Columbus, Ohio
       B. Dover, Delaware
       C. Montgomery, Alabama
    III. Marketing and distribution benefits
       A. Columbus, Ohio
       B. Dover, Delaware
       C. Montgomery, Alabama

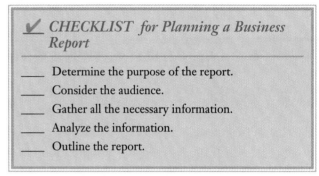

✔ **CHECKLIST** *for Planning a Business Report*

_____ Determine the purpose of the report.
_____ Consider the audience.
_____ Gather all the necessary information.
_____ Analyze the information.
_____ Outline the report.

An advantage of the topic order is its flexibility; it can be modified to meet the organization's structure. For example, if a company has three branches, the report can be built around those branches.

Topic order has the advantage of flexibility.

A second advantage of the topic order is that the author can organize the outline in descending or ascending order of importance, as in this first-degree outline:

    I. Introduction
    II. Most important topic
    III. Second most important topic
    IV. Least important topic
    V. Conclusions

Or you can reverse the order:

    I. Introduction
    II. Least important topic
    III. Second most important topic
    IV. Most important topic
    V. Conclusions

A third way to organize the body is the problem-solving order. Typically, this arrangement consists of several subparts: background, nature of the problem, solutions to the problem, and plan of action for implementing the solution. The problem-solving order is perfectly suited to Stephanie's needs because her purpose is to solve the employee relations problem. The first two major headings of her outline might look like this:

The problem-solving order is a third approach to organizing the report body.

    I.   Background: The importance of employee relations
       A. Employee relations in the industry
         1. Effects of good relations

   2. Consequences of poor relations
  B. Employee relations at Atlantic Electronics
 II. Nature of Atlantic Electronics' employee relations program
  A. Grievances
   1. Recent grievances
   2. Long-standing grievances
  B. Turnover
  C. Absenteeism
   1. By department
   2. By rank
  D. Morale
   1. Methodology
   2. Return rate
  E. Unionization

Key Terms

- **informational report**
- **interpretive report**
- **problem-solving report**
- **analytical report**
- **primary source**
- **secondary source**
- **population**
- **universe**

- **nonprobability sampling**
- **demographic question**
- **dichotomous question**
- **list question**
- **rank order question**
- **attitude question**
- **open-ended question**

Summary

Levels of contribution to decision-making process p. 280

Electronic databases p. 283

Questionnaires p. 286

Sampling pp. 286–287

Experiments p. 290

Interviews p. 291

Personal observation p. 292

Organization files p. 292

Outlining the report p. 293

Review Questions

1. Why are reports prepared? Which reasons are most important? Why?

2. Describe several characteristics of business reports.

3. What are the differences between informational, interpretive, and problem-solving reports?

4. What are the steps in planning the long report?

5. Identify some primary research methods. What are the strengths and weaknesses of each?

6. Differentiate between random, stratified, convenience, and systematic random samples.

7. What are the different levels of degree headings used in outlining?

8. Discuss the development of a questionnaire.

9. What are the differences between outlining and organizing a report?

10. What are the differences between direct and indirect arrangements of the parts of the report? Describe three approaches to organizing the body.

Exercises

1. Ask three business people in your area to define *communication*. Note their answers but also pay attention to problems of nonscientific inquiry. In other words, for what reasons should you discount the answers?

2. Through personal observation of students at your school, note the differences in behavior between boyfriends with girlfriends compared to behavior between other men and women students who are not so closely associated. What conclusions can you draw regarding gathering information from personal observation?

3. Select a brief essay in a periodical, such as "My Turn" in *Newsweek*, or a feature article in *The Wall Street Journal*. Outline the essay or article.

4. Use the Internet to research a project. Which techniques worked best?

CASE

Planning the Report

Kath Ralston, Chisholm Institute of Technology, Victoria, Australia

Sally Dixon is in her final year at business college. During the past two years she has worked part time at the local gymnasium and community center making appointments and scheduling classes conducted at the center. She enjoys working there, but she believes the management group is not very dynamic and does not take enough opportunities to promote the center's programs.

Recently Sally heard that the activities coordinator would be leaving at the end of the year. Sally would like to land the position and believes that with the combination of her practical work experience plus her business knowledge, she would make an excellent activities coordinator. She realizes that although the management group is pleased with her work, they would need more proof of her business ability if they were to consider her for the position of activities coordinator.

One evening when she arrived home she found a letter from her dentist reminding her of a dental checkup. This started her thinking about a promotional campaign for the community center in which each participant could be contacted in a short time after completing a class and advised of future activities at the center. This campaign would mean setting up a new record-keeping system, but she believed that the extra business the center would obtain would far outweigh any cost.

Sally decided this was her chance to show the management group that she could apply her study of business systems and marketing in a very practical way. She thought the best approach would be to present the proposal to the management group in a report.

Case Questions

1. What will be the purpose of the report?

2. What aspects of the receivers will Sally have to consider?

3. What information must Sally collect for her report? Where will she get it?

4. In outlining the report, which order do you think Sally should choose? Give the reasons for your choice.

CASE

Is This Course Really Important?

Robert J. Olney, Southwest Texas State University

As a member of the advisory board for your university's school of business, you and the school's dean are opposed to a move by other board members to remove business communication from the business curriculum. Although as a local business person and employer you are convinced of the importance of the course, you find that not all board members prioritize curriculum needs in the same way.

You have already found and reported a study in which business communication was rated very important in preparing people for leadership positions more often than any other of 13 business courses by 1,158 newly promoted executives (H. W. Hildebrandt et al., "An Executive Appraisal of Courses Which Best Prepare One for General Management," *Journal of Business Communication 19* (Winter 1982), 5-15). However, this article wasn't enough. In order to strengthen your case, you and the dean decide to conduct your own study to see whether the 1982 findings "hold up." How do today's executives, especially in your geographic area, feel about the importance of various courses and curriculum topics in preparing business leaders? You outline a plan of attack for the project:

1. Review secondary research sources. This review will help you establish a theoretical base for your study and determine how other individuals have approached similar research studies.

2. Design a questionnaire to aid in solving the research problem. Your questionnaire will contain:

   a. An introduction that identifies the purpose of the questionnaire.

   b. Instructions that explain exactly what the respondents should do.

   c. A list of the business core from your university and a rating scale that can be used by respondents to indicate the relative importance of each course.

   d. Other questions you design to solve the research problem.

3. Select a sample of business managers in your geographic area to participate in your study and distribute your questionnaire.

4. Evaluate the findings of the questionnaire.

5. Produce a report that contains a statement of the problem of the research, the methodology, the analysis of secondary and primary data, the conclusions based on this analysis, and recommendations. Follow a report format as specified by your instructor.

Case Questions

1. Are there other steps you believe should be added to your preliminary outline of this project?

2. From your review of the literature, which procedures used in similar research projects would be effective in assuring you objective results? How have data been analyzed?

3. What types of questions or combinations of questions will allow you to achieve appropriate depth in your research?

4. What sampling technique will yield an appropriately representative response for the population? What statistical tests are appropriate to your data to make them more meaningful?

5. What graphic aids will summarize your information best and create a more interesting flow for your report?

Note

1. Ed Krol, *The Whole Internet User's Guide & Catalog*, 2nd ed. *(Sebastopol, CA: O'Reilly & Associates, Inc., 1994), 187.*

Chapter 12

The Long Report: Writing

Stephanie looked at the business report just delivered by its author, Bill Wells, and thought back to a report she had written almost 10 years ago—a report that had influenced her career.

As new to Atlantic Electronics then as Bill is now, Stephanie had written a problem-solving report on employee relations. Unexpectedly, that report had been viewed by her superiors in the evaluation of her work as a personnel assistant. Although she was unsure of herself at the time, things worked out fine. The vice president had been impressed with her ability and potential. He recommended a promotion to personnel specialist a full year before most personnel assistants are promoted. He had even made a point of stopping by her desk to tell her how impressed he was by the report.

Much has happened since, Stephanie thought. Louise took over the vice president's job on his retirement. Stephanie's immediate boss, Scott Millan, took a job with a competitor, and she was selected to replace him. How proud she had been to be selected as the youngest person ever to hold the job of personnel director for the company.

Well, enough reminiscing, she thought. Let's see if this report from Bill will determine his future.

Two characteristics of business reports, as discussed in Chapter 11, are length and formality. Report formality is determined largely by language tone, such as using third-person singular versus first-person singular (*the author* instead of *I*), and by the number of formal parts included in the report. If the business report includes an authorization document or an abstract, for example, the report becomes more formal. The more parts, the greater the length will be. Therefore, formality and length are often related.

Chapter 11 ended with a discussion of how to outline three parts of the business report: introduction, body, and conclusion. In this chapter, they are treated together as one of the three major divisions of the report: the text. The other two major divisions, also presented in this chapter, are the preliminary parts and the supplementary parts.

THE TEXT

If the outline you have developed is thorough, writing the text should not be too difficult, although it may be time consuming. No matter in which order you have chosen to present the introduction, body, and conclusion, you should write the conclusion last. The act of writing is the first time you will think about your report material in detail, and your conclusions may change in the process.

The body is often written first. The introduction, regardless of when it is written, should conclude with a transition to the body of the report. In location as well as importance, the body is central to the report. About 75 percent of the report text should be body and the remaining 25 percent distributed between introduction and conclusion.

The body should flow from topic to topic in a logical, clear order. Use a variety of transitions, such as *next, consequently, fourth, on the other hand,* and *similarly* to function as guideposts to the reader. Give summaries periodically, such as at the end of each major section, to remind the reader where you are and where you are going.

The characteristics of effective written communication (discussed in Chapter 5) apply to long reports as they do to other forms of written communication.

1. *Tactful:* Avoid offensive language, don't insult your readers, and don't categorize them. Be especially careful to avoid sexist language.

2. *Personal:* Generally, do not use the "you" attitude when writing the text parts of a formal business report; these reports usually demand a more impersonal writing style. However, in some circumstances a report that contains formal report parts, such as an abstract or appendixes, can be made more readable by using the first or second person.

3. *Positive:* Use a positive tone whenever possible. (But remember that some ideas aren't adaptable to a positive approach.)

4. *Active:* Use the active voice as much as possible. Use passive voice only to de-emphasize an idea.

5. *Unified:* Be sure that each sentence and paragraph contain only one central idea.

6. *Coherent:* Use signposts, linking words, and enumerators to give smooth and logical transitions to the text. Proper headings help coherence.

7. *Clear:* Avoid unfamiliar words, and use jargon only if you're sure the reader can understand you.

8. *Concise:* Avoid trite expressions, wordy phrases, unnecessary repetition, and abstract words.

9. *Readable:* Consider the education level of your receiver. You might compute a readability index on your drafts to ensure that you've written them at the appropriate level.

10. *Mechanically sound:* Check and recheck for grammar errors.

Two of these characteristics, coherence and clarity, can be dramatically improved if you include headings, tables, and figures in the body of the report.

Headings

A single, generic outline of **headings** and subheadings for most business reports is impossible to prepare. You should follow your outline, presenting headings and material under them in a consistent fashion. Headings serve as signposts and improve the reader's speed and ease in comprehending your ideas.

Headings serve as signposts.

Many authorities discuss the relationship between the various levels of headings. Not all authorities agree, but a few principles emerge: (1) if a heading is centered, it is more important than a heading that is flush with the left margin; (2) if a heading is flush with the left margin, it is more important than a heading that is indented; (3) if a heading appears in all capital letters, it is more important than a heading that has only initial capital letters; (4) if a heading is underlined, it is more important than a heading that is not underlined; and (5) if a heading is placed on a line by itself, it is more important than a heading that is followed by text.

By using these principles, and intermixing them, we can develop the following hierarchy of headings and subheadings, ranging from highest to lowest:

THIS IS A FIRST-LEVEL HEADING

THIS IS A SECOND-LEVEL HEADING

This Is a Third-Level Heading

This Is a Fourth-Level Heading

THIS IS A FIFTH-LEVEL HEADING

This Is a Sixth-Level Heading

This Is a Seventh-Level Heading

   This Is an Eighth-Level Heading

   This is a Ninth-Level Heading. It is indented, followed by a period, and with text starting on the same line.

You will probably never need to use all nine levels of headings. However, most reports will use at least three levels. The levels you select need not be limited to the top three. You can use the principles discussed to make obvious and helpful headings. Here is an example of picking and choosing four different levels of headings for a report:

THIS MIGHT BE THE TITLE

OF THE REPORT

This Might Be a Second-Level Heading

This Might be a Third-Level Heading

   This Might Be a Fourth-Level Heading

Heading levels should be obvious and logical.

The important point to remember in using headings is that they must be immediately logical to your reader; which subheading is subordinate to others should be obvious.

There are other formats for headings. For example, a numerical approach uses numbers—either with or without a phrase after the number—such as 1, 3.4, and 7.5.1 for headings. The numerical approach is used more often in formal and governmental reports. The numbers are likely to occur in technical and scientific reports and in other situations as well.

As more and more reports are prepared on computers and printed with ink jet and laser printers, even more heading possibilities emerge. Now the report writer can use boldface, italics, expanded, condensed, or enlarged type, as well as changing typefaces. In terms of hierarchy (1) the larger the text, the more important, and (2) boldface is more important than normal text, while italics is usually seen as lower in importance. With the wide variety of typefaces available, the user may select a face for headings that is different from the text, but should select a face that is visually compatible. Here is how four levels might appear:

THIS IS THE HIGHEST LEVEL HEAD

This Is a Second-Level Head

This Is a Third-Level Head

This Is a Fourth-Level Head. And this is the text that follows it on the same line.

Be judicious in your use of type treatments and avoid the **creeping elegance** of too many divergent appearances. No matter which heading technique you use, apply it consistently and be logical in your visual differentiation.

Tables and Figures

The report text can be divided into its prose and nonprose parts; tables and figures are subdivisions of the nonprose parts. Both tables and figures are useful for summarizing a large amount of detailed information in a small space. They also break up the text material and create a more interesting flow.

Here are some guidelines for using tables and figures in the text of a business report. (An explanation of their importance and how to prepare them will be presented in Chapter 17.)

The reader should understand tables and figures without having to refer to the text.

- A table or figure that is one-half page or larger is placed on a page by itself. A table or figure that is less than one-half page can have text above or below it.
- A table or figure should be able to stand alone. That is, any viewer should be able to look at the table or figure and quickly understand the information. Reading the related text should not be necessary in order to understand the table or figure.
- Tables are numbered as a series, beginning with *1*. Figures are numbered in a separate series. The table number along with a descriptive phrase appear above the table body. The figure number and descriptive phrase are positioned below the figure.
- Sometimes it is unclear whether the table or figure should be located in the text or at the end of the report in an appendix. The material should be in the text if it is necessary for the reader to view it to understand the report. If the information might be helpful but is not required, it is usually placed in an appendix. If the material is lengthy—several pages or more—it is usually placed in an appendix.
- When a table or figure that was presented by someone else in published form is presented in your report, indicate that source, much as you would use a footnote. The source indication, however, is part of the table or figure.
- Each table or figure should be referred to in the text. The table or figure then appears at the end of the paragraph or—if it is to appear alone on a page—on the next page. In the latter case, fill out the page on which it was mentioned with text.
- If the table must be presented parallel to the long sides of the paper, place the heading along the inside margin or spine so that it is read from the outside page margin of the report.
- In both tables and figures, the time period (years, months, and so on) is usually presented on the top axis.

Documentation

The business report writer must attribute information obtained through secondary research to the source, rather than leave the reader to guess. In formal business reports, **attribution** usually appears as notes either at the bottom of the page or at the end of the text. In more informal reports, the attribution may be found solely in the text, such as "David Fenton, our St. Louis marketing manager, said sales should increase by 37 percent this year." Internal attribution is more likely to be used when there are only a few sources mentioned. Once you reach four or five citations—or when you are writing a formal business report—you will need to use notes and possibly a bibliography.

Footnotes

Footnoting is the most common form of attribution.

The footnoting approach is traditional and is widely used. With this approach, a number is placed at the end of the information you are citing in the text. The number is raised one-half line and is called a **superscript**. The first citation is numbered *1*, the next *2*, and so on sequentially through the report. Any information cited that is taken from someone else—including both direct quotations and your paraphrasing of ideas—receives a footnote number. A block of information taken from the same source in the same publication receives one number. Thus one paragraph might be attributed to one author.

On the other hand, one paragraph might include the ideas of a variety of sources. Even a single sentence can have more than one footnote, as shown here:

> Many experts in finance agree with the point we have been discussing. Included in this group are Lewis,[1] Jones,[2] Harris,[3] and McWilliams.[4]

Each time you cite information you need to use a footnote. This is true even if you have cited the author earlier in the report. We often use *Ibid.* in a footnote to indicate we are referring to information from the same author and source as the one in the last footnote cited. The author's name and *op. cit.* in a footnote mean the author and publication mentioned earlier but not the one immediately preceding. *Op. cit.* and, to a lesser extent, *Ibid.* are being phased out in favor of repeating the author's last name and the new page reference.

Either telephone or face-to-face interview attribution is handled as if the interview was a publication and the interviewee was the author. The observation in the text still receives a superscript number at the end of the quote or paraphrase, or by the author's (interviewee's) name.

As we use the superscript numbers in the text of the report, we must leave space at the bottom of the page for the footnote citation. If there are four superscript numbers in the text on page 7 of your report, there must be four footnotes at the bottom of the page.

This footnoting approach has both strengths and weaknesses. Besides being traditional and widely accepted, it is the most efficient approach for the reader. Attribution is made in the text, and the reader can look directly to the bottom of the page for the information. On the other hand, footnoting is tedious and time consuming for the typist. If you have ever typed a page of text and tried to leave adequate room for footnotes at the bottom only to run out of space, you know the frustration it can cause! Many word processing software packages overcome this problem and allocate appropriate space at the bottom of the page. They also can automatically renumber footnotes when a new citation is inserted among existing citations.

Endnotes

Footnotes grouped at the end of the report are called endnotes.

To avoid the frustration with footnotes, a modification of the standard technique is becoming widely used. Instead of presenting the footnotes at the bottom of each page as they occur, they are lifted from each page and placed in numerical order in the first of the supplementary pages, as in this text. The part containing these lifted footnotes is appropriately titled **Endnotes**. Other than their location, the endnote citations are the same as those placed at the foot of the page. A sample endnotes page appears in the sample business report in this chapter.

In addition to deciding between footnoting or endnoting, you must also contend with different ways of preparing the note (as well as your bibliography). Most periodicals select one style and ask authors to use it. In other cases you may select from the various styles. Three of the most widely used are the University of Chicago style, the

American Psychological Association style, and the Modern Language Association style. Table 12.1 illustrates these three styles for both footnotes and bibliography entries.

With the next attribution technique, there are no footnotes or endnotes. A bracketed number is placed at each location in the text where attribution is required. The numbers refer the reader to the bibliography, which is arranged alphabetically. Therefore, the bracketed numbers referring to items in the bibliography will not be sequential. Here are two sample sentences that use this attribution style:

> Jones is one of the best-known authorities espousing this philosophy [6]. There are, however, other authorities who disagree with Jones [17:50], [3:63-8], [9:121].

The reader can now turn to the bibliography, find the [6] before the Jones citation, and determine the balance of the information about this source. When a specific page or pages are cited, it is customary to include this information within the brackets and after a colon. In [17:50], the 50 means page 50 in reference 17.

Yet another approach to formal attribution differs from the ones already described but has some similarities, too. It tends to be used in academic writing, has many variations, and is rapidly gaining application. This approach eliminates the footnoting process entirely, yet delivers the information required for the appropriate attribution.

One style of attribution eliminates numbered notes entirely.

If you choose this approach, instead of using a superscript number, you present the author's last name, the year of publication, and, if appropriate, the specific pages that were used. Citations are presented in the same fashion regardless of whether the source is an article, a book, or an interview. An exception is when the author is not known—then you present the publication name, the year, and perhaps the page numbers. Here is some sample text that utilizes the author's name attribution approach. Notice the information appears in parentheses after the citation, but the author's name may be part of the sentence.

> As we continue to examine the effect of increased production on job satisfaction, it is necessary to consider classical management theory. Smith (1996, p. 307), for example, feels that production is all-important. Several other authorities agree with Smith (see, for example, McWilliams, 1956; Lewis, 1971; McAllister, 1989; Harris & Woffort, 1995; or Graber et al., 1990). Probably the most sweeping comment to the opposing view is, "Smith and her cronies are absolutely wrong! Job satisfaction is so much more important than production that it can't even be mentioned in the same breath!" (Horvath, 1994, p. 227).

The reader can locate the complete citation in the bibliography. A bibliography presents much of the same information as a footnote, but instead of being presented numerically, items are alphabetized by authors' last names. Thus, to find the Smith (1996, p. 307) citation, the reader would scan the bibliography to locate Smith.

If the bibliography is prepared using this attribution technique, it is the same as a standard bibliography; however, it is called references instead of bibliography.

Introduction and Conclusion

A typical introduction explains the importance of the report topic. The introduction may give a historical perspective and can discuss the organization of the balance of the body of the report. It may have sections for relevance, problem statement, scope, or purpose.

The introduction may also include a section on limitations of the study. The writer should be careful, however, not to supply ammunition to the reader to help discount the report. If relevant and defensible shortcomings exist, such as a shortage of research funds or concrete information, include them. Avoid mentioning a lack of interest in the topic, computer breakdowns at the last minute, or poor personal analytical abilities that destroy your credibility.

TABLE 12.1 NOTE AND BIBLIOGRAPHIC STYLES

	This Style Manual	**Two-Author Book**	**Two-Author Article**	**Sample Electronic Media Citations**
University of Chicago style	*Notes* 1. *The Chicago Manual of Style*, 14th ed. (Chicago: The University of Chicago Press, 1993), 101.	1. James M. Lahiff and John M. Penrose, *Business Communication Strategies and Skills*, 5th ed. (Upper Saddle River, N.J.: Prentice Hall, 1997), 101.	1. Carolyn M. Anderson and Matthew M. Martin, "Why Employees Speak to Coworkers and Bosses: Motives, Gender, and Organizational Satisfaction," *Journal of Business Communication*, Vol. 32, no. 3 (July 1995): 250.	1. Statistical Package for the Social Sciences Level M Ver. 8 (SPSS Lev. M 8.1), SPSS, Chicago.
American Psychological Association style	APA does not use citation-type notes; instead the information is found in References.	APA instead uses the author's last name and the year of publication in the text. Here are examples: According to Jones (1996), . . According to another source (Smith, 1997), . .		
Modern Language Association style	[1]Joseph Gibaldi, *MLA Handbook for Writers of Research Papers*, 4th ed. (New York: The Modern Language Association of America, 1995).	[1]James M. Lahiff and John M. Penrose, *Business Communication Strategies and Skills*, 5th ed. (Upper Saddle River, NJ: Prentice Hall, 1997).	[1]Carolyn M. Anderson and Matthew M. Martin, "Why Employees Speak to Coworkers and Bosses: Motives, Gender, and Organizational Satisfaction," *The Journal of Business Communication* 30 (July 1995): 250.	[1]Thomas Hardy, *Far from the Madding Crowd*, ed. Ronald Blythe (Harmondsworth: Penguin, 1978), online, Oxford Text Archive, Internet, 24 Jan. 1994.
University of Chicago style	***Bibliographical Citations*** *The Chicago Manual of Style*, 14th ed. Chicago: University of Chicago Press, 1993.	Lahiff, James M., and John M. Penrose, *Business Communication Strategies and Skills*. Upper Saddle River, N.J.: Prentice Hall, 1997.	Anderson, Carolyn M., and Matthew M. Martin. "Why Employees Speak to Coworkers and Bosses: Motives, Gender, and Organizational Satisfaction," *The Journal of Business Communication* 32, no. 3 (July 1995): 249–265.	Statistical Package for the Social Sciences Level M Ver. 8 (SPSS Lev. M 8.1). SPSS, Chicago.
(Title of page with references)	Bibliography			

TABLE 12.1 CONTINUED

	This Style Manual	Two-Author Book	Two-Author Article	Sample Electronic Media Citations
	Bibliographical Citations			
American Psychological Association style	Publication Manual of the American Psychological Association (4th ed.). 1994. Washington, DC: American Psychological Association.	Lahiff, J.M., & Penrose, J.M. *Business Communication Strategies and Skills* (5th ed.). Upper Saddle River, NJ: Prentice Hall, 1997.	Anderson, C. M., & Martin, M. M. (July 1993). Why employees speak to coworkers and bosses: Motives, gender, and organizational satisfaction. *Journal of Business Communication*, 32 (3), 249–265.	Funder, D.C. (1994, March). Judgmental process and content: Commentary on Koehler on base-rate [9 paragraphs]. *Psycholoquy*. [On-line serial], 5(17). Available FTP: Hostname: princeton.edu Directory: pub/harnad/Psycholoquy/1994.volume.5File:psycholoquy.94.5.17.base-rate.12.funder.
(Title of page with references)	References			
Modern Language Association style	Gibaldi, Joseph. *MLA Handbook for Writers of Research Papers*. 4th ed. New York: The Modern Language Association of America, 1995.	Lahiff, James M., and John M. Penrose. *Business Communication Strategies and Skills*. 5th ed. Upper Saddle River, NJ: 1997.	Anderson, Carolyn M., and Matthew M. Martin. "Why Employees Speak to Coworkers and Bosses: Motives, Gender, and Organizational Satisfaction," *Journal of Business Communication* 32 (July 1993): 249–265.	Russo, Michelle Cash. "Recovering from Bibliographic Instruction Blahs." *RQ: Reference Quarterly* 32 (1992): 178–83. *Infotrac: Magazine Index Plus*.
(Title of page with references)	Works Cited			

The conclusion section explains and summarizes what the reader has just read in the body of the report. The value of a conclusion lies in its focus and emphasis; the reader is told what were the most memorable points in the report. This section may bring together for the first time divergent ideas from the report and synthesize them. No new information should appear in the conclusion, however—only new perspectives on existing information.

No new information should be presented in the conclusion section.

The writer may wish to include recommendations as part of the conclusion or as a separate section. This should be done only when recommendations are a logical outgrowth of the material in the report and are obviously needed by the reader. For example, a lengthy analysis of safety conditions that concludes that hazards exist calls out for recommendations and perhaps even suggestions for implementation of the recommendations.

The conclusion section is much different from an abstract, although some people confuse the two.

THE SUPPLEMENTARY PARTS

The most common supplementary parts are the endnotes page, appendixes, bibliography, and the index. Supplementary parts are completed before the preliminary parts. The reason is that the page numbers for the parts at the end of the report are needed for the table of contents.

Endnotes

As previously discussed, endnotes are synonymous with footnotes; the only difference is they are grouped at the end of the text. The first page is titled *Endnotes*. Endnotes are listed in the numerical order in which they are cited in the report.

Appendixes

An **appendix** contains material that is useful to the report but that might slow the reader if it appeared in the body. Items that would be part of an appendix are questionnaires, copies of interview questions, letters, memos, and other related materials that are useful but not required for the text itself.

In a formal report, each appendix is preceded by a title page containing the label and the title of the appendix. Appendixes are lettered starting with *A* and placed in the order of their mention in the text. They are listed in the table of contents.

Bibliography

The bibliography is a list of the sources consulted in preparing the report, whether or not they are actually cited in the report. The bibliography assists the reader if additional information is needed; therefore, going beyond the sources cited can be useful. If all the sources are cited, the bibliography becomes a list of references or works cited.

Whether you use a bibliography or list of references, you can list your sources alphabetically, either under one heading or under several subheadings. Subheadings classify your types of sources, such as books, periodicals, and government publications. The main title may be bibliography, references, list of references, or works cited.

Index

Used only in lengthy reports, the index is an alphabetical list of key topics. This list includes the page numbers for each topic. The index to this book is an example of the format. Ask yourself whether the reader would benefit from an index before deciding to include one in your report. Many of today's word processors can automatically prepare an index.

THE PRELIMINARY PARTS

A variety of items can be presented in the preliminary parts; generally speaking, the more items that are included, the more formal the report is. Other items are dependent on the situation and content of the report—obviously a list of tables is used only when there are tables, for example. The following, although not an exhaustive list, includes most of the formal preliminary parts: title fly, title page, authorization document, transmittal document, table of contents, list of tables, list of figures (or a combined list of illustrations), and the abstract.

Title Fly

An optional part used in especially formal reports, the title fly (also called *half title*) contains only the report title. The title should be brief yet descriptive and should indicate either the report's depth or objective.

Title Page

Most business reports have a title page. This page contains at least the following information: the report title, the name (and perhaps the position) of the person the report was prepared for, the author of the report (perhaps with position), and the date.

Authorization Document

If your report was authorized in writing, a copy of the letter or memo authorizing you to undertake it should accompany the report. Showing authorization will add credibility to your work. This document is likely to be found in more formal reports.

Transmittal Document

The transmittal document is also likely to be seen in more formal reports. This document—a letter or memo—transfers the report to the reader. The report recipient is likely to be the author of the authorization document; the author of the transmittal document (and the report) is probably the person authorized to do the report. These two items are closely related.

Authorization and transmittal documents are likely to be found in more formal reports.

A transmittal document should include the following:

1. The transmittal itself (first paragraph)
2. An overview of the report (second paragraph)
3. Optional acknowledgments to people who assisted in preparing the report (third paragraph)
4. A courteous closing that might discuss the next steps, express pleasure at providing the report, or indicate willingness to discuss the report in more detail (fourth paragraph)

Table of Contents

A required part of the formal business report is the table of contents. It lists all of the parts of the report except those appearing before the table of contents—list of tables, list of figures, appendixes, and bibliography, for example—as well as the first- and second-level headings in the text. Dotted lines, called leader lines, can be used to lead the reader's eyes across to the page number. The first table of contents page is titled *Contents*.

List of Tables

If tables are included in the report, or even only one table, then a list of tables on a separate page should follow the table of contents. The list of tables includes table numbers, table titles, and numbers of the pages where they appear.

List of Figures

A list of figures is required if a figure or figures appear in the report. The list is not divided according to types of figures, such as graphs and charts. Rather, all figures are listed in order of their appearance in the report. The format is identical to the list of tables. The two lists are occasionally combined to create a list of illustrations.

Abstract

The **abstract**—which may also be called a synopsis or executive summary—provides the reader with a summary of the entire text. The abstract may be considered the report in miniature; it is not simply the conclusions. An abstract (on a separate page)

The abstract is normally single-spaced and should seldom exceed one page.

✔ *CHECKLIST for Writing Business Reports*

____ Meet your goals in the body of the report.

____ Use headings correctly and consistently.

____ Support the text with tables and figures as appropriate.

____ Attribute sources of information.

____ Include necessary preliminary and supplementary parts.

____ Achieve an appropriate level of formality.

____ Be consistent in page treatments.

____ Produce an aesthetically pleasing product.

---

may help the receiver understand the text material before he or she reads it. Or it may be used as a time-saving summary after the entire report has been read. The single-spaced abstract has about a one-to-ten relationship to the text of the report, but it should seldom exceed one page.

In writing your abstract, be informational and include some depth. Do not say, "Next we gathered some data and then analyzed them." Instead, give the reader a description with details, such as "Data were gathered by distributing by mail an anonymous questionnaire to 400 randomly selected employees. Of the 273 questionnaires returned, 63 percent *(n = 172)* were from blue-collar workers."

THE ASSEMBLED REPORT

The chapter so far has discussed the writing of the text and preparation of the preliminary and supplementary parts. Now we are ready to put the report together. A formal report will have the following items, in this order:

Preliminary Parts	Text (also sometimes referred to as the body)	Supplementary Parts
Title fly*	Introduction	Endnotes
Title page	Body	Appendixes
Authorization document*	Conclusion	Bibliography
Transmittal document*		Index*
Table of contents		
List of tables		
List of figures		
Abstract		

*Especially found in formal reports.

Some additional instructions that may affect your writing and typing of the report involve pagination, spacing, and a cover.

Pagination

Briefly, **pagination** is the placement of page numbers on the pages. Knowing when, where, and which type of number to place on a page is often a problem.

Roman numerals are used for the preliminary pages.

The preliminary parts are treated differently from the balance of the report. You should count every page, but start your numbering with the table of contents. Thus, if the table of contents is the fifth page (after the title fly, the title page, the authorization document, and the transmittal document, each of which was counted but not numbered), it would be given the number *v.* This small Roman numeral is centered at the bottom of the page. The rest of the preliminary pages are numbered.

If a part, such as the table of contents, has more than one page, the page number moves to the upper right corner on the second and succeeding pages. It is always a small Roman numeral. The first page of the body is numbered with an Arabic number centered at the bottom. All pages after page 1 are numbered at the top of the page, probably in either the right corner or, less likely, centered. In any case, be consistent. An exception to this rule occurs when you start a major new section, such as a new chapter. The page number then is placed at the bottom, centered, on that page.

Do not use any punctuation or words with the page number. Use just the number 2, for example, and not *Page 2, -2-, 2., two,* or *"2."*

Spacing

Business reports are a combination of single and double spacing, as you will see in the complete report later in this chapter (Figure 12.1). Footnotes, for example, are single-spaced, with a space between citations. The text of the report may be either single- or double-spaced, but be consistent.

A double-spaced text promotes readability and leaves space for comments between lines. It also uses more paper, which may be important if many copies of your report will be duplicated. A single-spaced text adds an air of formality and precision while being more efficient. In reports, paragraphs are usually indented with typically five or eight spaces of indention.

Many organizations have standard formats for their reports (and letters and memoranda as well). You may be directed on which spacing is desired.

Cover

You may want to package your completed report inside a binder or prepare it with a special cover. Your organization may have printed covers for all reports. Covers can add uniformity, protection, and attractiveness.

BOXED IN

AN ETHICAL DILEMMA

Margie learned the hard way about the supposed fair treatment of subordinates at Quality Products. She recalls many occasions when she worked long and hard on reports, only to have her name removed from the title page and replaced with her supervisor's name. Even for reports in which she initiated recommendations to upper management she received no recognition or credit; her name did not appear on them. Margie is still bitter about that supervisor's getting credit for her work and ideas.

As it turns out, she realizes, she did benefit indirectly. Her supervisor was promoted to a better position and Margie has moved up to the supervisor's job.

This morning Margie received a subordinate's report to review. She sees that it proposes some much-needed changes in the manufacturing process. It is sure to catch Vice President Wilson's eye.

Now, she reminds herself, it is her turn to get some free accolades. She types a replacement title page, with her own name on it. She remembers how many times her own supervisor must have done exactly that. When it is time to take her subordinate's report to a meeting, however, she has not yet switched title pages.

Margie feels boxed in. What would you do?

Questions

1. Since middle and upper management take responsibility for what they send forward, isn't it fair that they receive the praise for work their subordinates do?

2. Under what circumstances would you switch title pages on reports from your subordinates?

Correct Procedures

Experts do not always agree on how to put together a report.

As mentioned often in this chapter, two or more approaches may be acceptable or correct because authorities do not always agree and because organizations may have different goals for their reports. Different techniques have been presented when we thought they were important, such as the three attribution styles. There are, however, some other points on which experts differ. The bibliography is sometimes the first item in the supplementary parts. The abstract is sometimes placed before the table of contents in the preliminary parts; it is sometimes double-spaced. The table of contents does not always have leader lines and occasionally shows third- or even fourth-level headings. The page numbers for the additional levels may be given. There are other approaches to pagination, less often used, than the one described in this chapter. Some reports use numbers before headings, such as 1, 1.1, or 3.12. Other reports use a combination of numbers and letters before headings, such as I, C, 2, a. Still other reports do not use these systems, but rely on the levels of the headings to help the reader.

COMPUTER APPLICATIONS

With the widespread use of computers to prepare business correspondence, and especially business reports, the approach to preparing these reports and their appearance is changing. Even low-level word processing software allows authors to write sections of a report out of order and then use block moves to rearrange them. Sophisticated word processors enable the automatic generation of tables of contents, bibliographies, and indexes. The highest levels of word processors and desktop publishing packages facilitate multiple columns, varied typefaces and type sizes, and the inclusion of graphics within documents. Today, professional and attractive reports are the norm.

Computer technology is responsible for the trend toward increasingly attractive reports.

When using computers and word processors to prepare business reports, you should avoid using too many typefaces and sizes in your report. About four or five treatments is an upper limit. Make sure there is a good reason for including an element or feature. Do not include an index, for example, just because your computer system is capable of producing one.

Holding down a computer key repeats the character, making it easy to overdo characters. In preparing the leader lines in your table of contents, use period space period space rather than a series of periods, which overwhelm the viewer with unnecessary images. Use only a single question mark; more than one appears sophomoric. Use exclamation points sparingly or not at all. Running headers and footers, if used judiciously and appropriately, can improve the appearance and readability of lengthy reports. They should be unobtrusive.

If a report is to be duplicated on two sides of the paper, software can automatically modify the inside margin of varying left and right pages.

Perhaps most important of all, if you write sections of your report out of order and then rearrange them, be sure to prepare transitions for the newly sequenced items.

A SAMPLE BUSINESS REPORT

The complete business report in Figure 12.1 illustrates the writing principles discussed in this chapter. It does not present every part of a formal report, because some of them are incongruous and some duplicate others. Of the preliminary and supplementary parts, only the index—which is exemplified at the end of this book—is omitted.

Careful examination of the writing tone of the report, as well as the appearance of the parts, will guide you in preparing your business report.

This problem-solving report examines employee relations at Atlantic Electronics. Some items discussed earlier, such as outlines and tables, are used again in the report.

Figure 12.1
Example of a Long Report

EMPLOYEE RELATIONS PROBLEMS AT ATLANTIC ELECTRONICS:

NATURE, CAUSES, AND SOLUTIONS

Title Fly

Figure 12.1
Continued

EMPLOYEE RELATIONS PROBLEMS AT ATLANTIC ELECTRONICS:

NATURE, CAUSES, AND SOLUTIONS

Prepared for
Scott Millan, Personnel Director
Atlantic Electronics

by

Stephanie McQuiston, Personnel Assistant

January 30, 1997

Title Page

Figure 12.1
Continued

MEMO

TO: Stephanie McQuiston, Personnel Assistant

FROM: Scott Millan, Personnel Director

DATE: November 18, 1996

SUBJECT: Employee Relations Report Assignment

As explained in our conversation this morning, I am directing you to
research, analyze, and report on the current status of employee relations at Atlantic Electronics. As members of the personnel office, we
know there has been an increasing number of grievances reported to
us, and the company grapevine is carrying more negative information
than usual.

You are to conduct research, both formal and informal, to adequately
appraise the employee relations situation. If the situation warrants it,
analyze solutions to our problem and propose them to me.

This matter is of major and immediate concern. Therefore, I need your
report by the end of January 1997. You have a budget of $10,000 for
supplies and can use the steno pool for duplication needs. Bill Parsons,
the new management trainee, is also assigned to you for this project.

Do let me know if you encounter problems or have questions.

Letter of Authorization

Figure 12.1
Continued

MEMO

TO: Scott Millan, Personnel Director
FROM: Stephanie McQuiston, Personnel Assistant
DATE: January 30, 1997
SUBJECT: Employee Relations Report

Here is the report you directed me to prepare on November 18, 1996.
The report researches employee relations problems at Atlantic
Electronics, examines those problems, looks at solutions, and proposes
specific actions.

You will find that our employee relations problem is more serious than
you apparently thought when we discussed this project last November.
You'll want to pay particular attention to the implementation sections of
the report for ways to overcome these problems.

This has been a most interesting project. I'll be pleased to discuss it
with you, at your request.

Transmittal

Figure 12.1
Continued

CONTENTS

Table of Contents

Figure 12.1
Continued

LIST OF ILLUSTRATIONS

vi

List of Illustrations

Figure 12.1
Continued

ABSTRACT

In the past five years, Atlantic Electronics has lost its position of employee relations leadership in the electronics industry. The purpose of this report is to analyze the current employee relations situation, draw conclusions, and make recommendations for action. Investigation of the situation focused on comparisons with companies in the industry, on our existing records, and on an employee questionnaire. Atlantic Electronics employees are showing an increased turnover rate internally and as compared with the industry; they also cite a number of complaints. At the root of the discontent are inadequate rewards and poor supervisory methods. To overcome some of its employee disenchantment, Atlantic should offer more tangible and intangible rewards. Implementation of the recommendations would benefit from hiring a consulting firm, starting a job rotation system, initiating supervisor training, and planning future follow-up.

vii

Abstract

Figure 12.1
Continued

<u>EMPLOYEE RELATIONS PROBLEMS AT ATLANTIC ELECTRONICS:</u>

<u>NATURE, CAUSES, AND SOLUTIONS</u>

<u>Problem Statement</u>

For many years, Atlantic Electronics led the industry with its employee relations program. Recently, however, our leadership position is decaying. Our turnover rate is increasing, and many attributes associated with positive employee relationships are not being realized. The purpose of this report is to fully investigate the employee relations problem, to draw conclusions, and to recommend solutions to the problem.

<u>Background</u>

Atlantic Electronics is a mature and successful company. It has grown from 17 employees who produced vacuum tubes for radios to more than 2,000 employees who design and make 107 different electronics parts for home and commercial applications. Gross income has also increased dramatically: 1940 produced a gross income of only $140,000, compared to 1996's $17 million.

These increases have not been without inherent costs. President and founder Claude William Rasnor has reminisced about the good old days when the first employees were close socially as well as vocationally. Spouses of soldiers who died in World War II were voluntarily given pensions and other benefits.[1] Indeed, Atlantic Electronics was cited as a leader in the

1

Page 1 of Body

Figure 12.1
Continued

2

industry in low turnover rates only a few years ago.[2] As this report will show, however, employee relations are no longer at this high level.

<u>Employee Relations in the Industry</u>

One authority has stated that the electronics industry has led the country in positive employee relations for the last 50 years.[3] An examination of employee relations in the industry reveals the effects of good employee relations and the consequences of poor employee relations.

Effects of good relations. A company with good employee relations benefits both directly and indirectly. Direct results include higher quality,[4] harder work by employees,[5] fewer injuries and days lost,[6] and less absenteeism and tardiness.[7] Indirect benefits include cleaner work areas,[8] happier and more energetic employees,[9] and lower turnover rates.[10]

Consequences of poor relations. When a company does not have good relations, not only does it lose the positive benefits, but it also acquires negative consequences. Included among these negative consequences are employee-family problems,[11] poor public image,[12] sabotage of facilities,[13] leaks of corporate secrets,[14] and the likelihood of labor/management distrust and alienation.[15] Distrust and alienation break down the existing channels of communication. If no channels exist, a union is likely to seek admittance.[16]

Body (Continued)

Figure 12.1
Continued

3

Employee Relations at Atlantic Electronics

President Rasnor was always concerned with good employee relations. Since he started the company in 1940, he has maintained turnover rate records. Company records show three major clusters of turnover rates. For the 1940–1960 period, turnover was a mere 2 percent. For the 1961–1986 period, turnover rose to 6 percent, but this level was not considered especially serious.

Since 1993 our rate has been in the 20 percent and higher range. Because the rate had been creeping upward slowly since about 1973, the high level was not accurately recognized until recently. Particularly heavy demands on the company and the rapid changes in technology may have clouded the seriousness of the rate as well.

For the last seven years, under the direction of Louise Alexander, personnel manager, these rates have been compared with those of our three major competitors: Burns, Dominion, and Southern. The precise results of Alexander's record keeping are found in Table 1. Figure 1 illustrates the upward trend.

Table 1: Turnover Rates for Atlantic Electronics and Selected Competitors, 1990–1995

Company	1990	1991	1992	1993	1994	1995
Atlantic Electronics	13	17	18	21	21	23
Burns	18	21	16	12	11	7
Dominion	15	14	17	13	12	15
Southern	17	24	18	16	15	16

Body (Continued)

Figure 12.1
Continued

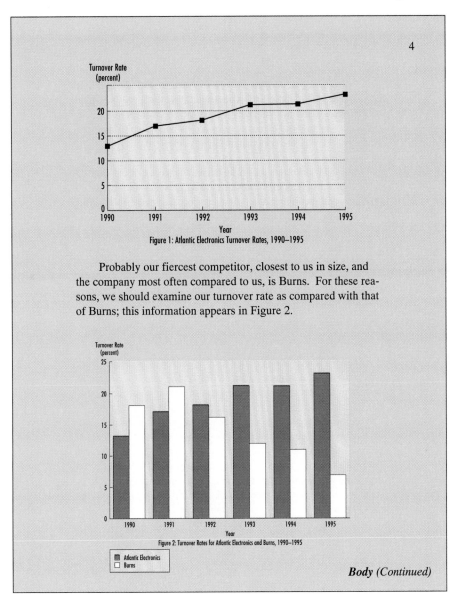

4

Figure 1: Atlantic Electronics Turnover Rates, 1990–1995

Probably our fiercest competitor, closest to us in size, and the company most often compared to us, is Burns. For these reasons, we should examine our turnover rate as compared with that of Burns; this information appears in Figure 2.

Figure 2: Turnover Rates for Atlantic Electronics and Burns, 1990–1995

Body (Continued)

Figure 12.1
Continued

5

One can conclude from the information presented so far that good employee relations are to be sought, that there has been a major increase in turnover rates at Atlantic Electronics in the last six years, and that our turnover rates are rising while our major competitor's rates are constant or slightly improving.

The balance of this report discusses the nature of the employee relations problem, examines its causes, presents solutions to the problem, and recommends implementation of specific solutions.

Nature of Atlantic Electronics' Employee Relations Problem

Our immediate problem has five major components: The number of grievances is high, turnover rates are excessive, absenteeism is unacceptable, morale is low, and unionization appears imminent.

Grievances

The personnel office is the destination for formal employee grievances. In addition to either acting on the grievance itself or directing it to the appropriate person, the personnel office codes the severity of the grievance. For example, 1 is for a valuable and legitimate grievance, a zero denotes a neutral grievance, and a –1 is given if the grievance has no apparent value, logic, or point. The office admits this system is extremely subjective, and the office has kept the tally for only three years. However, in that three-year period, the ratio of 1-rated grievances per 100 employees per year has increased from 27 in 1994, to 41 in 1995, to 57 last year.

Body (Continued)

Figure 12.1
Continued

6

Turnover

Just knowing the rates of turnover is not enough. We also
need to know the reasons for the turnover. Since the termination
procedure for employees who choose to leave the company
requires completion of separation forms, we know the stated reasons for turnover. The results of these inquiries are found in
Figure 3. Almost three-quarters (72 percent) of the stated reasons
for leaving were for one of three reasons: no job challenge, low
pay, or no chance for promotion.

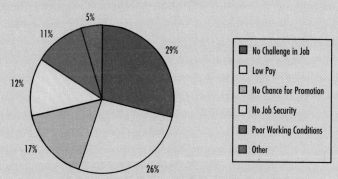

Figure 3: Reasons for Employee Separations at Atlantic Electronics

Absenteeism

We define absenteeism as missing a day or more of work
without authorization by a superior on a TP-8 form or without the
knowledge or consent of the company. An employee may receive
permission to miss work, for example, in an emergency, by phon-

Body *(Continued)*

Figure 12.1
Continued

7

ing a superior. If an employee misses work, even for an emergency, but does not notify a company representative, absenteeism
is reported to the personnel office.

This definition allows us to examine recent absenteeism
levels. Absenteeism rates from 1969 to 1989 did not vary from
the average for that period by more than 5 percent. In other
words, in that 20-year period, there was almost no variance in
absenteeism. Table 2 compares that rate to the last six years.

Table 2: Absenteeism Rates at Atlantic Electronics for
1990–1995, Compared to the Preceding 20 Years

Days Lost per Employee by Year

Mean Absenteeism Rate		Annual Rate					
1969–1989		1990	1991	1992	1993	1994	1995
4.4		4.6	5.1	5.4	6.0	6.8	7.2

Morale

In order to determine the current level of employee morale
and causes for employee dissatisfaction, a survey was distributed
to a random sample of 500 employees. (See Appendix A.)

Methodology. To select the 500 employees, we used our
computer file of all part- and full-time employees. The number
004 was drawn from a random number table. Every fourth name
was selected from the file.

Return rate. Surveys were mailed to employees' homes. Of
the 500 surveys distributed, 407 were returned completed, 9 were

***Body** (Continued)*

Figure 12.1
Continued

8

returned by the post office, and 3 were returned uncompleted. The ratio of completed surveys to delivered surveys (407/491) is 83 percent.

When respondents were asked to rate their current morale level on a scale of 1 to 5, with 1 being the lowest possible score, the mean for all respondents was 1.8. One interpretation is that any score less than 3.0, the mid-point on the scale, is low morale. Clearly the 1.8 figure is low.

Unionization

The electronics industry has relatively little unionization. There have been no overt efforts to keep unions out of the industry, and unions are most likely to emerge when conditions are poor; therefore we surmise that circumstances have not been ripe for unionization. However, in response to an open-ended survey question, 13 respondents mentioned unionization as the best way to improve working conditions and morale. Two comments stated that conversations have taken place with representatives of the Electronics Workers of America (EWA). For the first time in Atlantic's history, unionization appears a possibility. Studying the nature of the employee relations problem is not enough. Statistics about turnover and absenteeism are symptoms of more deeply rooted problems.

Causes of Atlantic Electronics' Employee Relations Problem

The employee survey focuses on the causes of employee relations problems. Two major categories of problems emerge

Body (Continued)

Figure 12.1
Continued

9

from the survey results: inadequate employee rewards and poor supervisory methods.

Inadequate Employee Rewards

Question 2 in the survey asked respondents to check any item in a ten-item list that they believed was evident and important at Atlantic Electronics. Of the ten items, three were checked by over 50 percent of the respondents. Those three are (1) pay and benefits unsatisfactory, 71 percent; (2) work unfulfilling, 57 percent; and (3) feedback about performance nonexistent, 51 percent.

Poor Supervisory Methods

The survey also uncovered two items of major concern about supervisory methods: (1) inconsistent application of company rules and regulations and (2) lack of communication between supervisors and employees. Together they received a 50 percent notation level.

Evaluation of these survey results leads us to conclude that although pay and benefits are seen as low, nonmonetary concerns such as meaningful work, communication, and praise are also important. Our review of the nature of the employee relations problem and its causes brings us to solutions to the problem.

Solutions to Atlantic Electronics' Employee Relations Problem

Employee concerns of unsatisfactory pay and benefits, unfulfilling work, lack of performance feedback, and inconsistent application of company rules and poor superior/subordinate communication are the causes of Atlantic Electronics' employee rela-

Body (Continued)

Figure 12.1
Continued

10

tions problems. These problems have surfaced in increased numbers of grievances, high turnover, high absenteeism, low morale,
and discussion of unionization. The solution to employee discontent has two parts: more intangible rewards and more tangible
rewards.

More Intangible Rewards

Intangible rewards are the most important aspect of the solution package. Most of the employee complaints and concerns, as
uncovered by the employee survey, focused on the intangible
aspects of their work. This finding is not surprising, because
extensive research has shown that once a worker's basic needs are
met, the worker seeks other forms of compensation, such as
friendly working conditions, praise from supervisors, respect
from peers, and so on.[17] In improving the employees' intangible
rewards, we need to improve the jobs and provide more feedback
about employee performance.

Improving jobs. There are two aspects to improving the
employees' jobs: job enrichment and job rotation.

Improving feedback. The feedback improvement solution
has three elements: formal quarterly performance reviews, monthly group feedback sessions, and informal daily feedback.

More Tangible Rewards

In addition to the improvements in intangible rewards,
Atlantic must provide increased pay and improved benefits.

Body *(Continued)*

Figure 12.1
Continued

Increased pay. The survey found that 71 percent of respondents checked low pay and poor benefits as major concerns. Although the survey presents clear-cut conclusions about the concern, it does not indicate the necessary amount of improvement. The average pay at Atlantic Electronics is somewhat lower than the industry average. For hourly employees, the industry average is $18.75 versus our average of $16.50. For salaried employees, we compare well with the industry: the industry average is $31,985 and our average is $44,985.[18]

The electronics industry is highly competitive and there are many professional associations where employees can meet with peers in other companies and compare their career situations. There is also substantial pride associated with pay in the industry. We might conclude that the high level of concern over a relatively small difference between Atlantic and the industry is the result of frequent cross-industry communication and personal pride. Therefore, although we need to improve the pay scale, the increases need not be exorbitant.

Fringe benefits. The situation with fringe benefits is closely aligned with that of employee pay: frequent comparisons with the industry and personal pride account for much of the employee concern. Less than one year ago the Atlantic benefits package was compared to that of the industry in an internal report.[19] This report concluded that Atlantic is competitive with the industry in all areas except dental care, which is not included in our health insurance. About half of the companies in the industry provide dental care.

Body *(Continued)*

Figure 12.1
Continued

12

Implementation of the Solutions

Although Atlantic has a history of more than 50 years, which is relatively long in the electronics industry, it is still a newcomer to the diverse problems of rapid growth, expanded product lines, and technology. The interests of our employees, once exemplified as closeness and team spirit, have been lost recently. To regain this position, we must implement improvements in both intangible and tangible rewards. However, we need expertise from outside our company to guide us.

Hire Consulting Firm

A first step in improving jobs is to seek counsel on job-enrichment strategies. No one in our personnel office professes experience in job enrichment or formal performance review systems. Initial contact has been made with Felix Graham & Associates, the consulting firm Atlantic has retained for four years. A copy of its response to our inquiry is in Appendix B.

Begin Job Rotation System

For some time we have been contemplating a job rotation system. For the past 18 months the supervisors have met to propose how such a system would work. Their conclusion is that the system would be applied to all employees who are not classified E-3 (engineering specialist) or higher, and who wish to be rotated. All employees would spend at least one week a year in a new job, to be determined jointly with their supervisor, and at least one week a year in seminars, short courses, and instruction for new jobs.

Body (*Continued*)

Figure 12.1
Continued

13

Initiate Supervisor Training

It is critical that we immediately initiate training sessions for our supervisors to learn how to give effective formal and informal feedback. Amanda Lewis, a recent Ph.D. in psychology and counseling whom we hired one month ago as an industrial psychologist, has expertise and interest in developing these sessions.

Implement Follow-Up

We must not allow Atlantic to come this close to disaster again. We hope the implementation of the solutions outlined will overcome the current crisis. But we must launch a three-part follow-up system so we will not be caught off guard again. We must (1) survey employees regularly, both through attitude surveys and informally through discussions and interviews, (2) pay attention to what is happening in our industry in terms of pay and benefits as well as other unexpected developments that might affect the dedication of our employees to Atlantic Electronics, and (3) stay even with—or even move ahead of—industry averages for pay and benefits.

Conclusions and Recommendations

Atlantic Electronics has a proud history of employee relations. Recently, however, those relations have disintegrated as evidenced by problems with grievances, absenteeism, morale, and discussion of unionization. These symptoms, our employee survey determined, are related to major concerns about intangible and tangible rewards. To solve these problems we need to

Body (Continued)

Figure 12.1
Continued

14

improve the employees' jobs, provide more feedback, and enhance their pay and benefits. Implementation of the solutions involves hiring a consulting firm, rotating jobs, training supervisors, and starting a follow-up system.

If these solutions are implemented as outlined, Atlantic should overcome its employee relations problems. The cost in achieving positive employee relations will be high in dollars, time, and effort. On the other hand, Atlantic cannot afford to allow the situation to continue.

Body (Continued)

Figure 12.1
Continued

15

ENDNOTES

1. Claude William Rasnor, <u>The History of Atlantic Electronics, 1940–1986</u> (New York: Executive Press, 1987), 25.

2. "A Review of the Industry," <u>Electronics Age</u>, December 1994, 134–145.

3. Mary Louise Harris, <u>Employee Relations in the Electronics Industry: A Review</u> (Chicago: A. J. Smith & Sons, 1995), 421.

4. Harris, <u>Employee Relations</u>, 521.

5. Henry Rosenblum, "Work and Working Relationships," <u>Labor Quarterly</u>, Spring 1992, 83.

6. Sherry S. Quillan and Herman A. Quillan, "Injury in the Work Place," <u>Labor-Management Review</u> 27 (March 1992): 330–340.

7. "Absenteeism and Tardiness," <u>Labor</u>, Fall 1993, 35–60.

8. Rosenblum, "Working Relationships," 85.

9. Harrison Smith, "An Examination of Happiness on the Job" (Ph.D. diss., University of Texas at Austin, 1991), 221–254.

10. Harris, <u>Employee Relations</u>, 390.

Endnotes
(University of Chicago Press Style)

Figure 12.1
Continued

16

11. "The Effect of Poor Employee Relations on Job Performance," in <u>Reflections on Employee Relations</u>, ed. Carlos S. Gonzalez (New York: Prestige Press, 1991), 121–129.

12. "The Effect of Poor Employee Relations," 135.

13. Francis Lewis et al., <u>The New Management</u> (San Francisco: Unicorn Publishers, 1995), 45.

14. William R. Armstrong, Vice President for Production, Atlantic Electronics, personal interview, 12 December 1996.

15. Rosenblum, "Working Relationships," 89.

16. "When Unions Prefer to 'Make Their Move,'" <u>The Hickory Times-Dispatch</u>, 18 April 1994, 3.

17. Smith, "Happiness on the Job," 207.

18. Company files and <u>U.S. Government Review of Employee Income</u>, no. 114, April 1994, 1092–1107.

19. Personnel Office, Atlantic Electronics, <u>Fringe Benefits Review</u> (Dover, Del., February 1996).

Endnotes (Continued)

Figure 12.1
Continued

APPENDIX A

Employee Attitude Survey

You are being asked to respond to a few questions about Atlantic Electronics. Only 500 employees are receiving this survey; therefore, your response reflects the opinions of many of your fellow employees. The survey will take about one minute to complete, and your responses are anonymous. Use the enclosed stamped, addressed envelope to return your survey.

The information we receive from this survey will be used to determine employee concerns. In turn, knowing these concerns will direct our attention to improving employee needs and benefits. Thank you for your help.

1. Please rate your current morale level on the following scale, with 1 as the lowest possible level and 5 as the highest possible level. Place a single check mark in one of the five locations. My current morale level is:

   ___   ___   ___   ___   ___
    1   2   3   4   5

2. Listed below are ten items that relate to work conditions at Atlantic. Place a check mark beside any item that represents your feelings about your job.

   ____ Feedback about performance nonexistent
   ____ Working conditions dirty

17

Appendix A

Figure 12.1
Continued

18

_____ Working conditions unsafe
_____ Not enough training sessions
_____ Pay and benefits unsatisfactory
_____ No choice in shift assignment
_____ Work unfulfilling
_____ Plant too far from home
_____ Poor parking situation
_____ Uniforms not supplied

3. Check any of the following items that you feel are current conditions at Atlantic.

_____ No time to talk to supervisors
_____ Lack of communication between supervisors and
       employees
_____ Not allowed to talk to peers
_____ Inconsistent application of company regulations
_____ Employees don't seem to know their jobs

4. On the back of this sheet, write any comments that you think might improve employee relations.

Appendix A (Continued)

Figure 12.1
Continued

APPENDIX B

<u>Letter from Felix Graham & Associates</u>

FELIX GRAHAM & ASSOCIATES   Management Consultants
1414 Eauclaire, Suite 100
Richardson, DE 18790

December 31, 1996

Ms. Stephanie McQuiston
Personnel Assistant
Atlantic Electronics
P.O. Box 138
Dover, DE 18717

Dear Ms. McQuiston:

As we discussed on the phone today, I am confirming our firm's interest in working with Atlantic Electronics on review, analysis, and redesign of a job enrichment program. I believe your president, Claude W. Rasnor, knows of our expertise in this area.

Our financial arrangements would follow our usual approach. Your annual retainer with us covers the first ten hours of consultation, and after that each hour is billed at $150.

We'll be pleased to visit you at the Dover location, at no cost to you, to discuss this project. Just let us know when you'd like to get together.

Cordially,

Felix Graham

Felix Graham
President

c: Claude W. Rasnor

19

Appendix B

Figure 12.1
Continued

BIBLIOGRAPHY

"Absenteeism and Tardiness." <u>Labor</u> (Fall 1993).

Armstrong, William R., Vice President for Production, Atlantic
    Electronics. Interview, Dover, Delaware, 12 December 1996.

"The Effect of Poor Employee Relations on Job Performance." In
    <u>Reflections on Employee Relations</u>, edited by Carlos S.
    Gonzalez. New York: Prestige Press, 1991.

Harris, Mary Louise. <u>Employee Relations in the Electronics
    Industry: A Review</u>. Chicago: A. J. Smith & Sons, 1995.

Lewis, Francis, Jean Berry, and Mark Grippando. <u>The New
    Management</u>. San Francisco: Unicorn Publishers, 1995.

Personnel Office, Atlantic Electronics. <u>Fringe Benefits Review</u>.
    Dover, Delaware, February 1996.

Quillan, Sherry S., and Herman A. Quillan. "Injury in the Work
    Place." <u>Labor-Management Review</u> 27 (March 1992):
    330–340.

Rasnor, Claude William. <u>The History of Atlantic Electronics,
    1940–1986</u>. New York: Executive Press, 1987.

"A Review of the Industry." <u>Electronics Age</u>, December 1994,
    134–135.

20

Bibliography
(University of Chicago Press Style)

Figure 12.1
Continued

21

Rosenblum, Henry. "Work and Working Relationships." <u>Labor Quarterly</u>, Spring 1992, 71–90.

Smith, Harrison. "An Examination of Happiness on the Job." Ph.D. diss., University of Texas at Austin, 1991.

<u>U.S. Government Review of Employee Income</u>, no. 114, April 1994.

Bibliography (Continued)

Key Terms

- **heading**
- **creeping elegance**
- **attribution**
- **superscript**
- **endnotes**
- **appendix**
- **abstract**
- **pagination**

Review Questions

1. Identify the treatments of the first four levels of headings.

2. Differentiate between the three frequently used attribution styles. What are their strengths and weaknesses?

3. What are the differences between a footnote, an endnote, and a reference?

4. What is pagination? How is it applied to a business report?

5. What are the differences between illustrations and appendixes?

6. Describe the preparation of an abstract.

7. What are some techniques for increasing or decreasing the formality of a business report?

8. What are the differences between a business report and a term paper?

Exercises

1. Working at the Grande Hotel in Miami Beach as a management trainee for the past four months has been exciting as well as educational. You enjoy your job and are pleased to be working with this hotel and in this fine location. Your business degree background and your specialization in hotel management, of course, helped prepare you for this position. But the on-the-job training is more beneficial than you had imagined.

   One of the reasons you are optimistic about this position is that you work under the supervision of Harold Fenton, the hotel manager and part owner. He is a professional and a pleasant person as well. He gives you quite a bit of latitude in your job and is earnestly guiding you into professional hotel management. He has even told you that any area of hotel management is within your jurisdiction; you can talk to him about any problem you observe.

   So far you have stayed fairly close to the problems and projects Fenton has assigned to you. Recently, however, you noticed a problem that you think should be brought to Fenton's attention.

   Water is rather expensive in Miami Beach and of course your hotel uses thousands of gallons a day. Much of this water usage is from guests bathing. You know that about 88 percent of the hotel's water usage is in the guest rooms; the remaining 12 percent occurs in the hotel's kitchens, administrative offices, air conditioners, and so on. The swimming pool is not included in your analysis. At 95 percent occupancy, which is the level at which your hotel operates 10 months of the year (about 85 percent the other two months), the hotel uses an average of 70,000 gallons of water a day. There are 623 units in the hotel.

Recently, you noticed in a hotel management magazine an advertisement for a Super Water Sav'r showerhead. The showerhead is supposed to function on one-third the water of a standard unit, and it can be quickly adjusted by the user to provide a refreshing, pulsating stream of water as well. There is a sliding scale in the cost of the items:

Units	Cost per Unit
1-50	$20.00
51-100	18.50
100-500	17.50
Over 500	17.00

The hotel was built and the shower/tubs were installed 18 years ago. You assume the existing showerheads are functioning satisfactorily, because you did not uncover an unusual number of complaints about them in the hotel files.

The hotel is billed monthly for water by the city at the following commercial rates:

Gallons	Cost per Thousand
0-25,000	$10.75
25,000-50,000	10.53
50,000-100,000	10.31
Over 100,000	10.10

In appropriate report form, analyze the data and present your findings. State whether or not you recommend purchasing the Super Water Sav'r.

2. Permian Storage Tank Manufacturing Co. of Odessa, Texas, builds large oil storage tanks for oil companies in west Texas. Recently, the board of directors at Permian, under the recommendation of Jimmy Womack, president, decided to expand operations. The expansion plan encompasses building new tank manufacturing plants in Longview, Texas, and near Carrizo Springs in south Texas. Located at the new plants will be branch offices.

Neither town is served by an airline. Permian Tank Corporation would like to purchase its own airplane to fly company executives and important customers between Odessa, Longview, and Carrizo Springs. You, as purchasing director for Permian, have been given the responsibility for conducting a survey and making a final recommendation.

For safety reasons, management would like to purchase some type of twin-engine, turboprop airplane. Because seven or more persons (not including pilots) may frequently be riding on the plane, management would like to have a cabin-class aircraft. Other required features are cabin pressurization, instrument flying capabilities, and the ability to take off and land on a runway with a length of 3,500 feet (which is the length of the strip at Carrizo Springs).

The following information has been collected on various aircraft, all of which are pressurized, cabin-class, twin-engine, turboprop airplanes.

Manufacturer or Model	Maximum Number of Passengers	Maximum Cruise Speed (knots)	Takeoff and Landing Distance (feet)	Fuel Consumption (gallons per hour)	Price
Screech King Air	8	222	2261	60	$692,000
Pepper Indian	6	283	2480	65	707,000
Welstone Jet Prop Leader	8	290	2030	65	839,000
Screech King Air 100	13	248	2681	80	985,000
Conquest 2000	9	295	2465	80	995,000
Sakatawi Solitaire	9	321	1950	90	1,095,000
Rodgers Swift IIIB	9	309	3240	85	1,290,000

The distances between airports in nautical miles are Odessa to Longview, 370; Longview to Carrizo Springs, 340; and Carrizo Springs to Odessa, 240.

Write a report to Womack informing him of the results of your analysis. Include a recommendation of which aircraft should be purchased.

3. The National Bank of Ohio is considering adding more drive-up teller windows. Presently all 10 windows are used only during peak periods, such as Mondays and Fridays. However, at least eight of the 10 tellers are busy at all times.

Questionnaires were given randomly to 800 customers inside the bank and in the drive-up area. Of these, 411 were returned. The response was as follows:

1. How long have you been doing business with the National Bank of Ohio?

0-1 year	32	4-6 years	158
1-2 years	52	6-9 years	34
2-4 years	123	9 or more	12

2. What is the most important feature of the bank?

Location	142	Financial Service	150
Size	21	Other	19
Personnel	89		

3. How would you rate the overall performance of the bank?

Excellent	56	Poor	32
Good	135	Bad	14
Fair	174		

4. What type of account(s) do you have?

Commercial	123	Checking	190
Savings	162	Loan	56
Other	44		

5. How long does it usually take you to travel from your home to the bank?

0-5 minutes	41	13-17 minutes	104
5-8 minutes	67	17-22 minutes	20
8-13 minutes	171	More than 22 minutes	8

6. Where do you usually conduct your banking business?

Drive-up window	251	Mail	40
Inside the bank	105	Other	9

7. When you conduct your banking business, how rushed are you?

Terribly rushed	179	In no hurry	104
Somewhat rushed	128		

8. If you use the drive-up window, what is your average wait?

0-2 minutes	5	7-10 minutes	110
2-4 minutes	41	10-15 minutes	81
4-7 minutes	161	More than 15 minutes	13

9. If you see a teller inside the bank, how long is a typical wait?

0-2 minutes	7	7-10 minutes	41
2-4 minutes	43	10-15 minutes	12
4-7 minutes	65	More than 15 minutes	6

10. How often do you bank at the drive-up windows?

Less than once a month	14	Once a week	92
1-2 times a month	25	Twice a week	109
2-3 times a month	29	Three times or more	41

11. How often do you come inside the bank to conduct business?

Less than once a month	17	Once a week	41
1-2 times a month	191	Twice a week	30
2-3 times a month	101	Three times or more	31

12. How do you prefer to conduct banking business?

Drive-up window	297	Mail	14
Inside the bank	92	Other	8

13. Which day or days do you usually bank?

Monday	187	Thursday	97
Tuesday	103	Friday	283
Wednesday	88	Saturday	220

14. How do you rate the present drive-up window service as compared to other banks?

Excellent	61	Poor	71
Good	163	Bad	9
Fair	107		

Write a report to Baily Davis, executive vice president of the National Bank of Ohio. Your report should analyze the survey and make recommendations concerning the drive-up windows.

4. The vice president of personnel for a medium-sized firm has examined the records of the company's 50 secretaries to determine how many days each was absent on sick leave during the prior year.

The vice president needs to give the accounting department an estimate for the budget of expenses for hiring temporary help, and he has asked you to analyze the data to produce this estimate. He is interested in knowing the total number of days missed, the average number of days missed, the variation from the average, the median number of days missed, and how many days were most commonly missed. The number of days missed is as follows:

5	3	15	21	3	28	17	16	13	1
20	1	0	3	8	2	9	19	15	0
6	9	3	5	10	0	11	2	3	3
10	2	8	4	5	1	3	0	9	12
10	8	10	4	1	3	6	3	8	5

Analyze the data and prepare it for a report.

CASE

Sunny Orange Juice
Robert J. Olney, Southwest Texas State University

As you arrive at Bennett Food Products on Monday morning, you cannot resist stopping to look at the sign on the door of your new office. Below your name is the title Assistant Advertising Manager. While you are admiring this visible evidence of your success, Mary Poplin, advertising manager, calls you into her office to confirm a rumor you have heard: the company wants to test the effectiveness of television advertising for Sunny Orange Juice. Sunny Orange Juice is a frozen concentrate of 100 percent natural juice and has had excellent acceptance in a limited test market. You are to make a media recommendation, and it is the first opportunity to prove yourself in your new position.

From your educational background and work experience, you know that such decisions normally require extensive study, but you also realize that the relatively young company cannot afford a costly study at this time. You spend only a few minutes in thought before outlining this plan of attack for the project:

1. Contact three area television stations that represent the three national networks to determine the advertising time periods that are available.

2. Determine the viewer popularity of the shows around the available time periods.

3. Determine characteristics of the audience you want to appeal to in your television campaign.

4. Informally analyze characteristics of the audience viewing programs during each of the available times. Include age, sex, and marital status in your analysis.

5. Analyze the products currently advertised on these shows to determine the buying motives that current product advertising appeals to.

6. Produce a report that analyzes secondary and primary data that will help top management make its decision.

You call the area television stations to determine the commercial time periods that are available and discover that each station has a 30-second time period (listed as Eastern Standard Time) available in the prime viewing time: ABC, 8:15 Monday; CBS, 9:45 Friday; and NBC, 8:15 Wednesday.

Case Questions

1. Using your preliminary outline, begin your investigation.

2. Add to your preliminary outline any other factors you believe should be considered in the analysis of a time period.

3. In determining viewer popularity for the shows in the available time slots, you may want to trust the Nielsen ratings of the shows (published weekly in Wednesday's edition of *USA Today*), or you may want to conduct your own telephone survey of the households in your area. If you elect the second alternative, carefully plan your telephone interview. Be prepared for a variety of responses.

4. Determine the cost for 30 seconds at the time available at each of the networks. This information is published in *Standard Rate and Data Service*.

5. Use as many sources as possible to get other information to support your recommendations.

6. Present your problem data, analysis, conclusions, and recommendations in a report format specified by your instructor.

C A S E

Breaking the Lockstep

James M. Lahiff, University of Georgia

Curriculum development is a controversial topic in many schools. Administrators and faculty members devote much time and energy to developing the curriculum, but the results rarely satisfy everyone.

You attend Midwest State, where students must take many required courses. The program, known as the lockstep sequence, has been the subject of many student complaints. Most students believe that the program should be more flexible and that students should be allowed to select more of their courses.

Midwest State has decided to seek ideas from the students regarding possible changes in the program. The idea of allowing students to structure more of their program is under consideration. You have been appointed to the program evaluation committee, a group assembled to provide student input on this matter.

As a member of the program evaluation committee, you must select eight courses you believe would make up a good program for you. Prepare a report to be sent to the chairperson of the program evaluation committee.

In this report describe eight specific courses and your rationale for including each one. Indicate what you consider to be the goal of your program and how each course contributes to that goal.

Use as many sources as possible to get the information necessary for this report. Interview professors, administrators, and other students. Perhaps someone in a field in which you hope to work would have some insights on the subject. Also, review the catalogs of other colleges that may be available in your college library. Use your imagination in developing your program. The courses that you suggest need not be presently available at your school.

Case Questions

1. Why did you organize your report the way that you did?
2. Describe one other way in which you might have organized it.

C A S E

Biking for Profit

David B. Parsons, Lakehead University, Thunder Bay, Ontario

For several years, the Brocklin brothers have been looking to start a family business in which all three can be actively involved. The brothers, ages 22, 24, and 26, have a variety of backgrounds. Bobby, the oldest, is a sheet-metal worker; Brian, the second oldest, is a small-motor mechanic; and Bruce, the youngest, is a bulldozer operator.

All three are reasonably successful in their careers, but they have always wanted to work together. Their problem was to find a business that offered a product or service attractive to their hometown residents.

Two things that all three have in common are that they hate sitting behind a desk and they love working out-of-doors. Three weeks ago, while waiting to tee off at their local public golf course, they overheard the foursome ahead of them complaining about the rising cost of courier service.

On the way home, Bruce suggested that they investigate the courier service business to see if there was room for some competition. They discovered that four courier companies serviced the area, but not one of them was a mountain-bike courier. A comprehensive market survey indicated that a mountain-bike courier company would do very well if the prices were attractive and the service fast and reliable.

The Brocklins then formed the Roadrunner Mountain Bike Courier Company. Their first problem was that they didn't know much about mountain bikes, so they hired your student consulting group to research the top five mountain bikes on the market and to recommend the best bike for Roadrunner to purchase.

Your task is to identify the top five mountain bikes on the market, select at least five criteria against which you can evaluate the bikes, and write a formal recommendation report to be submitted to Roadrunner Mountain Bike Courier Company.

Case Questions

1. What are the criteria that should be used in picking a brand and model of mountain bike?

2. What brands and models of mountain bikes should be considered?

3. Which is the best bike for the Brocklin brothers' needs?

Chapter 13

Instructions, Documentation, and Policy and Procedure Statements

"Pardon me. I'm new here. I'm trying to get to the mailroom and I'm lost. Which way is it?"

"Yes, you are lost, but no problem. Take the elevator to the basement, G-2, go left down a long hallway until you get to a door with a funny poster on it, then take the next right, go until you hear the noise from the envelope sorting machine, and you're there."

"Thanks, I think I can find it now."

You did find the mailroom, of course, but only after spending 25 minutes lost and frustrated by the instructions you received. As a new employee, how were you supposed to know that not all elevators go to the basement? What did the person mean by a "funny" poster? You saw several posters in the hallway. Some were humorous and others strange. And what does an envelope sorting machine sound like? If only you had been given good instructions. . . .

Anyone who has been frustrated by ambiguous **instructions** recognizes the importance of clearly conveying this form of information. On the job, instructions may be delivered orally from a superior on how to do a task, presented in a manual on how to use computer software, or given formally, in a policies and procedures booklet that details operations procedures. Whether written or oral, formal or informal, good instructions have common characteristics. This chapter discusses these characteristics and then relates them to two main applications: (1) documentation and (2) policies and procedures.

FIVE GUIDELINES FOR GIVING GOOD INSTRUCTIONS

Good instructions are unambiguous, understandable, complete, consistent, and efficient. Each of these characteristics is a guideline for the writer.

1. Avoid Ambiguity

The more concrete your instructions, the better. Rather than "Turn at the big tree," say "Turn left at the large oak tree that has a 'House for Sale' sign on it." Writing with clarity avoids words that have multiple meanings or little meaning. Precision is an important aspect of clarity.

2. Be Understandable

Instructions should relate to the receiver. Target your audience with your message. If you are preparing computer systems documentation, you need to decide on your audience's level of familiarity with the system. Jargon and acronyms may be appropriate with some audiences and inappropriate for others. Instructions can also be made more understandable with short sentences, familiar words, and good transitions.

3. Be Complete

Instructions can be clear and understandable but still fail if they are incomplete. Leaving out an important step in a task procedure may result in failure to complete the task. In addition to identifying all central steps or elements in your instructions, anticipate possible problems or questions that may arise.

The next time you read a newspaper or newsmagazine, note that most stories begin by answering many of these basic questions: Who? What? When? Where? How? Why? Here is an example:

> The U.S. Census Bureau unknowingly distributed a virus-infected floppy disk to 350 research libraries, the agency revealed last week. The disk, which allows IBM PC users to read data on the Census County and City Data Book CD-ROM, contained the Jerusalem-B virus, which infects any .COM or .EXE programs, according to a warning notice from the Government Printing Office.[1]

These sentences tell us who (Census Bureau), what (distributed), when (last week), where (from the printing office to 350 libraries), and how (unknowingly), and indirectly answer why (not on purpose).

As a partial test of the completeness of your instructions, you may wish to ask yourself these six questions.

4. Be Consistent

Much as parallel structure in sentences improves understanding, so does consistency in giving instructions. Know the different levels of your instructions and make those levels obvious to your receiver. For example, in written instructions, treat each major step similarly, each substep in a consistent fashion, and so on. Each major step might start a new page, have the same typeface treatment and white space, and start with an overview.

5. Be Efficient

Efficiency means to achieve the other four guidelines while holding the length of the instructions to an absolute minimum. Efficiency can be difficult because clear, unambiguous, understandable, consistent instructions are likely to be lengthy. Nevertheless, seek ways to minimize your instructions. For example, starting each of seven steps with the phrase, "Your next step in accomplishing your task is to . . ." is inefficient. Instead, use a similar phrase once, follow it with a colon, and then list all seven steps.

Efficiency can often be achieved through the use of overviews that give the parameters of the instructions, such as, "Installing this software involves three main steps and takes about eight minutes. Before you can install the software, however, you must know your serial number and the amount of RAM memory installed in your computer." Overviews avoid the inefficiency of getting part way through a set of instructions before learning you do not have the necessary equipment or information to complete the task.

Two types of relatively formal instructions you are likely to encounter in business are documentation and policies and procedures.

WRITING INSTRUCTIONAL DOCUMENTATION

The establishing of proof, information, evidence, or sequence, usually in written form, is called **documentation**. After a business trip, you will be asked to document your travel expenses, perhaps on an expense voucher, before you can be reimbursed. Or you may decide to protect yourself from challenges in the future by putting in writing your request to your superior for a quieter office because your clients cannot hear you on the phone, which reduces your performance.

Documentation usually is written.

The form of documentation of most interest here is instructional documentation. Instructional documentation might be computer systems operational guidelines, job or specific task instructions, or software manuals. The main purpose of instructional documentation is to teach a sequence of activities or to serve as a reference for instructions. Recent software manuals are typically divided into at least these two parts, often called "User's Manual" and "Reference Manual." In this way, information that is usually examined only once or twice during the learning process is kept separate from reference information used frequently over the long term.

As you organize your documentation assignment, in addition to applying the five guidelines, also consider how the information will be used by your audience. An airplane pilot refers to a list of necessary behaviors and conditions each time before takeoff. A word processing specialist refers to a "Quick Help" guide to recall a seldom-used keystroke command. A computer user looks up "Fatal Error #107" only when a certain system malfunction occurs. A new employee follows a tutorial prepared by his or her predecessor to learn a complicated task. A job applicant examines a job description to evaluate interest in the position. Each of these documents has a different, focused goal based on anticipated audience use.

In preparing documentation, you may wish to refer to this list of questions:

The quality of documentation should be checked.

- What is the goal of the documentation?
- Am I writing to a single user or a group of users?
- Will the user refer to this documentation more than once?
- How long should this version of the documentation be used? (What is its lifespan?)
- Would a glossary be helpful?
- Should I pilot test the documentation on a naive user?
- Is the writing level appropriate for the lowest level user?
- Should I include an index?
- What visual aids would help?

The second major application of instructions in business is policies and procedures statements.

THE NATURE OF OBJECTIVES, POLICIES, AND PROCEDURES

Objectives Defined

Every business is obviously concerned about its own success. In establishing and maintaining a successful operation, the owners or managers of the business set objectives and goals. **Objectives** are generalized purposes toward which the entire organization strives. Goals are the foundation upon which the organization is based. Examples of general objectives include these:

- Maximizing net profits
- Keeping employees satisfied
- Keeping customers satisfied
- Maximizing market share
- Being of service to the community

Not all organizations—nor authorities on organizations—agree on how specific objectives should be. All seem to agree, however, on the necessity of having objectives (which are also called goals, missions, principles, or purposes). Objectives may vary from one organization to another in terms of stability, constancy, and how well known they are.

Objectives perform five critical functions for the organization:

1. They provide orientation by depicting a desired future state of affairs.

2. They set down guidelines.

3. They constitute a source of legitimacy that justifies the organization's activities and its existence.

4. They serve as standards by which success can be assessed.

5. They represent a sought-after state, not one that is already available.

Figure 13.1 contains an example of corporate objectives. Although they change from time to time, objectives are intended to channel the efforts of all employees toward similar ends. Yet, because they are so generally worded, objectives do not provide much guidance to employees in terms of exactly how to meet them. There are many different means to one end. Thus, policies and procedures must be written.

Policy Defined

A **policy** is a general guide to decision making and reflects the organization's attempts to achieve its goals. Policies are the framework, consistent with organizational objectives, that helps managers make decisions. Yet a policy is only a guideline, as it usually gives the manager some degree of discretion in making decisions. Here are some examples of policies as they relate to objectives:

Policies help put objectives into operation.

Objective	Policy
Keeping customers satisfied	If any customer is dissatisfied with a purchase, then his or her money will be refunded.
Being of service to the community	Managers will use every opportunity to become involved in community services such as the United Way, the Heart Fund, and the American Cancer Society.
Keeping employees satisfied	All promotions to managerial positions will be from within the company.

As you examine these policy statements, notice that they provide for discretion or flexibility in decision making. For example, the community service policy does not tell the manager which or how many community organizations to join, nor does it specify how extensively the manager should be involved in any one organization.

You'll find that the higher you move in a business, the more discretion you will probably have. Policy statements for top-level management are usually worded more

Figure 13.1
General Motors' Mission
Statement

GENERAL MOTORS MISSION

The fundamental purpose of General Motors is to provide products and services of such quality that our customers will receive superior value, our employees and business partners will share in our success, and our stockholders will receive a sustained, superior return on their investment.

GENERAL MOTORS GUIDING PRINCIPLES

- We will establish and maintain a Corporation-wide commitment to excellence in all elements of our product and business activities. This commitment will be central to all that we do.

- We will place top priority on understanding and meeting our customers' needs and expectations.

- General Motors is its people. We recognize that GM's success will depend on our involvement and individual commitment and performance. Each employee will have the opportunity, environment, and incentives to promote maximum participation in meeting our collective goals.

- We recognize that our dealers, suppliers, and all our employees are partners in our business and their success is vital to our own success.

- We recognize that a total dedication to quality leadership in our products, processes, and workplaces is of paramount importance to our success.

- We are committed to sustained growth which will enable us to play a leading role in the worldwide economy.

- We will continue to focus our efforts on transportation products and services, both personal and commercial, but will aggressively seek new opportunities to utilize our resources in business ventures that match our skills and capabilities.

- We will offer a full range of products in the North American market and participate with appropriate products in other markets on a worldwide basis.

- We will maintain strong manufacturing resources at the highest levels of technology and be cost competitive with each manufacturing unit.

- We will operate with clearly articulated centralized policies with decentralized operational responsibilities to keep decisions as close to the operations as possible.

- We will participate in all societies in which we do business as a responsible and ethical citizen, dedicated to continuing social and economic progress.

Source: Courtesy of General Motors Corporation.

generally than those that are used at lower levels. Figure 13.2 shows the amount of discretion given management levels in a small manufacturing plant.

Advantages of Policies
Policies help to implement objectives. There are other advantages of policies as well, especially when they are in written form. First, policies enhance consistency in decision making. Second, conflict among employees may be prevented. Finally, policies can save time. Policies keep managers from having to make the same decision over and over again.

Policies have three main uses.

Disadvantages of Policies
Despite the advantages of policies, they are not usually created for every decision. First, it is almost impossible to write a policy for every set of circumstances. To do so

Figure 13.2

Example of Differing Amounts of Discretion Allowed by a Policy Statement

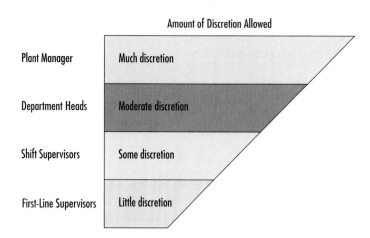

	Amount of Discretion Allowed
Plant Manager	Much discretion
Department Heads	Moderate discretion
Shift Supervisors	Some discretion
First-Line Supervisors	Little discretion

would require amazing foresight and would probably result in a policy manual hundreds of pages long (which many managers would not read). Second, although policies promote consistency in decision making, at the same time they reduce the amount of flexibility decision makers have. Exceptions to nearly every policy exist, and their existence often creates frustrated reactions.

Policies, then, are general guides to decision making. They are created to help a business accomplish its objectives. If more specific decision-making guides are wanted, then procedures are written.

Procedure Defined

A **procedure** is a specific guide to decision making, a tool for implementing a policy. While the general wording of a policy allows discretion in making decisions, procedures provide little or no discretion. When procedures give discretion, they are called **guides**. If no discretion is allowed, then the procedure is a **rule**. The example below shows this distinction.

Guides differ from rules.

Objective	Policy	Procedure (Guide)	Procedure (Rule)
Keeping customers satisfied	If any customer is dissatisfied with a purchase, then his or her money will be refunded.	Check the returned merchandise carefully to see if it has been misused.	The customer must sign the refund slip.

For this one objective we could develop a long list of both guides and rules. However, notice first that the guide listed gives the employee discretion, whereas the rule does not. Second, notice how the chart moves from the general (the objective) to the specific (the rule). The farther we go toward the right side of the chart, the more control we exert over the behavior of our employees.

Not all businesses have written policies and procedures.

You may have worked for a company that had no written policies or procedures: Many businesses do not. The larger a firm is, the more written policies and procedures (sometimes called standard operating procedures, or SOPs) the firm usually will have. You will also find that if the business has unionized employees, then no matter how large or small it is, most policies and procedures will be contained in what is called the labor agreement or contract.

AN ETHICAL DILEMMA

"Ralph, it's company policy," said Paul, leaning back in his chair. "I can't help what they do in other departments."

"But, Paul, I've got a lot of unhappy people down there," Ralph responded. "When they called in, I told them we'd pay them only for the hours they put in. And Jean is paying all of her people for a whole day. Some of her folks didn't get here till three o'clock."

"I know," Paul replied. "Look, Ralph, this happened once before—long before you got here. Must have been 15, maybe 16 years ago. We had a terrible storm. Ice on the roads . . . hanging from the trees. Believe me, the whole town was just dead. But you know, we had 10 or 15 faithful employees show up, some of them after lunch. And that's when the man upstairs decided to give a full day's pay in circumstances like this. Jean knew about it because she was one of those people who got paid."

"Is that written down somewhere?" Ralph asked.

"The policy?"

"Yeah."

Paul shook his head. "I doubt it. We've got enough company policy, rules of conduct, standard operating procedures, and the like in writing as it is. Look, Ralph, I'm sorry you didn't get the word. But it's simple. Your people stayed home. They get paid nothing. If they'd shown up at even four o'clock, we'd have paid them for the whole day. But they didn't. Now you're going to have to work this out with them as best you can."

Ralph feels boxed in. What would you do?

Questions

1. How much policy is "enough"? Too much?

2. Is this approach fair to the employees?

3. Must a policy be written down to be a policy?

Figure 13.3 shows part of a policy statement that includes procedures. Other terms than objectives, policies, and procedures may be used in corporate statements, and these three items may be written in a single statement, but the final test of the statement is whether it is clear, understandable, and ultimately followed.

WRITING POLICIES AND PROCEDURE STATEMENTS

As you pursue your career in business, you will most likely be involved in writing policies and procedures in one of three instances: (1) when a new business is formed; (2) when a new policy or procedure is needed; or (3) when old policies or procedures are being rewritten. You will probably have a chance to write policies and procedures on a variety of topics, including promotion and pay policies, actual work procedures for performing a task, and employee grievances and discipline.

Figure 13.3
Administrative Order
Source: Texas State
Department of Highways
and Public Transportation,
Austin, Texas, June 1, 1986.

STATE DEPARTMENT OF HIGHWAYS AND PUBLIC TRANSPORTATION

Administrative Order No. 17-86

SUBJECT	Department Written Communications
TO	Deputy Directors, District Engineers and Division Heads
REFERENCE	A.O. No. 35-81

Par. 1. Purpose
    2. Effective Date
    3. Supersedes
    4. General Information
    5. Engineer-Director Communications
    6. Department Correspondence
    7. Motor Vehicle Information Circulars
    8. Attachment

AO 17-86
June 1, 1986
D-7

1.	Purpose	To establish policy governing the format, intent and use of Department administrative written communications.
2.	Effective Date	Administrative Orders — June 1, 1986; Other - July 1, 1986
3.	Supersedes	Administrative Order No. 35-81.
4.	General Information	Intradepartment communications transmitting policy, procedures or instructional/informational data are to be prepared in the style used in this order. It will not apply to technical data changes or legal documents.
		Correspondence of a personal nature and Department external communications will be prepared in letter format.
		With exception of correspondence prepared for the Engineer-Director's signature, documents should bear the typed initials of the originator.
5.	Engineer-Director Communications	The documents listed below are published over Engineer-Director signature and are used to communicate directives and information within the Department. They are prepared on white paper stock with preprinted headings as shown on the Attachment and printed on the colors of paper described below. Detailed formatting guidance for the preparation of the documents shall follow by Administrative Circular.

Many organizations have policies and procedures for hiring new employees, ensuring employee safety, disciplining employees, hearing employee grievances, handling customers, dealing with employee absences, and evaluating employees. You can see from this list that most policies and procedures affect the internal operation of a company.

As you write your policies and procedures, apply the five guidelines presented earlier. Note how this partial policy-procedure is concrete, understandable, complete, consistent, and efficient:

Sick Leave Policy. As an employee of Burns Chemical Company you are allowed time off with pay when you are unable to work because of illness. Pay for sick leave is for the sole purpose of protecting you against loss of income when you are ill.

Figure 13.3
Continued

Engineer-Director Communications	• Administrative Orders are for use by the Engineer-Director to communicate Department directives and policies. Orders shall be typeset after approval and prior to Engineer-Director signature. Printing is on white paper stock.
	• Administrative Circulars are used for communicating procedures and guidance and are printed on pink paper.
	• Manual Change Transmittals are used to transmit revisions to Department and Division manuals and are printed on buff paper. A summary of changes is included in the text and/or as an attachment.
	• Newsletters are used by the Engineer-Director to communicate items of interest to employees of the Department such as personnel matters, promotions, retirements, etc. Printing is on green paper.
	• Department Management by Objectives documents are printed on yellow paper and are transmitted by Administrative Circular.
6. Department	The signature level for Department correspondence should be determined by the position or level of authority of the receiver. Consideration may also be given to the significance, impact or sensitivity of the subject matter on Department operations.
	Correspondence between Deputy Directors/Districts/Divisions shall be addressed to and carry the signature of the respective Deputy Director, District Engineer or Division Head. Exception is made when signature authority for such correspondence has been delegated or the correspondence is addressed below the executive manager level. The signature block on all correspondence should be that of the signer.
	Courtesy copies of correspondence addressed to ALL Districts and/or Divisions shall be provided the Engineer-Director, the Deputy Directors and the Internal Review and Audit Section.
7. Motor Vehicle Information Circulars	Instructions to county tax assessor-collectors are published and distributed by the Director, Division of Motor Vehicles.
8. Attachment	Preprinted headings.

M. G. Goode
M.G. Goode
Engineer-Director

Procedure

1. If you are sick and unable to work, you should call your supervisor at least one hour before your shift begins.
2. If you are unable to work for three or more days in a row, then you must bring a note from your doctor on the day you return to work. This note should be given to your supervisor.

Although this example is only part of a sick leave policy and procedure, it clearly tells the employee *who* is involved (the employee, the supervisor, and possibly a doctor). *What* is a telephone call and bringing a physician's note. Two *whens* are in the procedure—one hour before the shift begins and the day the employee returns to work. The *how* is implicit in this procedure because it links the answers to the first three questions. *Why* is answered in the policy statement. Note also that the statement is consistent.

An effective policy/procedure answers five basic questions.

The two characteristics of a policy and procedures statement format are (1) policies appear first, then procedures, and (2) procedures are listed step by step.

As you write policy and procedure statements, you will often find that more than one policy is covered by a given procedure. If this is the case, you will want to list all those policies first, then follow them with the procedures. The following example expands the sick leave policy we used earlier:

Sick Leave Policies. As an employee of Burns Chemical Company, you are allowed time off with pay when, because of illness, you are unable to work. Pay for sick leave is for the sole purpose of protecting you against loss of income when you are ill.

1. You are allowed 18 paid sick days per calendar year.
2. If you do not need all of your sick leave days during a year, then you may add the days you don't use to your next year's total. A maximum of 90 paid sick leave days can be saved.

Procedures

1. If you are sick and unable to work, you should call your supervisor at least one hour before your shift begins.
2. If you are unable to work for three or more days in a row, then you must bring a note from your doctor on the day you return to work. This note should be given to your supervisor.

In this example the first policy may seem to be a procedure because it appears to be a rule. However, remember that procedures are specific guides to decision making. They tell us how to take action to implement a policy.

When writing procedures, you should organize them step by step. Often, following procedures results in an end product of some kind. Therefore, to be sure that the product is correct, you should organize and label the steps clearly:

> ✔ **CHECKLIST** *of Indications That an Organization Would Benefit from Policy/Procedures Statements*
>
> _____ Does the organization have frequent personnel changes between jobs?
>
> _____ Is the turnover rate of employees high?
>
> _____ Do supervisors realize that people have memory limitations?
>
> _____ Are many activities complex and often repeated?
>
> _____ Do supervisors tend to formalize communication by "writing things down"?
>
> _____ Do supervisors or trainers have to repeat instructions?
>
> _____ Do employees forget important steps in complex tasks?
>
> _____ Do employees complain they did not know certain steps were required as part of a procedure?

Customer Refunds Policy. If any customer is dissatisfied with a purchase, then his or her money will be refunded.

Procedures

1. Check the customer's sales slip. Only the store manager may authorize returns on merchandise the customer has had for more than 30 days.
2. Fill out the customer refund slip, making sure that you enter:
   a. Customer's name and address
   b. Date of purchase
   c. Stock number and description of merchandise
   d. Sales number of salesperson who sold the merchandise
   e. Your sales number
   f. Reason for return
3. Take the customer refund slip to your immediate supervisor, who will approve the refund.
4. Have the customer sign the customer refund slip.
5. Refund the customer's money:
   a. If the purchase was by credit card, then tell the customer his or her account will be credited for the amount of purchase. Do not make cash refunds on credit card purchases.
   b. If the purchase was by cash, then refund the customer's money from your cash register drawer. Place the audit copy of the credit refund slip in the drawer.
6. Take the remaining copies of the credit refund slip and the returned merchandise to the customer service department.

Each step in the procedure requires a different action. Ideally, no two acts (unless they are closely connected, as in 5b) should be described in one step.

Within a procedure, if a specific sequence is to be followed, number (or perhaps letter) the steps. If an array of items is to be completed in no particular order, or choices are to be made from a list of options, use bullets in front of the items.

Typically, policies and procedures should follow this format:

- General policy
- Specific policies (1, 2, 3, etc.)
- Procedures (1, 2, 3, etc.)

As a business person, you will likely be aware of your organization's goals, will be required to align with its policies, and may take part in formulating its procedures. The better you understand the roles and interrelationships of these statements, the better you will respond to their purposes.

Key Terms

- **instructions**
- **documentation**
- **objective**
- **policy**
- **procedure**
- **guide**
- **rule**

Summary

Writing good instructions   pp. 349–350

Writing instructional documentation   p. 351

Recognizing objectives   p. 351

Recognizing policies   p. 352

Recognizing procedures   p. 354

Writing policy and procedures statements   pp. 355–359

Review Questions

1. What are the guidelines for giving good instructions?

2. What questions might you ask as you write documentation?

3. Explain the differences among an objective, a policy, and a procedure.

4. What is the role of discretion in writing policies and procedures?

5. Describe two basic kinds of procedures.

6. What questions does an effective policy and procedure statement answer?

7. What is the proper format for a policy and procedure statement? Describe it in detail.

Exercises

1. Locate some software instruction manuals that are five or more years old. Compare them to some recently written manuals. Is there a difference? Have manuals improved over time? How?

2. Locate a software instruction manual that gives poor instructions. Why is it poor? How would you rewrite it to improve it?

3. Find a policy and procedure statement in the student handbook for your college or university.
   a. Evaluate the statement using the guidelines in this chapter.

b. If the statement does not meet all the guidelines, rewrite it so that it does.

4. You work for a company that has decided to begin an employee suggestion system. Employees who submit useful suggestions will receive cash awards. Write a policy and procedure statement for all the hourly employees to follow in participating in the new system.

5. Write a set of instructions about one of the following:
   a. How to change an automobile tire.
   b. How to replace a printer ink cartridge.
   c. How to fold and place a letter in an envelope.

6. Write a policy statement for each topic:
   a. Employee vacations.
   b. Employee coffee breaks.
   c. Employee safety.

7. Choose one of the policy statements you wrote in Exercise 6 and write a set of procedures for it.

8. Write a set of instructions for some simple task one of your classmates might perform in class (for example, folding papers, working with columns of numbers). Give the procedures to a classmate and see how well that person can follow your instructions.

C A S E

What Is the Policy?

David B. Parsons, Lakehead University, Thunder Bay, Ontario, Canada

Varsity Sports Inc. is a local sporting goods store. During the last week of July, it was selling baseball equipment for half price. Grady Cowan stopped by the store after work to buy a catcher's mitt for his son. Cowan normally pays cash for everything he buys.

This time, however, he paid by check. He asked the cashier whether he could return the mitt for refund if it was the wrong size. Being assured that he could return the mitt as long as he had the receipt, Cowan wrote a check for $69.95.

When he returned the mitt the next day, a new cashier was on duty. She told Cowan that he would have to wait 10 days for his check to clear the bank before he could get a refund. Cowan told her that he would return in 10 days, and the cashier confirmed the date.

Ten days later, Cowan was told that the store policy required that 10 banking days had to elapse before he could get his refund. Rather upset, he asked why this policy had not been specified earlier. The reply was a shrug of the shoulders. The cashier did say, however, that if he returned on Monday, he would get his refund.

On Monday, Cowan returned for the third time, only to be told that the 10 banking days were not officially over until Tuesday morning. His subsequent appeal to the manager fell on deaf ears.

On his fourth visit to the store, Cowan finally received his $69.95. He vowed never to shop at Varsity Sports again. He also decided to write a letter of complaint to the owner of the store.

Case Questions

1. Who was at fault for the communication breakdown?

2. Assuming the role of Cowan, write the letter of complaint.

3. Assuming the role of the owner, write a reply to Cowan's complaint. Concentrate on selling Varsity Sports as a good place to shop.

4. What should have been done to avoid this situation?

CASE

Policy Changes from the Treasurer's Office

William C. Sharbrough III, The Citadel

Ralph, the controller, and John, the treasurer, the company's two top accounting officers, were discussing a problem that had just developed with employee accounts.

Ralph: We've had a real problem with employees not paying their employee accounts on time. These are the credit accounts that they use to buy our products for personal use. Some of them have run up bills of more than $300. To combat this problem, we did the same thing we do to customers. We implemented a $10 late fee.

John: To make sure the employees knew about this policy change, we made an announcement in the August company newsletter telling them it would go into effect on the October bills. Several employees still paid their October bills late. Now, here we are. The November bills have had the late charges added to them, and employees are screaming, "When did you make this change? You didn't notify us!" When we told them we had put the announcement in the newsletter, they responded, "We don't read the official announcements in the newsletter. They never apply to us." Further, they said that they didn't read the notice on the bills. They read only the amount owed.

Ralph: Well, we solved one problem. Employee accounts are paid on time now. But now we have another problem. We've got angry employees, and some of them had very small bills—less than $10—that were doubled by this first late penalty. How could something so simple develop into such a big problem?

Case Questions

1. What communication problems occurred here?

2. What could Ralph and John have done to prevent this whole set of problems from occurring?

3. What can they do now?

Note

1. Scott Mace, "Census Bureau Finds Virus in Research Disk," *InfoWorld*, February 5, 1990, 3.

Part 3

Strategies for Oral Communication

Oral communication in business is perhaps more widely used than written communication, and is at least as important. Knowing how to interact with others in oral settings, such as in business meetings and presentations, or interviews, is an important ability. Other important abilities are listening, using visuals, managing conflict, and understanding nonverbal communication.

Chapter 14

Listening as a Communication Tool

"Excuse me, Janet, are you listening to me?" Janet Weir's boss asked her. "Yes. Of course, Mr. Jones," Janet replied. Janet's boss never knew if she was concentrating on what he said or if she was a million miles away because Janet had an unfortunate habit of focusing in space when listening intently. She found staring at the speaker distracting. However, a large part of listening, especially in one-on-one situations, requires signaling to the speaker that you are paying attention and understanding.

Janet decided to improve her listening style consciously. She had a great opportunity that weekend because she went to a party, where there were a lot of people she didn't know. She met new people and, when listening, she nodded and made eye contact and affirmative noises such as, "uh-huh." She realized she should not overdo the nodding and "uh-huh-ing" because she remembered a doctor she had seen once who was such an aggressive listener that he gave the impression of either already knowing what she was going to say or of being bored.

At the party Janet also asked many questions of her new acquaintances so she would get more practice listening. As a result they did most of the talking and she learned a great deal about them. The next day her friend told her several people commented on how interesting she was. This was an unexpected benefit of being a good listener!

Recall a recent experience you had in which the outcome was influenced by bad listening. Were you at fault or was it the other person? Or were both of you at fault? We usually don't have to think back to the distant past to recall such experiences since outcomes are always being influenced by bad listening. Drivers fail to listen carefully to directions and lose their way. Students are denied credit for assignments not completed as instructed. Sometimes the consequences of bad listening are insignificant; other times they are not. A structural engineer, working on a stadium, designed a light tower to support a bank of 100 lights weighing 3,960 pounds, even though he had been told a year earlier to expect the lights to weigh at least 7 tons. Shortly after the tower was constructed the engineer discovered the error, and he informed his superiors. They had done nothing about it twelve days later when the tower collapsed, killing one worker and injuring another. An Occupational Health and Safety Administration (OSHA) official described the inaction as a "lack of realization of potential catastrophe."[1] Some might attribute the accident to bad listening.

The importance of listening cannot be overstated because it is crucial to the success of organizations and individuals alike. A study of communication preferences by first-line managers and supervisors has found that the predominantly used communication skills are listening and speaking, and that listening is perceived as the most important communication skill.[2] Based on an ongoing survey that has now covered a million workers, it appears that companies that encourage upward communication and listen to their employees perform better than other companies.[3] Research findings testify to the relationship between listening and organizational effectiveness.

Between 1987 and 1993 small and midsize companies created 6.5 million new jobs, while companies with more than 500 employees lost nearly 4 million jobs. Large organizations are often accused of becoming complacent and assuming continued success while small companies are aggressively pursuing customers and listening to what they say.[4] The authors of a popular book on organizational excellence recognized the importance of listening when they stated that corporate excellence was "built . . . on a bedrock of listening. . . ."[5]

Management is acknowledging the importance of listening by committing more resources to its improvement. In 1988, for example, 52.4 percent of the companies surveyed were providing employees with training in listening.[6] In 1991 that number had increased to 59 percent.[7]

Besides being critical to organizational effectiveness, listening is also a determinant of individual effectiveness. When evaluating an individual's competence as a communicator, that person's listening ability is a major consideration.[8] Without a demonstrated ability to listen well, a person is unlikely to be considered an excellent communicator. While investigating the link between communication and health, researchers had observed that a dog's blood pressure rises when the dog barks, and drops when the dog is quiet. Researchers later learned that the same holds true for humans, in that our blood pressure rises when we talk and rapidly drops when we listen. In short, listening is good for us.[9]

Many organizations offer employee training in listening, sometimes built around learning packages such as those of Nichols[10] or Spectra.[11] Employers are becoming increasingly aware that listening relates to almost all forms of business communication. It is a necessary skill, for example, in gathering information for a business report, in working in a small group, in interviewing as a management tool or to get a job, and in communicating effectively across cultures.

CHARACTERISTICS OF LISTENING

People retain 50 percent of what they hear, and 48 hours later that drops another 50 percent.

The average listener who hears a 10-minute presentation will hear, understand, and retain only half of what was said. Forty-eight hours later that portion drops another 50 percent. Put another way, we retain about 25 percent of what we hear.

Part of the reason for poor listening ability is the educational system, which emphasizes the speaker at the expense of the listener. The system focuses major attention on reading, writing, and speaking skills—not listening skills. Yet one study shows that 45 percent of total working hours are spent listening, 30 percent speaking, 16 percent reading, and 9 percent writing.

You have no doubt found yourself in the situation of talking to another person and suddenly becoming aware that the other person is not listening. Not a very good feeling, is it? The fact is that most people have no fundamental hearing deficiency, but they still do not listen very well. How can people become better listeners?

Several researchers have examined the potential relationships between effective listening and other individual characteristics. The research suggests several conclusions.

Sex

Although some research has shown that females comprehend slightly less from lectures than do males, the discrepancy is probably caused by the manner of testing, not inherent sex differences.

Personality

Generally speaking, researchers have discovered no marked relationship between listening comprehension and personality characteristics; that is, a good listener does not possess a certain type of personality.

Intelligence

Obviously, intelligence can be a determining factor in listening (aural) comprehension, but it is not the only element that affects aural proficiency. Intelligence alone does not produce listening skills.

Scholastic Achievement

Moderately positive correlations exist between listening ability and cumulative grade average. Such findings indicate that those who listen well get higher grades. Furthermore, because listening and reading have similar correlations with grade point average, it is reasonable to conclude that scholastic excellence depends equally upon aural and reading skills.

Verbal Ability and Vocabulary

Verbal competence is an important part of listening comprehension. An adequate vocabulary aids listening and word retention. In fact, the effective use of words, through both listening and speaking, is a definite business and social asset.

Note Taking

Because most listeners take poor notes, note taking does not have a noticeable effect on listening comprehension and retention. However, if you listen carefully and synthesize as you write, you will probably perform better on examinations.

Motivation

Motivation is one of the most significant elements of listening proficiency. Specifically, motivation—in terms of interest, emotional appeals and attitudes, and mind set—determines the level of aural competence. A listener's comprehension improves if there is interest in the topic before the speech, if interest is created during the speech, or if the listener is to be tested after the speech. Comprehension is also determined by the intensity of the listener's emotional reaction to what is being said. Finally, a listener's level of understanding is influenced by various methods of producing an **anticipatory mind-set**. For example, if you introduce your point by stating that it is going to be critical of, say, tax increases, your listeners are more apt to remember your criticisms. You have created, in the minds of your audience, a mind-set to anticipate criticisms.

Organizational Ability

Listening comprehension is directly related to the ability to organize and structure a message. The better organized the message, the higher the comprehension will be. This applies to speakers as well as listeners.

Environment

Research findings show that environmental factors influence comprehension. Good listeners will learn to allow for or adjust to distracting elements, such as poor lighting or extraneous noises, distance from the speaker, or other environmental shortcomings that the listener cannot control.

Hearing Ability

Many think that those who suffer some hearing loss therefore are not good listeners; actually just the opposite is true. Those with moderate hearing loss usually are better listeners than those who have normal hearing.

Usage

Writing skills and, to a lesser extent, speaking skills, improve with use, but this is not necessarily the case with listening. Just because people have been hearing the spoken word all their lives does not mean they are good listeners. Instruction and practice in effective listening are needed for listening improvement.

Listening ability depends on a complex combination of factors. No particular personality trait or intelligence level excludes anyone with a stable personality and average intelligence from being a good listener. Listening is a skill that can be learned; all of us can become better listeners and better teachers of listening skills.

BARRIERS TO EFFECTIVE LISTENING

Major barriers to effective listening are perceptual in nature.

In order for listeners to improve their listening skills, they need to be aware of the major barriers to effective listening.[12] Some barriers are perceptual in nature; others are more general.

Perceptual Barriers

Frame of Reference

People perceive stimuli according to their individual frames of reference. "Meanings are in people" means a message is composed solely of aural and visual stimuli. Although the speaker (message sender) may want to convey a particular meaning, it is the listener's individual frame of reference—that is, total life experience up to that point—that determines the actual meaning assigned to the message. As discussed in Chapter 2, the speaker and listener may share similar but never identical meanings through a given message.

Many aspects of culture determine our frame of reference and how we apply it to our listening behaviors. These cultural differences increase in importance as we expand into international markets and employ global trade. For example, the belch after a meal that is considered a compliment in Arabia is socially unacceptable in the United States.

Expectations

People perceive stimuli according to their own expectations. Expectations are based on experiences in similar situations. For example, picture two Americans in the headquarters of a large business in a Middle Eastern country. This is their first visit to the region, and they felt it was appropriate to arrive 15 minutes early for their appointment with a local executive. They have been waiting an hour and 15 minutes. They are frustrated and upset. Finally, the executive appears and says, "Oh, there you are. Won't you please come in?"

The Americans think, "How rude not even to apologize for the delay."

The executive thinks, "Perhaps I should have kept them waiting a bit longer to emphasize even more my position above them."

What occurred is a mix of cultural differences and forceful experiences that probably overrode much of what took place in the meeting. In this case, the listeners' past climate of communication determined their perceptions of the immediate listening situation, the speaker, and the messages being sent.

Particularly when position in a formal hierarchy is highly defined, vantage point may determine expectations. You may approach a situation in which you communicate with a superior differently than when communicating with a subordinate or a peer. For example, if you are a line person, you may communicate in a different tone with a manager than with another line person.

Attitudes and Beliefs

People perceive stimuli according to individual attitudes and beliefs. Most people have an almost innate ability to distort information so that it fits into their model of the world. This process is called **selective perception** and is relevant to listening activity. For example, some employees may conveniently filter out criticisms from a supervisor to support the belief that their work is acceptable. They refuse to hear negative comments about their work, thus avoiding an unpleasant confrontation with reality. Selective perception serves as a protective device against unwelcome aural stimuli.

People selectively remember certain experiences (selective retention). They selectively pay attention to those things they find of value (selective attention). They have comprehension skills in some areas and weaknesses in others (selective comprehension). Awareness of these attitudes is important if you are to overcome them.

Our communication behavior is selective.

Relationship with Speaker

The continuing relationship between speaker and listener plays an important role in perception. The relationship between superior and subordinate is the most relevant case in point. Subordinates will pay close attention to a respected, credible supervisor's comments and will be more conscious of how they perceive communication from that supervisor. However, subordinates are likely to attach minor importance to the comments of a supervisor with low credibility or little power.

Nonverbal Cues

Ineffective listeners are unaware of nonverbal cues, although they dramatically affect how people listen. As Chapter 15 shows, as much as 93 percent of people's attitudes are formed by nonverbal cues. Knowing this should help you avoid undue influence from nonverbal communication.

Influential Words

"Signal" words can cause anxiety or raise emotions. People have certain words that affect them in either a positive or a negative way. Check yourself and create an inventory of these influential words. Do not let specific words get in the way of effective listening.

> ### ✔ CHECKLIST *for Overcoming Perceptual Barriers*
>
> _____ Avoid perceiving stimuli according to your own frame of reference.
>
> _____ Avoid perceiving stimuli according to your own expectations.
>
> _____ Avoid perceiving stimuli according to your own attitudes and beliefs.
>
> _____ Do not allow your relationship with the speaker to detract from effective listening.
>
> _____ Be aware of nonverbal cues.
>
> _____ Watch out for "signal" words that can cause anxiety or raise emotions.

General Barriers

In addition to perceptual barriers, other barriers exist that are of a more general nature:

* *Faking attention.* All too many people know how to appear as though they are listening. Outward appearance and actual listening comprehension may be quite different.

• *Listening only for facts.* Although individual facts are important, check yourself to ensure that you are also clear on the overall goal of the message.
• *Avoiding difficult listening.* Difficult topics vary with individuals and depend on other circumstances such as the listener's physical alertness and the context. Be sure you do not turn off your listening when you encounter a topic that is difficult.
• *Dismissing the topic as uninteresting.* "I've heard it all before," is an attitude that is certain to affect listening detrimentally; so is the assumption that a topic is beneath you or beyond your sphere of interest.
• *Criticizing physical appearance on delivery.* If you have ever not listened to an individual because the speaker's looks, dress, age, mannerisms of speech, or slight speech defects bothered you, you will realize that this is a common barrier to effective listening.
• *Yielding easily to distractions.* People listen for many reasons. They listen for information, to evaluate the speaker, for esthetic appreciation of the voice, and to empathize with the sender. Research indicates that when they are not listening, they are likely to be daydreaming (about something totally unrelated to what is being said), detouring (from what was said to their own thoughts), debating (against what was said), or planning (what to say when it's their turn). To overcome distraction you need to concentrate.

Having considered some of the major barriers to effective listening, you are ready to examine ways to improve your listening ability.

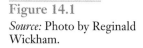
CHECKLIST *for Overcoming General Barriers*

____ Do not fake attention.

____ Listen for the overall message as well as facts.

____ Be receptive when topics require difficult listening.

____ Do not dismiss a topic as uninteresting.

____ Do not criticize physical appearance or delivery.

____ Avoid yielding to distractions.

THE ACTIVE LISTENING CONCEPT

When you think of a person listening, do you picture a passive activity? To improve your listening behavior, you must modify this view. The preferred approach pictures a good listener as actively involved in the listening process (Figure 14.1).

Several years ago Rogers and Farson introduced a concept of **active listening**.[13] Basically, it requires the listener to grasp, from the speaker's point of view, just what is

Figure 14.1
Source: Photo by Reginald Wickham.

being communicated. More than that, listeners must convey to the speaker that they are seeing things from the speaker's viewpoint.

Active listening entails grasping the speaker's point of view.

Listening for Total Meaning

Any message a person attempts to convey usually contains two important and meaningful elements: content and the attitude or feeling underlying this content. These two components make up the total meaning of the message, which is what listeners try to understand. To illustrate, machine operator Alan Morrison tells his foreman, "I have finished the production run." This message has definite content and may be interpreted as a request for another work assignment. Suppose, instead, that Alan says, "Well, I've finally finished that damned production run." The basic content is the same, but the total meaning of the message is quite different.

The difference in the meanings of the two statements has important implications for both the foreman and the machine operator. Listening sensitivity on the part of the foreman will determine whether this conversation is a successful exchange between the two parties. Suppose the foreman's reaction is simply to assign another production run. Would Alan believe that he had successfully communicated his total message? Would he feel free to talk to his foreman? Would he have a positive feeling about his work and be anxious to perform even better on the next job assignment?

On the other hand, the foreman could respond with such statements as "Worked under a lot of pressure, right?" or "Glad to have it over with, huh?" or "Guess I couldn't get you to do that again!" In this instance the foreman's listening sensitivity reacts in line with Alan's attitude or feeling about the completed task. In other words, the foreman responds from Alan's point of view. Such supportive replies do not mean that the next work assignment need be changed or that the way is open for the employee to complain about the pressure of the job. Listening sensitivity is simply a way to transform an average working climate into a more positive one.

Responding to Feelings

In some situations the message content is far less important than the feeling that underlies it. To interpret the full meaning of the message accurately, listeners must respond to the feelings or attitude component. For example, if Alan had told his foreman, "I'd like to disassemble the production machine and sell its parts to our competitor," responding to content would obviously be absurd. The meaning of any message contains various degrees of feeling; each time the listener must be sensitive to possible variations. What is this person trying to tell me? What does this mean to him or her? What is this person's view of the problem?

Noting All Cues

Communication is made up of verbal and nonverbal cues. Words alone do not reveal everything that the speaker is communicating. Sensitive listening requires an awareness of several levels of communication besides verbal. Voice inflection is one factor: A speaker may stress certain points loudly and clearly and only mumble others. The way a speaker hesitates reveals a great deal. The speaker's facial expressions, posture, hand gestures, eye movements, and breathing also help to convey the total message.

In addition to listening for total meaning, responding to feelings, and noting all cues, active listeners show their engagement with the speaker through certain observable behaviors and mental outcomes. Many active listeners convey interest through their posture, by leaning forward. They maintain appropriate eye contact, and they may periodically nod to show interest. These observable behaviors testify to the listener's involvement. Mental outcomes of active listening include comprehending what is being said and being able later to recall it. Figure 14.2 is a test of your self-reported listening skills in everyday conversations. The brief test may suggest some of your own strengths and shortcomings as an active listener. Class averages are usually in the mid-forties.

OTHER CONCEPTS RELATED TO LISTENING ABILITY

The concept of active listening has to do with the mental attitude that we should bring to the listening situation. In addition, several other basic concepts relate directly to our listening ability.

Concentration

Motivation and demotivation affect the listening experience.

People are motivated to listen in varying degrees to a variety of messages. Simultaneously, they are demotivated from listening for many of the same kinds of reasons. Effective listeners are continually and consciously motivated to listen. From the effective listener's viewpoint, whatever other individuals wish to communicate is important. Though it sometimes appears that nothing of great value may be gained through listening, effective listeners consciously strive to disprove this expectation. They become selfish listeners who look for potential economic benefits, personal satisfaction, or new interests and insights. In brief, each listener needs to say, "What is that speaker saying that I can use?"

A significant differential exists between average speaking rate (100 to 200 words per minute) and an average listener's ability to process messages (400 words per minute). Such a differential provides opportunities for mental tangents. Average lis-

Figure 14.2

Conversational Listening Test
Source: Blaine Goss, "A Test of Conversational Listening" *Communication Research Reports* 8, June 1991.

Read each item and circle one answer indicating whether you strongly disagree (SD), disagree (D), are neutral or unsure (N), agree (A), or strongly agree (SA) with the statement. Since there are no correct answers, please respond honestly.

1.	I have difficulty remembering what people say.	SD	D	N	A	SA
2.	I am polite when listening to others.	SD	D	N	A	SA
3.	I can't figure out what people are driving at.	SD	D	N	A	SA
4.	When listening to others, I rarely ask questions.	SD	D	N	A	SA
5.	I avoid making irrelevant remarks.	SD	D	N	A	SA
6.	When someone else is talking, I have trouble paying attention.	SD	D	N	A	SA
7.	I show interest in what the other person is saying.	SD	D	N	A	SA
8.	I have a fantastic memory for things people say.	SD	D	N	A	SA
9.	I jump to incorrect conclusions about what the other person means.	SD	D	N	A	SA
10.	When I'm talking, I link my comments directly to what the other person said.	SD	D	N	A	SA
11.	When listening, I give appropriate feedback.	SD	D	N	A	SA
12.	When reacting to others, I don't show much sympathy.	SD	D	N	A	SA

Scoring: The items can be scored 1–5 from SD to SA on all items, except for items 1, 3, 4, 6, 9, and 12. These items should be scored in reverse.

BOXED IN

AN ETHICAL DILEMMA

Ellen Berringer is intelligent, highly organized, and articulate. She can always be counted on to grade and return assignments promptly, and her grading system is fair and easily understood. She is well-prepared for her classes, and her lectures are generally quite interesting.

It sounds as though she is a good teacher, doesn't it? Well, she is, except for an idiosyncrasy that greatly reduces her effectiveness. When lecturing she says, "Be that as it may," after virtually every statement she makes. While that may seem harmless enough, her habit has become a source of considerable distraction. If a speaker makes such comments occasionally, the comments may go unnoticed. When a speaker does the same thing repeatedly, as Ellen does, the comments become a focal point for listeners.

It has come to the point where her students refer to Ellen as "Professor Be That As It May," and many of them keep count each day of the number of times she says it. All of her students are aware that the current record is thirteen "Be that as it may(s)" in a single class period.

It is obvious to Antonio Sanchez that Ellen's habit distracts students away from the subject matter, and the habit also detracts from her professional image. Ellen remains completely unaware of how her comments make it difficult for students to listen to her. Antonio believes that everyone would benefit if Ellen were to be told, but he is unsure how she would respond. Also, he does not want to jeopardize his grade in the class. Antonio feels boxed in. What would you do?

teners tend to tune in and out of conversations. As a consequence, they often fail to grasp what the speaker deems the important contents of a message.

Concentration is the key to avoiding such counterproductive tangents. The listener should be aware of the difference between the rate of speech and the rate of thought and should use the time lag effectively rather than let it destroy the listening process.

Concentration is an important determinant of listening ability.

Several tactics can be used both to maintain attention to the speaker's message and to aid retention. One of them is to anticipate what the speaker will say next. Whether or not the anticipations are confirmed, this activity focuses the listener's attention on the subject at hand. Another tactic is to focus on the message. Weighing the speaker's evidence and searching for the speaker's deeper meanings, particularly connotative ones, will help bridge the time gap created by the speech-thought differential. A third tactic is to review previous points. This involves mentally summing up the major points already covered. Reviewing points can help to reinforce the ideas the speaker is explaining.

> ✔ *CHECKLIST for Listening Concentration*
> _____ Anticipate what the speaker will say next.
> _____ Focus on the message.
> _____ Review previous points.

Questioning

In dyadic or paired communication, such as between a superior and a subordinate, asking questions may often be an effective listening tactic. Such activity serves two purposes: It encourages the speaker by demonstrating that the listener is, indeed, actively listening, and it can clarify and develop points, thereby enhancing the listener's chances of clearly understanding the speaker's message.

The use of questions is an effective listening strategy.

To improve listening capabilities, **probing questions** are highly useful types of questions. The listener simply asks questions that build on a speaker's words. Probing and other types of questions are discussed in Chapter 20.

Objectivity

Objectivity is a critical element in effective listening. Not only can lack of objectivity result in assigning distorted meanings to messages, but it may also jeopardize the relationship between speaker and listener. An effective listener knows how to overcome barriers to objectivity.

Emotion-Laden Words

Effective listeners minimize the impact of emotion-laden words. Quite often a listener's perceptual process goes awry simply because the speaker arouses an automatic emotional response. Words and phrases such as *sexism, reduction in force, strike,* and *grievance* can sometimes engender feelings of hostility or anxiety in a listener. When such feelings arise, the ability to think clearly and logically may be severely hampered.

Delivery

Effective listeners judge content, not delivery. Listeners often discount messages largely because of some distracting characteristic in the speaker's tone of voice, delivery, or pronunciation. Subjective impressions of the value of messages seriously endanger listening efficiency. An effective listener, therefore, focuses on what is said, not on how it is communicated.

Unfair Reaction

Effective listeners react fairly and sensibly. One of the most difficult listening functions is to avoid reacting too soon to what is heard. For example, a department head was informed by the plant manager that her staff must be reduced by two people. Rather than wait for an explanation or justification from her superior, she immediately responded defensively. She plunged right in, offering every reason imaginable for not cutting back the number of people in her department. Her attitude resulted only in the plant manager's defensive behavior as well as hostile feelings between them.

Effective listeners follow the timeworn advice, "wait your turn." They allow others sufficient opportunity to satisfactorily communicate their position or ideas. By adhering carefully to the rule of taking turns, the listener becomes a more effective communicator.

Distractions

Effective listeners overcome distractions. Listeners should not let environmental factors affect their listening. For example, you should turn down a stereo or television that keeps you from hearing.

Isolated Facts

Effective listeners detect the central message. Isolated facts are not allowed to get in the way of the total meaning. You should ask for clarification or rewording if you are unsure what is being said.

✔ *CHECKLIST for Objective Listening*

____ Minimize the impact of emotion-laden words.

____ Judge content, not delivery.

____ React fairly and sensibly.

____ Overcome distractions.

____ Detect the central message.

Note Taking

Note taking may be useful in some situations; it may be unnecessary in others; in some cases it may even be distracting. Your purpose in listening should determine whether or not you need to take notes. If you think you will need to refer to the information in the future, notes are probably necessary. If the information is for immediate use, you are probably better off to listen carefully and omit notes.

Appropriate note taking may nonverbally convey to the speaker that you are paying close attention to what he or she is saying. Such note taking shows respect for the speaker and earnestness on the part of the listener.

Feedback

Although feedback is important to listening, it is frequently overlooked. Listeners should provide feedback, at appropriate points, to a speaker, who is sometimes unsure what is actually getting through to the listener. The speaker may start repeating the same ideas if the listener does not appear receptive. At this point the listener shows even less interest and comprehension, the speaker repeats even more, and the entire communication process quickly deteriorates. This problem can be alleviated when the listener provides appropriate and timely feedback to let the speaker know that an idea has been understood.

Feedback is important in the listening process.

Appropriate feedback may be verbal or nonverbal. Examples of nonverbal response include nodding the head in agreement, appearing involved with the conversation, and maintaining eye contact. Verbal clarifiers might be "What you're saying is . . ." or "Let me see if I have this right. . . ."

KEYS TO EFFECTIVE LISTENING

Ten keys to effective listening demonstrate the major differences between good listeners and bad listeners. Lyman Steil, a well-known authority who serves as a listening consultant to major corporations throughout the country, has summarized these differences, as shown in Table 14.1.

TABLE 14.1 TEN KEYS TO EFFECTIVE LISTENING

Keys	The Bad Listener	The Good Listener
1. Find areas of interest.	Tunes out dry subjects.	Opportunizes; asks "What's in it for me?"
2. Judge content, not delivery.	Tunes out if delivery is poor.	Judges content, skips over delivery, errors.
3. Hold your fire.	Tends to enter into argument.	Doesn't judge until comprehension complete.
4. Listen for ideas.	Listens for facts.	Listens for central themes.
5. Be flexible.	Takes intensive notes using only one system.	Takes fewer notes. Uses four to five different systems, depending on speaker.
6. Work at listening.	Shows no energy output; attention is faked.	Works hard, exhibits active body state.
7. Resist distractions.	Distracted easily.	Fights or avoids distractions, tolerates bad habits, knows how to concentrate.

continued

8. Exercise your mind.	Resists difficult expository material; seeks light, recreational material.	Uses heavier material as exercise for the mind.
9. Keep your mind open.	Reacts to emotional words.	Interprets emotion-laden words; does not get hung up on them.
10. Capitalize on the fact that thought is faster than speech.	Tends to daydream with slow speakers.	Challenges, anticipates, mentally summarizes, weighs the evidence, listens between the lines to tone of voice.

Source: Lyman K. Steil, Larry L. Barker, and Kittie W. Watson, *Effective Listening: Key to Your Success,* pp. 72-73, 1983, Addison-Wesley Publishing Co. Reprinted with permission of Random House, Inc.

Key Terms

- **anticipatory mind-set**
- **selective perception**
- **signal words**
- **active listening**
- **probing questions**

Summary

Relationship between listening ability and individual characteristics pp. 366–368

Perceptual barriers to listening pp. 368–369

General barriers to listening pp. 369–370

Active listening pp. 370–371

Listening concentration pp. 372–373

Objective listening p. 374

Keys to effective listening pp. 374–375

Review Questions

1. On the average, how much of the workday do people spend in some type of communication? How much of that time is spent listening?

2. On the average, how much of what someone tells us do we remember immediately after we have heard it? Forty-eight hours after we have heard it? What do these facts tell you about the average person's level of listening retention?

3. Select what you believe are the six or seven more important individual characteristics that affect your ability to listen. Explain your selections.

4. Give an example in a business setting of each of the major perceptual barriers to listening.

5. What is active listening? Why is it so important?

6. What is a selfish listener?

7. What are the tactics a listener can use to facilitate concentration? In turn, how does concentration facilitate listening?

8. Is the use of questions an effective listening strategy? Explain.

9. Why is objectivity a critical element in effective listening? In terms of objectivity what should an effective listener do?

10. What are the major differences between good listeners and bad listeners?

11. Which one of the items in the Conversational Listening Test (Figure 14.1) presents the biggest problem for you as a listener? Describe two ways in which you might overcome the problem.

Exercises

Pair up with a member of your class and perform the following exercises:

1. Give your partner a two-minute description of your favorite restaurant. Why is it your favorite (i.e., atmosphere, food, price, service) and why might someone else enjoy dining there? The listener should then give a 30-second restatement on why an outside observer should try this restaurant. Reverse roles and repeat. What did you learn?

2. Tell your partner about a particular place, but do not use any names. Speak for at least two minutes before allowing the listener to speak. The listener should not reveal his or her guess until stating the information that led to the conclusion. Only after the information has been successfully repeated back to the speaker should the listener divulge his or her guess. If incorrect, was it an information problem or listening problem? Reverse roles and repeat. What did you learn?

3. Tell your partner about an argument you have had in the past where your position was unequivocally correct. The listener should then step into your shoes and make the same argument for your position. At this time, you should step into your shoes and make the same argument for your position. At this time, you should step into the shoes of the one you were originally arguing with and argue that person's perspective. When finished, discuss with your partner how well listening skills were used during the exercise. Were they used well in the original argument by both parties? Reverse roles and repeat with a new argument. What did you learn?

4. Give directions to your home from wherever you are now. Make the directions as specific as you can. The listener should then repeat the directions as closely as possible. Reverse roles and repeat. What did you learn?

5. Describe in detail your favorite weekend activity. The listener should then list reasons why that activity is fun to you, and then list reasons why he or she would find that activity fun. Reverse roles and repeat. What did you learn?

6. You, the listener, are an informant for the police, but you care more about getting paid than aiding justice. Describe a crime you witnessed, giving as many details as possible. The listener then must ask questions about the account to determine the credibility of the information. Reverse roles and repeat. What did you learn?

7. Tell an employee five things that should be done on the job. Emphasize the negative. The listener should then tell the employee those five directives in a positive way. Reverse roles and repeat. What did you learn?

8. Describe the perfect sunset, and the emotional feeling a perfect sunset brings (i.e., relaxation, nostalgia, romance). The listener should then tell from that description what key external stimuli might bring on that same emotion. Reverse roles and repeat. What did you learn?

9. You are a car buyer looking at a new model. Make positive and negative comments about the cars you have seen in the past. The listener is the seller and should determine what is important to the buyer (called "hot buttons" in sales) and then sell the buyer the perfect car. Did the seller "listen" to the buyer's interests? If so, congratulations to the listener for making the sale. Reverse the roles and repeat. What did you learn?

10. You and a classmate each choose a topic of considerable personal interest. Take turns discussing your topic for three minutes. After each discussion have the listener convey the content of the message and the attitude or feeling underlying the content.

11. As a variation of Exercise 10, the class can be divided into triads consisting of a speaker, a listener, and a referee who will evaluate the feedback by the listener and make suggestions for more active listening.

12. If some memorable event is scheduled and if all class members have access, each member should attend or watch. An appropriate event might be a presidential address on television, a presentation by a campus speaker, or an organization meeting. Students should listen but not take notes. The next day the instructor will quiz the class on what they heard.

13. Present a five-minute speech on a business-related topic to a friend majoring in the liberal arts. Ask your friend (the listener) to provide feedback at any point the speech is unclear. Reverse the roles so that you become the listener providing feedback to your friend's speech on some aspect of the liberal arts.

14. Which of your friends or classmates is a good listener? What makes you think so? Explain to that person that you are interested in knowing more about how he or she became a good listener. Try to improve your own listening skills by applying the same techniques.

15. Visit the library and search out information on listening improvement. Which skills are consistently perceived as important? Try to apply those techniques, even for a short period of time, such as for five minutes. See how much you can recall.

C A S E

Do You Know the Way to Midway?

Anji K. Roy, University of Wisconsin–Oshkosh

Sandy, a sophomore at Marquette University in Milwaukee, planned to visit her cousin in San Jose during the spring break. She checked all of the airlines and found that Popular Airlines offered the lowest fare. She would, however, have to change planes in Chicago and Los Angeles.

On the afternoon she was to leave, her 3:15 flight from Milwaukee to Chicago was canceled because of fog. Even if she were able to take the next flight to Chicago at 5:25, she could not make connections the rest of the way. She would have to stay overnight in Los Angeles before going on to San Jose the next day.

Sandy decided that she might as well stay in Milwaukee and leave the next morning. She was disappointed, because her cousin had already made special plans for the next day.

Sandy's sister, Simone, volunteered to drive her directly to Midway Airport in Chicago. Sandy might still make the earlier flight from there to Los Angeles.

The Popular Airlines agent gave Simone instructions to Midway. "Take I-94 East from Milwaukee to the 294 bypass south around Chicago. Leave the bypass at I-55. Take that to Cicero Avenue and exit south. Midway Airport is right on Cicero."

Simone followed the directions, but realized that they were headed south toward St. Louis on I-55. She turned around at the next exit and went back north on I-55. They reached Midway Airport five minutes after the flight had left.

Sandy had to take a later flight from Chicago to Los Angeles after all, and she stayed overnight in Los Angeles at her own expense.

Case Questions

1. Why did Simone take I-55 South instead of I-55 North?
2. What could Simone have done to be reasonably sure that Sandy would catch the flight?
3. What were the wrong assumptions on which this miscommunication was based?
4. What could the Popular Airlines agent have done to avoid the situation that Sandy found herself in?

CASE

Neglecting the True Customer?

Cara A. Curtis, University of Georgia, Athens, GA

Laura Thomas graduated cum laude from the state university with a degree in chemical engineering. Before graduation, she landed a job with Procter & Gamble in Cincinnati, and she began to plan her move to Ohio and arrange her personal finances. Laura secured a lease on a suburban apartment and determined her monthly expenses; based on her expected salary, she decided that she would have enough money to purchase a new car. After researching the possibilities within her price range, she narrowed her choices to five cars that she would further investigate. Since she did not feel comfortable with her knowledge about cars, and since she had never made such a significant purchase, Laura asked her father to visit car dealerships with her.

When Laura and Bill Thomas went to the first dealership, they strolled around the lot looking at different models and sticker prices. They were approached by a middle-aged salesman, who spoke directly to Mr. Thomas and asked him which model appealed to him. Mr. Thomas immediately deferred to his daughter, and Laura informed the salesman that she wanted to find a sporty car for under $15,000. While she recognized that the salesman originally thought that her father was shopping for this car, she felt that when she told the salesman about *her* needs, it would become clear that *she* was the customer.

The salesman continued to address Mr. Thomas and suggested that he come into the showroom to look at an engine and check out the possible paint and upholstery combinations. Again Mr. Thomas emphasized that his daughter would be purchasing the car, and he mentioned that Laura had just been hired into a fast-track position at Procter & Gamble, to give her more credibility in the salesman's eyes. For the fifteen or twenty minutes that the Thomases talked to this salesman, Laura became increasingly upset because it seemed that she was not being taken seriously. She was unable to communicate her frustration to the salesman, and she remained silent since it seemed easier to let her father do the talking.

Laura knew that she was just comparison-shopping at this point, but she worried that it might be much more difficult in the final stages of decision making, when she wanted to talk about financing options. She discussed the situation with her father after they left the dealership, and he agreed that the salesman was not acting appropriately. Mr. Thomas advised her to write a letter to the salesman to inform him that he would be losing a sale due to his inappropriate behavior. Laura wanted to deal with the situation as tactfully as possible, so she decided to write two letters, one to the salesman himself, and one to the owner of the dealership.

Case Questions

1. Identify and discuss the communication barriers involved in this situation.
2. If you were in Laura's position, how would you have acted differently?
3. Write the letter to the salesman.
4. Write the letter to the owner of the car dealership.

Notes

1. Michelle Hiskey, "Error Led to Deadly Tower Fall," *The Atlanta Constitution*, October 25, 1995, A1.

2. Martha Eaton Maddox, "First-Line Managers/Supervisors/Perceptions and Business Communication Faculty's Perceptions of Communication Skills Needed by First-Line Managers/Supervisors," unpublished dissertation, University of Georgia, 1989.

3. Susan Harte, "Listening Up Helps Firms Move Ahead," *Atlanta Constitution*, February 12, 1990, B2.

4. Robert F. Gault, "Large Companies, Are You Listening?", *Management Review*, September 1994, 42.

5. Tom Peters and Nancy Austin, *A Passion for Excellence* (New York: Random House, 1985).

6. Jack Gordon, "Who Is Being Trained to Do What?" *Training*, October 1988, 55–61.

7. Andrew D. Wolvin and Carolyn Gwynn Coakley, "A Survey of the Status of Listening Training in Some Fortune 500 Corporations," *Communication Education*, April 1991, 152–164.

8. John W. Haas and Christa L. Arnold, "An Examination of the Role of Listening in Judgments of Communication Competence in Co-Workers," *The Journal of Business Communication*, April 1995, 123–138.

9. James J. Lynch, *The Language of the Heart: The Body's Response to Human Dialogue* (New York: Basic Books, 1985).

10. Ralph G. Nichols, *Successful Listening* (St. Paul, MN: Telstar, 1985).

11. *We Are Listening* (New Orleans: Spectra, 1989).

12. The review of listening research is based on the following work: Charles B. Petrie, Jr., "Informative Speaking: A Summary and Bibliography of Related Research," *Speech Monographs 30* (January 1963), 79–91. See also Lyman K. Steil, Larry L. Barker, and Kittie W. Watson, *Effective Listening: Key to Your Success* (Reading, MA: Addison-Wesley, 1983); Paul Kaufmann, *Sensible Listening: The Key to Responsive Interaction* (Dubuque, IA: Kendal/Hunt, 1993); and Steven Golen, "A Factor Analysis of Barriers to Effective Listening," *The Journal of Business Communication*, Winter 1990, 25–35.

13. Carl Rogers and Richard Farson, "Active Listening," in *Readings in Interpersonal and Organizational Communication*, 3d ed., eds. Richard Huseman, Cal Logue, and Dwight Freshley (Boston: Holbrook Press, 1977), 561–586.

Chapter 15

Nonverbal Communication

Learning Objectives

1
TO UNDERSTAND THE IMPORTANCE OF NONVERBAL BEHAVIOR IN THE COMMUNICATION PROCESS.

2
TO LEARN HOW PARALANGUAGE CAN AFFECT THE MESSAGE.

3
TO IMPROVE YOUR PERCEPTION OF BODY MOVEMENT IN NONVERBAL COMMUNICATION.

4
TO LEARN HOW SPACE IS USED TO COMMUNICATE.

5
TO RECOGNIZE THE IMPACT OF DRESS AND APPEARANCE, COLOR, AND TIME ON THOSE AROUND YOU.

Guest Speaker: *Thanks for inviting me to speak to you today about effective strategies for enhancing long-term growth of your stock market portfolio. I welcome the opportunity to talk with you members of the South Side Rotary Club and always enjoy sharing my financial expertise.*

Tyler: *That speaker is lying. Lying like crazy.*

Henry: *What are you talking about? He's a well-known expert on investments and what's more, he's barely started talking.*

Tyler: *He's barely started talking but he's lying. His voice is trembling. He's wringing his hands when he's not white-knuckling the podium or jingling the change in his pocket. He won't look us in the eyes and he's nervously pacing behind the podium. Henry, that speaker is scared stiff, even if he did say he was pleased to be here.*

Tyler's observations are examples of the many ways that nonverbal communication influences people every day.

More and more writers on the subject of business communication stress the importance of nonverbal communication. For example, in your resume you communicate not only with words that describe your education and experience, but also with the quality and color of paper your resume is typed on, the neatness of the typing, and similar nonverbal qualities. Although this text separately analyzes several aspects of nonverbal communication, in practice the verbal and nonverbal aspects of the message together comprise the total message that is communicated.

Chapter 2, on the nature of communication, was primarily concerned with **verbal communication**—the transferring of information through messages encoded in words. This chapter focuses on **nonverbal communication**—the transferring of information without relying on word meaning. Many authorities maintain that the nonverbal aspects of communication are the key to most ordinary communication. However, verbal and nonverbal communication usually occur together.

THE IMPORTANCE OF NONVERBAL COMMUNICATION

One authority, Albert Mehrabian, believes that words convey a very small part of the message. He argues that 93 percent of the total impact of any

TABLE 15.1 COMPARISON OF VERBAL AND NONVERBAL COMMUNICATION

Message Impact	Type of Communication
7 percent	Words
38 percent	Tone of voice and inflection
55 percent	Facial expression, body position, gestures

Source: Adapted from Albert Mehrabian, "Communication without Words," *Psychology Today 2* (September 1968): 53-55.

More than 90 percent of the message may be communicated nonverbally.

given message consists of nonverbal factors, as shown in Table 15.1. If you carefully analyze the messages that others communicate, it may surprise you how much emphasis is placed on the nonverbal aspects of communication.

Nonverbal communication usually occurs *with* verbal communication and always as part of a situation that gives context. Listeners should be cautious of placing too much importance on a single, isolated nonverbal cue until they have compared it to other nonverbal cues, to the verbal message, to the immediate situation, and to the larger environment and culture.

THREE MAJOR CATEGORIES OF NONVERBAL COMMUNICATION

Researchers divide nonverbal communication into three major categories. The first involves voice qualities. The other two are communication through body language and communication through space.

Paralanguage—How You Say It

Paralanguage can reinforce or undermine the verbal message.

Of the three major categories of nonverbal communication, **paralanguage** is most akin to verbal communication. Language deals with what is said; paralanguage deals with how it is said. To realize the importance of paralanguage you can perform a simple test. The next time a friend asks you to do something—for example, to go to a movie or to a particular restaurant for dinner—respond, "Sure, I would love to go," but let your tone of voice betray your words and convey that you have little or no interest in going. Watch the reaction of your friend to your response.

At times people mean to communicate a particular message through the use of paralanguage. For example, the phrase "I would like to help you" can convey several meanings, depending upon the paralanguage employed. Note the following types of emphasis:

- *I* would like to help you.
- I would *like* to help you.
- I would like to *help* you.
- I would like to help *you.*

In each case the emphasized word changes the meaning of the message.

Paralanguage voice qualities include rate, volume, rhythm, pitch, and resonance.

Paralanguage can be better understood by looking at voice qualities, including volume, rate, rhythm, pitch, and resonance. Everyone at one time or another has been made aware of the quality known as rate—how fast or slow someone is speaking. Depending on the other messages that are being communicated, an increase in rate could indicate anger, impatience, or anxiety from the person sending the message. A decrease in rate can indicate thoughtfulness or a reflective attitude; on the other hand, it can indicate boredom or lack of interest.

Volume is another voice quality that frequently conveys meaning, especially in conjunction with rate. If a supervisor said softly, "I would like to talk with you in my office," you might feel somewhat at ease. But if your supervisor said loudly, "I would like to talk with you in my office!" you would feel disturbed and ill at ease.

The qualities of rhythm, pitch, and resonance are more difficult to understand than rate and volume. When you consider voice qualities, the major point to note is a change or deviation from the speaker's normal voice quality. Noting differences in the sender's rhythm, pitch, and resonance can often increase your understanding of the message.

The voice qualities of rate, volume, pitch, and resonance in combination with vocal qualifiers cause paralanguage to become most apparent. Vocal qualifiers include intensity (overloud to oversoft), pitch height (overhigh to overlow), extent (extreme drawl to extreme clipping), and accent. Accent was demonstrated earlier by changing the emphasis on words in a sentence.

The major function of paralanguage is to express emotions. Several researchers have demonstrated that it is possible to communicate various emotions solely with paralanguage. In a foundation study, actors who read the following ambiguous text made sure that the meanings communicated were solely the result of vocal cues rather than vocabulary.

Paralanguage conveys emotion.

> You've got to believe it in time to keep them from hanging me. Every night you ask me how it happened. But I don't know! I don't know! I can't remember. There is no other answer. You've asked me that question a thousand times, and my reply has always been the same. It always will be the same. You can't figure things like that. They just happen, and afterwards you're sorry. Oh, God, stop them . . . quick . . . before it is too late![1]

The actors repeated the statement to 64 student judges and attempted to convey contempt, anger, fear, grief, and indifference. The study concluded that all emotions could be communicated. Average accuracy of identification for the five emotions was 88 percent for indifference, 84 percent for contempt, 78 percent for anger and grief, and 66 percent for fear.

Several more recent studies have demonstrated that paralanguage—how we say something—does convey emotions. These studies indicate that some emotions are more accurately transmitted than others. Frequently, it is easier to convey impatience, fear, and anger than satisfaction and admiration.

Kinesics—Communicating through Body Movement

The second major category of nonverbal communication is **kinesics,** which means communicating through body movement. The face and eyes are the most expressive means of body communication. Dale Leathers has found that 10 basic classes of meaning can be communicated by facial expression.[2]

The face and eyes convey 10 different types of meaning.

1. Happiness	**6.** Disgust
2. Surprise	**7.** Contempt
3. Fear	**8.** Interest
4. Anger	**9.** Bewilderment
5. Sadness	**10.** Determination

The ability to interpret facial meaning is an important part of communication, because facial expressions can facilitate or hamper feedback. Leathers developed the Facial Meaning Sensitivity Test (FMST). Part I of the FMST contains photographs representing the 10 basic classes of meaning. To test your ability to perceive facial expression, study the 10 photos in Figure 15.1, which were originally used in facial research many years ago, and match them with Leathers' list.[3]

Eye Contact

The eyes play an especially important role in facial communication. Eye contact is one of the most powerful forms of nonverbal communication. Authority relationships as well as intimate relationships are frequently initiated and maintained with eye contact. In the United States, looking directly at your listener is usually thought to convey openness and honesty; people usually believe it is easier to trust someone who looks right at them. On the other hand, they tend to distrust those who don't look directly at them; less confidence is attributed to those who avoid eye contact. Prolonged eye contact can signal admiration, while brief eye contact usually means anxiety. On the other hand, direct eye contact of more than 10 seconds can create some discomfort and anxiety. The especially unusual behavior most people exhibit on elevators—being quiet, avoiding physical and eye contact, and concentrating on the floor indicator numbers—can be fascinating to study.

Gesture

Another important element of kinesic communication is the use of gestures. The language of gesture is usually thought of as hand and arm movements, but the entire body is capable of gesture. Ekman and Friesen have identified five types of body gesture.[4]

Emblems. Emblems are thought of as sign language and are the equivalent of words or phrases. For example, the thumb and forefinger held in a circle say *OK.* The index and middle fingers held up in the form of a *V* indicate victory.

Illustrators. Directly tied to verbal language, these gestures illustrate the words a speaker is saying. When a speaker says, "My third and final point is . . . " and holds up three fingers, this gesture is an illustrator. When a baseball umpire calls someone out at home plate, he uses an illustrator as he points his thumb up and quickly jerks his hand upward.

Regulators. Regulators control oral communication by alerting the sender to the need to hurry up, slow down, or repeat something. Examples are frequent glances at your watch or drumming your fingers on the table when someone is talking with you.

Figure 15.1
Facial Meaning Sensitivity Test, Part 1
Source: Reprinted by permission from Dale Leathers, *Nonverbal Communication Systems* (Needham Heights, MA: Allyn & Bacon, 1976).

Affect Displays. These indicate emotional states, such as anger or embarrassment, and usually occur in facial expressions. Affect displays differ from the three previous types in that people have far less control over them. Many people, for example, have felt their faces turning red because they were angry or embarrassed, but there is little they can do to control this affect display.

Adaptors. These are another type of gesture over which people have little control. Frequently people are not conscious of performing such gestures. Stifling a yawn or clasping the hands to the face in fear are adaptor gestures.

Posture

A person's general posture, even without specific gestures, communicates meaning. Posture frequently gives clues to self-confidence or status. For example, superiors usually take a more relaxed posture than their subordinates.[5] Posture is also a way to demonstrate interest in another person. Several writers have concluded that when you lean forward to the person you are speaking with, you demonstrate interest in that person. Sitting back, on the other hand, may communicate a lack of interest (see Figure 15.2).

Posture of superiors and subordinates conveys meaning.

Movement Analysis

It is difficult to assess exactly how important gesture and posture are as modes of communication. Apparently gesture and posture are assuming more importance in organizational life. A London-based management consultant, Warren Lamb, has developed his business based on the idea that a person's posture and gesture can tell much about how effectively the person will perform in an organization. Lamb claims that his program, called **movement analysis**, represents a new branch of applied behavioral science.[6] Corporations hire Lamb to help in the selection and promotion of managers. He conducts his work by holding an interview session and watching for three types of body movements.

Side-to-Side Movements. These are most evident when a person shakes hands. This person moves the arm in a sideways, circular motion and occupies a lot of space when talking. Such an individual is an effective informer and listener—in short, an effective communicator. According to Lamb, this individual is best suited for companies seeking a sense of direction in their business ventures.

Some firms make selection decisions primarily on the basis of posture and gesture.

Forward and Backward Movements. These movements occur when an individual extends the hand straight forward when shaking hands and leans forward during an interview. The person using these forward and backward movements is described as an

Figure 15.2
Nonverbal Communication of Interest Level
Source: Photo by Reginald Wickham.

operator. Lamb would assign this type of person to an organization that needs a dramatic change or an infusion of energy.

Vertical Movements. These take place during the handshake, when the person using vertical movements draws himself or herself up to the tallest posture possible. According to Lamb, this individual is the master salesperson or presenter, an expert at selling himself or herself or the company.

No single gesture can always be accurately interpreted. However, Lamb asserts that the three categories of gesture—side to side, forward and backward, and vertical—enable him to identify and place executives where they will function most effectively.

Classification of Body Movements

Most people will not make their living the way Lamb does, but on a daily basis they need to understand what other people are communicating with their posture and gestures. Knapp has provided a useful scheme for classifying major types of body movements.[7] The following classifications are based primarily on Knapp's work.

Attitudes. Everyone likes or dislikes particular elements in the environment. Many times these attitudes are reflected in body movement. The degree of like or dislike can be seen in terms of general body orientation by noting if the communicator's legs and shoulders are turned toward or away from the other person. When the body is turned fully toward the other person, it may indicate liking, whereas the body turned away may indicate a degree of dislike.

Status. Individuals in superior roles or positions have status. They frequently keep their heads raised when communicating with others. Those in lower or subordinate roles often lower their heads and shoulders when speaking.

Affective States of Moods. These occur in various degrees of emotional conditions and are associated with body movements. The head and face convey information about anger, joy, and happiness; other body movements convey the intensity of the particular emotional state.

Approval Seeking. People may nod their heads and smile to secure approval from another person. In general, their bodies are more active than when they are not seeking approval. Frequently, this type of bodily activity can be observed by watching a subordinate present an idea to a superior.

Inclusiveness. Inclusiveness involves cues as to whose side you are on. The positioning of the body, especially the way the legs are pointed, will communicate, "I am on your side and not on their side." It can also indicate whether someone is open-minded to the other person's ideas.

Interaction Markers. Certain body movements naturally accompany particular oral language. Frequently, at the end of a statement a person will move the head, eyelids, or hands downward. At the end of questioning statements, these movements will tend to be upward. Other types of interaction markers include leaning back when listening and leaning forward when speaking.

AN ETHICAL DILEMMA

Recruiter: I'm not inviting Harold back for another office interview. There's something about him that isn't quite right. I don't trust him.

Manager: How can you say that? He has the best credentials of any of the applicants so far. In looking over your notes, you will surely find that he said the right things in the interview, too. What's the problem?

Recruiter: I can't pinpoint anything he said or did but I know he's not right for us. I've been a recruiter for 17 years and I can tell when there's something wrong. Harold made me uncomfortable by sitting too close, looking at me too much, things like that. I think he's a con man who's going to take advantage of us.

Manager: Is it ethical to reject an applicant simply because he makes you uncomfortable?

Recruiter: I gave you my reason—his behavior. We are going to call back only three candidates for the position, and I think at least three others are more deserving of a second look.

Manager: It's your decision, of course, but . . .

The recruiter feels boxed in. What would you do?

Questions

1. How much influence in a job interview do such nonverbal elements as smiles, clothing, eye contact, and handshakes have?

2. Do you think you could pick the best or worst job applicant from a pool of applicants based mainly on nonverbal communication? What would you look for?

3. How much of our intuition about other people is based on nonverbal communication?

4. When someone says one thing in words and sends contradictory nonverbal information, which do we believe? Why?

Although it is easy to oversimplify the classifications, you should realize that kinesic behavior affects the communication process. Having some basic understanding of how people communicate with their bodies will make you a more effective communicator.

Proxemics—Communicating with Space

The third major category of nonverbal communication is **proxemics**, or how people communicate with space. How close or far they stand in relation to another person, where they sit in a room, or how they arrange the office furniture has a real impact on communication. One of the major writers on this type of communication is anthropologist Edward T. Hall. He has identified three major types of space: feature-fixed space, semifixed feature space, and personal space.[8]

People use the space around them to communicate.

Feature-Fixed Space

Feature-fixed space refers to buildings and other fairly permanent structures, such as walls. The manner in which buildings are laid out and the sequence of rooms and offices have a considerable influence on communication. You will probably communicate more with those individuals whose offices are closer to rather than farther from yours.

Semifixed Feature Space

The placement and arrangement of movable objects, such as desks and chairs, is referred to as semifixed feature space. Currently a great deal of emphasis is placed on how business offices are arranged. Frequently, the superior person will come from behind the desk and sit face-to-face with the subordinate to make it easier to communicate.

Personal Space

Communication zones determine social interaction.

The physical distance people maintain in their encounters with others is known as personal space. Hall has suggested four different zones or distances for different types of social interaction:

- *Intimate distance* ranges from actual physical contact to about 18 inches from another person. Communication and interaction within this distance are intimate activities. In organizations confidential information is often communicated within the intimate distance. The major form of intimate contact in business organizations is, of course, the handshake. Most people respond positively to men who give a firm handshake and negatively to men who give a limp handshake. Men respond positively to women who have either a firm or limp handshake. Many women, however, do not respond positively to a firm handshake from another woman.
- *Personal distance* ranges from 18 inches to four feet. Interaction in this zone includes casual and friendly conversation.
- *Social distance* ranges from four feet to about eight feet. Communication in this zone often occurs in the business setting. Much of the communication in organizations is done at social distance. The attention a teacher gives primarily to the front and middle section of the classroom is a unique form of interaction.
- *Public distance* ranges from 12 feet to the limits of visibility and hearing. Communication at public distance is considered public speaking. A good deal of communication within and outside an organization takes place at this range.

The space people occupy in the organization communicates much about their status in the organization.

Everyone is aware of some of the ways space is used to communicate in business organizations. Goldhaber has identified three basic principles about the use of space as it relates to status within the organization.[9]

First, the higher people are in the organization, the more and better space they are allotted. In many organizations the president has the most attractive office, while the vice president, the department heads, and lesser employees have succeedingly smaller offices. The number of windows in the office and the way the office is furnished are also commensurate with rank or position.

Second, the higher people are in the organization, the better protected their territory is. Many times the more status a person has in the organization, the more difficult it is to see that person. Outer offices and secretaries often are used to protect the high-status person.

Third, the higher people are within the organization, the easier it is for them to invade the territory of lower-status personnel. The supervisor usually can enter the subordinate's office at will. The supervisor also has the ability to phone the subordinate at almost any time. However, the subordinate usually does not have this same access to the supervisor.

Photographs illustrating these principles are reproduced in Figure 15.3.

OTHER CATEGORIES

Some areas that receive less attention than the three major categories of nonverbal communication nevertheless play an important role in communication.

Figure 15.3
Nonverbal Communication of Status
Source: Photos by Reginald Wickham.

Dress and Appearance

Everyone has heard the cliche, "Clothes make the person." However, many people are not aware of the impact that clothing has on those around them. John Molloy, a consultant on executive dress with major corporations, has conducted several experiments to see what various types of clothing communicate.[10] In one of his studies Molloy compared the impact of black and beige raincoats. He took a set of twin pictures with only one variable: the pictures showed the same man in the same pose dressed in the same suit, the same shirt, the same shoes, the same tie. The only difference was the raincoat—one black, the other beige. Participants were told the pictures were of twin brothers and were asked to identify the more prestigious of the two brothers. Over 87 percent of the 1,362 people in the study chose the man wearing the beige raincoat as the more prestigious.

In another set of experiments Molloy found a group of 27 restaurants in New York where ties were not required. In each restaurant he asked the headwaiter to divide the dining room into the most preferred seating areas and least preferred areas. Those areas near the street door and near the kitchen door were considered to be the least preferable. Invariably there was a disproportionate number of men who were not wearing ties in the less preferable areas; in fact, almost no men without ties were seated in the more preferable areas.

Although these experiments are interesting, the basic question remains: does the way a person dresses communicate something to others in the organization? The impact of dress is placed in perspective by Molloy in his book, *The New Dress for Success:*

> Twelve years ago I surveyed one hundred top executives in either medium-sized or major American corporations about their attitude toward corporate dress. With updated pictures I reran the survey for this version of the book.
>
> The first series of questions was designed to establish the most up-to-date attitudes on corporate dress.
>
> I showed the executives five pictures of men, each of them wearing expensive, well-tailored, but high-fashion clothing. I asked if this was a proper look for the junior business executive. Ninety-two of the men said no, eight said yes.

Clothing communicates much about the wearer to others.

Top executives have an unwritten code for corporate dress.

I showed them five pictures of men neatly dressed in obvious lower-middle-class attire and asked if these men were dressed in proper attire for a young executive. Forty-six said yes, fifty-four said no.

I next showed them five pictures of men dressed in conservative upper-middle-class clothing and asked if they were dressed in proper attire for the young executive. All one hundred said yes.

I asked them whether they thought the men in the upper-middle-class garb would succeed better in corporate life than the men in the lower-middle-class uniform. Eighty-eight said yes, twelve said no.

I asked if they would choose one of the men in the lower-middle-class dress as their assistant. Ninety-two said no, eight said yes.[11]

Uniforms—such as bankers' clothes, nurses' outfits, or your interviewing outfit—transmit special messages. Outside the business world, clothing communicates as well. For example, T-shirts, which have been called the graffiti of the 1980s, often are used to show allegiance to a favorite rock group, to identify where the wearer spent a vacation, to publicize college, club, or fraternity affiliation, or just to say something to the world.

Clothing styles and appearance change with time and depend on context. And picking the appropriate clothes for the office is getting more difficult. Corporate dress codes are crumbling, "casual Fridays" are spreading,[12] and Ford Motor Company now allows its 80,000 worldwide employees to dress casually any day of the week.[13]

You might guess a man's military vocation, even out of uniform, by his short haircut. The jeans worn by working people for years took on a new and almost universal appeal with the advent of designer jeans in the early 1980s. Not too long ago business women, particularly in executive roles, were encouraged by both fashion and some experts to wear the corporate uniform of the three-piece suit. Shortly afterward, the three-piece suit was no longer recommended, because the appearance was perceived as an invasion of the man's world, rather than an effort by women to be accepted in the corporate world. Furthermore, the look was unnecessarily and inappropriately unfeminine.

Whether or not people are correct in their evaluation of the wearer, certainly most of them are aware of others' clothing. Most clothing decisions are not made on exclusively functional grounds.

You can test your "image IQ" by answering the following questions:

1. What is the most effective raincoat color?
2. For which professionals are bow ties acceptable—and often preferred—attire?
3. What tie color makes men look sexy?
4. Should today's executive wear pants with cuffs—or without them?
5. Are shirts with contrasting collars acceptable in conservative companies?
6. "Old money" Americans are most likely to distrust a man who (a) has disheveled hair, (b) is wearing a wrinkled suit, (c) is wearing shoes that are unshined or worn at the heels, (d) drives an old car.
7. Should suspenders always have button fasteners?
8. Should you wear stripes or solids if you are going to appear on television?
9. If you are a small man, will a dark, pinstripe suit make you look smaller and ineffective?

Answers appear at the bottom of the page.[14]

Answers: 1. beige 2. waiters, clowns, college professors, and commentators 3. bright red 4. with cuffs 5. Yes, Lee Iacocca made them acceptable. 6. (c) 7. yes 8. solids 9. No, with the right accessories it will do the opposite.

Color

The communication involved in the choice of color can be related to dress because color in clothing affects communication. Some evidence indicates that a relationship exists between specific moods and color. This relationship, in terms of color, mood, and frequency of times chosen, is illustrated in Table 15.2.

The colors around people affect them. In rooms with warm or hot colors, such as reds or oranges, people are likely to be more creative, stimulated, and prone to quick decisions. Rooms with cooler colors, such as blues, will likely engender solitude; slow, deep, and methodical thinking; and detachment.

Men and women often describe colors with different language. Men may describe objects as purple, blue, and yellow, whereas women might describe the same objects as fuchsia, robin's egg blue, and canary yellow.

Check the colors of a fast-food establishment, a church, and a classroom. There's a good chance that colors enhance the desired image or mind-set. If your classroom is devoid of color, that absence is probably not an accident but a carefully planned effort.

Color is related to particular moods.

Warm or hot colors engender quick decisions.

Mood Tone	Color	Frequency of Times Chosen
Exciting, stimulating	Red	61
Secure, comfortable	Blue	41
Distressed, disturbed, upset	Orange	34
Tender, soothing	Blue	41
Protective, defending	Red	21
	Brown	17
	Blue	15
	Black	15
	Purple	14
Despondent, dejected, unhappy, melancholy	Black	25
	Brown	25
Calm, peaceful, serene	Blue	38
	Green	31
Dignified, stately	Purple	45
Cheerful, jovial, joyful	Yellow	40
Defiant, contrary, hostile	Red	23
	Orange	21
	Black	18
Powerful, strong, masterful	Black	48

TABLE 15.2 MATCHING COLORS WITH MOODS

Source: L.B. Wexner, "The Degree to Which Colors (Hues) Are Associated with Mood-Tones," *Journal of Applied Psychology* 38 (1954): 432-435. Table from Mark L. Knapp, *Nonverbal Communication in Human Interaction*, 2nd ed. (Ft. Worth, TX: Holt, Rinehart and Winston, Inc., 1978).

Time

Being early, on time, or late communicates much in our society. Setting and meeting deadlines is also important. The employee who is habitually late for work and misses deadlines communicates very little interest in the job. Another observation about time is that individuals with high status are usually able to get appointments sooner and their meetings with superiors usually last longer. They wait less in the waiting room. High-status people usually have more flexible work hours. We even hear about banker's hours as the working day for individuals with higher status. Today, of course, bankers no longer keep banker's hours.

The amount of time taken to provide or receive feedback communicates a message.

Another way in which time communicates is the amount of time it takes to provide or receive feedback. For example, someone who responds too quickly to a written request may not have carefully considered the request. On the other hand, if a long period of time elapses with no response, the person who made the request may believe it is because of a lack of interest even though formal communication has not taken place.

Visual Design of Communication

Even the typeface you select for your business letter, and the way you deliver that typeface, says something about your company. Of course, the words carry content, but the visual impact of the typeface influences our reception of it. Typefaces can elicit such feelings as modern, old-fashioned, luxurious, powerful, or serious. Historically, decisions on typefaces for printed matter, such as advertisements or brochures, were made by graphic artists. The balance of business people used typewriters that had a common type appearance. Today's computers, printers, and down-loadable typefaces have placed type decisions in the hands of the user. Knowledge of type can help users who are not designers avoid the pitfalls of poor type selection.

Type Categories

Type falls into **serif, sans serif,** and decorative styles. Serif types have small counterstrokes on letters that can create a feeling of horizontal flow and unity within word groupings. Often the width of individual serif letters varies (see Table 15.3). A sans serif type does not have serifs and typically the stroke of each letter is the same.

Both serif and sans serif typefaces are commonly used in business for body type and headings. Decorative types, however, are more likely used in specialized printing applications, such as wedding invitations or advertisements.

✔ CHECKLIST for Effective Use of Type

____ Use all capital letters judiciously.

____ Keep line length to about 12–14 words or 40–60 characters.

____ Select a serif typeface for wide lines.

____ Consider a ragged-right margin; flush right margins can create unusual spacing between words or too many hyphenated words.

____ Match the typeface to the content.

____ Limit the number of different typefaces in a document to two.

____ When in doubt about type treatments or selections, be conservative.

Type Qualities

In selecting a typeface, four qualities should be considered: legibility, readability, congeniality, and visual appeal.[15] Legibility is affected by type design (thick/thin, tall/short letters, large/small serifs), type size, and type style (italics, shadow, bold). Sans serif typefaces tend to be more legible.

Readability relates to the ease with which we can read wide blocks of type. The wider the line of type, the more serif typefaces are preferred. Lines too short or too long hinder readability, as does too little or too much space between words, too large a block of all-capitals, or a size that is too small or too large.

Congeniality is the connection between the meaning and the appearance of the words, and may even be a consideration when an organization interested in establishing a corporate identity selects its "standard" typeface. Match an

TABLE 15.3   SAMPLE TYPEFACES

Serif Types:	Comment:
New Century Schoolbook	Clean, easy to read
Courier	Typewriter appearance, legal-looking
Joulliard	Squarish, formal
Palatino	Roundish, modern
Times Roman	One of the most widely used fonts, faxes well, conservative
Sans-Serif Types:	**Comment:**
ANNA	AFFECTED, ALL CAPS, HARD TO READ, UNUSUAL
Helvetica	Clean, light, modern, widely used; faxes well
Avant Garde	Similar to Helvetica, but wider
Revue	**Dark, heavy, best for only a few words at a time**

annual report's delivery of disappointing financial information with a somber type, for example.

Blocks of type may have visual appeal if there is appropriate contrast and white space, as well as fit and suitability, between different typefaces.

If your organization follows a standard approach to its written documents, of course follow those guidelines. In the absence of such guidelines, avoid too much variation in type treatments and err on the conservative side. Use good judgment and a sense of aesthetics in your decisions.[16]

THE IMPACT OF COMBINED CATEGORIES

So far this chapter has looked at individual ways that nonverbal information is communicated. There are also occasions when categories are grouped and create nonverbal impact.

Power

Nonverbal indicators of power are prevalent in the business world. How you perceive others' indicators, react to those indicators, and pick indicators for yourself may have substantial impact on your business career.

In addition to using clothing for power, people adorn themselves with other power indicators, some of which may serve as clues to wealth or judgment as well. These three clues—power, wealth, and judgment—may stand alone but they often overlap and reinforce one another. For example, while you may be aware of a man's expensive cologne, you may also be offended by it. Conversely, you are likely to be impressed by a person in well-coordinated attire, with expensive but not gaudy accessories.

Examples of power indicators can be found in all of the nonverbal categories, such as standing tall, using expansive gestures, speaking in a loud voice, taking large strides, using a firm handshake, and looking away or walking while others talk. Physical examples of power with which people surround themselves are recognition plaques, memberships in honorary or exclusive organizations, photos of powerful people, large and well-appointed offices, and private secretaries.

Often people are only slightly aware of power symbols, but they are still cognizant of the presence of power and adjust their behavior. The high-status individual who does not have to face you but whose eyes you try to contact, even if you must back out of the person's presence, is establishing or exercising power.

People who know when, where, and with whom to use power symbols and actions can positively affect how others see and react to them. At all levels in the business world power is present; clearly some use it and others abuse it. Skillful understanding of the intricacies of nonverbal power can pay rich rewards.

The Professional Image

Some business people stand out in a crowd. They appear confident, attractive, well-dressed, personable, and in control. In short, some people transmit a professional image. They accomplish this through careful manipulation of what they write and say supported by effective nonverbal behavior.

In Control

People who are confident and in control are not afraid to look others in the eyes. Whether men or women, they often initiate firm handshakes. They speak up, aware that a strong voice suggests authority. They have something to say and, when opinions are sought, share theirs. Studies suggest that those who initiate conversations and who talk the most are seen as leaders, even when the content may be weak.

Well-Dressed

Traditional and conservative clothes are safe for most jobs.

Business people with a professional image dress meticulously, making sure that clothes are clean, pressed, and fit well; shoes are shined; and jewelry is tasteful. They avoid both fads and the appearance of being out-of-date. Traditional and conservative clothes are safe for most jobs and a professional image requires the best clothes the wearer can afford. Colors should enhance body color and size and, if possible, suggest power.

Attractive

A professional image demands good posture. It means avoiding negative images from perspiration, from too-strong perfume or after-shave cologne, or from strong foods. Conversely, appropriate perfumes and after-shave lotions, fresh-smelling hair, or the imagery brought about by the smell of a leather briefcase can be positive. A professional image may require enlisting help in caring for hair and nails.

Personable

Those with a professional image know that gestures suggest vibrancy and activity and that positive facial expressions are noticed—and are usually desirable.

THE MODIFYING OF NONVERBAL COMMUNICATION

People are taught, over many years, how to manipulate verbal communication. Some become quite adept at lying with words. However, few can manipulate their nonverbal behavior much beyond such obvious changes as clothing or the surrounding environment. If they are experiencing stage fright, for example, they find it hard to turn off nonverbal messages of perspiration, white knuckles, or a cracking voice.

People receive little practice or instruction in how to modify nonverbal communication, which makes the application of nonverbal communication to public presentations and speech making very important. Although speakers have little control over emotions that present themselves in recognizable nonverbal patterns, they can modify their behavior somewhat.

Here are some nonverbal behaviors associated with effective oral presentations, with some suggestions for overcoming nonverbal problems:

- A relaxed speaker tends to gesture, but not too much. A nervous speaker either avoids gestures and movement or tends to overdo it.
- The confident speaker does not show perspiration. The nervous speaker might consider dressing in light-weight clothes so as not to start out too warm.
- Visual contact with the audience enhances a presentation. This visual contact also scares many speakers. One well-known approach is to avoid direct eye contact by looking just above the eyes of your audience. Then, as you become more confident, you can work to effective direct eye contact. A similar technique for eye contact is to try to talk to and look at the audience one by one. Try not to think of the large group, but rather engage a person on one side of the room for a few seconds, then look at a person in the middle, and then one on the other side of the room. Most effective speakers use this technique not so much to overcome nervousness, but more for a personal touch.
- Effective voice control affects the impact of a speech greatly. An over-rehearsed speech often comes out in a monotone no matter how enthusiastic the speaker. On the other hand, an ill-prepared speaker is likely to exhibit the cracking voice, gasping, or swallowing that we associate with nervousness. Try to pace yourself in terms of speed. A speaker who lacks confidence is likely to change delivery speed by either speeding up or slowing down. Aim for a normal delivery rate.
- Hands and fingers are not obtrusive for the confident speaker; they tend to shake for the nervous speaker. This shaking is amplified many times over if you point with a pencil at a transparency during overhead projector use. If you plant your pencil solidly on the film, you won't shake.
- Some effective speakers move around behind the podium somewhat, but usually not much. Beware of the speaker's shuffle. This side-to-side balancing often can be overcome if you remember to put one foot forward and one backward diagonally.

> ✔ *CHECKLIST for a Professional Image*
>
> ____ Look people in the eyes.
> ____ Give a firm handshake.
> ____ Speak with a strong voice.
> ____ Avoid reticence.
> ____ Dress meticulously.
> ____ Do not slump or slouch.
> ____ Pay attention to cleanliness and neatness.
> ____ Allow yourself to gesture.
> ____ Smile.

An over-rehearsed speech is often delivered in a monotone.

THE MEASURING OF NONVERBAL FEEDBACK

Many instruments measure nonverbal communication and nonverbal behavior, but they are usually focused on a specific category, such as the FMST to measure facial expressions. An approach to measuring a larger portion of the nonverbal experience—and even the verbal message—is Leathers' Nonverbal Feedback Rating Instrument (LNFRI).[17] This instrument uses 10 semantic differential scales to measure a person, event, or behavior. Photographs may be used to depict the ends of the scales and to guide the novice evaluator, as shown in Figure 15.4. The LNFRI "provides the user with detailed information about the feedback to his own communication that suggests (1) whether any corrective action should be taken and (2) what types of corrective actions should be taken."[18]

The semantic differential approach yields a wealth of information. For example, a person's nonverbal behavior can be viewed as predominately positive or negative

Figure 15.4

Nonverbal Feedback Rating Instrument
Source: Adapted from Dale Leathers, *Nonverbal Communication Systems* (Needham Heights, MA: Allyn & Bacon, 1976), 24.
Photo source: Reginald Wickham.

depending on which half of the scale is checked. The behavior can also be compared to similar evaluations from another time period, thus showing change over time.

Three dimensions in a grouping of semantic differential scales are evaluation, potency, and activity. A person might be measured as being good (evaluation), offering potential (potency), and being passive (activity). When respondents react to a series—usually at least 10—of semantic differential scales, they will probably note that some of the scales are similar and that they answer those scales in about the same way. Using the LNFRI, we might evaluate an individual similarly on the attentive/unattentive scale, the responsive/unresponsive scale, and on the interested/disinterested scale. The grouping of these three scales broadens our understanding of the evaluation. Even clearer conclusions can be drawn through application of various statistical techniques.

Key Terms

- **verbal communication**
- **nonverbal communication**
- **paralanguage**
- **kinesics**
- **movement analysis**
- **proxemics**
- **serif**
- **sans-serif**

Summary

Paralanguage   p. 382

Kinesics   p. 383

Proxemics   p. 387

Dress and appearance   p. 389

Color   p. 391

Time   p. 392

Visual design of communication   p. 392

Power   p. 393

The professional image   p. 394

Modifying nonverbal communication   p. 394

Measuring nonverbal communication   p. 395

Review Questions

1. Why do nonverbal messages play such a critical role in communication?
2. How can paralanguage reinforce or undermine the verbal message?
3. Cite examples of how facial expressions attach emotional meaning to our messages.
4. In what ways is gesture an important means of kinesic communication?
5. How can posture provide clues to the self-confidence or status of a person in a business organization?
6. How is space used as a communication device?
7. In what ways might your dress and appearance and the way you handle time impress your business colleagues?
8. In using your computer to prepare a business letter, what typeface characteristics should be considered?
9. Can you think of an example of nonverbal business behavior from each of the following categories: music, kinesics, posture, proxemics, time, paralinguistics, animal

communication, clothing, body beautification, tactile communication, taste, smell, human-machine communication?

Exercises

1. Identify some nonverbal rules, such as books and a coat in a library chair marking a person's territory. Then break the rule, in this case by moving the books and coat and sitting in the chair.

2. Observe and record people's behavior in elevators. List as many nonverbal behavior patterns as you can. Compare these patterns to those of people using escalators. What are the differences? Why do you think these differences exist?

3. Most of us feel comfortable in a classroom and think little about its nonverbal aspects. Identify the nonverbal patterns of students and instructors in typical classrooms.

4. What is the appropriate dress and appearance in a typical business setting? How much can you vary from this standard without being penalized?

5. What are the nonverbal aspects of music? Does music create different moods in different people at different times? How? Give examples. How is music used in business?

6. Observe the proxemic behaviors of people in a room, such as a classroom or cafeteria. Do some sit or stand closer together than others? Why do you think this is? Can you categorize those people who are alone? Are there proxemic behavior differences by age or sex?

7. Observe members of another culture. What nonverbal things do they do differently from you? Are there differences in tone of voice (even if you don't understand the language), clothing, spacial differences between sender and receiver, or eye contact?

8. Many speakers of a romance language, such as Spanish or Italian, prefer to be closer to their listener than is comfortable for Americans. Test this theory by visiting with a person whose primary language and culture are from a romance country.

C A S E

The Telephone Answering Machine

Marcia Mascolini, Western Michigan University

Andy Smith runs Andy's Plumbing Service out of his home. His business is small and he does not have a secretary. Instead, he uses an answering machine on the family telephone to accept messages from customers when he is out on a call and his wife is at work. Andy believes that the answering machine is a necessity for anyone who runs a one-person operation like his; however, he is not happy with the recorded customer calls that he has been receiving.

This is the greeting, recorded by Andy's wife, that customers hear when they call Andy's number: "Hello. You've reached the Smiths'. When you hear the tone, please leave your message. We'll get back to you as soon as we can."

These are 10 typical calls recorded on the answering machine:

- Hi, Andy. This is Dave. Call me back when you get a chance.

- (no message)

- Hello . . . . Um. I'm having trouble . . . . You know that new pipe you put in the basement last week? The cold water pipe? Well, I think something's wrong with it. It looks sort of funny. I'm really worried. Should I shut off the water? I can't shut off the water because I just put a load of clothes in, and the kids are all home from school sick. I don't know what to do. It's getting wet, sort of dripping. I'm over on Main Street, the white house on the corner. Please come over as soon as you can.

- (no message)
- (no message)
- (no message)
- Hello? Andy's Plumbing? Please call me at 555-1212. Thanks.
- -2325. Please call this evening after 6 P.M.
- (no message)
- Hi, Andy. You were right about the faucet that you said was going to go out on me. It went. Give me a call when you get a chance. It's Charlie Ensminger. Call me at work if it's before five.

Case Questions

1. Analyze the greeting on Andy's phone. What specific suggestions could you give for improving it:?

2. What do you think accounts for the large number of calls that people place without leaving messages?

3. Analyze the messages people have left on Andy's answering machine. Why would each one cause Andy additional work?

4. If you had a plumbing problem that you wanted Andy to fix, what specific message would you leave to ensure his speedy response?

CASE

Body Language

Mildred W. Landrum, Kennesaw College

Mike Thornton was seething. Every time it looked as if he had finally straightened out his production supervisor, Steve Perkins, Steve managed to blow another situation with one of the workers. This time the worker had walked out, and the line had to be slowed down while a replacement was found.

This was a critical time for Mike. The vice president in charge of production was coming from New York for an inspection tour of the southeastern plant, and Mike wanted everything to go right. His future with the corporation depended on it.

For the third time he called in Steve to talk with him. Steve had better understand this time that he was really in trouble. Twelve years with the corporation gave Steve seniority, and the union would be difficult to handle if Mike fired Steve. Mike had to be sure Steve was impressed with the seriousness of the situation.

When the secretary buzzed Mike that Steve was in the waiting room, Mike said, "Let him cool his heels." Fifteen minutes later he asked Steve to come into the office. Mike did not raise his head and greet Steve nor did he rise to shake hands as he would normally have done. Steve stood at his desk several moments before Mike looked up and said, "Sit down." The telephone rang, and Mike talked five minutes before putting down the receiver. He then turned to Steve, folded his arms, leaned back, and said, "Well, tell me about this one."

Steve was upset by the extremely negative attitude he felt from Mike. He dropped his eyes, lifted his hands in a hopeless gesture, and said, "Well, what can you do with some of these guys who think they know everything?"

Case Questions

1. Describe the negative nonverbal messages Mike sent to indicate his displeasure with Steve.

2. Describe the submissive nonverbal messages Steve sent to Mike.

3. Suggest a positive movement for each negative movement named in this interaction.

References

Leathers, Dale G. *Successful Nonverbal Communication Principles and Applications.* New York: Macmillan, 1986.

Malandro, Loretta A., and Larry L. Barker. *Nonverbal Communication.* Reading, MA: Addison-Wesley, 1983.

Parker, R.C. *Looking Good in Print.* Chapel Hill, NC: Ventana Press, 1990.

Rubinstein, Ruth P. *Dress Codes—Meanings and Messages in American Culture.* Boulder, CO: Westview Press, 1995.

Notes

1. G. Fairbanks and W. Pronovost, "An Experiment Study of the Durational Characteristics of the Voice during the Expression of Emotion," *Speech Monographs* 6 (1939): 88.

2. Dale Leathers, *Nonverbal Communication Systems* (Needham Heights, MA: Allyn & Bacon, 1976), 24.

3. These facial expressions portray: I, disgust; II, bewilderment; III, happiness; IV, determination; V, fear: VI; anger; VII, surprise; VIII, interest; IX, contempt; and X, sadness.

4. Paul Ekman and Wallace V. Friesen, "The Repertoire of Nonverbal Behavior: Categories, Origins, Usage, and Coding," *Semiotics* 1 (1969): 63-92.

5. Randall Harrison, *Beyond Words: An Introduction to Nonverbal Communication* (Englewood Cliffs, NJ: Prentice-Hall, 1974), 132-133.

6. Jean Ross-Skinner, "Those Telltale Executive Gestures, "*Dun's Review,* March 1970, 66-67.

7. Mark Knapp, *Nonverbal Communication in Human Interaction,* 2d ed. (New York: Holt, Rinehart and Winston, 1978), 220-232.

8. Edward T. Hall, *The Hidden Dimension* (New York: Doubleday, 1966).

9. Gerald M. Goldhaber, *Organizational Communication,* 4th ed. (Dubuque, IA: William C. Brown, 1986), 202-206.

10. John T. Molloy, *Dress for Success* (New York: Peter Wyden, 1975).

11. John T. Molloy, *The New Dress for Success*, rev. ed. (New York: Warner Books, 1988), 27–28.

12. Teri Agins, "Between Suits and Jeans: The Corporate Casual Look," *The Wall Street Journal*, January 21, 1994, B-1.

13. "Casual Attire Is in at Ford Headquarters," *The Atlanta Journal/The Atlanta Constitution*, December 30, 1994, S2.

14. John T. Molloy, *The New Dress for Success*, rev. ed. (New York: Warner Books, 1988), i. Reprinted with permission.

15. Robin Williams, *How to Boss Your Fonts Around* (Berkeley, CA: Peachpit Press, 1994).

16. Williams.

17. Leathers, *Nonverbal Communication Systems*, 214-220.

18. Leathers, 215.

Chapter 16
Public Presentations

Learning Objectives

1

TO RECOGNIZE THE VALUE OF DEVELOPING EXCEPTIONAL PUBLIC PRESENTATION SKILLS.

2

TO UNDERSTAND THE NECESSITY FOR DEVELOPING A GENERAL AND SPECIFIC PURPOSE FOR EACH SPEECH.

3

TO APPRECIATE THE SIGNIFICANCE OF ESTABLISHING CREDIBILITY WITH THE AUDIENCE WHILE MEETING THEIR NEEDS.

4

TO LEARN THE ADVANTAGES OF USING VARIOUS METHODS OF ORGANIZING AND DELIVERING SPEECHES.

5

TO IDENTIFY TECHNIQUES THAT MINIMIZE THE IMPACT OF STAGE FRIGHT ON THE SPEAKER.

6

TO PRACTICE THE SYSTEMATIC APPROACH AND THUS LEARN TO GIVE A SUPERIOR PUBLIC PRESENTATION.

Taylor Collins's least favorite course in college was public speaking. He just couldn't seem to catch on. In preparation for a speech, he would conduct meticulous research, prepare a well-organized report, and then attempt to memorize it. He usually went over the information many times and tried to pack as many facts as possible into the allotted time. The more he went over the speech the more compact it became. To Taylor the goal was to give the audience as much information as possible. After all, the point of speech making was sharing information.

He went through the semester refining his technique, but his grades did not improve. This was particularly distressing for Taylor, a straight-A student, whose grades in public speaking were average or below average. Unfortunately, Taylor did not have a breakthrough before the class ended and wound up with a low grade. Taylor decided that he would just have to avoid public speaking in the future as he had no aptitude for it.

The next semester, Taylor was required to attend a series of professional lectures. The quality varied. Some were truly inspiring while others were deadly dull. Taylor wondered what the distinguishing characteristic was. All of the speakers were experts in their respective fields. They spoke intelligently and authoritatively, but there was a difference.

Slowly it dawned on Taylor. The effective speakers were conversational and emotionally involved with the audience. They weren't just spewing data at the audience; a connection had to be established first. Then the speech had to be given at a pace that a first-time listener could absorb. Speaking is a different form of communication from writing. A reader has the luxury of rereading a particularly dense passage and varying the speed at which he or she reads. However, during a speech the speaker has control and, therefore, must be sensitive to the audience. If they don't get it the first time, there's no second chance.

A survey of 2,500 Americans indicated that over 40 percent of those surveyed feared speaking before a group.[1] All 2,500 were shown a long list of items and asked to indicate which ones they were afraid of. The 10 items picked most often were:

- Speaking before a group   40.6%
- Height   30.0
- Insects   22.1

- Financial problems   22.0
- Deep water   21.5
- Sickness   18.8
- Death   18.7
- Flying   18.3
- Loneliness   13.6
- Dogs   11.2

The surprise is not that many people fear giving public speeches, but that the fear is so widespread. Since today's workforce is more sophisticated than it was when the survey was conducted, you might suspect that the fear of public speaking has diminished in significance. A recent national survey conducted by Dial Soap, however, should dash any such suspicions. The "Big Sweat" poll of 1,000 adults revealed that both males and females, regardless of age, income level, or region of the country, find the prospect of giving a public speech to be more frightening than any other activity. It was ranked first by 45 percent of the males and 53 percent of females, and it was the only stressful situation on which both sexes agreed on the ranking. Here are some of the other "sweaty situations":[2]

Females	**Males**
Interviewing for a job (43%)	Getting married (44%)
Going to the dentist (39%)	Interviewing for a job (44%)
Winning the lottery (39%)	Getting divorced (35%)
Getting married (38%)	A first date (34%)
A first date (32%)	

A systematic approach may reduce some of the uncertainties associated with public speaking.

Such fear can be overcome by learning to apply a systematic approach to the process of public speaking. Approaching the problem systematically removes much of the apprehension by replacing the uncertainty with a plan.

THE ROLES OF THE SPEAKER

Public speaking encompasses many aspects of people's lives. Over the years your public presentation skills will influence how well you function in your roles as an individual, an organization person, and a member of society.

The Individual

When you apply for a job, the employment interviewer evaluates you on the basis of certain characteristics. Your ability to communicate is one characteristic, and it comes across clearly in an interview. Employers realize that the ability to communicate often separates an exceptional employee from the average ones. Two recent surveys of employers identified communication skills and interpersonal skills as the most important nontechnical skills sought when hiring new employees.[3]

Being able to organize and present your thoughts is a significant determinant of your personal and professional success. When you speak and others listen and respond to your

Public speaking ability has a major influence on personal and professional success.

Figure 16.1
Identify These Top Motivational Speakers for Corporate Audiences
Source: (Photo 4): Jerry Wachter Photography Ltd.; (Photo 5): Michael Ponzini. All photos courtesy of Focus on Sports.

1

Bonnie Blair

2

Pat Riley

3

Dan Jansen

4

Mary Lou Retton

5

Greg Gumbel

comments, it affects the way you see yourself and how others see you. Being able to give an effective public speech enhances your self-esteem; you feel good about yourself.

Your message is more likely to be accepted if you have credibility with your audience. Source credibility pertains to both oral and written communication. Your credibility as a speaker and as a person will be recognized to the extent that you are perceived as expert, trustworthy, dynamic, objective, and well-intentioned.

The Organization Spokesperson

An organization, it has been said, is only as good as the individuals who comprise it. It might also be said that an organization communicates only as effectively as its individual members do. Business needs people who can effectively present the organizational viewpoint to the public. The average business organization does a poor job of acquainting the public with its contributions to society.

There have always been exceptions. For example, when Robert Blake entered a management training program 24 years ago, very little set him apart from the other trainees in terms of educational background and technical ability. However, he soon displayed a superior ability to organize his thoughts and to express himself. At the end of the training program he was awarded the choicest job assignment ever given to a trainee. Today he is president of the company. He recognizes the importance of technical ability, but as he sees it, "Unless a person is able to transmit information to others in a well-organized and convincing way, that person is likely to remain a technician—and a mediocre one at that."

From a communication standpoint it does not matter how pure the motives of the organization are. What does matter is what the public knows about such things and how the public responds to this knowledge. Unless the public is made aware of what business is doing and why, the best intentions of business will be to no avail.

Only through effective external communication can business present the information that is most likely to result in a desirable image. One of the most important and effective formats used to present that information is the public speech.

> ✔ *CHECKLIST for Establishing Credibility*
>
> ____ Be knowledgeable about your subject and well-prepared to speak. (expertise)
>
> ____ Develop and maintain a reputation for telling the truth. (trust)
>
> ____ Display an urge to communicate through your genuine involvement with both subject and audience. (dynamism)
>
> ____ Be open-minded to the views of others. (objective)
>
> ____ Be considerate of the feelings of others. (goodwill)

The Member of Society

The free expression of ideas is not merely tolerated but is encouraged in the United States. Issues are analyzed and points of view are presented in many different formats. Newspaper editorials, listener call-in shows on radio, town hall meetings, barroom discussions (or arguments), and now the Internet are a few ways in which opinions are shared.

A democratic society thrives on the free expression of ideas, for it is through such interchange that a balanced perspective is maintained. When a certain point of view ceases to be expressed, perhaps for the lack of someone willing and able to speak out, that viewpoint no longer influences society.

Through public speaking ideas are presented for public evaluation. This was as true in the preliminaries to the Declaration of Independence as it is today in election campaigns. It is as evident at an annual meeting of stockholders as at the monthly meeting of a local union.

For lack of an effective speaker a good idea may fail to be considered. A lack of articulate opponents may result in the passage of legislation of little merit. Our free society requires willing and articulate people of every viewpoint.

THE PURPOSES OF THE SPEECH

Many speakers seem unable or unwilling to determine in advance the purposes of their speech. Consequently, the response of listeners is likely to be:

- "I'm not sure exactly what he meant."
- "I couldn't find any point to the speech."
- "I don't know what she was getting at."
- "What was the purpose of the speech anyway?"

In planning a speech you should first decide what its purposes will be. This is a two-step process: determine first the general purpose and then the specific purpose.

General Purpose

Most authorities recognize three general purposes in public speaking: to inform, to persuade, and to entertain. Although the three general purposes are usually considered as if they were separate and distinct, that is not actually true. Very few speeches are

The three general purposes of public speaking are to inform, to persuade, and to entertain.

entirely informative, persuasive, or entertaining. Most speeches are a combination of two or more.

Informative

When you try to teach your listeners or to explain something to them, your general purpose is to inform. The classroom lecture is an example of an **informative speech**. Some informative speeches are intended to acquaint the listeners with something completely new to them. When Brenda White, a personnel director, explains to a group of new employees the company's benefits program, she is doing just that. Some informative speakers try to update listeners who are already somewhat knowledgeable about a subject. To give another specific example, when officers of credit unions attend the regional meeting of their trade association, they hear many informative speeches.

Persuasive

The second general purpose is to persuade the listener. **Persuasive speeches** range from those that seek to change the listener's beliefs or attitudes to those that attempt to get the listeners to act in a certain way.

The purpose for giving a persuasive speech is to elicit a covert response or an overt response. A **covert response** is, as the word implies, not readily apparent to the speaker or to an observer. When a union leader seeks to convince the members that the union has their interests at heart, the speaker is seeking a covert response, acceptance of an idea. It is usually difficult to evaluate a speaker's effectiveness when the response being sought is covert.

Evaluating a speaker's effectiveness is easier when the speaker is seeking an **overt response**, one that is observable and measurable. The manager who tries to get billing clerks to reduce their errors can check future error counts for evidence of effectiveness. The production manager who urges increased output from production workers can also measure results easily. In each of these specific examples, the speaker is seeking an overt response.

> Measuring effectiveness is easier with an overt response than with a covert response.

Entertaining

The third general purpose is to entertain—the response sought from the listeners is enjoyment. Many persons consider entertainment and humor to be synonymous, but that is not the case. Humor is certainly a common ingredient of entertainment, but it is not the only one. Perhaps you have had a teacher who thoroughly entertained and captivated the class with little or no humor. Others are able to entertain through their flair for drama or through their picturesque language.

Specific Purpose

The number of specific purposes for making a presentation is virtually infinite. The specific purpose of a speech is constructed with both the subject and the audience in mind.

The following examples suggest the relationship among subject, audience, general purpose, and specific purpose.

- *Subject:* The collection of delinquent accounts
- *Audience:* A class of undergraduate students of business administration
- *General purpose:* To inform
- *Specific purpose:* To explain techniques commonly used by business organizations to collect past-due bills from customers.

- *Subject:* The collection of delinquent accounts
- *Audience:* Professional association of collection officers
- *General purpose:* To inform

BOXED IN

AN ETHICAL DILEMMA

You are head of sales for a corporation that manufactures dyes for the textiles industry. Although you have worked extremely hard your whole career, you have learned through the grapevine that your performance over the last few years has been questioned due to declining company sales.

A large contract has just been tentatively agreed to with Elegante Inc., an international men's high-quality clothing manufacturer that is diversifying into the casual clothing market. This would be a ten-year contract that would result in a minimum increase of three times your present annual sales. Not only will this contract bring you job security and a possible promotion, it will result in a year end bonus for you of well over $100,000.

All details have been worked out, but the Board of Directors of Elegante would like you to give them a brief presentation on how the chemical by-products from the dyeing process will be disposed. Your company has received permission to bury the waste of this nature in steel drums on site, and the cost is well within their budget. As an expert in the industry, you know this is the only economically feasible method of disposal. The next cheapest alternative would push costs of manufacturing much higher. That alternative would entail a more expensive dyeing process using environmentally friendly dyes. You know that your company will not be breaking any laws by dumping on site, but you also know that within fifty years these drums will probably begin to leak and contaminate groundwater. This will result in lawsuits and cleanup costs that could bankrupt your company. Since Elegante has a record of concern for the environment, you think that its management would probably decide to use the more expensive, environmentally friendly dyeing process if you informed them of the possible future ramifications, but you also know that a loss of this contract would mean a loss of your job.

You feel boxed in. What would you do?

- *Specific purpose:* To explain the latest approaches for collection of delinquent accounts.

- *Subject:* Use of nuclear energy for generating electrical power
- *Audience:* Approximately 100 members of a neighborhood homeowners association
- *General purpose:* To persuade
- *Specific purpose:* To persuade listeners to write their senators and representatives to express their opposition to increased reliance on nuclear energy.

These examples indicate that, while the general purpose may remain the same, the specific purpose will vary according to the audience.

RESEARCH FOR THE SPEECH

Audience Analysis

The more the speaker can learn about the audience in advance, the more appropriate the speech should be. To illustrate, Congressman Lilburn was invited to address the

Wilbanks Employees Association. Seeking reelection, he was happy for the opportunity to promote his campaign theme, which was economy in government. He arrived at the auditorium barely in time. He spoke with vigor and emotion about the Social Security system and the absurdity of it. The audience numbered nearly 200, but only two people asked questions, and both were hostile. Had the congressman bothered to do research on the association in advance, he would have learned that most of the active members are retired employees.

A common shortcoming among speakers is a tendency to assume that what they find interesting will also interest their listeners. To be a good speaker you must adopt a **listener orientation.** When preparing a speech, ask yourself how you would feel if you were in the listener's place. Before being able to answer that, you must learn as much about your listeners as possible. This necessitates asking some basic questions immediately:

* How large will the audience be?
* How educated are the listeners?
* What occupations will be represented?
* What is the age range represented?
* To which social, political, or religious groups do the listeners belong?

The best way to analyze an audience is to talk personally with the group you will address. Ideally, you would accomplish this far enough in advance to give you ample time to tailor the material to the listeners. Unfortunately, this is an unrealistic approach to audience analysis—in most cases it would be difficult, time consuming, and impractical.

A satisfactory alternative is to talk to several people who are likely to be in the audience. Assuming that they are similar to the rest of the audience members, you will get accurate insights into the interests of your listeners. When it is not possible to talk with a likely member of the audience or even to talk with anyone familiar with the audience, you face a challenge. You will have to make some inferences about the audience from the information that is available.

The more similar your listeners are in terms of such factors as educational level, occupation, age, and group memberships, the easier it is to predict their attitudes toward you and your message. The more heterogeneous or diversified the audience is, the fewer inferences you can make about your listeners.

The audience for a business presentation is generally knowledgeable about the speaker's topic. Because the audience members are similar in interests, knowledge, and background, the speaker can make certain assumptions about them. As in any speaking situation, however, advance audience analysis is also important in making a business presentation.

Topic Research

Much more time should be devoted to preparing a speech than to giving it.

Just as an athlete spends much more time training and practicing than actually competing, you will devote more time to preparation than to speaking. After determining the general purpose and the specific purpose, and after analyzing the audience, you should then take inventory of the sources of information available on the topic.

In recent years many business organizations have developed speakers' bureaus comprised of employees who volunteer to speak before local community organizations. In most cases these employees speak on subjects related to their areas of specialization. For speeches of this nature the speaker is probably his or her own best source of information.

To illustrate, when Randall Best, assistant purchasing manager, was asked to speak to a civic club on purchasing and its effects on the local community, he spent hours in the library preparing his speech. Yet he was disappointed with the audience's response.

At the end of the speech he offered to answer questions, but no one asked any. There was courteous applause. The next day his boss was sympathetic but bluntly pointed out Randall's mistake: "As a purchasing agent you are recognized by these local groups as an expert. They want to learn what you think on the subject. They don't want some list of figures. They want your opinion."

Businesspeople who need more specific information for a speech can usually call on someone else in the organization for help. Either through personal observations and knowledge or with the assistance of colleagues, most business speakers can prepare an appropriate speech.

Most students do not have the appropriate personal experiences for source material, so the research process is complicated by the need to go beyond themselves for suitable ideas. This approach is not limited to students, because business speakers often look to outside sources for support of their ideas or to clarify knowledge of the subject. Students particularly, however, need to be aware of printed sources of information. These were described in Chapter 11, along with a discussion of the research process.

The most effective business presentations are based on thorough research. Waiting until the last minute to prepare usually results in a presentation that is shallow in its coverage and weak in its organization, and the lack of preparation is immediately obvious to listeners. Many aspects of our lives, in addition to presentations, could be enhanced through better research. For example, when Carlene Murphy Ziegler followed the advice of a stock broker and bought "a lot of shares" of stock in a bio-technology company at $7 each, the value of the stock quickly shot up to $15 per share; then the stock mysteriously disappeared from the market. She later learned that the success of the company had rested on a single cow on which cancer research was being done. When the cow died, the company did also.[4] If Carlene had done better research on the company, she would have saved her money; similarly, better research will save a presentation.

A knowledge of information sources will facilitate smooth and systematic progress from preparation to presentation of the speech. Throughout the preparation process keep in mind these questions to which your listeners will be seeking answers:

- What are your sources?
- Is this information accurate?
- How relevant is this?
- Why should I care about this?
- What should I do about this?

Of particular interest to speakers is a magazine called *Vital Speeches* devoted to significant recent public speeches. By reading it you can gain insights into the positions being taken by prominent speakers.

ORGANIZATION OF THE SPEECH

Speakers often make the mistake of believing that they are ready to speak once they have completed their research. What usually results is a speech that is unclear in purpose and inconsistent in direction. Such speakers have overlooked the necessity of organizing their material.

Speakers should have an overabundance of materials from which to select the most appropriate. Inexperienced speakers often question the value of doing more research than is absolutely necessary; however, after they have presented several speeches, the reasons will be obvious. It is uncomfortable to a speaker and obvious to the listeners when a speech is short on ideas, for a speaker is then likely to include digressions, redundancies, and irrelevant statements.

Business speakers may be their own best source of information.

The Body

A speech is made up of three main parts: the introduction, body, and conclusion. Although the body follows the introduction, most speakers develop the body first. The body of a speech presents its actual message and has three main components: central idea, main ideas, and supporting materials.

Central Idea

The central idea is the major theme of a speech; the speaker wants the listeners to remember it even if they forget all else. A campaigning politician may present many ideas in a campaign speech, but the central idea is usually "vote for me." Although central ideas are generally longer, they should be limited to one sentence. A training director recently gave an informative speech in which the central idea was this: A person should not be made a supervisor until he or she has satisfactorily completed a course in interpersonal communication. A good central idea is, like the example, brief and clear. The central idea represents the minimum that you want the listeners to remember.

Main Ideas

Several main ideas support the central idea.

After determining the central idea, you seek ideas to support it; these are the main ideas. The main ideas are secondary in importance only to the central idea, and speakers hope that the listeners will retain the main ideas, too. For that reason there should be many; four or five are sufficient for most speeches.

Supporting Materials

Once the main ideas have been selected, look for ways to support them. Because an argument that convinces some listeners will not necessarily convince others, you should seek enough supporting materials to reach all of the listeners.

Among the methods of support most frequently used are quotations, examples, analogies, and statistics. In deciding the appropriateness of a given form of support, the speaker should consider these questions:

1. *Quotations (or testimony)*
    a. Will the person being quoted be recognized by the listeners?
    b. Will the listeners regard the quoted person as an authority?
    c. Does the person being quoted have credibility with the listeners?

2. *Examples*
    a. Can the example be understood by the listeners?
    b. Is the example clearly related to the main point?

3. *Analogies*
    a. Is the analogy appropriate for the subject being considered?
    b. Will the listeners be able to grasp the relevance of the analogy?

4. *Statistics*
    a. Will the statistics be understandable to the listeners?
    b. Will the listeners recognize the relationship between the statistics and the main point the statistics are intended to support?
    c. Are the statistics recent and reliable enough to be acceptable to the listeners?

Sequence of Main Ideas

Once the central idea, the main ideas, and the supporting materials have been selected, the speaker must decide the sequence in which the main points will be presented.

Some of the most common organizational patterns are the chronological, topical, spatial, and logical sequences. The sequence that will be most appropriate depends on the topic, the purpose, and the listeners' interests. Effective speakers are equally adept in using any one of these sequential arrangements.

Chronological Sequence.   In the **chronological sequence** the speech progresses from one given point in time to another. This sequence is regularly used when explaining a process. For example, when a plant manager explained papermaking to a class of undergraduates, he started by explaining how the lumber is purchased and what is done to it in the wood room. He described the entire process for the listeners up until the time when the paper is packaged and shipped out of the mill.

The chronological sequence might be used to describe the evolution of an idea or to explain how to do something.

Topical Sequence.   When a topic is divided into several different parts, it is arranged according to the **topical sequence**. The more natural the divisions, the easier it is for the listeners to understand and retain what the speaker is presenting. To illustrate, a company president spoke at the annual meeting of stockholders on the declining productivity of employees. He first spoke about the causes of this problem as perceived by management, then he presented the causes as perceived by labor. He concluded by discussing those causes perceived differently by the two sides.

The topical sequence seems to be the one used most frequently. Some speakers tend to use it even though another sequence would be more effective.

Spatial Sequence.   As the name **spatial sequence** implies, the use of space determines the arrangement of ideas that the speaker presents. In the spatial sequence the speaker arranges the material according to physical location. One approach to the spatial sequence might involve describing something directionally, from east to west; another might be to describe a building from its first floor to the top floor. For example, when the city planner presented recommendations for a mass transit system, she talked about the unique ways each suburb would be affected by the system. She described the location of the main stations in the inner city and the system's accessibility to downtown office workers and shoppers. She also described the major northern, southern, eastern, and western routes and the terminus of each route.

> The spatial sequence involves presenting material according to physical location.

Speakers who use the spatial sequence describe the physical location of certain points and the relationship between them. The spatial sequence should enable the listeners to visualize what the speaker is telling them.

Logical Sequence.   Several different arrangement patterns are included within the logical sequence. Among the most common are the causal and the problem–solution patterns.

> The causal and the problem–solution patterns are examples of the logical sequence.

In using the causal approach, speakers have two options. One is to point out certain forces and the results that follow from them. For example, when a state chamber of commerce official spoke, he described the organized efforts made to attract new business to the state. He listed organizations that have moved to the state as a result of the efforts. In the presentation the efforts of the chamber were the forces and new business organizations the results.

The other option using the causal approach is to describe events and then to explain the forces that caused them. To illustrate, a representative of the Sierra Club discussing water pollution pointed out the growing health problems associated with it. She listed discharges from manufacturing plants and lax sewage control as the causes. In her argument she presented the results first, then the causes.

The problem–solution approach is quite similar to the causal approach because the speaker presents two main points. For example, in discussing an increase in customer complaints about sales personnel (the problem), the personnel director urged that greater emphasis be placed on employee training (the solution).

Introduction and Conclusion

Until you have decided what you will present in your speech, it is difficult to know how to get the listeners involved in it. For that reason the body of the speech should be developed before the introduction and the conclusion.

There are some speakers, however, who develop their ideas in the order they will present them. These speakers believe that by developing the introduction, body, and conclusion in that order, they will achieve better continuity between ideas.

An introduction should establish rapport with the listeners while gaining their attention.

The manner in which you introduce your speech will greatly influence the listeners' initial impressions. There are two purposes of the introduction: to establish rapport with the listeners and to gain the listeners' attention.

Among the approaches commonly used in the introduction are these:

1. Make a startling statement.
2. Refer to the audience.
3. Refer to the occasion.
4. Quote a recognized authority.
5. Ask a rhetorical question.
6. Use humor that is relevant.

Regardless of the approach you use, you should remember the purposes of the introduction and of the speech: to indicate your subject and to gain the acceptance of the listeners.

In concluding a speech you should, at a minimum, restate the central idea. A good conclusion indicates to the listeners that the topic has been thoroughly covered. These are some of the most common ways a speaker may conclude a speech:

1. Summarize the main points.
2. Propose a solution.
3. Quote a recognized authority.
4. Challenge the listeners to accomplish some specific goal.
5. Visualize the future if your proposal is or is not accepted.

OUTLINE FOR AN INFORMATIVE SPEECH

By outlining a speech, the speaker is able to clarify the relationship between ideas.

In outlining an informative speech, arrange its different parts into a sequence that allows an orderly presentation of ideas. Through the use of an outline you can determine whether the relationship between ideas is clear. An outline also helps the listener follow your train of thought. This is the outline of an informative speech given by a training director to an undergraduate professional management society:

I. Introduction
    A. Brief history of the training function within the business organization
    B. Increased specialization and automation changes as stimulants for training

II. Central idea: The job of the training director is varied enough to be challenging and very important to the organization.

III. Body (main ideas)
    A. The training director must learn the training needs of the organization
       1. Through observation of operations
       2. Through interviewing upper management
       3. Through interviewing line workers

B. The training director must develop training programs to meet organizational needs
1. Determine the target audience for the program
2. Locate and schedule competent instructors for the program
C. The training director must evaluate the effectiveness of the training programs
1. Test participants on the subject matter
2. Interview superiors of the participants and use other criteria to measure improvement

IV. Conclusion
A. Summary of speech body
1. Training director must learn training needs
2. Training director must develop appropriate training programs
3. Training director must evaluate the effectiveness of the programs
B. The job of the training director is important to the organization and challenging to the individual

OUTLINE FOR A PERSUASIVE SPEECH

Although the outline of the persuasive speech is similar to that of the informative speech, the two types are not developed in the same way. The informative speech is usually factual and not controversial, and so gaining the listeners' acceptance is ordinarily not difficult. To the persuasive speaker, however, gaining the listeners' acceptance is a challenge. The more a persuader's ideas conform to the way people think, the more likely it is that successful persuasion will occur.

The **motivated sequence** is a method of speech organization based on analysis of the thought process.[5] If you follow this sequence, you will present your ideas in the natural order that people follow when thinking through to a problem solution. Listeners who are led through these steps will be motivated to accept your proposition. The motivated sequence consists of five steps:

> In the motivated sequence ideas are presented in a natural order.

1. Getting attention
2. Showing the need
3. Satisfying the need
4. Visualizing the results
5. Requesting approval or action

Just as readers become oblivious to magazine and newspaper advertisements, listeners also become oblivious when speakers try to persuade them. This is certainly not surprising; during an average day most of us are bombarded by numerous attempts to persuade. For these reasons a persuader must first get the attention of the listeners. There are a number of options available. The most appropriate approach depends on many factors, including the occasion and the nature of the audience. The opening least likely to get the attention of the listeners is, "My topic today is . . . . "

In showing the need to the listeners, you describe a problem. Besides a mere description you may clarify the problem by using examples. The examples will be effective if they illustrate the seriousness of the problem. Moreover, listeners are more likely to recognize the need if you point out how the problem affects them.

In satisfying the need you present a solution to the problem raised in the previous step. You show how the solution will satisfy the need of which the listeners are now aware. At this point you clearly state the attitude or action the listeners are being asked to adopt. By using examples or other supporting materials, show that your proposal will work. As you explain how the solution will meet the need, you should anticipate likely objections and address them during this step.

By describing future conditions you help the listeners to visualize the results of the proposed solution. Some speakers describe the results likely if the solution is accepted.

Others approach it negatively and describe future conditions if the solution is not accepted. The intended result of the visualization step is to intensify the desire of the listeners.

In requesting approval or action you focus the thoughts of the listeners on the theme developed in the speech. The speaker's request should be brief, to the point, and unmistakably clear.

This is the outline of a persuasive speech given by a production manager to a group of supervisors. In addition to the ideas presented, the steps of the motivated sequence are also indicated:

I.   Introduction *(attention)*
    A. You have within you the power to grant yourself a pay increase.
    B. You are in a position to generate more business for the company.

II. Body *(main ideas)*
    A. Industrywide research shows that we trail competitors in two significant factors. *(need)*
        1. We have the highest rate of lost-time accidents in the industry.
        2. We have a worse than average rate of consumer complaints about product defects.
    B. There are some actions you can take that will increase your earnings and improve the company's position within the industry. *(satisfaction)*
        1. Always enforce all safety regulations.
        2. Stress constant quality control and make more spot checks yourself.
    C. If you follow our supervisory manual to the letter, lost-time accidents will be reduced by 50 percent and consumer complaints will be reduced by at least 30 percent. You will benefit directly in two ways. *(visualization)*
        1. Your earnings will increase.
        2. You will have less unproductive paperwork to complete concerning accidents.

III. Conclusion *(action)*
    A. Report all violations of safety regulations.

Developing a Coherent Presentation

A message in which ideas are connected logically and flow smoothly is said to be coherent. Coherence was identified as a characteristic of effective writing in Chapter 5, and it is equally important in presentations. In a coherent presentation, the structure is obvious and, consequently, the listeners will be more likely to retain the information. An additional benefit of a coherent presentation is that it is also easier for the speaker to remember simply because it makes more sense.

Enumeration and **parallelism** are devices that will enhance the coherence of a presentation. The speaker who tells her listeners how many points she intends to make, numbers each one ("My first point is . . . . "), and repeats those points in the conclusion is more likely to be remembered than is the presenter whose message does not include such cues.

Speakers who repeat similar phraseology in stating their ideas are using parallelism. The political candidate who says, "The citizens deserve safe streets; the citizens deserve well-paying jobs; the citizens deserve a clean environment," is using parallelism. Ann Richards, former Governor of Texas and an outstanding speaker as well as a recovering alcoholic, provided a vivid example of parallelism in a speech at Southern Methodist University. Sober for the past fifteen years, she spoke candidly about her drinking days:

> I drank to celebrate. I drank when it had been a bad day. I drank if I had a temporary, painful experience. I drank if I wanted to have a good time. I drank if I wanted to relax. I drank if I needed to stay up to party. I drank if I needed to get ready to party. There was

always a very good reason to drink—you get the idea. And I always had somebody to drink with me.[6]

Parallelism has a rhythm that is both easy to listen to and easy to remember. It enhances the coherence of a message.

The Human Dimension

Electronic communication and computerization have revolutionized the business organization. Information is transmitted at high speed and at relatively low monetary cost. Technological advances have led to downsized organizations, and mergers of competitors now routinely occur for reasons of efficiency and cost savings. The increased efficiency that results, however, is accompanied by a significant human cost: less human contact.

Their face-to-face nature is one of the strengths of most business presentations. While some organizations may justifiably be described as bland and impersonal, the same should not be true of presentations. In addition to strong content, an effective presentation should also have a personal touch. Better speakers will always reveal something about themselves, and their speeches will be more than a litany of facts. For example, when representatives of four major companies seeking a construction contract made presentations, each focused on key issues. One, however, " . . . . won not only the minds but the hearts of the decision makers when he personalized his presentation by saying: 'I have to drive right past this site every day on my way to the office. I can't stand the thought of seeing someone else's sign there'."[7]

Presentations and speeches provide an opportunity for speakers to convey a personal touch in an impersonal environment. Effective speakers will take advantage of the opportunity.

THE DELIVERY OF THE SPEECH

Many speakers believe if they have attended to all of the preliminaries leading up to a speech, the delivery will take care of itself. The advice they most likely give beginning speakers is, "Be natural." They tell speakers, "Imagine that you are carrying on a conversation with the audience and act accordingly." Such advice, although well-intended, is not helpful, because it is difficult to be natural in what is an unnatural situation.

Bodily changes usually occur when you are about to give a speech. Digestive processes slow down, hands tremble, and butterflies take flight in your stomach. Dr. Hans Selye, winner of the Nobel Prize for his research on the effects of stress on the human body, described the stress response as a **"fight or flight" syndrome**. According to his research, the perception of danger causes the secretion of adrenaline into the bloodstream. Adrenaline affects body functions in many ways: Muscles tighten, perspiration occurs, heart and breathing rates increase, and the mouth goes dry. At one time this stress response served as a survival mechanism for the human species.[8]

> ✔ *CHECKLIST for Reducing Stage Fright*
>
> ____ Select a topic that genuinely interests you.
> ____ Analyze your audience and the setting in advance.
> ____ Prepare thoroughly; use a notecard for your main points.
> ____ Practice, practice, practice—but do not memorize.
> ____ Go through the entire speech on six or seven consecutive days.
> ____ Always keep your main purpose in mind.
> ____ While waiting to speak, sit in a relaxed, even limp, position and breathe deeply.
> ____ Know your introduction especially well.
> ____ Refer to the notecard as necessary, but do not read.
> ____ Focus on your message and the response, not on yourself.
> ____ Use gestures and movement for emphasis.

Feeling nervous in a public-speaking situation is to be expected—it is completely normal. Even the most seasoned public speaker can get butterflies at the start of a presentation. The Checklist for Reducing Stage Fright presents some techniques to "make

Some nervousness is to be expected in giving a public speech, but much of it can be overcome.

your butterflies fly in formation."[9] As you become more experienced, such signs may become less apparent, but they never completely disappear. Even extreme nervousness—which you may be so aware of—is not nearly as noticeable to the listeners as you may think.

Nervousness has a positive aspect. It gives you a slight edge, which is evident in greater alertness and sensitivity to the listeners. In fact, speakers who are more anxious very often give better speeches than do speakers who are less anxious. All in all, delivering a speech is a challenge that can provide satisfaction.

Voice Qualities

Since noise pollution has become an issue in society, people have grown increasingly aware of loudness, or volume. Speakers addressing a group should adjust their volume according to such factors as room size and background noises.

A speaker who regularly speaks more softly toward the end of each sentence is probably practicing improper breath control. Fred Rosen, for example, is a well-organized and an articulate speaker with one overriding fault that greatly reduces his effectiveness. He begins each sentence with enough volume to be easily heard, then reduces his volume until many of the listeners are unable to hear the end of each sentence. This practice has led his subordinates to call him Half-a-Sentence Rosen. If you have this problem, use shorter sentences or else consciously pause at natural breaks in the expression of your ideas to take a breath.

Rate of speech and pitch contribute to the impression made by a speaker.

The speed, or rate, at which you speak influences the way others respond to you and your message. Inexperienced speakers sometimes speak too quickly due to nervousness, and this causes other problems. Speaking too rapidly results in breath-control difficulties and a tendency to give all ideas equal emphasis. Your main ideas should leap out at the listener, but this will not happen unless you slow down—but not to extremes. By speaking much too slowly some people err in the opposite direction.

The high or low sound level of the voice is referred to as pitch. No one pitch is correct, but individuals have a certain pitch level at which their voice is most effective.

Variety is the key to the successful use of these voice qualities. By varying your volume, rate, and pitch you will become more interesting to hear, and your message will be more memorable.

Modes of Delivery

The four main modes of delivery used in public speaking are (1) impromptu, (2) extemporaneous, (3) memorized, and (4) manuscript. The impromptu speech is delivered with little opportunity to prepare. Its main virtue is that it is spontaneous; its main shortcoming is that it is usually not well planned. When you are urged to say a few words without any advance warning, what results is an impromptu speech.

Extemporaneous speaking is somewhat more formal than impromptu speaking. You have an opportunity to plan, and the resulting speech is better organized than an impromptu speech. You will usually rely somewhat on notes, but you will not read to the listeners. Most public speeches are delivered extemporaneously.

A memorized speech allows for a well-planned expression of ideas. When presenting a speech from memory, however, speakers tend to lose a certain amount of naturalness and sometimes sound and look quite wooden. The possibility of memory lapse is another negative aspect of the memorized speech.

Manuscript speaking is relied on for more formal occasions. Speaking from a manuscript, you are able to be very precise, and you can carefully control the exact message the listeners receive. Of course, it takes longer to develop a manuscript speech, and frequently the manuscript becomes a barrier between you and the audience.

Visual Support

Visual support, which will be discussed in Chapter 17, can help the communicator in at least four ways: by crystallizing vague ideas, by helping listeners remember information, by overcoming boredom and day-dreaming, and by serving as signposts to keep the listener and speaker on track.[10]

Photographs, charts, graphs, handouts, chalkboards, bulletin boards, and overhead projectors are frequently used by the speaker as visual aids. However, they are also frequently misused. Visual support is not a substitute for the speech itself. The burden is still on you to convey the message. Very good support material will not compensate for a mediocre speech.

Visual aids help keep the speaker and listeners on track.

> ### ✔ CHECKLIST *for Delivery*
>
> ____ Record your speech at least once while practicing and carefully evaluate it.
>
> ____ Vary your rate, pitch, and volume so that you emphasize your main points.
>
> ____ Avoid vocalized pauses ("uh," "uhm," etc.): silence is preferable to unnecessary *uhs*.
>
> ____ Maintain eye contact with your listeners.
>
> ____ Develop an urge to communicate by selecting a topic in which you are interested.
>
> ____ Lessen the distance between yourself and your listeners.

Team Presentations

Although individual presentations are much more frequent, presentations by teams of individuals are not unusual. Continuity is especially important in a team presentation. The presentation should appear as a unified whole rather than as a series of individual presentations. Through careful planning the team members should avoid repetition and should structure the presentations so that each speaker paves the way for the succeeding speaker.

To illustrate, a chamber of commerce that sought to attract a major league baseball team assembled a group to present the city's case to the owners of the ball clubs. The first speaker described the area from which the team would draw spectators. Through the use of flip charts the makeup of the population according to educational level was described. The second speaker presented the findings of a wage survey done in the community. The various income levels were described, and the amount of discretionary income at each level was estimated. Transportation facilities were described by the third speaker. Information about the airport and flight schedules was presented, as was a description of the city bus system. The urban freeway system was also shown with graphics. The fourth speaker described the sports complex where the team would play and listed the specific financial incentives and tax benefits the city would provide the team that accepted its offer. After agreeing to move to the city, the team officials cited the attractive package and persuasive presentations as major reasons.

> ### ✔ CHECKLIST *for Team Presentation*
>
> ____ Plan the team presentation as a group, and divide the topics into logical and well-balanced divisions.
>
> ____ Anticipate questions and be prepared to respond to them.
>
> ____ Unless you are the first speaker, begin by referring to the previous speaker.
>
> ____ Direct your speech primarily to the larger audience rather than to the other speakers.
>
> ____ Refer where appropriate in your speech to the speeches of those who preceded you.
>
> ____ Do not infringe on the time of the speakers who follow you.
>
> ____ Do not lose sight of the goal of the team.

The team presentation makes all the demands of an individual presentation, and it also requires coordination with your colleagues. Planning, therefore, is especially important. Be sure to practice with visual aids and to time each speaker's presentation, because a limited amount of time often is scheduled for team presentations.

Planning and coordination are especially important in team presentations.

People react differently to the stress of public speaking, making it difficult to know exactly how much time each speaker may take. In their anxiety, some speakers speed up their delivery rate by as much as one-third or more. Others do just the opposite; they slow down and therefore put pressure on other members to cut their presentations so that the team ends on schedule. Some system, such as placing a watch on the lectern or signaling the time remaining, can help keep the presentation from continuing too long.

All of the principles of effective communication by individual speakers pertain to the team presentation as well.

Key Terms

- **informative speech**
- **persuasive speech**
- **covert response**
- **overt response**
- **listener orientation**
- **chronological sequence**
- **topical sequence**
- **spatial sequence**
- **logical sequence**
- **motivated sequence**
- **enumeration**
- **parallelism**
- **fight or flight syndrome**

Summary

Factors of credibility   p. 405

Possible purposes of a speech   p. 405

Audience analysis   p. 407–408

Parts of a speech   p. 410

Types of supporting materials   p. 410

Sequential arrangements of ideas   p. 411

Motivated sequence   p. 413

Coherence, enumeration, and parallelism   p. 414

Techniques for reducing stage fright   p. 415

Modes of delivery   p. 416

Team presentations   p. 417

Review Questions

1. Why is public speaking so important to the individual, the organization, and society?
2. Describe the two-step process used to arrive at the purposes of a speech.
3. What are the differences between a covert response and an overt response? Give three examples of each.
4. What is audience analysis?
5. What are the five basic questions you should consider when analyzing an audience?
6. Explain the relationship between the central idea, the main idea, and supporting materials in a speech.
7. What are four commonly used forms of support?
8. What are four commonly used sequences of main points?

Exercises

1. Give a five-minute presentation describing a particular episode of your favorite television sitcom. Make sure you first describe the major cast members to those who may not be familiar with the show.
2. Give a five-minute presentation describing your favorite movie.
3. Pick a particular volunteer community service activity. Give a five-minute presentation describing why your audience should participate.

4. You are the Executive Director of your hometown Chamber of Commerce. Prepare a five-minute presentation to give to a group of English-speaking tourists who are considering visiting your town. Describe what they should see and do while there.

5. With a partner, each pick a topic and videotape a three-minute presentation to each other. Critique each other's presentation and redo with the suggested improvements in mind.

6. Give a speech to motivate your class to be more productive. Try to use positive language.

7. Pick a company you would like to work for and give a five-minute presentation describing why others would enjoy working for that company.

8. You are running for an elected office. Identify the office and give a campaign speech.

9. Select a speech from *Vital Speeches* magazine and analyze it to determine its general purpose, main ideas, and supporting materials.

10. Develop a five-minute informative speech to present to your class. Encourage comments and questions from the class members. Write a one- or two-page paper in which you describe the changes you would make in the speech if you gave it again.

11. Do a written audience analysis of your communication class. Detail the ways in which class members are similar and ways they are different.

12. Develop a five-minute persuasive speech on a subject about which you feel strongly. Describe those factors from your audience analysis (as in Exercise 11) that most influenced your approach.

13. Give a one-minute impromptu speech on a topic selected by someone else in your class. Try to present one main idea and support it as well as you can.

14. In groups of four or five prepare a team presentation to be given before the class. Select a subject, and divide it among the team members. Each team member should have a specific role, and the other class members should be told the kind of group they are to represent. Following each team presentation ask the class to do an evaluation.

15. Name two public figures whom you have seen give a speech (either in person or on television). Describe what you think each should do to become a better public speaker.

CASE

Central Telephone Company

John D. Stegman, The Ohio State University

Central Telephone (CTC) is an independent communications company, not connected with any of the Baby Bells. It is large enough to maintain a profitable enterprise and provide the service that is required by the state's Public Utilities Commission (PUCO). The company provides telephone service to homes and businesses. Like all utilities, CTC must obtain the approval of the PUCO for a rate increase. The reason for a recent request for a 2 percent increase in rates is that CTC's previous increases have not been enough to keep pace with inflation. CTC, like most other companies, has shareholders to please. In addition to the requested rate increase, CTC has proposed an aid package for those who are below the federal poverty level and therefore cannot afford local phone service.

In order to sell the proposed rate increase, CTC is sending spokespersons to give free "coffee and donut" sessions to the opinion leaders of various towns. The towns are not picked at random. They are those that the company expects to oppose the increase. The company spokespersons are usually local service reps, and so the townspeople know them well. Unfortunately, the service that CTC provides is not always good. Many complaints have been made about noisy lines, billing problems, and high rates. The company will use the welfare proposal as an argument against the complaint about high rates. Recent advances in service levels and office improvements (digital conversion of central offices) should help CTC to counter other complaints.

One of the meetings is scheduled at the Hillyerds Grade School. You represent CTC as the local service representative and spokesperson. Jerry Neal, your division manager, will also attend the meeting. In the audience will be the Hillyerds mayor and council members plus several extremely disgruntled local customers. You know that anyone who favors a telephone rate increase will not likely attend such a meeting. You realize that this is a crisis communication situation. Accordingly, your planning must include speaking to a hostile audience.

Case Questions

1. What is your purpose for this presentation to this particular audience?
2. What elements of the audience makeup are important to you and how do you tailor your message?
3. What tone and style should you use to speak to this group?
4. Will you involve your boss, the division manager? If so, how?
5. How are your strategies different from normal speaking situations?

CASE

The City Council Meeting

Julie C. Burkhard, Charlottesville, Virginia

Jeffrey Faught is the director of the chamber of commerce in Eastman. The town has a population of approximately 3,000 but is growing.

Jeffrey has been working for about two years to bring industry to Eastman. Presently the town has no industries at all. Most of the people in Eastman are local business people or farmers. Jeffrey believes the town needs some industry. It would not only strengthen the economy but would also create more jobs. With jobs come people, and people need homes to live in; therefore, real estate would gain from the industry as well.

Jeffrey has been talking with someone who might be interested in moving a light-manufacturing branch to Eastman. The problem is that many townspeople want a park and recreational area where the plant would be built. The city council must decide whether to grant a zoning change for the new industry or the new park.

The second Tuesday night of every month, the city council meets. The public is invited, and so anyone may attend. This particular Tuesday Jeffrey decides he must make his stand known to both the town and the people who want the park. He has not given many speeches, but he knows this presentation must be very persuasive.

Many townspeople have wanted a park for their children for years. They believe the town is doing just fine without industry. In the past, the town council has shared this view. Jeffrey is faced with the job of convincing both the council and the people to change their views.

Case Questions

1. What should Jeffrey take into consideration when analyzing his audience?
2. How might he organize his presentation to accomplish his persuasive purpose?
3. In view of the fact that Jeffrey has to overcome the objections of the council and the people, what modes of proof should he attempt to employ?

CASE

The Parent/Teacher Association Meeting

Mary A. Gowan, The University of Texas at El Paso

Soon after completing college, Janice went to work for Highland Pacific Bank. She has just completed Highland Pacific's management training program and has been appointed as manager of the Western Hills branch of Highland Pacific. Western Hills is a small town—population 18,000—located 100 miles north of San Francisco, California. Most of the residents of Western Hills have lived there their entire lives.

The Western Hills branch of Highland Pacific is only three years old and has as its major competitor the locally owned Western Hills Bank. Janice knows that her bank offers more types of financial services than Western Hills Bank. For instance, her bank can approve loan applications within 24 hours, something Western Hills cannot do. In addition, Highland Pacific offers special programs with incentives to encourage children and young people to start saving at an early age. People in the community have told her, however, that they like the "down home touch" they get at Western Hills, and that they "will never change banks."

Janice has been asked to speak to the Parent/Teacher Association at the local middle school. The president of the organization requested that she speak about how to teach children the importance of money management. The president also mentioned that, in her opinion, many of the parents needed to understand the importance of money management more than the children did!

Janice will have 20 minutes for her presentation. A short question and answer session will follow. The president said that she would tell the parents which bank Janice represents, but also stressed that she didn't want Janice to use the time to "sell" Highland Pacific.

Case Questions

1. What type of speech would be most appropriate for this occasion?
2. What would be the general purpose of this speech? The specific purpose?
3. Why would a carefully conducted audience analysis be critical to the success of this presentation?
4. What tone and style should Janice use to speak to this group?

Notes

1. David Wallechinsky and Irving Wallace, *The Book of Lists* (New York: William Morrow, 1977), 469–470.

2. From a press release from Robert Marston Marketing Communications, Inc., 485 Madison Avenue, New York, NY, March 1994.

3. Kimberly F. Kane, "MBAs: A Recruiter's-Eye View," *Business Horizons*, January–February 1993, 65–71; and Charles C. DuBois, "Portrait of The Ideal MBA," *The Penn Stater*, September/October 1992.

4. "Bad Investment Milked Young Analyst," *The Milwaukee Journal*, August 14, 1994, D2.

5. Alan H. Monroe and Douglas Ehninger, *Principles of Speech Communication*, 8th ed. (Glenview, IL: Scott, Foresman, 1978), 252.

6. "People in The News," *Athens Daily News/Athens Banner-Herald*, October 1, 1995, 2A.

7. Wicke Chambers and Spring Asher, "Getting Ahead," *The Atlanta Journal/The Atlanta Constitution*, April 28, 1991, H4.

8. Paul Karasik, *National Underwriter*, "How to Get Your Butterflies to Fly in Formation," October 4, 1993, 10.

9. Karasik, 10.

10. Paul R. Timm, *Functional Business Presentations* (Englewood Cliffs, NJ: Prentice-Hall, 1981), 131.

Chapter 17

Visual Support

"I'm worried about this presentation, Henry. My research is thorough and my conclusions are solid, but there's so much data that the managers may not be able to follow my analysis or they may get bored. I'd really like to use some flashy 3-D pie graphs. Can you help me?"

"That's our job in Media Services—to help employees who are writing reports or making oral presentations. We all know that visual support can add interest, precision, and clarity to the presentation. On the other hand, we have to be careful not to mislead the audience or obscure important information. And too much 'flash' can call undue attention to the visual support itself.

"Our job, Jeannie, is to apply solid principles of visual communication to enhance primary messages. I need to find out from you the goals, the main points, and areas of potential confusion in your presentation. We might ultimately use a 3-D pie graph, but there are many important steps to take first. Visual support is a process, not just an end result."

Jeannie's request for a specific form of visual support, without knowing the underlying principles, is not unusual. Many finished reports and presentations are weakened by this approach.

Chapter 12 was devoted to the writing of effective reports, and Chapter 16 discussed the effective delivery of oral presentations. This chapter examines how to make them more effective through the use of carefully executed visual support.

PREPARATION OF TABLES AND FIGURES

Most types of **visual support** can be incorporated in a written report or delivered as part of an oral presentation equally well. In fact, written reports often precede oral reports on the same topic, and written information is often distributed as part of the oral presentation. Of the two categories of visual support, **tables** are more likely to be used in written reports because of the amount of precise data they contain. On the other hand, the category referred to as **figures**—which includes graphs, charts, maps, drawings, and photographs—has at least as many applications in oral presentations as in written reports.

Tables provide a relatively large amount of precise data.

Figure 17.1
Parts of a Table

Table 1: Turnover Rates for Atlantic Electronics and Selected Competitors, 1990-1995

Company	1990	1991	1992	1993	1994	1995
Atlantic Electronics	13	17	18	21	21	23
Burns	18	21	16	12	11	7
Dominion	15	14	17	13	12	15
Southern	17	24	18	16	15	16

Labels shown in figure: Title, Spanner Head, Column Heads, Rules, Stub Head, Stub Data, Footnotes: a b c, Data.

Turnover Rate per Year

Footnotes: a
b
c

Source: Full citation must be given, using the same form as a footnote.

Tables

Their tabular format gives tables a rather standard appearance, as discussed in Chapter 12. Tables are valuable for delivering precise data. Organizations that use computers to store, retrieve, and analyze data use database and spreadsheet software, and the initial output from this software is usually in tabular form.

The appearance of tables may vary somewhat, but they typically have these parts: title, spanner head, stub head, column heads, rules, and data. They may have totals, footnotes, source information, and a caption in addition to the title. A series of tables may be numbered. Figure 17.1 shows the position of typical elements. Although not shown in the figure, data that include decimals should be aligned vertically on the decimal points. Rules are lines that separate portions of the table. A double line or bold line separates the title from other information. A single line of normal weight separates spanner heads from column heads. Data are then placed in rows and columns.

When used in oral presentations, tables need to be simple enough so that the main concept can be quickly grasped. Adding shading or a change in color to important columns or rows, such as subtotals, can dramatically improve the speed of comprehension. Note in Figure 17.2 how shading, italics, and different type sizes improve the appearance of the same information as in Figure 17.1.

Figures

The data available in table form from your spreadsheet or database can be entered into presentation graphics software to produce graphs, charts, maps, drawings, or other visual support forms. Use these treatments to summarize information, add clarity, illustrate relationships, or to add vividness. Among the most popular types of figures you might use in a long report are graphs, charts, and maps.

Graphs can sometimes present information more effectively than tables.

Graphs

Like tables, **graphs** are used to present quantitative data. You will often discover that information you intended to put into table form can be shown more effectively in a

Figure 17.2
Table Using Shading, Italics, and Different Type Sizes

Table 1: Turnover Rates for Atlantic Electronics and Selected Competitors, 1990-1995

Company	1990	1991	1992	1993	1994	1995
Atlantic Electronics	13	17	18	21	21	23
Burns	18	21	16	12	11	7
Dominion	15	14	17	13	12	15
Southern	17	24	18	16	15	16

Turnover Rate per Year

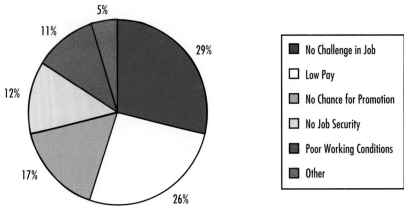

Figure 17.3
Sample Pie Graph

Figure 3: Reasons for Employee Separations at Atlantic Electronics

graph. Graphs show trends, comparisons, or sometimes both trends and comparisons. Four basic kinds of graphs are pie graphs, line graphs, bar graphs, and pictographs.

Pie Graphs.   Pie graphs, also called circle graphs, show comparisons only. They contain a comparison of parts to a whole. You will recall the pie graph in the long report in Chapter 12, reproduced here as Figure 17.3. These simple rules should help you construct a good pie graph:

1. Always begin your pie graph at the 12 o'clock position.
2. Enter the largest percentage first, and work clockwise around the graph entering the remaining percentages in descending order according to size. If there is a "miscellaneous" or "other" category, it may appear last, regardless of size.
3. To compute the exact space needed for each percentage, multiply 360 (the number of degrees in a circle) by the percentage. Your product is the number of degrees the percentage should represent. (For example: 360 × 29% = 104 degrees.)
4. Use a protractor and ruler to draw the graph.

Line Graphs.   Single line graphs show trends. Multiple line graphs show both trends and comparisons. Multiple line graphs usually contain no more than three or four lines; too many will confuse the reader. One line—usually the lowest, the primary, or the earliest—should be a solid line. Other lines, added above the solid one, are often dotted and dashed. Another option is to use colors for the lines. In any case, the treatment selected should allow quick differentiation. Figure 17.4 is a line graph reproduced from the long report in Chapter 12. Figure 17.5 is an example of a multiple line graph.

Bar Graphs.   The third kind of graph, the bar graph, best shows comparisons. Again, the example (Figure 17.6) is from Chapter 12.

In preparing a bar graph, make the bars wider than the space between them. If the x-axis has a logical progression, such as time units, use that progression and plot the bars as the data dictate. If no logical sequence exists, however, arrange the items so the bars either increase or decrease in height.

Grid lines and tick marks can be helpful to the viewer. Grid lines are light horizontal, or occasionally vertical, lines that lead the eyes from the value on the y-axis across to—and behind—the bars. Tick marks on either the x- or y-axis appear at major divisions of the axis, such as at 500, 1,000, 1,500, and 2,000 units.

In Figure 17.6, bars for Atlantic Electronics and Burns are grouped for each of the six years. This type of bar graph is thus called a grouped or clustered bar graph. Had

Figure 17.4
Sample Line Graph

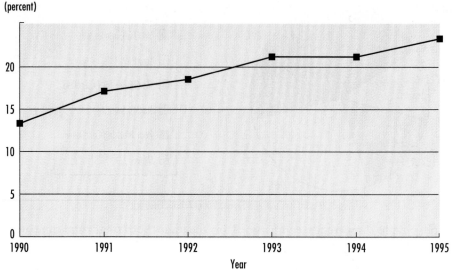

Figure 1: Atlantic Electronics Turnover Rates, 1990–1995

Figure 17.5
Multiple Line Graph

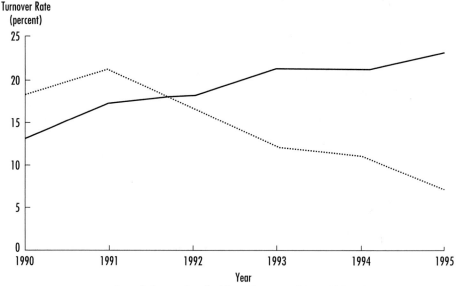

Figure 1: Turnover Rates for Atlantic Electronics and Burns, 1990–1995

only Atlantic Electronics' bars been shown, for example, it would have been known as a simple vertical bar graph.

If the bars extend from left to right, the graph is called a horizontal bar graph. Another type, the subdivided bar graph, can be used if you have more specific information about the contents of each bar. For example, in Figure 17.7, we see that the information about turnover rates has been subdivided by sex.

A final type of bar graph can show both positive and negative qualities. This graph is called a bilateral bar graph. If the information in Figure 17.7 for 1995 (23 percent turnover rate) is broken down by plant location, we develop the bilateral graph shown in Figure 17.8.

On a bilateral bar graph, typically the zero point is drawn through the middle of the graph. Positive quantities are entered first, beginning with the largest positive quantity. Negative quantities are on the right side of the graph, with the smallest negative quantity shown first. An exception to this arrangement is when the *x*-axis has an inherent order, such as years. In that case, the bars would be plotted in year order regardless of positive or negative order.

Three special types of bar graphs are horizontal, subdivided, and bilateral.

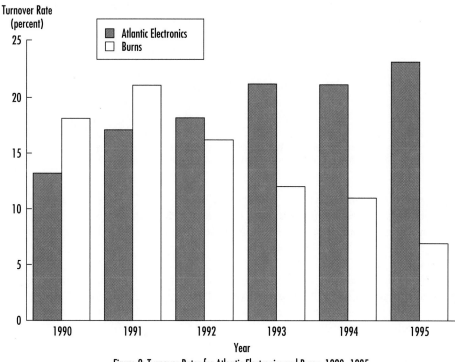

Figure 2: Turnover Rates for Atlantic Electronics and Burns, 1990–1995

Figure 17.6
Sample Bar Graph

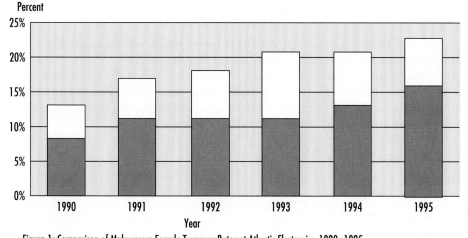

Figure 1: Comparison of Male versus Female Turnover Rates at Atlantic Electronics, 1990–1995

Figure 17.7
Subdivided Bar Graph

Figure 17.8
Bilateral Bar Graph

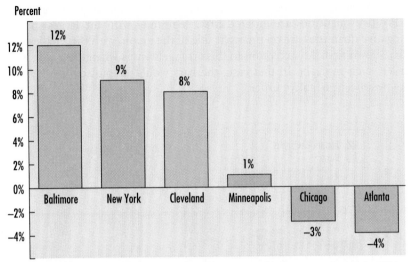

Figure 1: Breakdown of 1995 Atlantic Electronics Turnover Rate by Plant Location Compared to 1994

Pictographs.   Another type of graph is the pictograph. This is similar to the bar graph except symbols rather than bars represent the quantities shown. The symbols can vary widely, from coins representing money to tractors representing farmers.

Charts

Charts show nonquantitative information.

Unlike graphs, which contain quantitative data, **charts** and diagrams show nonquantitative information. The differences between charts and diagrams are not always clear-cut. However, most diagrams show some kind of process, whereas charts contain static information.

BOXED IN

AN ETHICAL DILEMMA

Marie: I'm not too comfortable about submitting this bar graph to George. I think it's misleading.

Paul: It looks fine to me. I really like the vivid red for our company. It makes us look better than our competitors with the drab-colored bars.

Marie: That's my point. The graph is supposed to reflect the actual data. But using a bright color for us—and drawing the three-dimensional graph so that we have more area than the competitors—seems as if we're tricking the viewer. The graph makes us look much bigger and better than we are.

Paul: I like it. George will like it. What's your problem?

Marie feels boxed in. What would you do?

Questions

1. How much influence can colors have for such elements as bars or slices of a pie graph?

2. Under what circumstances is it acceptable to "massage" the data in a graph to strengthen your position?

3. What is it about 3-D graphs that often misleads?

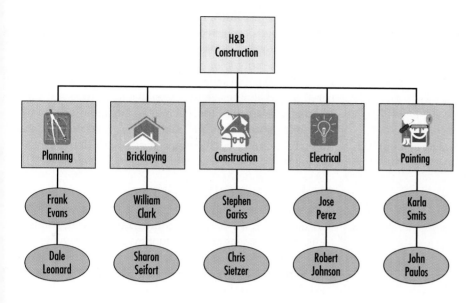

Figure 17.9
Organizational Chart
Prepared with MORE II
Software
Source: Courtesy of
Symantec Corporation.

The organizational chart used by many businesses is a picture of the organization. It shows (1) the various positions in the hierarchy and (2) the lines of authority among these positions. An organizational chart for a small construction firm with five functional areas might be very simple, as shown in Figure 17.9.

The variety of charts and diagrams you might use in long reports is unlimited—although all of them would not appear in a single report, of course. During the planning stage for a report, you might even put together a kind of checklist, called a needs chart, for your own use. A sample needs chart was shown in Chapter 11 (Table 11.1).

These brief guidelines should help you prepare charts and diagrams:

- Keep the chart or diagram as simple as possible. Do not slow your readers down by forcing them to spend unnecessary time trying to understand your drawing.
- If you are diagramming a process, add arrows between steps or stages in the process. Arrows will help readers follow the process itself.
- Give the chart or diagram a number and a title. Place this information directly beneath the drawing (for example, "Figure 1: Steps in Computing Compound Interest"). Typically, an Arabic number is used.
- Place the chart or diagram on the page as you would a table. Introduce it, present it, and interpret it.
- Do not rule out the use of color. If you only have the one copy of the report to prepare, it is easy to add color, which itself adds clarity, understanding, and interest.

Maps

In writing long reports, maps are used less frequently than graphs, charts, and diagrams. However, maps are an interesting way to present the geographical distribution of a variety of information. For example, you might use a map of the United States to show the dollar sales for a particular company in each state. You might also break the map into territories or regions and show increases or decreases in sales for each region. Generally, you can use any map of a city, state, region, country, or larger area if it fits your report material.

Drawings and Photographs

Occasionally, a report can be improved by adding a drawing or photograph. Drawings could include floor plans, artistic illustrations, or medical and anatomical drawings. Figure 17.10 is an example of an engineering drawing prepared with computer-assisted design and drafting software. Photographs are used for much the same purposes as drawings, but photographs add realism and precision because they are pictures of the actual item. Both drawings and photographs, of course, can be presented in color.

Computer-Generated Visual Support

As business increasingly relies on computers for text editing and data analysis, it will also integrate special graphics tools. Besides saving time and money, computer-generated visual support can be produced in color. The report writer or oral presenter processes, examines, and manipulates the data, prepares and edits the text, and designs the maps, graphs, and drawings, all at the same computer terminal.

Microcomputer-generated graphics are created in four ways: from statistical packages, from spreadsheets, from graphics packages, and from packages that are combinations of other packages. One of the major types of combination packages is the presentation graphics software group. Figure 17.11 shows 16 categories of typical output. These packages usually import data from the database or spreadsheet of a personal computer and produce graphic output. Figure 17.12 depicts this process. The more expert the user and the more powerful the software, the more impressive the results will be.

Savings in both time and money result when visual support material is computer generated.

Computer graphics are created in four ways.

MODES OF DELIVERY

The placement of visual support in a written report was discussed in Chapter 12. For oral reports, the media used to deliver the images include transparencies, 35mm slides, flip charts, blackboards, and computer-driven color projection systems.

Business is placing increasing emphasis on high-quality, visually supported presentations, and the design of conference rooms is changing accordingly. Computer and photographic equipment is available in increasing variety for both the preparation and projection of images. These developments underscore the importance of mastering techniques for the delivery of high-quality, well-executed visual support. Table 17.1

Figure 17.10
Sample Drawing
Source: Prepared in Drafix CAD Ultra, courtesy of Foresight Resources Corporation, Kansas City, Missouri.

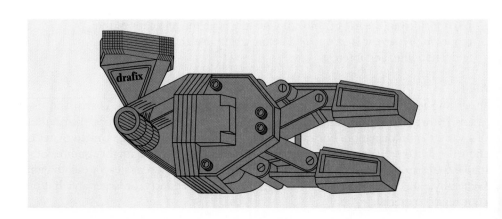

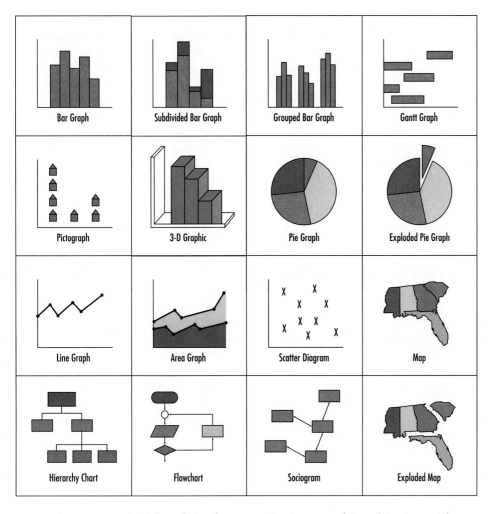

Figure 17.11
Typical Graphics Output of a Combination Software Package
Source: Figure 13-12 from *Understanding Computers and Information Processing: Today and Tomorrow*, Third Edition, by Charles S. Parker, p. 426, copyright 1990 by The Dryden Press, a division of Holt, Rinehart and Winston, Inc., reprinted by permission of the publisher.

summarizes some principles of visual communication, matching objectives with support forms. It also provides solutions to application concerns.

Transparencies

Transparencies are widely used in academic settings and for quick, informal presentations. The overhead projectors for transparencies are easy to use, inexpensive, work well for small and large audiences, and do not require a totally darkened room. Black-on-white original images can be transferred to transparencies as black-on-clear, black-on-color, or color-on-clear film. Several transparencies can be made for a dollar, and preparation requires only a few minutes. Most laser printers can provide black-on-clear transparencies instead of paper originals. Computer images can be transferred to color transparencies with high quality at low cost.

Laser printers can provide black-on-clear transparencies.

When using the overhead projector, avoid leaving the projector on with no image showing, leaving an image on longer than necessary, standing in front of the screen, looking at the screen rather than the audience, and relying too heavily on the visual portion of your presentation. Instead, use transparencies to add continuity and interest to your presentation and to clarify data. Consider covering part of the transparency and disclosing items as you discuss them. Also consider using pens with either permanent or removable ink to add on to transparency images. For example, you may wish to have a prepared *x*- and *y*- axis grid to which you add, with different colors, the lines of a line graph as you discuss each one.

Figure 17.12

Graphics Package Process

Source: Figure 13-13 from *Understanding Computers and Information Processing: Today and Tomorrow,* Third Edition, by Charles S. Parker, p. 427, copyright 1990 by The Dryden Press, a division of Holt, Rinehart and Winston, Inc., reprinted by permission of the publisher.

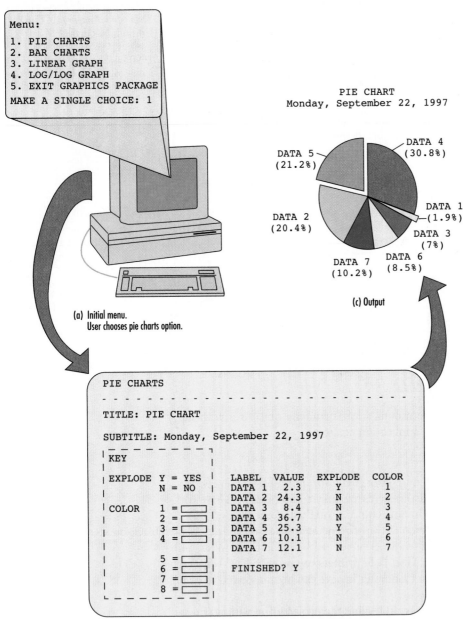

35mm Slides

Slides tend to be used in more formal situations with larger audiences than transparencies. The recent marriage of photography and computer text and images is increasing the quality and speed of preparation of 35mm slides. A color photograph

Primary Objective	Best Support Form	Primary Application Concerns	Secondary Application Concerns
Deliver Precision	Table	Accuracy, heads, rules, totals	Spacing, placement on page or in report
Deliver Complex Documentation	Table	Thoroughness of information	Spacing, placement on page or in report
Achieve Retention	Combine oral and visual messages	Balance of oral and visual	Timing
Enhance Comprehension: Show Trends	Line graphs	Differentiating lines	Grid lines, tick marks, legend
Enhance Comprehension: Show Comparisons	Bar graphs	Selection of correct type of bar graph	Grid lines, tick marks, legend
Enhance Comprehension: Show Relationships	Pie graphs, Venn diagrams	Avoiding too much complexity	Showing secondary relationships
Illustrate Technical Detail	Engineering drawing	Accurate representation	Avoiding too much detail
Create Interest	3-D graphics, colors, pictures, drawings	Avoiding inappropriate emphasis of items	Creating too much interest in support
Maintain Continuity	Text selections, icons	Achieving consistency	Producing too much information

Table 17.1

Summary of Visual Communication Principles

can be scanned and sent to a computer screen, where text or graphics can be added or the photograph modified, and output sent to an on-the-spot processing machine (or delivered digitally to a slide preparation service). Another machine can print a sequence number and title on the slide carrier to ease slide show organization. The total time required is only a few minutes.

For most preparers, several days are needed for film processing, and slides cost more to prepare than transparencies. The projection of slides requires an almost dark room.

Flip Charts

Widely used for small business presentations because of their flexibility and low cost, **flip charts** are the large tablets of plain or gridded paper fastened to an easel. Information can be added with a marking pen during the presentation and pages can be flipped or removed as clean sheets are needed. Another approach is to place packaged presentations on tablets for repeated use.

Use flip charts only for informal presentations and be sure that each member of the audience can see the chart. Write legibly. Use various colors of markers to add interest and variety.

Speakers may write on flip charts during the presentation—or prepare the pages in advance.

✔ *CHECKLIST for Delivery of Visual Support*

____ Make sure everyone can see the visual.

____ Don't talk to the visual; look at your audience.

____ Display the visual only when you refer to it; for example, turn off an overhead projector when you have made your point.

____ Learn in advance the most appropriate time to use a visual.

____ Be familiar with your equipment; practice beforehand if you need to.

____ Be sure the equipment is operable.

____ Have a back-up machine if the aid is integral to your presentation.

Blackboards

The reasons why blackboards have been used in educational settings for so many years are that they allow spontaneous sharing of information, are inexpensive, and are easy to use. Businesses today are moving more to whiteboards that are marked on with erasable, colored pens. Some portable whiteboards can electronically capture the image on the screen and provide a photocopy immediately. Modern conference and presentation rooms are often equipped with built-in boards, screens, projectors, lighting control, and even computer image projectors.

Computer-Driven Color Projection Systems

As the cost of computer technology rapidly decreases and the ease of software use and the power of software increase, computer-driven color projection systems are being widely used in such settings as classrooms, sales presentations, and boardroom briefings.

In such presentations, the user prepares computer slides of text or graphics enhanced with vivid colors, photographs, or clip art. Bulleted items in a list can appear one by one as the items above are shaded. The emerging items can move in from any direction or can fade in. New lines or bars on a graph can appear with existing lines or bars. Each new item or effect can be timed in seconds; additional slides can also be timed to form an automatic slide show. Or, each effect or slide can be advanced manually.

The user can select from dozens of dissolve or transition treatments between slides.

Lighting requirements are similar to those of an overhead projector. The building of lists and transitions between slides can be quite attention grabbing. However, users need to be cautious of overdoing the special effects and mindful of preparing logical, clear, helpful images that don't overshadow the theme of the presentation.

Key Terms

- **visual support**
- **figure**
- **table**
- **graph**
- **chart**
- **flip chart**

Summary

Review Questions

1. What is the difference between tables and figures?

2. What are the major types of figures?

3. What are the categories of graphs?

4. Which type of graph is best for comparison of parts?

5. Which type of graph is best for showing trends?

6. What are the major media employed in business to support oral presentations? Describe the strengths and weaknesses of each.

Exercises

1. As an accountant at Briggs Manufacturing, you have been able to isolate the utilities costs incurred in the operation of the research building that was completed and occupied four years ago. Your superior, Henrietta Starling, has asked you to gather this information so that she can analyze it. You know this information will be part of a report she is preparing for the board of directors, and you want to present as clear and understandable a report as possible. If you can take some of the burden of the report preparation off Starling, so much the better.

   You have decided that you will present the information in a variety of ways. You will supply both charts and tables; in some cases this will be a duplication so that Starling may choose between alternatives. The data are as follows:

Monthly Electricity Usage in Kilowatt Hours				
	1994	**1995**	**1996**	**1997**
J	2,500	2,575	2,495	2,600
F	2,500	2,600	3,000	3,200
M	3,000	3,100	3,200	3,500
A	3,800	3,800	3,700	4,000
M	4,800	4,775	4,975	5,000
J	5,025	5,000	5,600	5,250
J	5,100	5,200	5,750	5,200
A	5,600	5,500	6,000	5,800
S	4,800	4,800	4,900	5,000
O	3,900	3,700	3,700	3,800
N	3,000	3,000	3,200	3,200
D	2,400	2,275	2,700	2,700

Fuel Oil Usage in Gallons				
	1994	**1995**	**1996**	**1997**
J	4,900	4,800	5,000	5,010
F	4,500	4,550	4,600	4,750
M	2,500	2,250	2,500	2,000
A	1,000	1,100	950	1,100
M	600	750	600	550
J	200	210	190	200
J	210	195	200	195
A	850	1,000	900	1,000
S	3,000	2,950	1,500	2,500
O	4,200	4,000	3,250	3,950
N	4,500	4,500	4,350	4,275
D	4,950	4,775	5,010	5,040

Water Usage in Thousands of Gallons				
	1994	**1995**	**1996**	**1997**
J	100	110	105	101
F	98	100	101	104
M	102	100	97	102
A	88	90	103	100
M	97	100	102	98
J	100	101	96	94
J	89	92	96	100
A	91	102	107	100
S	103	100	98	98
O	92	94	94	93
N	101	93	100	98
D	97	95	102	104

a. Prepare, for insertion in a report, a single table showing a year-by-year unit total (gallons, kilowatt hours) for electricity, fuel oil, and water.

b. Prepare one line graph showing month-by-month electricity, fuel oil, and water usage fluctuations for a 12-month period. (Sum the four Januaries, the four Februaries, and so on.)

c. Prepare one pie graph for electricity that indicates the percentage of the whole for each of the four years.

d. Prepare a bar graph for fuel oil only that shows the percentage of change from the preceding month for all four years. That is, compare the total of four Januaries to four Februaries, and so on.

e. Combine electricity (at a constant $.08 per kilowatt hour), fuel oil (at a constant $.80 a gallon), and water (at a constant rate of $5.00 per 1,000 gallons) into a segmented (or subdivided) bar graph that has four bars—one for each of the four years.

2. As the student member of the president's building committee at your university, you have been given a report from the building's architects. The report shows the sizes of the existing and the proposed classrooms for Jefferson Hall and the adjoining Sloane Hall. Additionally, the report presents the proposed numbers of classrooms for the small addition that will be built between, and connecting, Jefferson and Sloane Halls.

The committee will meet tomorrow, and you must be prepared to interpret the data.

Classroom Capacity	Jefferson Hall Existing	Proposed	Sloane Hall Existing	Proposed	New Construction	Total Existing	Proposed
1–19	10	1	13	13	0	23	14
20–39	14	2	11	15	4	25	21
40–59	28	2	4	11	8	32	21
60–99	7	0	9	9	6	16	15
100–199	3	3	2	2	18	5	23
200+	1	0	0	0	2	1	2

a. Decide how much visual support is needed to deliver this information.

b. Prepare the visual support for the meeting.

CASE

Memorable Graphics

Lecia Archer, University of Colorado, Boulder

"Hi Al."

Al Wyborg turned around to see Mary Flannery, a friend and classmate from college, entering the cafeteria. "Hi Mary. Are you eating alone?"

"Not if you join me. What looks good today?"

Al and Mary worked for companies located in the same building and occasionally ran into each other at lunch. Mary's company, Barker, Carroll & Associates Architects, designed commercial buildings in the fast-growing southern California market. Al's company, Seismic Simulations Inc., conducted complex computer simulations to test the effects of earthquakes on commercial buildings. This very rigorous testing was required to ensure that new buildings conformed to state code and, although most architectural firms conducted their own preliminary testing, an independent firm was required to conduct simulations also.

Because of the need for technical expertise and expensive computer equipment, only six firms in the area competed for testing contracts. They submitted proposals outlining the type of tests they planned to conduct as well as individuals' and corporate technical expertise. The proposals were often quite technical as a result, offering a great deal of complex, quantitative information to readers.

Seismic Simulations had recently submitted a proposal to test a new building design for Barker, Carroll & Associates. Al had been part of the proposal writing team for this contract and was disappointed to learn that a competitor, Blake & Company, had been awarded the contract.

Al decided to ask Mary why. "I understand Blake got the contract for your new design. What made you decide to go with them? Was it their price?"

"Their price was on a par with most," Mary replied. "I can't quite put my finger on it, Al. All I know is that everyone that read Blake's proposal understood the explanations of the proposed analyses, and the proposal seemed to stand out in our minds."

"Our proposal was written in an easy-to-read style with several visuals to ease understanding. I wonder what they did that was different," said Al.

"I remember yours, Al; it was easy to read. But so were several others. Maybe it was Blake's color graphics," suggested Mary. "I can't say that Blake had more graphs than others, but they certainly were easy to read, and memorable."

On the way back to his office, Al thought about the conversation. Was it possible that the use of color graphics in proposals could give his company a competitive edge? He decided to investigate.

Case Questions

1. Conduct an experiment: Find a high-quality color graphic and a similar black and white graphic. Show both to a group of people. Which seems easier to understand? Which will be remembered?

2. Prepare a report on the following problem statement: Readers perceive reports with color graphics to be more professional looking or of higher quality than their black and white counterparts.

3. Determine whether Al's company should buy a state of the art color printer. What capabilities should such a printer have? Write a report on your findings.

4. Prepare a report analyzing the use of color. Specifically, address the issue of clutter and distraction caused by color in a graphic aid. How many colors are too many? Which colors are best? Should some color combinations be avoided? Which? Why?

CASE

Marketing Presentation for the Board of Directors

Marie Flatley, San Diego State University

As the marketing director for an expanding shoe company, you formulate market forecasts and expansion recommendations. This year you've been asked to present your report orally to the board of directors. For this presentation, you've decided to use a variety of graphics to supplement both the written and oral reports.

You've determined that you need three different types of graphics for this report. The first will be a world map; it will show, through the use of colors or shading and hatching, where you are doing business now, where you propose to be doing business five years from now, and where you recommend to be doing business ten years from now. The second graphic will be line graphs. In these graphs you'll show the estimated population trends in the countries where you are proposing to do business in the next five years and the next ten years. The third graph will be a stacked bar graph showing the components of income and income projections for ten years ago, five years ago, current, five years ahead, and ten years ahead.

Choose any countries you like for this report. Use your library and references such as almanacs for the population data and population growth rates projections for your countries. Then use statistics from the shoe industry along with your company's current market share to determine income projections. You'll find spreadsheet software helpful in creating the data-generated line and bar charts, and drawing or clip art software will be helpful in creating the world map. Be sure to include all the components necessary for each graphic as discussed in the chapter.

Case Questions

1. Do your illustrations clearly show the data?
2. Have your illustrations met all the principles presented in this chapter?
3. Could any of your illustrations be challenged as misleading?

References

Auvil, Mary S., and Kenneth W. Auvil. *Introduction to Business Graphics: Concepts and Applications.* Cincinnati, OH: South-Western Publishing Co., 1992.

Hoadley, Ellen D. "Investigating the Effects of Color." *Communications of the ACM* 33 (February 1990): 120-125.

Tufte, Edward R. *The Visual Display of Quantitative Information.* (Cheshire, CT: Graphics Press, 1983).

Tufte, Edward R. *Envisioning Information.* (Cheshire, CT: Graphics Press, 1990).

Chapter 18

Meetings: Small Group Communication

"I've got a million things to do today," Tim was thinking as he entered the conference room. "The last thing I need is another meeting." The purpose of this meeting was to explain to the supervisors the new worker involvement program the company was about to implement.

Ron Ryan, the plant manager, conducted the meeting with the assistance of an outside consultant. In the first part of the meeting the consultant described the benefits other companies experienced through worker involvement programs. After that the consultant explained the process and the critical role that the supervisor played. Tim found the concept of worker involvement interesting. He was skeptical, however, about its working in his company.

Following through on what he had been taught, but with considerable apprehension, he called a meeting of the people in his unit. He explained the worker involvement program and described how everyone stood to benefit from the program's success.

"Concentrate on quality control," he told the workers. "What are some things you think should be done to improve quality control?" After an awkward silence a few members made halfhearted suggestions. Fortunately, the time had come to end the meeting. "Same time next week," Tim reminded his people, all the while dreading the prospect of another such meeting. "Between now and then, keep thinking of ways to improve quality control," he said.

At the next meeting, Tim realized that his fears had been unfounded. The group members required no prodding to participate. The members obviously had given some thought to quality control, and they were no longer hesitant about expressing their thoughts.

Tim was pleasantly surprised by the transformation of a collection of individuals into a group. As a result of his experience with the worker involvement program, Tim began to recognize the many values to be derived from working with groups.

THE ROLE OF GROUPS IN TODAY'S BUSINESS ORGANIZATION

Groups have played a major role in U.S. society since the nation's inception. The Declaration of Independence and the U.S. Constitution were forged through painstaking discussion and debate, which is also true of virtually every piece of legislation at both state and national levels.

Business management, also, traditionally has made extensive use of groups. In the past, however, the makeup of such groups was exclusively managerial; that is, only managers and staff participated in the meetings designed to find facts and make decisions. Plans were developed and policies were determined by groups that rarely included any of the individuals affected by them. Business leaders considered these activities to be the province of management alone.

Today the use of groups pervades all levels of the organization. In the quest for greater productivity and employee satisfaction, many companies have moved toward **participative management**. This means that employees at every level become involved in job-related decision making.

In modern organizations decision making involves people at all levels.

The growth of the quality circle movement in Japan, the United States, and many European nations mirrors the growing emphasis on participative management. **Quality circles** are small groups of workers (and managers) that meet regularly to discuss and resolve problems of productivity, quality, and the workplace in general. The impact of quality circles appears to be significant in terms of employee commitment to the organization as well as in organizational productivity and development.

Employees also often function in a **matrix environment** that uses their skills and expertise in both vertical and horizontal directions. A manager, for example, might supervise subordinates in an area of expertise, but also be a representative to a horizontal committee of peers with mixed functions that responds to suggestions for new products. In American business today, the "lone wolf" worker who in the past was often rewarded for individual effort is rapidly being transformed into an effective team member.

Whatever job you eventually assume in a business organization, you will become a part of various work groups. Your ability to work and to interact effectively in groups will significantly determine your occupational success. A knowledge of the contents of this chapter will not in itself turn you into a polished team player, but it will help you move in that direction.

BASIC CHARACTERISTICS OF SMALL GROUPS

Imagine that you participated in two groups today. The first group gathered in the plant cafeteria 30 minutes before starting work. It consisted of you and five friends who meet most mornings and discuss such topics as sports and politics. The second group was the plant grievance committee, consisting of seven members who meet weekly to consider employee grievances. You represent the shipping department. Only one of these groups meets all of the criteria necessary to be designated a small group for our purposes.

A Common Purpose

The members of the plant grievance committee gather with a common purpose to consider the grievances of employees. The individuals who meet in the cafeteria do not share a common purpose. Some enjoy talking about sports, some like to talk about current events, and others have their own interests. They enjoy each other's company and so they continue to meet.

Group members must share a common purpose.

A Small Number of Participants

The size of a group has a significant impact on productivity as well as on the satisfaction of group members. A group that is too small will be limited in the quantity of information it can generate. Individual members may, however, have greater opportunities to participate because of the small size of the group. The increased opportunities will often result in more satisfied members.

With greater size a group can generate more ideas. There will be fewer opportunities for individual participation, however, and members may be less satisfied with their groups. Although there is no magic number at which groups automatically achieve greatest effectiveness, groups of five members are often regarded as the ideal.

Interdependency among Members

Groups are assembled with the intent of capitalizing on the combined efforts of the members. Members not only influence one another, but they also rely on one another for information and support. A bond develops between the members that leads to an interdependence that facilitates communication within the group. Members remain aware of the collective nature of the group.

Face-to-Face Interaction

Interaction among group members is traditionally face to face.

Another characteristic of a small group is that the members interact face to face. The members meet and exchange information verbally and nonverbally. To an extent, this characteristic has been modified by the introduction of computer conferencing and other types of electronic meetings.

Roles

The type of group as well as members' individual characteristics determine their roles.

The roles that group members assume are a function of the type of group as well as the characteristics of the individual group member. If group members belong to a command group of superior and subordinates, the roles they play will depend on their organizational position as well as their relationship with the group's formal and informal leaders. If the group were a friendship group, the role and role expectations would be entirely different.

In any group, individuals can choose whether to play a task or a maintenance role. A **task role** focuses on accomplishment of the task set before the group. Conversely, a **maintenance role** centers around the emotional and psychological needs of the group members. Both roles are essential for effective group functioning.

A **small group** may therefore be defined as a collection of a few individuals who interact face to face, verbally and nonverbally, for a common purpose, and with interdependency among the members. The grievance committee possesses all of the characteristics. The cafeteria group does not, because it lacks both a common purpose and interdependence among its members.

ADVANTAGES OF GROUP DECISIONS

The complaints most often voiced against group meetings are that there are too many meetings, that meetings take too much time, and that most meetings do not achieve any worthwhile results. The obvious question is, therefore, why do managers schedule so many meetings? The answer is that a decision made at a small group meeting has several potential advantages.

Higher Quality of Decisions

A group decison is usually superior to the decision of an individual, provided the members of the group have appropriate knowledge and expertise. Obviously a group of sales managers cannot be expected to deliver a quality decision regarding the implementation of a new computer system for the accounting department. In general, however, groups will bring a greater sum of knowledge and a greater number of approaches to a given problem. This is especially true when no one is an acknowledged expert.

Acceptance

Subordinates who are included in the decision-making process will usually accept the decision more readily than if it is simply handed down. By getting people together to discuss an issue or problem you may expect there to be a greater understanding of others and their ideas and a greater involvement in the arrival at an acceptable solution. For example, suppose that the clothing manager in a retail store is faced with requests from three full-time salespeople for the same week of vacation. One of the three must be asked to reschedule so that the business can function normally. This is not a decision about quality—any one of these three salespeople could perform adequately alone. If the department manager makes the decision, the unlucky salesperson will be upset and may become hostile. However, if the three salespeople are asked to work out a decision among themselves, each has the opportunity to discuss his or her own viewpoint. A group decision in this instance improves the chances that all the salespeople will accept the final agreement.

> Subordinates being involved makes decisions easier to accept.

Commitment

The elements of acceptance and commitment are closely related. Commitment, however, goes beyond acceptance. When individuals are directly involved in analyzing and solving a problem, they become more committed to the effective implementation of the decision. Greater enthusiasm is likely for the broader group goals. Thus, a company considering such motivational tools as job enrichment, wage incentives, or profit sharing might benefit from involving employees in selecting the appropriate program.

Status

Participants gain a sense of heightened status and recognition from the responsibility and interaction in group decision making. This advantage is often one of the keys to effective participatory management in that it gives group members the very real sense that they share an active role in the management of the organization.

DISADVANTAGES OF GROUP DECISIONS

Decision making by small groups has several potential disadvantages.

Time

The typical manager may spend 69 percent of his or her daily communication time in meetings.[1] In addition to the time spent in each meeting, the leader and the participants need time to prepare for it. All of this is time taken away from other duties.

Cost

Surveys indicate that business meetings cost the organizations that sponsor them more than $8 billion a year. A manager's time may be worth over $50 an hour if allocated overhead costs are included. A two-hour meeting of 10 such managers would cost the company more than $1,000. When you consider that business people spend more than 1.5 billion hours a year in meetings, you can see what is at stake. Table 18.1 gives an easy way to calculate how much a meeting might cost just in terms of participant salaries.

> Meetings are expensive.

Unclear Individual Accountability

When an individual is assigned a task, that person is accountable for its satisfactory completion. When a group is assigned a task, accountability is less clear. **Accountability** means the expectation that someone will do some specific things to accomplish a specific goal. When a group pursues a task, accountability is blurred.

> Group decisions blur individual accountability.

Number of Participants	Average Annual Pay			
	$50,000	**$40,000**	**$30,000**	**$20,000**
10	$240	$192	$144	$96
8	192	154	115	77
6	144	115	87	58
5	120	96	72	48

TABLE 18.1 MEETING COSTS PER HOUR

Someone once said, "Success has a thousand fathers; failure has none." Although it was not meant to refer specifically to groups, the quotation suggests a disadvantage of groups. When a group effort is successful, individual members will often try to take credit for the success. When a group effort is unsuccessful, individual members will often seek to disassociate themselves from the results. From the standpoint of individual members, unclear accountability may be viewed as an advantage of small groups. From the standpoint of group productivity, unclear accountability is a definite disadvantage.

Undue Conformity

The mere gathering of different people into a group does not guarantee an ideal result. Sometimes, a group is dominated by one individual and the other members acquiesce in order to speed the decision or to avoid conflict. At other times, a group may perceive a member as more knowledgeable than is actually the case and, therefore, go along with that person's opinions. Less outgoing group participants may hesitate to speak out, especially when a supervisor is in the room.

A related problem has to do with a phenomenon called **group polarization**.[2] In some instances, a group may take a riskier position on an issue than any one individual would take working alone. In other cases, the group might be inclined to a more cautious position. These extremes are typically dependent on the decision to be made and the nature of the participants themselves.

Finally, there is the problem of excess cohesion. The more often a group meets or interacts, the greater the pressures on members to conform. Peer pressure—the influence of the other members—is likely to ensure conformity. The greater the conformity, the less likely a group will benefit from all members' expertise. At the extreme, such conformity is called groupthink, which is discussed later in the chapter.

TYPES AND PURPOSES OF MEETINGS

Small groups are used in a wide variety of situations. However, the two basic purposes of small groups are to share information and to solve problems. Frequently, these purposes are combined within the same group; for example, a group usually exchanges information before it reaches a decision about a problem.

Information-Sharing Meetings

A major purpose of some meetings is to transmit or share information.

The major purpose of information-sharing meetings is to transmit information, ideas, programs, or decisions from one person or group to another person or group. Specifically, these meetings might be held for any one or more of the following purposes.

Report Presentation
The report presentation is an uncomplicated meeting. For example, you may have asked the sales manager of a new territory to give an update on efforts to break into the new market. The marketing staff is gathered to hear this report and perhaps to give feedback that might be useful in the development of the new area.

Training Session

The overall purpose of a training session is to see that essential information is transmitted to an appropriate group. As an example, assume that you are the supervisor of safety and training for a medium-sized manufacturing firm. Your company has just purchased $8 million worth of highly sophisticated, numerically controlled, metal-working lathes. The operations manager for the firm asks you to coordinate a number of hands-on training sessions for the operators of the new machine. Another use for this type of meeting would be to demonstrate a new product for the current sales force.

Brainstorming Session

The purpose of this type of gathering is to generate new ideas or concepts. The discussions are necessarily freewheeling, with the exchange of information among group members as a major goal. When brainstorming is the sole function of a group meeting, a problem-solving meeting often follows. Brainstorming will be discussed in more detail in the section on special techniques for conducting a meeting.

Problem-Solving Meetings

The problem-solving meeting reaches a group judgment or decision or solves a particular problem. Sometimes this type of group may be designated as a committee or task force. In any event, problem-solving groups may come together for any of the following purposes.

Another major purpose of meetings is to solve problems.

Decision Making

In the business setting a wide range of strategic decisions require group attention. A bank or savings and loan, for example, might need to decide whether to open a branch in a large new shopping center. An automobile manufacturer may be faced with deciding whether to discontinue a product line when sales decline.

Problem Analysis

Perhaps the group's most difficult task in reaching an appropriate solution is to determine the real problem. Groups have often decided on a course of action that, once taken, leaves the problem still there. A number of techniques to help analyze and define the question are discussed later in the chapter.

Conflict Resolution

In any organization, various personalities or issues come into conflict. The issues may involve overlapping authority, unequal workloads, impending layoffs, company policies, and the like. The object of bringing together appropriate parties in a group setting is to try to make decisions that will placate the opposing factions. Disgruntled employees need the opportunity to air differences and come to a better understanding of other points of view.

Alternatives to Meetings

The manager's prime obligation in terms of small group communication is to call a meeting only when absolutely necessary. Managers should take advantage, whenever possible, of all alternatives to meetings. For instance, a phone call to the right person or persons (perhaps a conference call) can often resolve a problem, generate an idea, or ratify a decision. For simple information sharing, a memo to all concerned parties can be used to provide the facts and solicit comment. Managers should approach the calling of a meeting with the same concern for cost that they show for the purchase of new equipment or supplies.

A phone call or memorandum might take the place of a meeting.

PREPARATION FOR THE MEETING

Both the group leader and group participants must assume significant roles in getting ready for a meeting.

Leader Responsibilities

The 4 Ws for meeting planning are who, when, where, and why.

Meeting leaders may find the 4 Ws—who, when, where, and why— to be useful in making basic decisions about their meetings. They must determine who will attend, inviting only those necessary to make the meeting productive. They must decide when the meeting will be held so that time is allowed for adequate preparation and there is minimum conflict with other activities. Where the session will convene must be considered in terms of convenience to participants and isolation from disturbances. Finally, and most important, leaders must come to grips with the why of the meeting—the most important purpose, the singular issue, or precisely what is to be accomplished.

Defining the Objective or Purpose

Clarity of purpose is the key ingredient in determining a meeting's success. If you have any doubt about what you wish to accomplish, you are unlikely to accomplish it. Look ahead to the conclusion of the meeting and what it is you wish to have achieved. Are you looking for a final decision? Are you wanting key people to be informed about a policy change? Once defined, this purpose should be conveyed to all invited participants.

Studying the Issues to Be Discussed

Leaders should thoroughly study the general subject area on which group help is sought. Such study will better equip them to guide the group process and ask questions of a reasonable quality.

Selecting the Participants

Careful study of the issues will go a long way in helping leaders determine the composition of the group that they plan to convene. Only those who have something to share or those who have a stake in hearing what is shared should be invited to attend. You may occasionally want to include someone who is likely to oppose a decision reached by the group simply because he or she was not invited. However, as the number of participants increases, the opportunity for quality discussion decreases. You should also be aware of Wolf's law of decision making:

> Major decisions are rarely decided by more than four people. If you think a larger meeting you're attending is really "hammering out" a decision, you're probably wrong. Either the decision was agreed to by a smaller group before the meeting began, or the outcome of the larger meeting will be modified later when three or four people get together.[3]

Setting the Date and Time

If leaders cannot get together with everyone they need, they may not attain the purpose of the meeting. They should therefore set both date and time for the convenience of participants. The date should be far enough in advance so that the group members can prepare for the meeting and adjust their schedules as needed. When planning a meeting, the leader should establish an ending time as well as the starting time. This allows participants to budget appropriately the time block needed for the session.

Notifying the Participants

Notice of the meeting should include the time and place, a complete agenda, specific preparation guidelines for the group members or key participants, the purpose or objective of the meeting, perhaps a list of participants, and any necessary background information. The more you can tell group members prior to the meeting, the more thoroughly they will be able to prepare for it and the more likely they will be to contribute to the desired outcome.

Writing the Agenda

The leader will probably find it useful to furnish each participant with an order of business or list of things to be done. This is the agenda. Most often, business meetings call for the consideration of only one topic. In that case, the meeting notice will likely suffice as the agenda. In a multi-item gathering, however, invited participants should have a list of the topics in the order in which they will be approached. You may want to arrange your agenda so that complex topics are taken up at the most appropriate point in the meeting. Following John E. Tropman's "rule of the agenda bell" illustrated in Figure 18.1, the group moves through discussion items in ascending and then descending order of complexity so that group energy and intensity can be properly focused.[4] Because the best meetings last no more than 1 or 1½ hours, however, an extremely complex or controversial item might be best relegated to a separate meeting.

Microsoft Word contains a meeting agenda template that queries the user on a variety of issues, and then prints the agenda. Sample output appears in Figure 18.2.

Setting up the Meeting Room

Given a choice of meeting rooms, the leader should select a room that is as far away as possible from noise and interruptions. However, the choice of location should not make it difficult for group members to attend. The room should be well lighted and equipped with comfortable chairs and sturdy tables.

The table and seating arrangement should be based, to some degree, on the nature of the meeting. In all cases, the ideal layout provides for eye contact among all participants. In a general discussion session that calls for equal participation on the part of each person present, a square, round, or wide-oval table is best (see Figure 18.3). If, on the other hand, you are leading a problem-solving meeting that requires rather strong leadership to help the group stay on task, you might consider an arrangement that provides a dominant position. Typically, this may be achieved with a rectangular or narrow-oval table (see Figure 18.4). Whichever layout is selected, you should always ensure ample elbow room for each participant. For more on the importance of this arrangement, you might review the section on personal space in Chapter 15.

At least a day or two before the meeting the leader should make the necessary arrangements for any special audiovisual aids that may be used in the meeting room.

Figure 18.1
Tropman's Agenda Bell

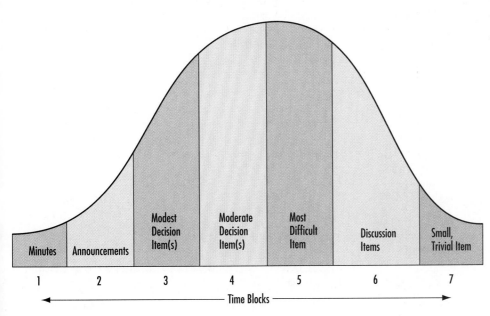

| Minutes | Announcements | Modest Decision Item(s) | Moderate Decision Item(s) | Most Difficult Item | Discussion Items | Small, Trivial Item |

| 1 | 2 | 3 | 4 | 5 | 6 | 7 |

◄———————— Time Blocks ————————►

Figure 18.2
Weekly Quality Circle
Meeting

10/07/97
2:00 PM to 3:10 PM
Building 1, Conference Room

Meeting called by:	Margaret	**Note taker:**	Caitlin
Type of meeting:	Information sharing	**Timekeeper:**	Alberto
Facilitator:	John		

Attendees: Margaret, Toshiko, Alberto, Caitlin, Morgan, Gregory, John, and Kwai
Please read: Last week's minutes (attached)
Please bring: New proposal on selling surplus materials earlier; last week's minutes

Agenda Topics

1. Meeting Overview	Margaret	2:00–2:10 PM
2. Unresolved issues from last week	Toshiko	2:10–2:25 PM
3. Paperwork reduction suggestion	Alberto	2:25–2:35 PM
4. Selling surplus materials earlier	Caitlin	2:35–2:55 PM
5. New suggestions review	Margaret	2:55–3:05 PM
6. Assignments for next meeting	Margaret	3:05–3:10 PM

Other Information

Observers: None for this meeting
Resource persons: Gloria will be in her office if we need to call her
Special notes: Be on time; we don't have much time this week

Figure 18.3
Seating Arrangement to
Promote Discussion

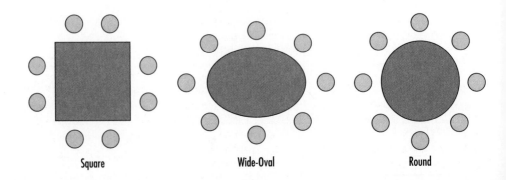

Square   Wide-Oval   Round

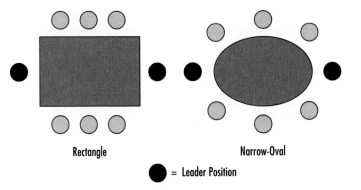

Rectangle Narrow-Oval

● = Leader Position

Figure 18.4
Seating Arrangement
to Provide Strong Leader
Position

Generally, an overhead projector and screen, chalkboard, and flipchart will cover most group needs.

Finally, the leader must check just prior to the meeting to make sure that the meeting room is neat, clean, and orderly and that all audiovisual equipment is in good working condition. Pads and pencils for participants should be in place before they arrive.

Naming of the Recorder

Often overlooked aspects of meeting preparation are the naming of an individual to take notes and the preparing of the minutes of the meeting. The recorder's function is very similar to that of a club secretary. In appointing the recorder, the meeting leader should select a person who knows enough about the subject to summarize rather than record word for word what takes place. The recorder should note who is in attendance and the decisions that were made. The information summarized by the recorder will provide the basis for all follow-up activities. Of course, if every word becomes important, an audio or video recording may be used in lieu of minutes.

The recorder should have some knowledge of the subject.

Participant Responsibilities

Participants should carefully review the agenda and study any other premeeting materials or background materials, keeping in mind the precise objective or purpose of the meeting. They should make careful notes on ideas, comments, questions, or suggestions as they occur in addition to gathering information and sources related to their own area of expertise. Participants who plan to propose a certain solution or strongly support a certain position should make clear and concise notes in order to be prepared to articulate their side of the argument. If the presentation will include visual support (see Chapter 17), the group leader should be alerted to the need for a projector or other equipment.

Overall, the leader selects a group member for a particular reason. It has to do with the individual's role in the organization and how that role may affect the outcome of the group's efforts. Therefore, when you are asked to participate in a group, in all your preparations you should look for ways to support the leader's stated purpose or objective.

✔ **CHECKLIST for Leader Preparation Responsibilities**

_____ Define the meeting's objectives or purpose.

_____ Study the issues to be discussed.

_____ Select the necessary participants.

_____ Choose an appropriate date and time for meeting.

_____ Notify all participants.

_____ Prepare and distribute a complete agenda.

_____ Set up the meeting room.

_____ Appoint a recorder.

✔ **CHECKLIST for Participant Preparation Responsibilities**

_____ Review the agenda.

_____ Study all premeeting materials and background.

_____ Write down ideas, comments, and questions on the topic.

_____ Gather necessary information to present at the meeting.

_____ Prepare any position statement carefully.

_____ Look for ways to support the group's purpose and objective.

THE GROUP LEADER'S ROLE DURING THE MEETING

A key role in every group is that of the group leader. Because of the importance of leadership, a great deal of research has been done on it.

Styles of Leadership

Researchers have identified four styles of group leadership.

Authoritarian Leadership

Authoritarian leaders exercise strong control.

Authoritarian leaders usually determine the specific task for each participant because they often believe that group participants are limited in ability and need strict guidance and control. This style of leadership, therefore, is rigid and inflexible. Authoritarian leaders often dominate discussions and are usually reluctant to acknowledge those who disagree with them. Such leaders discourage member participation, causing members to resign themselves to the fact that the leader will make all the decisions no matter what anyone else might have to contribute. Leaders who employ the authoritarian style may very quickly reach the solution they want, but in terms of group morale the costs are high.

The emotional consequences of authoritarian leadership are serious. You might wonder, why would any group leader use this style of leadership? In many situations, leaders want the group to know beyond any doubt that they are in control. Because they so completely dominate their groups they remain unaware or unconcerned about the members' perception of them as leaders.

Authoritarian leadership would be appropriate for some situations—for example, in a crisis or when time is extremely limited or when the matter under discussion is trivial. Authoritarian leadership, however, is overused and counterproductive.

Supervisory Leadership

Supervisory leaders are slightly more flexible than authoritarian leaders.

Supervisory leadership, which stops short of autocratic control, is useful when efficiency is critical. Supervisory leaders almost always introduce the problem for discussion with a lengthy description. They usually decide the problem that will be discussed in the meeting and frequently summarize what has taken place in the group. Such leaders are not as formal or as rigid as the authoritarians, but they give little attention to the needs of the group.

Participative Leadership

Participative leaders relinquish some control and encourage group participation.

Both authoritarian and supervisory leaders depend on methods that limit the participation and freedom of other group members. Participative, or democratic, leaders encourage group members to participate actively in discussion. Rather than restrict group members, this style of leadership has a positive effect. Meetings conducted in the participative style can be characterized as follows:

- All group members participate freely.
- Communication is directed to all members, not just the leader.
- Group decisions are perceived as group achievements.
- Group members are able to satisfy some personal needs in the group environment.
- Group members are able to identify with the group.

Employing the participative style is difficult. The leader must balance the need to achieve the desired task with the aim of encouraging uninhibited group interaction. This type of leadership is the most frequently used because it promotes a high degree of group cohesion and at the same time spurs the group toward accomplishing the task.

Group-Centered Leadership

Group-centered, or laissez faire, leaders expect group members to be self-directed. They refrain from structuring the group in any way. They listen but do not show approval or disapproval, and although they may clarify on occasion, they are careful not to inject their own thoughts. The group atmosphere is extremely permissive. The leader of a group-centered gathering always tries to view the discussion from the frame of reference of the member who is speaking.

Group-centered leaders are permissive.

Relationship between Styles

The relationship between the styles of leadership can be seen on the continuum in Figure 18.5. Participative leadership is usually desirable. Although the group often takes longer to reach a consensus, member satisfaction is highest. Each group has its own needs, however, and each leader will want to select a style that is in keeping with these needs and with his or her personality.[5]

Basic Duties of the Group Leaders

Regardless of the leadership style, several basic duties are essential to attaining the group's purposes. They can be most easily understood by dividing the meeting into three parts.

The Beginning.   Arrive early. As leader, you should make sure that the room is set the way you want and that all necessary equipment and materials are on hand. Start on time. Keep in mind the high costs associated with meetings. If you respect participants' time, you are more likely to gain respect for your time in return. Make your opening count:

A responsibility of the group leader is to start and end the meeting on time.

- Establish the right tone—usually serious and positive.
- Be sure to identify any participants unknown to the group.
- Offer any background comments that might prove useful to the group.
- Review the objectives of the meeting in terms of items on the agenda.
- Identify any time constraints not already expressed on the agenda—for example, when the meeting must end.[6]

The Principal Task.   The actual conduct of the meeting should reflect your primary purpose (or purposes) for calling it. Keep to the planned agenda. As leader, you will probably have to prod the group, from time to time, to return to the task at hand. You may want to periodically restate the purpose of the meeting. Ask the recorder to summarize points made or decisions completed as you progress through the agenda. Above all, you will want to balance the discussion between those who tend to dominate meetings and those who are always reluctant to speak. This will help you remain impartial and diffuse controversies to the end that all of the individuals you have gathered will have the opportunity to express their thoughts. Finally, you will want to set a good example by listening attentively to all speakers and thus take advantage of the expertise they bring to the meeting.

Figure 18.5
Styles of Leadership

The Closing.   As leader, you should make every effort to end on time. Nothing can more easily destroy the atmosphere of a well-run meeting than to have people get up to leave because they have another commitment. As you approach the ending time, you should summarize all the decisions made. Emphasize specifically the action that should be taken, by whom, and when.

Special Techniques for Meeting Conduct

Maximum and proper participation on the part of all group members produces the most useful results. Toward this end, the leader can employ a number of skills and techniques for encouraging and channeling participation.

Problem-Participant Methods

Timid participants must be treated differently from overtalkative ones.

In any group setting you, as leader, may encounter individuals whose behaviors are counterproductive to the overall mission. You should know some of the methods for dealing with them. The timid participant, for example, may be brought out with an occasional question or by soliciting information that he or she holds exclusively. At the opposite extreme is the person who always seems to have too much to say about everything. Appropriate actions include interrupting the person at the end of a sentence and asking for comments from another member, changing the topic to consider another point, or reminding the group of the need to move on because of a crowded agenda.

The private conversationalists are a special problem because their talking among themselves makes it difficult for other participants to hear the discussions on the topic at hand. You might ask them to continue their conversation after the meeting or invite them to share their comments with the rest of the group. In all cases, you should try to remain calm, understanding, and tactful and maintain a good sense of humor.

The Dewey Reflective Thinking Process

Nearly every small group brought together to solve a problem finds it useful to follow a set format or agenda. The most widely used format is based on John Dewey's Reflective Thinking Process.[7] These six steps are based on Dewey's work:

> **✔ CHECKLIST *for Leading a Meeting***
>
> ____ Arrive early and start on time.
>
> ____ Make your opening count. Be sure to define the purpose and state the timetable for the meeting.
>
> ____ Keep to the planned agenda.
>
> ✔ Remain impartial.
>
> ____ Balance the discussion.
>
> ✔ Restate the purpose/objectives periodically.
>
> ____ Listen attentively to other group members.
>
> ✔ Summarize the group's decisions or progress at intervals during the meeting.
>
> ✔ Diffuse hot controversies.
>
> ✔ End with a summary of decisions made.
>
> ✔ Highlight the action that should be taken, by whom, and when.

The most widely used format for problem solving is the Reflective Thinking Process.

1. Defining and Analyzing the Problem.   During the initial meeting the precise nature of the problem should be specified and its underlying causes investigated. Consider, for example, a small retail firm that has low employee morale, a decline in sales, and an unusually high rate of employee turnover. The conference leader might begin by describing these problems and delineating them with available facts. By concisely depicting the present state of affairs, the leader is defining the problem.

Once each conference participant understands the nature and scope of the problem, the group can investigate potential causes. This is the crux of the first step in problem solving. In the example, group members would offer their perceptions of what might be causing the morale, sales, and turnover problems. These perceptions are discussed, modified (if necessary), and recorded by a leader or appointed group member. Suppose the group perceives the following four possible causes: (1) lack of communication between superiors and subordinates; (2) poor motivational programs,

(3) conflict between the sales and delivery departments; and (4) insufficient advertising. After analyzing information from attitude surveys or grievance and exit interviews, the group might decide that inadequate motivation is the major cause of the problem. When the problem is defined and the suspected cause is identified, the group can move to Step 2.

2. Establishing Criteria for a Solution.   The criteria step in the problem-solving sequence is optional and may be postponed until solutions are actually evaluated. Suppose, however, that this group determines the criteria that any potential solution must meet. The criteria might be that the solution: (1) must include all nonmanagement employees; (2) must become effective within two months; and (3) must cost no more than 2 percent of the company's gross profits.

These criteria are derived from discussion among the conference members. Some proposed criteria were altered slightly, while some were rejected. In any event, the group has arrived at three criteria and is ready to begin Step 3 of the problem-solving process.

3. Proposing Possible Solutions.   In this step participants suggest as many potential solutions as possible. Each participant attempts to propose solutions that meet the specified criteria. Although members may amend the solutions offered by others, no solutions are evaluated at this time. The third step is essentially brainstorming.

Suppose that the group suggests the following five potential solutions: (1) better fringe benefits; (2) increased commissions; (3) profit sharing; (4) a sales contest; and (5) wage incentives. The group can now move to Step 4.

4. Evaluating Possible Solutions.   In Step 4 the conference members evaluate each of the proposed solutions. Each solution is weighed against any criteria outlined in Step 2 as well as against other proposed criteria. The group's aim is to identify the advantages and disadvantages of each solution. For example, the wage incentives might be pertinent to all nonmanagement employees and easily set up within two months but, nevertheless, too costly and irrelevant to the needs of the commission salespeople.

Once the advantages and disadvantages have been assigned to each solution, the group can proceed to Step 5.

5. Selecting a Solution.   A critical point to keep in mind is that the group is not obligated to select only one of the proposed solutions. The most effective decision might combine two or three proposed solutions or an altered version of only one solution. Whatever the outcome, during Step 6 a final decision must be made concerning the best possible solution. The precise details of the solution should also be decided. Suppose, in this example, that the group chooses to increase commissions by one percent across the board. In addition, the group decides on a three-month sales contest between hard- and soft-line divisions, and the winners are to receive cash bonuses and gift certificates. The participants are now ready for the final step in the problem-solving sequence.

6. Plotting a Course of Action.   This final step concentrates on how best to execute the solution. Before the conference can end, the participants must agree on a specific, detailed method for enacting the solution. Conference members may volunteer to assume responsibility for certain aspects of the program, or the leader may assign specific tasks to group participants. Whatever approach is chosen, agreement must be reached before the problem-solving process can terminate.

For the sake of illustration, suppose that two department heads have volunteered to direct the sales contest. Together they will work out the details and report to the store manager within one week. Finally, the store manager announces that the one percent commission increase will become effective at the beginning of the next month.

The Ideal Solution Format

Although Dewey's six-step format is the best known and most widely used approach to problem solving, there are other formats in use. One is the ideal solution format, which was developed from observing the problem-solving process followed by many business groups. In the ideal solution format, group discussion follows this sequence of questions:

The ideal solution format for solving problems originated in business.
起源

- Are we all agreed on the nature of the problem?
- What would be the ideal solution from the point of view of all parties involved in the problem?
- What conditions within the problem could be changed so that the ideal solution might be achieved?
- Of the solutions available to us, which one best approximates the ideal solution?

The Single Question Format

The single question format is another approach to group problem solving. Groups that follow the single question format focus on a single objective and thereby are less likely to pursue digressions. In the single question format this sequence of questions is followed:

The single question format for problem solving discourages digressions.
离题

- What single question will yield the answer that is all the group needs to know to accomplish its purpose?
- What subquestions must be answered before this single question can be answered?
- Do we have sufficient information to confidently answer the subquestions? (If yes, answer them. If not, continue.)
- What are most reasonable answers to the subquestions?
- Assuming that our answers to the subquestions are correct, what is the best solution to the problem?

The ideal solution format and the single question format appear to be more direct and to the point than the Dewey approach. The Dewey approach, however, is more thorough and is more likely to develop the group members' analytical skills. As a group matures and remains intact over long periods of time, it adopts a more abbreviated approach to problem solving. Its new approach may be the ideal solution format or the single question format, or the group may adopt another approach specifically tailored to its environment and needs.

The Nominal Group Procedure

Sometimes groups are dominated by individuals with powerful personalities. These individuals often keep others from actively participating in the group process. You may encounter a group member who digresses and consumes valuable group time talking about unrelated topics. On other occasions, individuals in the group may press for a quick decision before all the important aspects of the problem have been thoroughly considered. In numerous other ways, also, individuals can dilute the decision-making potential of groups. One way to overcome some of these problems is to employ the nominal group procedure. The nominal group procedure can be briefly outlined in three stages, which are discussed in terms of analyzing possible problem causes.

The nominal group procedure avoids problems caused by aggressive or unfocused members.

冲淡

In the first stage, the members who are going to participate in the small group session are brought together and are asked not to speak to each other; thus the term **nominal group** is used because the members are in a group setting but no verbal interaction is permitted. After the participants are seated, they are asked to write on a piece of paper what they believe are the major causes of the problem under consideration. This task should take approximately 10 to 15 minutes. For example, if the problem-solving group has been brought together to discuss a high rate of absenteeism, each group member would be asked to list as many causes for the absenteeism as possible. Throughout this first stage it is important that individuals in the nominal group not talk to each other.

In the second stage, after the members of the nominal group have had enough time to list the causes of the problem, the group leader asks a member to read one of the items he or she listed. As the person reads the cause aloud to the group, the leader writes the cause on a large pad of paper or blackboard so that all group members can read it. The group leader proceeds to the next person and asks for another cause, continuing around the group until everyone's list has been read. When a cause is put on the master sheet that other members have also included on their lists, they cross that item off their lists. In this way each cause is listed only once on the master list. If there is a question whether an item overlaps with an item already on the list, that item should be placed on the master list.

In the final stage, all members examine the master list carefully and rank-order the causes of the problem. If the list is long, the group members are asked to select the top five by secret ballot. After all individuals have completed their rankings, the information is collected and tabulated.

All three stages of this process can be completed in about one hour. When employed this way, the nominal group process can identify the major causes of the problem. The procedure also allows for the establishment of the most important causes. Because individuals rank the causes by secret ballot, the probability is high that the priority causes of the problem are accurately established.

When used as described here, the nominal group format enhances the advantages and minimizes the disadvantages of the interacting group format. The following are some major advantages of the nominal group:

- Members' influence is more equal.
- Members accept ideas more readily.
- Members need not be acquainted for the group to be productive.
- Premature evaluation of ideas is avoided.
- Time is spent more effectively.
- The format can be used to involve very large groups.

Brainstorming

This is a well-known technique for reaching creative solutions to a variety of problems. In the brainstorming session, the leader states the problem. The recorder writes down the ideas for solving the problem as fast as the group members can call them out. The main purpose of this method is to generate as many novel solutions as possible. Participants are encouraged to be creative without regard to whether what they propose is actually feasible. No group member may explain or criticize any proposal. This activity continues as long as group members have ideas. The theory is that creativity will build as one idea triggers another. Only when participants have exhausted their ideas on the subject is evaluation allowed. The basic rules of brainstorming are these:

- Ideas are expressed freely without regard to quality. The emphasis is on quantity.

- Criticism of ideas is not allowed until the brainstorming session is over.
- Elaboration and combinations of previously expressed ideas are encouraged.

A record of the ideas generated is kept by the recorder or other appointee.

Circular Response Method

The circular response method ensures that everyone contributes to the meeting.

This technique is an ideal way of seeing to it that all participants are given the opportunity to speak on the given subject. As the topic is announced, the leader begins by soliciting a comment from one member of the group. The next person on the right or left is then directed to comment, and so on around the entire group. This pattern continues until everyone has spoken. The basic rule is that no one can speak a second time until every member of the group has had the opportunity to comment at least once. Like the nominal group procedure, this technique is useful in reducing the dominance of one strong participant.

Groupthink Avoidance

Groupthink hampers decision making.

Groups that are overly cohesive suffer from **groupthink**.[8] Groupthink occurs when agreement becomes more important than critical thinking. Under conditions of groupthink, a group may make decisions that the individual members, acting alone, would probably not have made. A sentiment that often prevails in groups beset by groupthink is expressed by the cliche, "Don't make waves."

Here are the symptoms of groupthink:

- An illusion of invulnerability, shared by most or all the members, which creates excessive optimism and encourages taking extreme risks
- Collective efforts to rationalize in order to discount warnings that might lead members to reconsider their assumptions before they recommit themselves to their past policy decisions
- An unquestioned belief in the group's inherent morality, inclining the members to ignore the ethical or moral consequences of their decisions
- Stereotyped views of opposition leaders as too evil to warrant genuine negotiations or as too weak and stupid to counter whatever risky attempts are made to defeat their purposes
- Direct pressure on any member who expresses strong arguments against any of the group's stereotypes, illusions, or commitments, making clear that dissent is contrary to what is expected of all loyal members
- Self-censorship of deviations from the apparent group consensus, reflecting each member's inclination to minimize the importance of any doubts and counterarguments
- A shared illusion of unanimity concerning judgments conforming to the majority view (partly resulting from self-censorship of deviations and augmented by the false assumption that silence means consent)
- The emergence of self-appointed mindguards—members who protect the group from adverse information that might shatter their shared complacency about the effectiveness and morality of decisions[9]

Groupthink is prevalent and is destructive to genuine group efforts. Its presence defeats the main reason for assembling groups—critical thinking.

Decision-making groups can take measures to prevent groupthink.[10] As a first step, the leader should assign the role of critic to each member. Doubts and objections are thus more likely to be exposed and discussed rather than suppressed. Group leaders must set an example by accepting criticism of their ideas and thoughts. Acceptance of criticism does not often come naturally; it may have to be learned by group members.

Second, when assigning a decision-making mission to a group, the leader should be impartial rather than state preferences. When executives in an organization give guidance to decision-making groups, many times they introduce bias unwittingly by being too specific in outlining what they want accomplished. If the time is short, more guidance will hasten the decision. However, less guidance will lessen the chance that the executive's preconceived notions will unduly influence the group's decision. Certainly the leader should not be so specific as to indicate which of several alternatives is personally preferable. A delicate balance is needed between enough guidance to get the job done and so much guidance that group members believe they have been manipulated. A good group leader should strive for that balance.

BOXED IN

AN ETHICAL DILEMMA

Claire Watson is in her tenth year as director of management information systems (MIS) for a major firm headquartered in Charlotte, North Carolina. Although she holds an important position, she feels that she has not always received recognition for her efforts. She has built what is, perhaps, the most comprehensive MIS division in the industry. For the past year, Claire has responded to overtures from one of her company's top competitors to become vice-president for MIS.

This morning Claire accepted the competitor's job offer by phone. Her calendar shows a marketing meeting scheduled after lunch. She decides that, immediately after the meeting, she will get together with her boss and discuss her transition out of the company. She has kept him apprised of negotiations regarding the new position, but she is confident that he will be surprised.

The company president himself called the special marketing meeting, which is held in his luxurious conference room. Shortly into the meeting, he announces a significant change in marketing strategy—a change based primarily on the firm's strategic advantage of having a state-of-the-art MIS division and a dynamic MIS director. Claire squirms uncomfortably, as the meeting seems to focus on how critical she will be to the success of this new venture. Her boss is beaming because his best division head is finally being recognized in grand fashion. As Claire looks at the timetable for implementation, she knows that the changes in marketing thrust cannot be effected on schedule if the company must search for a new director of MIS.

Claire feels boxed in. What would you do?

Questions

1. Should Claire renege on her decision to change jobs?

2. Is it fair to her new company to try to help out her current company by delaying her departure?

3. How appropriate was it for the president to steep his praise on Claire at the meeting? Should he have spoken with her before the meeting and shared his intentions?

Third, members of the decision-making group should seek advice and counsel from trusted associates in their own departments within the organization. Fresh perspectives on a problem can be gained by introducing thoughts from outside the group. When the decision involves highly confidential planning of goals or policies, discretion must be used in implementing this suggestion, of course.

Finally, the tendency to seek consensus could be thwarted effectively by using a devil's advocate at each group meeting. The role of devil's advocate, to be most effective, should be rotated among the group members, and in some cases more than one may be desirable. Criticisms by the devil's advocate should be taken seriously and discussed to the satisfaction of all present.

PARTICIPANTS' ROLES DURING THE MEETING

You may not always be cast in the role of leader in a small group situation but, rather, as a participant who is present because of certain expertise you possess. In that role, you should take equal responsibility for the attaining of the group's purpose. Several behaviors of participants contribute to the group's success.

Arriving on Time

Participants have a primary responsibility to arrive at a scheduled meeting at the appointed time, perhaps even a little before. By arriving late, you disrupt the proceedings and extend discourtesy to those who arrived on time.

Following the Agenda

You should make every attempt to restrain yourself from making comments that do not relate to the items on the agenda. The objectives and purposes of the meeting must be regarded as uppermost in importance.

Contributing Information

The problem-solving group needs information to reach a decision. Effective group members bring information they have gathered about the topic. Some participants have a tendency to divulge all their information the first time they have the opportunity to speak; this leads to disorganization. People need to develop the ability to see where their information on the topic applies. Timing is a critical element in presenting information.

Evaluating the Information

Group participants need to bring several critical skills to the problem-solving situation. One of the most important is the ability to carefully examine all information presented to the group. Participants should offer additional supporting evidence when they have it and contradictory evidence when it is available. Fallacious reasoning and unsupported assertions should be exposed. Good reasoning and accurate information are essential to the problem-solving process. Participants should resist the tendency to accept everything that is said during the discussion.

Asking Questions

Group participants perform an important function by asking pertinent questions at appropriate times. Such questions help to expose inaccurate information or to clarify a point that one of the other members is attempting to make. The use of questions encourages feedback, aids the understanding of all group members, and helps keep the participants on the main subject of the discussion. The attention of the entire group can be focused on the central issue of the discussion by a well-phrased, pertinent question.

Listening Empathetically

Effective group participants listen to the content of what other members are saying and also "listen between the lines." The empathetic listener tries to see the topic from the other members' frames of reference as they speak. The listener should be sensitive to the attitudes and feelings of other group members.

Avoiding Side Discussions

A participant may on occasion be stimulated to discuss a topic with the group member in the adjacent seat. Such discussions obviously disrupt the deliberations of the rest of the group. The best action to take is to simply make note of the side issue and plan to bring it up in another setting after the meeting is over.

Thinking as the Group Thinks

The group member needs to be aware that thinking as the group thinks is different from individual thinking. Participants need to relate their comments to the group's thinking. People should refer to what their fellow group members have said and what has already been agreed on. The more often people participate in a group, the more skilled they usually become in group thinking. Also, to try to move ahead too quickly is not a good idea. For the group to function effectively, the group must think together.

Encouraging Others

Equal to your responsibility to share your expertise is your obligation to encourage others to share theirs. You may stimulate the reticent participant by simply stating, "We haven't heard from Susan on this issue. Susan, what do you think about this proposal?" Try to follow up by positively reinforcing the suggestions of your fellow group members.

> ✔ *CHECKLIST for Participating in a Meeting*
>
> ____ Be on time.
> ____ Follow the agenda.
> ____ Contribute information.
> ____ Evaluate information.
> ____ Ask questions.
> ____ Listen empathetically.
> ____ Avoid side discussions.
> ____ Think as a group member.
> ____ Encourage others to participate.
> ____ Keep your comments brief.
> ____ Take notes to retain specific information.

THE MEETING FOLLOW-UP

Follow-up activities are often as important as the preparation for the meeting. At this stage the decisions, suggestions, and solutions are implemented. Both leaders and participants share the responsibility for the implementation.

A successful meeting requires a successful follow-up.

Leader Activities

Follow-up activities should be swiftly executed. A coordinated effort by the group leader and the recorder is necessary to assemble and reproduce copies of the meeting record, or minutes. The record should not be long or formal. It should, however, include the date and place of the meeting; the names of the group leader, the recorder, and all participants; the purpose of the meeting; the alternatives considered; the decisions made; and the action required, by whom, and when. Ideally, the record is in the hands of all participants within two or three days after the meeting.

The leader is responsible for following up with individuals regarding implementation of the solutions generated at the meeting.

Participant Activities

Basic follow-up activities for the participants are twofold. First, group members who have been appointed to do special tasks should immediately plan and move on the implementation. Any uncertainty about these tasks should be cleared up in the meeting record. The second responsibility of each participant is to review the meeting record and forward to the leader any corrections or clarifying comments. The meeting has not been a success until all follow-up activities are completed.

THE ELECTRONIC MEETING

Electronic meetings break with tradition in that participants are not face to face.

One of the traditional characteristics of small groups is that members interact face to face. To this extent, electronic meetings differ from what is customarily considered to be small group communication. The individuals involved may, at best, see only images of faces.

One useful form of electronic group interaction involves the linking of compatible personal computers at either local or distant sites. To illustrate, James Cox is international materials manager for a large manufacturer of parts for the aerospace industry. His company has eight regional manufacturing facilities located in various parts of the United States, Spain, and Brazil, all linked by computers. Lately, several of the plants have been experiencing erratic, unexplained fluctuations in spare parts inventories. James uses his desktop computer to transmit an E-mail message to all eight regional managers. Before long (accounting for the widespread time zones involved), all eight managers have read the message and are inputting their own suggestions as well as comments on suggestions made by others. By the end of the next day, as his supporting managers have dropped in and out of his electronic meeting and back in again, James Cox is ready to decide on a solution to the inventory problem.

Computers may be employed in other unique ways. A relatively recent development is known as Collaborative Work Support Systems (CWSS), or sometimes alternatively as Group Decision Support Systems. The possibilities that result from merging of CWSS and the traditional group session are virtually unlimited.

Suppose, for example, that a group of managers is linked electronically to a local CWSS. A meeting is called for a week in the future. The managers begin brainstorming ideas into their office computers, entering information at random times prior to the meeting. These ideas may or may not be attributed to the respective sources. When they convene for the face-to-face meeting, a compiled list of all the ideas is retrieved from the networked computer in the meeting room. The ideas are available for all of the group members to view, discuss, and evaluate—perhaps projected onto a larger screen.

Savings in travel costs and time have been mentioned as an obvious advantage of electronic meetings. Electronic conferencing can work well when routine decisions are made among managers located some distance from one another. A disadvantage is the lack of a sense of interpersonal interaction among participants. Doubt still exists as to whether the quality of decisions produced can match the quality of those produced in a face-to-face encounter.

A spin-off of electronic meetings and an extension of telecommuting—working from one's home via phone lines and a computer—is the emerging concept of the virtual office. The virtual office is actually a nonoffice. Workers visit customers and clients face to face at their business location, use portable phones and computers, and may meet with colleagues on the train during a morning commute or at an airline hospitality suite at the airport. When they do go to the headquarters, they have no individual location. They might be issued a computer cubicle, use the company's media library, or meet with others in a conference room. The closest thing to a private desk might be an employee locker for storage of limited business-related items.[11]

A comparison of face-to-face meetings with various types of electronic meetings is shown in Table 18.2. In simplest terms, electronic meetings can be classified as audio, commonly via telephone; audiographic, which adds a device for transmitting diagrams,

---

TABLE 18.2   MEETING COMPARISON CHART

Features	Audio	Audiographic	Type Video	Computer Conferencing	Face-to-Face
Does everyone have to be on line at the same time?	Yes	Yes	Yes	No	Yes
Can graphics be exchanged?	No	Yes	Yes	Yes	Yes
Can facial expressions and other nonverbal clues be exchanged?	No	No	Yes	No	Yes
Is a written record immediately available?	No	No	No	Yes	No
Does everyone have to be in the same location?	No	No	No	No	Yes

Source: Adapted from Robert Johansen, Jacques Vallee, and Kathleen Spangler, *Electronic Meetings: Technical Alternatives and Social Choices* (Reading, MA: Addison-Wesley, 1979).

maps, charts, and sketches; video, or telecommunicating; and computer conferencing, represented by the James Cox example. Chapter 4 was devoted to electronic equipment used in business.

Key Terms

- **participative management**
- **quality circle**
- **matrix environment**
- **task role**
- **maintenance role**
- **small group**
- **accountability**
- **group polarization**
- **nominal group**
- **groupthink**

Summary

Review Questions

1. Discuss the major advantages and disadvantages of reaching decisions in small groups. Give an example of each.

2. What are the basic identifying characteristics of a small group?

3. Define and discuss the two basic types of small group meetings. Give examples of each.

4. What are some of the most useful alternatives to the calling of a meeting?

5. Describe some of the duties required of the leader in preparing for a meeting.

6. Discuss the basic principle underlying Tropman's "rule of the agenda bell."

7. Why is the simple arrangement of tables and chairs important in the conduct of a meeting?

8. What are the major styles of group leadership? Which style best fits your personality? Why?

9. Most of the time, the participative leadership style is the most desirable. Why?

10 Describe some of the basic leader duties essential to the conduct of each part of a successful meeting.

11. Discuss the six steps involved in the Dewey Reflective Thinking Process.

12. In what ways is the nominal group approach to problem solving superior to the interacting group approach?

13. What is brainstorming and why is it useful in the problem-solving process?

14. What is groupthink? How does it contribute to irrational and poorly formulated decisions? What are some of the ways of avoiding groupthink?

15. Describe some of the behaviors that group members can exhibit that can contribute to a meeting's success.

16. Why is follow-up important to a group process?

17. What are some of the advantages and disadvantages of the various types of electronic meetings?

Exercises

1. As a class, divide into groups of five or six and use the brainstorming technique to generate solutions to a problem that confronts your school.

2. Attend a meeting of the local city council and observe the interaction of council members. Record your observations.

3. Critically evaluate a meeting connected with your interests at school—student government, fraternity or sorority, professional honor society, or the like. Include both pros and cons of the proceedings in your evaluation.

4. Select a problem that you have in common with a peer group. Reach a decision on your own, then discuss it with the group. Record any new viewpoints that the group brought up that you overlooked in your original decision.

5. Lead a group discussion about a pertinent issue such as job placement or course curriculum degree requirements. How did your role as a group leader differ from that of a participant? Rotate the leadership role among other group members and describe how individual styles produced various types of interaction.

6. Assemble two groups of four to six people. Discuss an issue. How did the conclusions and decision-making procedures differ between the two groups?

7. Form a group with 12 classmates. Split up into two subgroups of four and eight, then attempt to resolve the same problem as in Exercise 6. Did the size of the two groups affect the communication process and the eventual outcome? How?

8. As a class, divide into three groups and select a single problem in which the participants are interested. Assign each group a different approach to solving the problem. One group uses the steps of reflective thinking; another uses the single question format; the third uses the ideal solution format. Following the exercise, discuss the differences and similarities of the three approaches.

9. Each person in the class should make a list of the problems experienced as a new member of an established group. As a class, divide into groups of five or six and construct a master list for each group using the individual lists. Each group should then identify ways in which group members can overcome these problems.

10. Using the problem lists generated in Exercise 9, identify ways that group leaders can assist members in overcoming those problems.

CASE

The Realty Tangle

Doris D. Phillips, University of Mississippi

Kilgore and Mitchell, Realtors, is a Mississippi real estate firm that has been in business for 15 years and has a strong local and regional reputation. Partners James J. Kilgore and Donald O. Mitchell are assisted by six full-time salespeople, two part-time salespeople, and two full-time secretaries. Until recently they had enjoyed a harmonious office atmosphere.

Virginia Bolt has been with the firm in part-time sales for about five years and has built a reasonably large clientele. Before joining Kilgore and Mitchell she worked a total of 25 years in various clerical positions in banks and with governmental agencies. She had excellent clerical skills but was unable to remain long in any job because of an inability to get along with people.

Her recent actions indicate a renewal of the old people problem. In addition to antagonizing other salespeople in the firm by undercutting and backstabbing, she has allegedly violated an important point in realty ethics by advertising property in her own name with no reference to Kilgore and Mitchell as her employers.

Mitchell wants to release Virginia from her position with the firm. He believes that her unethical actions could damage the firm's good name. He also thinks that her personality is disrupting an otherwise smooth operation.

Kilgore wishes to give Virginia another chance. His reasoning is that her successful record in sales outweighs her shortcomings in other areas.

Case Questions

In groups of five, analyze the case.

1. Make the management decision about Virginia's future with the firm.

2. Decide how to communicate the decision to Virginia and to others in the office so as to provide the greatest degree of acceptance and harmony.

3. Draft messages to Virginia and to the other employees informing them of the decision reached.

C A S E

The Springwood Drive Plaza

Judith V.A. Dietrich, R.N.,M.S.N., formerly Sessional Lecturer, University of British Columbia, Vancouver

The United States is facing new problems related to a phenomenon called the "graying of America." A decrease in infant mortality and improvements in the diagnosis and treatment of disease have helped reduce mortality rates and extend life expectancy. Greater numbers of Americans are living longer. Some 28 million people, or 12 percent of the population, are 65 or over; at least 21 percent, or 66 million people, will be 65 or over by the year 2030.[12]

As people age, they often become less able to care for themselves. The elderly frequently must either obtain help within the home or move into some type of institutional setting. Society has the responsibility of ensuring that the home help services and care facilities are available. Presently they are inadequate, however, and a definitive plan for meeting the needs of the year 2030 still must be addressed.

The Springwood Drive Plaza is one facility that offers a unique approach to these problems. It provides apartments for the elderly individual or couples, support services on site, and supervision by caring, skilled personnel.

The Plaza is managed by Marie, Susan, and Dennis. Marie and Susan are registered nurses; Dennis is a social worker. The three of them have worked extensively with the aged population in a variety of settings. Their combined skills and backgrounds provide the expertise required to accurately assess, plan, carry out, and evaluate strategies designed to meet the needs of the tenants. In addition, they are familiar with and know how to cope with the type of stress generated from caring for the elderly.

Marie, Susan, and Dennis have maintained an effective and satisfying working relationship during the three years their business has been in operation. Though they consider themselves to be partners, Marie is considered to be the leader of the group and is officially recognized as the administrator of the organization.

The relationship has been characterized by the use of open communication lines. The three of them chat over coffee and meet informally during the week to discuss any problems that arise. Once a month, they and their families get together for a supper or barbecue. There is also a formal meeting once a month to review major problems and the success of the program in helping the elderly tenants retain independence and meaning in their lives.

Eight months ago, an additional service was added to the package offered to the tenants. Tom, a massage therapist and physiotherapist, had convinced Marie, Susan, and Dennis that a program of massage and exercise would help the tenants feel better and maintain the physical strength needed to carry out the activities of daily living. The results of the program have been positive in both of these areas.

Gradually, Tom began to spend more time talking to Dennis. He had mentioned to Dennis over coffee one day how satisfying it was to work independently and not have to deal with the restrictions of a hospital bureaucracy. The fact that Dennis had two women for partners and that one of them was the administrator of the Plaza seemed to surprise Tom.

During Tom's fourth month at the Plaza he asked Dennis if he could participate in the monthly meetings. Dennis discussed the request with Marie and Susan, and as a group they made the decision to include Tom in the meetings.

Tom has attended two of the meetings. At the first meeting he contributed little to the discussion. When he did speak, it was to boast about the success of his massage program. At the second meeting, he spoke in an authoritarian manner when addressing Marie and was openly critical of how the status of the tenants was assessed.

Case Questions

1. What factors fostered the cohesiveness within the small group consisting of Marie, Susan, and Dennis?

2. What type of leadership style would you use with a group member such as Tom?

3. What are the different types of individual roles a group member may play?

4. What can be done when a group member has adopted an individual role that hinders the progress of the group?

References

Janice, Elizabeth. "Manager's Meeting: 9 a.m. Sharp." *Black Enterprise*, March 1995, 58-59.

Scannel, Edward E. "We've Got to Stop Meeting Like This: Effective Business Meetings." *Training and Development*, January 1992, 70-75.

Shafroth, Morrison. "Creative Conferencing: How to Have a Successful Business Meeting." *California Business*, January 1993, 44-46.

Notes

1. Henry Mintzberg, *The Nature of Managerial Work* (New York: Harper & Row, 1973).

2. Marvin E. Shaw, *Group Dynamics*, 3d ed. (New York: McGraw Hill, 1981).

3. Paul Dickson, *The Official Rules* (New York: Delacorte Press, 1981), 187.

4. John E. Tropman with Gersh Morningstar, *Meetings: How to Make Them Work for You* (New York: Van Nostrand Reinhold, 1985).

5. This discussion of leadership styles is adapted from Charles R. Gruner, Cal M. Logue, Dwight L. Freshley, and Richard C. Huseman, *Speech Communication in Society*, 2d ed. (Boston: Allyn & Bacon, 1977), 258-260.

6. John M. Penrose, Jr., et al., *Advanced Business Communication*, 2d ed. (Belmont, CA: Wadsworth Publishing Co., 1993), 278.

7. John Dewey, *How We Think* (Boston: D.C. Heath, 1933).

8. Irving L. Janis, *Groupthink*, 2d ed. (Boston: Houghton Mifflin, 1982).

9. Ibid., 197-198.

10. Ibid., 198-199.

11. Phil Patton, New York Times Service, "Virtual Office Is the Latest in Work Styles," *The San Diego Union-Tribune*, November 1, 1993, E-3.

12. Joseph A. Califano, Jr., *America's Health Care Revolution—Who Lives? Who Dies? Who Pays?* (New York: Random House, 1986), 177.

Chapter 19

Communication and Conflict

We become aware of conflict through some form of communication.

Ken McBride gazed blankly at the softly rolling hills as he traveled the short distance to the plant. His mind was working double time. During his many years with the company he had learned to dread Fridays. Every week ended with a planning session. Ken was the firm's production scheduler. His decisions caused constant clashes with the marketing manager, Pat Francis.

Pat's staff did a good job, but frequently the salespeople promised customers delivery dates the production department found difficult to meet. The success of the firm's latest line was compounding the problem. For the first time Ken was finding it absolutely impossible to juggle the production schedule to meet delivery dates, and he needed to state his case emphatically.

Ken dreaded the upcoming confrontation. He knew previous arguments about the same subject would serve to intensify the current conflict. As the guard waved him through the gate he felt his stomach tighten; another week was going to come to an uncomfortable close.

All of us experience some type of conflict in our daily lives. Tensions, antagonisms, and frustrations always occur when people work together. Think about any part-time or summer jobs you have held. You will probably remember disagreements, perhaps even fights, between employees and the supervisor or between coworkers. Aside from personality clashes, people simply have different viewpoints about the way things should be done.

Conflict is an appropriate topic for a business communication text because it relates directly to communication. Although we can have communication without conflict, we cannot have conflict without some form of communication. More important, through communication we can minimize the impact of conflict when it occurs. Both verbal and nonverbal communication can soothe tempers, settle misunderstandings, and get the organization back on a normal work schedule.

THE NATURE OF CONFLICT

When conflict occurs, the adrenal glands deliver extra energy. The individual is in a state of tensed readiness in which hearing and vision become more acute. Properly channeled, this type of stress can stimulate a person to put forth superior effort. In fact, conflict is an inevitable by-product of an interesting and challenging job. Many active people thrive on conflict, and it can have a beneficial effect on physical and mental health. For example, competition between two companies can be healthy for the members of both organizations and beneficial to the companies as well.

On the other hand, conflict can be damaging. Too much conflict can be harmful when your overstimulated body refuses to relax and assume normal activity. Your blood pressure remains high, your back muscles develop spasms, and your judgment is impaired. Excessive conflict over time could make you unable to work.

Competition within an organization is potentially dangerous because it can divide loyalties and hamper cooperation. Even competition as apparently harmless as an interdepartmental bowling league should be examined carefully.

Conflict is like one of the modern miracle drugs: The correct dosage can be good for you, but too much can bring damage. One level of conflict may key you up for superior performance—that is, moderate conflict can be **constructive conflict**. Too much conflict may cause worry or fear, hamper your work performance, and in some cases lead to ulcers and other forms of physical and mental illness. Thus intense or prolonged conflict is **destructive conflict**.

Conflict can be constructive or destructive.

Conditions Leading to Conflict

Certain social relationships characterize various kinds of conflict behavior. Each one could occur in your work area. As future managers, the more aware you are of these conflict settings, the better your chances of correcting them and running a smooth operation.[1]

Ambiguous Jurisdictions

Conflict is greater when the lines that set forth each employee's jurisdiction (area of job responsibility) are unclear. When two people have related job tasks with ambiguous boundaries, the potential for conflict between them increases. For example, consider the case of a department head to whom three first-line supervisors report. Each of these supervisors should have clearly defined job responsibilities so that the potential for overlap among the three is reduced. Otherwise, confusion and conflict result as each of the supervisors tries to do all of the jobs. The boundaries between the department head and the supervisors must also be clearly spelled out; otherwise the supervisors may resent the department head's interference in their work responsibilities. The result is a department full of discord and conflict over unclear limits of authority. Such an antagonistic situation can be avoided if job descriptions are clarified so that all employees know the extent of their work responsibilities.

Conflict of Interest

Conflict will be greater when people's interests diverge. For example, consider the conflict between the marketing manager and the plant production manager of a leading producer of chocolate. Each manager would like to have more control over the factors that affect the company's profitability. In the face of fierce competition from other chocolate manufacturers, the marketing manager occasionally wants to run a sampling campaign to support a new candy bar. This manager needs to act fast before competitors match the new product. However, when the marketing manager asks for sharply increased production capacity during the sampling campaign, the plant production manager refuses. The hiring and training of new workers would only be temporary. After the sampling campaign is completed, the company would lay off the new workers. The result is a conflict of interest between the marketing and plant production managers, and a competitive edge for rival chocolate manufacturers.

Communication Barriers

Conflict will be greater when barriers to communication exist. If parties are separated from each other physically or by time—for example, the day shift versus the night shift—the opportunity for conflict is increased. To illustrate, suppose a company employs only one plant supervisor, who works the day shift and leaves orders at the beginning of each week for the workers on the night shift. By the end of the week, however, these orders have been only partially carried out. The supervisor cannot figure out why. Obviously, the supervisor's absence from the night shift has posed a communication barrier, which in turn causes decreased output. Space or time separations can promote isolated group interests rather than advance a common effort toward joint goals.

Dependence of One Party

Conflict will be greater when one party is dependent on another. When parties are dependent, they must rely on each other for performance of tasks or for provision of resources. For example, a supervisor who depends on the preparation of a cost-effectiveness report by a subordinate in order to make a marketing decision may monitor the subordinate's progress. The subordinate resents this close supervision and in retaliation takes a long time to prepare the report. The supervisor, in turn, reminds the subordinate of a forthcoming performance evaluation. The interdependence of supervisor and subordinate fuels the potential for serious conflict.

Differentiation in Organizations

Conflict will be greater as the degree of differentiation, or the division of labor, in an organization increases. When people work together in a complex organization, there is evidence that conflict is related to the number of organizational levels, the number of distinct job specialties represented, and the degree to which labor is divided in the organization. For example, consider the administrators in your college: Most likely there is a dean, an associate dean, department heads, program advisors, and secretaries. All of these people administer some aspect of your curriculum and other educational needs. However, they are at different levels of the organizational hierarchy and handle specialized tasks. Although these university employees share a common focus, their different positions and job concentrations can lead to overlap and conflict.

Association of the Parties

Conflict will be greater as the degree of interaction of the parties increases. As used here, degree of association, or interaction, refers both to the parties' participation in decision making and to informal relations between them. When parties make decisions jointly, the opportunity for conflict is greater, which may explain why some managers are reluctant to involve others in decision making. These managers would prefer to make decisions on their own rather than risk a difference of opinion with a colleague. However, there is a trade-off between the possibility of gaining valuable suggestions and the possibility of an argument. The association of parties has constructive and destructive possibilities.

Need for Consensus

Conflict will be greater when consensus between the parties is necessary; that is, when all parties must agree on a decision so that no individual believes the decision is unacceptable. It is possible to avoid conflict by having mechanisms such as voting to make decisions without the confrontation of consensus. However, such mechanisms themselves may have undesirable consequences. They may offer an easy way out of the immediate conflict but may not solve the problem. Settling the matter by majority rule may only postpone the conflict until a true crisis occurs. When consensus is difficult to achieve, the resultant conflict should not be avoided but used in a constructive manner.

Behavior Regulations

Conflicts will be greater when behavior regulations are imposed. Regulating mechanisms, which include standardized procedures, rules, and policies, seem to do two things at once. On the one hand, they reduce the likelihood of conflict because they make relationships predictable and reduce the need for arbitrary decisions. Some individuals need specific guidelines explaining how to perform their jobs. They are only comfortable making routine decisions about their work. Other individuals have a greater need for autonomy and self-control. Regulating mechanisms that increase the degree of control may be resisted by some workers and welcomed by others. For either type of individual, if the adherence to or the imposition of rules becomes discretionary, further sources of disagreement are created. If behavioral regulations fail to match individual needs of employees, conflict is bound to occur.

Unresolved Prior Conflicts

Conflicts will be greater as the number of unresolved prior conflicts increases. That is, the longer problems are ignored or postponed, the worse new conflicts become. Suppression of conflict through the use of power or compromises to which the parties are uncommitted creates conditions and expectations that may lead to further conflict.

Suppose the people in an office want to streamline operating procedures and rearrange desks and other office furniture to fit a new office reorganization. The workers are not content with the present office organization and their lack of input into

BOXED IN

AN ETHICAL DILEMMA

Tim Fields is leaving his office to start his daily round of sales calls when the phone rings. His morning's plans go awry as the angry voice on the other end of the line demands to know the status of an order. The order represents Tim's biggest sale to date and the first his company has made with a major franchise.

Tim quickly contacts Ken McBride. Ken feels his breath catch in his chest. As he had predicted earlier in the month, production has fallen behind schedule. Now he has a unique part on hand that is needed for two different orders. He has to decide whether to use it to fill a regular customer's order, which is legitimately far ahead of the one in question and urgently needed, or to honor Tim's frantic request.

Ken could reduce his immediate stress level and save Tim's day by bumping the regular customer's order. This move would cause serious problems for the valued old customer, however. No business would be lost, of course, because the old customer would have no way of knowing that its order had been set aside to accommodate a new customer in the hope of generating future sales.

Ken feels boxed in. What would you do?

Questions

1. Which of the nine characteristics that lead to conflict are present here?
2. Does there appear to be any possibility for compromise?
3. Let's assume Ken decides to reject Tim's request. How should he present this decision to Tim to minimize conflict?

office policy. For some time their complaints have been ignored by the division manager, who hoped they would tire of asking for changes and drop the matter once and for all. Together with their supervisor, the employees seek permission from the division manager to draw up reorganization plans. In an effort to placate them, the manager approves their request. The office members and their supervisor earnestly devise new guidelines for office rearrangement. They submit the guidelines to the division manager, who rejects their proposals because he lacks sufficient time to review the plans properly and he fears unsatisfactory changes. The staff becomes very angry and seeks outside help in organizing a union. The manager's attempt to suppress conflict by the use of power has increased the original conflict to a crisis point. This example underscores the idea that unresolved prior conflicts are active breeding agents for future crises.

The conditions that can lead to conflict need not always do so. However, these conditions create the opportunity for conflict to occur. Being aware of the conditions for discord will help you to avoid some potential conflicts and to understand other conflicts once they become apparent.

The Conflict Episode

The conflict episode provides a perspective for viewing the conflict situation.

When people experience a particular conflict, they may feel frustration or even anger. Sometimes it is difficult for them to know exactly why they experience this conflict. Furthermore, they are not sure exactly how to remedy the situation.

A convenient perspective for examining conflict is what Pondy has termed the conflict episode, which consists of five distinct stages.[2]

Latent Conflict Stage

Latent conflict has underlying sources. In an organizational setting, these sources include competition for scarce resources (such as materials, money, and labor), drives for autonomy, and differing subunit goals within the organization.

As an example of latent conflict on a personal level, assume you attend a university that has a very limited number of tennis courts. During the past few years more and more students have started playing the game. You have become an avid tennis player and two or three nights a week you try to play.

Perceived Conflict Stage

Perceived conflict can occur whether or not latent conflict is present. When no latent conflict exists but conflict is nevertheless perceived, it is said to be the result of the parties' misunderstandings of one another's true positions. When latent conflict exists but fails to reach the level of awareness, it is not because such conflict is not actually perceived, but because certain individual defense mechanisms tend to suppress it.

To continue the personal conflict episode, on Monday evening you and a friend decide to play tennis. As the two of you take your rackets and get in the car, your friend remarks, "Boy, I sure hope we can get a court." You glance at your watch and notice that it is almost 6:30—a time when the few tennis courts are likely to be available. Suddenly, you perceive a conflict situation.

Felt Conflict Stage

Felt conflict may also be termed personalization of conflict, because at this stage the conflict actually affects the individual directly. Felt conflict is normally a function of either (a) individual anxieties created by organizational demands that the individual perceives as limiting personal growth or (b) total involvement in a relationship, making an individual necessarily more aware of the occurrence of conflict.

To continue the example, as you approach the tennis courts you observe that all the courts are occupied. Then you notice that the group on the last court has apparently finished and the players are leaving the court. Just then another car speeds into the parking lot. Two players quickly jump out and rush toward the court. You and your partner also make a dash for the court.

Manifest Conflict Stage

Manifest conflict is identified simply as the actual occurrence of conflicting behavior. It may range from aggression to apathy or even extremely rigid adherence to rules with the intention of frustrating another party to the relationship. So long as both parties perceive a specific behavior to be conflicting, and so long as the party indulging in the behavior persists, a clear case of manifest conflict has developed.

Again, to continue the example, your partner wins the race and secures the court. As you and your partner begin play, the two players that lost the footrace come onto the court and sit down close to the playing area. During the match the two other players make comments when you or your partner misses a shot. Your match stands one set to one set. As you begin the third set, the two unwanted visitors stand up and start bouncing tennis balls with their rackets. On your first serve you double fault. You eventually lose the set 6–4.

Conflict Aftermath Stage

Conflict aftermath is a function of how well the entire episode or sequence of episodes has been resolved. Perhaps this stage will reveal that bases for a more cooperative relationship have been established; or it may suggest how newly perceived problems might be handled; or, if the latent conditions were merely suppressed instead of resolved, they may emerge at this time to foster more serious difficulties. The aftermath stage suggests the dynamic nature of conflict; that is, a conflict between or among two or more individuals in an organization is not likely to consist of only one episode, but it is made up of a sequence of such episodes. Each one results from the resolution of conflict in the previous episode.

To conclude the personal conflict episode, you and your friend discuss the possibility of trying to play tennis again on Thursday. Neither of you displays much interest as you both recall the conflict that frequently results from the limited number of courts available. Early the next morning your tennis friend calls you and excitedly tells you that his parents have just given him a birthday present—a membership in a new tennis club. The membership guarantees six hours of court time each week. Suddenly your interest in the game of tennis is renewed.

PERCEPTION AND CONFLICT

The adage, "beauty is in the eye of the beholder," makes the point that what one person perceives as beauty may not be thought beautiful by another. You have no doubt watched two people observe the same event, yet later describe two different situations. People do not behave according to the facts as other people interpret them. The behavior of individuals is based on their unique perceptions of themselves and the world in which they live. Indeed, all behavior is completely determined by the way people perceive the events around them.

In conflict situations perception also plays a major role. In some cases perception may be the cause of conflict. Whatever the cause of a conflict situation, those involved must be aware of the conflict in order for it to exist. Perception as it relates to conflict can be illustrated by five conflict levels.

Conflict must be perceived for it to exist.

1. *Intraindividual conflict* occurs when the perceiver experiences conflict within himself or herself. Such conflict may arise from personal or job responsibilities and may influence, either directly or indirectly, job performance.

2. *Interindividual conflict* exists between the perceiver and another individual within the organization. Although the other person need not be aware of the conflict, the perceiver of the conflict situation recognizes the present or future impact the conflict can have on job performance.

3. *Intragroup conflict* occurs between the perceiver and his or her immediate group within the organization. The immediate group can consist of a work team, department, or union. Whether fully or only superficially aware of the conflict issue, the perceiver realizes that the conflict can directly or indirectly affect job performance.

4. *Intergroup conflict* arises between the perceiver's immediate group and another group within the organization. Again, the perceiver's involvement may not be critical, but he or she must be aware of the situation and the potential impact the conflict can have on work performance.

5. *Organization-environment conflict* arises between the perceiver's organization and the environment it is part of. Environment may refer to the city, country, or world in which the organization exists. For example, if the environment consists of a main office and a number of branches, each branch may be viewed as a single entity within its local environment or as part of the entire organization within a state, nation, or worldwide setting. Whatever the context, the environmental boundary should be defined so that the conflict situation is accurately understood. As with the other four conflict circumstances, the perceiver may be acutely or only casually aware of the conflict and its effect on job performance.

To illustrate these five levels of perceiving conflict, take the case of the second-year business student at a leading two-year college. Jan has worked hard throughout her college career and maintained a high grade point average. As she nears graduation, she is anxious about getting a good job. She has recently received a very low grade in one of her courses and is worried that the grade will lower her overall average. Furthermore, she believes that the grade is unfair because she always completed her assignments on time and had worked hard to write an excellent term paper. Jan wants to discuss with her professor the possibility of a grade change, but she wonders if she dares take the time away from job hunting (intraindividual conflict). Furthermore, her professor is known to be an insensitive person who reacts poorly to any student's request for a grade change (interindividual conflict). If Jan gets her grade changed, then her classmates might start squabbling about who else deserves a raise in grade (intragroup conflict). If several grades are changed and word gets back to students from previous semesters, they might complain about unequal grading standards among the different classes (intergroup conflict). Finally, if word of the discrepancy gets to the board of examiners that accredits the college's business program, the business department risks having its accreditation reviewed (organization–environment conflict).

Table 19.1 provides an analysis of the five levels of conflict involved in Jan's deciding whether to ask the professor for a grade change. Although Jan's case does not provide entries for each column of the table, it is easy to imagine other cases that would illustrate those areas.

An example in a business setting involves the assistant manager of production for a medium-sized company that makes pleasure sailboats. Jeff, although not a yacht designer, sees a modification to the keel of his company's top-of-the-line boats as an idea with potential. He prepares a proposal and submits it to his immediate supervisor.

Jeff receives no response to his proposal for four months. Then he hears through the grapevine that some major modifications are to be made to the larger boats. The production line is halted for those models.

When Jeff asks about what is going on, his supervisor is evasive. The following week, the company announces a breakthrough in keel design for its large offshore

TABLE 19.1   An Analysis of Conflict as Perceived by a College Student

Perceived Source of Conflict	Perceived Impact of Source of Conflict			
	Direct (Impact on Student)		Indirect (Impact on Extra-Organizational Concerns)	
	Current (Operating Now)	Potential (Likely to Operate)	Current	Potential
Intraindividual	Student wonders whether to spend time getting grade changed.			Student loses time for job search.
Interindividual		Student and professor disagree over grade change.		Student's relationship with professor is strained.
Intragroup	Furor erupts in class over changing only one student's grade.	Students argue among themselves about who deserves a higher grade, and the conflict becomes worse.	Low ticket sales to end-of-school party result from tension caused by grade controversy.	
Intergroup	Class groups from previous semesters quarrel over why their grade changes weren't granted.	Class groups from different semesters may complain to dean about unfair grade distribution.		
Organization-Environment	Board of examiners has the power to investigate irregular grading policies.	Angry students contact board of examiners.		Business department loses accreditation by board of examiners.

boats. This design will be incorporated immediately in selected models. At the same time the company announces that Jeff's boss will be promoted to vice president.

Jeff is unsure whether to do or say anything about his report (intraindividual conflict). He is tempted to speak to his boss, who is the only person to whom he had given his report. Jeff knows there is potential here for interindividual conflict because he believes his idea has been stolen.

Jeff doesn't want to let others in the department know of his anger for he realizes it could create unrest (intragroup conflict). He also is wary of talking to acquaintances in the yacht design department, which has been mentioned as deeply involved in the keel design project (intergroup conflict). Jeff considers going to the editor of the employee newspaper, the trade journal, or even the local daily newspaper, but reconsiders (organization–environmental conflict).

BENEFITS OF CONFLICT

While we have alluded to potential benefits of conflict, a closer examination of them may encourage us to be better conflict managers. Here are some benefits.

- Awareness of individuals' positions. Being able to identify who feels strongly about certain issues is beneficial and may influence how we interact with them in other situations.
- Awareness of problems, issues, and conflict. Problems need exposure, discussion, and examination or else they grow and ultimately get out of control.
- Open debate. When problems are openly challenged and discussed, research into the problems and solutions occurs. Such research is less likely to happen with behind-the-scenes gossip, grapevine communication, or anonymous comments.
- Managed conflict. Conflict that is managed, as opposed to "swept under the rug," is more efficient in terms of energy and time.
- Self-acceptance. For some people, letting out their thoughts and frustrations about an issue is important. They may also benefit from having others listen to them.
- Organizational improvement. Organizations need to change over time. Bringing conflict out in the open can identify illogical procedures and outmoded hierarchies.
- Empowerment. People like to be informed and included in decision making and conflict resolution. For some it may be fun, for others power. They may be more accepting of the positions of others if they are involved in the discussion.
- Group synergy. As individuals work together to resolve problems, they are more likely to come up with solutions that are better than any one individual might have contributed. Groups benefit from an enlarged knowledge and expanded creativity base.
- Team spirit. When people work together to solve conflicts and problems, there can be a bonding of the members. Their joint success creates a positive relationship.

CONFLICT MANAGEMENT

Conflict management can improve performance.

Managers need to distinguish between conflict that is useful and conflict that should be reduced or eliminated. The objective of conflict management is to see that conflict remains creative and productive. Besides requiring managers to be able to distinguish between functional and dysfunctional conflict, conflict management requires that managers develop individuals who can work under conflict and tension and still be productive members in the organization.

Method for Analyzing Conflict Situations

Analyzing conflict situations can aid in conflict management.

In deciding how to handle a particular conflict situation, the manager first needs to understand it. The following suggestions comprise a method for analyzing conflict situations.

1. *Assess the importance and impact of the conflict.* Is the conflict useful and motivational in nature and likely to improve the performance of one or several members of the organization? Or is the conflict damaging and in need of resolution? If the conflict is harmful, the remaining steps of analysis should be used.

2. *Identify the type of conflict.* As previously discussed, intraindividual conflict is conflict individuals experience within themselves. Interindividual conflict is conflict the individual experiences with another. Intragroup conflict is conflict between the individual and his or her immediate group within the organization. Intergroup conflict is conflict between the individual's immediate group and another group within the organization. Organization–environment conflict is conflict between the individual's organization and the larger outside environment.

3. *Select an overall strategy for dealing with the conflict.* Controlling the conflict may be preferable—perhaps at this time it is either impossible to resolve completely or it would take too much time and energy to do so. Resolving the conflict is another strategy—if the conflict is serious, you will want to resolve it.

4. *Identify methods for reducing the conflict.* Decide on the basic approach to conflict resolution. Select particular communication strategies.

Styles of Conflict Management

In every conflict situation there are at least two major concerns. The first is the extent to which an individual wants to meet personal goals. The second is the extent to which the individual wants to maintain a relationship with another individual or group or wants to be accepted by the individual or group.[3] The way these two concerns interact is demonstrated in Figure 19.1. Concern for personal goals is scaled from 1 to 9 representing the increasing degree of importance in the mind of the individual (1 = low concern; 9 = high concern). The concern for relationships is also scaled from 1 (low concern) to 9 (high concern). Given this scale, Blake and Mouton identify the following styles: high concern for personal goals and low concern for relationships (9,1); low concern for personal goals and high concern for relationships (1,9); low concern for personal goals and low concern for relationships (1,1); moderate concern for personal goals and moderate concern for relationships (5,5); and high concern for personal goals and high concern for relationships (9,9). With this overview, each style can be examined in more detail.

> Two major concerns exist in every conflict situation.

- *Tough Battler Style:* The win-lose style (9,1) is the trademark of the tough battler who seeks to meet goals at all costs without concern for the needs of others. For this type of individual losing means the loss of self-image. This type of person is willing to sacrifice individuals or groups to be a winner.
- *Friendly Helper Style:* The yield-lose style (1,9) involves the friendly helper who overvalues relationships with others and undervalues the achievement of personal goals. People of this type desire acceptance by others so much that they give in to the desires of others almost all the time. They always avoid conflict in favor of harmony.
- *Loser Style:* The lose-leave style (1,1) is used by the person who sees conflict as a hopeless and useless experience. Rather than be a part of any conflict, this type of person simply withdraws, either physically or mentally, from the conflict.
- *Compromise Style:* The compromise style (5,5) is exemplified by the middle-of-the-roader who takes the position that half a loaf is better than none. The person using this style looks for a position that allows each side to gain something. This individual always looks for the middle ground when confronted with a conflict situation.
- *Problem-Solver Style:* The integrative (9,9) style is the approach of the problem solver, who seeks to satisfy his or her own goals as well as the goals of others.

Figure 19.1
The Conflict Grid
Source: Reprinted by special permission from Robert R. Blake and Jane Srygley Mouton, "The Fifth Achievement," *Journal of Applied Behavioral Science 6,* No. 4 (1970): 418; NTL Institute for Applied Behavioral Science.

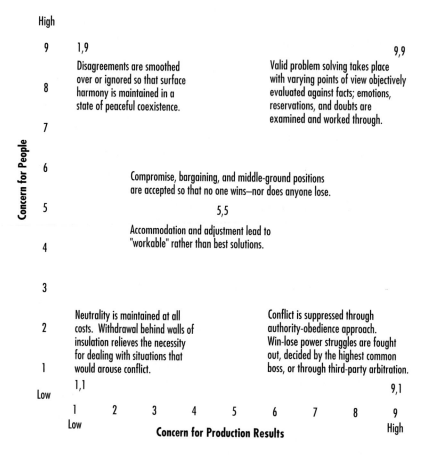

The individual who takes the problem-solving approach has the following views: (1) Conflict is natural and helpful and can even lead to a more creative solution if handled properly. (2) The attitudes and positions of everyone need to be aired when attempting to resolve conflicts. (3) No one is ever sacrificed simply for the goal of the group.

Filley reports on research that shows the relative effectiveness of three different conflict styles. He cites the work of Cummins, who identified three types of bargainers: the tough bargainer, the soft bargainer, and the equalizer. Filley points out that the tough bargainer is equivalent to the tough battler (9,1); the soft bargainer equates to the friendly helper (1,9); and the equalizer is like the problem solver (9,9).

Filley also describes the consequences when the tough battler, the friendly helper, and the problem solver interact with one another. This is his summary of the interaction of these conflict styles:

Interaction of conflict styles results in various consequences.

- When one tough battler meets another tough battler, a stalemate results 80 percent of the time.
- When the tough battler meets the friendly helper, the battler wins 90 percent of the time.
- When the tough battler meets the problem solver, the battler wins over 50 percent of the time.
- Strangely enough, when two friendly helpers meet, a stalemate results 80 percent of the time.
- When a friendly helper meets a problem solver, the problem solver usually wins.
- When two problem solvers interact, they frequently arrive at an agreeable solution.[4]

Filley concludes that the problem-solving style of conflict resolution is the preferred style in that it provides advantages relative to possible agreements reached through the use of other styles.[5]

Given that the problem-solving approach has the greatest potential for resolving conflict, we can now offer some specific suggestions for communicating in conflict situations. The suggested pattern for communication in conflict is based on Rapoport's Region of Validity Technique.[6] It is illustrated by a common scenario that you may have experienced as a college student. Whether you communicate orally or in writing, the following is useful as an overall approach to communicating with someone in a conflict situation.

A problem-solving approach is the preferred style.

Step 1. Communicate to the other people that they have been carefully heard and that understanding exists. If misunderstanding still exists, ask the other party to express his or her position again. Keep in mind that it is important that the other people are convinced that you understand their exact positions.

As an example, suppose you have spent hours writing a term paper for your favorite class. You are expecting a high grade for your extra effort, hence you are very upset when the paper is returned with a low mark. You decide to communicate to the professor that you would like him to reread your paper and raise the grade or at least provide a critique. The professor thinks you are criticizing his grading standards and reacts defensively. To clear up this misunderstanding, you reiterate that you are asking the professor simply to reread the paper and change the grade only if he feels it is justified. The professor relaxes and is more open to discussion about your paper.

Step 2. At this point you enumerate the valid points in the other person's position. Concentrate on the valid points, not the inadequacies of the position.

To continue the example, you explain your paper's content. You want to make sure the professor understands that you followed his instructions. You avoid criticizing the inadequacies of his assignment and concentrate instead on enumerating his instructions and the corresponding points in your paper.

Step 3. At this stage in the process you invite the other party to participate in the process, as you did in Steps 1 and 2.

To conclude the example, you hope that you have convinced the professor of your sincere scholarly interest. You ask if you correctly understood his instructions. After he answers this question, ask him to discuss the valid points of your paper to make sure he understood your explanation. The conflict is resolved through open communication about both parties' perceptions of the term paper.

You should be able to differentiate these same three stages in this incident:

You have been called to the director of personnel's office, and you know that several others in your department have also been called in. They were reprimanded for making personal calls on the company's long-distance telephone line. They had to reimburse the company, and a disciplinary letter was placed in their personnel files.

You have never used the telephone system for personal calls. Once you did find a colleague using your extension for a private call and although you made it clear he was not to use your extension again, you let the matter slide because other employees were taking advantage of the system.

The personnel director brings you into the office, points to a chair, and coldly states, "I'm sure you're aware of the policy statement of November 12 about inappropriate use of the company phone system. That policy is the subject of this conversation." You volunteer your position regarding personal use of the system and explain that you have never misused the system. Indeed, you believe in the policy and support it.

You mention that you know of the disciplinary actions taken on the others and that on one occasion you found someone misusing your extension. You don't volunteer the person's name.

You then say, "I suppose you want to discipline me, too, because an inappropriate call showed on my extension. Is this the purpose of this meeting?"

"Yes and no," is the response. "Alicia told me last week that she misused your phone. To get to the bottom of this situation, I asked the others who were involved about your participation. I'm pleased to report that they all verify your story. Congratulations—you're one of the few in the department to follow company policy. I just wanted you to know we appreciate your honesty and loyalty. I'm sorry I don't sound more enthusiastic with my praise. I've got a toothache that's killing me!"

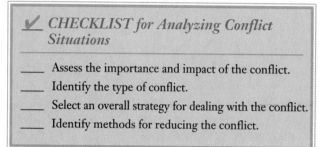

✔ *CHECKLIST for Analyzing Conflict Situations*

_____ Assess the importance and impact of the conflict.
_____ Identify the type of conflict.
_____ Select an overall strategy for dealing with the conflict.
_____ Identify methods for reducing the conflict.

The accompanying checklist can be applied to a number of communication situations that you will face using both written and oral formats. It is essential to understand how the other party perceives the conflict situation. After this perception, communication needs to be directed openly and honestly in a manner that promotes trust and confidence from the receiver.

Key Terms

- **constructive conflict**
- **destructive conflict**

Summary

Conditions leading to conflict   p. 467

The conflict episode   p. 470

Perception and conflict   p. 471

Benefits of conflict   p. 474

Method for analyzing conflict situations   p. 474

Styles of conflict management   p. 475

Review Questions

1. Comment on the statement, "All conflict is harmful and should be reduced or eliminated whenever possible."

2. You manage a large department of employees with different backgrounds, skills, and job responsibilities. Within the context of the nine characteristics of social relationships associated with conflict behavior, provide an example of each kind of conflict situation that could arise in your department.

3. Discuss the five distinct stages of a conflict episode.

4. How does perception play a major role in conflict situations? Provide original illustrations of the five possible conflict circumstances that could occur in a business organization.

5. What is conflict management? What steps might a manager take to analyze a particular conflict situation?

6. What are some benefits of conflict? Which are most valuable?

7. Describe the different styles of conflict management. Which style is preferred? Why?

Exercises

1. The next time you have a disagreement with a friend, see if you can identify the various stages of the conflict. Does this identification process help you better understand how the conflict arose?

2. Conflict can occur in student work groups. The next time you observe group conflict, see if you can help resolve that conflict by following the guidelines presented in this chapter.

3. Identify as many situations from your experience as you can in which conflict was beneficial. Are there similarities among these positive experiences? What are they?

4. Of the various styles of conflict management, which would be easiest for you to assume? The most difficult? Why do you lean in the direction you do? Will this leaning hinder your ability to be an effective conflict resolver?

5. Review recent articles in a local newspaper and identify an article dealing with a conflict between two or more parties. How many underlying causes of the conflict can you identify?

CASE

The Hemphill Company

Elizabeth Plunkett, West Georgia College

One of the nation's leading shirt manufacturers, the Hemphill Company, a moderate-sized, family owned business, has recently acquired a highly sophisticated Japanese pressing system. Because Hemphill's purchase represents the introduction of this technology into the United States, the Japanese electronics manufacturer will provide specialized training for Hemphill's mechanics. The Japanese firm will assume all costs—except for transportation to and from Japan—for an unlimited number of Hemphill's mechanics to participate in a three-week program.

The company president called a meeting to determine who should attend this training program. Present at the meeting are: Jim Hemphill, the company president/general manager; Tom Cates, the production manager, who assists the president with many management decisions (he is ambitious to become general manager and considered by Mr. Hemphill to be capable); Dave Day, the personnel manager, whose responsibilities uniquely but appropriately include overseeing maintenance personnel, equipment needs, and small parts procurement; Susan Miller, the research and development manager, who is responsible for managing training programs; and Jackie Lee, the chief engineer, who is responsible for setting rates and payback figures on new equipment.

The management group considers six employees to be possible candidates. Brian Finch, the mechanics' foreman, respected by his subordinates, has refused previous training opportunities, believing that they required too much personal time. Joan South was stationed in Japan in the military, and her familiarity with Japan is considered an asset. Even though Joan is highly skilled on manual equipment, electronic machines under her supervision have not performed well. Ed Crawford has consistently been Hemphill's top performer in training programs, and while extremely successful with electronic equipment, he appears to be negligent in routine maintenance of equipment. Karlene Miles has previously received additional training to become the company specialist on one piece of electronic equipment. Bill Hatfield works exceptionally well with Karlene Miles, and the electronic machinery under their joint supervision has attained optimal productivity. A dedicated employee, Bill has had personal problems with drug addiction and marital difficulties. Although he appears to have conquered his drug problem, his marital situation still conflicts with his job. Recently, his wife objected to his absence while he attended a two-day training session. Despite this conflict, he excelled in the course. All of the above candidates are from 28 to 34 years of age, except Finch and Hatfield, who are 40 to 42 years old.

The managers agree that Brian Finch should be included in the program, in spite of his previous reluctance to accept training. They feel that he needs updating in this technology and that his leadership could influence the success of this program. Brian enthusiastically accepts the challenge of this important project. When asked for his suggestions regarding the other candidates, Brian responds that he has no preference among them and that he has no additional names for consideration.

After much deliberation, the managers reach a standstill in the decision-making process. Jim Hemphill is adamant that performance and teamwork are essential factors in candidate selection. Karlene Miles and Bill Hatfield meet these particular requirements. Faced with the issue of Bill's marital conflict, Jim Hemphill emphasizes that management must be careful about making decisions for subordinates based on how the managers judge subordinates' nonwork environment. He feels that Bill Hatfield should have the opportunity to choose whether or not to accept the assignment.

Tom Cates supports Joan South and Ed Crawford, believing that Joan's knowledge of Japan is invaluable and that Ed's proficiency and success with electronics equipment make him a natural choice. On the other hand, Dave Day suggests that the foreman should make the final decision but that personally he would eliminate Ed Crawford and Karlene Miles from consideration. He objects to Ed's maintenance record and stresses that Karlene, with her specialized training, could not be spared. Dave also indicates that the company's extensive investment and dependence on any single individual could create unnecessary vulnerability.

Conversely, Susan Miller proposes that Ed Crawford and Karlene Miles are the only logical selections based on their strong training performance records. Jackie Lee, however, firmly believes that all the candidates should attend the course because this solution not only would assure the payback on this expensive system but also would resolve the deadlock in this discussion.

Case Questions

1. What could be done to facilitate the decision-making process?

2. What interpersonal factors influence the decision makers in their selections?

3. Which candidates would you select to participate in the training program? Support your recommendations.

C A S E

A Touchy Situation

Margaret Fitch-Hauser, Auburn University

Ellen Jones is an attractive woman in her mid-30s. She has worked for 14 years in public relations. Six months ago she began a new job that represented a major career advancement for her. She began work for a large industrial firm as their chief public relations officer. During the brief time that she has been on the job, she has worked very hard to establish a sound image for the company and a reputation for herself. The reactions to her efforts have been very favorable. Much of her success has been due to the fact that Ellen finds the job both challenging and rewarding. However, a situation has arisen that she feels threatens her job performance and may force her to resign.

The situation involves the behavior of Rex Dycus, a senior vice president with the firm. On a number of occasions he has made comments or behaved in a manner that Ellen perceives to be condescending or to contain obvious sexual overtones.

Several times when she went to get a cup of coffee, Rex was also at the coffee maker. On two of those occasions, he placed his hand on her back as if to pat her on the back but then let his hand slide on down until it brushed her seat. Not knowing exactly what to do, she simply stepped away and returned to her office as soon as she could. Lately, she has begun to avoid the coffee room.

On other occasions, Rex has come into her office to talk about certain projects of mutual interest. For the most part, Ellen has enjoyed their conversations because Rex is a good problem solver. She has found him to be very insightful about the company's various public relations problems. In fact, several times she has been able to more clearly understand a particular situation because of his observations. Clearly, he is a valuable information resource for her. Unfortunately, he nearly always manages to drop a comment or two about helping her advance in the company if she is willing to do some favors for him. He has even suggested that the two of them get together after work some evening for dinner and "whatever" so they can discuss how they might be of mutual benefit to one another. On these occasions Ellen has been embarrassed and angry but has managed only to stammer some type of joking response. However, she does not feel that Rex is joking. She is afraid that if she responds in anger, she will come across as a pushy, defensive woman and consequently undermine her hard-earned credibility as well as lose a valuable information source.

Ellen has also become aware that Rex seems to go out of his way to be in the corridor when she arrives at work in the mornings. On these occasions he always compliments her appearance. Although the attention is flattering, the content of his compliments disturbs Ellen. He has said things like, "What a lovely suit. It really shows your womanly build." On another occasion he commented that a particular garment was especially attractive as she walked down the hall because it moved with her hips. Not wanting to appear ungrateful for the compliments, Ellen has simply said thank you and walked quickly away. On at least two occasions she heard some of the other men in the hall snicker as she left.

The entire situation has really disrupted Ellen's ability to work. She finds that she is spending much of her time trying to avoid Rex or trying to figure out how to handle the situation without damaging either one of their positions with the company. The problem is compounded by the fact that she is currently working on a major project for Rex's division and has to consult with him regularly on several matters. These meetings are always in one of their offices, and she feels especially vulnerable when she is in either office alone with him. At this point Ellen is so frustrated that she is ready to tender her resignation.

Case Questions

1. What type of conflict is described in this case?
2. Should Ellen report Rex's behavior to her superiors?
3. Should Ellen confront Rex about his behavior?
4. What is the best approach Ellen can take in handling this problem?
5. Should Ellen resign, or can the situation be resolved?

References

Hebdon, R., and M. Mazerolle. "Mending Fences, Building Bridges: The Effect of Relationship by Objectives on Conflict." *Industrial Relations* 50, 164.

Popham, A. "Conflicts Can Become Positive Business Opportunities." *New Tribune*, May 22, 1994, C-8.

Ralston, F. "Keeping Hot Buttons from Taking Control." *Supervisory Management* 40 (1995), 1.

Ray, G.R., J. Hines, and D. Wilcox, "Training Internal Facilitators." *Training and Development* 48 (1995), 45.

Tjosvold, Dean. *Learning to Manage Conflict.* New York: Lexington Books, 1993.

Weigand, Rolf E. "Managing Beliefs, Managing Silence: Silence Is Not Always the Best Method of Dealing with Volatile Issues in the Workplace." *Business Horizons* 37 (1994), 58.

Notes

1. These nine characteristics of conflict are adapted from Alan C. Filley, *Interpersonal Conflict Resolution* (Glenview, IL: Scott, Foresman, 1975), 9-12. Reprinted by permission.
2. L.R. Pondy, "Organizational Conflict Concepts and Models," in *Management of Change and Conflict*, eds. John M. Thomas and Warren Bennis (Middlesex, England: Penguin Books, 1972), 360-366.
3. The remainder of this section is based on Robert R. Blake and Jane Srygley Mouton, "The Fifth Achievement," *Journal of Applied Behavioral Science* 6, no. 4 (1970): 413-426; and Jay Hall, *Conflict Management Survey* (Houston: Teleometrics, 1968).
4. Filley, *Interpersonal Conflict Resolution*, 55-56.
5. Ibid., 56.
6. Anatol Rapoport, *Fights, Games, and Debates* (Ann Arbor: University of Michigan, 1960).

Chapter 20

Interviewing as a Management Tool

Brenda Morris and Bob Lustberg started working for Continental Enterprises on the same day. Both were twenty-two years old and had graduated from the same college with degrees in accounting. Beyond those similarities, however, they had little in common. Brenda was rather reserved and bookish; she had graduated with a GPA of 3.8 in her major courses. Bob was outgoing and gregarious, and he had a GPA of 3.0 in his major courses. While Brenda was regarded as brilliant, Bob was considered slightly above average. Brenda had been the more highly recruited of the two, and she had been at the top of Continental's "wish list." Bob had been ranked seventh of their top ten candidates. Candidates two through six had been hired elsewhere.

Both Brenda and Bob made steady progress and, at the end of three years, had firmly established themselves with the company. Brenda continued to be slightly more proficient technically than Bob, but Bob was now the more productive of the two. While Brenda would seek solutions to problems in books and manuals, Bob was more likely to ask co-workers. Brenda had to call clients back more frequently for additional information. Bob, on the other hand, seemed to ask the right questions the first time. Although their approaches differ, both Brenda and Bob are solid employees. It has become obvious to management, however, that Bob excels as an interviewer and that his interviewing skills will take him a long way.

PURPOSES AND CHARACTERISTICS OF INTERVIEWS

As used by management, the interview has a wide variety of purposes. Job applicants are hired on the basis of interviews. Employees who experience personal problems may be counseled in an interview. In many organizations managers evaluate the performance of their workers in regularly scheduled appraisal interviews. Disciplinary interviews are conducted with workers who are involved in job-related problems. Through an exit interview program a company seeks to learn the reasons why employees leave. New employees are often oriented to their duties through an interview. Through the interview management acquires and transmits much of the information necessary for efficient operations.

Figure 20.1
Interviews must often be conducted in less-than-desirable settings.
Source: John Coletti, Stock Boston.

Business people no longer believe that anyone who can carry on a conversation can conduct an interview. To understand the need for trained interviewers, they need only look within their organizations. A large number of employment interviews have resulted in the selection of unsuitable individuals. Counseling interviews often do not resolve problems, and disciplinary interviews may not result in changed behaviors.

Although one usually associates the interview with such functions as selection, counseling, and appraisal, the range of the interview process extends much further. For example, in the weeks after Dana Brewster was promoted to correspondence coordinator, following the sudden death of Chuck Lambert, she spent many hours meeting with her boss and learning everything that the job entailed. Many of their meetings consisted of little more than Dana asking specific questions and listening carefully to what she was told. These sessions were actually interviews rather than meetings.

No matter how well educated a new jobholder is, that person does not possess all the information necessary to succeed at the job. Success will be strongly influenced by the jobholder's ability to elicit accurate and thorough information from co-workers. Being able to recognize and ask the right questions is all-important. Tom Peters, internationally renowned consultant and author, criticized his graduate education, "... I crunched a zillion numbers. But I never had 30 seconds worth of counsel about conducting interviews." He described interviewing as "essential to the success of high-priced consultants and inquisitive managers."[1]

Physicians have been maligned for years on the basis of lack of interviewing skills. They are often accused of dominating conversations with patients and of overusing medical terminology and thereby confusing patients. One study had shown that, although the average patient had three different problems in mind, the physician would interrupt the patient's statements within the first eighteen seconds. In most cases only the first problem was considered. Other studies have shown that when patients were taught to ask forthright questions, they received better medical care.[2]

Today's business environment is one of ongoing and rapid change, and skills in interviewing are essential if one is to contribute to it. The importance of these skills, however, extends beyond business into all other occupational and social arenas.

Some characteristics of an interview clearly differentiate it from a conversation. An interview is purposeful, whereas a conversation may not be. Interviewers must draw out

An interview is a purposeful exchange of information for a predetermined purpose in a structured situation.

the desired information while motivating the interviewee to cooperate. Because the interview has a predetermined purpose, it is more formal than a conversation. Interviews are clearly structured. They are comprised of an opening, a body, and a closing, and the participants have specific roles. In contrast, many conversations appear formless. Conversations may involve an exchange of information, but the exchange is a universal and essential characteristic of the interview.

TYPES OF QUESTIONS USED BY INTERVIEWERS

Generations of schoolchildren have been taught that the verb is the motor of the sentence. Without a good verb, a sentence will wander rather than move purposefully. An interview also has a motor—the question. Without appropriate questions an interviewer accomplishes little. Unless interviewers are able to recognize and use the variety of questions available, they will not utilize the full potential of the interview.

Open and Closed Questions

Questions fall into two general categories—open and closed. **Open questions** allow the interviewee much freedom to answer. An open question is broad in scope and usually requires more than a few words in response. When you ask an open question, you are often merely specifying the topic to be covered. The interviewee may decide on the quantity and the type of information to provide.

Open questions allow the interviewee more freedom to respond.

Open Questions

Open questions are not all alike. They may differ in their degree of openness. The following questions are very open:

* Tell me about yourself.
* What are you seeking in a career?
* How do you feel about the present candidates?

Other questions are less broad. Although still open, they restrict the interviewee's response somewhat:

* What do you like about your present job?
* Tell me how you feel the problem developed.
* Why did you apply for this job?

Open Questions	
Advantages	**Disadvantages**
Provide interviewer greater opportunity to observe	Take more time
Are considered nonthreatening because they are usually easy to answer	Are more difficult to record or the information is difficult to quantify
Suggest interest by the interviewer	Make controlling the interview more difficult

Closed Questions
Closed questions are somewhat restrictive in nature and generally call for a brief and limited response. By using closed questions you limit the answer options available to the interviewee. The following questions are moderately closed as they call for only a brief bit of information:

Closed questions are more restrictive than open questions.

- Who is Peter Drucker?
- What is your main duty on your present job?
- For what reason do you wish to leave?

Questions may be very closed in that the interviewer has few answer options. These are some very closed questions:

- Rank the following courses in terms of their value to you: business mathematics, English composition, American history.
- How would you rate the present governor in terms of his concern for the unemployed: very concerned, neutral, or unconcerned?
- Do you drink alcoholic beverages?

Closed Questions	
Advantages	**Disadvantages**
Require less training of interviewers	Provide too little information
Take less time	Sometimes inhibit communication
Make it easier for the interviewer to exert control	Provide little opportunity for the interviewee to offer additional information
Make tabulation of the answers easier	

Neutral and Leading Questions

Neutral questions are completely unbiased.

When you ask a neutral question, you make no attempt to direct the interviewee's response. Because neutral questions do not exert any pressure, they may elicit more accurate responses. **Neutral questions** are phrased so that possible responses are not indicated, and alternatives are presented in a balanced fashion. These are typical:

- How would you feel about work that requires a considerable amount of traveling?
- Why are you leaving the company?
- Who do you think is responsible for the problem?
- Which one of the following sports do you enjoy participating in most—baseball, football, basketball, tennis, or soccer?

Through leading questions an interviewer can guide the interviewee in a certain direction.

On the other hand, **leading questions** enable the interviewer to obtain accurate information quickly by guiding the interviewee in a certain direction. They are especially useful when trying to verify factual information. Leading questions are sometimes regarded negatively because, when used carelessly, they may result in biased responses. These are some leading questions:

- You have a driver's license, don't you?
- You are at least 16 years of age?
- You have a telephone, don't you?
- Do you believe, as most students do, that you are overworked?

Loaded Questions

Loaded questions are strongly directional.

A **loaded question** is even stronger in direction than a leading question, which may be somewhat subtle. A loaded question tends to be hard-hitting. Some interviewers use loaded questions to create stress by using language likely to draw an emotional response or by inquiring into topics about which the interviewee feels strongly. No need exists in most interviews for loaded questions. They should be left to skilled interviewers for the exploration of emotional issues. These are examples of loaded questions:

- What do you think of the government's foolish waste of the tax dollar?
- Do you mean to tell me that you have no work experience? (asked of a new college graduate who has been rejected by other interviewers for lacking experience)
- How do you like the company's ridiculous policy about vacations?

Mirror Questions

A **mirror question** reflects an interviewee's previous answer with the intent of drawing out additional information. Through the use of mirror questions more information can be obtained without biasing the interviewee's responses. When you believe a response is incomplete, you may draw the interviewee out more by simply restating that response. This is called mirroring a response. When you do it, you are trying to get the interviewee to elaborate on a particular topic. Mirror questions are employed in these examples:

A mirror question can get an interviewee to elaborate.

Interviewee:	I liked my last job a lot. It was interesting and the pay was good. I'd still be there if it weren't for my problems with my supervisor.
Interviewer:	Problems with your supervisor?
Interviewee:	You'll see that I do good work so long as people don't hassle me.
Interviewer:	Hassle you?

Probing Questions

A **probing question** is stimulated by the interviewee's previous response. Some interviewers prepare a schedule, or list of questions, in advance. No probing questions could be included in such a list, for probing questions are unplanned. For example, if a job applicant says, "In my present job I had to learn how to assume responsibility," the interviewer might then ask probing questions such as these:

Probing questions are stimulated by the interviewee's previous response.

- Exactly how did you assume responsibility?
- How much responsibility did you assume?
- Why did you have to learn that?

Through probing questions the interviewer may elicit important information that had not been anticipated.

Pauses

Although it is not actually a question, the **pause** may serve the same purpose. When you want the interviewee to elaborate, you may simply remain silent. The pause is the most neutral approach of all, because it does not structure the answer or even suggest a topic for discussion. At some point your pause may turn into an embarrassing silence, which the interviewee will find threatening. With experience, however, you will become comfortable and proficient in the use of pauses to stimulate the interviewee.

By pausing, the interviewer can draw out the interviewee.

THE INTERVIEW STRUCTURE

Although they differ in purpose, all interviews are very much alike in structure. Awareness of this structure makes interviewing more productive and more pleasant. The interview process is continuous, with no apparent separation between phases. An interview has five distinct phases, however, and your strategy should be different for each one.

Planning

Planning is vital to the success of the interview. It should include the following steps:

1. Determine the purpose or purposes of the interview.
2. Identify the type of responses being sought from the interviewee.
3. Learn as much about the interviewee and about the subject in advance as possible.
4. Determine the amount of structure to employ, and on that basis develop whatever questions are necessary.
5. Select an appropriate setting for the interview and communicate this information to the interviewee.

The extent of planning to be done depends on the purpose of the interview. Before a performance appraisal interview some managers spend several hours familiarizing themselves with the interviewee's work records. An employment interviewer should read the completed application form. In contrast, the clerk in a clothing store may have no advance information about a customer—but will be prepared to discuss the merits of the clothing.

Establishing Rapport

For many individuals an interview is an infrequent occurrence and as such is a cause of tension. In order to reduce the tension and make it easier to exchange information, the interviewer should strive to establish rapport with the interviewee. Rapport is simply a harmonious relationship. Greeting the interviewee graciously and extending simple courtesies will help to establish rapport. Many interviewers engage in small talk at the start about topics of mutual interest.

More time for establishing rapport is needed in some types of interviews than others. The success of a counseling interview, for example, depends on the climate established. The relationship between the interviewer and the interviewee is also a factor. People who work together ordinarily have little need to devote attention to establishing rapport.

Even after an interview has started smoothly, the interviewer should remain aware of the importance of rapport. Differences of opinion may surface, or tension may increase for other reasons. In any case, through rapport, a climate conducive to open communication can be developed and maintained.

Stating the Purpose

Interviewers often assume that they and the interviewee have the same understanding of the purpose of the interview. An employment interviewer, for example, may explain the duties of a level-1 secretary at great length to an applicant for a level-2 job. Such problems could be prevented by establishing the purpose of an interview at the outset.

Even when people work together, the purpose of an interview may not be clear. To illustrate, in her job as a programmer Jan Rowan has had the same boss for two years. A couple of weeks ago he asked her to reserve an hour so he could talk with her. At the end of the hour Jan left without knowing what the purpose of the interview had been. He asked questions about how she liked her job, problems in the organization, the conditions of the lunchroom, and even her vacation plans. As Jan said, "It's nice to have a boss who is interested in you, but it would also be nice to know what he is getting at."

Asking Questions

The nature of the interview will determine the type of questions chosen as well as the strategy the interviewer will employ. If control of the interview is very important, then the interviewer may choose to ask primarily closed or even loaded questions and to employ a directive strategy. This strategy involves a highly structured question-and-answer format and allows the interviewer to control the direction the interview takes. This strategy is most appropriate when the interviewer has a purpose to accomplish (such as correcting an employee about a particular behavior) and does not want the interview to deviate from that purpose.

On the other hand, if the interview is a device for fact finding, the interviewer would ask more open questions, probes, mirror questions, and neutral questions to employ a nondirective strategy. Counseling interviews, complaint handling, and problem solving are situations in which these types of questions and this strategy are most appropriate. The use of these questions in the nondirective strategy underscores the necessity for freedom of exchange and the interviewer's desire not to control the direction of the interview.

This phase constitutes the largest part of the interview. The interviewer comes into it having already determined the types of questions to ask and the sequence in which to ask them.

Summarizing

During the questions phase, interviewer and interviewee usually exchange a considerable amount of information. Some of the information may be highly relevant, and some may be less so. Irrelevancies, redundancies, and unanticipated interruptions may blur some of the conclusions, with the result that the interviewer and the interviewee may not perceive the conclusions identically. The interviewer should clarify what he or she considers these conclusions to be. Without such a summary the interview may end with the parties unaware that differences exist.

At the end of an interview the interviewer should summarize the conclusions that were reached.

ALLOCATION OF INTERVIEW TIME

The amount of time appropriate for a particular phase of the interview structure varies with the type of interview. In a 30-minute employment interview, for example, the first two phases—establishing rapport and stating the purpose—are vitally important to the success of the interview. Together, they should consume only 4 to 5 minutes. In all types of interviews the third phase—asking questions—should take the majority of the time available. In the employment interview applicants should have some time to ask questions of interviewers in order to determine if the organization is the one best suited to meet their needs. This step of the employment interview should take approximately 80 percent of an interview.

Asking questions will consume approximately 80 percent of an employment interview.

Summarizing is a critical last step in the actual interview, but it should consume proportionally little of the employment interview time. In fact, summarizing what has occurred during the interview and any further actions either party will take as a result of the interview should usually take only about 2 minutes of a 30-minute interview.

TYPES OF INTERVIEWS

Interviews are often classified as information getting, information giving, or problem solving. However, they can be more clearly identified on the basis of specific purpose. This section will review the types of interviews conducted most frequently in business organizations.

The Employment Interview

The employment interview is an important tool in the selection process of most organizations and is, in fact, the basis of most selection decisions. Yet top management

The interview is used more than any other method for selecting employees.

often fails to realize the importance of the interviewer's job. The way applicants feel about a company is influenced by their impression of the company's representative. As far as most applicants are concerned, the interviewer is the company.

As an example, Wanda Metcalf had met with 20 employment interviewers by the time she graduated from college. Most of them represented large national organizations. Some were well-organized and businesslike: others were not. A recruiter for a paper company said little beyond "Tell me all about yourself." A chemical company recruiter must have asked 100 questions, all of them of the yes or no variety. Several interviewers did not seem to know anything about the job they were trying to fill. Although none was actually unfriendly, a few interviewers did not seem to be at all interested in Wanda. She wondered why they had bothered with the interviews.

Computerization has had a growing impact on the selection process. Companies as diverse as Pic 'n Pay Stores,[3] Shoney's, and Neiman Marcus are using computerized interviews for screening purposes.[4] After a computer scores the applicant's answers, those applicants with the highest number of desirable responses are selected to participate in a traditional interview.

Employment Interview Goals

As an interviewer your main goal should be to determine an applicant's suitability for the job. You should also tell interviewees enough about the job so that they will clearly understand its scope and duties. Usually the applicant's knowledge of the job is slight, probably based on a newspaper ad or a brief job description posted on a bulletin board. Therefore you must educate the applicant about what the job actually entails. The more thorough you are in performing this function, the less likely it is that new employees will quickly grow disillusioned with their jobs.

You should also be aware of the importance of good public relations. Seek to create and maintain goodwill for the company. Often numerous applicants are interviewed before anyone is hired. You have the opportunity to influence how the applicant, whether successful or not, will view the company and its products or services in the future. The level of attraction that a position holds for an applicant can be affected greatly by the interaction that occurs during an interview. An applicant who finds communicating with the interviewer to be satisfying will often view the vacant position as more desirable than had been true prior to the interview.[5]

As an employment interviewer you should have three goals: (1) principally, to determine a person's suitability for employment; (2) to present an accurate description of the job to the applicant; and (3) to create and maintain goodwill for the company.

Topics usually covered in an employment interview are:

- Work experience, emphasizing jobs recently held
- Educational background, including both formal and informal training
- Outside interests, especially those that might affect the individual's job performance
- Physical characteristics, if such factors are important for the job

In order to comply with the guidelines of the Equal Employment Opportunity Commission you should ask questions that are directly related to the job being sought and ask the same questions of all the applicants.

Employment interviews are more structured and more behavioral in nature than was formerly the case. An approach taken by many major corporations today is called Behavior Description Interviewing.[6] These interviews focus on actual behaviors, things that the applicant has done, rather than on personality characteristics or hypothetical questions. This approach to interviewing more accurately predicts how effective each applicant would be on the job.

Team-oriented business organizations involve greater numbers of employees in the selection of new workers. Human resources specialists usually screen and test applicants, but other team members will often conduct the interviews and make the selection decision. There seems to be less turnover among team members when selection is done in that way.[7]

Throughout the interview you should encourage the applicant to ask questions, and you should respond to the questions with as much detail as necessary. In closing the interview you should briefly summarize the main points covered as well as clearly indicate to the applicant what will follow. At the end of the interview the applicant should know exactly what to expect. If the applicant will be expected to take further tests, you should explain that. If some organizational policy dictates the next step in the selection process, you should make the applicant aware of that. It is an interviewer's responsibility to remove as much of the applicant's uncertainty as possible.

In closing the employment interview the interviewer should tell the interviewee what to expect next.

After the Employment Interview

Interviewers often meet many applicants in a single day and should therefore record the findings from each interview as soon as possible after the interview. Many companies provide forms on which interviewers rate applicants. If forms are not available, you should develop one of your own so that you are sure to note your reactions immediately following the interview.

> ✔ *CHECKLIST for an Employment Interview*
>
> ____ Learn the applicant's background by reading the completed application form and the applicant's resume (if it's available).
>
> ____ Know enough about the job so that its most important requirements are clear to you.
>
> ____ Schedule the interview so that sufficient time is available and so that there will be no interruptions.
>
> ____ Scan the topics to be covered early in the interview, and proceed through each topic in an organized manner.
>
> ____ Determine that the interviewee is aware of the most important aspects of the job.
>
> ____ Relate your questions to the job the interviewee is applying for, and ask the same questions of each applicant.
>
> ____ Summarize what has been accomplished at the close of the interview and indicate specifically what the interviewee can expect next.

The Performance Appraisal Interview

In many organizations **performance appraisal interviews** are conducted on a regular basis, often annually or semiannually. The interview is conducted by a worker's immediate superior. It is intended to provide the worker with feedback concerning how the company thinks the worker is performing.

Performance appraisal interviews are usually conducted by a worker's immediate superior.

The performance appraisal interview is strongly evaluative in nature and is sometimes difficult to conduct. Adding to the sensitivity of the situation is the effect that the appraisal could have on the subordinate's pay. The specific goal of each performance appraisal interview depends on how the interviewee has been performing on the job.

To illustrate, Werner Nelson is required to conduct 10 performance appraisal interviews a year. Evaluating 10 subordinates is a difficult and a time-consuming process. No two workers are exactly alike, and the goals of each interview differ according to the nature of the individual worker.

As Werner sees it, this year he conducted three different types of appraisals. In interviewing five of the subordinates he believed his main task was to recognize their good work and to express the company's appreciation. At the same time he attempted to point out ways they could improve. He was trying to develop two other subordinates for higher level jobs, and he used the appraisal interviews with them mainly for that purpose. The other three subordinates were still on probation and had been performing poorly. Werner warned each one of them that some improvement was necessary. These appraisals consisted of discussing specific ways each interviewee could improve.

Werner said of the appraisal interviews, "My people seem to think that I like evaluating them, but they're dead wrong. I don't like it any better than they do. No one likes to play God, but it's a method of developing people, of helping them become better at their jobs."

Before the Performance Appraisal Interview

You must decide what the specific purposes of a performance appraisal will be on the basis of what the interviewee's performance has been.

After determining the purposes, you decide the extent to which the interviewee should participate in the preliminaries. In some organizations employees are given copies of the evaluation forms in advance and are requested to evaluate themselves. They return their completed forms to their superior or bring them to the interview so there can be discussion of how the supervisor's rating differs from their own and the possible reasons for the differences. At the very least, workers are told well in advance of the pending appraisals so they can organize their thoughts.

During the Performance Appraisal Interview

Goal setting is an important aspect of the performance appraisal interview.

The evaluation form should certainly not be the sole focus of the performance appraisal interview. Emphasis should be on involving the subordinate in two-way communication rather than telling the subordinate what is to be done. If the discussion of problems is to be meaningful, the subordinate must first acknowledge that problems exist. In setting goals for the future there must be agreement between the superior and the subordinate. The main strength of the performance appraisal process lies in human interaction.

In closing the performance appraisal interview you should summarize the main points covered. By now there should be agreement on (1) the areas in which the subordinate is performing well; (2) the areas in which the subordinate needs improvement; and (3) what the subordinate must do to attain that improvement. If disagreement exists between the parties after the summary, the interview should not end until the points of disagreement are resolved.

After the Performance Appraisal Interview

You must follow up the interview in whatever way has been agreed upon. In some organizations the subordinate is given a copy of the final evaluation form. If additional paperwork is to be completed, you should do it immediately. If the subordinate complained during the interview about the standards used for measurement, you should look into the matter immediately rather than wait for it to surface again in the next appraisal interviews.

> ✔ *CHECKLIST for a Performance Appraisal Interview*
>
> ____ Notify subordinates well enough in advance to allow them to prepare for the interview.
>
> ____ Encourage written or oral self-evaluation by the subordinates.
>
> ____ Involve the subordinates in every aspect of the discussion.
>
> ____ Separate salary matters and discussion of promotional possibilities from the appraisal itself.
>
> ____ Identify and solve, together with the subordinate, any performance problems.
>
> ____ Set specific, short-term objectives with the subordinate and discuss methods of attaining them.

The Correction Interview

Managers who dislike conducting performance appraisal interviews react even more negatively to the **correction interview**. In this type of interview the superior seeks to get the subordinate to substitute some desirable behavior for behavior that is undesirable. Even though negative information might be presented to the interviewee in the performance appraisal interview, at least it is a regularly scheduled event in which all employees routinely participate. The correction interview, however, is not a part of every employee's schedule. The irregular nature of the correction interview adds to the suspicion and hostility that usually accompany it.

Before the Correction Interview

Correction interviews deal with sensitive matters. For that reason before the interview the supervisor should collect as much information as possible concerning the employee's alleged infraction. The supervisor should also be aware of what corrective measures might be appropriate and should then schedule the interview as soon as possible.

During the Correction Interview

A correction interview is a serious matter, and both parties know it. Little time need be devoted to establishing rapport, because both parties, especially the subordinate, are anxious to get on with it. The interviewer should state the interview's purpose and describe the violation in as much detail as necessary. The subordinate should be encouraged to describe his or her version of the problem, and both parties should work together to arrive at a solution. In closing the correction interview, the interviewer should summarize what has been accomplished and restate the corrective action to be taken.

Openness and candor are vital for an effective correction interview.

To illustrate, Ellen noticed that George's productivity was dropping and began to observe him more closely. George did not manage time well. When he arrived at work at exactly 8:00 A.M., he would devote 15 or 20 minutes to straightening up his desk. Each afternoon he quit work 15 minutes early to prepare to leave. For several weeks Ellen kept records of all her subordinates' time usage habits. She concluded that the misuse of time was causing George's decreased productivity.

Following her research Ellen conducted a correction interview in her office with George. At first George disputed Ellen's findings; however, her carefully kept records soon convinced him that a problem existed and that his misuse of time was the cause. Ellen and George agreed that George would become more aware of how he used his time. Within three weeks George had regained his previous high level of productivity.

After the Correction Interview

If a description of the violation should be put in the employee's file, this should be done immediately. The manager should ascertain not only that corrective action is being taken, but also its apparent effect. This might be accomplished through any or all of the following: observation, judicious discussion with the associates of the subordinate, or discussion with the subordinate.

> ✔ **CHECKLIST for a Correction Interview**
>
> _____ Obtain all of the relevant facts in advance and get verification when possible.
>
> _____ Conduct the interview out of earshot of others.
>
> _____ Concentrate on the subordinate's behavior in describing the problem, and avoid any discussion of personality traits.
>
> _____ Encourage the subordinate to describe the infraction as it occurred.
>
> _____ Discuss possible corrective actions with the subordinate.
>
> _____ Summarize what has occurred during the interview and the corrective action that will be taken.

The Counseling Interview

Because **counseling interviews** are directed at personal problems, many people believe that only social workers and psychologists conduct them. Although counseling is not always recognized as a manager's duty, most managers do counsel their subordinates. Even if a problem is personal or family related, it will have some effect on the employee's job performance.

To illustrate, when Bob Wiggins became a supervisor he assumed that on-the-job problems would mainly involve equipment, raw materials, and the manufacturing process. He had not expected the high incidence of personal problems among workers. Bob found that personal problems make many workers less effective than they would otherwise be. He estimates that he devotes 10 percent of his work week to counseling employees with problems. "It's time well-spent if it results in a more productive worker," he has said.

Because of the personal nature of the subject, the climate that is established is very important. The interviewer should try to create a situation that will allow a free exchange of information. Such a climate is more likely if the interviewer does the following:

AN ETHICAL DILEMMA

BOXED IN

Your company is facing a patent infringement lawsuit that could take up to two years to settle. Although a federal judge has ordered both sides of the suit not to discuss the case with anyone, many upper level managers have learned through the grapevine that if the company loses, the fines imposed will send the company into bankruptcy. As time goes on, word has it that the outcome looks bleak.

As Director of Human Resources, you are interviewing a highly qualified candidate to replace a production manager who has recently quit rather than wait for the outcome of the legal action. You would like to hire this candidate, but he is concerned with job security. He is willing to relocate with his wife and three children, but is afraid to leave the security of his old job. He relaxes a bit when you write the salary figure on a piece of paper and hand it to him, but when he asks you why the last person left, you are at a loss for words.

You feel boxed in. What would you say?

1. Secures the trust of the interviewee, possibly by assuring that what the interviewee says will remain confidential

2. Creates an atmosphere in which the interviewee will feel free to bring up any subject without fear of offending or alienating the interviewer

3. Maintains a nondirective approach so that the interviewee, rather than the interviewer, determines the subjects to be considered

4. Refrains from evaluating, either verbally or nonverbally, what the interviewee is saying

The Orientation Interview

The purpose of **orientation interviews** is to acquaint new employees with their jobs and with the range of duties involved. A good orientation interviewer will provide the new employee with a desire to learn and an interest in succeeding. This type of interview is unique because the interviewer's primary role is that of information giver. The interviewer tells the new employee about the job and the company. Organizational policies and procedures may be discussed, as will any other subject that is pertinent to orienting a new worker to the environment. Initial opinions, attitudes, and expectations are formed, at least partly, as a result of orientation interviews.

The orientation interview can profoundly affect the way a new employee views the job and the organization.

The initial expectations formed at the orientation interview can significantly influence the behavior of the new employee. As an example, the most memorable of a dozen or so typist jobs Bob Porter has held was the one with Allied Industries. On his first day, Mae Rosen, his supervisor, told him that she hoped Bob would like his job. "The only really bad thing about this work," she said, "is that it is so repetitive. You do the same thing from nine until five. Until you learn how to think about other things while typing, you'll be pretty bored." Bob soon discovered what Mae had meant. He probably never gave the job a chance because he was led to expect to be bored and he immediately was bored. He quit the job after the longest two weeks he could remember.

The Exit Interview

An **exit interview** is conducted in order to learn why employees who leave voluntarily are doing so. The interview is usually conducted by a personnel specialist, who also may use the opportunity to explain the organization policies on such matters as letters of recommendation and continuation of insurance.

The exit interviewer intends to discover if the employee's reasons for quitting indicate some organizational problem that merits investigation. For example, if several departing employees cite the supervision on the night shift as their reason for leaving, an actual problem exists.

This is a difficult interview to conduct because of several obstacles to frank disclosure of the true reasons for leaving. Interviewees are often suspicious of the company's sudden show of interest. The chance always exists that the employee may want to return to the organization and therefore is unwilling to speak negatively of it.

The exit interviewer must overcome such obstacles by securing the interviewee's trust. The suggestions for creating an appropriate climate for the counseling interview are equally pertinent to the exit interview. A good exit program can be the source of information that leads to significant organizational improvements.

Rarely a week goes by that Charlie Bennings, as assistant personnel manager, does not conduct several exit interviews. Some of these interviews last for an hour or more. "After doing several exit interviews, I have a tendency to stick to the company interview form and rush through it. If I take my time in establishing rapport and keep the interview conversational, I get more helpful information," he has observed.

The exit interview can yield information that is useful in improving the organization.

The Information-Getting Interview

Many of the interviews conducted in organizations do not fall into any of the major categories. Instead, they are conducted to elicit information for a specific purpose. An interviewer from the news media would conduct an information-getting interview with witnesses to an accident. An interviewer for a public opinion poll would conduct an information-getting interview, as would an automobile service manager when talking with the owner of a car that requires service.

Numerous such interviews are routinely conducted, many of them so unstructured that they resemble conversations rather than interviews. Jerry Sloan, for example, is a project coordinator who is currently responsible for keeping three construction projects on schedule. Most of his time is spent talking to each of the three site managers to ensure that deadlines will be met. When bottlenecks seem likely, Jerry talks with the subcontractor responsible and tries to solve the problem. "I'm a coordinator," says Jerry, "and coordination is communication; I'm also an interviewer, because I get most of the information I need through interviews."

Styles of Interviewing

Styles of interviewing can be thought of in terms of two concepts: freedom and control. The extent to which these two concepts are balanced determines interviewing style. The three distinct styles of interviewing are (1) highly directive, (2) directive, and (3) nondirective. They are not unique and separate; rather they should be thought of as existing on a continuum. The differences among styles are matters of degree and are determined by the extent that the interviewer emphasizes freedom and control. This continuum is illustrated in Figure 20.2.

The three styles of interviewing are highly directive, directive, and nondirective.

In the **highly directive interviewing style** the interviewer exerts strong control. Typically, little time is devoted to establishing rapport. Most of the questions are closed, and the responses elicited are often recorded. The highly directive style is frequently used for gathering factual information. Many, if not all, of the questions asked by the highly directive interviewer may be prepared in advance.

The **directive interview style** is characterized by the interviewer's balance between freedom and control. A more flexible approach allows the interviewer more

Figure 20.2
Interview Styles as Related to Freedom and Control

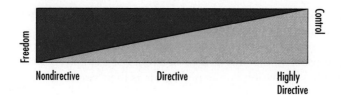

leeway in terms of approach. Directive interviewers usually prepare their main questions in advance and they rely on a balance of open and closed questions.

In the **nondirective interviewing style**, open questions are used almost exclusively. The nondirective interviewer may list in advance some topics for discussion, but the style is mainly an unstructured one. Considerable control of the interview is given to the interviewee, who does most of the talking. This style is appropriate only for skilled interviewers; otherwise it takes much time and the results are largely unclear.

Key Terms

- **open question**
- **closed question**
- **neutral question**
- **leading question**
- **loaded question**
- **mirror question**
- **probing question**
- **pause**
- **performance appraisal interview**
- **correction interview**
- **counseling interview**
- **orientation interview**
- **exit interview**
- **highly directive interviewing style**
- **directive interviewing style**
- **nondirective interviewing style**

Summary

Types of questions used by interviewers   pp. 485–487

Advantages and disadvantages of question types   pp. 485–486

Conducting an employment interview: before, during, and after   pp. 489–491

Performance appraisal interview   pp. 491–492

Correction interview   pp. 492–493

Counseling interview   pp. 493–494

Orientation interview   p. 494

Exit interview   pp. 494–495

Information-getting interview   p. 495

Interviewing styles   p. 496

Review Questions

1. What is an interview?

2. How does an interview differ from a conversation?

3. How do open questions differ from closed questions?

4. How do leading questions differ from loaded questions?

5. What are the five phases of the interview structure?

6. What must you do when planning an interview?

7. Why does the importance of rapport vary with the purpose of the interview?

8. What are the four main topics usually covered in an employment interview?

9. In what types of interview would the time allocation differ from that of the employment interview? Give reasons for your answer.

10. By the end of the performance appraisal interview there should be agreement between interviewer and interviewee regarding three main points. What are these three points?

11. What are the three main styles of interviewing? Describe each style.

Exercises

1. You are conducting a survey to determine what people like about their hometowns. Interview three students on that subject, and continue each interview until you have learned at least five things the interviewee likes. Then divide into groups of four or five interviewers and compile the results.

2. Choose a partner and determine what your partner likes and dislikes about your particular college or university so you can prepare a report on the pros and cons of that institution.

3. You work for a large advertising agency and you are asked to research consumer preferences in regard to automobiles. Develop a set of questions to help you prepare a report on what consumers look for when buying a new car.

4. You are hiring an executive from a pool of highly qualified applicants. The person hired will receive a one-year assignment overseas. Because of the remoteness of the overseas location and the undependable communication technology there, this particular position requires honesty, self motivation, and an ability to make decisions independent of guidance from company headquarters. Develop a set of questions that will aid you in finding the right person.

5. You have been granted unlimited time to interview your favorite public figure or celebrity, but you will be allowed to ask only three questions. Your goal is to get as much information as possible, given the fact that these questions will be answered as fully as the interviewee is able to do so. Who would you select to interview, and what would your questions be?

6. You are interviewing potential jurors for a civil suit. You are the lawyer representing a consumers' action group that is suing a utility company for 500 million dollars for polluting a local river and damaging the ecosystem. You are forbidden to discuss the details of the case directly or indirectly, but you are seeking someone who would be sympathetic to your cause. What questions would you ask to determine if a potential juror would be acceptable to you?

7. Interview someone who has a job in which you are interested. In the interview emphasize such aspects of the job as qualifications necessary to do the job, opportunity for growth and advancement, and likely starting salary and future earning potential. Describe your findings in a letter report for the director of the placement office at your school.

8. Conduct two interviews, one with a person who works primarily with his or her hands and another with someone who mainly uses his or her mind. Determine what they like and dislike about their respective jobs. Prepare a report in which you compare and contrast your two interviewees.

9. Conduct an interview with a person in business concerning that person's letter-writing practices. Find out the kind of writing that your interviewee does most. What is the purpose of it? What are the most important principles in doing that

kind of writing? Prepare a brief informational report for your professor. Prepare an oral report to present before your business communication class.

10. Interview someone who graduated within the past three years. Find out what your interviewee considered the strengths and shortcomings of his or her college program. Find out any changes that your interviewee would suggest. Prepare a short informational report for your professor.

11. Your business communication professor has a policy of conducting performance evaluation interviews with each student midway through the term. Prepare a form that would ensure that the same topics are covered with every student.

12. Form a pair with another student. Participate in two interviews, once as interviewer and once as interviewee. Each interview should last five minutes. Each interviewer should try to learn as much as possible about the other person's background and interests. The first interviewer should ask only closed questions; the second interviewer should ask only open questions. Write a one-page report on the interview you conducted and the effect of asking only one type of question.

13. Interview someone who conducts employment interviews. Try to learn the interviewing techniques that your interviewee uses. Compare what your interviewee says to what is presented in this chapter. Write a one-page report.

14. Visit a factory or office in your community and learn the performance appraisal techniques used. Interview someone who conducts performance appraisal interviews and write a report on the approach used.

15. Keep a diary for one day of all your contacts with others. How many of these were interviews? How many were conversations? Write a report explaining what made you label some interviews and others conversations.

16. Select a national figure and make a list of 20 questions you would like to ask this person.

17. Have another student role-play the part of the interviewee in Exercise 16. Ask that person your 20 questions. After each response, ask two probing follow-up questions.

18. Select a topic about which people are concerned. Write two lists of closed questions— one of 10 neutral questions; the other, 10 leading questions. Ask five persons your 10 neutral questions and record their answers. Ask five other persons your 10 leading questions and record their answers. Write a one-page report in which you compare the responses to the neutral questions with the responses to the leading questions.

19. Interview someone in a personnel office who conducts exit interviews. Find out the purpose of the exit interviews and the kinds of information obtained from them. Prepare a report on this topic.

C A S E

A Hair-Raising Situation

Amanda Copeland, Southwestern Oklahoma State University
Kathy B. White, University of North Carolina at Greensboro

Jean entered a nationally franchised hair-care center in a town of approximately 30,000 population and asked for the owner.

Marie, who was at the desk, noted the young woman's self-confident and poised manner. "I'm the owner," she said, "What can I do for you?"

Jean explained that she was new in town and was looking for a job. She offered proof of her ability and previous employment by producing paycheck stubs from a hair-care center of the same franchise in a large city. Substantial earnings, as shown on the stubs, indicated that Jean was a good hairdresser. As the conversation continued, Marie became more and more favorably impressed with Jean's personality and apparent skill.

Although impressed, Marie decided to defer any positive commitment. She told Jean that she had no immediate opening, but that things looked promising and that she would let her know in a week's time whether business would let her afford another hairdresser.

The next morning Jean returned to the shop and asked for Marie. Sue, the shop manager, came forward and told Jean that Marie would not be in that day and asked if she might help.

Jean drew some papers out of her purse and asked Sue to complete them for her so that she could return them immediately. The papers were from a local apartment complex, asking for confirmation on Jean's employment date and salary.

Sue told Jean that she could not complete the papers, because she knew nothing of the hiring. Jean insisted that she had to have the papers, that she had talked with Marie the day before, and that she was going to work there. She was so insistent that Sue felt inept; she did not know what to do about the papers or how to handle the situation. Finally she told Jean that she really was sorry but that she could do nothing except take the papers and ask Marie to take care of them when she returned to the shop the following day. Plainly perplexed and exasperated, Jean left and left the papers for Marie.

The following day, Sue gave Marie the papers and told her about the incident. Marie was dumbfounded. She could not imagine what had gone wrong or why Jean would think that a job offer had actually been made.

Case Questions

1. What do you think went wrong?

2. Who failed to communicate what properly or adequately and to whom?

3. What could be done to ensure that no similar incident occurs again?

Notes

1. Tom Peters, "Peters on Excellence," *Atlanta Business Chronicle*, September 30–October 6, 1994, 29A.

2. Daniel Coleman, "Doctors Don't Interview Well, Researchers Say," *Atlanta Constitution*, January 22, 1988, C1.

3. "Automatic Interview," *Atlanta Constitution*, March 9, 1994, D2.

4. David Stamps, "Cyberinterviews Combat Turnover," *Training*, April 1995, 43.

5. Steven M. Ralston and Robert Brady, "The Relative Influence of Interview Communication Satisfaction on Applicants' Recruitment Interview Decisions," *The Journal of Business Communication* 31, No. 1, 1994, 61–77.

6. Tom Janz, Lowell Hellervik, and David C. Gilmore, *Behavior Description Interviewing* (Boston: Allyn and Bacon, 1986).

7. Shari Caudron, "Team Staffing Requires New HR Role," *Personnel Journal*, May 1994, 77–83.

Part 4

CAREER
STRATEGIES

Knowing how to market yourself is an important aspect of getting your first job and in long-term career planning. Many of the principles examined throughout this text apply to the written elements of job-seeking: application letters, resumés, follow-up letters, and so on. The principles also relate to the oral side of job-seeking: presenting yourself well in the many types of job interviews.

Writing a Resumé

Doug Mills has been a successful recruiter for one of the Big Six accounting firms for 12 years. He prides himself on his ability to screen college students, based on their resumés, and to select good candidates for introductory interviews. Doug knows that accounting is a profession built on accuracy and precision. He believes resumés need to reflect those characteristics. He therefore looks for high grades—at least a 3.0 overall. He also seeks indications of involvement in the profession beyond majoring in accounting, such as membership in an accounting club. Finally—and he applies this rule rigorously—if he sees a misspelled word or uncorrected typo, he discards the resumé immediately and does not even send an acknowledgment letter.

Whether you are a student about to finish school, a person reentering the job market after a period of time, or someone simply wanting to find a more attractive position than the one you have now, you will find that people use a variety of techniques to find a job:

- Personal contacts through family and close friends
- Personal contacts through acquaintances
- Employment agencies
- College placement centers
- Mass mailings
- Newspaper advertisements
- Unannounced visits to businesses
- Community surveys of employers

No matter which technique you use, your success in convincing a company to hire you instead of someone else depends on three factors: your background, your effectiveness in presenting that background, and your performance in the job interview.

THE USES AND CHARACTERISTICS OF RESUMÉS

The resumé and the cover or application letter that accompanies the resumé are usually the first contact between you and the organization; therefore, you will be evaluated through these documents. In reading a resumé and letter of application, the recruiter seeks three types of information: (1) Do you have the basic credentials for the job, such as a business degree for a business job? (2) Do you have background that elevates you beyond the basic qualifications, such as related job experience? and (3) Are you good at what you do?

This third type of information is the most important to most recruiters. Many recruiters prefer an applicant who is good at ditch digging, for example, to one who is only mediocre in a related job. The enthusiasm, leadership, or responsibility that emerges when you hold a job indicates your effectiveness. This effectiveness is sometimes referred to as your track record. If you can show a history of winning, recruiters will anticipate your continued success. Most resumés transmit the first type of information; many transmit the second type. Few, however, take full advantage of the third type.

> *Recruiters are particularly interested in whether applicants are good at what they do.*

Three characteristics define **resumés**: they are factual, categorized, and tabulated. The information in resumés can be substantiated and is not opinion. The location of your high school and the date of your graduation, for example, can be verified. On the other hand, your belief that you are enthusiastic cannot be verified. The information is categorized or grouped under headings, such as education or job experience. The headings tend to be mutually exclusive. Information in a resume is not presented in sentence form; it is tabulated much like a balance sheet, with headings and subheadings and responses to queries, such as *Interests: writing programs for home computer, playing tennis.*

Whether or not you use a resumé to obtain interviews, you will need one at some time during the job-hunting process. Interviewers refer to the resumé during the interview. Resumés are often used later to compare applicants for a position or for further evaluation.

COMPONENTS OF AN EFFECTIVE RESUMÉ

The order of the components in a resumé may determine the image or tone of the message. Just as we organize persuasive letters differently from positive letters, we need to plan the organization of the resumé. It will benefit from moving stronger components to positions of strength and emphasis and playing down weaker components by either omitting them or placing them near the end.

The most effective resumé is one that presents factual data in an enticing, clear, positive, and individualized fashion. The effective resumé writer does not think in terms of just filling in blanks on a form; instead he or she decides which information has the most value and how it can be phrased for maximum effect.

Heading

A required part of every resumé, the heading should contain your name, address, and telephone number. The word *resumé* is an optional part of the heading, although it is being included less often than in the past. If you have two addresses, one at school and one at home, put both in the heading. Listing your home address will help an employer contact you when you are no longer in school. Here is an example:

ROBERT J. ANDERSON

(until June 1, 1997)	(after June 1, 1997)
134 Ansley Street	1897 Clearwater Road
Atlanta, GA 30324	Duran, IA 52242
(404) 863-2717	(319) 422-5799

If you have only one address, place it either to the far left or directly beneath your name. Some people add their E-mail address.

> *Resumés should not include a photograph.*

You may wonder why no photograph is used with a resumé. In times past pictures were usually included. However, federal laws now prohibit employers from discriminating on the basis of several factors, including race, sex, and age. If you put your picture on your resumé, someone at the company that receives it will likely feel obliged to obscure it. Rather than put a potential employer in an embarrassing position, omit the picture.

Availability Date

Companies budget many of their entry-level openings to coincide with graduation dates. For example, Doug Mills' organization at the beginning of this chapter might have five openings beginning July 1 (for May and June graduates), two September 1 openings (for August graduates), and two January 1 openings (for December graduates).

Openings may occur in every month of the year, of course. As a convenience to the potential employer, however, place your date of availability on the resumé. This will enable the employer to more easily fit you into a budgeted position. Give both the month and year and, if possible, the specific day:

AVAILABLE: June 2, 1997

If you are available for a position at the time you complete your resumé, you might write the availability component like this:

AVAILABLE: Immediately

If you know that the availability date is not important to the company, place this information near the end, perhaps with personal data, or omit it.

Objective

The impression you make on your potential employer is due in large part to how clearly defined your goals are. As Chapter 22 explains, interviewers will normally ask about both your short-term and your long-term goals. To many interviewers applicants with clear-cut goals show more maturity and readiness to pursue a profession than applicants who have no clear goals in mind. This is an example of a goal statement:

OBJECTIVE: Responsible career position in accounting or finance

The objective shows potential employers that the applicant has set goals.

Choose your words carefully. The word "responsible" says that you want and are willing to assume responsibility. The word "career" says that you want to stay with the company. Employees are expensive to replace. In some organizations the cost of hiring and training a replacement could be many thousands of dollars. Therefore, at the front of an interviewer's mind may be the question, how long will this applicant stay with this company?

Be sure that the position you mention in the goal statement is as specific as you can make it. Accounting and finance are fairly closely related. Try to avoid general statements or statements that represent you as the proverbial jack of all trades. On the other hand, when using one resumé for many openings, some generality may be necessary. Perhaps you will even omit this component.

Are you willing to relocate or to travel? If so, state your willingness along with your objective:

OBJECTIVE: Responsible entry-level position in personnel management with opportunity for advancement. Willing to relocate and travel.

The reason for placing relocation and travel information with your objective is that every reader will notice it.

This information is tremendously important to some businesses. In recent years many managers in large companies have turned down promotions and salary increases simply because relocation was involved. If you are willing to relocate, let the reader know as soon as possible. Such willingness is critical for many sales positions. No matter what position you seek, however, some traveling may be involved, especially during the training and orientation period.

A willingness to relocate and travel helps to make a good impression.

Education

The education section of your resumé should contain these important items:

1. When you received your degrees or diplomas
2. Where you earned your degrees or diplomas
3. Your major or field of concentration
4. Relevant course work taken, or skills or knowledge acquired
5. Your grade point average, if appropriate

Where you place the education component in your resumé will depend on which format you decide to use. However, most students just finishing school place education directly beneath the objective.

If you have or are expecting to receive a four-year degree, you might write your education component like this:

EDUCATION:

June 1997	Bachelor of Business Administration, Southern University, Atlanta, Georgia. Major in personnel management. Minor in marketing. Course work included wage and salary administration, personnel selection, personnel administration, EEO, and ERISA. GPA of 3.8 on a 4-point scale. Graduated summa cum laude.
June 1993	Graduated with honors from Southwestern High School, Roanoke, Virginia.

If the location of your college or university is well known, then omit the city and state, but always include the city and state for your high school entry.

The course work you list should be related to the objective stated in your resumé. Be careful about listing courses by name, as often the name of a course is misleading or ambiguous. For example, if a course called Human Resource Management focused primarily on such topics as Equal Employment Opportunity (EEO) and the Occupational Safety and Health Act (OSHA), then your course work statement should read "EEO and OSHA."

Finally, list your grade point average (GPA) only if you want to call attention to it. Many employers are more interested in your major, work experience, and activities than in your GPA. Be sure to show the scale on which your GPA is computed (for example, 3-point scale, 6-point scale). Also, if your overall GPA is not high but the GPA of your major is, then state, "GPA in major of 3.6 on a 4-point scale."

If you are a graduate of a two-year college, then you might use this format for your education component:

EDUCATION:

June 1997	Associate of Arts in Business Administration, Atlanta Junior College, Atlanta, Georgia. Concentration in general business. Forty hours of business course work, including Administrative Practices, Business Communication, Marketing Principles, and Accounting Theory. GPA of 3.4 on a 4-point scale.
June 1995	Graduated with honors from Central High School, Atlanta, Georgia.

Finally, if you have a four-year degree but also attended a two-year school during your college career, you can work both colleges into your resumé like this:

EDUCATION:

June 1997 (expected)	Bachelor of Business Administration, Southern University, Atlanta, Georgia. Major in personnel management. Minor in marketing. Course work included wage and salary administration, personnel selection, personnel administration, EEO, and ERISA. GPA of 3.8 on a 4.0 scale. Graduated summa cum laude.

Grade point averages are listed only if the applicant wants to call attention to them.

September	Attended Wolfson Junior College, Roanoke, Virginia.
1992 to	Concentration in general business. GPA of 3.9 on a 4.0 scale.
June 1995	
June 1993	Graduated with honors from Southwestern High School, Roanoke, Virginia.

If you write your resumé before you receive your final degree, you can place "expected" beneath the date shown. If that date is only two or three months away, however, most potential employers reading your resumé will understand that the degree is expected.

If you are short of space—and especially if you do not have high school honors—consider omitting or reducing the high school information.

> High school information is often omitted from the resumé.

Work Experience

For every full-time or part-time job that you list, include the following information:

1. When you held the job
2. Your job title
3. Who your employer was
4. Your responsibilities
5. Your accomplishments

Here is an example:

WORK EXPERIENCE:

| September 1995 to present | <u>Part-time Registration Clerk,</u> Holiday Hotel, Atlanta, Georgia. Responsibilities include registering hotel guests, making reservations, processing checkouts, and handling guest problems. Earned approximately 30 percent of college expenses. |
| Summer 1995 | <u>Sales Representative,</u> Eastern Book Company, Baltimore, Maryland. Responsibilities included calling on potential customers, processing orders, and delivering merchandise. Was top salesperson in 12-person territory. Earned 70 percent of college expenses for 1995-1996 year. |

First, notice that the jobs are listed in reverse chronological order—most recent job first. Second, if you held a number of jobs during college and high school, you may not want to list them all. Choose those most related to your objective. Remember that no matter how menial the job seemed to you, to a potential employer your having worked says two things: (1) this applicant has been out in the real world and therefore has actual business experience and (2) this applicant shows initiative and responsibility.

> The applicant who has held a number of part-time jobs might list only the goal-related ones.

Dates of Employment
The dates in the example are not exact—you do not need to list the actual days you began and ended your employment. If you held the same job at different times, you can state "Summers 1995, 1996" or "Summers 1995, 1996 and Christmas 1996."

Job Title
Some jobs do not have specific titles. If you had such a job, simply make up a descriptive title for it. For example, if your job was serving customers at the counter of a fast-food restaurant, then you can call your position "counter clerk." Each job title is underlined so that it stands out.

Name of Employer
When you list employers, show their names and locations. If your potential employer wants to call for a reference or verify your employment, this will make it easier to do so.

Responsibilities

The key word is responsibilities, not duties. Again, your purpose is to show that you are capable of assuming responsibility. You need not list all of your responsibilities, just those you think are the most important.

Accomplishments

Any accomplishment that your potential employer can verify belongs in your list of accomplishments. The work-experience example illustrates two kinds of accomplishments: earning money to attend school and succeeding as a salesperson. Other types of accomplishments you can list include supervising other people or training your replacement, both of which show leadership skills to many potential employers. If you assumed your supervisor's duties while he or she was absent, include that information. Perhaps you made some suggestion that was adopted by your employer. If so, then list it. Even seemingly minor accomplishments, such as an employee-of-the-month award, being placed in charge of other student summer help, or being assigned security or cash-handling duties, can impress the person who reads your resumé.

The accomplishments section—also called results—spotlights your track record, the third and most important type of information found in a resumé.

Accomplishments help set the applicant apart from others.

Honors

Any school-related honor you received belongs in an honors section of your resumé. If you have only one honor, however, you should consider including it in the activities section and renaming that section honors and activities. You can look outside school activities for honors as well. Here is a sample honors section:

HONORS: College
Sigma Iota Epsilon (National Management Honorary, 1997)
Phi Kappa Phi (Scholastic Honorary), 1997
Cardinal Club (Freshman Honorary), 1994
High School
Beta Club (Scholastic Honorary), 1993
National Honor Society (Languages), 1993
Others
Selected social director of neighborhood bicycling group.
Chosen to represent senior high-school students from area at national church convention.

A brief explanation of each honor is provided as well as the year the honor was received. Never list your honors in paragraph form because an interviewer is likely to forget them. If you list them as in the example, the interviewer might at least remember how many honors you have received.

Activities

The activities in which you have been involved constitute an important part of your resumé. Activities differ from honors in that honors are bestowed upon you by others; activities are things you yourself decide to do. To most potential employers, activities you list show interest in other people, practice in developing interpersonal relationships, and social skills. If you have served as an officer in some organization, you may also have leadership skills. Include organizations at school as well as religious, volunteer, and other outside activities.

ACTIVITIES: College
Delta Sigma Pi, Professional Business Fraternity (vice president, 1995-1997).
Member, Democrats in Action, 1995-present.
Chairperson, Red Cross blood drive on campus, 1996.

Interests

You may have wondered, when filling out an application for a job, why you were required to list your hobbies or interests. To many potential employers your interests are as important as your activities. Many employers seek a person who has a balance of individual and group interests. Consider the following:

INTERESTS: Reading, jogging, skiing, photography.

Some interviewers will perceive a person with interests like these to be an isolate. There are no real group activities listed. Other interviewers will have an equally negative perception of:

INTERESTS: Tennis, basketball, swimming, backgammon.

Interests such as these might depict a total group orientation. The interviewer may perceive you as too dependent upon others.

Your interests should include a mix of group and individual activities. However, do not list interests that you do not actually have. An interviewer will ask you to discuss the most recent book you have read or how often you jog. If you do not actually read or jog, you have placed yourself in an embarrassing predicament.

The resumé should show a mix of group and individual interests.

You may include hobbies instead of interests, if you wish, or you may combine the two. Interests are things that interest you, even though you may not do them often. Hobbies are usually done with some regularity or frequency.

In presenting hobbies or interests, keep these points in mind:

- Seek a balance between individual and group activities. For example, include "read science fiction" with "play intramural football."
- Seek a balance between athletic and more cerebral activities. Contrast "avid jogger" with "enjoy hearing classical piano concertos."
- Avoid items that appear average, or make you appear average, such as "watch TV" or "go to football games."
- Try to find job-related items, such as writing programs for a home computer or charting marketing trends in some industry.
- Be specific in your description if possible. "Sorority tennis team co-captain" is better than just "tennis."
- Job-oriented organizations, such as a business fraternity or a real estate club, are valuable assets. Volunteer work, such as blood drive worker, or hospital candy striper, also carries a positive message.
- Do not overdo it. A list of too many items suggests you may not have enough time or interest for the job. A total of about six hobbies, interests, or activities is probably the maximum.

Be aware that because a resumé is often but one page in length, you may not have the luxury of presenting hobbies or interests. These suggestions, however, may still be applied to the application form if it asks for such data, or they may be used in the job interview.

Achievements

If you have at least three major achievements, consider illuminating them. These achievements might be found in more depth elsewhere on your resume but are highlighted here.

Make sure your items are true achievements. To emphasize achievements and then present weak items is quite negative. Similarly, having only one or two items under the heading shows a weakness in achievements, not a strength. Five or six items should be the most you present, however; more tend to diminish your entries.

Here are some sample achievements entries:

ACHIEVEMENTS: Earned 90 percent of college expenses. Achieved 3.8 GPA (on 4.0 system) for four-year period.
Elected president of Finance Club.
Dean's list (three semesters).
Reemployed each of four summers by same company.
Selected by (college/dean/fraternity/sorority/business organization/church group, etc.) as representative at (convention, meeting, seminar, etc.)

Personal Data or Background Information

Businesses are prohibited from making selection decisions based on your age, race, sex, marital status, and other personal data unless the data are bona fide occupational qualifications. Thus, this section of your resumé is optional. You should include personal data only if you think it will help you get the position.

Personal data are an optional component of the resumé.

With ongoing pressure to keep resumés brief, constant concern by companies to avoid making discriminatory hiring decisions, and a hesitancy by many applicants to disclose personal details, clearly the trend is away from including the personal data section—or at least from including much information in it.

However, a personal data section may be helpful in some instances. For example, if you are an unmarried female who is also willing to relocate, then your marital status might help you, although legally it should not. You may wish to check with your placement office for guidance on local or regional approaches to this component.

Personal data on a resumé may include the following:

PERSONAL: Age: 22   Birth Date: August 15, 1975
Health: Excellent

With both age and birth date provided, you do not need to update your age if a birthday occurs during the job-seeking process.

Other items sometimes included as background information are the following:

- Geographic preference
- Date of availability
- Percentage of college expenses earned
- Family background (number of children, information about spouse or parents, etc.)

Many of these items are inconsequential to the job—you would only include items you believe might reflect favorably on you. You should also be aware that you are volunteering this information. Current laws are clear that you are not required to give information about such items as religion or family background.

Military Service

An entry pertaining to your military service is appropriate only if you received an honorable discharge. Also, persons with military service receive bonus points on aptitude tests when applying for many civil service positions.

If your military service is extensive (more than two years) and relates closely to your objective, you might enter it as part of your work experience component. Otherwise, the entry should be brief:

MILITARY SERVICE: U.S. Navy, 1994-1996. Served as supply officer on a destroyer.
Discharged as lieutenant (junior grade).

AN ETHICAL DILEMMA

"George, you're misrepresenting yourself on your resumé and you're going to get caught."

"People stress their best qualities on resumés, Juanita. It's assumed you're going to try to make yourself look good."

"That's probably true up to a point, but it's dishonest to say your grades are 3.0 and that you have related job experience."

"I just rounded 2.86 to a 2.9 and 2.9 is almost 3.0. Besides, by the time I graduate I'll probably have a 3.0. And who's to say that my work serving hamburgers doesn't have managerial overtones? Companies want people who have an optimistic outlook and who can see the bright side of things. I'm just improving the perception they'll have of me."

"You're pushing the 'facts' too far. You're being unethical."

"And you're confusing me. I wish you had kept your ideas on business ethics to yourself."

George feels boxed in. What would you do?

Questions

1. How far can you stretch your facts on a resumé without going too far?

2. If an organization uncovers an exaggeration on a resumé, what is it likely to do? What if the organization perceives it as an outright lie?

Licenses and Other Accreditations

Possessing a license or some professional certificate may be important to your getting a position. For example, if you are applying for a real estate salesperson's position, having a real estate license would be important. Other examples of licenses or accreditations that might be entered on your resumé are licensed practical nurse, registered nurse, certified public accountant, certified nuclear safety engineer, certified life underwriter, and any teaching certificate relevant to your objective. An entry for this component can appear like this:

PROFESSIONAL LICENSES: Licensed Practical Nurse, State of Illinois
                         Certified Nurse-Midwife, State of Illinois
CERTIFICATION: Certified Netware Engineer (CNE)

Special Skills

Some jobs you may apply for require special skills. For example, many computer programmers are expected to know several computer languages as well as different types of computer systems. Their special skills component might appear as follows:

COMPUTER SKILLS: Languages: COBOL, FORTRAN, SYSTEX
                    Operating Systems: Unix, Windows, OS/2

Many applicants for positions in international business must know one or more foreign languages. These special skills can appear on the resumé in the same format as the computer skills:

Special skills include computer languages and foreign languages.

FOREIGN LANGUAGES: Speak and read German and Spanish fluently.
Read and write Italian.

Any special skill you possess that is relevant to your objective should be entered on your resumé.

Professional Memberships

Many college students are members of campus chapters of professional organizations. Your membership in such organizations can be listed under the activities component, unless you would like to draw special attention to it, as in this example:

PROFESSIONAL MEMBERSHIPS: American Marketing Association, 1995-present
American Society for Personnel
Administration, 1995-present

References

Unless you are changing jobs and want to keep your decision private as long as possible, consider listing your references on your resumé. Phrases such as "references available upon request" are inconvenient to the personnel specialist, who must either call or write you, ask for your references, and then contact them. You'll save the specialist time if references are on the resumé. If your references are easy to check, he or she may be more inclined to consider you. Be aware, however, that listing references takes valuable space.

Categories of references are professional, character, and educational.

References are supplied for possible verification of the facts you have presented on the resumé or for additional information. References fall into three main categories: (1) professional references, who can speak about your professional ability for this job, such as your knowledge of accounting or computer science; (2) character references, who know your personality, such as your industriousness or ambition; and (3) educational references, who can respond to questions about your scholarly achievements and background, such as your performance in a management class.

Former employers are frequently used as professional references; friends, neighbors, or colleagues are used as character references; and teachers are used as educational references. Keep in mind, though, that how they know you determines the category of reference. A boss may be a friend (character reference), for example. Of course, one reference may be found in several categories. Never list a person as a reference until you have obtained permission to do so.

Some types of people should generally be avoided as references. Family members, clergy, or fellow students are assumed to be biased in your favor. Their opinions, therefore, are discounted.

You may wish to categorize your references under subheadings in the references component. Because educational references are close to professional references in the type of information they supply, the two can be combined under the professional references subheading.

When you use references subheadings, supply an equal number of references under each subheading for balance. That is, supply two professional references to equalize two character references. Here is an example of a reference section from a resumé:

REFERENCES

Professional	Character
Dr. Lillian Patterson	Ms. Betty Weatherford
Department of Business	Department of English
Southern University	Southern University
P.O. Box 3561	P.O. Box 3561
Atlanta, GA 30723	Atlanta, GA 30723
(404) 731-8265	(404) 731-8143
Mr. William Lucey	Dr. John L. Harper, D.D.S.
Distribution Manager	Harper Dental Center
Eastern Book Company	Maguire, GA 30703
4324 Brownsboro Road	(404) 737-2245
Baltimore, MD 13426	
(301) 926-5333	

Be sure each of your references has a title (for example, Dr., Mr., Mrs., or Ms.) so that the personnel specialist who telephones them will know how they are to be addressed. Give the complete business address and telephone number. Never list the reference's home address unless the reference prefers it.

What your references say about you will not—unless it is negative—have a great impact on your evaluation. Some potential employers will not even contact your references, although others will. Employers expect that anyone you list as a reference will support your application. Nevertheless, you will be required normally to submit at least three names of people who are willing to recommend you.

Should you decide, because of limitations of space, not to list your references on the resumé, you might use one of the following statements:

REFERENCES:	Excellent references available upon request.
REFERENCES:	Excellent references available at:
	Career Planning and Placement Center, Southern University,
	Atlanta, GA 30723

A word of caution regarding references: Today's electronic databases, search capabilities, and computers on the Internet permit ready access to people's background information. And the ease and depth of this access is far greater than most people are aware. Therefore, be sure of the accuracy of the information you supply—including data about references—and know that some companies conduct data searches on applicants.[1]

You can choose from among the 15 components those that you think will best show your accomplishments. The balance of the chapter will be devoted to packaging these components in a compelling format.

RESUMÉ FORMATS

From a variety of formats, you can select the one you think presents your resumé components in the best way. The formats presented here will meet most needs, but creating your own format for a specific company may be even more effective. Keep your resumé balanced, clean, and esthetically pleasing.

Figure 21.1
Typical Resumé for a
Graduating Student

HOLLY M. CLARK
1554 Westside Drive
Atlanta, GA 30110
(404) 638-2176

AVAILABLE: July 1, 1997

OBJECTIVE: Responsible entry-level position in computer programming. Willing to relocate.

EDUCATION: Associate of Arts in Computer Sciences, Northrup Junior College, East
June 1997   Point, Georgia. Concentration in Computer Analysis and Design. Course
(expected)   work included Computer Design, Computer Programming, COBOL, and
              FORTRAN. GPA in concentration of 3.4 on a 4-point scale.

June 1995   Graduated from Southwest High School, East Point, Georgia.

WORK   Part-Time Computer Programmer, Northrup Junior College Computer
EXPERIENCE: Center. Responsibilities include programming, checking system malfunc
September 1996 tions, assisting students with computer jobs, keeping time-sharing records
to present   on all users.

Summer and   Salesperson, Annette's Dress Shop, East Point, Georgia.
Christmas   Responsibilities included assisting customers, stocking merchandise,
Vacations   creating displays, and inventory. Trained replacement at the end of
1995 to 1996 Summer 1996.

ACTIVITIES: Baptist Student Union, 1996 to present
              Staff writer, The Blue and Gold (Northrup Junior College newspaper)

COMPUTER   Languages: COBOL, FORTRAN
SKILLS: Systems: Windows '95, Apple Macintosh System 7

PROFESSIONAL National Computer Science Association, 1996 to present
MEMBERSHIPS: Computer Users of America, 1996 to present

INTERESTS: Writing computer programs for home computer
              Singing in church choir
              Playing intramural tennis (doubles)

PERSONAL: Age: 20   Birth Date: August 15, 1977
              Health: Excellent

REFERENCES: Available on request

Resumé Format for New Graduates

A resumé format tailored to a student about to receive an associate degree and enter the job market with little work experience is shown in Figure 21.1.

In this example most section headings are capitalized, underlined, and set apart in the left-hand margin. A reader can quickly find the information that is most important.

ROBERT J. ANDERSON

<table>
<tr><td>(until June 1, 1997)</td><td>(after June 1, 1997)</td></tr>
<tr><td>134 Ansley Street, Apt. 4-B</td><td>1897 Clearwater Road</td></tr>
<tr><td>Atlanta, GA 30723</td><td>Duran, IA 63217</td></tr>
<tr><td>(404) 863-2717</td><td>(612) 422-5799</td></tr>
</table>

AVAILABLE:

June 1, 1997

OBJECTIVE:

Responsible career position in accounting or finance.

EDUCATION:

Bachelor of Business Administration, Southern University, Atlanta, Georgia. Major in Accounting. Minor in Finance. Course work included Accounting Principles, Tax Accounting, Accounting Law, Financial Analysis, and Financial Planning. GPA of 3.7 on a 4-point scale (4.0 in major). Graduated summa cum laude, June 1997.

WORK EXPERIENCE:

Part-Time Registration Clerk, Holiday Hotel, Atlanta, Georgia. Responsibilities include registering hotel guests, making reservations, processing check-outs, and handling guest problems. Have earned approximately 30 percent of college expenses. September 1995–present. Sales Representative, Eastern Book Company, Baltimore, Maryland. Responsibilities included calling on potential customers, processing orders, and delivering merchandise. Was top salesperson in 12-person territory. Earned 70 percent of college expenses for 1996–1997. Summer 1996.

HONORS:

College
Beta Alpha Psi (National Accounting Honorary), 1997
Phi Kappa Phi (National Scholastic Honorary), 1997
Cardinal Club (Freshman Honorary), 1994
High School
Beta Club (Scholastic Honorary), 1993
National Honor Society (Languages), 1993

Figure 21.2
Typical Resumé for a Graduating Senior

For example, some will want to read about work experience first; others, about education. The information is blocked attractively, several spaces in from the section headings. The appearance of a resumé is almost as important as its contents.

Another example, this one for a graduating senior, is shown in Figure 21.2. It has several additional components and carries over to a second page. Note that the references are listed across, not down, the page to save space and to make them easier to identify.

Figure 21.2
Continued

Robert J. Anderson, p. 2

ACTIVITIES:

College
Alpha Kappa Psi Business Fraternity
(Vice President, 1996)
Member, Democrats in Action, 1995–present
Chairperson, campus Red Cross blood drive, 1996
High School
Spanish Club (President)
Tennis team (lettered three years)

INTERESTS:

Reading, tennis, basketball, photography

REFERENCES:

Professional
Dr. Lillian Patterson
Department of Business
Southern University
P.O. Box 3561
Atlanta, GA 30723
(404) 731-8265

Ms. Betty Weatherford
Department of English
Southern University
P.O. Box 3561
Atlanta, GA 30723
(404) 731-8143

Character
Mr. William Lucey
Distribution Manager
Eastern Book Company
4324 Brownsboro Road
Baltimore, MD 21426
(301) 926-5333

Dr. John L. Harper, D.D.S.
Harper Dental Care
Maguire, GA 30703
(404) 737-2245

Chronological Resumé Format

Chronological or functional resumé formats are appropriate when work experience is extensive.

Both the chronological and the functional resumé formats are typically used by people with extensive work experience. In the **chronological resumé** the work experience component appears early and describes each position in detail. An example appears in Figure 21.3.

Figure 21.3
Chronological Resumé
Format

WILMA G. PETERSON

4255 Tufts Road
Troy, IL 62234
(316) 614-8432

OBJECTIVE: Responsible and challenging management position in health-care
administration.

EXPERIENCE:

May 1996   Assistant Administrator, Cowans County Medical Center,
to present   Troy, Illinois
                Responsibilities
                - Directly responsible for hiring all hourly employees to staff 100-
                  bed hospital
                - Administer wage and salary program for all staff members
                - Write policies and procedures for employee handbook
                - Supervise four department heads, two clerical workers
                Accomplishments
                - Implemented technical training program for all health-care
                  employees; received highest possible rating from Hospital
                  Accreditation Board
                - Implemented employee suggestion system that has resulted in net
                  savings to hospital of $75,327

September 1995 Nursing Supervisor, Cowans County Medical Center, Troy, Illinois
to April 1996   Responsibilities
                - Scheduled working hours for all nursing staff
                - Supervised three shift supervisors
                Accomplishments
                - Promoted use of paraprofessionals to assist nursing staff
                - Awarded the Illinois Nurses' Association "Supervisor of the Year
                  Award," 1996

June 1992   Nurse, Groveland Hospital, Chicago, Illinois
to August 1995 Responsibilities
                - Patient care and medication, intensive care unit
                - In charge of 12 other nurses on night shift (June–August 1995)
                Accomplishments
                - Promoted to nurse-in-charge after three years
                - Recommended changes in patient care were implemented
                - Salary increased 110 percent in 39-month period

With this resumé format the individual's work experience consumes the most
space. Work experience also precedes education, because it is more important.

Functional Resumé Format

The **functional resumé** emphasizes kinds of work. Using the functional format, you
can choose the qualifications you think are important for the position you want, list

Figure 21.3
Continued

Wilma G. Peterson, p. 2

EDUCATION:

1996 to present   Working toward a Master's Degree in Hospital Administration, Acton College, St. Louis, Missouri. Have completed 35 hours of course work.

June 1992   Bachelor of Science Degree in Nursing, St. Mary's School of Nursing, Chicago, Illinois. Graduated with high honors.

PROFESSIONAL
MEMBERSHIPS:
- National Association of Hospital Administrators
- Illinois Association of Health Care Administrators
- National Association of Nursing Administrators

COMMUNITY
ACTIVITIES:
- American Cancer Society
- American Red Cross
- United Way (Campaign Chairperson, 1995)

INTERESTS:
- Collecting antiques
- Playing golf
- Listening to light opera

REFERENCES:
- Available upon request

them separately, and show how you possess each of the qualifications. In Figure 21.4 an individual with little formal education and work experience was able to show himself to be highly competent.

There are five dimensions in effectively preparing your resumé that set you apart from—and above—the crowd.

1. Present positive information with positive phrasing.

2. Order your components and the items under the components with most important (to the reader) information first.

Figure 21.4
Functional Resumé Format

HAROLD D. WILLIAMS

25 Clarkston Place
Salem, OR 80135
(817) 236-5926
E-mail: hdwilliams.937@aol.com

OBJECTIVE:	Responsible general management position in textile or related field. Willing to travel or relocate.
EXPERIENCE:	
General Management	Supervised more than 100 hourly workers in two textile plants. Responsible for scheduling and employee-relations problems.
Quality Assurance	Met or exceeded quality standards 95 percent of the time. Helped establish quality standards for new product.
Production	Assisted in introduction, set-up, and operation of new machines. Am familiar with Crossland and Weaveright equipment.
Motivation	Used MBO, goal-setting, and piece-rate systems.
WORK HISTORY:	1993 to present: Production Manager, Bostick Mills, Salem, Oregon 1989–1993: Production Supervisor, Quality Fabrics, Inc., Salem, Oregon
EDUCATION:	
June 1989	Graduated from Owen Technical School, Salem, Oregon (two-year program). Concentration in Textile Management. Course work included Production Planning, Quality Control, Supervision, Machine Design, and Human Factors Engineering.
COMMUNITY ACTIVITIES:	Lion's Club, 1994 to present Toastmaster's International, 1989–1992
SPECIAL QUALIFICATIONS:	Four years' related job experience Supporting technical education Record of achievement
INTERESTS:	Hunting with bow and arrow, Pente, old movies
REFERENCES:	Available on request

3. Show your track record. Indicate that you're good at what you do, whatever it may be.

4. Avoid being average or saying average things. Look for information that sets you apart from the crowd.

5. Aim for consistency and balance. Try to present equal numbers of items or to handle items similarly.

Resumé Formats for Unusual Backgrounds

Each individual should try to transmit his or her unique personality when writing a resumé. Some people, however, have especially unusual backgrounds that may affect resumé preparation. Among them are the older-than-average student and the international student.

For the older-than-average student, the resumé should emphasize maturity, judgment, and drive. Because this person may have large gaps between high school and college graduation, some explanation may be necessary. If the void is filled by job experience, the reason for returning for the college degree may be given. Other activities, such as unemployment while raising a family, form a desirable rationale. Figure 21.5 is an example of a resumé for an older-than-average student.

The international student studying in the United States, graduating, and seeking a job here faces some concerns different from native students. Prospective employers will want to know the answers to the following questions:

- Are you seeking permanent, full-time employment (or will you have to leave the country in several years)?
- What is your language ability, especially with English? How are your writing and speaking abilities?
- What is your citizenship situation? Do you hold dual citizenship? Do you hold a visa? What kind? Do you plan to apply for American citizenship? When?
- Does your country expect you to serve some obligation, such as in the military? Have you served yet?
- Is there any reason to be concerned about security clearances? Have you been cleared before? By whom?
- Do you have family in your country? How often do you visit them? Do you have relatives in this country?

The international student may wish to address these questions in the resumé or in the letter of application. Figure 21.6 illustrates an international student resumé in which some of these issues are confronted.

> ✔ *CHECKLIST for an Effective Resumé²*
>
> _____ Forget the fancy stuff. The person reading the resumé wants information pertinent to the job vacancy, not an elaborate format or colored paper.
>
> _____ Keep it simple and hard-hitting. Flowery language and literary affectations are a waste.
>
> _____ Lead off with work experience, going back from your current job. Education comes next. It's the easiest kind of resumé to write—and read.
>
> _____ Stick to two pages. A single page is even better.
>
> _____ Customize. Emphasize one job experience over another, depending on the position you're seeking.
>
> _____ Don't blow your horn too loud. When you accomplished something as part of a team, say so.

THE COMPUTER-PREPARED RESUMÉ

Traditionally the final versions of resumés were prepared on a typewriter. Copies were then made on professional offset printers. Now more and more resumés are being written on a computer and the finished product is output from a laser printer. The computer provides easier corrections and updates as well as design options that

Figure 21.5
Resumé of the Older-Than-Average Student

JUDITH KASTON BERRY

Bachelor of Business Administration
May 1997

Permanent Address
1717 Royal Court
Chicago, IL 60681
(312) 771-1003

EDUCATION: Roosevelt University, 1989–1997
                 Degree: Bachelor of Business Administration
                 Major: Dual major in accounting and finance
                 Grades: Overall, 3.71/4.0; accounting, 3.6/4.0;
                 finance, 3.75/4.0
                 Honors: Dean's list (seven semesters); graduation with honors
                 anticipated; highest score ever achieved on mock CPA exam

RELATED
EXPERIENCE: Treasurer, Church of the Good Shepherd
                 Accountant/bookkeeper, part-time, Lion's Club Women's Auxiliary
                 Treasurer, Cub Scout Pack #214
                 Bookkeeper and tax work, part-time (in home) for Green Laundry,
                 10 months

VOLUNTEER
WORK: St. Margaret's Children's Hospital, Chicago, work in cafeteria
                 Church of the Good Shepherd, teach Sunday school
                 American Heart Association, fund-raiser
                 KCHI, public broadcasting station, auction volunteer

PERSONAL
BACKGROUND: Age: 46
                 Family: Husband is employed in city transportation department;
                 three children (one senior in high school, one junior at Roosevelt
                 University, one employed in St. Paul)

OTHER: Geographic requirement: Chicago or northwest suburbs
                 Position sought: full-time job in accounting or finance with an
                 established company

REFERENCES: References available on request

can be used to improve appearance. An inexpensive dot matrix printer is useful for draft copies, but you should always prepare the resumé you send to a prospective employer with a high-quality printer.

A variation on using the computer is to prepare the resumé with desktop publishing software or advanced word processing software. The packages often can slightly

Figure 21.6
Resumé of International
Student

CARLOS LUIS RODRIGUEZ

Present address:
1324 Halfhill Court
Phoenix, AZ 60990
(602) 691-8891

Permanent address:
Monterrey 893 Col. Mexico
Nuevo Laredo, Tamps., Mexico
Phone: 7.27.21

OBJECTIVE

Full-time position in data processing or systems management

EDUCATION

Arizona State University 1993–1997, Bachelor of Business Administration
Majors: Data Processing and Analysis, General Business
Grades: Overall GPA, 3.31/4.0; DPA, 3.5/4.0

Saltillo Escuela Preparatoria, Saltillo, Mexico 1991–1993

EMPLOYMENT

Arizona State University 1996–1997
Registration supervisor for university registration; in charge of 15 student workers;
responsible for security and student traffic flow.

College of Business Administration 1994–1996
Computation center PC laboratory assistant and mainframe computer operator; proctored
lab; distributed printed mainframe output.

COMPUTER SKILLS

Languages: COBOL, FORTRAN, BASIC, C++
Software Familiarity: Microsoft Office Suite
Hardware Familiarity: IBM compatibles, Apple Macintosh, Novell networks

ACTIVITIES

Data Processing Management Association
Delta Sigma Pi National Professional Business Fraternity
Chicano Business Students Association

OTHER

Speak and write fluent English and Spanish
Mexican citizen; hold student visa (since 1993); plan practicum and then application for
U.S. citizenship
Brother, a Chicago banker and legal alien; rest of family is in Mexico
Geographic preference: Southwest United States

REFERENCES

Available on request

increase or decrease a typeface size to expand or contract text to fit better on the
printed page. Although you must be careful of overdoing the visual treatments, the
goals of an esthetically pleasing, balanced, and neat final product are more attainable

Figure 21.7
Resumé Prepared Using
Desktop Publishing
Computer Program

Samuel G. Toliver   1569 West College Avenue
                                       San Diego, CA 92183
                                       (619) 594-3241
                                       Internet: sgt0012@powerlaser.com

Summary of Qualifications
Worked for four years as assistant manager of shoe department for a major San Diego
retailer; joined Retailing Club at San Diego State University in 1994; maintained high
grades for full college experience; applied retailing experience with social fraternity at
SDSU as part of fund-raising campaign to help homeless people of the community.

Experience
Assistant Manager, Softstride Shoe Department of Federated Stores, San Diego,
1993–present.
Shift Supervisor, Homer's Hamburgers, 25 hours a week, Summer 1993.
Held following part-time jobs while in high school: paperboy, gas station cashier, cut
grass for neighbors, worked in family grocery store.

Education
Bachelor of Business Administration, San Diego State University, May 1997. Majored in
marketing (GPA: 3.2) and minored in communication. Overall GPA: 3.0/4.0. Took elec-
tive marketing courses in advanced retailing principles. Internship in retailing under
Dr. Ron Carruth, national retailing expert.

Honors
One of top ten marketing students in class of 1991 on the basis of grades. "Best
Salesperson," Shoe Department at Federated, May 1996.

Special Skills
Computer skills (Macintosh, VAX minicomputer): word processing, spreadsheets, and
database.
Oral presentations: class and on-the-job experience making business presentations supported by graphics.

Activities
Retailing Club: San Diego State University: vice president (1996–97), head of sales force
selling light bulbs in community to raise money for homeless people (Fall 1996), head of
speaker selection committee (Spring 1996).
Sigma Phi Nu Social Fraternity: president of pledge class (1994), vice president for cere-
monies (1995), assistant house manager (1996).

Hobbies and Interests
Intramural athletics with fraternity, mountain bicycling, reading Retailing News and
Advertising Age.

with this software. See Figure 21.7 for an example of desktop publishing treatment
applied to a resumé.

A third option is to use software that prepares the resumé, usually with a choice of
formats, on the basis of your responses to questions. You can accept the output or

Resumé software is available for both IBM and Macintosh computers.

modify the spacing, typefaces, or content, or make other adjustments with your word processor. Resumé software for both the IBM platform and Apple Macintosh computers often includes additional elements, such as a word processor, spelling checker, database for tracking contacts, mail-merge of network names and form letters, calendars for scheduling interviews, questionnaires for self-assessment, help with developing weekly action plans, lists of major companies, and extensive how-to manuals.

Related to a computer preparation of your resumé is selecting a typeface. Many companies—especially ones that receive a high volume of applications—scan resumés into a database. Because of this procedure, you should select a typeface that scans—and also faxes—well, such as 12-point Times Roman or Helvetica.

Key Terms

- **resumé**
- **chronological resumé format**
- **functional resumé format**

Summary

The uses and characteristics of resumés   p. 503

Components of an effective resumé   p. 504

Resumé formats   p. 513

The computer-prepared resumé   p. 520

Review Questions

1. What does the education component of a resumé contain? The work experience component?

2. What is meant by a balance of interests on the resumé? Why is this balance important?

3. Describe and differentiate among three different resumé formats.

4. What are special skills on a resumé?

5. Briefly discuss the final printing and copying of a resumé.

Exercises

1. Write a draft of your own resumé using the format for recent graduates. Exchange resumés with a classmate. Evaluate one another's drafts, suggesting changes you think will help.

2. Rewrite your resumé using either the chronological or the functional format. Do you see any advantages in this format for your resumé?

3. Make an appointment to interview a personnel officer in a company in your community. Your purpose is to find out the following:

   a. What does he or she consider to be most important in a resumé?

   b. How does he or she use the resumé in making selection decisions?

   c. What does he or she not like in a resumé?

   Write a brief report summarizing your interview findings.

4. Visit the placement center at your school. Ask to see the resumés of students who have left them for distribution to companies or that are otherwise available for public viewing. What things about these resumés are well done and what are some common mistakes?

5. Ask the placement office director at your school to speak to your club or business organization about effective resumé techniques. What inside advice can that person share to help your group?

C A S E

Why Larry Can't Get an Interview

Anita S. Bednar, Central State University, Edmond, Oklahoma

Your friend Larry is despondent because he is unable to get an interview in his chosen career field of accounting. He has asked you to take a look at his resumé and his accompanying cover letter and tell him what is wrong. Looking at them, you cannot find much that is right. You have learned in

Figure 21A.1
Cover Letter of Larry Gray

116 Walnut Street
Stinnett, TX 78903
September 1, 1997

Dear Sir,

My name is Larry Gray. I am interest in the Accounting position you advertise about in the Amarillo Daily Globe.

I graduated this past May from North Central University in Big Foot, Texas. I major in accounting and graduated with a 2.98 grade point in my accounting subjects and a 3.01 overall grade point.

I am 23 years old and single. I am a hard worker and willing to learn. I have no experience in accounting, becuase all of my spare time during college was taken up by football.

I am very interested in accounting and would like an opportunity to grow in this field. I hope you will consider me for the job.

Cordially yours,

Larry Gray
Larry Gray

PERSONAL SATA

Name:	Larry Gray
Address:	116 Walnut St.
	Stinnett, Tex.　78903
Phone:	806-943-9345
Marital Status:	Single
Age:	23

High School

I graduated from Stinnett High in Stinnett, Texas in 1993. I had a grade point average of ab about 3.4 upon graduation.

College

I graduated from North Central in May of this Year. My degree was in accounting. I had a 2.98 grade point average in my accounting subjects and a 3.01 overage grade point average.

My only activity in college was football. I recieve a scholarship upon graduation from high school from North Central. I was a four-year starter at fullback. I earned several honors while playing:

> 2nd-team all-conference fullback as a sophomore
> 2nd-team all-conference fullback as a junior
> 1st-team all-conference fullback as a senior
> 1st-team all-district fullback as a senior

Here are a list of my summer jobs I had during college. They were all in the oilfield and had nothing to do with accounting.

company	address	phone
Jefferson Tool & Supply	N of town	229-1430
	Stinett, Tex. 78903	
Riley & Marshall	5 A Sw	223-8311
	Borger, Tx. 78110	
Hank's Wldg & Mch Shop	201 E. Vine	229-1167
	Stinnett, Tex. 78903	

your business communication class how to write an effective resumé. Larry's cover letter and resumé (Figures 21A.1 and 21A.2) are not only ineffective; they are unacceptable.

Case Questions

1. List everything in both the resumé and the cover letter that might keep Larry from getting a job interview in accounting.
2. Think about a better approach for Larry to use. He is from a small town, attended a small college on a football scholarship, and wants to work as an accountant in a mid-sized city. With no experience in accounting, what can he do to emphasize the positive and present himself in the best light?

CASE

Resumé for an Average Student

Richard Pompian, Boise State University

When a student has a good academic and work record, writing an effective resumé is often just a matter of not making a mistake. By definition, most students are average, however, and they need special help in presenting themselves honestly but effectively. Generally, techniques center around emphasizing the positive and deemphasizing the negative.

John Demetrius Smith is a senior at Washington College. He expects to graduate next May with a Bachelor of Business Administration degree in management. John wants to work for a large automobile manufacturer. National Motor Company will have a representative on campus and has invited potential interviewees to submit a resumé for prescreening. John decides to apply even though his 2.8 grade point average is below the "preferred" 3.0; it puts him just barely in the upper half of his class. He also knows that many other students with higher GPAs will apply. His current resumé shows that he has considerable experience with cars; in fact, he calls himself a car psychologist because he is quite good at diagnosing car problems and buyers' needs even when the customers are unclear about them.

However, John has been involved with little else except cars (except for some mechanical drafting and building construction). Academically, the best he can offer is a 3.05 in his major, though he is fluent in modern Greek and can converse in Spanish. Outside of management, his grades were best in personnel management, organizational behavior, and marketing. His extracurricular activity has been limited by the need to work. He plans to marry soon after graduation.

Knowing that you are majoring in business communication, John asks for your opinions and suggestions concerning his resumé, which appears in Figure 21B.1.

The purpose of the resumé is to get an interview, not the job itself. Accordingly, John should focus on presenting himself as a person who is interesting enough for the interviewer to want to meet. That means that he should emphasize qualifications, deemphasize negatives, and avoid looking like just another (in this case, weak) applicant. An analysis of his resumé reveals the following:

- *Graphics:* John's resumé is satisfactory overall but could benefit from some bold type for headings and main ideas, or at least from some underlining.
- *Name:* Should John use a middle name that reflects a possible ethnic origin? That could be an advantage in some circles, and in any case plain John Smith in not very exciting. A reasonable compromise might be to use the middle initial.
- *Address:* Fine, but will the reader know where to reach John when? A phrase such as "through June 3," shown with the local address, will be helpful to the recipient.
- *Objective:* Improvements would be "Entry-level management position" and "major automobile manufacturer" rather than "car company." John should probably say what area of the company is of interest to him.

Figure 21B.1
Resumé of John Demetrius
Smith

JOHN DEMETRIUS SMITH

Local Address: 422 Fourth St., Rydal, PA 19046 / (215) 998-0405
Permanent Address: 312 Ford Rd., Falls, NY 14303 / (919) 245-0090

OBJECTIVE: Management position with major car company; eventual
                      move into senior management.

EDUCATION: Washington College, School of Business Administration,
                      major in management, 1993–1997

                      Glen Sigforce High School, Falls, New York, 1989–1993

EXPERIENCE: Night manager, Mel's Auto Parts,
                      Rydal, Pennsylvania, 1995–1996

                      Bought, repaired, and sold wrecked cars,
                      Falls, New York, 1991–1994

                      Salesman, Good Deal Used Cars,
                      Falls, New York, 1989–1991

                      Mechanic's helper, Al's Service Station,
                      Falls, New York, 1983–1985

ACTIVITIES: High school varsity baseball
                      Lettermen's Club
                      Auto Club (treasurer)

INTERESTS: Sports, cars, hunting and fishing, rock music

HONORS: Mechanical Arts Award, Auto Club
                      Employee of the Month, Good Deal Used Cars

AVAILABILITY: June 1997

REFERENCES: On request

- *Education:* The positioning of this item is a mistake. John has nothing
special to offer here: his degree is similar to that of his competitors (fellow applicants), and he has no special honors, GPA, or class standing.
John's experience should come first because it establishes greater relevance and a high degree of interest in automobiles.
Within the education section, items should begin with the credential
earned. Lack of this specific mention may make the reader wonder if
John successfully completed the program.
John was wise not to mention his grade point average because it was below the 3.0 mentioned by the recruiter. To show that he is not totally
lacking academically, he could and probably should add: Grade point
average in major: 3.0+.
- *Experience:* John needs to be a bit less modest. He should tell what he
did and what he accomplished in each position. He will achieve greater

credibility by mentioning specific facts and numbers: number of cars
and dollar value sold, skills learned, and so on.
- *Activities:* John should mention at least one college activity to round out
  the list. He should put his titles, if any, first. Some interviewers will
  want to know which sport he lettered in.
- *Interests:* This list is satisfactory, but John might want to find out a little
  about his reader. Will this reader be impressed (positively or negatively)
  by entries such as "rock music"? John may want to delete one or more
  items, depending on what he finds out about the interviewer.
- *Availability:* Satisfactory, but "Available June 1997" could be placed at
  the end of the objective entry unless other items are added under the
  availability heading.
- *References:* John needs credibility, and his references should be listed in
  order to help achieve that. His references should be as impressive as
  possible—ideally, one or two each of the best business, academic, and
  personal references. John should get permission first.
- *Other Items:* Does John have location needs or preferences? Is he willing
  to travel? Unless he is inflexible, these items should be mentioned tactfully;
  for example, "New York or Northeast preferred; up to 30 percent travel
  acceptable." These items too can be placed under objective or availability.

John appears to have participated very little in extracurricular activities
during college. If this is because he worked his way through, he could include the entry, "Percentage of college expenses earned: 65 percent." This
emphasizes his commitment and at least partially explains his lack of extracurricular activities. John could also join a professional association or two
and list them in an affiliations section.

Case Question
1. What could be done to improve Smith's resumé? Be specific.

CASE

The Resumé: Path to an Interview—and a Job
Richard J. Barnhart, San Francisco State University

Now that you are familiar with the theory of resumé writing, you should be
able to pinpoint the devices that distinguish an acceptable resumé from a
truly effective one.

Figures 21C.1 and 21C.2 show two resumés prepared by a young marketing graduate with a few years of business experience who set for himself
the goal of landing a job in sales with IBM.

He updated the resumé he had used in his senior year in college and
mailed it directly to IBM's San Francisco area marketing manager. When he
received no reply after two weeks, he phoned and learned from the secretary
that the company had no sales openings.

Using his marketing experience—he was, after all, selling himself—he
revised his resumé and resubmitted it. This time he received a phone call
from the marketing manager asking him to come in for an interview. And he
did get the job he wanted.

Figure 21C.1

Original Resumé of Wilson Paray

Wilson Paray

140 Crossroads
Hayward, California   81001

(415) 775-0179

EXPERIENCE:

1992 to
present

American Greetings Corporation
Hayward, California
Accounts Manager: Promoted from sales representative in
supermarket division to accounts manager of a top national
drug chain. Maintain customer satisfaction with successful
sales through the development of innovative merchandising
techniques and analysis of market trends. Supervise six
employees.
Accomplishments
Over forecast in 1994 by 32 percent and in 1995 by 71 percent with 11 new accounts opened. Percentage of new stores
successfully prospected is up 40 percent in 1995 over previous two years.

1986 to 1992

Magic Chef Delicatessen
Daly City, California
Night Manager: Worked up from apprentice clerk to night
manager with responsibilities for preparing and closing the
store. Paid for all school and traveling expenses with money
earned.

EDUCATION:

Bachelor of Arts in International Business from San
Francisco State University, June 1992. Member of the
Student World Trade Association.

AWARDS:

Earned Business Achievement Award from the Bank of
America in 1990 on the basis of scholastic accomplishments
and debating skills.

INTERESTS:

Building fine furniture, playing golf and racquetball.

REFERENCES:

References available upon request

Case Questions

1. Place yourself in the marketing manager's position. You do not have a current opening, but you can make room for an exceptional applicant. Which version would arouse your interest enough to call the applicant for an interview?
2. Why? Defend your selection with specific examples.

Wilson Paray   Telephone
140 Crossroads   (415) 775-0179
Hayward, California   81001

Occupational
Objective: To be an active participant in sales with a progressive company

Experience
Highlights:
1992 to   American Greetings Corporation
present   Hayward, California
                Accounts Manager: Initially employed as a sales representative in
                the supermarket division. Promoted to accounts manager, requir-
                ing supervision of merchandisers, sales analysis, development of
                innovative merchandising techniques and customer relations.

1986 to 1992   Magic Chef Delicatessen
                Daly City, California
                Night Manager: Worked up from apprentice clerk to night manag-
                er with responsibilities for preparing and closing the store. Paid
                for all school and traveling expenses with money earned.

Education: B.A. in International Business from San Francisco State
                University, June 1992.
                Played on college golf team. Member of the Student World Trade
                Association. Earned Business Achievement Award from the Bank
                of America in 1990.

Military
Service: Completed six years of service in the California National Guard

Personal
Interests: Building fine furniture, playing golf and handball

Personal
Data: Age 26; married, no children, height 6'0''; weight 170 lbs.;
                excellent health

References: Personal and business references available upon request.

Reference

Kennedy, Joyce Lain and Thomas J. Morrow, *Electronic Resumé Revolution*. New York: John
    Wiley & Sons, Inc., 1994.

Notes

1. R.J. Ignelzi, "'References Available Upon Request' Doesn't Quite Cut It Anymore," *The San
    Diego Union-Tribune*, July 3, 1995, D-4.

2. Mark Silver, "Selling the Perfect You," *U.S. News & World Report*, February 5, 1990, 70-72.
    Reprinted with permission from U.S. News & World Report.

Chapter 22

Interviewing for a Job

Learning Objectives

1

To learn different techniques for getting job interviews.

2

To learn how to write job search letters.

3

To learn how to write interview follow-up letters.

4

To learn how to plan for the job interview.

5

To understand the kinds of questions job interviewers typically ask.

6

To learn how to improve performance during a job interview.

The more interviews an applicant has, the greater the chances of finding an attractive position.

About to graduate with a degree in business, Phil Parton does not yet have a job. He has been through three interviews at the campus placement center, each of which he thought had gone well. Yet in the past week he has received rejection letters from all three companies. The letters said much the same thing: "You have fine qualifications, but at present you don't fit the position we are filling. Please keep us in mind in the future."

"So much for a college degree," Phil thought, as he packed his now huge collection of textbooks in boxes for shipment home. "Here I am, a 3.5 average, and I can't even get a job. Maybe I should go to graduate school."

Each year thousands of junior college and senior college students have an experience like Phil's. Desperation sets in as graduation approaches and no job offers appear.

Some students find jobs more easily because they majored in a field in which jobs are relatively more available. Most students, however, find attractive entry-level positions in business because they carefully plan and carry out a strategy to find the best possible job. Their primary goal is to schedule as many job interviews as they possibly can. There are two reasons for this strategy: experience and probability.

Most students have little or no experience in interviewing for a career position. Such interviews can be ego threatening and even traumatic, especially when an interviewer asks a question the applicant is not prepared to answer (for example, "What is your major weakness?"). As applicants progress through a number of interviews, however, they will become more confident and be able to sell themselves because they have learned from practice and from their own mistakes.

The more interviews applicants have, the greater the probability that they will be offered a job. Phil, in our story, had only three job interviews. He will be offered a job only when his qualifications match the position being filled and he is better qualified than all the other individuals who have applied for that position.

STRATEGIES IN GETTING INTERVIEWS

Job interviews come from many sources. Perhaps someone you know tells you about a job opening or you may apply to a company for which you have worked before. Most job openings, however, are found through direct-mail approaches, newspaper advertisements, networking, or college placement offices.

Direct-Mail Campaigns

The **direct-mail approach** most often involves writing unsolicited letters, which are also called surveying or prospecting letters. They are sent to companies without known job openings. This is in contrast to the letter of application—a solicited letter—sent to a company with a known job opening.

The direct-mail approach is a "shotgun" approach. Even though you may write to many companies, your chances of actually acquiring an interview are not particularly good. Nevertheless, if jobs are scarce in your major or if you wish to maximize your chances for acquiring interviews, a direct-mail campaign might be explored.

Direct mail is a "shotgun" approach.

The three steps in the direct-mail campaign are these:

1. Select the companies.
2. Prepare and mail a cover letter and resumé.
3. Follow up as necessary.

You cannot mail your resumé to every existing company, and so in Step 1 you should narrow your list of prospects down to companies that fit your job objective and, if important, your geographic preference. For example, if you want to work for an insurance company in Chicago, you might search the yellow pages in the Chicago telephone directory for the names of prospective employers. Should you want a personnel position, you might consult *Personnel Administrator*. Published by the American Society of Personnel Administrators, this journal prints an annual directory of its membership. Other key sources for selecting companies are:

- *College Placement Annual.* Contains a list of companies in both the United States and Canada that are seeking college graduates. Published by the College Placement Council.
- *Dun & Bradstreet Million Dollar Directory.* Provides information about more than 30,000 companies whose net worth exceeds $1 million.
- *Dun & Bradstreet Middle Market Directory.* Similar to the *Million Dollar Directory*, but information is about more than 30,000 companies whose net worth is between $500,000 and $999,999.
- *Moody's Manual of Investment.* Contains information about a variety of companies, including banks, public utilities, insurance firms, and industrial firms.
- *Standard & Poor's Register of Corporations, Directors, and Executives.* Contains an alphabetical listing of more than 35,000 corporations in the United States and Canada. Provides listing of products and services, officers, and telephone numbers.
- *Thomas' Register of American Manufacturers.* Contains a list of manufacturers under headings of 70,000 products. Information includes addresses and telephone numbers of manufacturers.

Some students select as many as 500 companies for their direct-mail campaign; more typically, 100 or fewer key prospects are chosen. If you send your application to 100 such firms, you can expect a rejection rate of approximately 85 percent. You will not hear at all from some of the other companies. However, should you get six or seven job interviews from such a campaign, your strategy has been successful.

Much of the reason for the low number of positive responses in a direct-mail campaign lies in the breadth of the approach. The more you narrow the focus of your campaign, the greater your success. You can do this in a number of ways: (1) Pick companies that offer the type of job in which you are interested. (2) Select companies with jobs for which you are qualified. (3) Locate companies that are known to provide advancement in your field. (4) Find companies that are centered or have branches in geographical locations of interest to you. (5) Omit companies where you are sure you would not accept a job. In the direct-mail campaign, your **cover letter** is just as important as the resumé. First, get the name and address of the person to whom you intend to mail your letter. Never send campaign letters to *Dear Sir or Madam* or *To Whom It May Concern*. A personal touch is critical in your campaign. Usually, the person whose name you want is the personnel officer of the company. Often you can obtain this name by consulting the sources already listed or by calling the firm and asking for the name and title of the personnel officer (for example, personnel manager, vice president for personnel, or recruiting officer).

Preparing an effective cover letter is essential in a direct-mail campaign.

Second, decide on a reason for applying with each specific company. You can include this reason in your cover letter as a way of showing interest in the firm. You can also get this type of information from the sources listed earlier.

Third, write the actual letter. Because it is a persuasive letter, you might use the format discussed in Chapter 8. Make the reader want to check your written personality (the cover letter) and your factual background (the resumé) against your face-to-face persona. As always, you should use the "you" attitude as well as the other strategies for effective communication.

One authority suggests that the cover letter used in a direct-mail campaign should accomplish these things:

1. Ask for a job; be specific about what you want.
2. Explain how your experience, as outlined on your resumé, relates to the desired job and to the company.
3. Tell how you were attracted to the company.
4. Ask for the interview. Tell the reader you would like to arrange a meeting at a time and place convenient for the employer.[1]

Another authority says to work into the first paragraph what you will contribute—and use that word—and emphasize your accomplishments and revise your letter to eliminate any negative phrases. Be brief—certainly no more than one page.[2] An example of a cover letter is shown in Figure 22.1.

Usually responses from your prospects arrive about two weeks after you mail your letter and resumé. If you do not hear from a company after about 14 days, you might consider following up by phone or letter. The phone call is quicker, but it may be perceived as too aggressive. If you decide to call, try to reach the person to whom you addressed the letter. Ask about the progress of your application. If you use a letter, you can organize your thoughts to achieve your goal.

A sample follow-up letter is provided in Figure 22.2. Notice first that the writer uses tact by mentioning the earlier contact without placing blame for inaction. Second, another resumé is enclosed in case the original is misplaced. Third, another summary of relevant qualifications is provided. New information can be added at this time as it is another opportunity to emphasize your qualifications. Finally, optimum times for receiving phone calls are repeated.

Response to Newspaper Advertisements

When you respond to a help wanted advertisement in a newspaper, be assured that scores of other applicants are responding to the same ad. You must prepare a most con-

Figure 22.1
Campaign Cover Letter

1065 Locust Drive
Fayetteville, AR 72701
March 12, 1997

Ms. Patricia Markham
Personnel Manager
Able Computers, Inc.
P.O. Box 1511
Columbus, OH 43216

Dear Ms. Markham:

The reputation and growth of Able Computers have led me to apply for a position in your management trainee program. Information in the University of Arkansas <u>Placement Annual</u> indicates that you hire college graduates with business degrees. The <u>Annual</u> states you prefer computer, management, and sales or marketing majors.

The fact that you were rated number one in a poll as the most promising company of the 1990s by <u>Electronic Industry Magazine</u> is impressive. The challenge of helping you maintain your position of leadership in the volatile computer industry is especially exciting and a contribution I believe I can make.

My BBA degree from the University of Arkansas incorporates a major in management and a minor in marketing. Further, my two years of part-time work for the Bank of New England in the data processing department utilized capabilities acquired in my three college computer classes.

As you will note on my attached resumé, I am willing to accept challenges and carry them through to successful completion. Grover Jefferson, of the Bank of New England, has offered to support this view. His address, and the names and addresses of other references, are on the resumé.

May I have an interview at your convenience? I am available at the phone at (501) 555-4567 between 2 p.m. and 6. p.m., weekdays.

Sincerely,

Jules Steiner
Jules Steiner

Encl.

---

vincing cover letter and resumé. Cover letters about known job openings differ somewhat from letters in a direct-mail campaign. You need to accomplish six things:

1. Identify the job opening, tell where you learned of it, and state that you are applying.
2. Describe the job opening as you understand it. This description clarifies your immediate aspirations and allows the reader to correct misunderstandings. It also sets up item 3. In writing item 2, try to show a void in the company that you (and your abilities and skills) can fill, with item 3. This combination can have a strong persuasive effect.
3. Pick selected items from your background to show how you meet the qualifications outlined in item 2.
4. Enter some human interest information. You may include details about why you are interested in this company or industry. Consider telling the reader of your

A convincing cover letter and resumé are essential when responding to newspaper ads.

Figure 22.2
Follow-Up Letter

> 1065 Locust Drive
> Fayetteville, AR 72701
> April 1, 1997
>
> Ms. Patricia Markham
> Personnel Manager
> Able Computers, Inc.
> P.O. Box 1511
> Columbus, OH 43216
>
> Dear Ms. Markham:
>
> Several weeks ago I wrote you applying for a management traineeship with Able. I do wish to ensure that you know of my enthusiasm for Able. As my March 12 letter stated, I am impressed with your position of leadership in your industry.
>
> You are interested, I understand, in recruits with computer, management, and marketing abilities. My management major, marketing minor, and data processing job experience meet those qualifications. Last week I was honored as the most promising senior in the University of Arkansas Management Club, a group of over 120 students.
>
> The enclosed resumé presents more information about how my education, job, and extracurricular activities well prepare me for your traineeship.
>
> An interview with you, at your convenience, is still my goal. My schedule remains the same; I am available by phone weekdays from 2 p.m. until 6 p.m.
>
> Sincerely,
>
> *Jules Steiner*
> Jules Steiner
>
> Encl.

enthusiasm or belief that you are a valuable asset. This is the only location in the letter (or the resumé) where you should express any opinions.

5. Mention one of your references as a source of verification of your credentials and abilities. Mention that you have enclosed a resumé.

6. Ask for the interview. Make it easy for the reader to respond to your request: offer to meet at the reader's convenience, give hours you can be reached by phone, mention your address, or volunteer to travel on certain days.

An example of an expanded cover letter is shown in Figure 22.3.

Again, be sure to follow up if the firm does not respond to your letter within two weeks.

If a firm grants you an interview as a result of your direct-mail campaign or your response to a newspaper advertisement, then you might write a letter confirming the date, time, and place for the interview and expressing your appreciation for being given the interview. Here's an example of the body of such a letter:

> Thank you for scheduling an interview with me about opportunities in Able Computer's manager trainee program. I am looking forward to our meeting.
>
> As you requested during our telephone conversation [or As you requested in your letter], I'll be in Room 117 of the Able Building at 10:00 A.M. on Thursday, August 7.
>
> I appreciate your interest in my application. If you need additional information, please let me know.

The direct-mail campaign and responding to newspaper advertisements are only two approaches to getting job interviews. Other strategies you might consider, especially if the job market in your particular field is tight, include: (1) calling personnel officers

Figure 22.3
Expanded Cover Letter

1065 Locust Drive
Fayetteville, AR 72701
March 12, 1997

Ms. Patricia Markham
Personnel Manager
Able Computers, Inc.
P.O. Box 1511
Columbus, OH 43216

Dear Ms. Markham:

Please consider me an applicant for the management trainee position you advertised in the March 11 issue of The Wall Street Journal.

The ad states you seek a person with a college degree and that you prefer a business major and some related experience. The job would include a six-month training period in Columbus and then placement in one of your three Ohio offices. The training class starts July 1.

My May 1997 BBA degree from the University of Arkansas, with a management major and marketing minor, meets your requirements. Having worked each summer for the last six years, I have acquired some related experience. This last summer I sold computers and did some hardware trouble-shooting for Computek.

Your job is especially interesting to me since it would allow me to make use of my management and marketing knowledge and pursue my personal interest in computers. Here at the university I was cofounder of the Computer Users Group and am just finishing my term as president. My skills, interest, and proven enthusiasm for hard work would serve me well as your management trainee.

Professor Paul Jarston, the club's faculty adviser and a member of the data processing faculty, has agreed to serve as a reference. Other references are found on the enclosed resumé.

May I have an interview at your convenience? Reach me by phone most afternoons at (501) 555-4567. I can travel to Columbus at most any time.

Sincerely,

Jules Steiner

Jules Steiner

Encl.

directly and asking for an interview; (2) making unannounced visits to the firms where you seek employment; (3) placing your own ad in a newspaper; (4) attending conventions or trade shows of industries you have selected as potential employers, and (5) networking. **Networking** is contacting friends, fraternity or sorority members (including recent graduates), family members, neighbors, former employers, and others who may know of job openings. Some experts estimate that as many as 90 percent of positions are filled through word-of-mouth announcements.

However, the people with whom you network are busy, especially as more and more people network and as organizations tighten their staffs. Minimize the time you seek from these individuals and improve your chances of finding the job you want by practicing **precision networking**.[3] This involves a thorough self-appraisal: Know your strengths, weaknesses, preferences, and goals. Next, be ruthless as you remove companies from your list of possibilities. Research the companies that remain to further focus your list. Now, network to seek help in getting your "foot into the door" with those companies.

Networking is likely to increase in importance as you move through your career and make more business contacts. Nevertheless, networking can be a valuable technique, even for entry-level positions.

Use of the College Placement Office

The college placement office sometimes leads directly to an interview.

Using the placement office in acquiring interviews is much different from direct-mail or newspaper advertisement techniques. The direct-mail and newspaper advertisement approaches are general in tone, frequently cannot be personalized, and are used on the assumption that if you apply to enough companies, you will receive some interviews.

The placement office, on the other hand, is more individualized and, in some cases, leads directly to an interview. The placement office is a valuable location to find the latest publications. Often recent publications on how to interview or write resumés are available. Many companies send placement offices their annual reports and other recruiting literature. In addition to the library function, workers in the placement office often can help you with career decisions or know the most recent trends in industries. They may also know of the latest job openings. Some placement offices maintain your records, including letters of reference and resumé. The workers can even review your resumé or application letter.

A second major activity of the placement office is scheduling on-campus job interviews. Companies frequently visit the campus to interview 13 to 15 students a day in a series of 30-minute interviews. The placement office coordinates room scheduling and time-period assignments, makes company literature available, and gathers interviewees' resumés.

Signing up for an interview through the placement office is far easier than having to use the letter of application to schedule an interview. For this reason, as well as the other benefits mentioned, regular communication with your placement office is usually wise.

Search of On-Line Want Ads

Job announcements are accessible with your computer. Many governments and universities post their openings, and may offer a database of openings other than their own. Another approach is to scan the "home pages" of companies on the World Wide Web. These **home pages** are prepared by the company and have interconnected information, often including job openings. An example of such an announcement from Hewlett Packard is shown in Figure 22.4. Yet another approach is to use an on-line service, such as CompuServe, which offers a program called E-Span (also on the Internet). E-Span is a listing of want ads that can be searched by occupation or geographical area.

Employment Opportunities		Figure 22.4 Finding a Job

 Finding a job

HP Job Opening

Job Number   32456

Job Title   Information Technology Solutions
Department   Information Technology
Division   TMIT-Management
City   Sunnyvale
State   California

Job Description
  Provide system administration and support of HP9000 Series 800
  servers. This includes disk management, performance tuning and
  HP-UX installation and HP-UX administration. Project leader in
  the implementation of NIS in the SC domain and VID servers.
  Project leader in the implementation of TMO IT Web server which
  includes writing HTML documents, configuration, PC proxy set-up
  and Mosaic/Netscape configurations for the HP-UX and PC platforms.
  Installation and support of Windows NT 3.5 server. Collaborate
  with other TMO IT entities and work in a team-based environment
  in the design of TMO IT-wide server processes, tools and technology.

Minimum Qualifications
  Three years project lead experience. BS in CS or equivalent,
  five years in-depth knowledge of HP-UX, development SW tools
  and strong trouble-shooting skills. Proactive person and
  innovative thinker.

Desired Qualifications
  HTML document writing experience. Mosaic configuration experience.
  Knowledge of various HW architecture. Risk taker. Knowledge of
  NT 3.5 server.

INTERVIEW PLANNING

Throughout this text we have emphasized planning in every business communication situation. Planning is of paramount importance to the job interview.

Reviewing Your Qualifications

Your job search will be successful when the employer's representative realizes that there is a match between your qualifications and the requirements of the position being filled. The question, "Is this person qualified?" is always uppermost in every interviewer's mind. Your goal is to show this match during the interview, to demonstrate that the pieces of this job selection puzzle do fit together. Figure 22.5 suggests the complexity of the matching process.

The interviewer looks for a match between company and job applicant.

Figure 22.5
Matching Process during
the Job Interview
Source: Pizza Hut.

Your Qualifications		Job Requirements
College Degree Good Grades Experience Honors Enthusiasm	Match?	Self-Starter Good "Track Record" Education Honest Hardworking

Your qualifications for a job include not only your previous applicable work experience, education, and extracurricular activities, but also any salable personal characteristics you have. Figure 22.6 provides a list of qualities that employers consider to be important. As you rate yourself on each quality by placing a check mark in the appropriate column, do not forget to consider all of your work and school-related experiences.

Be able to document your best qualities.

You should be able to justify clearly any high rating you have given yourself. Trained interviewers are not interested in statements, such as "I am a self-starter," unless you can give evidence of your initiative. Be prepared to show that you are dependable, adaptable, mature, and so on.

Any activity in which you have been involved can provide the necessary evidence. For example, playing basketball or any other team sport requires the ability to work with others. Earning part or all of your college expenses shows initiative. A clear and logical explanation of why you changed majors or transferred from one school to another can indicate decision-making ability and, perhaps, adaptability. Leadership skills can be shown through various activities, including offices in organizations, working as a counselor in a summer camp, or training your replacement for a job you left.

In short, pick your major qualifications, document them, review them, and be prepared to talk about them during the interview.

Researching the Company

The applicant should know as much as possible about the company.

One of the most important steps in preparing for an interview is to research the company. You need to know the size of the company, its products or services, position in the

Figure 22.6
Qualifications Checklist

Am I Qualified?	Superior	Above Average	Average	Below Average	Poor
Leadership Skills	___	___	___	___	___
Initiative (self-starter)	___	___	___	___	___
Decision-Making Abilities	___	___	___	___	___
Written Communication Skills	___	___	___	___	___
Oral Communication Skills	___	___	___	___	___
Adaptability	___	___	___	___	___
Professional Appearance	___	___	___	___	___
Working with Others	___	___	___	___	___
Enthusiasm	___	___	___	___	___
Dependability	___	___	___	___	___
Self-Confidence	___	___	___	___	___
Maturity	___	___	___	___	___

industry, some historical perspectives, locations from which it operates, financial considerations, employment situation, types of jobs being filled, the subsidiary situation, and its plans for the future. Articles by or about recruiters that discuss major problems or errors in interviews inevitably point to the interviewee's lack of knowledge about the company as a serious shortcoming. One recruiter for a nonprofit institution received comments about his company's products. Another recruiter was startled that an $80,000-a-year executive did not bother to read a prospective employer's annual report.[4]

In addition to the sources mentioned earlier in the direct-mail campaign, look also to *The Wall Street Journal,* the company annual report, recruiting literature, and the *Business Periodicals Index.*

You may also want to research your organizations on-line. In addition to reviewing home pages as mentioned earlier, you can find company information on Lexis/Nexis or on CompuServe's Business Database Plus, which, in early 1996 offered 192,880 company profiles and 1,134,491 articles about companies. A sample profile appears in Figure 22.7.

Anticipating What Will Happen in the Interview

Knowing what to expect will help you prepare for the interview and reduce your anxiety as well.

Types of Interviews.   Most interviews or interview situations fit into one or more of these classifications: (1) screening interview, (2) open-ended interview, (3) panel interview, (4) group interview, (5) stress interview, (6) office visit interview, (7) videotape interview, and (8) computer interview.

Interviews fit into one or more of eight classifications.

```
Company name:  GERS (San Diego, California)
               9725 Scranton Rd.
               San Diego, California 92121
               United States
               Tel: (619) 457-3888
               Fax: FX_(619)457-2145

Variant name: Gers Retail Systems_DBA

-------------------------------------------------

Business: Retail: Computer systems.
SIC codes: 5734_Computer & Computer Software Stores
Annual sales: $40.0 M Sales, Source: Verification Letter
Employees: 290, Source: Verification Letter
Sales/Employee: $137,931
Year Founded: 1974
Fiscal Year: Dec 31, 1994
Features: Private company, Headquarters location

SMSA code: 7320_San Diego, CA

Officers: Gary Reif - President
          Mike Larkin - Vice President, Finance
          Dennis Conforto - Vice President
          Richard Harmatiuk - Vice President
          Jill Kobrin - Human Resources Manager

Update Date: Mar 29, 1995
Reference #: C346290

     -End-
```

Figure 22.7
A Sample of CompuServe's Business Database Plus

AN ETHICAL DILEMMA

This morning Shawna received a phone call about a second interview. "We're quite interested in you," the personnel assistant explained, "but we need more information. We'd also like you to meet Annette Mead. She was unavailable during your first visit. Will 10 A.M. Friday be acceptable?"

"Yes, of course," Shawna said.

She begins thinking about how to make a great impression. "Let's see," she muses, "Last time they seemed interested in my accounting and bookkeeping skills. I can probably get away with saying that I'm the accountant rather than the bookkeeper at Wilson's Grocery. Instead of saying I worked there from late June to the end of July, I can say I have been there all summer. And I can say that at Happy Lanes Bowling Center I was in charge of all other part-time college students. There was only one, but it will sound impressive."

That should do it, she decides. They are sure to hire someone with more experience than she really has.

She wonders if employers check references even for little part-time jobs. If it turns out that they do, then she is not being very smart after all—and not very honest either. "If you have to worry about getting caught, what you're doing can't be right," she reminds herself. However, she is sure she will do well if she can only get the job.

Shawna feels boxed in. What would you do?

Questions

1. What are some ways a person might slip up in an interview and get caught exaggerating information?

2. What are some reasons why employment counselors always say, "It's safer to be honest with the information you share"?

The **screening interview**, as its name implies, screens prospects into groups to interview further, to reject, or to hold for future decision. These interviews usually occur before other categories of interviews and typically last about 30 minutes.

An **open-ended interview** (or unstructured or nondirective interview) follows no discernible pattern. Your answer to an initial question may determine the next question. The interactions and responses form the direction of the interview.

A **panel interview** involves one interviewee and more than one interviewer. Occasionally you may feel overwhelmed when there is only one interviewer; imagine the pressure you might feel with several people questioning and observing you. On the other hand, if the company believes an interview with you is important enough to justify the time of two or more recruiters, perhaps they are already impressed with you.

The **group interview** is the antithesis of the panel interview—several interviewees are presented with one interviewer. You are likely to encounter a group interview in a social setting, such as a party to which many job prospects are invited, or a mass screening when there is a large number of applicants for few positions. Because these interviews may not last long, each interviewee seeks to make a quick and positive impression—often at the expense of other applicants. Do try to impress your interviewer, but avoid direct comparison to others in the room if possible.

The **stress interview**, probably the most unpleasant of the eight categories, places the interviewee in a stressful situation that the interviewer then carefully observes. Inviting you to smoke but not supplying an ashtray or putting you in a lengthy business simulation full of tricks and pitfalls are examples of stress activities. Questions the interviewer knows to cause stress may also be used. At one time stress questions and stress interviews were fairly common. Today they are less frequent. For high-level, high-stress executive jobs and positions (high-pressure sales, for example) you are more likely to encounter stress interviews.

The stress interview is meant to be unpleasant.

The **office visit interview** (or plant or headquarters visit), is not a single interview but a series of interviews that may incorporate many of the other categories. Some interviews may be stressful, others may be conducted by a panel, and still others may be open-ended. A six- or seven-hour day, including lunch and coffee breaks with company officials, is not unusual. Although the day will range from formal interviews to casual, informal discussions, you are constantly being evaluated; never let down your guard. Other activities you may encounter include psychological or ability testing, building tours, discussions with potential peers or subordinates, and completion of application or travel reimbursement forms.

The **videotape interview** occurs in one of two ways. In some cases, the job applicant, on his or her own initiative, may submit a videotape showing performance, describing personal characteristics, explaining interest in the field and background strengths, and perhaps providing some personal data. In other cases, companies ask applicants to respond to a list of questions while being taped, either at the company or at a place of the applicant's choosing. The videotape can reduce recruiter time, allow replays, save travel expenses, and still transmit important applicant characteristics, such as preparation, enthusiasm, and communication ability. As with other forms of interviews, videotape interviews require thorough preparation.

The **computer interview** requires the applicant to complete a survey of direct and indirect questions. The computer interview may be part of a lengthy interview sequence or it may be an initial screening device. It allows development of a database and statistical analysis and minimizes costly face-to-face interaction. Computer ability and careful self-assessment before the computer interview are valuable attributes.

Types of Interviewers. Just as there are many types of interviews, there are also different types of interviewers; the major categories are the practitioner and the personnel office representative. These categories may be encountered in either a screening interview, which is usually the first interview, or the office visit, which is usually the culmination interview.

Most interviews are conducted by a practitioner or a personnel office specialist.

The practitioner is a person who is currently doing the type of job for which you would be hired. The term field interviewer is also used. For example, an accountant interviews prospective accountants, and so on. The practitioner may be the person who would be the immediate superior of the new hiree. The practitioner is not likely to have formal training in interview procedures; therefore, it is difficult to predict the course of the interview. The area of expertise and background about the job are likely to be discussion topics. Because of their naivete, practitioners are more likely to ask stress questions at inappropriate times or to ask questions deemed illegal by Equal Employment Opportunity Act guidelines.

The representative of the personnel office or personnel recruiter probably has, as part of his or her job description, the role of recruiter. Training in selection methods, appraisals, and interviewing prepare these people for this role. Because of their training, representatives of personnel offices are difficult to read. They will be pleasant and courteous, but seldom will you be certain what impression you have made.

A typical screening interview lasts 30 minutes.

Flow of the Interview.   A description of a typical screening interview will help you prepare for it. The interview may last from 15 to 45 minutes, but 30 minutes is traditional. A typical 30-minute period might be broken down as follows:

First 5 minutes:	Introductions, small talk, questions of low priority
Next 10 minutes:	Focus on interviewee's abilities and responses to interviewer's questions
Next 10 minutes:	Responses by interviewer to interviewee's questions and description of the company and job
Last 5 minutes:	Closing comments, explanation of next steps

A full-day office visit depends on the organization and type of job. However, a visit to an office for a management job might proceed through these steps:

9–10 A.M.:	Breakfast with the interviewer who conducted the screening interview
10:15–11 A.M.:	Introductions to other personnel office employees
11 A.M.–12 P.M.:	Meeting with vice president of related area
12–1:30 P.M.:	Lunch with two members of personnel office and prospective immediate superior
1:30–2:30 P.M.:	Meeting with prospective immediate superior
2:30–4 P.M.:	Half-hour meetings with three potential peers
4–5 P.M.:	Completion of company forms and tour of facilities with personnel office representative
5 P.M.:	Depart with screening interviewer for the airport for flight home

As you can see, by the time you get home, you will have had a long, tiring, and eventful day.

Most trained interviewers begin by asking a few ice-breaking questions.

Types of Questions.   Four types of questions may be asked during an interview—inconsequential questions, important-answer questions, stress questions, and inappropriate questions. Most interviewers start off with questions to which the answers—that is, the content per se—are really inconsequential. Their purpose is to break the ice and get the interview moving. Trained interviewers know that you will be anxious about the interview. After all, much rides on how you perform in a short period of time; you will be in a strange and perhaps bleakly appointed interview room; you are meeting a total stranger and talking, in some cases, about personal thoughts and feelings.

For these reasons questions about the weather or last Sunday's football game occur first. The recruiter does not care much about what you say but rather about how you say it. Your enthusiasm for a certain football team is more impressive than which team you prefer.

Shortly after you start to relax, the questions will focus on your interests, knowledge of the company or the job, and why you think you can do the job. The recruiter will listen carefully to your responses to these important-answer questions and is likely to build on your answers with related follow-up questions. You are evaluated on the speed, depth, and quality of your answers, as well as other ingredients. These questions may be subdivided into three types: goal questions ("What do you see yourself doing five years from now?" or "Which is more important to you, the money or the job?"); skills and qualifications questions ("Why should I hire you?" or "Describe your most rewarding college experience."); and personal qualities questions ("How would you describe yourself?" or "How do you determine or evaluate success?").

Stress questions may occur at any time in an interview, but they are most likely to follow some important-answer questions. Planning on how to respond to stress questions is difficult; their intent is to catch you off guard. Still, just knowing they may occur should help you.

Inappropriate questions are either illegal or unrelated to the job. Rules keep interviewers from asking questions that might discriminate against you. For example, questions about your age, marital status, or religion are seldom allowed. Exceptions occur when this or other information is directly related to the job, such as hiring a parent instead of a childless person for a child-care center. Other questionable topics include race, political affiliation, club memberships, handicapped status, national origin, and veteran status.

What should you do when you are asked one of these questions? You have several options. If you do not find the question offensive or the answer potentially damaging, you can answer it. If the answer to the question is personal or you think it is not related to the job, politely tell the recruiter so. Perhaps you will wish to ask the purpose of the question; there may be a good reason for it that you did not anticipate.

Most interviewers allow time for the applicant to ask questions about the job and the organization. Two reasons exist for asking truly valuable questions: the better the question, the better its reflection on you; and you should have some questions to which the answers are important. Prepare yourself before the interview with five or six questions. The interviewer may answer some of them in the company or job description segments of the interview. Then, when given the opportunity, you can raise several probing questions. Avoid trite or shallow questions. Aim for open-ended questions rather than those that yield only a yes or no answer. Consider questions about the extent of responsibility you would be given, the types of assignments encountered, and even queries about the negative aspects of the job. Here are some example questions you might ask:

The interviewee is usually allowed time to ask questions.

1. What positions do your typical manager trainees hold after five years with the company?
2. How important are advanced degrees, such as an M.B.A. or a law degree, to advancement?
3. Do you normally promote from within the company?
4. What kind of orientation program or training do you provide for new employees?

Be sure to avoid questions that might threaten the interviewer's ego or cause other negative feelings. For example, "Are you having much trouble with EEOC?" is inappropriate unless you are interviewing for a personnel job. "Will I have to work much overtime?" might categorize you as having little initiative. You should avoid questions about salary unless starting salaries are the same for all incoming employees (for example, some teaching positions, government jobs, and even management trainee programs).

As part of interview planning you will also find it valuable to review three categories of interview questions discussed in Chapter 20: open-ended questions, direct or closed questions, and indirect questions.

Listed in Figure 22.8 are 23 questions that are frequently asked by college recruiters. Examination of the questions will give you the flavor of an interview. Some of these questions are likely to be asked of you, and you may want to think of answers to them. As you read the questions you will notice that many seek your opinions and others ask for facts. Most interviewees have much more difficulty with the opinion questions because there is no one correct answer.

College recruiters often ask similar questions.

Here are some suggestions for dealing with two of the questions that students have found difficult:

What percentage of your college expenses did you earn? How? A paradox of our society is that most of us envy the wealthy, such as a college student who does not need to work during

Figure 22.8

Questions Most Frequently
Asked by Recruiters
Interviewing College
Students

1. What are your future vocational plans?
2. In what school activities have you participated? Why? Which did you enjoy most?
3. How do you spend your spare time? What are your hobbies?
4. In what type of position are you most interested?
5. Why do you think you might like to work for our company?
6. What jobs have you held? How were they obtained? Why did you leave?
7. What percentage of your college expenses did you earn? How?
8. Why did you choose your particular field of work?
9. What course did you like best? Least? Why?
10. How did you spend your vacations while in school?
11. What do you know about our company?
12. Do you feel that you have received a good general training?
13. What qualifications do you have that make you feel that you will be successful in your field?
14. What extracurricular offices have you held?
15. What are your ideas on salary?
16. How interested are you in sports?
17. If you were starting college all over again, what courses would you take?
18. Can you forget your education and start from scratch?
19. Do you prefer any specific geographic location? Why?
20. How much money do you hope to earn at age 30? 35?
21. Why did you decide to go to this particular school?
22. How did you rank in your graduation class in high school? Where will you probably rank in college?
23. Do you think your extracurricular activities were worth the time you devoted to them?

the summer or after school hours. However, job experience and indications of industriousness are paramount in employee selection. All things being equal, the recruiter is more impressed with a student who works to pay education expenses, even doing menial work or activities that are not job related, than with the wealthy student who does not indicate a willingness to work. Therefore, the stronger a case you can build for yourself in percentage of expenses earned, the better your evaluation. If your parents give you all your expenses, you earned 0 percent. If your spouse is paying the expenses, you can claim 100 percent. If you are using a loan that you will repay, claim that as a percentage from you.

Can you forget your education and start from scratch?   Your goal in answering this question is to underline the importance of your education but at the same time to show a willingness to learn new things. Thus an answer such as this might be appropriate: "I can't really forget my education, because I think I've learned some things that will be helpful to me in my work. However, I know that my education isn't completed yet. I'm willing and eager to learn new things."

Knowing What the Recruiter Is Seeking

You can prepare for an interview better if you have some feeling about how and on what you will be evaluated. Many students are surprised to learn that often they are not evaluated for what they know. Instead, recruiters assume that your college degree has given you some basic information and shows you have the ability to learn. It also indicates an interest in specific areas. If the recruiter hires you, the company supervisor will teach you, in depth, the specifics that he or she wants you to know. Therefore, few questions are asked about your knowledge of subjects, such as the difference between municipal bonds and corporate bonds or the application of Maslow's theory to a management trainee job. Questions are asked to determine such characteristics as tact, enthusiasm, industriousness, maturity, human relations skills, leadership ability, motivation, congeniality, or communication ability. How directed you are and your initiative, competitiveness, and intelligence will be scrutinized as well.

Most companies use an interviewee evaluation form that the recruiter completes after the interview. Because attributes of importance differ by company, no standard form exists. To understand better the content of these forms, visit your college placement office. The sample form in Figure 22.9 is typical in the type of attributes evaluated and the length and depth of response requested.

Name _____   School _____

Campus Address _____   Phone Number _____

Post Graduation
Mailing Address _____   Phone Number _____

Availability   Geographical   Career

Date _____   Preference _____   Interests _____   G.P.A. _____

Selection Standard	Observations	Relates to selection standards and to information reported by applicant or	Exceeds	Meets	Does Not Meet
Presentation	Forcefulness, Organization, Conciseness—ask related questions.				
Achievements	Academic, Technical, Professional Contributions to previous employers. Do they relate to our needs?				
Ambitions	Career Goals, Financial Goals—are they realistic?				
Contributions	Long- and short-term, what can the candidate add to the organization?				
Is Candidate Sold on Pizza Hut	Understands Career Opportunity.				
Overall Reaction					

Highly Recommended _____
Recommended _____
Reject _____

_____
Recruiter's Signature

Figure 22.9

Interview Appraisal Form
Source: Pizza Hut

Considering Your Appearance

One survey of practicing interviewers found that in a 20-minute interview the average interviewer had made a selection decision within the first four minutes of the interview.[5] Some interviewers claim that they can decide whether an applicant is suitable for a job the very instant that applicant enters the room. Obviously, these early decisions are based in large part on physical appearance.

Generally, you should dress as you would in the job for which you are applying. This guideline means that, as graduates of a two- or four-year college, males wear a coat and tie and females a dress or suit and appropriate shoes. If you are not sure how to dress, it is probably better to dress simply in business attire, giving consideration to what is socially acceptable in the area.

Preparing for the Unusual

Stories abound about tricks that interviewers use to catch an applicant off guard. Although it is unlikely that you will be confronted with any of these tricks, you should nevertheless be aware of and be prepared for them. Examples are:

- *Silence:* The interviewer says absolutely nothing at the beginning of the interview. Instead, he or she simply looks at you. You, therefore, must begin the interaction.
- *Sell me:* If you are interviewing for any kind of sales or marketing position, the interviewer slides an ashtray or pencil across the desk to you and says, "Here. Sell this to me."
- *Turnabout:* The interviewer says, "I've been interviewing people all day. I'm tired. Why don't you interview me?"
- *No smoking:* You are a smoker. You are nervous. The interviewer asks, "Would you like to smoke?" You light a cigarette and discover that there is no ashtray in the room.
- *Choose a chair:* When you enter the interviewer's office, two chairs are available from which to choose. One is near the interviewer's desk, the other is several feet away from the desk. The interviewer says simply, "Have a seat," but does not tell you which chair.

If these examples seem frightening to you, remember that very few interviewers use such tricks. Most contemporary interviewers are highly trained, competent business people who want to evaluate your qualifications in a straightforward manner.

INTERVIEW PERFORMANCE

For many years companies used two basic approaches to selecting new employees: the job interview and psychological testing. Now, however, many companies no longer use psychological testing because of federal laws; a company must be able to provide evidence that a psychological test can differentiate between good and poor performers on the job. Because gathering such evidence is difficult, especially for smaller companies, the job interview is now the major selection tool for most organizations.

Your actual, face-to-face interaction with a representative of the company is the most critical step in your job search process. Be sure to arrive on time—or even a little early. Being late for a job interview shows lack of dependability (one of the qualities discussed earlier). If you must be late, call the interviewer and explain why. Consider making a trial run prior to the interview to determine travel time, parking facilities, and exact location of the interview. Arriving late will put unneeded pressure on you.

Shake hands with the interviewer. A handshake is a sign of acceptance and greeting in a business situation. Have a firm handshake. A weak fishlike handshake is perceived by some interviewers to be characteristic of a similarly weak personality. Do not be afraid to offer your hand first. The job interview is not a social situation steeped in rules of etiquette. Many interviewers have expressed the same uneasy feeling about the handshake as you might experience: Do I shake hands first?" You can relieve much interviewer uneasiness and show some assertiveness if you simply extend your hand as you approach the interviewer.

Establish and maintain eye contact with the interviewer. Like the weak hand-shake, an absence of eye contact connotes a weak personality to many interviewers. To a few of them it also indicates that the interviewee may be lying. Interviewers will also sometimes unconsciously form negative perceptions of applicants who slouch in a chair, cross their arms or legs, or face away from them. Sit erect, facing the interviewer. Do not cross your legs and arms at the same time. Some interviewers believe that people who sit in such a closed position are trying to shut the other person out.

Playing with objects (for example, a pen or pencil) during the interview communicates unusual nervousness to many interviewers. Often they will translate nervousness during the interview to mean that you cannot perform well in stress situations on the job. In particular, do not pick up objects on the interviewer's desk.

An interviewer can interpret your criticism of past employers as an indication that you are a complainer who criticizes all your employers. Also, such criticism can be interpreted as a rationalization for the real (and damaging) reasons you left your previous employers. Similarly, do not evaluate previous jobs—simply describe them. Because many college students have work experience they consider to be simple or menial, they are often inclined to communicate that perception during the interview: "Well, really all I did was fry hamburgers," or "The job really wasn't much—I just waited on people." No matter how unimportant you think a job might have been, an interviewer will ask questions about it in order to assess a number of qualities, among them dependability, leadership skills, working with others, and initiative.

Two common mistakes are to criticize previous employers and to belittle menial jobs.

During interview planning you prepared questions about the company. Remember to ask them before the interview ends.

Do not try to be someone or something you are not. Allow your true personality to emerge and try to make a good impression, but avoid developing an image that is inaccurate. Recruiters are making hiring decisions on what they see in the interview. Problems may occur if the real you who shows up for work is substantially different.

As the interview closes and you are about to leave, remember to thank the interviewer for discussing employment opportunities with you. If possible, express appreciation for any constructive suggestions the interviewer has made, especially if you think you will not be considered for the job.

Interviewing requires polished, professional behavior. You can gain the needed skills by practicing with anyone (classmates, friends, relatives) who will take the time with you.

✔ *CHECKLIST for Interview Performance*
____ Arrive on time.
____ Shake hands firmly.
____ Use effective eye contact.
____ Be attentive to posture.
____ Avoid playing with objects.
____ Refrain from criticizing former employers.
____ Describe but do not evaluate previous jobs.
____ Ask questions about the company.
____ Remain honest.
____ Express appreciation for the interview.

INTERVIEW FOLLOW-UP
Immediate Follow-Up

As soon as possible after the interview, write the interviewer a follow-up letter. Basically, this letter consists of three paragraphs. In the first paragraph express appreciation for the interview and your continued interest in the position. In the second paragraph add any important information about yourself that you failed to mention during the interview. Or

Follow-up should occur within one to two days after your interview.

emphasize one of your qualifications that the interviewer stressed as being important, especially if you feel personally confident about the qualification. Or emphasize some information you learned about the company during the interview that impressed you. Finally, in the third paragraph, communicate your willingness to answer further questions about your qualifications. Assume a positive attitude toward hearing from the interviewer.

Try to say something in the follow-up letter that will remind the reader of you and the interview; pick something that would not have been discussed with other interviewees. You may mention also, as appropriate, that you have completed and enclosed an application form. An example of such a follow-up letter appears in Figure 22.10.

Most companies use their own standard application forms that ask for much of the same information supplied on your resume. Your resume is used to catch the recruiter's eye and to achieve an interview. You may be asked to complete the organization's form before a screening interview, immediately after the screening interview, or at the office visit. Frequently, at the completion of a successful screening interview, you will be asked to take a form with you and return it by mail. This is an indication

Figure 22.10
Follow-Up Letter
to an Interview

1065 Locust Drive
Fayetteville, AR 72701
May 12, 1997

Ms. Patricia Markham
Personnel Manager
Able Computers, Inc.
P.O. Box 1511
Columbus, OH 43216

Dear Ms. Markham:

Thank you for the time you spent with me on Thursday discussing employment opportunities in Able Computers' manager trainee program. Your description of Able's program is impressive and reinforces my serious interest in the position.

You mentioned during the interview that Able is interested in individuals who can assume responsibility. Both my work experience (where I trained new employees and replaced the manager when she was out of town) and my extracurricular activities (where I assumed leadership positions in three different campus groups) show the kind of responsible experiences you might be seeking in an applicant.

If you wish to further discuss my qualifications for the manager trainee position, please call. I look forward to hearing from you.

Sincerely,

Jules Steiner
Jules Steiner

that you are proceeding through the hiring process. As you complete the form, keep in mind that neatness, spelling, grammar, and punctuation are important. A sample application form appears in Figure 22.11.

Delayed Follow-Up

Most interviewers will close a job interview by telling you how soon a selection decision will be made: "We'll let you know something by the 15th of next month." If you do not hear from the company by the deadline they specify, then telephone the interviewer to check on the progress of your application. If a decision has not yet been made, you will have gained the advantage of immediate follow-up. If a decision has been made and you have not been chosen, you will at least know where you stand.

If you are turned down, you have little to lose by remaining diligent. Perhaps you can revise your application to a different area of the company, ask for a reevaluation, or seek to have your file remain active in case another position opens. Recruiters sometimes talk about the employee they hired whom they could not shake—who would not take no for an answer.

> **✔ CHECKLIST for Interview Follow-Up**
>
> ____ Complete and return application forms or other requested materials.
>
> ____ Write a letter of appreciation for the interview.
>
> ____ Write notes to yourself regarding what was covered, names of people you met, and upcoming deadlines.

Whether by letter or telephone, the follow-up serves two purposes. First, it is a public relations device designed to enhance your relationship with the interviewer. Second, it is a means of bringing your name back to the interviewer's attention. Many interviewers, especially those who visit your school's placement center, will interview as many as 15 applicants in one day. You will want your name to stand out among the applicants as a qualified person who is genuinely interested in the position.

Follow-Up to Letters of Acceptance or Rejection

You will probably get both of these kinds of letters—some offering you a position and others turning you down. You should respond to both. If made an offer, either accept or refuse the position.

Letters of acceptance and rejection both require a response.

Letter of Acceptance

A letter of acceptance should formally accept the position, express appreciation for the offer, and confirm the details of the offer, including salary, starting time, location, and the name of the person to whom you will be reporting. In addition, it should show anticipation of doing good work. Here is an example of such a letter:

> Your offer of a position in Able Computers' manager trainee program is enthusiastically accepted. Thank you for your confidence in my potential to perform well in the program.
>
> In confirming your letter offering the position, I understand that the starting salary is $27,000 per year to be paid monthly. I will report to Room 236 of the Able Building at 8 A.M. on Monday, January 4, and ask for Phillip Slone, who is to be my training coordinator.
>
> As we discussed earlier, I am impressed with the opportunities Able Computers provides qualified applicants. I will do all I can to justify your trust in my potential.

Letter of Refusal

If you refuse a position offered by a company, your letter should express appreciation for the offer, compliment the interviewer or the company offering the position, clearly refuse the position and explain your refusal, and repeat your appreciation for the offer. Here is an example of a letter refusing a job offer:

> Thank you for your letter of September 23 offering a position in Able Computers' manager trainee program. I am sincerely impressed by both your confidence in my potential and the opportunities Able offers to qualified applicants.

Figure 22.11
Application Form
Source: Reprinted with permission from Sears, Roebuck and Co.

PLEASE PRINT

Personal Data

Print Name in full

(Last) (First) (Middle)

Social Security Number

Home address

(Street) (City) (State) (Zip Code)

Telephone

Temporary Address

(Street) (City) (State) (Zip Code)

Telephone

If hired, can you furnish proof of age? ☐ YES ☐ NO   Licensed to drive car? ☐ Yes ☐ No   Is license valid in this State? ☐ Yes ☐ No
(Answer only if position for which you are applying requires driving.)

Are you a U.S. Citizen ☐ YES ☐ NO or Resident Alien ☐ YES ☐ NO

Have you ever been employed by Sears? ☐ Yes ☐ No   If so, when and where last employed?

Former employees of Sears and certain subsidiaries may be entitled to service credit under the Pension Plan based on prior employment with Sears, Roebuck and Co., Homart Development Co., Sears Investment Management Co., Sears, Roebuck Acceptance Corp., Sears, Roebuck de Puerto Rico, Inc., Sears, Roebuck Overseas, Inc., Terminal Freight Handling Co., Allstate Insurance Company and their subsidiaries, Lifetime Foam Products, Pacific Installers, and Sears, S.A. (Central America).

Are any of your relatives employed by Sears in the unit(s) where you want to work? _____

Position _____

Type of position desired?   State salary you will consider _____

Are you willing to relocate?   Date available for work _____

What initial location would you prefer? _____

Have you been convicted during the past seven years of a serious crime involving a person's life or property?   NO ☐   YES ☐
If yes, explain.

Physical Data

A PHYSICAL DISABILITY OR 'HANDICAP WILL NOT CAUSE REJECTION IF, IN SEARS MEDICAL OPINION YOU ARE ABLE TO SATISFACTORILY PERFORM IN THE POSITION FOR WHICH YOU ARE BEING CONSIDERED.

Do you have any physical condition which may limit your ability to perform the job applied for? If so, please give details._____

To protect the interests of all concerned, applicants for certain job assignments must pass a physical examination before they are hired. Alternative placement of an applicant who does not meet the physical standards of the job for which he/she was originally considered is permitted.

Education

	No. of Years	Name of School	City and State	Course or College Major	Average Grades	Did you Graduate?	Type of Degree
Senior High School							
College							
Graduate Studies							
Other— Give Type							

Military Service

	Date Entered Service	Date of Discharge	Service Related Disability	Highest Rank Held	Branch of Service	City and State	Service-Related Skills and Experience Applicable to Civilian Employment
Branch of Service			YES ☐ NO ☐				

Activities

Professional Organizations _____

What are your hobbies or special interests? _____

Experience

Please give a detailed account of your previous experience and training. Specify the type of work done and the type of work you would prefer to do. If more space is needed, continue on a supplementary page.

RECORD OF EMPLOYMENT AND REFERENCES

LIST BELOW YOUR FOUR MOST RECENT EMPLOYERS, BEGINNING WITH THE CURRENT OR MOST RECENT ONE. IF YOU HAVE HAD LESS THAN FOUR EMPLOYERS, USE THE REMAINING SPACES FOR PERSONAL REFERENCES. IF YOU WERE EMPLOYED UNDER A MAIDEN OR OTHER NAME, PLEASE ENTER THAT NAME IN THE RIGHT HAND MARGIN. IF APPLICABLE, ENTER SERVICE IN THE ARMED FORCES ON THE REVERSE SIDE.

☐ It is satisfactory to contact my present employer.   ☐ It is not satisfactory to contact my present employer.

1 NOTE: State reason for and length of inactivity between present application date and last employer.

Name _____ Tel. No. _____
Address _____
City _____ State _____ Zip Code _____

What kind of work did you do? | Starting Date | Starting Pay | Date of Leaving | Pay at Leaving | Nature of Employer's Business | Why did you leave? Give details | Name of your Supervisor
Month / Year | $ ☐ Mo. ☐ Wk. ☐ Hr. | Month / Year | $ ☐ Mo. ☐ Wk. ☐ Hr.

2 NOTE: State reason for and length of inactivity between last employer and second last employer.

Name _____ Tel. No. _____
Address _____
City _____ State _____ Zip Code _____

What kind of work did you do? | Starting Date | Starting Pay | Date of Leaving | Pay at Leaving | Nature of Employer's Business | Why did you leave? Give details | Name of your Supervisor
Month / Year | $ ☐ Mo. ☐ Wk. ☐ Hr. | Month / Year | $ ☐ Mo. ☐ Wk. ☐ Hr.

3 NOTE: State reason for and length of inactivity between second last employer and third last employer.

Name _____ Tel. No. _____
Address _____
City _____ State _____ Zip Code _____

What kind of work did you do? | Starting Date | Starting Pay | Date of Leaving | Pay at Leaving | Nature of Employer's Business | Why did you leave? Give details | Name of your Supervisor
Month / Year | $ ☐ Mo. ☐ Wk. ☐ Hr. | Month / Year | $ ☐ Mo. ☐ Wk. ☐ Hr.

4 NOTE: State reason for and length of inactivity between third last employer and fourth last employer.

Name _____ Tel. No. _____
Address _____
City _____ State _____ Zip Code _____

What kind of work did you do? | Starting Date | Starting Pay | Date of Leaving | Pay at Leaving | Nature of Employer's Business | Why did you leave? Give details | Name of your Supervisor
Month / Year | $ ☐ Mo. ☐ Wk. ☐ Hr. | Month / Year | $ ☐ Mo. ☐ Wk. ☐ Hr.

I certify that the information contained in this application is correct to the best of my knowledge and understand that any misstatement or omission of information is grounds for dismissal in accordance with Sears, Roebuck and Co. policy. I authorize the references listed above to give you any and all information concerning my previous employment and any pertinent information they may have, personal or otherwise, and release all parties from all liability for any damage that may result from furnishing same to you. In consideration of my employment, I agree to conform to the rules and regulations of Sears, Roebuck and Co., and my employment and compensation can be terminated with or without notice, at any time, at the option of either the Company or myself. I understand that no unit manager or representative of Sears, Roebuck and Co. other than the President or Vice-President of the Company, has any authority to enter into any agreement for employment for any specified period of time, or to make any agreement contrary to the foregoing. In some states, the law requires that Sears have my written permission before obtaining consumer reports on me, and I hereby authorize Sears to obtain such reports.

Applicant's Signature _____

Just this morning Stover Chemicals offered me a training position in its employee relations department. Because of Stover's closeness to my home and the immediate opportunity to work directly in the employee relations field, I have decided to accept their offer.

Your interest in me and your consideration of my application are appreciated.

Response to a Rejection Letter

If you receive a letter rejecting your application for a position, you should follow it up, especially if you might reapply with the company in the future. Such a letter should express appreciation for considering your application, express appreciation for the learning experience the application process has provided you, and introduce future application possibilities. Here is an example of a response to a letter of rejection:

> Your letter of September 23 indicating that I will not be offered a position in Able Computers' manager trainee program arrived today.
>
> Your time and effort in considering my application are appreciated. Interviewing with you has also been a learning experience that provided me with valuable insight into my qualifications and opportunities for improvement.
>
> As we discussed earlier, I am genuinely impressed with the opportunities Able provides qualified applicants. Therefore, as my qualifications you mentioned in your letter become better, I intend to reapply for a position with Able. Please keep my application on file.

THE DELAYED JOB DECISION

Sometimes you may receive a job offer from one company but will want to wait to see if you receive other, better offers. When this is the case, you may wish to write a letter seeking a delay in your decision. Recruiters assume you are interviewing elsewhere and are not embarrassed nor disconcerted by a request for a delay. On the other hand, they often have deadlines to meet or other applicants to whom they would like to offer the job. Therefore, your request must be tactful:

Recruiters will sometimes allow the applicant a little extra time to consider a job offer.

1. Express appreciation for the offer.
2. Indicate that your goal is to select the company in which you can be of the most benefit and your career will be most enhanced.
3. Explain that your interviewing process is not quite complete and you wish an extension of the decision date (state when you will be able to make a decision).
4. Do not explain that if forced into an immediate decision you would turn the offer down; this is better left unsaid.
5. Reaffirm your interest in the job and the company.

Here is a sample delay request letter:

> Last week you offered me a position at Able Computers as a management trainee, starting June 1, at a salary of $27,000. I am pleased to receive this offer and am giving it much thought. With your offer, you asked that I decide by February 1.
>
> As discussed during my visit to Columbus, I am seeking a position where I can make a valuable contribution while moving toward my career goal of high-level management. To be fair to myself and the company I will work for, I need to explore the job market fully. My exploration is not quite complete.
>
> Would it be convenient to delay my decision about your offer from February 1 until February 20?
>
> Your job offer impresses me and I am excited by it. This delay will enhance the quality of my decision—a decision that is important to both of us.

We hope that you will have the opportunity to compare many job offers, although it is sometimes difficult to weigh the organizations evenly. One company, realizing this, supplies a form for comparison. Its form is shown in Figure 22.12.

Figure 22.12

Form for Recording Comparative Data on Prospective Employers
Source: Main Hurdman.

The Main Hurdman

Career Guide

Despite the fact that accounting opportunities are expanding rapidly, there are many accounting graduates who never fully examine the range of options which are open to them.

From a student's viewpoint, the major accounting firms bear a striking resemblance to each other. Most of the well-known firms were founded within a decade of each other. All have a number of appealing but similar qualities—a record of growth, expanding opportunities, and attractive clientele.

Sorting it out.

A key to effectively planning your career lies in developing a systematic approach to assessing a variety of firm attributes. Certainly, this is no easy task. The Main Hurdman career guide on the next two pages should help you place into perspective various firms and to compare career options.

Before you begin.

The Main Hurdman career guide suggests several important variables, and provides space for applying these variables to different accounting firms. One column, which contains facts about Main Hurdman, has been completed.

Answers in many of the categories will require subjective judgments based upon your own experiences. When you are finished, you will have a set of organization profiles for comparison, analysis and further consideration.

It's Your Decision

If you have made an effort to use this guide, you will have organized some of your thoughts about the firms which you are considering. But there are many variables which cannot be compared objectively. Such qualities as reputation and leadership in the profession are difficult to assess on your own. Speak with your professors, your career counselors, or friends in the profession. They may be able to provide you with specific insights into the firms you are considering.

There is not a great deal of advice we can give you about analyzing the profiles you have developed. You must compare your own goals, values, and abilities with what a firm has to offer,

and then make your own decision. This is an intensely personal process and one that can never be accurately structured, except on an individual basis.

Each firm has a distinctive personality which will become evident to you during the recruitment process as you talk with various firm representatives. If you feel comfortable and interface well with these representatives you will probably be able to achieve maximum self-development in that firm's environment. In the final analysis a firm is nothing more or less than its people.

KMG Klynveld Main Goerdeler-International firm

(Continued)

Figure 22.12
Continued

	Main Hurdman	Firm A	Firm B	Firm C	Firm D	Firm E
Firm image	Recognized for its high quality work and leadership in the profession.					
Professional environment	Staff accountants are highly visible members of their local offices. They work directly with partners and managers. Firm stresses individual development and judgment.					
Firm growth	Dramatic growth over the last decade. Outstanding opportunities available as firm attains its growth goals.					
International scope	Services are provided throughout the world. Opportunities are available for international assignments at advanced levels.					
Firm size	An international accounting firm, but not so large as to lose sight of the individual.					
Client orientation	Main Hurdman provides professional services to a wide range of organizations, from "Fortune 500" multinational firms to small businesses, unions, governmental bodies and other entities.					
Career development	Staff members at all levels participate in an active career counseling and development program. Specialization is available.					
Evaluation and advancement	Promotion solely on merit. Comprehensive written evaluations after assignments.					
Professional education	Formal national professional education programs, regional and local office seminars and intensive on-the-job training.					

Key Terms

- **direct-mail approach**
- **cover letter**
- **networking**
- **precision networking**
- **home page**
- **screening interview**
- **open-ended interview**

- **panel interview**
- **group interview**
- **stress interview**
- **office visit interview**
- **videotape interview**
- **computer interview**

Summary

Direct-mail campaigns   p. 533

Response to newspaper advertisements   p. 534

Use of the college placement office   p. 538

Reviewing your qualifications   p. 539

Interview performance   p. 548

Immediate interview follow-up   p. 549

Delayed follow-up   p. 551

Follow-up letters of acceptance or rejection   p. 551

The delayed job decision   p. 553

Review Questions

1. What steps are involved in the direct-mail campaign? Describe them.

2. What are the steps in planning for a job interview?

3. Describe five nonverbal behaviors you should be conscious of during the job interview.

4. Discuss the importance of follow-up as it applies to job interviews.

5. What are three situations in which you would be likely to use a follow-up?

6. What are some ways you can use your computer to assist you in getting the job you want?

Exercises

1. You are a campus recruiter for Goldwin's, a chain of department stores with locations in Dallas, Atlanta, Chicago, and New York. You are looking for an applicant who shows three major qualities: dependability, initiative, and willingness to assume responsibility. The chosen applicant will become a manager trainee at Goldwin's in Atlanta.

   a. Interview one of your classmates for this position.

   b. Write a brief (no more than two pages) report that summarizes the following:

      i. How you assessed your classmate against the three qualities.

      ii. What your classmate said that made you believe that he or she possessed each of the qualities.

      iii. How your classmate's nonverbal communication affected your perception of him or her.

2. Form a trio with two of your classmates. Person A is the interviewer, Person B is the interviewee, and Person C is the observer. A should interview B for approximately 10 minutes, asking any of the 23 interview questions in Figure 22.8. A and C should give feedback to B about both his or her answers and nonverbal communication. Allow B to practice answering difficult questions. Then switch roles for the next 20 minutes, making sure that each member of your trio plays each person in the exercise.

3. Fill out the qualifications checklist presented in Figure 22.6. Then write a brief report justifying your rating on each qualification. Use your work experience, activities, honors, and interests as evidence.

4. Make an appointment to interview the personnel officer of a local company. Your purpose in this interview is to find out the following:

   a. The kinds of questions the person likes to ask in job interviews.

   b. The role this person thinks nonverbal communication plays in the job interview.

   c. The most difficult problem this person has in selecting among applicants.

   d. What qualities this person looks for in people with your level of education. Write a brief report or make a short oral presentation to the class summarizing your findings.

5. Use the Internet to locate job openings.

CASE

Multiple Offers

Mary Dehner, University of Georgia

John Behn, a senior at State University, put down the phone and let out a loud "Yahoo." He had just received his first job offer. The salary wasn't as high as he had hoped, and the firm wasn't his first choice; but it was a real job. And he would finally be able to get a decent car and get on with his life. He had accepted the offer on the phone and planned to start in June.

The next day, the company that had been John's first choice telephoned with a job offer. The job was in Tampa, right near the beach. The salary was higher, and the company offered a signing fee of $2,000. The recruiter even suggested that if he accepted immediately, he could get an extra $500. John was tempted to accept right away, but he told the recruiter he would have to think about his decision.

John called the company whose offer he had accepted and said, "I know I accepted your offer, and I am very excited about working with you. Something has come up, however, that I would like to discuss with you. Another firm has made a very attractive offer that I feel I must seriously consider. This firm offers a management career track that would put me in charge of a small operating unit right away. As you may recall from our interview, this is just the kind of opportunity I've been looking for."

John paused, waiting for an indication from the other end of the phone that he hadn't gone too far out on a limb. None came; he plunged ahead. "I will be happy to honor my commitment with you, yet if you would feel comfortable with my making another choice, I would accept the offer from the other company. While I am very excited about the opportunity to work with your firm, the other offer also represents strong challenges that are closely aligned with my career interests in marketing and management."

The manager of the original firm said that he was impressed with John's presentation of the problem, but he still expected John to honor his acceptance. It looked like the dream job was down the tubes.

Case Questions

1. What do you think John should do?

2. Was John's phone call to the original firm appropriate?

3. How could John have prevented this problem?

4. Why do you think the manager was impressed with John's presentation of the problem? What characteristics did John communicate to the manager about himself? How would these characteristics be productive if John were a manager?

C A S E

Who's Interviewing Whom?

Jim Stull, San Jose State University

Carla Chavez landed an interview with Tom Coates, regional sales manager for Nirvana Computers. During the interview, he asked, "Why do you want to work for Nirvana?"

Carla replied, "Well, Mr. Coates, that's why I asked for the opportunity to meet with you. I want to be sure that Nirvana *is* the right company for me. I've read a great deal of literature about Nirvana. I've met a few of your employees. I listened to a presentation by one of your campus recruiters. Everything that I've heard and read has been extremely positive. I'm especially impressed by your concern for employees and service to customers.

"But I need to see some of this for myself. I'm not sure that I can get a true feeling for the Nirvana culture without visiting and finding out how I would fit the profile of a Nirvana sales representative. I have a few questions that I need answered before I can be sure."

Tom said, "Go ahead and ask."

Carla had specific questions about Nirvana policies, and she probed until she was satisfied that she had received the information she needed.

Tom leaned back in his chair. "I like your style, Carla, and I think you've got the makings of a top-notch Nirvana sales representative."

Case Questions

1. What do you think it is in Carla's verbal behavior that Tom likes? Be specific and identify some of Carla's words that you believe were particularly effective in winning Tom over.

2. Some interviewers might perceive Carla's statement, "I want to be sure

that Nirvana *is* the right company for me," as threatening. Why do you think that they might?

3. Carla used an information-getting technique called probing. Explain why this is effective when used by the interviewee. Why is this technique especially effective for Carla, in view of her objective to be a sales representative? Write a brief dialogue between Carla and Tom showing how Carla would use the probing technique.

CASE

Lost Opportunity

Michael T. O'Neill, Personnel Finders of Arlington, Inc.

On the advice of his college placement center, Sid Flaccus called Data Preparation Associates to set up an interview for the entry-level technical writing position DPA advertised in the placement center's *Job Hot Line*.

Flaccus is 22 years old and has a B.A. in English. He works part-time for Personnel Service of Arlington, Texas, where he writes manuals, letters, memos, and reports.

Sid arrived 15 minutes early for his interview with Betty Boman, the chief editor at DPA. He had dressed in a suit and tie and had even shined his shoes. Two days earlier he had had his hair cut short and styled.

Betty was dressed casually and appeared relaxed. Sid could see that she was an experienced interviewer. She let Sid do most of the talking, but interrupted his digressions about his writing experiences to ask pointed questions about Sid's knowledge of computers and computer software.

Sid knew a little about computers from his required course in computer science, and he added that he "didn't see much difference between journalism and tech writing." He even recommended a recent article to Betty that took computer software writers to task for their jargon. Sid quoted several humorous examples from it.

When the conversation turned to Sid's writing, he quickly pointed out that he had published a short story in the campus magazine and was writing a scholarly paper on poetry. He also mentioned that his English professors had praised his writing and encouraged a writing career.

The interview lasted nearly an hour; for the last half hour Betty asked no questions. She and Sid discussed the novels of William Faulkner, in whose work they shared an interest. The interview ended cordially, and Betty told Sid to call in about a week.

When Sid called a week later, he was surprised to find that another applicant had been offered the job.

Case Questions

1. What do you suspect caused Betty to turn Sid down?

2. What would you have done differently at the interview that might have changed its outcome?

3. Would you tell Sid to do anything differently at his next interview? What?

C A S E

Who Needs a Job?

Margaret Fitch-Hauser, Auburn University

Jackie spent many hours as a student thinking about the type of career she wanted to enter when she graduated from college. As a senior she had an opportunity to do a public relations internship with a hospital. During her term with the hospital, she decided that she wanted to be involved with health care public relations and marketing.

The hospital with which Jackie interned was located in a small town and had a very casual atmosphere. Many of the staff wore nice, but casual clothes to work. However, the work was always very professionally done and Jackie was able to build quite a portfolio of her efforts. Unfortunately, the hospital did not have the resources to offer Jackie a job upon the completion of her internship and graduation from college. Consequently, she had to begin the process of searching for a job at the end of the internship.

Not too long after she graduated, her internship supervisor informed her about a marketing/PR position with a hospital in the third largest community in the state. It seemed that Jackie's career dreams were about to come true.

The hospital was located in a predominately white collar community. Much of the population were highly educated and employed in the aerospace industry. The hospital prided itself in maintaining a highly visible and professional image. Therefore, the employees were urged to reflect that image in their behaviors and their appearance.

Jackie's interview went very well. She addressed every question with sound judgment and well-thought-out answers. Her portfolio clearly demonstrated that she had the knowledge and the skill to meet the challenges of the job. However, something didn't seem to be right. Jackie could sense that the people that she interviewed with had some reservations about her.

The day after her interview, Jackie's former internship supervisor received a call from the personnel director at the hospital. The director asked if there were any extenuating circumstances which they should take into account in making any hiring decisions about Jackie. The internship supervisor said that she didn't know of any and inquired about the nature of the question. At that time the personnel director informed her that Jackie had interviewed very well but had come to the interview wearing a very nice, stylish sweater and slacks. The hospital staff was very concerned that Jackie would not be able to adequately represent them to the public in the manner that they desired. Therefore, they probably would not make her a job offer.

Case Questions

1. What mistakes did Jackie make in her preparation for the interview?
2. Should the internship supervisor call Jackie and give her advice?
3. What advice would you give Jackie?
4. Is there anything that Jackie can do to salvage her job opportunity?

References

Bolles, Richard Nelson. *What Color Is Your Parachute?* Rev. Ed. Berkeley, CA: Ten Speed Press, 1990.

Gonyea, James C. *The On-Line Job Search Companion.* New York: McGraw-Hill, Inc., 1995.

Smith, Carter. *America's Fastest Growing Employers.* Holbrook, MA: Bob Adams, Inc., 1992.

Yate, Martin. *Knock 'em Dead: The Ultimate Job-Seekers Handbook.* Holbrook, MA: Adams Publishing, 1995.

Notes

1. "Goof-Proof Your Resumé," *Changing Times,* September 1983, 43-46.

2. Vince Kowalick, "Good Cover Letter Puts Best Foot Forward," *The Atlanta Journal/The Atlanta Constitution,* September 9, 1990, 47-R.

3. "Networking II: The Sequel," *Training,* April 1992, 10-12.

4. "Goof-Proof Your Resumé."

5. Robert L. Dipboye, Richard D. Arvey, and David E. Terpotra. "Equal Employment and the Interview," *Personnel Journal* 55 (October 1976): 521.

Appendix A

Recognizable Patterns of Language

Learning Objectives

AFTER READING AND UNDERSTAND-
ING THIS SECTION, YOU WILL BE ABLE
TO WRITE A CORRECT SENTENCE.
MORE SPECIFICALLY, YOU WILL
BE ABLE:

1
TO IDENTIFY GRAMMATICAL
PATTERNS.

2
TO FOLLOW THE FORMAL GUIDELINES
FOR USAGE.

3
TO PUNCTUATE IN ACCORDANCE
WITH ESTABLISHED GUIDELINES.

4
TO SPELL CORRECTLY.

RECOGNIZABLE PATTERNS

A knowledge of grammar is necessary in order to communicate efficiently. Grammar provides the logical, mutually recognizable patterns in which the language operates.

Consider the following two sequences of numbers:

a. 5   3   9   1   4   0   8   2   7   6.

b. 9   8   7   6   5   4   3   2   1   0.

Which sequence puts less burden on the reader? Which sequence is easier to remember? Why? Sentence b is the answer, of course, because it follows a recognizable pattern. People look for such patterns in every aspect of life—in their daily schedules, in professors' lectures, in the music they listen to, in the way they drive cars, in certain matters of social protocol, and in the grammar of language.

Take a look at the following two sentences:

c. audited accountant ledger The the.

d. The accountant audited the ledger.

Which of these sentences communicates more efficiently? Which is easier to remember? Why? The answer is sentence d, because it follows the grammar (recognizable patterns) of the English language, whereas sentence c is nonsense.

Of course, not all the problems discussed in this chapter are as flagrant as those in the nonsense sentence, but readers do look for recognizable patterns. Further, the burden is on the writer (or speaker) to adopt the "you" attitude, that is, to identify with the reader's (or listener's) interests and concerns and to make the grammar everything that it should be for the reader's (or listener's) ease.

As it is actually used, the language has four levels of formality:

- *Standard.* This is what the textbooks teach, the highest level. You should use this level in contexts like job interviews and written reports.

- *Informal.* This is the level of most conversations around the office.
- *Colloquial.* This is the level of the company picnic or fishing trip.
- *Substandard.* This is the level of small children and others who have yet to learn the rules.

You should try to use the level appropriate to the situation. The grammar of the fishing trip will keep you from getting a job in an interview; the grammar of the interview will seem stilted on a fishing trip. Learn the standard rules so that you can rise to them when the occasion demands. A basic assumption is that the audience in business is usually literate; that is, the audience will be most favorably disposed toward the message and the product if the message follows the recognizable patterns (guidelines) of standard English. There are times when educated business people break some of these guidelines; they should do so deliberately, not ignorantly. For example, advertising sometimes uses actors saying such things as, "There just ain't nothing better." Perhaps the writers reasoned that the audience wouldn't really care about grammatical formalities.

UNITS IN GRAMMAR

"Give me a place to stand," said the Greek mathematician Archimedes, "and I will move the world." By analogy, the writer might say, "If I can write a sentence, I can move the world." A complete sentence has at least one clause, a clause has at least one phrase, and a phrase has at least one word.

Complete Sentence

A sentence may be of any length provided that it contains the following:

- A capital letter on the first word
- An independent clause
- A period or other appropriate ending punctuation mark

Clause

A clause must contain both of the following:

- *A subject.* In commands, the subject is often understood, as in "[*You*] type this letter."
- *A verb.* This must be a full verb, such as *audit*, not an infinitive, such as *to audit*.

Clauses may be of two kinds, independent or dependent.

Independent Clause
An independent clause can stand alone. It does not depend on another thought to make a statement. *The accountant audited the ledger* is an example.

Dependent Clause
A dependent clause begins with a subordinating word. It may function as an adverb, an adjective, or a noun within a sentence. In this sentence, the dependent clause functions as an adverb: *When the accountant audited the ledger,* the judge dismissed the lawsuit. In this sentence it functions as an adjective: The accountant *who audited the ledger* is Laurie Sosebee. In this sentence it serves as a noun: The judge could see *that the accountant had audited the ledger.* In the dependent clause used as a noun, the "subordi-

nating word" is often understood and omitted: The judge could see *the accountant had audited the ledger.*

Phrases

A phrase is a cluster of words that work together grammatically and that function as a single word might serve, if available. Some of the more common types of phrases are as follows:

- **Noun** (nominal). Noun phrases always function as nouns; for example: *The accountant* audited *the ledger.*
- **Verb.** Verb phrases always function as verbs; for example: The accountant *is auditing* the ledger.
- **Infinitive.** An infinitive phrase may function as a noun; for example: Laurie decided *to audit the ledger* (infinitive plus object of infinitive). An infinitive phrase may function as an adjective; for example: The accountant *to audit the ledger* is Laurie. It may function like an adverb; for example: *To audit the ledger,* you will need to see the bursar.

  Sometimes the *to* preposition does not appear in front of the infinitive; the most common instance is an infinitive after a modal verb *(can, may, must, shall, will):* I can pass the CMA examination; not, I can to pass the CMA examination.
- **Participial.** Participial phrases always function as adjectives (modifiers of the meanings of nouns or pronouns). The present participle always ends in *ing;* for example: *Auditing the ledger,* the accountant had difficulty with some entries. The past participle of most verbs ends in *ed;* for example: *Audited in accordance with the specifications,* the ledger was returned to the file.
- **Gerundive.** A gerundive phrase always contains an *ing* word formed from a verb and used as a noun; for example: *Working late* is something that accountants often do during the first two weeks of April. Compare this with the present participle, which is used as an adjective. The gerund (*ing* word used as a noun) is identical to the present participle in form but not in function.
- **Prepositional.** A prepositional phrase may function as an adverb; for example: The accountant testified *on the witness stand.* Alternatively, it may function as an adjective; for example: The accountant *on the witness stand* is Laurie Sosebee.

Words

Words serve various functions. Some of the most common of these functions are the following.

Substantives

Nouns and pronouns are classified as substantives.

1. *Nouns* serve as subjects and complements of verbs and as objects of prepositions. Nouns generally form the plural by adding an *-s* to the singular (*girl → girls*), but a few are irregular (*woman → women, datum → data, series → series*).
2. *Pronouns* are stand-ins for nouns. There are at least four common pronoun types.
   a. *Personal pronouns* are summarized in Table A.1. Note the three forms (cases). The nominative case is used for the subject of the verb (*I* saw John), the

objective case for the object of the verb (John saw *me*). The possessive case denotes possession.

b. *Relative pronouns* appear in clauses used as adjectives, to relate the clause to the noun antecedent. There are five relative pronouns: *that*,[1] *which*, and *who*, plus a possessive form, *whose*, and an objective form, *whom*. (Can you find the relative clause you are now reading?)

c. *Interrogative pronouns* ask questions: *Who, whose, whom,* and *which* appear here as well as in the list of relative pronouns. Another interrogative pronoun is *what*.

d. *Indefinite pronouns* include *one, anybody, anyone, everybody, everyone, somebody,* and *someone*. They are the only pronouns that use the apostrophe to form the possessive (*one's, anybody's,* and so on).

Verbs

Verbs express action or states of being. Each verb has three parts: the stem (*audit/write*), the past (*audited/wrote*), and the past participle (*audited/written*). Verbs have two basic tenses—present (*audit*) and past (*audited*). With the use of auxiliaries, verbs can express future time (*is going to audit, will audit*) as well as shades of present time (*is auditing*) and past time (*has audited, had audited*). Most verbs have a passive form (*is audited*), which differs from the active in that the passive contains (a) some form of *be* (*be/am/is/are/was/were/being/been*) plus a past participle and (b) directs its action toward the grammatical subject (*the ledger was audited*).

If a verb ends its past tense in *ed* and uses the same form for its past participle, the verb is regular (*audit → audited*). Any other verb is irregular (*write → wrote, written*). A verb that takes an object is called transitive, because its action goes across to the object. (The Latin prefix *trans* means across.) A verb that takes no object is intransitive. *Raise* and *lay* are transitive; their intransitive cognates are *rise* and *lie*. You raise the desk [object]. The desk rises [no object]. Only transitive verbs can go into the passive voice.

TABLE A.1 PERSONAL PRONOUNS

	Singular			Plural		
	Nominative	**Objective**	**Possessive**	**Nominative**	**Objective**	**Possessive**
First Person	I	me	my/mine	we	us	our/ours
Second Person	you (thou)	you	your/yours	you[a]	you[a]	your/yours
		(thee)	(thy/thine)	(ye)		
Third Person						
Neuter	it	it	its	they	them	their/theirs
Feminine	she	her	her/hers	same as neuter		
Masculine	he	him	his	same as neuter		

[a]Common regional variants in speech are *y'all* (contraction of *you all*), *yous* (pluralizing *you* like a noun), and *you guys,* all of which have possessive forms as well. In speech these forms compensate for the distinction lost several centuries ago when *you,* historically plural, replaced *thou* and *thee,* which have always been singular.

Modifiers

Adjectives and adverbs are classified as modifiers.

1. *Adjectives* modify or clarify nouns and pronouns.

    a. *Descriptive* adjectives often precede the word they modify; for example: I audit *red* ledgers. However, they can take a position far from the noun or pronoun modified; for example: Ledgers I audit are *red*. Descriptive adjectives can usually be compared *(red, redder, reddest)*.

    b. *Demonstrative* adjectives *(this, that, these, those)* must always precede the noun they modify. They also differ from descriptive adjectives in that they must agree with the noun in number. *(These book* is not grammatical English.)

    c. *Articles (a, an, the)* follow the same rules as demonstrative adjectives. They must always precede the noun and agree in number. *(A books* is not grammatically correct.)

2. *Adverbs* modify verbs, adjectives, and other adverbs, as illustrated in these examples:

    I wrote *fast*. (The adverb *fast* modifies the verb.)

    I wrote *unusually* fast. (The adverb *unusually* modifies another adverb.)

    He is *unusually* tall. (The adverb modifies the adjective *tall*.)

    Some analysts put *very* into a separate category, intensifiers. The reasons are that *very* is historically an adjective, is often used as an adjective (the very idea), and is not a pure adverb in that it cannot modify verbs (you can run fast, but you can't run very).

Prepositions

Prepositions are the headwords in prepositional phrases. They always connect a substantive to the rest of the sentence. The combination of preposition with substantive is a prepositional phrase (I went *into my office* to audit the ledger).

Conjunctions

The most important class of conjunctions is the coordinating conjunction, so named because it conjoins two or more units that are grammatically equivalent (two prepositional phrases, two verbs, two nouns, and so on). The coordinating conjunctions are *and, or, nor,* and *but*. When used to combine two independent clauses, the coordinating conjunction should be preceded by a comma; for example: The ledger contained mistakes, *and* the accountant had to work overtime to find them.

Expletives

The two common grammatical expletives are *it* and *there*. Both serve merely to get a clause moving:

It is raining.

There is one ledger on the table.

There are two ledgers on the desk.

Note that *there* can never be the subject of a sentence.

Interjections

These include *oh* and *well* used at the beginning of a clause.

QUIZ

This quiz may help you ascertain how well you apply specific guidelines for use of the English language. For each of the 25 sentences, indicate the type of error that you find, if any, by entering in the blank one letter from the following list. Correct each sentence in which you find an error.

A. Error in grammar or usage

B. Error in punctuation

C. Correct, no error

D. Error in spelling or capitalizing

E. Erroneous statement about grammar or punctuation

1. _____ The chapter on loans was entitled "Principal and Interest".

2. _____ The ledger was kind of illegible.

3. _____ A comma should appear before the coordinating conjunction joining two independent clauses.

4. _____ According to Mark Lester, "Grammar is a way of talking about how words are used to make units that communicate a meaning." (*Introductory Transformational Grammar of English*, 2d ed. [New York: Holt, Rinehart and Winston, 1976], 13).

5. _____ The city's four industries, Unisys, Data General Datapoint, and Halliburton, were expanding rapidly.

6. _____ The financial planner applied the new formula and the long-term forecast became much more optimistic.

7. _____ John's writing 32 instead of 23 in the last column caused the total to be $9 too high; however, he found the error quickly.

8. _____ B. F. Skinner was born in Susquehanna, Pennsylvania in 1904.

9. _____ Susan B. Anthony and Carrie Nation both supported womens' suffrage.

10. _____ Rensselaer Polytechnic Institute is a technological university. The oldest one in the United States.

11. _____ Metathesis is when someone transposes or reverses the letters in a word.

12. _____ The speaker's habit of inserting "You know" into virtually every sentence of the presentation weakened it's overall effect.

13. _____ I would urge you to sell that stock now and you should reinvest the money in a computer company.

14. _____ A worker must pay their union dues by payroll deduction.

15. _____ The accommodations were inadequate.

16. _____ On Sunday the "Daily Star" had a circulation of 35,003.

17. _____ Attending the class, a cadaver was used for experiments.

18. _____ Jill claimed, in her resumé, that she had taught at the University of Leeds, England, from 1995–1997.

19. _____ The passive voice in grammar is a combination of some form of *be* plus a past participle.

20. _____ After receiving fair warning from the instructor, George finally learned to separate *a lot* into two words.

21. _____ The contract is to expire at noon on July 1, 1997, when the new contract takes effect.

22. _____ You should remember to add in the deposits that have arrived by mail, you should never send out notices of bad checks until you have considered all deposits for the day.

23. _____ Attending the meeting were Joseph Biggs, Laramie, Wyoming, president, David L. Carson, Troy, New York, secretary, and Allen White, Duncan, Oklahoma, treasurer.

24. _____ Laurie felt badly about the erroneous entries in the ledger.

25. _____ Now that we have finished the quiz, is there any questions?

Answers and Corrections

1. **B.** The chapter on loans was entitled "Principal and Interest."

2. **A.** The ledger was rather illegible.

3. **C.**

4. **B.** According to Mark Lester, "Grammar is a way of talking about how words are used to make units that communicate a meaning" (*Introductory Transformational Grammar of English*, 2d ed. [New York: Holt, Rinehart and Winston, 1976], 13).

5. **B.** The city's four industries—Unisys, Data General, Datapoint, and Halliburton—were expanding rapidly.

6. **B.** The financial planner applied the new formula, and the long-term forecast became much more optimistic.

7. **B.** John's writing *32* instead of *23* in the last column caused the total to be $9 too high; however, he found the error quickly.

8. **B.** B. F. Skinner was born in Susquehanna, Pennsylvania, in 1904.

9. **B.** Susan B. Anthony and Carrie Nation both supported women's suffrage.

10. **B.** Rensselaer Polytechnic Institute is a technological university—the oldest one in the United States.

11. **A.** Metathesis is the transposing or reversing of the letters in a word. *Or* Metathesis occurs when someone transposes or reverses the letters in a word.

12. **B. or D.** The speaker's habit of inserting "You know" into virtually every sentence of the presentation weakened its overall effect.

13. **A.** I would urge you to sell that stock now and to reinvest the money in a computer company.

14. **A.** Workers must pay their union dues by payroll deduction. *Or* A worker must pay his or her union dues by payroll deduction.

15. **D.** The accommodations were inadequate.

16. **B.** On Sunday the *Daily Star* had a circulation of 35,003.

17. **A.** Attending the class, I used a cadaver for experiments. *Or* When I attended the class, a cadaver was used for experiments.

18. **A.** Jill claimed, in her resumé, that she had taught at the University of Leeds, England, during 1995 and 1997. *Or* from 1995 to 1997.

19. **C.**

20. D. The correct spelling is *receiving;* the other frequently misspelled expressions—*separate* and *a lot*—are correct as given.

21. B. The contract is to expire at noon on July 1, 1997, when the new contract takes effect.

22. B. You should remember to add in the deposits that have arrived by mail; you should never send out notices of bad checks until you have considered all deposits for the day.

23. B. Attending the meeting were Joseph Biggs, Laramie, Wyoming, president; David L. Carson, Troy, New York, secretary; and Allen White, Duncan, Oklahoma, treasurer.

24. A. Laurie felt bad about the erroneous entries in the ledger.

25. A. Now that we have finished the quiz, are there any questions?

GUIDELINES

These guidelines, if followed, will enhance your ability to communicate, especially in writing, so that the reader can understand you more easily. Remember that the "you" attitude minimizes the burden on the reader (or listener).

Proofreading Symbols

The symbols shown in Figure A.1 are often used in proofreading to correct various errors.

The rest of this Appendix is in three sections: "Guidelines for Usage," "Guidelines for Punctuation," and "Guidelines for Spelling and Capitalization." Usage has to do with choice of words in speaking or writing. Punctuation and spelling and capitalization are issues only in writing.

Symbol	Meaning
⌒	Close up, as in *partner ship.*
⫙	Delete material slashed and close up, as in *judgement.*
⸂	Delete the material circled, as in *July, 1974 was President Nixon's last full month in office.*
¶	Start a new paragraph.
No ¶	Do not begin a new paragraph.
∨∧	Insert missing material, as in *The TVA began during the Presidency of Roosevelt.*
⊏	Move the item to the left.
⊐	Move the item to the right.
Sp	Correct the spelling error.
(Sp)	Spell out the abbreviation in the text. (This notation usually appears in the margin.)

Figure A.1
Proofreading Marks

Guidelines for Usage

A/An Confusion

A/An

Use *a* before consonant sounds, *an* before vowel sounds:

Colloquial:	The company requested *a* audit.
Standard:	The company requested *an* audit.
Standard:	The word begins with an *f*.

Adjective/Adverb Confusion

Adj/Adv

Do not misuse an adjective for an adverb or an adverb for an adjective.

Misleading:	Laurie felt *badly* about the erroneous entries in the ledger.
True:	Laurie felt *bad* about the erroneous entries in the ledger.
Colloquial:	You did *real* good.
Standard:	You did *really well*.
Nonstandard:	I could *sure* use a new calculator.
Standard:	I could *surely* use a new calculator.

Some of the pairs of words that are often confused, cited later in guidelines for Word Misuse and for Spelling, are adjective/adverb confusions (for example, *because of/due to* and *all together/altogether*).

Adverbial Noun

Do not use an adverb clause where a noun clause is needed. The words *if* and *because* are adverbs and in standard English should not be used to introduce noun clauses. *When* and *where* are also subject to this error when they are used in definitions.

Instead of:	I'll see if she is here.
Use:	I'll see whether she is here.
Instead of:	The reason is because I'm penniless.
Use:	The reason is that I'm penniless.
Instead of:	Metathesis is when two letters are transposed.
Use:	Metathesis is the transposition of two letters. *Or:* Metathesis occurs when two letters are transposed.

Dangling Expressions

Make sure that a participle has a substantive logically to modify. Participles are verbal forms ending in *ing* (present) and *ed* (past) and used as adjectives. If the substantive that the participle is to modify is not actually named, the participle is said to dangle. See also guidelines for Misplaced Modifiers.

DglP

Dangling participle:	Rejected by management, a strike began at midnight.
Correct:	Rejected by management, the union went on strike at midnight.

The most vexing problem is with a present participle at the beginning of a sentence (often passive). Here is how such a dangling participle develops:

$$\begin{cases} \text{I attended the class.} \\ \text{I used a cadaver for experiments.} \end{cases}$$

$$\begin{cases} \text{Attending the class } \textit{(present participle).} \\ \text{A cadaver was used for experiments.} \end{cases}$$

The passive sentence, in eliminating the need to mention the doer of the action, simultaneously eliminates the word that *attending* needs to modify. See the guideline on Passives, Needless.

Dangling participle:	Attending the class, a cadaver was used for experiments.
Correct:	Attending the class, I used a cadaver for experiments.
Correct:	When I attended the class, a cadaver was used for experiments.
Correct:	In one of my classes, a cadaver was used for experiments.

Name the doer of the action of a gerund.

| **Dangling gerund:** | By standing on the riverbank, a steamboat could be seen. | DglG |
| **Correct:** | By standing on a riverbank, I could see a steamboat. | |

Double Negative

To express a negative concept, use *one* negative word. Observe that *hardly* and *merely* are negative in effect.

Colloquial:	I can't hardly sleep well, because of the money I lost in the canal.
Standard:	I can't sleep well, because of the money I lost in the canal.
Standard:	I can hardly sleep well, because of the money I lost in the canal.

Double negatives can be used in standard English if the intent is to express a positive concept. This behavior, technically known as litotes, is in fact *not uncommon*.

Incomplete Constructions

Do not leave out any word that is necessary to make a statement or a comparison log-   IC
ical and complete.

Incomplete:	Richard wanted to pass not only the CPA examination but the bar examination.
Complete:	Richard wanted to pass not only the CPA examination but also the bar examination.
Incomplete:	Be specific as possible.
Complete:	Be as specific as possible.

Misplaced Modifiers

Position a modifier and the word modified as close together as possible. See also   MM
guidelines for dangling expressions.

Misplaced:	It is unwise to carry an electromagnet into a computer center that is activated.
Better:	It is unwise to carry an electromagnet that is activated into a computer center.
Better still:	It is unwise to carry an activated electromagnet into a computer center.

A particular problem arises with the use of certain words such as *almost, just, nearly,* and *only*. Observe how *only* effects a different meaning in each of the following positions noted by the caret (⌄):

```
1     2      3     4        5
 ⌄The ⌄house ⌄cost ⌄$90,000 ⌄.
```

1. You'll pay an additional fortune for the garage!
2. There's no other house on the block.
3. The house really isn't worth that much.
4. The house doesn't cost any more than that.
5. There's no additional charge in pesos or yen.

Mood

Use the moods of verbs correctly. English verbs have three moods: indicative, subjunctive, and imperative. The indicative, used for statements and questions about facts, is by far the most common.

1. Use the subjunctive mood for statements contrary to fact and for resolutions under parliamentary procedure. (You look as if I *were* from Mars. I move that the budget *be adopted.*)

2. Use moods consistently. A common problem occurs when an untrained writer shifts needlessly from the indicative to the imperative (command); this shift usually involves a simultaneous shift in person, because the imperative mood can by definition be only in the second person.

Parallelism, Faulty

//

Make concepts that are parallel in thought parallel in grammatical form. In particular, because a coordinating conjunction must coordinate, be careful to keep coordinate elements on either side of it.

Faulty:	Keyboarding the data and to write the program might take all week.
Parallel:	To keyboard the data and to write the program might take all week.
Parallel:	Keyboarding the data and writing the program might take all week.

Also, be sure to follow each member of correlative pairs (*both . . . and, either . . . or, neither . . . nor, not only . . . but also*) with the same grammatical structure as the other member of the pair.

Faulty:	Both in cost and size, this computer is best.
Parallel:	In both cost and size, this computer is best.
Parallel:	Both in cost and in size, this computer is best.

Passives, Needless

PX

Avoid needless use of the passive voice (which may sound stilted) when the active voice (which is specific and often dynamic) will do the job. Use of the passive may also contribute to the construction of a sentence that begins with a dangling participle (see Dangling Expressions).

Passive:	The audit was conducted.
Active:	The accountant conducted the audit.

Preposition at End of Sentence

PrepX

Prepositions at the end of a sentence are native to the English language; avoid them only if you gain some rhetorical advantage by doing so.

Flat:	This is the desk our best accountant worked herself to death at.
Better:	This is the desk at which our best accountant worked herself to death.

If nothing will be gained by a change, this is a rule that you can just forget *about*.

Pronoun Problems

PRef

Give each pronoun a specific noun (antecedent) to refer to. The problem occurs most often with *it, that, this, they,* and *which.*

Vague:	The accounts had not been audited. This brought about many problems with the Internal Revenue Service.
Proper:	The accounts had not been audited. This failure brought about many difficulties with the Internal Revenue Service.
Proper:	Failure to audit the accounts brought about many difficulties with the Internal Revenue Service.

PAgr

Make each pronoun agree with its antecedent in number and gender.

1. Use a plural pronoun to refer to a plural noun and a singular pronoun to refer to a singular noun (see also guidelines for Subject-Verb Disagreement).

2. If the antecedent is two substantives joined by *and* (as in *X and Y*), make the pronoun plural (such as *they*), unless X and Y form a single unit, as in *bacon and eggs (it)*.

3. If the antecedent is two substantives joined by *or* or *nor*, make the pronoun agree with the nearer antecedent.

4. Use a singular pronoun (such as *it*) if a collective noun antecedent is unitary.[2]

   Unitary: It [the committee] agrees with the union about the need for a stock option plan.

   Individual: They [the committee] are going to the meeting in separate cars and airplanes.

   If the use of a plural pronoun with a collective noun antecedent is awkward, you may wish to recast the sentence.

5. Avoid sex bias in the use of pronouns. See Chapter 5 for examples of how to avoid sexist language.

6. Treat words following *every (everybody, everyone)* as singular (*every man, woman, and child* has *his or her* problems).

7. Treat foreign plurals *(data, memoranda)* as plural in English, too.

Use the proper case of pronoun.   PCase

1. Remember that a pronoun takes the case it has in its own clause.

   Instead of: Give the file to whomever asks for it.
   Use: Give the file to whoever asks for it. (*Whoever* is the subject of *asks;* the object of the preposition *to* is the entire clause *whoever asks for it*.)
   Instead of: This is her you're speaking with.
   Use: This is she you're speaking with. (The object of *with* is an understood *whom* or *that*.)

2. In the formal context use nominative pronouns for all nominative uses.

   Say: Susan and I wrote the program.
   Say: This is he, speaking.

3. Use objective pronouns for all objective uses.

   Say: The secretaries gave a party for John and me.
   Say: Between you and me there is an understanding.

4. Use the possessive case before a gerund.

   Don't say: I was displeased with him resigning so abruptly.
   Say: I was displeased with his resigning so abruptly.

5. Be conscious of courtesy in sequence of pronouns; if you can put yourself last, do so.

   Say: Janice and I are the top salespeople.

Split Infinitive
A split infinitive is often awkward; if it is, try to avoid it.   SInf

   Awkward: Virginia decided to, at the last minute, take the CPA review course.
   Better: At the last minute, Virginia decided to take the CPA review course.

Subject-Verb Disagreement
Make each subject and verb agree in number and person. See also guidelines for   SVAgr
Pronoun Problems.

1. Use a singular verb with a singular subject, a plural verb with a plural subject.

2. If the subject is two substantives joined by *and*, as in *X and Y*, make the verb plural unless *X and Y* forms a single unit (for example: *Ham and eggs is a common breakfast*).

Don't say:	Dallas and Houston is the largest cities in Texas.
Say:	Dallas and Houston are the largest cities in Texas.

3. If the subject is two substantives joined by *or* or *nor*, make the verb agree with the nearer substantive. For verbs, this rule applies to agreement in person as well as to agreement in number.

Don't say:	Either the accountants or the manager have objected to the new policy.
Say:	Either the manager or the accountants have objected to the new policy.

4. Use a singular verb (such as *is*) if a collective noun subject is unitary. If a collective noun subject is acting as individuals and a plural is awkward, you should recast the sentence. Instead of *The committee have*, say *The committee members have*.

Unitary:	The committee has remained firm in its resolve.
Individual:	The committee have argued all morning. *Or:* The committee members have argued all morning.

5. In sentences beginning with *there* or *here*, be careful to make the verb agree with the logical subject.

Colloquial:	There is too few accounting professors.
Formal:	There are too few accounting professors.

6. Treat words after *every (everybody, everyone)* as singular; for example: *Every man, woman, and child was present.*

7. Treat foreign plurals *(data, memoranda)* as plural in English, too.

Don't say:	This data is . . .
Say:	These data are . . .

8. Make the verb agree with the real subject, not with the object of an intervening prepositional phrase.

Not this:	Yesterday's balance of the accounts were correct.
But this:	Yesterday's balance of the accounts was correct.

Tense Problems

Tns

1. Use English tenses properly with regard to time.

   a. The present tense describes current happenings *(I am studying accounting)*, facts that are always true *(Only women can give birth)*, or historical events discussed in present time *(Hildebrand goes to Canossa and begs for mercy)*.

   b. The past tense describes events in past time.

   c. English expresses future time by using the present tense with an adverb of time *(I study accounting tomorrow)*, with modal *will* or *shall* *(I will study accounting)*, or through other means, usually the present participle of go *(I am going to study accounting)*.

2. Use tense consistently.

Don't say:	Geraldine adds up the columns and advised her supervisor about the overrings.
Say:	Geraldine added [or adds] up the columns and advised [or advises] her supervisor about the overrings.

3. If events happen at different times, use auxiliary verbs logically.

Not this:	Peri has been a good skier before she has broken her leg.
But this:	Peri had been a good skier before she broke her leg.

Word Misuse

1. Use logical comparisons. Some adjectives and adverbs are absolute in meaning and do not logically submit to comparison. Examples are *complete*, *full*, *perfect*, and *unique*. Instead of saying *fuller/fullest* or *more/most unique*, use *more/most nearly full* or *unique*.　　WL

2. Avoid wordiness.　　Wordy

Don't write:	Due to the fact that . . .
Write:	Because . . .
Don't write:	Fill the tank up.
Write:	Fill the tank.
Don't write:	Utilize
Write:	Use
Don't write:	The ledger that was returned to me was Tom's.
Write:	The ledger returned to me was Tom's.
Don't write:	Consensus of opinion
Write:	Consensus
Don't write:	Whether or not
Write:	Whether
Don't write:	And etc.
Write:	Etc.

3. Use standard expressions.　　WW

   a. There is no *s* in *anywhere*, *nowhere*, or *a long way*.

   b. The adverbial *kind of* and *sort of* (or *kinda*, *sorta*) should be omitted or changed to a standard expression such as *rather*, *somewhat*, or *a little*. *Kind of* and *sort of* are correct if the *of* preposition has an object (*Jane is the best kind of consultant*). *Kind of* and *sort of* are correct if you can use *type of* in the same position.

   c. The infinitive sign *to* is preferable to *and* after *try* (*try to come*, not *try and come*).

   d. Some words in colloquial speech are out of place in business situations where you are expected to use standard English.

Colloquial	*Standard*
Complected	Complexioned
Enthused	Enthusiastic
Irregardless	Regardless or irrespective
Yourn, Yous	Yours
Illiterate past tenses and past participles, such as brung, clumb, knowed, have went, nad have wrote	*Correct past tenses and past participles, such as brought, climbed, Knew, have gone, and have written*

Inexact	*Exact*
Contact	Communicate with, telephone, visit
Good	Delicious, effective, fitting, pious, well-behaved, wholesome
Great	Famous, large, wonderful
Nice	Attractive, congenial, easygoing, thoughtful

   e. Some words are more specific than others. Use exact language.

   f. Some expressions that seem alike in some way are actually different. Learn to discriminate between the following pairs:

Almost	Most
Among	Between
Amount	Number
An	And

As . . . as	So . . . as
(with positive comparison)	*(with negative comparison)*
Because of	Due to
Can	May
Continual	Continuous
Each other	One another
Fewer	Less
Farther	Further
Imply	Infer
In	Into
Lay *(transitive verb*	Lie *(intransitive verb*
meaning to put or place)*	meaning to recline)*
Oral	Verbal
Set *(transitive verb*	Sit *(intransitive verb*
meaning to put or place)*	meaning to seat oneself)*
Shall	Will
Whereas	While

Many people have difficulty with the difference between *lay* and *lie*. No native speaker misuses *raise* and *rise*, where the issue is the same. Observe the following:

	Transitive	Intransitive
Stem	raise/lay	rise/lie
Past Tense	raised/laid	rose/lay
Past Participle	raised/laid	risen/lain

Guidelines for Punctuation

Apostrophe

Apos

1. For all nouns, use the apostrophe to indicate possession. If a noun ends in *s*, add only the apostrophe. If the noun does not end in *s*, add *'s* for the singular possessive or end the word with *s'* for the plural possessive.

Singular		Plural	
Nominative	**Possessive**	**Nominative**	**Possessive**
Thomas	Thomas'	Thomases	Thomases'
Jane	Jane's	Janes	Janes'
company	company's	companies	companies'
woman	woman's	women	women's
attorney general	attorney general's	attorneys general	attorneys general's *(or* of the attorneys general)

2. Use the apostrophe with only the last noun in a series citing joint ownership.

   Individual ownership: John's and Mary's clothes
   Joint ownership: Derrill and Suzanne's advertising agency

3. Use the apostrophe with indefinite pronouns to indicate possession (*everybody's, one's*).

4. Use the apostrophe to stand for the missing elements in contractions (*doesn't, don't, aren't*).

5. Do not use needless apostrophes. The most flagrant violation of this rule is the confusion of the contraction *it's* (for *it is*) with the possessive pronoun *its*. Although some educated people use apostrophes in simple plurals of letters or numbers, the following is preferable: *1920s* or *CPAs*.

Brackets

1. Use brackets to insert material into a quotation, as in the following example. See also guidelines for Ellipsis Marks.

Brack

> Senator Fogbound claimed that "unemployment is no longer an anecdote [*sic*, antidote] to inflation."

2. Except in mathematics and in computer languages, substitute brackets for parentheses used inside parentheses, as in this example:

> According to Mark Lester, "Grammar is a way of talking about how words are used to make units that communicate a meaning" *(Introductory Transformational Grammar of English*, 2d ed. [New York: Holt, Rinehart and Winston, 1976], 13).

Colon

1. Use a colon to introduce an enumeration, explanation, list, or long quotation (particularly one that contains commas).

Col

2. Use a colon in the following particular places:

  a. Between title and subtitle, as in Grinder and Elgin's *Guide to Transformational Grammar: History, Theory, Practice.*

  b. Between place of publication and publisher in a citation, as in *Fort Worth, TX: Holt, Rinehart and Winston, 1997.*

  c. Between hours and minutes, as in *11:05 A.M.*

  d. Between sentences, if there is a cause-effect relationship. (This situation is similar to guidelines for the Semicolon and should be used sparingly.)

  e. After the salutation in a business letter—except when an open style of punctuation is used.

3. Do not use a colon that interrupts the syntax.

Unnecessary colon:	We sent technicians to: Birmingham, Leeds, and Manchester.
Correct:	We sent technicians to Birmingham, Leeds, and Manchester.
Correct:	We sent technicians to the following: Birmingham, Leeds, and Manchester.

Comma

1. Do not use a comma to join two independent clauses unless the comma is followed by a coordinating conjunction. This error, called a *comma splice* (or *comma fault*), is one of the most serious in punctuation. The comma splice, in other words, misuses the comma as if it were a period or semicolon.

Com

Wrong:	John did not study, therefore he did not pass.
Right:	John did not study, and therefore he did not pass.

2. Do not use a comma merely because it "feels good." There are rules that govern the use of commas. In particular, do not use a comma needlessly between subject and verb or between verb and complement (object, predicate nominative, etc.).

Not this:	Anne and Tyrone, studied together.
But this:	Anne and Tyrone studied together.

3. Do not use a comma before an indirect quotation or before a direct quotation that runs on with the sentence:

Indirect quotation:	Eleanor said that she would not go.
Running text:	Paul urged the Romans to be "Not slothful in business" (Rom. 12:11 KJV).

4. Use a comma before a coordinating conjunction (*and, or, nor, but*) joining two independent clauses. For example:

The financial planner applied the new formula, and the long-term forecast became much more optimistic.

Rule 4 is especially useful when the subject of the second independent clause may momentarily be confused as an object of the verb in the first independent clause. The comma in the sentence above presents this problem. Remember to adopt the "you" attitude and make things easy for the reader.

5. Use a comma after any verbal material that precedes an independent clause.

Correct:	When Bonnie finished the examination, she forgot to hand in the answer sheet.
Correct:	In preparing this form, you should write everything in ink.

6. Use the comma to set off an appositive—a noun explaining or defining another noun. See also guidelines for the Dash.

Correct:	Kimberly Shipman, our last supervisor, transferred to Alaska.

If the appositive is essential to the sense, the commas are not used. This type of appositive is called an "identifying appositive."

Correct:	The futurist Alvin Toffler wrote *Future Shock* and *The Third Wave*.

7. Use the comma to set off a nonrestrictive clause—that is, a clause not essential to the meaning of the sentence.

Correct:	Thomas Darden Willis, who sits in the back row, gave an excellent presentation.

8. Use the comma to separate words in a series.

Correct:	Mark wrote the C++ program quickly, neatly, and accurately.

Do not be confused by newspaper style, which usually eliminates that last comma. Most business writers retain it to ensure absolute clarity.

9. Use the comma to separate adjectives that independently modify a noun.

Correct:	Gretchen became involved in a long, expensive lawsuit.

10. Use the comma to set off a noun of address.

Correct:	What do you think, Trevor, about this solution?

11. Use the comma before a short direct quotation.

Correct:	John Paul Jones said, "I have not yet begun to fight."

12. Use the comma to separate contrasted elements.

Correct:	Take the blue form, not the red one, to the bursar.

13. Use the comma for the following purposes:

   a. To set off *yes* or *no* from the rest of a sentence.

   b. To set off conjunctive adverbs—particularly *however*.

   c. To set off tag questions. (*Thaddeus is stupid, isn't he?*)

d. To separate certain items in dates.

> **Correct:** July 1997 is the termination date.
> **Correct:** July 1, 1997, is the termination date.

e. To separate items in addresses (except state and zip code) when they are run in a sentence.

f. To stand for nonrepeated elements. *(The red form goes to the registrar; the blue one, to the bursar).*

g. To aid clarity as needed.

14. Remember that a comma on one side of an item to set it off generally requires a complementary comma on the other side of the item.

> **Correct:**   Baton Rouge, Louisiana, is the capital.

Dash

1. Use the dash to set off an appositive that (a) has commas inside it or (b) is separated from the substantive to which it refers.

> **Correct:**   John's book was widely read—a bestseller for months.

2. Use dashes, instead of parentheses, if the material set off is to be emphasized.

3. Remember that a dash on one side of an item to set it off requires a complementary dash on the other side of the item, unless the sentence ends there.

4. Observe that the dash and the hyphen are two different marks of punctuation, with no uses in common. On a keyboard, the dash is formed by typing two hyphens, with no spaces before, between, or after.

Dash

Ellipsis Marks

1. Use ellipsis marks (spaced periods) to show an omission within a quotation. See also guidelines for Brackets.

2. Type ellipsis marks to conform to the following:

a. Three spaced periods show an omission within a sentence.

b. Four periods show an omission that crosses over a sentence boundary; one period marks the end of the sentence, and it is followed by three spaced periods.

c. An entire line of spaced periods indicates the omission of at least a paragraph.

El

Exclamation Point

Use the exclamation mark only occasionally to show strong emotion.

Excl

Hyphen

1. Use the hyphen to separate the whole number from the fraction in a mixed number, as 3-5/16.

Hyph

2. Use the hyphen in compound words, such as *self-actualization.*

3. Use the hyphen between compound (unit) modifiers *(36-inch pointer* or *computer-scored answer sheet).*

4. Use a "suspension" hyphen after each item in a hyphenated series *(The company needs fewer mid- and upper-level managers).*

5. Do not use the hyphen between words that merely follow each other:

> **Compound modifier:**   20-dollar bills (= $20 x quantity)
> **Separate modifier:**   20 dollar bills (= 20 x $1)
> **Compound modifier:**   A deep-dredged canal

    Adverb and adjective: A deeply dredged canal

6. Do not hyphenate words at the ends of lines in these instances:

   The entire word is less than seven letters.

   The division does not occur between syllables.

   The word is part of a proper name.

   The line is at the end of a page.

   The hyphenated word comes immediately after or before another hyphen or dash.

   There are several other hyphenated words on the page.

   The manuscript is to be submitted to a publisher.

Parentheses

Paren

1. Use parentheses for supplementary remarks or for references in the text (Joseph N. Ulman Jr. and Jay R. Gould, *Technical Reporting,* 3d ed. [New York: Holt, Rinehart and Winston, 1972], 197–198).

2. If the sentence element before the parentheses requires a mark of punctuation, place the mark of punctuation after the closing parenthesis. Ulman and Gould (page 197), while discussing parentheses, also cite this rule.

3. Use parentheses to enclose the area code for a telephone number: (504) 345-2063.

4. Use parentheses in pairs.

      Not this: 1)
      But this: (1)

Period

Pd

1. Use the period at the end of a statement or a polite *would you please* request.

2. Use the period with certain abbreviations *(U.S., f.o.b., I.0.0.F., P.D.Q.)*, but not with others *(CIA, CYA, GAAP, NCR, TVA).* Most dictionaries include frequently used abbreviations. There are dictionaries of abbreviations that include less common abbreviations. If use of the period is optional, then be consistent (if *AM,* then *PM;* if *a.m.,* then *p.m.).*

3. Use the period for a decimal point.

Question Mark

QM

1. Use the question mark for a direct question, but not for an indirect question.

      Correct: Judy asked, "Did I hurt someone's feelings yesterday?"
      Correct: Judy asked whether she hurt someone's feelings yesterday.

2. Use the question mark in parentheses to express doubt about the material preceding the parentheses.

      Correct: John's new (?) car was a Model T.

3. Do not follow the question mark immediately with a comma, a period, or a semicolon.

Quotation Marks

Quo

1. Use quotation marks to enclose a speaker's or writer's exact words.

2. If a quotation extends over more than one paragraph, use opening quotation marks before each quoted paragraph, closing quotation marks only at the end of the quotation.

3. Use quotation marks to enclose the title of a work that is published as part of a book—for example, the titles of short stories, chapters, and poems. See also guidelines for Underlining.

4. Position the closing quotation marks as follows if there is an immediately adjacent mark of punctuation:

   a. The comma or the period always goes inside (to the left of) the closing "quotation marks."

   b. The colon or the semicolon always goes outside (to the right of) the closing "quotation marks":

   c. The exclamation point or the question mark goes inside if part of the quotation and outside if part of the sentence surrounding the quotation.

Correct:	Mary said, "When will I see you again?"
Correct:	Did Mary say, "I will see you again tomorrow."?
Correct:	Did Mary say, "When will I see you again?"?

5. Use single quotation marks for quotes within quotes; inside the single quotes revert to double quotation marks.

Correct:	John said, "Bill claimed, 'I have read the section entitled "Recognizable Patterns of Language."'"

6. Use quotation marks sparingly to indicate words used in a special (sometimes satiric) sense; do not use quotation marks as decorations.

7. Do not use quotation marks as an abbreviation for *inches* and *feet*. Spell the words out or use the standard abbreviations *in.* and *ft.*

8. Do not use quotation marks to surround blocks of quoted material that are separated from the text, indented, and single spaced unless these quotation marks are in the original quote. (The layout by itself indicates that the material is being quoted; quotation marks are therefore redundant.)

Semicolon

1. Use the semicolon to separate independent clauses that are intimately joined in logic.

   Semi

Correct:	Semicolons are one thing; commas are another.

2. Use the semicolon to join clauses or items that have internal commas.

Confusing:	Attending the meeting were Joseph Biggs, Laramie, Wyoming, president, David L. Carson, Troy, New York, secretary, and Allen White, Duncan, Oklahoma, treasurer.
Clear:	Attending the meeting were Joseph Biggs, Laramie, Wyoming, president; David L. Carson, Troy, New York, secretary; and Allen White, Duncan, Oklahoma, treasurer.

   This guideline sometimes works together with guidelines for the Comma (item 4):

Correct:	Suzanne, afraid of the final examination, studied frantically while drinking tea, coffee, and cola; and, in the end, she fell asleep during the test.

3. Use the semicolon only between grammatically equal units. Do not use it, for example, between a dependent clause and an independent clause:

Wrong:	While Sara studied to be a CPA; her boyfriend found a new lady.
Right:	While Sara studied to be a CPA, her boyfriend found a new lady.

Sentence Fragment

Sfrag

Give each sentence a subject and verb that do not have any initial subordinating word to prevent them from forming a complete sentence.

Fragment: Because the bookkeeper was drunk.
Sentence: The bookkeeper was drunk.

Many times a fragment is actually a clause or phrase that belongs with the preceding sentence but has erroneously been punctuated as a sentence by itself. The dash is useful in correcting the problem.

Not this: Rensselaer Polytechnic Institute is a technological university. The oldest one in the United States.

But this: Rensselaer Polytechnic Institute is a technological university—the oldest one in the United States.

Sentence Punctuation Error

SPE

Use only a period, a semicolon, a colon, a dash, a question mark, an exclamation point, or a comma plus coordinating conjunction between two independent clauses (see Figure A.2). See also guidelines for the Comma.

Figure A.2
Independent Clauses

S_1
This is the first
independent clause

S_2
This (or this) is the
second independent
clause

Slash (Virgule)

Slash

Use the slash to indicate alternative possibilities.

Correct: One may telephone the message to Richard at (504) 345-2682/2063.

Spacing

#

In typewritten work be careful to use spaces as follows:

1. Space twice at the end of a sentence.

2. Insert spaces between the dots in ellipses.

3. Space twice between the state and ZIP code (or postal code) in an address.

Correct: The vendor is The Bible Shop, Post Office Box 2491, Hammond, LA 70404-2491.

Correct: W. R. O'Donnell lectures in the Department of Linguistics and Phonetics, The University of Leeds, West Yorkshire LS2 9JT, England.

4. Do not space before or after the dash.

Underlining

Und

Use underlining (underscoring) for the same functions as italicizing in print.

1. Underline the titles of separately published works such as books and periodicals. See also guidelines for Quotation Marks.

2. Underline expressions used as themselves.

    Correct: The word <u>word</u> should be underlined when used as a word.

    Correct: John's writing <u>32</u> instead of <u>23</u> in the last column caused the total to be $9 too high.

3. Underline foreign words and expressions that have not become fully anglicized.

    Correct: The evaluator claimed that Ian's argument was <u>post hoc, ergo propter hoc.</u>

4. Underline the names of vehicles, particularly ships.

    Correct: David received valuable business experience while serving as disbursing officer aboard the USS <u>Berkeley.</u>

    Correct: Charles Lindbergh's <u>Spirit of St. Louis </u>is now in the Smithsonian Institution.

5. Italics may be substituted for underlines but be consistent throughout the manuscript.

Guidelines for Spelling and Capitalization

Spelling

1. Spell words in accordance with the dictionary. English spelling is more or less regular, but rules to describe it usually become submerged in exceptions. People who read a lot tend to spell well; the reason is partly a matter of pattern recognition. Some of the most troublesome words are listed in Table A.2.

    Sp

2. Differentiate between expressions that are alike in pronunciation but different in meaning or syntactic function (role in the structure of the sentence). The following similar-sounding words or expressions are sometimes confused:

- Accept/except
- Affect/effect
- All ready/already
- All together/altogether
- Any one/anyone
- Capital/capitol
- Cede/seed
- Cite/sight/site
- Every one/everyone
- Faze/phase
- Its/it's
- Led/lead
- May be/maybe
- Passed/past
- Principal/principle
- Right/write
- Some one/someone
- Some time/sometime
- Stationary/stationery
- Their/there/they're
- To/too/two
- Who's/whose
- Your/you're

3. Spell out expressions that, in the situation, may be misunderstood. Pronounce expressions in full if the audience is unfamiliar with the acronyms (*Students in Free Enterprise* instead of *SIFE*). The problem is particularly likely to occur in multinational business, where Americanisms like *ID* (for *identification*) are meaningless or misleading *(Idaho)*. Spell out all words in international correspondence, especially addresses (*LA* may mean *Los Angeles*, not *Louisiana*, to foreigners answering your letter).

TABLE A.2 POTENTIAL SPELLING DIFFICULTIES

a lot	chose	environment	license	paralyze	ptomaine	superintendent
absence	coming	equipped	lose	part-time	pursue	supersede
accessible	committee	exaggerate	loose	pastime	quantity	supposed
accidentally	comparative	exceed	losing	performance	questionnaire	surprise
accommodate	conscience	excellence	maintenance	permissible	quiet	technique
accommodation	conscientious	existence	maneuver	persistent	realize	than
accurate	conscious	existent	marriage	personal	receipt	then
achievement	consensus	experience	mere	personnel	receive	thorough
acquaintance	consistent	explanation	misspelling	picnic	receiving	through
acquire	controversial	fascinate	moral	picnicking	recommended	tragedy
among	controversy	forty	morale	possession	referred	transferred
analogous	convenience	government	mortgage	possible	referring	tries
analyze	coolly	grammar	necessary	practical	relevant	truly
apparent	cylinder	grievous	newsstand	precede	renowned	undoubtedly
appropriate	decision	guarantee	ninety	predictable	repetition	unnecessary
arguing	definitely	height	noticeable	preference	rhythm	until
argument	definition	holiday	occasionally	preferred	ridiculous	using
assistant	define	imagine	occurred	prejudiced	schedule	vacuum
attorneys	describe	immediately	occurrence	prepare	seize	varies
balloon	description	incidentally	occurring	prevalent	sense	vicious
beginning	desirable	indispensable	offered	privilege	separate	villain
belief	despair	insistent	offering	probably	separation	weird
believe	development	interest	omitted	procedure	sergeant	woman
beneficent	disappear	interface	opinion	proceed	sheriff	writing
beneficial	disappoint	interpret	opportunity	profession	shining	written
benefited	disastrous	irresistible	original	professor	similar	
carburetor	discriminate	irritable	paid	prominent	studying	
category	drunkenness	laboratory	pamphlet	pronunciation	succeed	
changeable	efficiency	ledger	panicky	propeller	succession	
choose	embarrassment	leisure	parallel	psychology	suddenness	

Note: Thirty of the most troublesome words are underlined.

4. Spell out the words for symbols unless you really need to save space.

> **Not this:**   @, ¢, #, %.
> **But this:**   At, cent or cents, number (or pounds), percent.

The # symbol has different meanings and in any case is often redundant before a number. Why write *Apartment #B*727 when *Apartment B*727 will suffice?

5. Leave the name of an organization exactly as it is officially—for example, *Texas Tech University*, not *Texas Tech. University* and not *Texas Technological University*. (This guideline also applies to punctuation—for example, *Holt, Rinehart and Winston*, not *Holt, Rinehart, and Winston*.)

6. Use apostrophes correctly in spelling of possessives (singular possessive *woman's*, plural possessive *women's*). See also the guideline for Apostrophe.

Numbers and Numerals

Use numbers and numerals according to the business writing conventions. The fol-   Num
lowing guidelines are arranged in increasing power or importance.

1. Write as numerals all numbers of two digits or more (10 and up) whether positive or negative.

2. Express all numbers containing decimals as numerals.

3. Use a cipher (even if *0*) to fill decimal notation (that is, write 1.0, not 1., and 0.1, not .1).

4. As a general rule use numerals with any unit of measure, even if below 10. Units of measure include money, time, dates, addresses, age, volume numbers, and arithmetic calculations, in addition to bushels, inches, meters, and so on.

5. Differentiate series running together. *(George had five 12-column ledgers and twelve 9-column ledgers.)*

6. Spell out any number coming immediately at the beginning of a sentence. (There are no capital numerals.)

7. Be consistent. For example, if you type a paper that has the fractions 1/2 and 3/16, you must type the 1/2 as 1/2, not by using the 1/2 key on the typewriter, because there is no 3/16 key.

Capitalizing

1. In material to be capitalized, except in headings and other situations in which you will use all capitalization (ALL CAPS), capitalize the first letter of nouns, verbs, adjectives, and adverbs.

  a. Capitalize the first letter of the first word in such material even if the word is not a noun, verb, adjective, or adverb.

  b. You may capitalize prepositions longer than four letters, if you wish, but be consistent.

> **Inconsistent:**   *Communicating through Letters and Reports* was written after the War Between the States.
> **Consistent:**   *Communicating through Letters and Reports* was written after the War between the States.
> **Consistent:**   *Communicating Through Letters and Reports* was written after the War Between the States.

2. Capitalize the following:

    a. Names of deities and of titles of scripture books.

    b. Works such as books, articles, poems, and stories.

    c. Important documents *(the Magna Carta, the Declaration of Independence)*.

    d. Days, holidays, months, and historical periods *(the Industrial Revolution)*.

    e. First word in a sentence.

    f. Languages.

    g. Organizations *(IBM, Rotary International, European Community)*, but preserve the capitalization that the organization uses officially (for example, *E. I. du Pont de Nemours & Co., Inc.*, not *E. I. DuPont De Nemours and Company*).

    h. Places and regions *(the Sahara, the South)*.

    i. Names of streets and other thoroughfares.

    j. Title when followed by a name *(Miss Alice Young, Professor Yaney)*.

    k. *President* when referring to the chief executive of the United States of America.

    l. Certain nouns if followed by numbers, as in *Apartment B727*.

3. Be consistent in capitalization of comparable words.

Wrong:	The officers present were President Elizabeth Carter and treasurer Pat Underwood.
Correct:	The officers present were President Elizabeth Carter and Treasurer Pat Underwood.
Also correct (consistent):	The officers present were Elizabeth Carter (president) and Pat Underwood (treasurer).

4. Use lowercase (small) letters for

    a. Seasons of the year *(winter)*.

    b. Academic subjects not otherwise capitalized.

Correct:	Brenda, Dee, and Terry respectively studied management, Roman history, and English.

    c. Simple directions, as on a compass.

Correct:	When John worked in the North, his office was on the south side of a busy street.

When you have finished studying this appendix, you may want to return to the quiz on page 567 to see how much you have improved.

Notes

1. Additionally, *that* may function to introduce a clause used as a noun or may be used as a demonstrative adjective. In this sentence, *that* is a relative pronoun: The ledger *that I audited* is on the desk. In this sentence, it introduces a noun clause: I saw *that the ledger was audited*. In this sentence, it is a demonstrative adjective: *That* ledger is the one I audited.

2. British standards differ from American standards in some pronunciations and in several other ways. A few examples:

   a. British collective nouns (such as *committee, government*) are always plural.

   b. British occasionally exercises different syntactical choices *(Have you got the time?* and *Is our policy different to yours?* as opposed to American *Do you have the time?* and *Is our policy different from yours?).*

   c. Certain vocabulary items in British are unknown in American, and vice versa. Examples are *bloke* and *zebra crossing* (crosswalk) in British and *sidewalk* and *automobile* in American.

   d. Words have different meanings in the two dialects. In American, *to table a motion* usually means, in effect, to kill it; but in British *to table a motion* means to schedule it for a vote.

   e. British punctuation uses single quotation marks where American uses double quotation marks, and vice versa.

   f. Spelling is often different *(civilization/civilisation, color/colour, connection/connexion, maneuver/manoeuvre).*

   We should be aware of these and other differences and exercise special care in international business communications. Multinational managers should be particularly careful to design advertising slogans that can be used throughout the English-speaking world.

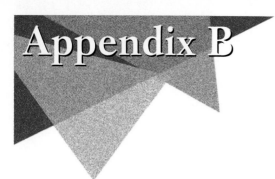

Appendix B

Letter Parts and Appearance

If, when talking with someone, you closed your eyes, you would miss a large part of the message. The same principle applies to business writing. The reader has access to many cues in addition to the verbal message. These cues, which together constitute appearance, create the first impression that the reader forms of the message and of its writer.

Too often business people overlook the importance of appearance in written communication. The effect of hours of effort spent developing a logical and coherent message may be neutralized by a displeasing appearance. Such factors as quality and color of paper, spacing, margins, and size of type will influence a reader's receptivity to a message.

Authors using today's fast computers, multi-faceted word processors, and full-featured laser printers have more control than ever over the appearance of their correspondence.

The content of a message is certainly more important than its appearance, but an appropriate appearance increases the likelihood of its being read. A written message must meet certain expectations if it is to be read and seriously considered. A cardinal rule in business writing is that appearance should not call attention to itself. Instead, it should subtly facilitate communication.

This appendix is divided into six sections: Stationery, Business Letter Parts and Formats, Additional Parts of a Business Letter, Memo Parts and Formats, Other Forms of Business Correspondence, and Computer Considerations.

STATIONERY

One of the first things a reader notices when opening a letter is the stationery on which it is typed. One characteristic of stationery is that it is both seen and felt.

Paper and Envelopes

Stationery should be the quality used in most business organizations. Good paper will meet public expectations and enhance the image of the organization. The same quality should be used for envelopes.

The most common paper size is 8½ -by-11-inch sheets, but some executives use Monarch-size sheets of 7¼-by-10½ inches. Half sheets, 8½-by-5½ inches, are often used for brief internal messages such as memos or notes. In other parts of the world, much different "standard" paper sizes are common. Stationery weight is expressed in pounds. Business stationery ranges from 16 to 20 pounds. If lighter than 16 pounds, it is too fragile, and if heavier than 20 pounds, it is too bulky and hard to fold, as well as expensive.

White continues to be the standard color for business stationery, although greater use is being made of pastels. Colored paper is used more often in sales letters than in other types of correspondence. Many companies personalize their stationery with a watermark, which is impressed on the paper during production. A watermark is a faint design that can be seen when the paper is held up to the light. The company logo, or some other identifying symbol, is often used as a watermark.

Paper for most computer printers meets the characteristics just mentioned, but also falls into two other categories: tractor fed paper and sheetfed paper. Tractor paper has holes on the left and right sides to enable the paper to be pulled through the printer—usually a dot matrix printer. Once printed, the edges of the paper with the holes can be removed at a perforation. "Sheetfed" means loose paper sheets placed in a paper tray. Laser printers use sheetfed stationery.

Paper for facsimile machines may be in rolls—often heat- or light-sensitive— or sheetfed.

In most routine business communication the role of the envelope is innocuous. In direct-mail advertising, however, the envelope greatly influences the effectiveness of the advertising enclosed. The perfect envelope is the one that is always opened. Research in direct-mail advertising has shown that the right envelope can double or triple the number of responses. Envelopes that resemble those used by Federal Express and other overnight mail companies, or government agencies such as the IRS, are more likely to be opened than are plainer envelopes. For purposes other than sales, a company's envelopes should be consistent with its desired image.

The *1995 Zip Code and Post Office Directory* urges the use of all capital letters for envelope addresses.

The Printed Letterhead

The printed heading on stationery is called a **letterhead**. A letterhead lends legitimacy to any business organization. Virtually all business organizations, whether one-person operations or much larger, use letterhead stationery.

At one time the letterhead took up a large part of a sheet of stationery. Often it included names of company officers and pictures of the plant along with routine identifying information. A modern letterhead has no extraneous details and usually occupies about two inches at the top of the sheet. Some companies print their letterhead on each letter as it is laser printed by merging a letterhead template with the message.

The modern letterhead includes the company name, address, and ZIP code. Most firms also give their telephone number, including the area code. Facsimile numbers now appear in many letterheads, as do E-mail addresses. Companies engaging in international business often show the country in which they are located and include a code address for cablegrams.

BUSINESS LETTER STANDARD PARTS AND FORMATS

Compare letters from a number of companies and you will notice obvious differences. They may vary considerably in such stylistic features as size of type, margins, and general appearance.

All, however, will contain the same basic parts. Regardless of the purpose of the letter, the reader has certain information needs that the following parts satisfy:

- Return address of sender
- Date letter was written
- Inside address of receiver
- Salutation
- Attention line
- Body of letter
- Close
- Signature block

Return Address

The return address of the sender consists of the street number and name or a post office box number, city, state, and ZIP code. On letterhead stationery, this is usually printed at the top. On plain paper, it is typed at least 1½ inches from the top of the sheet. It can be positioned horizontally in either of two ways: (1) begin each line at the center of the sheet or (2) position the return address so that the longest line ends at the right margin. It thus establishes the top and right margins.

Date

The date is an important part of any business letter.

All letters and reports should be dated. The date tells the reader something about the context in which the letter was written. It also simplifies filing; correspondence in a file folder is usually arranged chronologically. The standard form for dates is month, day, and year—for example, November 19, 1997. Companies with international business, military organizations, and foreign companies often use a day, month, year sequence, such as 19 November 1997. The date should be typed three line spaces below the sender's address, whether or not there is a letterhead.

Inside Address of Receiver

Information in the receiver's address is arranged from specific to general.

The inside address includes the name, title, and address of the person to whom the letter is being sent. Be very careful that all of this information is correct. Letter writers create unnecessary obstacles to their intended goal when they misspell receivers' names or use incorrect job titles.

Information in the receiver's address is arranged in descending degrees of specificity. The most specific information, the receiver's name, if known, is presented first and followed by the receiver's professional title, the name of the organization, mailing address, city, state, and ZIP code. It is customary, although not mandatory, to abbreviate the names of states, districts, and territories. The U.S. Postal Service recommends the abbreviations presented in Table B.1. The two-letter state abbreviation should be separated from the ZIP code by a double space.

Inside addresses are typically arranged in this manner:

Dr. John Robinson
Affirmative Action Officer
Central States College
Administration Building
Macon, MO 63552

Modern Office Supply
2226 Main Street
Buckeye, NM 88212

The first line of the inside address determines the left margin for the letter.

Salutation

Many writers of business letters today fret over what constitutes an appropriate **salutation**—the word or phrase of greeting that precedes the body of the letter. Some authors use gentle-people, Gentlefolk, Gentlepersons, and even Gentle/wo/men. Others prefer salutations such as Dear Colleague, Dear Professional, Dear Compatriot, and Dear Executive. A few use single-word salutations, ranging from Greetings to Hail to Howdy. Some authors even omit the salutation.

TABLE B.1 RECOMMENDED ABBREVIATIONS FOR STATE, DISTRICT, AND TERRITORY NAMES					
Alabama	AL	Kentucky	KY	Ohio	OH
Alaska	AK	Louisiana	LA	Oklahoma	OK
Arizona	AZ	Maine	ME	Oregon	OR
Arkansas	AR	Maryland	MD	Pennsylvania	PA
California	CA	Massachusetts	MA	Puerto Rico	PR
Panama Canal Zone	CZ	Michigan	MI	Rhode Island	RI
Colorado	CO	Minnesota	MN	South Carolina	SC
Connecticut	CT	Mississippi	MS	South Dakota	SD
Delaware	DE	Missouri	MO	Tennessee	TN
District of Columbia	DC	Montana	MT	Texas	TX
Florida	FL	Nebraska	NE	Utah	UT
Georgia	GA	Nevada	NV	Vermont	VT
Guam	GU	New Hampshire	NH	Virgin Islands	VI
Hawaii	HI	New Jersey	NJ	Virginia	VA
Idaho	ID	New Mexico	NM	Washington	WA
Illinois	IL	New York	NY	West Virginia	WV
Indiana	IN	North Carolina	NC	Wisconsin	WI
Iowa	IA	North Dakota	ND	Wyoming	WY
Kansas	KS				

By asking yourself how well you know your correspondent, you should be able to select an appropriate salutation. Some frequently used salutations in business letters are Dear Mr., Dear Ms., or Dear Mrs. The better you know the correspondent, the more informal you may be. By the time you have written several times and perhaps talked on the telephone with the person, you will probably be on a first-name basis. This familiarity is reflected in the salutation, such as Dear MaryLou, Dear Carlos, or Dear H.L.

In the past, salutations of Gentlemen, Sirs, and Madam were not only acceptable but widely used. These terms are used less today, even when a letter is addressed to a company. Instead a writer, unaware of an individual's name, may address a job title or use a subject line:

Purchasing Agent	Twin Cities Software, Inc.
Kennan Paper Company	14162 Perimeter Road
Hoffman, NC 28347	Groton, VT 05046
Dear Agent:	SUBJECT: Cash Discounts

The following are examples of plural salutations:

- Dear Mr. Dooley and Mr. Paterno
  or
  Dear Messrs. Dooley and Paterno

- Dear Mrs. Ross and Mrs. Warwick
  or
  Dear Mmes. Ross and Warwick

- Dear Ms. Landers and Ms. Manners
  or
  Dear Mses. Landers and Manners

When little is known about the intended recipient, determining an appropriate salutation can be troublesome. Salutations to women, to mixed-sex groups, or to organizations present special challenges. These challenges are best met by learning as much as possible about the correspondent. When you are responding to a letter, the correspondent's signature block should be your guide.

Mistaking the sex of the correspondent is sometimes possible. Names such as Jerry, Terry, Stacy, and Kelly are used interchangeably. The problem is even more widespread in England, where the bearers of names such as Leslie, Sydney, and Marion may be either male or female. Greeting a male with "Dear Ms." or a female with "Dear Mr." does little for the goodwill that letter writers strive to achieve. If you are uncertain as to an appropriate salutation, you may omit the salutation by following the simplified letter format described later in this chapter. See the discussion in this appendix under Computer Considerations about problems with computerized salutations.

A business letter writer has the choice of two styles of punctuating the salutation and the close of a letter. Open punctuation omits punctuation following the salutation and the close. Mixed punctuation uses a colon following the salutation and a comma following the close.

Open:	Dear Sir	Sincerely
Mixed:	Dear Ms. Ladd:	Cordially,

A recipient's title should be used in the salutation (Dear Captain Waterson). Deciding how to address high-level officials in government or dignitaries in the church is sometimes difficult. Table B.2 illustrates appropriate forms of address and salutation for some of them.

TABLE B.2	FORMS OF ADDRESS	
Addressee	**Address (envelope and letter)**	**Salutation**
U.S. Officials		
The President	The President The White House Washington, DC 20500	Dear Mr. (or Madam) President
The Vice President	The Vice President United States Senate Washington, DC 20510	Dear Mr. (or Madam) Vice President
Senator	The Honorable (full name) United States Senate Washington, DC 20510	Dear Senator (surname)
Representative	The Honorable (full name) House of Representatives Washington, DC 20515	Dear Mr. (or Madam) (surname)
Canadian Officials		
Member of House of Commons	Mr., Ms., Miss, or Mrs. (full name), M.P. House of Commons	*Formal:* Dear Sir (or Madam) *Informal:* Dear Mr., Ms., Miss, or Mrs. (surname)
Canadian Minister	Mr., Ms., Miss, or Mrs. (full name) Canadian Minister to (city or country)	*Formal:* Sir: (Madam:) *Informal:* Dear Mr., Ms., Miss, or Mrs. (surname)
Members of Provincial Governments	Mr., Ms., Miss, or Mrs. (full name), M.L.A. Member of the Legislative Assembly (name) Building (city, province)	*Formal:* Dear Sir (or Madam) *Informal:* Dear Mr., Ms., Miss, or Mrs. (surname)
Mayor	His or Her Worship (full name) City Hall (city, province)	Dear Sir (or Madam)
Religious Leaders		
Minister, Pastor, or Rector	The Reverend (full name) (title, name of church) (local address)	Dear Mr., Ms., Miss, or Mrs. (surname)
Rabbi	Rabbi (full name) (local address)	Dear Rabbi (surname)

Some writers use what we call a **salutopening** instead of a traditional salutation. A salutopening presents the first few words of the opening paragraph and the reader's name in place of the salutation.

Yes, Ms. Jefferson:

You are right to expect extended service . . .

The sentence continues into the letter body, which is a double space below the name line.

Addressee	Address (envelope and letter)	Salutation
Catholic Bishop	The Most Reverend (full name) Bishop of (diocese) (local address)	*Formal:* Your Excellency *Informal:* Dear Bishop (surname)
Catholic Priest	The Reverend (full name), (initials of order, if any) (local address)	*Formal:* Reverend Sir *Informal:* Dear Father (surname)
Protestant Episcopal Bishop	The Right Reverend (full name) Bishop of (name) (local address)	*Formal:* Right Reverend Sir (or Madam) *Informal:* Dear Bishop (surname)
Protestant Episcopal Dean	The Right Reverend (full name) Dean of (church) (local address)	*Formal:* Very Reverend Sir (or Madam) *Informal:* Dear Dean (surname)
Anglican Archbishop	The Most Reverend Archbishop of (archdiocese) (local address)	*Formal:* Most Reverend (full name) *Informal:* Dear Archbishop
Anglican Bishop	The Right Reverend (full name) Bishop of (name) (local address)	*Formal:* Right Reverend Sir *Informal:* Dear Bishop
Anglican Canon	The Reverend Canon (full name) (local address)	*Formal:* Reverend Sir *Informal:* Dear Canon
Methodist Bishop	The Reverend (full name) (local address)	*Formal:* Reverend Sir *Informal:* Dear Bishop (surname)
Miscellaneous		
President of University or College	Dr., Mr., Ms., Mrs., or Miss (full name) President, (name of institution) (local address)	Dear Dr. or President (surname)
Dean of College or School	Dean (full name) School of (name) (name of institution) (local address)	Dear Dean (surname)
Professor	Professor (full name) Department of (name) (name of institution) (local address)	Dear Professor (surname)

Salutopenings eliminate the artificiality of greeting strangers as "Dear." Conventional salutations, however, continue to be used much more frequently than salutopenings.

Attention Line

The **attention line** indicates the specific person who should read the letter. The letter is not addressed to that person, however, nor is that person named in the salutation. In fact, the attention line and the salutation are rarely used simultaneously. Either may be used with or without a subject line. One occasion to use the attention line is when your main goal is to have your message reach the organization, and your secondary goal is to have the message reach a specific individual, if he or she is still part of that organization.

Allied Lenses, Inc.
1418 Industrial Drive
Carbondale, IL 62901

Attention: Mr. Robert Jenkins

Subject: Insurance plans for lenses

Some writers use an attention line when they know the receiver's name but do not know the receiver's sex. For example:

Quality Printing Co.
124 East Frontage
Lobo, TX 79855

Attention: W. C. Brown

The attention line is placed below the inside address of the receiver. A salutation, if also used, is below the attention line.

The Body

The main message of a letter is contained in the body. The body should answer all significant questions but should be no longer than necessary. Many writers believe they are obligated to fill an entire sheet even when a shorter message would do.

Use short paragraphs. They make it easy for a reader to scan a letter and identify important points. Some authorities consider an average of four to six lines per paragraph to be reasonable.

The body begins a double space below the salutation or attention line. Use a single space within paragraphs and double space between paragraphs.

The Close

The close should match the salutation in formality or informality. An exception is form letters, especially sales messages, which frequently do not match salutations and closes. For example, one may contain the salutation Dear Resident and close with Sincerely.

The words most commonly used in closing letters are truly, sincerely, respectfully, and cordially. Each may be used with *yours* and sometimes with *very*. Some common and appropriate closes are:

The close and the salutation should be of equal formality.

- Yours truly
- Cordially
- Sincerely yours
- Sincerely
- Respectfully
- Respectfully yours

A double space separates the close from the last line of the letter body.

Signature Block

The **signature block** consists of the writer's name, typed and signed, and job title. The job title can be typed on the same line as the name if both are short. Otherwise it is typed directly below. In some organizations, the name of the company is also included in the signature block. This is to clarify the company's legal responsibility for the letter. It is no longer considered necessary, and the practice is diminishing.

The writer's name and job title comprise the signature block.

Through the signature block, correspondents may indicate how they prefer to be addressed:

Sincerely,   Yours truly,

PHOENIX INDUSTRIES   *Wanda L. Sinclair*

                                              Wanda L. Sinclair, Editor

Kenneth E. Booth

Kenneth E. Booth
Director of Public Relations

The signature block is separated from the close by four lines of space. If the company name is included, however, it is separated from the close by only two lines, and the four lines of space follow. Usually the handwritten portion matches the typed name, but some authors blend formality with informality by typing their full name, but signing only their first name.

ADDITIONAL PARTS OF A BUSINESS LETTER

The standard parts just described are routinely found in business letters. You should also be familiar with some additional parts that you may need to use on occasion.

Subject Line

The subject line alerts the reader to what the message is about. Subject lines assist in the proper filing of correspondence as well as in its transfer to an appropriate recipient. Regular use of subject lines enhances efficiency and paper management. The subject line is placed two lines below the salutation either along the left margin, indented the same as the paragraphs, or centered on the page.

Reference Initials, Enclosures, and Copies

The sender's initials in unspaced capital letters precede the typist's initials, which are lowercase. A colon, dash, or slash separates the two sets of initials. The sender's initials are often omitted, however, because the name is typed in the signature block. Reference initials appear at the left margin a double line space below the last line of the signature block.

If something in addition to the letter is included in the envelope, an enclosure notation should be made one or two line spaces below the reference initials. The word enclosure may be spelled out or abbreviated *Encl.* or *Enc.* If more than one enclosure is sent, the number should be indicated. Enclosures may be identified although this is not required.

If someone other than the intended receiver will be sent a copy of a letter, that person should be identified at the very end of the letter. List the names of those who are to receive copies after the single letter *c.* This notation refers to copies made by any means such as carbon, photocopy, or laser.

JTD:nvp   pnp
Enclosures 3   Enclosures: 1. Brochure
                                                 2. Registration Form

c: Mr. Jenkins   c: B. Kelly
   Ms. Phillips

Copies of letters may be sent out without the receiver or addressee being made aware that this is being done. Such copies are called **blind copies** and noted with a *bc*. This notation is typed on the copies but not on the original and appears directly below the usual copy notation.

Information about copies appears one or two spaces below the reference initials, enclosure notation, or signature block.

Postscripts

A postscript conveys thoughts added to a letter after it has been completed. If a message is planned and well-organized, a postscript would not be necessary. Postscripts are not often used today; when used, they are usually for emphasis. A postscript is often preceded by "P.S.," but this is not necessary. A postscript should appear at the bottom of the letter, one or two spaces below the last line typed on the page.

Second-Page Headings

When a letter continues beyond one page, each subsequent page should be headed by the receiver's name, page number, and date. The first page may be typed on letterhead stationery, but subsequent pages should be on plain paper.

Two or more lines of the body must be carried over to warrant a second page; never begin a second page solely for the signature block. These second-page headings are commonly used:

Wilcox Tool Company   -2-   May 14, 1997

Mr. Frank Settles, July 31, 1997, page 2

Ms. Tanya Berancourt
March 15, 1997
Page 2

The date that appears in the heading of the second and subsequent pages should be the same as the date on the first page. This is true even though subsequent pages may be typed on a different date from the first page.

Second-page headings should be typed one or two inches from the top of the page. The body of the letter should resume four spaces below the heading.

LETTER FORMATS

Planning is necessary so that letters will appear attractive and organized. An unattractive or disorganized appearance is likely to detract from the message itself. The placement of the letter on the page is an important determinant of appearance.

A letter that is balanced on the page is more attractive than one that is not. By surrounding your message with ample margins you can achieve a framing effect. Side margins are commonly 1½ inches, and top and bottom margins are approximately 2 inches. By varying the top and bottom margins on the basis of the message length, you can produce a letter with eye appeal. Space may be varied above and below the date; the spacing between other letter parts is constant.

Companies differ in the format of letters. In general, however, writers single-space within the parts of a letter and double-space between the parts. Some organizations provide employees with a manual or style sheet prescribing a certain format. The writer has four main formats from which to choose: full-block, modified-block, traditional (a modification of full-block), and simplified. (If your organization has its own style, follow it.)

In the **full-block** (see Figure B.1), every line begins at the left margin including the date, close, and signature block. Because of the focus on the left margin, a typist need not make many adjustments on the typewriter; thus it is fast. Critics of this

Figure B.1
Full-Block Format

Quad States College
P.O. Box 1412
Boise, ID 83707

January 8, 1997

Tina Rodriguez
President
Rodriguez & Associates
Jacksonville, FL

Dear Ms. Rodriguez:

All lines begin at the left margin.

The innovative management style you employ has made the news in recent months. I have followed the success of Rodriguez & Associates with great interest.

The full-block format facilitates fast typing.

I have taught courses in management to two generations of college students and am always seeking input from professionals. I would be very interested to know what management theory has most influenced you and would also appreciate any practical tips or examples you could share from the workplace. "Real world" examples help students better grasp management theories.

A major complaint is that the full-block format looks unbalanced.

Would you also please share this letter with your colleagues for their views on modern management approaches. I realize you are a busy person and hope that you will take the time to respond.

Sincerely,

Signature

Katherine Black
Katherine Black
Professor of Business

jam

format contend that it results in an unbalanced, left-leaning appearance and feels rather formal.

In the **modified-block format,** the date begins at the center of the page. The close and the signature block are normally aligned with the date. This format is shown in Figure B.2.

Figure B.2
Modified-Block Format

Rodriguez & Associates
Post Office Box 1412
Las Vegas, NV 89114

January 8, 1997 ——————————— *Date begins at center of page.*

Professor Katherine Black
Quad States College
P.O. Box 1412
Boise, ID 83707

Dear Dr. Black:

I am pleased that you have followed the progress of Rodriguez & Associates. Throughout my career I have kept informed of the trends and developments in management style. The approach I have developed and used in my public relations firm is most anal-ogous to participative management.

This method is usually extremely effective because some —————— *Although not indented here,* decision-making authority is given to employees. The benefits of *paragraphs may be indented in* increasing subordinates' role in the decision-making process are *modified-block format.* numerous. For example, I have found it increases morale, loyalty and productivity. It also results in decreased turnover. Most importantly, sharing decision-making power promotes a sense of ownership among employees.

This management style effectively gives me power by relinquish-ing power. The organization as a whole gains an advantage because the pooled knowledge of all employees is utilized.

Figure B.2
Continued

Modified-block is more
balanced than full-block.

Rodriguez & Associates
January 8, 1997
Page 2

I believe that communication is critical in a business that espouses
participative management. Employees need full information to
make intelligent decisions, which can only be accomplished
through open dialogue. Information flows in all directions—not
just from the top down.

However, there are situations when one leader's vision is needed
to make sound decisions. Quick action is necessary when a crisis
arises. Sometimes there simply isn't enough time to come to a
decision by committee. Also, there are some decisions that
should be made by the primary leader to maintain consistency.

Ultimately, success in business is measured by the bottom line,
and participative management leads to this success.

I have passed along your request to my colleagues. I wish you the
best in educating new generations of business leaders.

Sincerely,

Tina Rodriguez
Tina Rodriguez

Signature

Close and signature block
begin at center of page.

In the **traditional format**, each paragraph is indented five spaces or 1/2 inch.
Except for that, traditional is identical to modified-block. They are the most popular
formats both in the United States and abroad. The traditional format is shown in
Figure B.3.

P.O. Box 540
Mobile, AL 36603
January 14, 1997

Dr. Katherine Black
Quad States College
P.O. Box 1412
Boise, ID 83707

Dear Professor Black:

Tina Rodriguez informed me you are asking professionals for input about management theories they practice. I understand Ms. Rodriguez is enthusiastic about participative management. Here at Advantage Advertising we also believe in the merits of participative management. However, team building is a prerequisite for participative management and is the building block of effective modern organizations.

Each paragraph is indented five spaces or 1/2 inch.

Some researchers report over 75% of workers in the U.S. are directed to work in teams. Part of the reason for the popularity and necessity of team building is the continuing trend of downsizing. For instance, the staff of Advantage Advertising has been reduced 25% in the last five years despite the growth of our clientele. With reduced staff and increased work we needed a way to increase productivity. We found teamwork was the answer.

Except for indenting paragraphs, this is like the modified-block format.

Working effectively in a team requires the development of special skills. For one thing, the team needs to share common goals. In our organization, teams are organized to work on an account together. This arrangement gives the team a common goal: to please the client. It also increases tension in the team because the members come from different departments and have different orientations. However, because the client's interest comes first, this tension is used productively and brings out the best in each department.

To ensure participation, each member should feel respected and certain ground rules should be set. Successful team building also takes a commitment of time and energy from employees and management. Management's philosophy should be compatible with the team approach.

Good luck with your research.

Sincerely,

Jonathan Chang
Jonathan Chang

Signature

jam

In the **simplified format**, developed by the Administrative Management Society, neither a salutation nor a close is used.[1] A subject line replaces the salutation. As in the full-block format, all lines begin at the left margin. The simplified format is becoming

Figure B.4
Simplified Format

A subject line is used ————————
instead of a salutation.

All lines begin at the ————————
left margin.

Simplified format ————————
makes typing efficient.

No complimentary ————————
close is used.

Signature ————————

Printing Professionals

January 21, 1997

Dr. Katherine Black
Quad States College
P.O. Box 1412
Boise, ID 83707

POPULAR MANAGEMENT APPROACHES

My good client, Tina Rodriguez, mentioned to me that you were seeking feed-back about popular management approaches in practice. I understand she supports participative management, and another client of mine, Jonathan Chang, favors team building. The approach I endorse emphasizes quality. Emphasis on quality encompasses both participative management and team building.

Printing Professionals places emphasis on quality because high quality is necessary to compete. Obviously, if our product is inferior or inconsistent we will lose customers. They demand the job be done right the first time. In the printing business this precision is a challenge because there are so many variables. Printing is not a commodity; each job is different.

To accomplish high quality we utilize participative management. I know from experience that employees who feel a sense of ownership are more involved in their work. This feeling leads to more conscientious attention to quality. We also integrate the principle of team building to form quality circles. These circles consist of eight to ten people in our company and meet about once a week.

When I started in this business 22 years ago, there was not as much emphasis on quality. The goal was to produce as much as possible in the least amount of time. Today quick turnaround is still crucial, but customers have higher standards. Therefore, we have used and continue to use these techniques to continuously improve quality.

I hope these comments are useful. If you need a guest lecturer I have spoken to groups in the past on the subject of quality management and I would be happy to speak at your school.

I have enclosed two brochures we use to communicate our emphasis on quality. What do you think of the brochures?

Vincent Mancuso
Vincent Mancuso
Quality Manager

jam
Enclosures 2

---

increasingly popular because it contributes to greater keyboarding efficiency. The simplified format is shown in Figure B.4.

Most of the business letters you will send or receive use one of the four formats just discussed. Writers will sometimes devise special formats to get the reader's atten-

Figure B.5
Spacing Layout

RELIABLE TRUCKING, INC. —————————————————— *Letterhead*
4100 Madison Road, Cincinnati, OH 45227

February 3, 1997 ————————————————————————— *Date*
——— *Receiver's address*
Precision Plastic Parts ————————————————————
P.O. Box 1542
Hammond, LA 70402

Attention: Traffic Manager ——————————————————— *Attention line*

Dear Manager: ——————————————————————————— *Salutation*

REVISED PICKUP SCHEDULE ————————————————— *Subject line*

Your recent letter was forwarded to me by Brenda Bishop, Vice President of
Operations. Because your continued satisfaction is important to us, we intend to
accommodate your need for a different daily pickup schedule for the spring and
summer months.

On February 18 and 19 our customer service agent, Carmella Bryant, will be in —— *Body*
the Hammond area. One week before that she will phone you to arrange a
specific time to meet with you.

We appreciate your contacting us well in advance of the time when your pickup
needs will change. Carmella will be able to offer several different pickup and
delivery options, one of which is sure to be appropriate.

I have enclosed a brochure describing some additional services we will soon
introduce in the Hammond region. Please contact me if I may be of further service. ————————————————————————————————————
——— *Close*
Sincerely,

Shane R. Ellington ——————————————————————— *Signature block*
Shane R. Ellington
Operations Supervisor ——————————————————————
—— *Reference initial*
af ——
——— *Enclosure*
Enc.
——— *Copies*
c: B. Bishop
   C. Bryant

tion by using devices such as unusual margins, color, and boxes that enclose important
information. Sales letters frequently have unusual formats, but even they are comprised
of the standard parts. The parts of a letter and appropriate spacing are illustrated in
Figure B.5.

MEMO PARTS AND FORMATS

Memos differ from letters by having some different parts, by having a different appearance, and by often having a different verbal content or tone. Here we'll look at the parts and the formats.

Memo Parts

Some of the parts described under Business Letter Standard Parts and Formats are used similarly in memos: attention line, body, reference initials, enclosures, copies, and second page headings. The following parts, though, are unique to memos.

Imprinted "Memo." Most organizations do not use a letterhead for their memos, but may use the organization's name. They are likely to imprint "Memo" or "Memorandum" at the top of the page, much like a letterhead.

To, From, Subject, Date. Typically, organizations drop from memos the return address, inside address, salutation, closing, and signature block that are used with letters. Instead they use:

To:
From:
Subject:
Date:

Following the "To:" is the name, and perhaps the title, of the person to whom the memo is directed. You may send the memo to an individual, a list of individuals, or to a group, such as the Finance Committee. After "From:" is the author's name and maybe the title, especially if the audience doesn't know the person's title. Usually "Subject:" is next, and after it appear about three to five words of description. Finally, the date appears after "Date:." Some companies place the date between "Memo" and the "To:," or immediately after "From:."

Within most organizations, the signed name of the author used with letters is omitted and the author instead initials his or her name in the To/From/Subject/Date block.

Headings

Some memos are many pages in length, and such length calls for the use of headings and even subheadings to break up large blocks of text and to signpost the flow of information.

Keep in mind that headings (and subheadings) must be at least two in number, and consistently formatted. Review Chapter 11 for a discussion of headings, and for sample formats.

Memo Formats

Because memos are used internally, the guidelines for their appearance are not as established as with letters. Further, many organizations establish their own culture and identity, and have their own memo style as part of it. Finally, the power of the computer to modify the appearance of documents has blurred some of the long-standing guidelines. Nevertheless, memos have a rather common appearance, such as described above.

OTHER FORMS OF BUSINESS CORRESPONDENCE

Letters and memos make up the vast majority of written business messages. Other forms, though, include documentation, policies and procedures, reports, and electronic mail. Discussion of these different forms appears in Chapters 4, 10, 11, and 12. Among the similarities across these forms are:

- Use of headings and subheadings in a clear and consistent fashion.
- Delivery of single-spaced paragraphs, with a blank line between paragraphs.
- Selection of tasteful, readable typefaces and type sizes.
- Application of uniform margins (unless printed pages face each other, in which case left and right page margins alternate to produce a large center margin).
- Use of a common indent or no-indent decision for paragraphs.

COMPUTER CONSIDERATIONS

As business people have moved from typewriters to computers for the preparation of their correspondence, and from typewriters to daisywheel and dot matrix printers to laser printers for the final document, many of the old guidelines regarding appearance have fallen aside. Some comments that relate to computerized output have already appeared in this appendix; this final section discusses some additional considerations that supplement earlier discussions.

Time Stamps

A time stamp, or time-and-date stamp, is merely the placement of the time/date somewhere on a version of a document to serve as a reminder of when it was created or modified. Such a stamp is especially valuable in documents that go through multiple versions. The stamp may be on each page, or on just the first or last page. Wherever you place the stamp, it should be unobtrusive and perhaps in a smaller, less noticeable type size. Many word processors automatically update the time/date stamp each time you print the document.

Type Size and Face

The size of type should allow for easy reading. Although some people use 10-point type, more common is 12-point type for body copy. To add emphasis or to differentiate levels of headings and subheadings, size may be used. Titles of papers or reports may be 18 point, major headings 14 point, and subheadings 12, for example.

Care should be taken in picking a typeface that is appropriate to the organization and to the subject at hand. Times Roman is commonly used and is a conservative, safe selection. Courier looks like typewriter output and therefore may give your document a dated appearance. Cursives and scripts should be avoided in most applications. Avoid large blocks of all capitals, and consider a serif typeface instead of sans serif if maximum readability is desired. If you are likely to be faxing the material, consider either Times Roman or Helvetica, since they fax better than most typefaces.

Salutations

When personal computers were first being used to merge messages with mailing lists for computerized letters, some strange and sometimes irritating outcomes occurred. Women would receive letters addressed to their last name, with a "Dear Mr." in front of it. People who use an initial in front of their name or just initials (G. Gordon Liddy or B. J. Smith) might be addressed awkwardly (Dear G. or Dear B.). If a title instead of a name was in the mailing list, it sometimes produced such strange salutations as Dear Ass. Plant Mgr.

In an effort to avoid some of these undesired outcomes, many people started merging the entire name, as in Dear John J. Smith. While the intent is to sidestep some of the early salutation errors and, ideally, to produce an individualistic sounding salutation, such salutations are clearly inappropriate. They don't follow established guidelines and sound impersonal and computerish.

Running Headers and Footers

Most word processors allow, and make easy, the addition of information at the top or bottom of a page. Such material might include document title, page number, date, version, section or chapter, or name of person to whom the message is written. Some of these items, such as page number, can change automatically on each page. Lengthy documents can benefit from some of this information. Few guidelines exist beyond common sense for application of headers or footers, or for the information in them. Generally, select a header or a footer, not both, if it is really needed. Then place only what might benefit the reader in that location. The header or footer should not be obtrusive.

Orphans and Widows

In multipaged documents, sometimes the computer software produces odd-looking text. One such occasion occurs when the first line of a paragraph is the last line on a page (a *widow*) and another occurs when the last line of a paragraph appears by itself at the top of a page (an *orphan*). If your software has widow and orphan control, use it, since it makes reading easier. If not, try to control them yourself.

Justification

Text that is smooth or lined up on the left and/or right margins is called justified. Seldom do you want a left margin that is unjustified (or "ragged"), but an unjustified right margin can add readability since fewer words need to be hyphenated. Further, sometimes a justified right margin creates too much space between words on some lines.

Column Widths

Many of today's word processors can easily produce pages with multicolumns., which can add a published look or be valuable for such documents as newsletters or advertising brochures. One handy guideline in selecting column width (or selecting a type size for an existing column) is that about two and one-half alphabets of the type made a good column width.

Templates

Templates are packages of instructions to the word processor to speedily set up such document characteristics as type face and size, number of columns, margins, or automatic time stamp or page numbers. Fancier templates might automatically insert the corporate logo or start a new message with questions to the author, such as receiver's name and address, which are then inserted in the address and salutation.

People who write a great deal might create multiple templates. They might have templates for each of the following: business letter, internal memo, policy and procedure, company report, meeting agenda and announcement, and training materials.

Notes

1. *The Simplified Letter*, a brochure published by the American Management Society, Willow Grove, PA.

GLOSSARY

abstract Summary of the text of a report, presented idea by idea, that can serve to assist the receiver in understanding material before it is read or may provide a synopsis upon completion; may be considered the report in miniature.

accountability The expectation that someone will do some specific things to accomplish a specific goal.

acronym A word comprised of the first letters from each of a series of words in a phrase.

active listening Approach to listening with the goal of grasping what is being communicated from the speaker's point of view and being able to convey this understanding to the speaker.

advertising A highly structured form of external communication, including television commercials, printed ads, and mailed brochures.

AIDA sequence Four basic steps to be followed in seeking to persuade someone (get attention, stimulate interest, awaken a desire, and encourage action).

analytical report *See* problem-solving report.

announcement memorandum A memorandum used to announce personnel transfers, meetings, or policy changes; may be circulated widely or to only a select few.

anticipatory mind-set Mental attitude that can be created in a listener through statements made in introducing a topic.

appendix Information that is useful to the reader of a report but that is not required in the text itself.

arithmetic-logic unit (ALU) The part of the central processing unit of a computer that carries out the actual processing of information.

attention line Line in a business letter, placed below the inside address, indicating the specific person who should read it.

attitude question Question in a research questionnaire that seeks a respondent's attitude toward a statement.

attribution Use of footnotes, endnotes, or other sourcing techniques to indicate the origin of information obtained in secondary research.

bad-news letter Letter with a message that the receiver will consider bad news; a letter of refusal.

blaming style Style of communication that focuses on finding fault or discovering who is to blame for a problem.

blind copy Copy of a letter that is sent out without the knowledge of the receiver or addressee; indicated with the notation *bc* on the copy but not on the original.

boilerplate Standard paragraphs of text that are used repeatedly in documents; also called form paragraphs.

bottom-up style Managerial style whereby the role of the group in decision making is emphasized and subordinates are actively involved in all phases of arriving at decisions.

burnout Exhaustion caused by excessive demands on one's energy or strength.

CD-ROM (Compact Disk–Read–Only Memory) A form of optical storage in which a laser is used to "read" information from a disk very similar to an audio CD.

cell address The identification of a cell in a spreadsheet by its column and row number.

cellular telephone A wireless telephone that can be carried in the automobile, a briefcase, or a pocket.

central processing unit (CPU) The "brain" of a computer, where the processing of information occurs.

central selling point The prime reason a person would want what a seller is offering.

channel selection The careful weighing of benefits before choosing channels for shaping behavior.

chart Type of figure that shows trends or relationships for nonquantitative data.

chronological resumé format Style of resume that presents information by date, with most recent first.

chronological sequence The progression of a speech from one point in time to another.

clicking The process of giving instructions to a computer by pushing a button on a mouse.

closed question Type of question that is somewhat restrictive in nature and generally calls for a brief and limited response.

coherence A logical connection between ideas, as well as a smooth flow of ideas within a document.

collaborative writing A message prepared by and reflecting the views of a team, as opposed to a message prepared by an individual.

Commerce Business Daily (CBD) Publication of the U.S. Department of Commerce containing requests for proposals from various units of the federal government.

compatible computers Computers based on a computer architecture developed by IBM.

computer interview Completion of a series of direct and indirect questions via computer screen by the job applicant; may be an initial screening device or part of a lengthy interview sequence.

computer monitor The medium by which the instructions and data that are input using a keyboard or a mouse are displayed.

computer network A combination of two or more computers and other devices that allows information to be exchanged between the devices.

conciseness Saying what you want to say in the fewest possible words.

constructive conflict Moderate conflict that may key the individual up for superior performance.

contact cultures Cultures in which people tend to touch often and stand close together when interacting; include Latin America, southern Europe, and the Arab states.

control unit That part of the central processing unit that guides information processing by supplying the data and instructions to the arithmetic-logic unit.

copy machine Photocopier for reproducing paper documents—text, drawings, or pictures.

correction interview Type of interview in which a superior seeks to motivate a subordinate to substitute some desirable behavior for behavior that is undesirable.

counseling interview Type of interview directed at personal or family-related problems of a subordinate.

cover letter A personally addressed letter that accompanies a mailed resume.

covert response Response that is not readily apparent to either the speaker or an observer.

credibility The quality of inspiring belief; based on the overall image of the message sender.

creeping elegance Phrase that describes the divergent appearance resulting from the use of unrelated type treatments in published materials.

culture The total pattern of human behavior and its products embodied in thought, speech, action, and artifacts.

database A body of information that is stored in a way that makes it easily manipulated and retrieved by a user.

decisional roles Managerial roles focusing on the essential managerial activity of decision making.

decoding The process of translating a message into an idea; done by the receiver.

deductive arrangement Order of presentation of ideas that begins with the main idea and then gives secondary details.

demographic question Question in a research questionnaire that seeks information on characteristics of respondents such as age, sex, income, and race.

desktop publishing High-quality word processing, made possible by faster personal computers and lower cost, high-quality laser printers.

destructive conflict Intense or prolonged conflict that may cause worry or fear, hamper work performance, and in some cases lead to physical and mental illnesses.

dichotomous question Question in a research questionnaire that has only two possible answers; for example, yes/no, male/female.

direct sequence Order of presentation characterized by the presentation of ideas from the specific to the general.

direct-mail approach The writing of unsolicited letters, also called surveying or prospecting letters, aimed at achieving a particular goal—such as securing job interviews at companies with no known job openings.

directing style Style of communication that focuses on telling others, particularly subordinates, how to do their jobs or how to solve problems.

directive interviewing style Style of interviewing characterized by the interviewer's balance between freedom and control.

director of communication An individual responsible for managing the flow of information within an organization and solving communication problems.

documentation Establishing of proof, information, evidence, or sequence, usually in written form.

DOS Disk operating system, so named because of the PC's use of secondary storage devices.

downsizing Organizational restructuring that involves layoffs, hiring freezes, and early retirement as means of reducing headcount.

draft A preliminary version of a written message.

Electronic Data Interchange (EDI) A method for exchanging data with customers and suppliers by way of a computer network.

electronic mail (E-mail) Generic name for noninteractive communication of text, data, image, or voice messages utilizing telecommunications links.

emotional appeal Appeal directed to the feelings, rather than the intellect, of the receiver.

empowerment A movement toward increased employee involvement by allowing workers to make decisions rather than merely providing input to managers.

encoding The process of translating an idea into a message; done by the sender.

endnotes Notes, usually in the form of footnotes, grouped at the end of a report and providing attribution to original sources.

enumerating Assigning a specific numeric or chronological label to each idea in a paragraph to improve coherence.

enumeration Device whereby a speaker numbers each point and presents them by count: "My second point is...."

ergonomics The science that studies the relationship between efficiency and comfort in a worker's use of machines.

European Economic Community (ECC) An organization formed in 1993 that eliminated long-standing trade barriers by creating a free-trade zone comprised of twelve European countries.

European Union (EU) A coalition, founded in 1958, of France, West Germany, Italy, Belgium, The Netherlands, Luxembourg, and later Denmark, Great Britain, Ireland, Greece, Portugal, and Spain (broadened to include Austria, Sweden, and Finland) formed to improve economic activities and political relationships as well as to foster improved cooperation in science, education, and cultural matters.

exit interview Interview conducted to learn why an employee is voluntarily leaving the organization.

external communication Interaction with many individuals or groups outside the organization.

facsimile (fax) machine Equipment now commonplace in offices and many homes that is used to send copies of a document from one place to another electronically.

fax-modem A device that can be combined with circuitry to enable a computer to send and receive documents from facsimile machines.

feedback The reaction that the listener has to the sender's verbal and nonverbal message.

fight or flight syndrome The stress response by the human body to the perception of danger; secretion of adrenaline into the bloodstream results in tightened muscles, perspiration, increased heart and breathing rates, etc.

figure Visual support, including graphs, charts, maps, drawings, and photographs.

file transfer protocols (FTP) A set of signals that allow users to download documents and programs using a standard set of methods.

flip chart Large tablet of plain or gridded paper fastened to an easel for use during informal oral presentations.

floppy disk A small, plastic magnetic disk that is used for external storage of computerized information; it is the most widely used method of external storage.

form letter A very general letter that may be sent to a variety of people without change.

form report Short report presented in a predetermined format; the most common type of short report.

formal communication Messages sent through organizational channels developed by management.

full-block format A business letter format in which every line begins at the left margin, including the date, close, and signature block.

functional resumé format Style of resume that emphasizes job functions.

gateway A special device used with a leased phone line to connect a wide area network.

General Agreement of Tariffs and Trade (GATT) An international commercial treaty whose purpose is to sponsor trade negotiations.

good-news letter Letter with a message that the receiver will perceive as good news.

Gopher A means of accessing information on the Internet; uses a method based on menus to move from site to site.

graph Type of figure used to simplify and present numerical data in order to show trends or relationships.

group interview Interview in which several individuals are presented with one interviewer; likely to occur in a social setting.

group polarization In a group, concentration of opinion around a more extreme position than would be taken by individual members.

groupthink Tendency of group members to conform rather than to think independently and critically.

groupware Software developed for computer networks that helps people work together.

guide Type of procedure that allows discretion in making decisions; compare with rule.

hard disk A secondary storage device, a metal disk, that is usually housed in the system unit of the computer and utilizes the hard drive.

hardware The physical, electronic machinery employed in information processing.

heading Words or phrases displayed in written reports that act as signposts to improve the reader's speed and comprehension.

hierarchy of needs Maslow's theory that needs progress from lower to higher order, ranging from survival needs to self-actualization.

highly directive interviewing style Style of interviewing in which the interviewer exerts strong control.

home page Presentation by a company, organization, or individual of interconnected information, often including job openings, on the World Wide Web.

horizontal communication Communication between peers, or people on the same level in the organization.

host culture The culture of the country in which the firm seeks to do business.

hot link A feature that can be incorporated into web pages enabling the user to point, click, and be connected to another page from the same site or a site located on a computer anywhere in the world.

idiom An expression whose meaning cannot be derived from the meanings of individual words.

indirect sequence Order of presentation characterized by the presentation of ideas from the general to the specific.

informal communication Exchanges between individuals who, although not formally connected, interact by telephone, social, or chance meetings.

information explosion The proliferation of information, and sometimes inundation of management, as a result of computer storage and processing.

information overload The problem of having too much information to make intelligent use of it.

information superhighway A worldwide computer network that links together the large commercial on-line services (Prodigy, America Online, CompuServe) with thousands of smaller networks.

information tool Term applied to the computer because of its ability to process information in numerous ways.

informational report Business report that presents data without interpretation; has little application in decision making.

informational roles Managerial roles focusing on the receipt and dissemination of information.

informative speech Speech with the general purpose of teaching or explaining.

instructions Form of written or oral information pertaining to how to perform a task or presenting policies and procedures.

integrated services digital network (ISDN) A high-speed telephone connection that operates over existing phone lines and allows a single line to handle a voice call and send computer information simultaneously.

internal communication Messages sent and received within an organization.

Internet A collection of interconnected mainframe computers, personal computers, LANs, and WANs that serve as a global information network for consumers and business.

interpersonal roles Managerial roles focusing on interpersonal relationships.

interpretive report Business report that presents and examines data, thereby allowing implications to be drawn.

jargon A verbal shortcut that allows specialists to communicate more easily among themselves.

justification report Short report to justify an action or lack of action—a change in procedure, a budget increase, or reasons for resisting a new policy.

keyboard One of the most common devices for computer input; similar to a typewriter keyboard but contains special function keys, cursor control keys, and/or a numeric keypad.

kinesics Communication through body movement.

laptop computers Small versions of personal computers that are about the size of a phone book and weigh from 5 to 9 pounds; so named because they can be operated while sitting on one's lap.

laser printer Probably the most popular printer for the office; uses a laser beam to write dots on a drum that is coated with light-sensitive material, then transfers the dots to paper using ink.

leading question Question phrased so as to guide the response in a certain direction.

letter report Short report using a letter format; usually less formal than longer reports and intended for external communication.

letterhead The printed heading on company stationery; contains company name, address, ZIP code, telephone and facsimile numbers, and often E-mail address.

linking words Words that serve as transitions or bridges between ideas; examples are "also," "consequently," and "therefore."

list question Question in a research questionnaire for which the respondent selects from a list of answers.

listener orientation Focus by a speaker on the interests of listeners and learning as much about them as possible.

listserv A group electronic mail program that allows users to subscribe to special-interest electronic mailing lists.

loaded question Question phrased so that it is strongly directional; tends to be hard-hitting and can create stress in the interviewee.

local area networks (LANs) A small telecommunications network for connecting computers that are located close together.

logical appeal Appeal directed toward the receiver's rational thinking.

machismo Managerial style characterized by a strong sense of power and pride and conveyed through forceful and self-confident dealings with others.

macros Programs in connection with spreadsheets that create the ability to automate often-used commands.

magnetic tape A thin ribbon (often plastic) coated with a magnetic material on which information may be stored.

maintenance role In a worker group, the role played by one who focuses on the emotional and psychological needs of group members; compare with task role.

management by walking around (MBWA) Management technique intended to enable managers to increase their contact time with subordinates, suppliers, and customers.

mass emphasis The technique of using repetition for emphasis in a piece of writing; a positive message might be repeated in both similar and different ways.

matrix environment Utilization of employee skills in both vertical and horizontal directions; a manager might supervise subordinates in an area of expertise but also participate in a horizontal committee of peers with mixed functions.

memorandum A message written for use within the organization.

memorandum report A report using a memorandum format but generally more structured in that it has an introduction, body, and conclusion.

microprocessor A computer chip on the main circuit board in the computer's system unit on which the central processing unit is located.

mirror question Question in which the interviewer reflects the interviewee's previous answer with the intent of drawing out additional information.

mobile office Location of one's worksite in airplanes, client's office, or automobiles through the use of cellular technology.

modem A device used by a computer to communicate information over a phone line.

modified-block format A business letter format in which the date begins at the center of the page and the close and signature block are normally aligned with it.

motivated sequence Method of speech organization based on analysis of the thought process; results in presentation of ideas in the natural order that people follow when thinking through to a problem solution.

mouse A small device that is connected to a computer by a long cord and which can be moved over a flat surface—usually a mouse pad—to manipulate a pointer on the screen.

movement analysis Program developed by Warren Lamb, London-based management consultant, for predicting how a person will perform in an organization based on his or her kinesic behavior.

multimedia The use of multiple forms of media, such as video, animation, and audio, in a published document.

network card A circuit board that allows a computer to connect to a computer network.

networking Contacting friends, fraternity or sorority members, family members, neighbors, and former employers for the exchange of information regarding job openings.

neutral letter Letter that presents a message that is neither good nor bad.

neutral question Question phrased so that possible responses are not indicated and alternatives are presented in a balanced fashion.

nominal group Group that meets to solve a problem without engaging in verbal interaction.

nondirective interviewing style Style of interviewing in which open questions are used almost exclusively.

nonprobability sampling A form of convenience sampling in which there is a good chance that the sample selected does not represent the larger population.

nonverbal communication The transferring of information without relying on word meaning.

North American Free Trade Agreement (NAFTA) A mutual governmental action that eliminated trade barriers between the United States and its major trading partners.

objective Generalized purpose toward which an entire organization strives.

office visit interview Usually a day-long series of interviews that may incorporate many of the other categories; also called plant or headquarters visit.

open question Type of question that is broad in scope and allows much freedom in the response offered.

open-ended interview An interview that follows no discernible pattern; also called unstructured or nondirective.

open-ended question Question in a research questionnaire that sets no limit on the time or space the respondent may use in answering; strength is the richness of answers and weakness is the difficulty of statistical analysis.

operating system A type of software that provides the basic instructions to the computer for controlling the hardware, providing an interface between the user and the computer, handling files and storage, and running other software.

optical character recognition A means of converting an electronic document into standard text, through the use of special software.

orientation interview Interview intended to acquaint new employees with their jobs, the range of their duties, and the company.

overt response Response that is both observable and measurable.

pager A small device, worn on the belt or carried in a pocket, that signals the user of a message.

pagination Placement of page numbers on the pages of a report, following standard rules.

palmtop computers Hand-held computers that weigh a pound or less and fit into a jacket pocket.

panel interview Interview in which one individual is interviewed by more than one person at a time.

paperless office An automated business system used for the storage and transmission of information.

paralanguage Nonverbal component of the spoken message that includes such voice attributes as pitch, volume, rate, and resonance; the "how" as opposed to the "what" of communication.

parallel structure The repetition of sentence patterns in a piece of writing for improving paragraph coherence.

parallelism Repetition of similar phraseology by a speaker in stating ideas.

participative management Management style in which employees at every level become involved in job-related decision making.

pause Temporary silence observed by the interviewer, intended to encourage elaboration on a response by the interviewee.

perception Our unique understanding of the way things are; an integral part of both the sender's and receiver's involvement in the communication process.

performance appraisal interview Type of interview conducted by an immediate superior, on a regular basis, to provide the worker with feedback about his or her performance.

periodic report Short report issued on a regular basis (daily, weekly, monthly) to keep others informed about some aspect of operations.

personal digital assistants Another name for palmtop computers.

personal information managers (PIMs) Software with the capabilities of scheduling appointments, tracking to-dos, managing calendars, and an electronic Rolodex feature.

persuasion The art of getting people to do something that they would not ordinarily do if you did not ask.

persuasive letter Letter that seeks to modify the thought and action of others in a certain direction.

persuasive speech Speeches that range from those seeking to change the listener's beliefs or attitudes to those that attempt to get the listeners to act in a certain way; purpose is to elicit either an overt or a cover response.

persuasive style Style of communication that employs information sharing and acceptance techniques.

place emphasis Placing information either at the beginning or end of a message, the locations of maximum emphasis.

planning process Also referred to as prewriting, consists of four steps: (1) Determine the objectives, (2) Consider the audience, (3) Choose the ideas to include, and (4) Select the appropriate medium.

policy A general guide to decision making that reflects the organization's attempts to achieve its goals.

population A definable group from which a sample will be taken in order to conduct primary research; also called a universe.

precision networking Through thorough self appraisal—knowing one's strengths, weaknesses, preferences, and goals—and sharpened focus on companies, identifying those firms that are the most appropriate and desirable employers.

presentations graphic software Software packages that aid the user in preparing professional-quality slides and graphics for business presentations.

primary source Source of information in conducting research; includes questionnaires, interviews, and personal observations and is generally unpublished.

primary storage The working memory for the computer; consists of ROM and RAM.

printer Equipment utilized when the user desires a permanent printed copy of computer output.

probing question Question stimulated by the response to a previous question.

problem-solving report Business report that informs with data, interprets the data, analyzes the situation, and makes recommendations; also referred to as an analytical report.

problem-solving style Style of communication that seeks mutual acceptance from both sender and receiver of the final action; often involves compromise.

procedure A specific guide to decision making; a tool for implementing a policy.

progress report Ordinarily sent upward in the organization, a short report that provides rate of progress on a project as well as goals for subsequent time periods.

proposal An attempt, usually written, to persuade the management of one organization that the writer's organization is especially qualified to fill a need in exchange for compensation.

protocols A set of standard signals necessary for communication between very different machines.

proxemics Spatial relationships between speakers and listeners.

quality circle Small group of workers (and managers) who meet regularly to discuss and resolve problems of productivity, quality, and the workplace in general.

query A question about the database that is presented to the database software in a format that it can understand.

RAM Random access memory, used to store the data and instructions required for immediate tasks when the computer is working.

rank order question Question in a research questionnaire for which the respondent places a list of items in some order, such as best to worst or most important to least important.

reengineering A process of changing basic business procedures in order to make more efficient use of people, technology, and information resources.

request for proposal (RFP) Formal solicitation for a proposal.

resumé Factual, categorized, tabulated information about an applicant that is used in obtaining a job interview.

return on quality (ROQ) A company philosophy whereby any corporate spending on improving quality must contribute to financial performance.

reversal words Words that identify the change of direction or tone of a message from positive to negative or from negative to positive.

revision An altered version of a draft, involving additions, deletions, substitutions, and correction of errors in grammar and word usage.

ROM Read-only memory, or a set of chips that stores the instructions needed for the computer to start when the power is turned on.

rule Type of procedure that allows no discretion in its implementation; compare with guide.

salutation The word or phrase of greeting that precedes the body of a letter.

salutopening Presentation of the first few words of a letter, together with the reader's name, in place of a traditional salutation.

sans serif Family of typefaces that do not have serifs and in which the stroke of each letter is the same.

scanner A computer peripheral that is used for making an image of a hard, paper copy and storing it in the computer as an electronic image.

screen resolution A measure of the quality of the computer screen picture; calculated by the number of picture elements, or pixels, that the screen contains.

screening interview A brief, first interview to identify job prospects for further interview, rejection, or delayed decision.

secondary source Published information source for research including newspapers, government documents, books, and magazines.

secondary storage A means of saving work for the future, utilizing floppy disks, hard disks, magnetic tape, and CD-ROM.

selective perception Perception of stimuli in terms of individual attitudes and beliefs, thereby distorting the information.

self-directed work team (SDWT) A major component in many empowerment programs whereby a team leader oversees team activities but does not exercise veto power over decisions.

serif Family of typefaces that have small counterstrokes on letters that can create a feeling of horizontal flow and unity within word groupings.

signal words Certain influential words that affect individuals in either a positive or a negative way; can prevent effective listening.

signature block Writer's name, typed and signed, and job title as they appear in a business letter.

signposting Assigning brief headings to major ideas in a piece of writing to improve coherence.

simplified format A format for business letters in which all lines begin at the left margin, a subject line replaces the salutation, and no close is used.

small group A collection of a few individuals who interact face to face, verbally and nonverbally, for a common purpose, and with interdependency among the members.

smart machine An item of office hardware that contains a small computer, which enables it to make simple decisions and provide information to the user.

software A generic term for the programs and instructions provided to the computer by the user.

software suites Integrated packages of selected projects that are generally used as a group—for example, word processing, spreadsheet, database, presentation, and scheduling software.

solicited proposal A proposal written in answer to a request.

spatial sequence Arrangement of ideas by a speaker according to physical location and progressing from one physical location to another.

spreadsheet software The most popular form of software for business calculations and financial management; common uses are financial analysis, budgeting, and forecasting.

stress interview Interview in which the candidate is intentionally placed in a stressful situation so that the interviewer can carefully observe his or her responses.

superscript Number or letter typed a half line above normal text and used to cite a reference.

System 7 The standard operating system for Macintosh computers.

table Visual support consisting of tabular presentation of data.

task role In a worker group, the role played by a member who focuses on the task; compare with maintenance role.

telecommunications The use of technology such as phone systems, facsimile machines, modems, and cellular communications to enable a large organization to share resources and communicate as if operating from a single location.

telecommuter A worker who performs some or all of his or her responsibilities at home, through the use of a personal computer and advanced telecommunication technology.

telephone answering system An answering device that allows callers to leave messages in individual voice mailboxes.

topical sequence Division of a topic by a speaker into several different parts and progressing from one part to another.

Total Quality Management (TQM) A customer orientation that makes excellence the norm; for example, by initiating "zero-defects" programs and emphasizing quality improvement.

traditional format A business letter format that is identical to modified-block, except that each paragraph is indented five spaces or ½ inch.

transitory communication Communication such as phone calls, postcards, and form letters—as contrasted with personalized letters and personalized telegrams.

transmittal memorandum A covering memorandum introducing the reader to a longer, accompanying message.

turnaround time The time it takes for business firms to provide customers with their goods and services.

universe *See* population.

unsolicited proposal A proposal initiated by the proposer; no motivation is provided by the intended recipient.

Usenet News Group A group electronic mail program for on-line discussions about particular topics; accessed using special programs that can be used to maintain, monitor, access, and post to the discussion.

verbal communication The transferring of information through messages encoded in words.

vertical communication Communication between superiors and subordinates in the organization.

videoconferencing The use of video technology for group meetings when visual cues and body language are important.

videotape interview Interview in which an interviewee is taped either describing his or her qualifications or answering specific questions as part of the job-application procedure.

videotext An interactive two-way system for sending and receiving graphic or textual information through a computer interface by electronic means.

"virtual office" A business strategy through the use of telecommunications that allows people to work where and when they work best.

virtual reality The use of computer technology to create a simulated environment.

visual support Tables and figures used to support written or oral presentations.

voice mail Computer-based form of electronic mail that processes voice rather than text messages.

voice mail Voice processing technology in which users are assigned a personal mailbox from which they can access information at any time; users can also place detailed messages in the mailboxes of other subscribers without having to telephone them directly.

voice processing A collective term that encompasses voice messaging, speech recognition, speech synthesis, and interactive voice response services.

wide area networks (WANs) A telecommunications network for connecting computers that are located across the world.

Windows An operating system from Microsoft for IBM-compatible computers.

word processing software A package used on a personal computer for the generation and editing of business documents, letters, and memos.

workaholic An individual who becomes obsessed with work to the point that other aspects of life suffer.

World Wide Web A rapidly growing area of the Internet that provides information in a multimedia environment including text, images, sound, and video.

writer's block An inhibition or "freezing up" that prevents a communicator from writing.

INDEX